# Statistics for Economics, Accounting and Business Studies

Visit the *Statistics for Economics, Accounting and Business Studies, fourth edition* Companion Website at www.pearsoned.co.uk/barrow to find valuable **student** learning material including:

- Additional explanation of some topics with further references
- Excel worksheets and demonstrations
- Annotated links to other useful websites

**PEARSON**
Education

We work with leading authors to develop the strongest educational materials in Accounting, bringing cutting-edge thinking and best learning practice to a global market.

Under a range of well-known imprints, including Financial Times Prentice Hall, we craft high quality print and electronic publications which help readers to understand and apply their content, whether studying or at work.

To find out more about the complete range of our publishing, please visit us on the World Wide Web at: www.pearsoned.co.uk

**Fourth Edition**

# Statistics for Economics, Accounting and Business Studies

## Michael Barrow

University of Sussex

**FT** Prentice Hall
FINANCIAL TIMES

*An imprint of* **Pearson Education**
Harlow, England • London • New York • Boston • San Francisco • Toronto • Sydney • Singapore • Hong Kong
Tokyo • Seoul • Taipei • New Delhi • Cape Town • Madrid • Mexico City • Amsterdam • Munich • Paris • Milan

**Pearson Education Limited**

Edinburgh Gate
Harlow
Essex CM20 2JE
England

and Associated Companies throughout the world

*Visit us on the World Wide Web at:*
www.pearsoned.co.uk

———————————

First published 1988
**Fourth edition published 2006**

© Pearson Education Limited 1988, 2006

ISBN-13: 978-0-273-68308-7
ISBN-10: 0-273-68308-X

**British Library Cataloguing-in-Publication Data**
A catalogue record for this book is available from the British Library

**Library of Congress Cataloging-in-Publication Data**
Barrow, Michael.
    Statistics for economics, accounting, and business studies / Michael Barrow.— 4th ed.
        p. cm.
    Includes index.
    ISBN-13: 978-0-273-68308-7
    ISBN-10: 0-273-68308-X
        1. Economics——Statistical methods.   2. Commercial statistics.   I. Title.

    HB137.B37 2006
    519.5024'33—dc22

                                                                    2005056640

10 9 8 7 6 5 4 3 2
10 09 08 07 06

Typeset in 9/12pt Stone Serif by 35
Printed and bound by Ashford Colour Press, Gosport, Hants.

*The publisher's policy is to use paper manufactured from sustainable forests.*

For Patricia, Caroline and Nicolas

# Contents

# Preface to the fourth edition

This text is aimed at students of economics and the closely related disciplines of accountancy and business, and provides examples and problems relevant to those subjects, using real data where possible. The book is at an elementary level and requires no prior knowledge of statistics, nor advanced mathematics. For those with a weak mathematical background and in need of some revision, some recommended texts are given at the end of this preface.

This is not a cookbook of statistical recipes; it covers all the relevant concepts so that an *understanding* of why a particular statistical test should be used is gained. These concepts are introduced naturally in the course of the text as they are required, rather than having sections to themselves. The book can form the basis of a one- or two-term course, depending upon the intensity of the teaching.

As well as explaining statistical concepts and methods, the different schools of thought about statistical methodology are discussed, giving the reader some insight into some of the debates that have taken place in the subject. The book uses the methods of classical statistical analysis, for which some justification is given in Chapter 5, as well as presenting criticisms which have been made of these methods.

## Changes in this edition

There have been some substantial changes to this edition in the light of my own experience and comments from students and reviewers. There has been some rearrangement of the chapters of the book, although the content remains similar with a few changes to encourage better learning of the subject. The main changes are:

- The old Chapters 2 (Index numbers) and 7 (Data collection and sampling methods) have been moved to the end of the book. This allows a continuous development from descriptive statistics, through probability concepts, to statistical inference in the first part of the book. This will suit many courses which concentrate on the use of statistics and which do not wish to focus on data collection. Index numbers and data collection now form the final two chapters which may be thought of as covering the collection and preparation of data.
- The previous edition's final chapter on time-series methods (covering seasonal adjustment) has been dropped, but this chapter is available on the website for those who wish to make use of it. It was apparent that not many teachers used this chapter, so it has been dropped in order to keep the book relatively concise.
- In most chapters, exercises have been added within the chapter, at the end of each section, so that students can check that they have understood the material (answers are at the end of each chapter). The previous edition's exercises (at the end of each chapter) are renamed 'Problems' and are mostly

unchanged (with answers to odd-numbered problems at the end of the book). The new exercises are relatively straightforward and usually require the student to replicate the calculations in the text, but using different data. There is thus a distinction drawn between the *exercises* which check understanding and the *problems* which encourage deeper thinking and discussion.

■ Some of the more challenging problems are indicated by highlighting the problem number in colour. This warns that the problem might require some additional insight or effort to solve, beyond what is learned from the text. This may be because a proof or demonstration is demanded, or that the problem is open-ended and requires interpretation.

■ In a few places I have included some worked examples, but, in general, most of the book uses examples to explain the various techniques. The new exercises may be treated as worked examples if desired, as worked-out answers are given at the end of each chapter.

■ Where appropriate, the examples used in the text have been updated using more recent data.

■ There is a website (**www.pearsoned.co.uk/barrow**) accompanying the text. For this edition the website contains:
  – Powerpoint slides for lecturers to use (these contain most of the key tables, formulae and diagrams, but omit the text). Lecturers can adapt these for their own use.
  – An instructor's manual giving hints and guidance on some of the teaching issues, including those that come up in response to some of the problems.
  – Answers to even-numbered problems (available to lecturers).
  – The chapter on seasonal adjustment of time-series data, mentioned above.

## Mathematics requirements and texts

No more than elementary algebra is assumed in this text, any extensions being covered as they are needed in the book. It is helpful if students are comfortable manipulating equations so if some revision is required I recommend one of the following books:

I. Jacques, *Mathematics for Economics and Business*, Prentice Hall, 2003.

E.T. Dowling, *Mathematics for Economists*, Schaum's Outline Series in Economics, McGraw-Hill, 1986.

J. Black and J. Bradley, *Essential Mathematics for Economists*, 2nd edn, Wiley, 1980.

# Author acknowledgements

I would like to thank the anonymous reviewers who made suggestions for this new edition and the many colleagues and students who have passed on comments or pointed out errors or omissions in previous editions. I would like to thank all those at Pearson Education who have encouraged me, responded to my various queries and reminded me of impending deadlines! Finally, I would like to thank my family for giving me encouragement and the time to complete this new edition.

# Publisher's acknowledgements

We are grateful to the following for permission to reproduce copyright material:

Crown copyright material is reproduced with the permission of the Controller of HMSO and the Queen's Printer for Scotland for the following under a click user licence Figure I1; Figure I2; Table p3; Table 1.1; Figure 1.1; Figure 1.2; Figure 1.3; Table 1.2; Figure 1.4; Figure 1.5; Figure 1.6; Table p15; Table 1.3; Figure 1.7; Figure 1.8; Table 1.4; Figure 1.9; Table 1.12; Figure p23; Figure 1.3 p23; Table p60; Table p61b; Table p326: Table 10.22; Table 10.24; Table 7.1 Todaro's data on birth rate, GNP, growth and inequality and table p45. Data to analyse birthrate from *Economic Development for a Developing World*, 3rd ed, Pearson Education (Todaro, M); 'Cohabitation: not for long but here to stay' from *Journal of Royal Statistical Society*, Series A, 163 (2), Blackwell Publishing (Ermisch J and Francesconi M, 2000); Tab 10.26 from Real GDP per capita for more than one hundred countries *Economic Journal*, Vol. 88 (350) p215–242 Blackwell Publishing (Kravis, Heston and Summers 1978); Table p197 'Road accidents and darkness from some effects on accidents of changes in light conditions at the beginning and end of British Summer Time', *Supplementary Report 587*, Transport and Road Research Laboratory (Green H, 1980).

In some instances we have been unable to trace the owners of copyright material, and we would appreciate any information that would enable us to do so.

# Introduction

Statistics is a subject which can be (and is) applied to every aspect of our lives. A glance at the annual *Guide to Official Statistics* published by the UK Office for National Statistics, for example, gives some idea of the range of material available. Under the letter 'S', for example, one finds entries for such disparate subjects as salaries, schools, semolina(!), shipbuilding, short-time working, spoons, and social surveys. It seems clear that whatever subject you wish to investigate, there are data available to illuminate your study. However, it is a sad fact that many people do not understand the use of statistics, do not know how to draw proper inferences (conclusions) from them, or mis-represent them. Even (especially?) politicians are not immune from this – for example, it sometimes appears they will not be happy until all school pupils and students are above average in ability and achievement.

## Two types of statistics

The subject of statistics can usefully be divided into two parts, descriptive statistics (covered in Chapters 1 and 10 of this book) and inferential statistics (Chapters 4–8), which are based upon the theory of probability (Chapters 2 and 3). Descriptive statistics are used to summarise information which would otherwise be too complex to take in, by means of techniques such as averages and graphs. The graph shown in Figure I.1 is an example, summarising drinking habits in the UK.

The graph reveals, for instance, that about 43% of men and 57% of women drink between 1 and 10 units of alcohol per week (a unit is roughly equivalent to one glass of wine or half a pint of beer). The graph also shows that men tend to drink more than women (this is probably no surprise to you), with higher proportions drinking 11–20 units and over 21 units per week. This simple graph has summarised a vast amount of information, the consumption levels of about 45 million adults.

Even so, it is not perfect and much information is hidden. It is not obvious from the graph that the average consumption of men is 16 units per week, of

**Figure I.1
Alcohol consumption
in the UK**

women only 6 units. From the graph, you would probably have expected the averages to be closer together. This shows that graphical and numerical summary measures can complement each other. Graphs can give a very useful visual summary of the information but are not very precise. For example, it is difficult to convey in words the content of a graph; you have to see it. Numerical measures such as the average are more precise and are easier to convey to others. Imagine you had data for student alcohol consumption; how do you think this would compare to the graph? It would be easy to tell someone whether the average is higher or lower, but comparing the graphs is difficult without actually viewing them.

Statistical inference, the second type of statistics covered, concerns the relationship between a sample of data and the population (in the statistical sense, not necessarily human) from which it is drawn. In particular, it asks what inferences can be validly drawn about the population from the sample. Sometimes the sample is not representative of the population (either due to bad sampling procedures or simply due to bad luck) and does not give us a true picture of reality.

The graph was presented as fact but it is actually based on a sample of individuals, since it would obviously be impossible to ask everyone about their drinking habits. Does it therefore provide a true picture of drinking habits? We can be reasonably confident that it does, for two reasons. First, the government statisticians who collected the data designed the survey carefully, ensuring that all age groups are fairly represented, and did not conduct all the interviews in pubs, for example. Second, the sample is a large one (about 10 000 households) so there is little possibility of getting an unrepresentative sample. It would be very unlucky if the sample consisted entirely of teetotallers, for example. We can be reasonably sure, therefore, that the graph is a fair reflection of reality and that the average woman drinks around 6 units of alcohol per week. However, we must remember that there is some uncertainty about this estimate. Statistical inference provides the tools to measure that uncertainty.

The scatter diagram in Figure I.2 (considered in more detail in Chapter 7) shows the relationship between economic growth and the birth rate in 12 developing countries. It illustrates a negative relationship – higher economic growth appears to be associated with lower birth rates.

Once again we actually have a sample of data, drawn from the population of all countries. What can we infer from the sample? Is it likely that the 'true'

Figure I.2
**Birthrate vs growth rate**

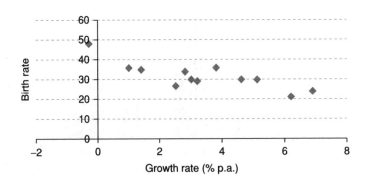

relationship (what we would observe if we had all the data) is similar, or do we have an unrepresentative sample? In this case the sample size is quite small and the sampling method is not known, so we might be cautious in our conclusions.

**Statistics and you**

By the time you have finished this book you will have encountered and, I hope, mastered a range of statistical techniques. However, becoming a competent statistician is about more than learning the techniques, and comes with time and practice. You could go on to learn about the subject at a deeper level and learn some of the many other techniques that are available. However, I believe you can go a long way with the simple methods you learn here, and gain insight into a wide range of problems. A nice example of this is contained in the article 'Error Correction Models: Specification, Interpretation, Estimation', by G. Alogoskoufis and R. Smith in the *Journal of Economic Surveys*, 1991 (vol. 5, pp. 27–128), examining the relationship between wages, prices and other variables. After 19 pages analysing the data using techniques far more advanced than those presented in this book, they state 'the range of statistical techniques utilised have not provided us with anything more than we would have got by taking the [ . . . ] variables and looking at their graphs'. Sometimes advanced techniques are needed, but never underestimate the power of the humble graph.

Beyond a technical mastery of the material, being a statistician encompasses a range of more informal skills which you should endeavour to acquire. I hope that you will learn some of these from reading this book. For example, you should be able to spot errors in analyses presented to you, because your statistical 'intuition' rings a warning bell telling you something is wrong. For example, the *Guardian* newspaper, on its front page, once provided a list of the 'best' schools in England, based on the fact that in each school, every one of its pupils passed a national exam – a 100% success rate. Curiously, all of the schools were relatively small, so perhaps this implies that small schools get better results than large ones. Once you can think statistically you can spot the fallacy in this argument. Try it. The answer is at the end of this introduction.

Here is another example. The UK Department of Health released the following figures about health spending, showing how planned expenditure (in £m) was to increase.

|  | 1998–99 | 1999–00 | 2000–01 | 2001–02 | Total increase over 3-year period |
|---|---|---|---|---|---|
| Health spending | 37 169 | 40 228 | 43 129 | 45 985 | 17 835 |

The total increase in the final column seems implausibly large, especially when compared to the level of spending. The increase is about 45% of the level. This should set off the warning bell, once you have a 'feel' for statistics (and, perhaps, a certain degree of cynicism about politics!). The 'total increase' is the result of counting the increase from 98–99 to 99–00 *three times*, the increase from 99–00 to 00–01 *twice*, plus the increase from 00–01 to 01–02. It therefore measures the *cumulative* extra resources to health care over the whole period, but not the year-on-year increase, which is what many people would interpret it to be.

You will also become aware that data cannot be examined without their context. The context might determine the methods you use to analyse the data, or influence the manner in which the data are collected. For example, the exchange rate and the unemployment rate are two economic variables which behave very differently. The former can change substantially, even on a daily basis, and its movements tend to be unpredictable. Unemployment changes only slowly and if the level is high this month it is likely to be high again next month. There would be little point in calculating the unemployment rate on a daily basis, yet this makes some sense for the exchange rate. Economic theory tells us quite a lot about these variables even before we begin to look at the data. We should therefore learn to be guided by an appropriate theory when looking at the data – it will usually be a much more effective way to proceed.

Another useful skill is the ability to present and explain statistical concepts and results to others. If you really understand something you should be able to explain it to someone else – this is often a good test of your own knowledge. Below are two examples of a verbal explanation of the variance (covered in Chapter 1) to illustrate.

| *Good explanation* | *Bad explanation* |
|---|---|
| The variance of a set of observations expresses how spread out are the numbers. A low value of the variance indicates that the observations are of similar size, a high value indicates that they are widely spread around the average. | The variance is a formula for the deviations, which are squared and added up. The differences are from the mean, and divided by $n$ or sometimes by $n - 1$. |

The bad explanation is a failed attempt to explain the formula for the variance and gives no insight into what it really is. The good explanation tries to convey the meaning of the variance without worrying about the formula (which is best written down). For a (statistically) unsophisticated audience the explanation is quite useful and might then be supplemented by a few examples.

Statistics can also be written well or badly. Two examples follow, concerning a confidence interval, which is explained in Chapter 4. Do not worry if you do not understand the statistics now.

| *Good explanation* | *Bad explanation* |
|---|---|
| The 95% confidence interval is given by $$\bar{x} \pm 1.96 \times \sqrt{s^2/n}$$ Inserting the sample values $\bar{x} = 400$, $s^2 = 1600$ and $n = 30$ into the formula we obtain $$400 \pm 1.96 \times \sqrt{1600/30}$$ yielding the interval [385.7, 414.3] | $95\%$ interval $= \bar{x} - 1.96\sqrt{s^2/n} = \bar{x} + 1.96\sqrt{s^2/n} = 0.95$ $= 400 - 1.96\sqrt{1600/30}$ and $= 400 + 1.96\sqrt{1600/30}$ so we have [385.7, 414.3] |

In good statistical writing there is a logical flow to the argument, like a written sentence. It is also concise and precise, without too much extraneous material. The good explanation exhibits these characteristics whereas the bad explanation is simply wrong and incomprehensible, even though the final answer is correct. You should therefore try to note the way the statistical arguments are laid out in this book, as well as take in their content.

When you do the exercises at the end of each chapter, try to get another student to read your work through. If they cannot understand the flow or logic of your work then you have not succeeded in presenting your work sufficiently accurately.

**Answer to the 'best' schools problem**

A high proportion of small schools appear in the list simply because they are lucky. Consider one school of 20 pupils, another with 1000, where the average ability is similar in both. The large school is highly unlikely to obtain a 100% pass rate, simply because there are so many pupils and (at least) one of them will probably perform badly. With 20 pupils, you have a much better chance of getting them all through. This is just a reflection of the fact that there tends to be greater variability in smaller samples. The schools themselves, and the pupils, are of similar quality.

# 1

# Descriptive statistics

| Contents | |
|---|---|

**Learning outcomes**

By the end of this chapter you should be able to:

■ recognise different types of data and use appropriate methods to summarise and analyse them

■ use graphical techniques to provide a visual summary of one or more data series

■ use numerical techniques (such as an average) to summarise data series

■ recognise the strengths and limitations of such methods

■ recognise the usefulness of data transformations to gain additional insight into a set of data

# Introduction

The aim of descriptive statistical methods is simple: to present information in a clear, concise and accurate manner. The difficulty in analysing many phenomena, be they economic, social or otherwise, is that there is simply too much information for the mind to assimilate. The task of descriptive methods is therefore to summarise all this information and draw out the main features, without distorting the picture.

Consider, for example, the problem of presenting information about the wealth of British citizens (which follows later in this chapter). There are about 17 million households on which data are available and to present the data in raw form (i.e. the wealth holdings of each and every family) would be neither useful nor informative (it would take about 30 000 pages of a book, for example). It would be more useful to have much less information, but information which was still representative of the original data. In doing this, much of the original information would be deliberately lost; in fact, descriptive statistics might be described as the art of constructively throwing away much of the data!

There are many ways of summarising data and there are few hard and fast rules about how you should proceed. Newspapers and magazines often provide innovative (though not always successful) ways of presenting data. There are, however, a number of techniques which are tried and tested and these are the subject of this chapter. These are successful because (a) they tell us something useful about the underlying data, and (b) they are reasonably familiar to many people, so we can all talk in a common language. For example, the average tells us about the location of the data and is a familiar concept to most people. For example, my son talks of his day at school being 'average'.

The appropriate method of analysing the data will depend on a number of factors: the type of data under consideration, the sophistication of the audience and the 'message' which it is intended to convey. One would use different methods to persuade academics of the validity of one's theory about inflation than one would use to persuade consumers that Brand X powder washes whiter than Brand Y. To illustrate the use of the various methods, three different topics are covered in this chapter. First, we look at the relationship between educational attainment and employment prospects. Do higher qualifications improve your employment chances? The data come from people surveyed in 2003, so we have a sample of cross-section data giving a picture of the situation at one point in time. We look at the distribution of educational attainments amongst those surveyed, as well as the relationship to employment outcomes.

Second, we examine the distribution of wealth in the United Kingdom in 2001. The data are again cross-section, but this time we can use more sophisticated methods since wealth is measured on a ratio scale. Someone with £200 000 of wealth is twice as wealthy as someone with £100 000 for example, and there is a meaning to this ratio. In the case of education, one cannot say with any precision that one person is twice as educated as another (hence the perennial debate about educational standards). The educational categories may be ordered (so one person can be more educated than another) but we cannot measure the 'distance' between them. We refer to education being measured on an ordinal scale. In contrast, there is not an obvious natural ordering to the three employment categories (employed, unemployed, inactive), so this is measured on a nominal scale.

Third, we look at investment over the period 1970 to 2002. This uses time series data, since we have a number of observations on the variable measured at different points in time. Here it is important to take account of the time dimension of the data: things would look different if the observations were in the order 1970, 1983, 1977, . . . rather than in correct time order. We also look at the relationship between two variables, investment and output, over that period of time and find appropriate methods of presenting it.

In all three cases we make use of both graphical and numerical methods of summarising the data. Although there are some differences between the methods used in the three cases these are not watertight compartments: the methods used in one case might also be suitable in another, perhaps with slight modification. Part of the skill of the statistician is to know which methods of analysis and presentation are best suited to each particular problem.

## Summarising data using graphical techniques

**Education and employment, or, after all this, will you get a job?**

We begin by looking at a question which should be of interest to you: how does education affect your chances of getting a job? With unemployment at high levels in many developed and developing countries around the world, one of the possible benefits of investing in education is that it reduces the chances of being out of work. But by how much does it reduce those chances? We shall use a variety of graphical techniques to explore the question.

The raw data for this investigation come from *Education and Training Statistics for the U.K. 2003*. Some of these data are presented in Table 1.1 and show the numbers of people by employment status (either in work, unemployed, or inactive, i.e. not seeking work) and by educational qualification (higher education, A-levels, other qualification, or no qualification). The table gives a cross-tabulation of employment status by educational qualification and is simply a count (the frequency) of the number of people falling into each of the 12 cells of the table. For example, there were 8 224 000 people in work who had experience of higher education. This is part of a total of just over 37 million people of working age.

**The bar chart**

The first graphical technique we shall use is the bar chart and this is shown in Figure 1.1. This summarises the educational qualifications of those in work, i.e.

**Table 1.1** Economic status and educational qualifications, 2003 (numbers in 000s)

|  | Higher education | A levels | Other qualification | No qualification | Total |
|---|---|---|---|---|---|
| In work | 8 224 | 5 654 | 11 167 | 2 583 | 27 628 |
| Unemployed | 217 | 231 | 693 | 303 | 1 444 |
| Inactive | 956 | 1 354 | 3 107 | 2 549 | 7 966 |
| Totals | 9 397 | 7 239 | 14 967 | 5 435 | 37 038 |

**Figure 1.1 Educational qualifications of people in work in the UK, 2003**

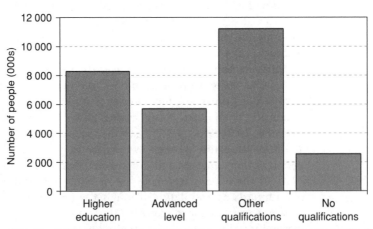

*Note*: The height of each bar is determined by the associated frequency. The first bar is 8224 units high, the second is 5654 units high, and so on. The ordering of the bars could be reversed ('no qualifications' becoming the first category) without altering the message.

**Figure 1.2**
**Educational
qualifications by
employment category**

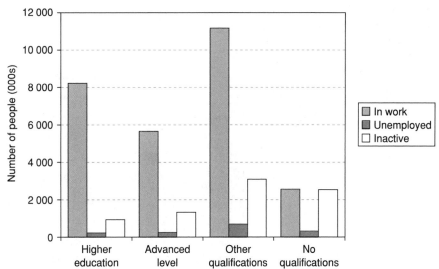

*Note*: The bars for the unemployed and inactive categories are constructed in the same way as for those in work: the height of the bar is determined by the frequency.

the data in the first row of the table. The four educational categories are arranged along the horizontal (*x*) axis, while the frequencies are measured on the vertical (*y*) axis. The height of each bar represents the numbers in work for that category.

The biggest group is seen to be those with 'other qualifications' which is nearly as big as the 'higher education' and 'A-level' categories put together. The 'no qualifications' category is the smallest though it does make up a substantial fraction of those in work.

It would be interesting to compare this distribution with those for the unemployed and inactive. This is done in Figure 1.2, which adds bars for these other two categories.

This multiple bar chart shows that the sizes of the unemployed and inactive categories get larger, the lower the level of educational qualification obtained. The 'no qualifications' category is numerically unimportant relative to the others, so is difficult to compare directly, but the unemployed and inactive are large compared to those in work.

Figure 1.3 shows an alternative method of presentation: the stacked bar chart. In this case the bars are stacked one on top of another instead of being placed side by side.

A clearer picture emerges if the data are transformed to (column) percentages, i.e. the columns are expressed as percentages of the column totals. This makes it easier to directly compare the different educational categories. We can then see, of those in higher education, what proportion are in work (88%), and so on. These figures are shown in Table 1.2.

Having done this, it is easier to make a direct comparison of the different education categories (columns). This is shown in Figure 1.4, where all the bars are of the same height (representing 100%) and the components of each bar

**Figure 1.3**
**Stacked bar chart of educational qualifications and employment status**

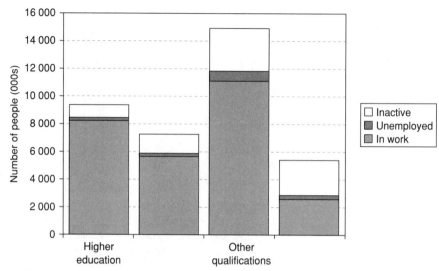

*Note*: The overall height of each bar is determined by the sum of the frequencies of the category, given in the final row of Table 1.1.

**Table 1.2 Economic status and educational qualifications: column percentages**

|  | Higher education | A levels | Other qualification | No qualification | All |
|---|---|---|---|---|---|
| In work | 88% | 78% | 74% | 48% | 75% |
| Unemployed | 2% | 3% | 5% | 6% | 4% |
| Inactive | 10% | 19% | 21% | 47% | 21% |

*Note*: The column percentages are obtained by dividing each frequency by the column total. For example, 88% is 8224 divided by 9397; 78% is 5654 divided by 7239, etc.

**Figure 1.4**
**Percentages in each employment category, by educational qualification**

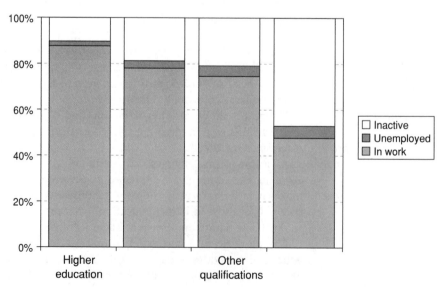

now show the *proportions* of people in each educational category either in work, unemployed or inactive.

It is now clear how economic status differs according to education and the result is quite dramatic. In particular:

■ The probability of unemployment increases rapidly with lower educational attainment (this interprets proportions as probabilities, i.e. if 10% are out of work then the probability that a person picked at random is unemployed is 10%).
■ The biggest difference is between the no qualifications category and the other three, which have relatively slight differences between them.

Can we safely conclude therefore that the probability of your being unemployed is significantly reduced by education? Could we go further and argue that the route to lower unemployment generally is via investment in education? The answer *may* be 'yes' to both questions, but we have not proved it. Two important considerations are as follows:

■ Innate ability has been ignored. Those with higher ability are more likely to be employed *and* are more likely to receive more education. Ideally we would like to compare individuals of similar ability but with different amounts of education; however, it is difficult to get such data.
■ Even if additional education does reduce a person's probability of becoming unemployed, this may be at the expense of someone else, who loses their job to the more educated individual. In other words, additional education does not reduce total unemployment but only shifts it around amongst the labour force. Of course, it is still rational for individuals to invest in education if they do not take account of this externality.

**The pie chart**

Another useful way of presenting information graphically is the pie chart, which is particularly good at describing how a variable is distributed between different categories. For example, from Table 1.1 we have the distribution of people by educational qualification (the first row of the table). This can be shown in a pie chart as in Figure 1.5.

**Figure 1.5**
**Educational qualifications of those in work**

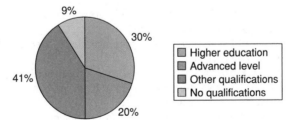

*Note*: If you have to draw a pie chart by hand, the angle of each slice can be calculated as follows:

$$\text{angle} = \frac{frequency}{total\ frequency} \times 360$$

The angle of the first slice, for example, is

$$\frac{8224}{27\ 628} \times 360 = 107.2°$$

Figure 1.6
**Educational
qualifications of the
unemployed**

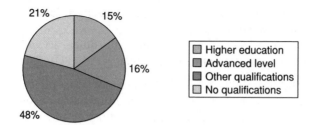

The area of each slice is proportional to the respective frequency and the pie chart is an alternative means of presentation to the bar chart shown in Figure 1.1. The percentages falling into each education category have been added around the chart, but this is not essential. For presentational purposes it is best not to have too many slices in the chart: beyond about six the chart tends to look crowded.

The chart reveals that around 40% of those employed fall into the 'other qualification' category, and that just 9% have no qualifications. This may be contrasted with Figure 1.6 which shows a similar chart for the unemployed (the second row of Table 1.1).

The 'other qualification' category is about the same size, but the 'no qualification' group is bigger and now accounts for 21% of the unemployed. Further, the proportion with a degree halves from 30% to 15%.

Using such graphs we are able to present the main features revealed by the data in an arresting way. If done correctly it is an extremely effective way of getting a message across.

---

### Producing charts using Microsoft Excel

Most of the charts in this book were produced using Excel's charting facility. Without wishing to dictate a precise style, you should aim for a similar, uncluttered look. Some tips you might find useful are:

■ Make the grid lines dashed in a light grey colour (they are not actually part of the chart, hence should be discreet).

■ Get rid of the background fill (grey by default, alter to 'No fill'). It does not look great when printed.

■ On the x-axis, make the labels horizontal or vertical, not slanted – it is then difficult to see which point they refer to. If they are slanted, double click on the x-axis then click the alignment tab.

■ Colour charts look great on-screen but unclear if printed in black and white. Change the style type of the lines or markers (e.g. make some dashed) to distinguish them on paper.

■ Both axes start at zero by default. If all your observations are large numbers this may result in the data points being crowded into one corner of the graph. Alter the scale on the axes to fix this – set the minimum value on the axis to be slightly less than the minimum observation.

Otherwise, Excel's default options will usually give a good result.

The following table shows the total numbers (in millions) of tourists visiting each country and the numbers of English tourists visiting each country:

|  | France | Germany | Italy | Spain |
|---|---|---|---|---|
| All tourists | 12.4 | 3.2 | 7.5 | 9.8 |
| English tourists | 2.7 | 0.2 | 1.0 | 3.6 |

(a)  Draw a bar chart showing the total numbers visiting each country.

(b)  Draw a stacked bar chart, which shows English and non-English tourists making up the total visitors to each country.

(c)  Draw a pie chart showing the distribution of all tourists between the four destination countries. Do the same for English tourists and compare results.

# Looking at cross-section data: wealth in the UK in 2001

**Frequency tables and histograms**

We now move on to examine data in a different form. The data on employment and education consisted simply of frequencies, where a characteristic (such as higher education) was either present or absent for a particular individual. We now look at the distribution of wealth, a variable which can be measured on a ratio scale so that a different value is associated with each individual. For example, one person might have £1000 of wealth, another might have £1 million. Different presentational techniques will be used to analyse this type of data. We use these techniques to investigate questions such as how much wealth does the average person have and whether wealth is evenly distributed or not.

The data are given in Table 1.3 which shows the distribution of wealth in the UK for the year 2001 (the latest available at the time of writing), taken from *Inland Revenue Statistics* 2003. This is an example of a frequency table. Wealth is difficult to define and to measure; the data shown here refer to *marketable* wealth

Table 1.3 **The distribution of wealth, UK, 2001**

| Class interval | Numbers (thousands) |
|---|---|
| 0–9 999 | 3 417 |
| 10 000–24 999 | 1 303 |
| 25 000–39 999 | 1 240 |
| 40 000–49 999 | 714 |
| 50 000–59 999 | 642 |
| 60 000–79 999 | 1 361 |
| 80 000–99 999 | 1 270 |
| 100 000–149 999 | 2 708 |
| 150 000–199 000 | 1 633 |
| 200 000–299 000 | 1 242 |
| 300 000–499 999 | 870 |
| 500 000–999 999 | 367 |
| 1 000 000–1 999 999 | 125 |
| 2 000 000 or more | 41 |
| Total | 16 933 |

(i.e. items such as the right to a pension, which cannot be sold, are excluded) and are estimates for the population as a whole based on taxation data.

Wealth is divided into 14 class intervals: £0 up to (but not including) £10 000; £10 000 up to £24 999, etc. and the number of individuals (or frequency) within each class interval is shown. Note that the class widths vary up the wealth scale: the first is £10 000, the second £15 000; the third £15 000 also, and so on. This will prove an important factor when it comes to graphical presentation of the data.

This table has been constructed from the original 16 933 000 observations on individuals' wealth, so it is already a summary of the original data (note that all the frequencies have been expressed in thousands in the table) and much of the original information is lost. The first decision to make when drawing up such a frequency table from the raw data is how many class intervals to have, and how wide they should be. It simplifies matters if they are all of the same width but in this case it is not feasible: if 10 000 were chosen as the standard width there would be many intervals between 500 000 and 1 000 000 (50 of them in fact), most of which would have a zero or very low frequency. If 100 000 were the standard width there would be only a few intervals and the first (0–100 000) would contain 9947 observations (59% of all observations) so almost all the interesting detail would be lost. A compromise between these extremes has to be found.

A useful rule of thumb is that the number of class intervals should equal the square root of the total frequency, subject to a maximum of about 12 intervals. Thus, for example, a total of 25 observations should be allocated to five intervals; 100 observations should be grouped into 10 intervals; and 16 933 should be grouped into about 12 (14 are used here). The class widths should be equal in so far as this is feasible, but should increase when the frequencies become very small.

To present these data graphically one could draw a bar chart as in the case of education above, and this is presented in Figure 1.7. Before reading on, spend some time looking at it and ask yourself what is wrong with it.

**Figure 1.7**
**Bar chart of the distribution of wealth in the UK, 2001**

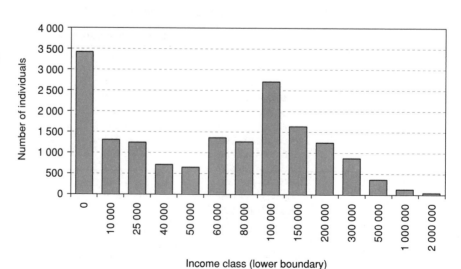

**Figure 1.8**
**The wealth distribution with different class intervals**

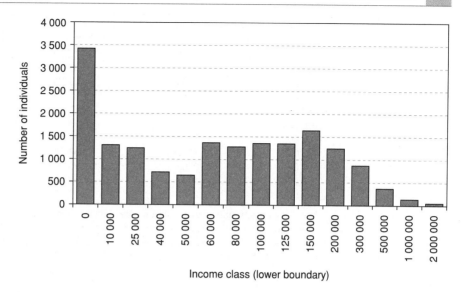

The answer is that the figure gives a completely misleading picture of the data! (Incidentally, this is the picture that you will get using a spreadsheet computer program, as I have done here. All the standard packages appear to do this, so beware. One wonders how many decisions have been influenced by data presented in this incorrect manner.)

Why is the figure wrong? Consider the following argument. The diagram appears to show that there is a concentration of individuals above £60 000 (the frequency jumps from 642 to 1361) and above £100 000 (a jump from 1270 to 2708). But this is just the result of the change in the class width at these points (to 20 000 at £60 000 and to 50 000 at £100 000). Suppose that we divide up the £100 000–£150 000 class into two: £100 000 to £125 000 and £125 000 to £150 000. We divide the frequency of 2708 equally between the two (this is an arbitrary decision but illustrates the point). The graph now looks like Figure 1.8.

Comparing Figures 1.7 and 1.8 reveals a difference: the hump at £100 000 has now disappeared. But this is disturbing – it means that the shape of the distribution can be altered simply by altering the class widths. If so, how can we rely upon visual inspection of the distribution? A better method would make the shape of the distribution independent of how the class intervals are arranged. This can be done by drawing a histogram.

**The histogram**

A histogram is similar to a bar chart except that it corrects for differences in class widths. If all the class widths are identical then there is no difference between a bar chart and a histogram. The calculations required to produce the histogram are shown in Table 1.4.

The new column in the table shows the frequency density which is defined as follows:

**(1.1)**    $frequency\ density = \dfrac{frequency}{class\ width}$

Table 1.4 **Calculation of frequency densities**

| Range | Number | Class width | Frequency density |
|---|---|---|---|
| 0– | 3417 | 10 000 | 0.3417 |
| 10 000– | 1303 | 15 000 | 0.0869 |
| 25 000– | 1240 | 15 000 | 0.0827 |
| 40 000– | 714 | 10 000 | 0.0714 |
| 50 000– | 642 | 10 000 | 0.0642 |
| 60 000– | 1361 | 20 000 | 0.0681 |
| 80 000– | 1270 | 20 000 | 0.0635 |
| 100 000– | 2708 | 50 000 | 0.0542 |
| 150 000– | 1633 | 50 000 | 0.0327 |
| 200 000– | 2645 | 3 800 000 | 0.0007 |

*Note*: As an alternative to the frequency density, one could calculate the frequency per 'standard' class width, with the standard width chosen to be 10 000 (the narrowest class). The values in column 4 would then be 3417; 868.7 (= 1303 ÷ 1.5); 826.7; etc. This would lead to the same shape of histogram as using the frequency density.

Using this formula corrects the figures for differing class widths. The principle behind this correction is that if the class width doubles, then we halve the frequency to compensate. If the width quadruples, we divide by four, and so on. The simple way to carry out this correction is to divide each frequency by the class width. Thus 0.3417 = 3417/10 000 is the first frequency density, 0.0869 = 1303/15 000 is the second, etc. Above £200 000 the class widths are very large and the frequencies small (too small to appear on the histogram), so these classes have been combined.

The width of the final interval is unknown, so has to be estimated in order to calculate the frequency density. It is likely to be extremely wide since the wealthiest person may well have assets valued at several £m. (or even £bn); the value we assume will affect the calculation of the frequency density and therefore of the shape of the histogram. Fortunately it is in the tail of the distribution and only affects a small number of observations. Here we assume (arbitrarily) a width of £3.8m. to be a 'reasonable' figure, giving an upper class boundary of £4m.

The frequency density is then plotted on the vertical axis against wealth on the horizontal axis to give the histogram. One further point needs to be made: the scale on the wealth axis should be linear as far as possible, e.g. £50 000 should be twice as far from the origin as £25 000. However, it is difficult to fit all the values onto the horizontal axis without squeezing the graph excessively at lower levels of wealth, where most observations are located. Therefore the classes above £100 000 have been squeezed and the reader's attention is drawn to this. The result is shown in Figure 1.9.

The effect of taking frequency densities is to make the *area* of each block in the histogram represent the frequency, rather than the height, which now shows the density. This has the effect of giving an accurate picture of the shape of the distribution.

Having done all this, what does the histogram show? The highlights are:

**Figure 1.9**
**Histogram of the distribution of wealth in the UK, 2001**

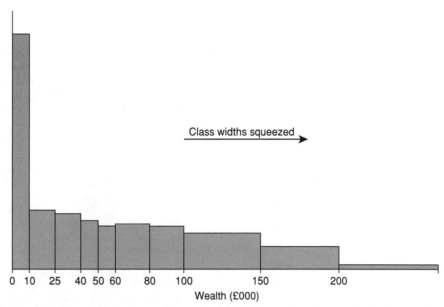

*Note*: A frequency polygon would be the result if, instead of drawing blocks for the histogram, one drew lines connecting the centres of the top of each block.

■ The histogram is heavily skewed to the right (i.e. the long tail is to the right). Most people have modest levels of wealth; a few have a great deal.
■ The modal class interval is £0–£10 000 (i.e. has the greatest density: no other £10 000 interval has more individuals in it).
■ The majority of people (51.2% in fact) have less than £80 000 of marketable wealth.
■ About 16% of people have more than £200 000 of wealth.[1]

The figure shows quite a high degree of inequality in the wealth distribution. Whether this is acceptable or even desirable is a value judgement. It should be noted that part of the inequality is due to differences in age: younger people have not yet had enough time to acquire much wealth and therefore appear worse off, although in life-time terms this may not be the case. To get a better picture of the distribution of wealth would require some analysis of the acquisition of wealth over the life-cycle. In fact, correcting for age differences does not make a big difference to the pattern of wealth distribution (on this point and on inequality in wealth in general, see Atkinson (1983), chapters 7 and 8).

**Relative frequency and cumulative frequency distributions**

The wealth distribution may also be illustrated using relative and cumulative frequencies of the data. These values are calculated in Table 1.5.

The relative frequencies show the *proportion* of observations that fall into each class interval, so, for example, 4.2% of individuals have wealth holdings

---

[1] Due to the compressing of some class widths, it is difficult to see this accurately on the histogram. There are limitations to graphical presentation.

### The AIDS epidemic

To show how descriptive statistics can be helpful in presenting information we show below the 'population pyramid' for Botswana (one of the countries most seriously affected by AIDS), projected for the year 2020. This is essentially two bar charts (one for men, one for women) laid on their sides, showing the frequencies in each age category (rather than wealth categories). The inner pyramid (in the darker colour) shows the projected population given the existence of AIDS; the outer pyramid assumes no deaths from AIDS.

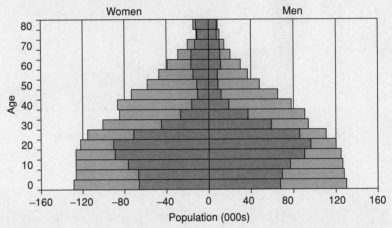

Original source of data: US Census Bureau, *World Population Profile 2000*. Graph adapted from the UNAIDS website at http://www.unaids.org/epidemic_update/report/Epi_report.htm#thepopulation.

One can immediately see the huge effect of AIDS, especially on the 40–60 age group (currently aged 20–40), for both men and women. These people would normally be in the most productive phase of their lives but, with AIDS, the country will suffer enormously with many old and young people dependent on a small working population. The severity of the future problems is brought out vividly in this simple graphic, based on the bar chart.

between £40 000 and £50 000. Relative frequencies are shown in the third column, using the following formula:[2]

$$(1.2) \qquad relative\ frequency = \frac{frequency}{sum\ of\ frequencies} = \frac{f}{\Sigma f}$$

The sum of the relative frequencies has to be 100% and this acts as a check on the calculations.

The cumulative frequencies, shown in the fourth column, are obtained by cumulating (successively adding) the frequencies. The cumulative frequencies show the total number of individuals with wealth *up to* a given amount; for example, about ten million people have less than £100 000 of wealth.

---

[2] If you are unfamiliar with the $\Sigma$ notation then read Appendix 1A to this chapter before continuing.

**Figure 1.10**
The relative frequency distribution of wealth in the UK, 2001

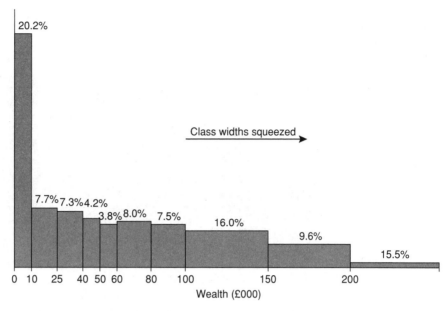

**Table 1.5** Calculation of relative and cumulative frequencies

| Range | Frequency | Relative frequency (%) | Cumulative frequency |
|---|---|---|---|
| 0– | 3 417 | 20.2 | 3 417 |
| 10 000– | 1 303 | 7.7 | 4 720 |
| 25 000– | 1 240 | 7.3 | 5 960 |
| 40 000– | 714 | 4.2 | 6 674 |
| 50 000– | 642 | 3.8 | 7 316 |
| 60 000– | 1 361 | 8.0 | 8 677 |
| 80 000– | 1 270 | 7.5 | 9 947 |
| 100 000– | 2 708 | 16.0 | 12 655 |
| 150 000– | 1 633 | 9.6 | 14 288 |
| 200 000– | 1 242 | 7.3 | 15 530 |
| 300 000– | 870 | 5.1 | 16 400 |
| 500 000– | 367 | 2.2 | 16 767 |
| 1 000 000– | 125 | 0.7 | 16 892 |
| 2 000 000– | 41 | 0.2 | 16 933 |
| Totals | 16 933 | 100.0 | |

*Note*: Relative frequencies are calculated in the same way as the column percentages in Table 1.2. Thus for example, 20.2% is 3417 divided by 16 933. Cumulative frequencies are obtained by cumulating, or successively adding, the frequencies. For example, 4720 is 3417+ 1303, 5960 is 4720 + 1240, etc.

Both relative and cumulative frequency distributions can be drawn, in a similar way to the histogram. In fact, the relative frequency distribution has exactly the same shape as the frequency distribution. This is shown in Figure 1.10. This time we have written the relative frequencies above the appropriate column, though this is not essential.

**Figure 1.11**
**The cumulative frequency distribution of wealth in the UK, 2001**

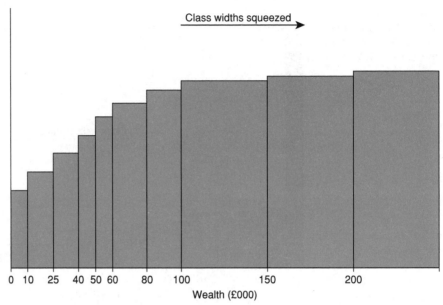

*Note*: The *y*-axis coordinates are obtained by cumulating the frequency densities in Table 1.4 above. For example, the first two *y* coordinates are 0.3417, 0.4286.

The cumulative frequency distribution is shown in Figure 1.11, where the blocks increase in height as wealth increases. The simplest way to draw this is to cumulate the frequency densities (shown in the final column of Table 1.4) and to use these values as the *y*-axis coordinates.

**Worked example 1.1**

There is a mass of detail in the sections above so this worked example is intended to focus on the essential calculations required to produce the summary graphs. Simple artificial data are deliberately used to avoid the distraction of a lengthy interpretation of the results and their meaning. The data on the variable *X* and its frequencies *f* are shown in the following table, with the calculations required:

| X | Frequency, *f* | Relative frequency | Cumulative frequency, *F* |
|---|---|---|---|
| 10 | 6 | 0.17 | 6 |
| 11 | 8 | 0.23 | 14 |
| 12 | 15 | 0.43 | 29 |
| 13 | 5 | 0.14 | 34 |
| 14 | 1 | 0.03 | 35 |
| Totals | 35 | 1.00 | |

*Notes*:
The *X* values are unique but could be considered the mid-point of a range, as earlier.
The relative frequencies are calculated as 0.17 = 6/35, 0.23 = 8/35, etc.
The cumulative frequencies are calculated as 14 = 6 + 8, 29 = 6 + 8 + 15, etc.
The symbol *F* usually denotes the cumulative frequency in statistical work.

The resulting bar chart and cumulative frequency distribution are:

**Bar chart of variable X**

and

**Cumulative frequency distribution of X**

Given the following data:

| Range | Frequency |
| --- | --- |
| 0–10 | 20 |
| 11–30 | 40 |
| 31–60 | 30 |
| 61–100 | 20 |

(a)  Draw both a bar chart and a histogram of the data and compare them.

(b)  Calculate cumulative frequencies and draw a cumulative frequency diagram.

# Summarising data using numerical techniques

Graphical methods are an excellent means of obtaining a quick overview of the data, but they are not particularly precise, nor do they lend themselves to further analysis. For this we must turn to numerical measures such as the average.

There are a number of different ways in which we may describe a distribution such as that for wealth. If we think of trying to describe the histogram, it is useful to have:

■ A measure of location giving an idea of whether people own a lot of wealth or a little. An example is the average, which gives some idea of where the distribution is located along the x-axis.
■ A measure of dispersion showing how wealth is dispersed around (usually) the average, whether it is concentrated close to the average or is generally far away from it. An example here is the standard deviation.
■ A measure of skewness showing how symmetric or not the distribution is, i.e. whether the left half of the distribution is a mirror image of the right half or not. This is obviously not the case for the wealth distribution.

We consider each type of measure in turn.

**Measures of location: the mean**

The arithmetic mean, commonly called the average, is the most familiar measure of location, and is obtained simply by adding all the observations and dividing by the number of observations. We denote the wealth of the ith household by $x_i$ (so that the index $i$ runs from 1 to $N$, where $N$ is the number of observations). As an example, $x_3$ is the wealth of the third household. The mean is then given by the following formula:

$$(1.3) \qquad \mu = \frac{\sum_{i=1}^{i=N} x_i}{N}$$

where $\mu$ (the Greek letter mu, pronounced 'myu') denotes the mean and $\sum_{i=1}^{i=N} x_i$ (read 'sigma x i, from $i = 1$ to $N$', $\Sigma$ being the Greek capital letter sigma) means the sum of the x values. We may simplify this to

$$(1.4) \qquad \mu = \frac{\sum x}{N}$$

when it is obvious which x values are being summed (usually all the available observations). This latter form is more easily readable and we will generally use this.

Formula 1.3 can only be used when all the individual x values are known. The frequency table does not show all 17 million observations, however, but only the range of values for each class interval and the associated frequency. In this case of grouped data the following formula may be used:

$$(1.5) \qquad \mu = \frac{\sum_{i=1}^{i=C} f_i x_i}{\sum_{i=1}^{i=C} f_i}$$

or, more simply,

$$(1.6) \qquad \mu = \frac{\sum fx}{\sum f}$$

In this formula:

- $x$ denotes the mid-point of each class interval, since the individual $x$ values are unknown. The mid-point is used as the representative $x$ value for each class. In the first class interval, for example, we do not know precisely where each of the 3417 observations lies. Hence we *assume* they all lie at the mid-point, £5000. This will cause a slight inaccuracy – because the distribution is so skewed, there are more households below the mid-point than above it in every class interval except, perhaps, the first. We ignore this problem here, and it is less of a problem for most distributions which are less skewed than this one.
- The summation runs from 1 to $C$, the number of class intervals, or distinct $x$ values. $f$ times $x$ gives the total wealth in each class interval. If we sum over the 14 class intervals we get the total wealth of all individuals.
- $\Sigma f_i = N$ gives the total number of observations, the sum of the individual frequencies. The calculation of the mean, $\mu$, for the wealth data is shown in Table 1.6.

Hence we obtain:

$$\mu = \frac{2\,225\,722.5}{16\,933} = 133.443$$

Note that the $x$ values are expressed in £000, so we must remember that the mean will also be in £000; the average wealth holding is therefore £131 443. Note that the frequencies have also been divided by 1000 but this has no effect upon the calculation of the mean since $f$ appears in both numerator and denominator of the formula for the mean.

The mean tells us that if the total wealth were divided up equally between all individuals, each would have £131 443. This value may seem surprising,

**Table 1.6** The calculation of average wealth

| Range | x | f | fx |
|---|---|---|---|
| 0– | 5.0 | 3 417 | 17 085.0 |
| 10 000– | 17.5 | 1 303 | 22 802.5 |
| 25 000– | 32.5 | 1 240 | 40 300.0 |
| 40 000– | 45.0 | 714 | 32 130.0 |
| 50 000– | 55.0 | 642 | 35 310.0 |
| 60 000– | 70.0 | 1 361 | 95 270.0 |
| 80 000– | 90.0 | 1 270 | 114 300.0 |
| 100 000– | 125.0 | 2 708 | 338 500.0 |
| 150 000– | 175.0 | 1 633 | 285 775.0 |
| 200 000– | 250.0 | 1 242 | 310 500.0 |
| 300 000– | 400.0 | 870 | 348 000.0 |
| 500 000– | 750.0 | 367 | 275 250.0 |
| 1 000 000– | 1500.0 | 125 | 187 500.0 |
| 2 000 000– | 3000.0 | 41 | 123 000.0 |
| Totals | | 16 933 | 2 225 722.5 |

*Note*: The *fx* column gives the product of the values in the *f* and *x* columns (so, for example, 5.0 × 3417 = 17 085.0, which is the total wealth held by those in the first class interval). The sum of the *fx* values gives total wealth.

since the histogram clearly shows most people have wealth below this point (approximately 70% of individuals are below the mean, in fact). The mean does not seem to be typical of the wealth that most people have. The reason the mean has such a high value is that there are some individuals whose wealth is way above the figure of £133 443 – up into the £millions, in fact. The mean is the 'balancing point' of the distribution – if the histogram were a physical model, it would balance on a fulcrum placed at 133 443. The few very high wealth levels exert a lot of leverage and counter-balance the more numerous individuals below the mean.

---

**Worked example 1.2**

Suppose we have 10 families with a single television in their homes, 12 families with two televisions each and three families with three. You can probably work out in your head that there are 43 televisions in total (10 + 24 + 9) owned by the 25 families (10 + 12 + 3). The average number of televisions per family is therefore 43/25 = 1.72.

Setting this out formally, we have (as for the wealth distribution, but simpler):

| $x$ | $f$ | $fx$ |
|---|---|---|
| 1 | 10 | 10 |
| 2 | 12 | 24 |
| 3 | 3 | 9 |
| Totals | 25 | 43 |

This gives our resulting mean as 1.72. Note that our data are discrete values in this case and we have the actual values, not a broad class interval.

---

**The mean as the expected value**

We also refer to the mean as the expected value of $x$ and write:

**(1.7)**    $E(x) = \mu = 133\ 443$

$E(x)$ is read 'E of $x$' or 'the expected value of $x$'. The mean is the expected value in the sense that if we selected a household at random from the population we would 'expect' its wealth to be £133 443. It is important to note that this a *statistical* expectation, rather than the everyday use of the term. Most of the random individuals we encounter have wealth substantially below this value. Most people might therefore 'expect' a lower value because that is their everyday experience; but statisticians are different, they always expect the mean value.

The expected value notation is particularly useful in keeping track of the effects upon the mean of certain data transformations (e.g. dividing wealth by 1000 also divides the mean by 1000); Appendix 1B provides a detailed explanation. Use is also made of the E operator in inferential statistics, to describe the properties of estimators (see Chapter 4).

**The sample mean and the population mean**

Very often we have only a sample of data (as in the worked example above), and it is important to distinguish this case from the one where we have all the possible observations. For this reason, the sample mean is given by:

(1.8)    $\bar{x} = \dfrac{\Sigma x}{n}$ or $\bar{x} = \dfrac{\Sigma fx}{\Sigma f}$ for grouped data

Note the distinctions between $\mu$ (the population mean) and $\bar{x}$ (the sample mean), and between $N$ (the size of the population) and $n$ (the sample size). Otherwise, the calculations are identical. It is a convention to use Greek letters, such as $\mu$, to refer to the population and Roman letters, such as $\bar{x}$, to refer to a sample.

**The weighted average**

Sometimes observations have to be given different weightings in calculating the average, as the following example. Consider the problem of calculating the average spending per pupil by an education authority. The figures for spending on primary (ages 5 to 11), secondary (11 to 16) and post-16 pupils are given in Table 1.7.

Clearly, significantly more is spent on secondary and post-16 pupils (a general pattern throughout England and most other countries) and the overall average should lie somewhere between 890 and 1910. However, taking a simple average of these three values would give the wrong answer, because there may be different numbers of children in the three age ranges. The numbers and proportions of children in each age group are given in Table 1.8.

Since there are relatively more primary school children than secondary, and relatively fewer post-16 pupils, the primary unit cost should be given greatest weight in the averaging process and the post-16 unit cost the least. The weighted average is obtained by multiplying each unit cost figure by the proportion of children in each category and summing. The weighted average is therefore

(1.9)    $0.444 \times 890 + 0.389 \times 1450 + 0.167 \times 1910 = 1277.8$

The weighted average gives an answer closer to the primary unit cost than does the simple average (1416.7 in this case) of the three figures, which would be misleading. The formula for the weighted average is

(1.10)    $\bar{x}_w = \Sigma_i w_i x_i$

where $w$ represents the weights, *which must sum to one*, i.e.

(1.11)    $\Sigma_i w_i = 1$

and $x$ represents the unit cost figures.

**Table 1.7** Cost per pupil in different types of school (£ p.a.)

|  | Primary | Secondary | Post-16 |
|---|---|---|---|
| Unit cost | 890 | 1450 | 1910 |

**Table 1.8** Numbers and proportions of pupils in each age range

|  | Primary | Secondary | Post-16 | Total |
|---|---|---|---|---|
| Numbers | 8000 | 7000 | 3000 | 18 000 |
| Proportion | 44.4% | 38.9% | 16.7% |  |

---

### Calculating your degree result

If you are a university student your final degree result will probably be calculated as a weighted average of your marks on the individual courses. The weights may be based on the credits associated with each course or on some other factors. For example, in my university students taking law, with one year spent abroad, had their degree mark (the grand average, G) calculated as

$$G = \frac{0.75L + 0.25S + 0.25Y}{1.25}$$

where $L$ represents the mark on their law course, $S$ the mark on the school (non-law) course, and $Y$ is the mark for the year-abroad dissertation.

Note that the weight on the major course is actually $0.75/1.25 = 0.60$, not 0.75, but it is felt easier to express the formula in the form above. In my experience many people (including some faculty and administrators) have difficulty calculating a weighted average, so you may want to check that yours has been done correctly! You clearly have an interest in learning how to calculate the weighted average.

---

## The median

Returning to the study of wealth, the unrepresentative result for the mean suggests that we may prefer a measure of location which is not so strongly affected by outliers (extreme observations) and skewness.

The median is a measure of location which is more robust to such extreme values; it may be defined by the following procedure. Imagine everyone in a line from poorest to wealthiest. Go to the individual located halfway along the line. Ask her what her wealth is. Her answer is the median. The median is clearly unaffected by extreme values, unlike the mean: if the wealth of the richest person were doubled (with no reduction in anyone else's wealth) there would be no effect upon the median. The calculation of the median is not so straightforward as for the mean, especially for grouped data. The following worked example shows how to calculate the median for ungrouped data.

---

**Worked example 1.3**

### The median

Calculate the median of the following values: 45, 12, 33, 80, 77.

First we put them into ascending order: 12, 33, 45, 77, 80.

It is then easy to see that the middle value is 45. This is the median. Note that if the value of the largest observation changes to, say, 150, the value of the median is unchanged. This is not the case for the mean, which would change from 49.4 to 63.4.

If there is an even number of observations, then there is no middle observation. The solution is to take the average of the two middle observations. For example:

Find the median of 12, 33, 45, 63, 77, 80.

Note the new observation, 63, making six observations. The median value is halfway between the third and fourth observations, i.e. $(45 + 63)/2 = 54$.

For grouped data there are two stages to the calculation: first we must identify the class interval which contains the median person, then we must calculate where in the interval that person lies. To illustrate, we will find the median of the wealth data:

1  To find the appropriate class interval: since there are 16 933 000 observations, we need the wealth of the person who is 8 466 500 in rank order. The table of cumulative frequencies (see Table 1.5 above) is the most suitable for this. There are 7 316 000 individuals with wealth of less than £60 000 and 8 677 000 with wealth of less than £80 000. The middle person therefore falls into the £60 000–80 000 class. Furthermore, given that 8 466 500 is quite close to 8 677 000 it follows that the median is close to the upper boundary of the class interval. We now go on to make this statement more precise.

2  To find the position in the class interval, we can now use formula (1.12):

$$(1.12) \qquad median = x_L + (x_U - x_L) \left\{ \frac{\frac{N+1}{2} - F}{f} \right\}$$

where:

$x_L$ = the lower limit of the class interval containing the median

$x_U$ = the upper limit of this class interval

$N$ = the number of observations (using $N + 1$ rather than $N$ in the formula is only important when $N$ is relatively small)

$F$ = the cumulative frequency of the class intervals up to (but not including) the one containing the median

$f$ = the frequency for the class interval containing the median.

The expression in the large bracket tells us how far through the interval we need to go to arrive at the median.

For the wealth distribution we have:

$$median = 60\ 000 + (80\ 000 - 60\ 000) \left\{ \frac{\frac{16\ 933\ 000}{2} - 7\ 316\ 000}{1\ 361\ 000} \right\} = £76\ 907$$

This alternative measure of location gives a very different impression: it is not much more than half the mean. Nevertheless, it is equally valid despite having a different meaning. It demonstrates that the person 'in the middle' has wealth of £76 907 and in this sense is typical of the UK population. Note that the median is indeed near the upper boundary of this interval. The large bracket evaluates to 0.84, indicating that the median is 84% of the way through the interval. Before going on to compare these measures further we examine a third, the mode.

**The mode**

The mode is defined as that level of wealth which occurs with the greatest frequency, in other words the value that occurs most often. It is most useful and easiest to calculate when one has all the data and there are relatively few distinct observations. This is the case in the simple example below.

---

### Generalising the median – quantiles

The idea of the median as the middle of the distribution can be extended: quartiles divide the distribution into four equal parts, quintiles into five, deciles into ten, and finally percentiles divide the distribution into one hundred equal parts. Generically they are known as quantiles. We shall illustrate the idea by examining deciles (quartiles are covered below).

The first decile occurs one-tenth of the way along the line of people ranked from poorest to wealthiest. This means we require the wealth of the person ranked 1 693 300 (= $N/10$) in the distribution. From the table of cumulative frequencies, this person lies in the first class interval. Adapting formula (1.12), we obtain:

$$first\ decile = 0 + (10\ 000 - 0) \times \left\{ \frac{1\ 693\ 300 - 0}{3\ 417\ 000} \right\} = £4956$$

Thus we estimate that any household with less than £4956 of wealth falls into the bottom 10% of the wealth distribution. In a similar fashion, the ninth decile can be found by calculating the wealth of the household ranked 15 239 700 (= $N \times 9/10$) in the distribution.

---

Suppose we have the following data on sales of dresses by a shop, according to size:

| Size | Sales |
| --- | --- |
| 8 | 7 |
| 10 | 25 |
| 12 | 36 |
| 14 | 11 |
| 16 | 3 |
| 18 | 1 |

The modal size is 12. There are more women buying dresses of this size than any other. This may be the most useful form of average as far as the shop is concerned. Although it needs to stock a range of sizes, it knows it needs to order more dresses in size 12 than in any other size. The mean would not be so helpful in this case (it is $\bar{x} = 11.7$) as it is not an actual dress size.

In the case of grouped data matters are more complicated. It is the modal class interval which is required, once the intervals have been corrected for width (otherwise a wider class interval is unfairly compared with a narrower one). For this, we can again make use of the frequency densities. From Table 1.4 it can be seen that it is the first interval, from £0 to £10 000, which has the highest frequency density. It is 'typical' of the distribution because it is the one which occurs most often (using the frequency densities, *not* frequencies). The wealth distribution is most concentrated at this level and more people are like this in terms of wealth than anything else. Once again it is notable how different it is from both the median and the mean.

The three measures of location give different messages because of the skewness of the distribution: if it were symmetric they would all give approximately the same answer. Here we have a rather extreme case of skewness, but it does serve to illustrate how the different measures of location compare. When the

Figure 1.12
The histogram with
the mean, median and
mode marked

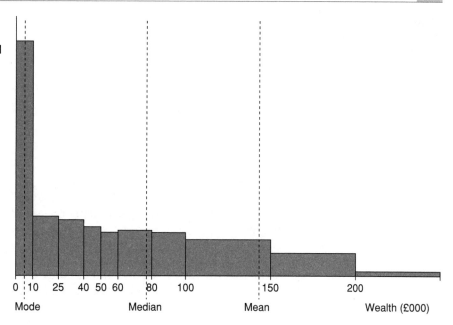

distribution is skewed to the right, as here, they will be in the order mode, median, mean; if skewed to the left the ordering is reversed. If the distribution has more than one peak then this rule for orderings may not apply.

Which of the measures is 'correct' or most useful? In this particular case the mean is not very useful: it is heavily influenced by extreme values. The median is therefore often used when discussing wealth (and income) distributions. Where inequality is even more pronounced, as in some less developed countries, then the mean is even less informative. The mode is also quite useful in telling us about a large section of the population, although it can be sensitive to how the class intervals are arranged. If there were a class interval of £5000 to £15 000 then this might well be the modal class, conveying a slightly different impression.

The three different measures of location are marked on the histogram in Figure 1.12. This brings out the substantial difference between the measures for a skewed distribution such as for wealth.

**Exercise 1.3**

(a)   For the data in Exercise 1.2, calculate the mean, median and mode of the data.

(b)   Mark these values on the histogram you drew for Exercise 1.2.

**Measures of dispersion**

Two different distributions (e.g. wealth in two different countries) might have the same mean yet look very different, as shown in Figure 1.13 (the distributions have been drawn using smooth curves rather than bars to improve clarity). In one country everyone might have a similar level of wealth (curve B). In another, although the average is the same there might be extremes of great wealth and poverty (curve A). A measure of dispersion is a number which allows us to distinguish between these two situations.

The simplest measure of dispersion is the **range**, which is the difference between the smallest and largest observations. It is impossible to calculate

**Figure 1.13**
**Two distributions with different degrees of dispersion**

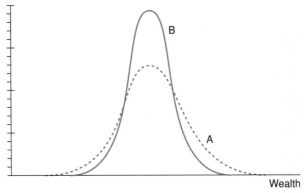

Wealth

*Note*: Distribution A has a greater degree of dispersion than B, where everyone has similar levels of wealth.

accurately from the table of wealth holdings since the largest observation is not available. In any case, it is not a very useful figure since it relies on two extreme values and ignores the rest of the distribution. In simpler cases it might be more informative. For example, in an exam the marks may range from a low of 28% to a high of 74%. In this case the range is $74 - 28 = 46$ and this tells us something useful.

An improvement is the **inter-quartile range** which is the difference between the first and third quartiles. It therefore defines the limits of wealth of the middle half of the distribution. To calculate the first quartile (which we label $Q_1$) we have to go one-quarter of the way along the line of wealth holders (ranked from poorest to wealthiest) and ask the person in that position what their wealth is. The answer is the first quartile. The calculation is as follows:

■ one-quarter of 16 933 is 4233.25
■ the person ranked 4233.25 is in the £10 000–£25 000 class
■ adapting formula (1.12):

$$\textbf{(1.13)} \quad Q_1 = 10\,000 + (25\,000 - 10\,000)\left\{\frac{4\,233.25 - 3417}{1303}\right\} = 19\,396.58$$

The third quartile is calculated in similar fashion:

■ three-quarters of 16 933 is 12 699.75
■ the person ranked 12 699.75 is in the £150 000–200 000 class
■ again using (1.12):

$$Q_3 = 150\,000 + (200\,000 - 150\,000)\left\{\frac{12\,699.75 - 12\,655}{1633}\right\} = 151\,370.18$$

and therefore the inter-quartile range is $Q_3 - Q_1 = 151\,370 - 19\,396 = 131\,974$.

This gives one summary measure of the dispersion of the distribution: the higher the value the more spread-out is the distribution. Two different wealth distributions might be compared according to their inter-quartile ranges therefore, with the country having the larger figure exhibiting greater inequality. Note that the figures would have to be expressed in a common unit of currency for this comparison to be valid.

| Worked example 1.4 | **The range and inter-quartile range** |

Suppose 110 children take a test, with the following results:

| Mark, X | Frequency, f | Cumulative frequency, F |
|---|---|---|
| 13 | 5 | 5 |
| 14 | 13 | 18 |
| 15 | 29 | 47 |
| 16 | 33 | 80 |
| 17 | 17 | 97 |
| 18 | 8 | 105 |
| 19 | 4 | 109 |
| 20 | 1 | 110 |
| Total | 110 | |

The range is simply $20 - 13 = 7$. The inter-quartile range requires calculation of the quartiles. $Q_1$ is given by the value of the 27.5th observation ($= 110/4$), which is 15. $Q_3$ is the value of the 82.5th observation ($= 110 \times 0.75$) which is 17. The IQR is therefore $17 - 15 = 2$ marks. Half the students achieve marks within this range.

Notice that a slight change in the data (three more students getting 16 rather than 17 marks) would alter the IQR to 1 mark ($16 - 15$). The result should be treated with some caution therefore. This is a common problem when there are few distinct values of the variable (eight in this example).

## The variance

A more useful measure of dispersion is the **variance**, which makes use of all of the information available, rather than trimming the extremes of the distribution. The variance is denoted by the symbol $\sigma^2$. $\sigma$ is the Greek lower-case letter sigma, so $\sigma^2$ is read 'sigma squared'. It has a completely different meaning from $\Sigma$ (capital sigma) used before. Its formula is:[3]

$$(1.14) \quad \sigma^2 = \frac{\Sigma(x_i - \mu)^2}{N}$$

The variance is the average of all the squared deviations from the mean. A more dispersed distribution (such as A in Figure 1.13) will tend to have larger deviations from the mean, and hence a larger variance. In comparing two distributions with similar means, therefore, we could examine their variances to see which of the two has the greater degree of dispersion. With grouped data the formula becomes:

$$(1.15) \quad \sigma^2 = \frac{\Sigma f(x_i - \mu)^2}{\Sigma f}$$

The calculation of the variance is shown in Table 1.9, and hence we obtain:

$$\sigma^2 = \frac{895\ 418\ 240.28}{16\ 933} = 52\ 880.07$$

---

[3] $x_i - \mu$ measures the **deviation** of $x_i$ from the mean. These deviations are first squared and then summed. Dividing by $N$ gives the variance.

Table 1.9 **The calculation of the variance of wealth**

| Range | Mid-point x (£000) | Frequency, f | Deviation $(x - \mu)$ | $(x - \mu)^2$ | $f(x - \mu)^2$ |
|---|---|---|---|---|---|
| 0– | 5.0 | 3 417 | −126.4 | 15 987.81 | 54 630 329.97 |
| 10 000– | 17.5 | 1 303 | −113.9 | 12 982.98 | 16 916 826.55 |
| 25 000– | 32.5 | 1 240 | −98.9 | 9 789.70 | 12 139 223.03 |
| 40 000– | 45.0 | 714 | −86.4 | 7 472.37 | 5 335 274.81 |
| 50 000– | 55.0 | 642 | −76.4 | 5 843.52 | 3 751 537.16 |
| 60 000– | 70.0 | 1 361 | −61.4 | 3 775.23 | 5 138 086.73 |
| 80 000– | 90.0 | 1 270 | −41.4 | 1 717.51 | 2 181 241.95 |
| 100 000– | 125.0 | 2 708 | −6.4 | 41.51 | 112 411.42 |
| 150 000– | 175.0 | 1 633 | 43.6 | 1 897.22 | 3 098 162.88 |
| 200 000– | 250.0 | 1 242 | 118.6 | 14 055.79 | 17 457 288.35 |
| 300 000– | 400.0 | 870 | 268.6 | 72 122.92 | 62 746 940.35 |
| 500 000– | 750.0 | 367 | 618.6 | 382 612.90 | 140 418 932.52 |
| 1 000 000– | 1500.0 | 125 | 1 368.6 | 1 872 948.56 | 234 118 569.53 |
| 2 000 000– | 3000.0 | 41 | 2 868.6 | 8 228 619.88 | 337 373 415.02 |
| Totals | | 16 933 | | | 895 418 240.28 |

This calculated value is before translating back into the original units of measurement, as was done for the mean by multiplying by 1000. In the case of the variance, however, we must multiply by 1 000 000 which is the *square* of 1000. The variance is therefore 52 880 070 000. Multiplying by the square of 1000 is a consequence of using squared deviations in the variance formula (see Appendix 1B on E and V operators for more details of this).

One needs to be a little careful about the units of measurement therefore. If the mean is reported at 133.443 then it is appropriate to report the variance as 52 880.07. If the mean is reported as 133 443 then the variance should be reported as 52 880 070 000. Note that it is only the presentation which changes; the underlying facts are the same.

**The standard deviation**

In what units is the variance measured? Since we have used a squaring procedure in the calculation we end up with something like 'squared' £s, which is not very convenient. Because of this, we define the square root of the variance to be the standard deviation, which is therefore back in £s. The standard deviation is therefore given by:

(1.16)     $$\sigma = \sqrt{\frac{\Sigma(x_i - \mu)^2}{N}}$$

or, for grouped data:

(1.17)     $$\sigma = \sqrt{\frac{\Sigma f(x - \mu)^2}{\Sigma f}}$$

These are simply the square roots of (1.14) and (1.15). The standard deviation of wealth is therefore $\sqrt{52\ 880.07} = 229.957$. This is in £000, so the standard deviation is actually £229 957 (note that this is the square root of 52 880 070 000, as it should be). On its own the standard deviation (and the variance) is not easy to interpret since it is not something we have an intuitive feel for, unlike the mean. It is more useful when used in a comparative setting. This will be illustrated later on.

**The variance and standard deviation of a sample**

As with the mean, a different symbol is used to distinguish a variance calculated from the population and one calculated from a sample. In addition, the sample variance is calculated using a slightly different formula from the one for the population variance. The sample variance is denoted by $s^2$ and its formula is given by equations (1.18) and (1.19) below:

$$(1.18) \qquad s^2 = \frac{\Sigma(x - \bar{x})^2}{n - 1}$$

$$(1.19) \qquad s^2 = \frac{\Sigma f(x - \bar{x})^2}{n - 1}$$

where $n$ is the sample size. The reason $n - 1$ is used in the denominator rather than $n$ (as one might expect) is the following. Our real interest is in the population variance, and the sample variance is an estimate of it. The former is measured by the dispersion around $\mu$, and the sample variance should ideally be measured around $\mu$ also. However, $\mu$ is unknown, so $\bar{x}$ is used instead. But the variation of the sample observations around $\bar{x}$ tends to be smaller than that around $\mu$. Using $n - 1$ rather than $n$ in the formula compensates for this and

---

**Worked example 1.5**

## The variance and standard deviation

We continue with the previous worked example, relating to students' marks. The variance and standard deviation can be calculated as:

| X | f | fx | $x - \mu$ | $(x - \mu)^2$ | $f(x - \mu)^2$ |
|---|---|----|-----------|---------------|----------------|
| 13 | 5 | 65 | -2.81 | 7.89 | 39.45 |
| 14 | 13 | 182 | -1.81 | 3.27 | 42.55 |
| 15 | 29 | 435 | -0.81 | 0.65 | 18.98 |
| 16 | 33 | 528 | 0.19 | 0.04 | 1.20 |
| 17 | 17 | 289 | 1.19 | 1.42 | 24.11 |
| 18 | 8 | 144 | 2.19 | 4.80 | 38.40 |
| 19 | 4 | 76 | 3.19 | 10.18 | 40.73 |
| 20 | 1 | 20 | 4.19 | 17.56 | 17.56 |
| Totals | 110 | 1739 | | | 222.99 |

The mean is calculated as $1739/110 = 15.81$ and from this the deviations column $(x - \mu)$ is calculated (so $-2.81 = 13 - 15.81$, etc.).

The variance is calculated as $\Sigma f(x - \mu)^2/(n - 1) = 222.99/109 = 2.05$. The standard deviation is therefore 1.43, the square root of 2.05. (Calculations are shown to two decimal places but have been calculated using exact values.)

For distributions which are approximately symmetric and bell-shaped (where the observations are clustered around the mean) there is an approximate relationship between the standard deviation and the inter-quartile range. This rule of thumb is that the IQR is 1.3 times the standard deviation. In this case, $1.3 \times 1.43 = 1.86$, close to the value of 2, calculated earlier.

the result is an unbiased[4] (i.e. correct on average) estimate of the population variance.

Using the correct formula is more important the smaller is the sample size, as the proportionate difference between $n - 1$ and $n$ increases. For example, if $n = 10$, the adjustment amounts to 10% of the variance; when $n = 100$ the adjustment is only 1%.

The sample standard deviation is given by the square root of equation (1.18) or (1.19).

**Alternative formulae for calculating the variance and standard deviation**

The following formulae give the same answers as equations (1.14) to (1.17) but are simpler to calculate, either by hand or using a spreadsheet. For the population variance one can use

$$(1.20) \qquad \sigma^2 = \frac{\sum x^2}{N} - \mu^2$$

or, for grouped data,

$$(1.21) \qquad \sigma^2 = \frac{\sum fx^2}{\sum f} - \mu^2$$

The calculation of the variance using equation (1.21) is shown in Figure 1.14. The sample variance can be calculated using

$$(1.22) \qquad s^2 = \frac{\sum x^2 - n\bar{x}^2}{n - 1}$$

or, for grouped data,

$$(1.23) \qquad s^2 = \frac{\sum fx^2 - n\bar{x}^2}{n - 1}$$

The standard deviation may of course be obtained as the square root of these formulae.

**Figure 1.14**
**Descriptive statistics calculated using *Excel***

---

[4] The concept of *bias* is treated in more detail in Chapter 4.

> ## Using a calculator or computer for calculation
>
> Electronic calculators and (particularly) computers have simplified the calculation of the mean, etc. Figure 1.14 shows how to set out the above calculations in a spreadsheet (*Microsoft Excel* in this case) including some of the appropriate cell formulae.
>
> The variance in this case is calculated using the formula
>
> $$\sigma^2 = \frac{\sum fx^2}{\sum f} - \mu^2$$
>
> which is the formula given in equation (1.21) above. Note that it gives the same result.
>
> The following formulae are contained in the cells:
>
> D5:  = C5*B5            to calculate $f$ times $x$
> E5:  = D5*B5            to calculate $f$ times $x^2$
> C20: = SUM(C5:C18)   to sum the frequencies
> H6:  = D20/C20         calculates $\sum fx / \sum f$
> H7:  = E20/C20–H6^2  calculates $\sum fx^2 / \sum f - \mu^2$
> H8:  = SQRT(H7)        calculates $\sigma$
> H9:  = H8/H6            calculates $\sigma/\mu$

**The coefficient of variation**

The measures of dispersion examined so far are all measures of absolute dispersion and, in particular, their values depend upon the units in which the variable is measured. It is therefore difficult to compare the degrees of dispersion of two variables which are measured in different units. For example, one could not compare wealth in the UK with that in Germany if the former uses £s and the latter euros for measurement. Nor could one compare the wealth distribution in one country between two points in time because inflation alters the value of the currency over time. The solution is to use a measure of relative dispersion, which is independent of the units of measurement. One such measure is the coefficient of variation, defined as:

$$(1.24) \qquad coefficient\ of\ variation = \frac{\sigma}{\mu}$$

that is the standard deviation divided by the mean. Whenever the units of measurement are changed, the effect upon the mean and the standard deviation is the same, hence the coefficient of variation is unchanged. For the wealth distribution its value is 229.957/131.443 = 1.749, that is the standard deviation is 175% of the mean. This may be compared directly with the coefficient of variation of a different wealth distribution to see which exhibits a greater relative degree of dispersion.

**The standard deviation of the logarithm**

Another solution to the problem of different units of measurement is to use the logarithm[5] of wealth rather than the actual value. The reason why this works can best be illustrated by an example. Suppose that between 1994 and 2001 each individual's wealth doubled, so that $X_i^{2001} = 2X_i^{1994}$, where $X_i^t$ indicates the wealth of individual $i$ in year $t$. The standard deviation of $X^{2001}$ is therefore

[5] See Appendix 1C if you are unfamiliar with logarithms.

**Table 1.10 The calculation of the standard deviation of the logarithm of wealth**

| Range | Mid-point x (£000) | ln (x) | Frequency, f | fx | fx² |
|---|---|---|---|---|---|
| 0– | 5.0 | 1.609 | 3 417 | 5 499.4 | 8 851.0 |
| 10 000– | 17.5 | 2.862 | 1 303 | 3 729.4 | 10 674.4 |
| 25 000– | 32.5 | 3.481 | 1 240 | 4 316.7 | 15 027.6 |
| 40 000– | 45.0 | 3.807 | 714 | 2 718.0 | 10 346.3 |
| 50 000– | 55.0 | 4.007 | 642 | 2 572.7 | 10 309.7 |
| 60 000– | 70.0 | 4.248 | 1 361 | 5 782.2 | 24 565.7 |
| 80 000– | 90.0 | 4.500 | 1 270 | 5 714.8 | 25 715.3 |
| 100 000– | 125.0 | 4.828 | 2 708 | 13 075.1 | 63 130.6 |
| 150 000– | 175.0 | 5.165 | 1 633 | 8 434.1 | 43 560.3 |
| 200 000– | 250.0 | 5.521 | 1 242 | 6 857.7 | 37 864.3 |
| 300 000– | 400.0 | 5.991 | 870 | 5 212.6 | 31 231.0 |
| 500 000– | 750.0 | 6.620 | 367 | 2 429.6 | 16 083.9 |
| 1 000 000– | 1500.0 | 7.313 | 125 | 914.2 | 6 685.4 |
| 2 000 000– | 3000.0 | 8.006 | 41 | 328.3 | 2 628.2 |
| Totals | | | 16 933 | 67 584.6 | 306 673.6 |

*Note*: Use the 'ln' key on your calculator or the =LN() function in a spreadsheet to obtain natural logarithms of the data. You should obtain ln 5 = 1.609, ln 17.5 = 2.862, etc.

twice that of $X^{1994}$. Taking (natural) logs, we have $\ln X_i^{2001} = \ln 2 + \ln X_i^{1994}$, so that the distribution of $\ln X^{2001}$ is the same as that of $\ln X^{1994}$ except that it is shifted to the right by $\ln 2$ units. The variances (and hence standard deviations) of the two logarithmic distributions are the same, indicating no change in the *relative* dispersion of the two wealth distributions.

The standard deviation of the logarithm of wealth is calculated from the data in Table 1.10. The variance is therefore:

$$\sigma^2 = \frac{306\ 673.6}{16\ 933} - \left(\frac{67\ 584.6}{16\ 933}\right)^2 = 2.181$$

and the standard deviation $\sigma = 1.477$. See below for a comparison of the 2001 distribution with one for 1979, just prior to the election of a Conservative government which ruled throughout the 1980s and much of the 1990s.

**Measuring deviations from the mean: z scores**

Imagine the following problem. A man and a woman are arguing over their career records. The man says he earns more than she does, so is more successful. The woman replies that women are discriminated against and that, relative to women, she is doing better than the man is, relative to other men. Can the argument be resolved?

Suppose the data are as follows: the average male salary is £19 500, the average female salary £16 800. The standard deviation of male salaries is £4750, for women it is £3800. The man's salary is £31 375 while the woman's is £26 800. The man is therefore £11 875 above the mean, the woman £10 000. However, women's salaries are less dispersed than men's, so the woman has done well to get to £26 800.

One way to resolve the problem is to calculate the z score, which gives the salary in terms of standard deviations from the mean. Thus for the man, the z score is

(1.25)    $z = \dfrac{x - \mu}{\sigma} = \dfrac{31\,375 - 19\,500}{4750} = 2.50$

Thus the man is 2.5 standard deviations above the male mean salary. For the woman the calculation is

(1.26)    $z = \dfrac{26\,800 - 16\,800}{3800} = 2.632$

The woman is 2.632 standard deviations above her mean and therefore wins the argument – she is nearer the top of her distribution than is the man and so is more of an outlier. Actually, this probably won't end the argument, but is the best the statistician can do! The $z$ score calculation is frequently encountered in statistics and will be used again later in the book when we cover hypothesis testing (Chapter 5).

## Chebyshev's inequality

Use of the $z$ score leads on naturally to **Chebyshev's inequality**, which tells us about the proportion of observations that fall into the tails of any distribution, regardless of its shape. The theorem is expressed as follows:

(1.27)    At least $(1 - 1/k^2)$ of the observations in any distribution lie within $k$ standard deviations of the mean

If we take the female wage distribution given above we can ask what proportion of women lie beyond 2.632 standard deviations from the mean (in both tails of the distribution). Setting $k = 2.632$, then $(1 - 1/k^2) = (1 - 1/2.632^2) = 0.8556$. So at least 85% of women have salaries within ±2.632 standard deviations of the mean, i.e. between £6800 (= 16 800 – 2.632 × 3800) and £26 800 (= 16 800 + 2.632 × 3800). At most, 15% of women therefore lie outside this range and one might expect about 7.5% of women, at most, to have salaries above £26 800. This presumes the salary distribution is roughly symmetric, which may not be the case.

Chebyshev's inequality is a very conservative rule since it applies to *any* distribution; if we know more about the shape of a particular distribution (for example, men's heights follow a Normal distribution – see Chapter 3) then we can make a more precise statement. In the case of the Normal distribution, over 99% of men are within 2.632 standard deviations of the average height, because there is a concentration of observations near the centre of the distribution.

We can also use Chebyshev's inequality to investigate the inter-quartile range. The formula (1.27) implies that at least 50% of observations lie within $\sqrt{2} = 1.41$ standard deviations of the mean, a more conservative value than our previous 1.3.

## Exercise 1.4

(a)  For the data in Exercise 1.2, calculate the inter-quartile range, the variance and the standard deviation.

(b)  Calculate the coefficient of variation.

(c)  Check if the relationship between the IQR and the standard deviation stated in the text is approximately true for this distribution.

(d)  Approximately how much of the distribution lies within one standard deviation either side of the mean? How does this compare with the prediction from Chebyshev's inequality?

**Table 1.11 Calculation of the skewness of the wealth data**

| Range | Mid-point x (£000) | Frequency f | Deviation x − μ | (x − μ)³ | f(x − μ)³ |
|---|---|---|---|---|---|
| 0 | 5.0 | 3 417 | −126.4 | −2 021 544 | −6 907 616 944 |
| 10 000 | 17.5 | 1 303 | −113.9 | −1 479 319 | −1 927 552 150 |
| ⋮ | ⋮ | ⋮ | ⋮ | ⋮ | ⋮ |
| 1 000 000 | 1500.0 | 125 | 1 368.6 | 2 563 237 059 | 320 404 632 317 |
| 2 000 000 | 3000.0 | 41 | 2 868.6 | 23 604 266 037 | 967 774 907 513 |
| Totals | | 16 933 | 4 674.8 | 26 419 423 675 | 1 382 901 383 966 |

## Measuring skewness

The skewness of a distribution is the third characteristic that was mentioned earlier, in addition to location and dispersion. The wealth distribution is heavily skewed to the right, or positively skewed; it has its long tail in the right-hand end of the distribution. A measure of skewness gives a numerical indication of how asymmetric is the distribution.

One measure of skewness, known as the coefficient of skewness, is

$$(1.28) \qquad \frac{\Sigma f(x - \mu)^3}{N\sigma^3}$$

and it is based upon *cubed* deviations from the mean. The result of applying formula (1.28) is positive for a right-skewed distribution (such as wealth), zero for a symmetric one, and negative for a left-skewed one. Table 1.11 shows the calculation for the wealth data (some rows are omitted for brevity). Thus:

$$\frac{\Sigma f(x - \mu)^3}{N} = \frac{1\,382\,901\,383\,966}{16\,933} = 81\,669\,012.2$$

and dividing by $\sigma^3$ gives

$$\frac{81\,669\,012.2}{12\,160\,125} = 6.716$$

which is positive, as expected.

The measure of skewness is much less useful in practical work than measures of location and dispersion, and even knowing the value of the coefficient does not always give much idea of the shape of the distribution: two quite different distributions can share the same coefficient. In descriptive work it is probably better to draw the histogram itself.

## Comparison of the 2001 and 1979 distributions of wealth

Some useful lessons may be learned by comparing the 2001 distribution with its counterpart from 1979. This covers the period of Conservative government starting with Mrs Thatcher in 1979 up until the first four years of Labour administration. This shows how useful the various summary statistics are when it comes to comparing two different distributions. The wealth data for 1979 are given in Problem 1.5 (see p. 61 below), where you are asked to confirm the following calculations.

Average wealth in 1979 was £16 399, about one-eighth of its 2001 value. The average increased substantially therefore (at about 10% per annum, on average), but some of this was due to inflation rather than a real increase in the quantity of assets held. In fact, between 1979 and 2001 the retail price index rose from 59.9 to 183.2, i.e. it increased approximately three times. Thus the nominal[6] increase (i.e. in cash terms, before any adjustment for rising prices) in wealth is made up of two parts: (i) an inflationary part which roughly tripled wealth and (ii) a real part, consisting of a 2.6-fold increase (thus $3 \times 2.6 = 8$). Price indexes are covered in Chapter 10 where it is shown more formally how to divide a nominal increase into price and real (quantity) components. It is likely that the extent of the real increase in wealth is overstated here due to the use of the retail price index rather than an index of asset prices. A substantial part of the increase in asset values over the period is probably due to the very rapid rise in house prices (houses form a significant part of the wealth of many households).

The standard deviation is similarly affected by inflation. The 1979 value is 25 552 compared to 2001's 229 957, which is about nine times larger. The spread of the distribution appears to have increased therefore (even if we take account of the general price effect). Looking at the coefficient of variation, however, shows that it has increased from 1.56 to 1.75 which is not quite such a dramatic change. The spread of the distribution *relative to its mean* has not changed quite so much. This is confirmed by calculating the standard deviation of the logarithm: for 1979 this gives a figure of 1.31, slightly smaller than the 2001 figure (1.48).

The measure of skewness for the 1979 data comes out as 5.723, smaller than the 2001 figure (6.716). This suggests that the 1979 distribution is less skewed than is the 1994 one. Again, these two figures can be directly compared because they do not depend upon the units in which wealth is measured. However, the relatively small difference is difficult to interpret in terms of how the shape of the distribution has changed.

## The box and whiskers diagram

Having calculated these various summary statistics we can now return to a useful graphical method of presentation. This is the box and whiskers diagram (sometimes called a box plot) which shows the median, quartiles and other aspects of a distribution on a single diagram. Figure 1.15 shows the box plot for the wealth data.

Wealth is measured on the vertical axis. The rectangular box stretches (vertically) from the first to third quartile and therefore encompasses the middle half of the distribution. The horizontal line through it is at the median and lies less than halfway up the box. This tells us that there is a degree of skewness even within the central half of the distribution, though it does not appear very severe. The two 'whiskers' extend above and below the box as far as the highest and lowest observations, *excluding outliers*. An outlier is defined to be any observation which is more than 1.5 times the inter-quartile range (which is the same

---

[6] This is a different meaning of the term 'nominal' from that used earlier to denote data measured on a nominal scale, i.e. data grouped into categories without an obvious ordering. Unfortunately, both meanings of the word are in common (statistical) usage, though it should be obvious from the context which use is meant.

as the height of the box) above or below the box. Earlier we found the IQR to be 131 974 and the upper quartile to be 151 370, so an (upper) outlier lies beyond 151 370 + 1.5 × 131 974 = 349 331. There are no outliers below the box as wealth cannot fall below zero. The top whisker is thus substantially longer than the bottom one, and indicates the extent of dispersion towards the tails of the distribution. The crosses indicate the outliers and in reality extend far beyond those shown in the diagram.

A simple diagram thus reveals a lot of information about the distribution. Other boxes and whiskers could be placed alongside in the same diagram (perhaps representing other countries) making comparisons straightforward. Some statistical software packages, such as *SPSS* and *STATA*, can generate box plots from the original data, without the need for the user to calculate the median, etc. However, spreadsheet packages do not yet have this useful facility.

## Time-series data: investment expenditures 1970–2002

The data on the wealth distribution give a snapshot of the situation at particular points in time, and comparisons can be made between the 1979 and 2001 snapshots. Often, however, we wish to focus on the time-path of a variable and therefore we use time-series data. The techniques of presentation and summarising are slightly different than for cross-section data. As an example, we use data on investment in the UK for the period 1970–2002. These data were taken from Statbase (http://www.statistics.gov.uk/statbase/) although you can find the data in *Economic Trends Annual Supplement*. Investment expenditure is important to the economy because it is one of the prime determinants of growth. Until recent years, the UK economy's growth record has been poor by

**Table 1.12  UK investment, 1970–2002**

| Year | Investment | Year | Investment | Year | Investment |
|------|-----------|------|-----------|------|-----------|
| 1970 | 10 036 | 1981 | 43 331 | 1992 | 100 583 |
| 1971 | 11 243 | 1982 | 47 394 | 1993 | 101 027 |
| 1972 | 12 347 | 1983 | 51 490 | 1994 | 108 314 |
| 1973 | 15 227 | 1984 | 58 589 | 1995 | 117 448 |
| 1974 | 18 134 | 1985 | 64 400 | 1996 | 126 291 |
| 1975 | 21 856 | 1986 | 68 546 | 1997 | 133 776 |
| 1976 | 25 516 | 1987 | 78 996 | 1998 | 150 540 |
| 1977 | 28 201 | 1988 | 96 243 | 1999 | 154 647 |
| 1978 | 32 208 | 1989 | 111 324 | 2000 | 161 210 |
| 1979 | 38 211 | 1990 | 114 300 | 2001 | 166 691 |
| 1980 | 43 238 | 1991 | 105 179 | 2002 | 169 972 |

*Note*: Time-series data consist of observations on one or more variables over several time periods. The observations can be daily, weekly, monthly, quarterly or, as here, annually.

international standards and lack of investment may be a cause. The variable studied is total gross (i.e. before depreciation is deducted) domestic fixed capital formation, measured in £m. The data are shown in Table 1.12.

It should be remembered that the data are in current prices so that the figures reflect price increases as well as changes in the volume of physical investment. The series in Table 1.12 thus shows the actual amount of cash that was spent each year on investment. The techniques used below for summarising the investment data could equally well be applied to a series showing the volume of investment.

First of all we can use graphical techniques to gain an insight into the characteristics of investment. Figure 1.16 shows a time-series graph of investment. The graph plots the time periods on the horizontal axis and the investment variable on the vertical.

**Figure 1.16**

**Time-series graph of investment in the UK, 1970–2002**

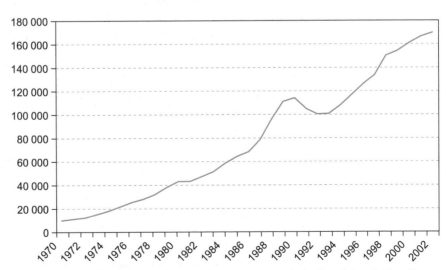

*Note*: The x, y coordinates are the values {year, investment}; the first data point has the coordinates {1970, 10 036}, for example.

Plotting the data in this way brings out clearly some key features of the series:

- The trend in investment is upwards, with only a few years in which there was either no increase or a decrease.
- There is a 'hump' in the data in the late 1980s/early 1990s, before the series returns to its trend. Something unusual must have happened around that time. If we want to know what factors determine investment (or the effect of investment upon other economic magnitudes) we should get some useful insights from this period of the data.
- The trend is slightly non-linear – it follows an increasingly steep curve over time. This is essentially because investment grows by a *percentage* or *proportionate* amount each year. As we shall see shortly, it grows by about 9% each year. Therefore, as the level of investment increases each year, so does the increase in the level, giving a non-linear graph.
- Successive values of the investment variable are similar in magnitude, i.e. the value in year $t$ is similar to that in $t-1$. Investment does not change from £40bn in one year to £10bn the next, then back to £50bn, for instance. In fact, the value in one year appears to be based on the value in the previous year, plus (in general) 9% or so. We refer to this phenomenon as serial correlation and it is one of the aspects of the data that we might wish to investigate. The *ordering* of the data matters, unlike the case with cross-section data where the ordering is usually irrelevant. In deciding how to model investment behaviour, we might focus on *changes* in investment from year to year.
- The series seems 'smoother' in the earlier years (up to perhaps 1986) and exhibits greater volatility later on. In other words, there are greater fluctuations *around* the trend in the later years. We could express this more formally by saying that the variance of investment around its trend appears to change (increase) over time. This is known as heteroscedasticity; a constant variance is termed homoscedasticity.

We may gain further insight into how investment evolves over time by focusing on the *change* in investment from year to year. If we denote investment in year $t$ by $I_t$ then the change in investment, $\Delta I_t$, is given by $I_t - I_{t-1}$. Table 1.13

**Table 1.13** The change in investment

| Year | Δ Investment | Year | Δ Investment | Year | Δ Investment |
|------|-------------|------|-------------|------|-------------|
| 1970 | 970 | 1981 | 93 | 1992 | −4 596 |
| 1971 | 1207 | 1982 | 4 063 | 1993 | 444 |
| 1972 | 1104 | 1983 | 4 096 | 1994 | 7 287 |
| 1973 | 2880 | 1984 | 7 099 | 1995 | 9 134 |
| 1974 | 2907 | 1985 | 5 811 | 1996 | 8 843 |
| 1975 | 3722 | 1986 | 4 146 | 1997 | 7 485 |
| 1976 | 3660 | 1987 | 10 450 | 1998 | 16 764 |
| 1977 | 2685 | 1988 | 17 247 | 1999 | 4 107 |
| 1978 | 4007 | 1989 | 15 081 | 2000 | 6 563 |
| 1979 | 6003 | 1990 | 2 976 | 2001 | 5 481 |
| 1980 | 5027 | 1991 | −9 121 | 2002 | 3 281 |

*Note*: The change in investment is obtained by taking the difference between successive observations. For example, 1207 is the difference between 10 036 and 11 243.

**Figure 1.17**
**Time-series graph of the change in investment**

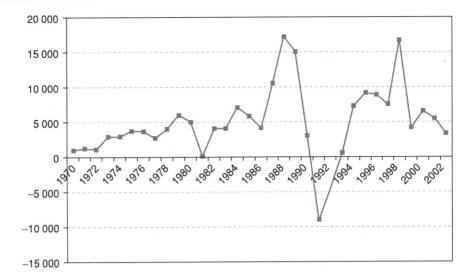

shows the changes in investment each year and Figure 1.17 provides a time-series graph.

The series is made up of mainly positive values, indicating that investment increases over time. It also shows that the increase grows each year, with perhaps some greater volatility (of the increase) towards the end of the period. The graph also shows dramatically the change that occurred around 1990.

### Outliers

Graphing data also allows you to see **outliers** (unusual observations). Outliers might be due to an error in inputting the data (e.g. typing 97 instead of 970) or because something unusual happened (e.g. the investment figure for 1991). Either of these should be apparent from an appropriate graph. For example, the graph of the change in investment highlights the 1991 figure. In the case of a straightforward error you should obviously correct it. If you are satisfied that the outlier is not simply a typo, you might want to think about the possible reasons for its existence and whether it distorts the descriptive picture you are trying to paint.

Another useful way of examining the data is to look at the logarithm of investment. This transformation has the effect of straightening out the non-linear investment series. Table 1.14 shows the transformed values and Figure 1.18 graphs the series. In this case we use the natural (base e) logarithm.

This new series is much smoother than the original one (as is usually the case when taking logs) and is helpful in showing the long-run trend, though it tends to mask some of the volatility of investment. The slope of the graph gives a close approximation to the average rate of growth of investment over the period (expressed as a decimal). This is calculated as follows:

$$(1.29) \quad slope = \frac{change\ in\ (\ln)\ investment}{number\ of\ years} = \frac{12.043 - 9.214}{32} = 0.088$$

Table 1.14 **The logarithm of investment and the change in the logarithm**

| Year | ln Investment | Δ ln Investment | Year | ln Investment | Δ ln Investment | Year | ln Investment | Δ ln Investment |
|------|------|------|------|------|------|------|------|------|
| 1970 | 9.214 | 0.102 | 1981 | 10.677 | 0.002 | 1992 | 11.519 | −0.045 |
| 1971 | 9.328 | 0.114 | 1982 | 10.766 | 0.090 | 1993 | 11.523 | 0.004 |
| 1972 | 9.421 | 0.094 | 1983 | 10.849 | 0.083 | 1994 | 11.593 | 0.070 |
| 1973 | 9.631 | 0.210 | 1984 | 10.978 | 0.129 | 1995 | 11.674 | 0.081 |
| 1974 | 9.806 | 0.175 | 1985 | 11.073 | 0.095 | 1996 | 11.746 | 0.073 |
| 1975 | 9.992 | 0.187 | 1986 | 11.135 | 0.062 | 1997 | 11.804 | 0.058 |
| 1976 | 10.147 | 0.155 | 1987 | 11.277 | 0.142 | 1998 | 11.922 | 0.118 |
| 1977 | 10.247 | 0.100 | 1988 | 11.475 | 0.197 | 1999 | 11.949 | 0.027 |
| 1978 | 10.380 | 0.133 | 1989 | 11.620 | 0.146 | 2000 | 11.990 | 0.042 |
| 1979 | 10.551 | 0.171 | 1990 | 11.647 | 0.026 | 2001 | 12.024 | 0.033 |
| 1980 | 10.674 | 0.124 | 1991 | 11.563 | −0.083 | 2002 | 12.043 | 0.019 |

*Note:* For 1970, 9.214 is the natural logarithm of 10 036, i.e. ln 10 036 = 9.214.

**Figure 1.18**
**Time-series graph of the logarithm of investment expenditures**

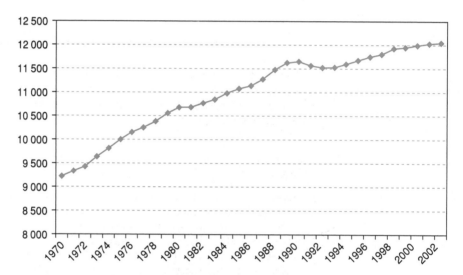

that is 8.8% per annum. Note that although there are 33 observations, there are only 32 years of growth. A word of warning: you must use natural (base e) logarithms, not logarithms to the base 10, for this calculation to work. Remember also that the growth of the *volume* of investment will be less than 8.8% per annum, because part of it is due to price increases.

The logarithmic presentation is useful when comparing two different data series: when graphed in logs it is easy to see which is growing faster – just see which series has the steeper slope.

A corollary of equation (1.29) is that the change in the natural logarithm of investment from one year to the next represents the *percentage* change in the data. For example, the natural logarithm of investment in 1970 is 9.214, while in 1971 it is 9.328. The difference is 0.114, so the rate of growth is 11.4%. You can verify this using the original data. This approximation is good as long as the growth rate is around 20% or less.

**Figure 1.19**
**Time-series graph of the difference of the logarithmic series**

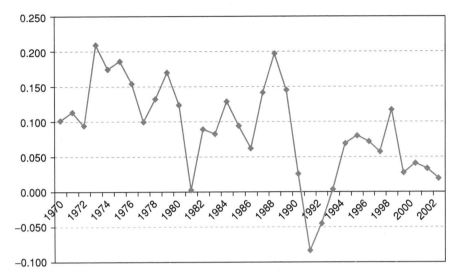

Finally we can graph the difference of the logarithm, as we graphed the difference of the level. This is shown in Figure 1.19 (the calculations are in Table 1.14).

This is quite revealing. It shows the series fluctuating about the value of approximately 0.10 (the average calculated in equation (1.29) above), with a slight downward trend. Furthermore, the series does not seem to show increasing volatility over time, as the others did. The graph therefore demonstrates that in *proportionate* terms there is no increasing volatility; the variance of the series around 0.10 does not change much over time (though 1991 still seems to be an 'unusual' observation). We may loosely refer to this series as being stationary – it has a constant mean and variance. This is not a formal definition of the statistical term, which imposes stricter conditions on the series, but it is a useful one to refer to.

**Graphing multiple series**

Investment is made up of different categories: the table in Problem 1.14 presents investment data under different headings: dwellings; other buildings and works; transport; machinery; and intangible fixed assets. Together they make up total investment. It is often useful to show all of the series together on one graph. Figure 1.20 shows a multiple time-series graph of the investment data.

Construction of this type of graph is straightforward; it is just an extension of the technique for presenting a single series. It is easily, though laboriously, done by hand but most computer software can produce this type of chart very quickly. The only complication arises when the series are of different orders of magnitude and it is difficult to make all the series visible on the chart. In this case you can chart some of the series against a second vertical scale, on the right-hand axis. An example is shown in Figure 1.21, plotting the investment data with the interest rate, which has much smaller numerical values.

Returning to the investment categories, Figure 1.20 shows that 'machinery' and 'other buildings' are the two largest categories and are of approximately

**Figure 1.20**
**A multiple time-series graph of investment**

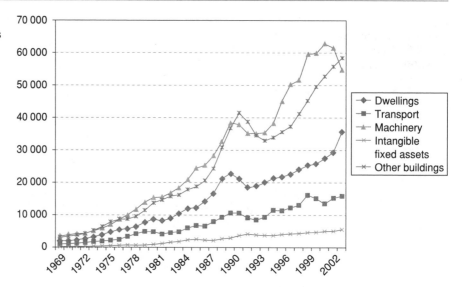

equal size. This has not altered much over the period. All the series demonstrate generally similar patterns of behaviour over the time period. (One could also produce multiple plots of the logarithm of investment and of the change.)

## Overlapping the ranges of the data series

The graph below, taken from the *Treasury Briefing*, February 1994, provides a nice example of how to plot multiple time-series and compare them. The aim is to compare the recessions and recoveries of 1974–78, 1979–83, and 1990–93. Instead of plotting time on the horizontal axis, the number of quarters since the start of each recession is used, so that the series overlap. This makes it easy to see the depth of the last recession and the long time before recovery commenced. By contrast, the 1974–78 recession ended quite quickly and recovery was quite rapid.

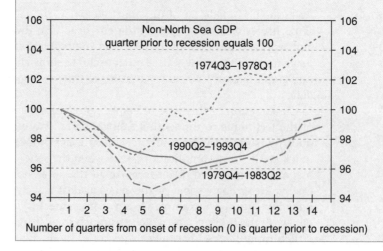

**Figure 1.21**
**Time-series graph using two vertical scales: investment (LH scale) and the interest rate (RH scale), 1982–2002**

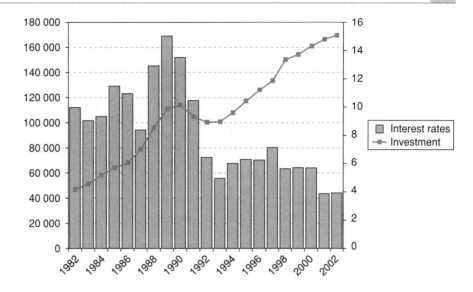

**Figure 1.22**
**Area graph of investment categories, 1969–2002**

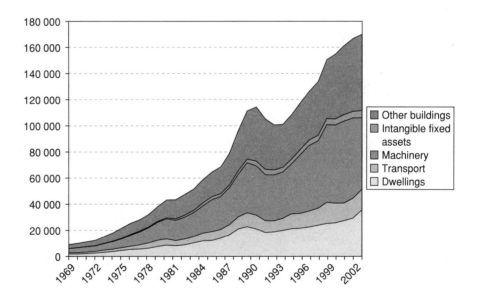

These series may also be illustrated by means of an area graph, which plots the five series stacked one on top of the other, as illustrated in Figure 1.22.

This shows, for example, that construction (of all types) makes up over half of all investment and that this proportion has not changed significantly over the period shown.

## 'Chart junk'

With modern computer software it is easy to get carried away and produce a chart that actually hides more than it reveals. There is a great temptation to add some 3-D effects, liven it up with a bit of colour, rotate and tilt the viewpoint, etc. This sort of stuff is generally known as 'chart junk'. As an example, look at Figure 1.23 which is an alternative to the area graph in Figure 1.22 above. It was fun to create, but it doesn't get the message across at all! Taste is, of course, personal, but moderation is usually an essential part of it.

**Figure 1.23**
**Over-the-top graph of investment**

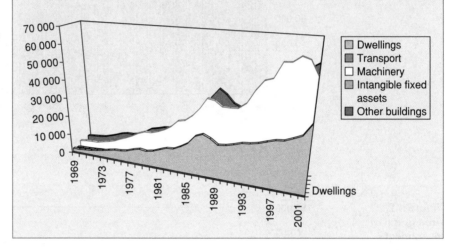

**Exercise 1.5**

Given the following data:

|        | 1990 | 1991 | 1992 | 1993 | 1994 | 1995 | 1996 | 1997 | 1998 | 1999 |
|--------|------|------|------|------|------|------|------|------|------|------|
| Profit | 50   | 60   | 25   | −10  | 10   | 45   | 60   | 50   | 20   | 40   |
| Sales  | 300  | 290  | 280  | 255  | 260  | 285  | 300  | 310  | 300  | 330  |

(a) Draw a multiple time-series graph of the two variables. Label both axes appropriately and provide a title for the graph.

(b) Adjust the graph by using the right-hand axis to measure profits, the left-hand axis sales. What difference does this make?

**Numerical summary statistics**

The graphs have revealed quite a lot about the data already, but we can also calculate numerical descriptive statistics as we did for the cross-section data. First we consider the mean, then the variance and standard deviation.

**The mean of a time series**

We could calculate the mean of investment itself, but would this be helpful? Because the series is trended, it passes through the mean at some point between 1970 and 2002, but never returns to it. The mean of the series is actually £78.379bn, which is not very informative since it tells nothing about its value today, for instance. The problem is that the variable is trended, so that the mean is not typical of the series. The annual increase in investment is also trended, so is subject to the same criticism.

It is better to calculate the average growth rate, since this appears stationary (Figure 1.19 above). This was calculated in equation (1.29) as 8.8% per annum by calculating the slope of the graph of the investment series. We can get an accurate value in the following way:

1 Calculate the overall growth factor of the series, i.e. $x_T/x_1$ where $x_T$ is the final observation and $x_1$ is the initial observation.
2 Take the $T - 1$ root of the growth factor.
3 Subtract 1 from the result in the previous step, giving the growth rate as a decimal.

For the investment data we have:

1 $\dfrac{x_T}{x_1} = \dfrac{169\ 972}{10\ 036} = 16.93$, i.e. investment expenditure is 17 times larger in 2002 than in 1970.

2 $\sqrt[32]{16.936} = 1.092$

3 $1.092 - 1 = 0.092$.

Thus the average growth rate of investment is 9.2% per annum, rather than the 8.8% calculated earlier. (Step 2 can be performed on a scientific calculator by raising 16.936 to the power 1/32, i.e. $16.936^{(1/32)} = 1.092$.)

   (Note that we could have obtained the accurate answer from our earlier calculation as follows:

- the slope of the graph is 0.088 (equation (1.29) above);
- calculate the anti-log ($e^x$) of this: $e^{0.088} = 1.092$;
- subtract 1, giving a growth rate of $1.092 - 1 = 0.092 = 9.2\%$ p.a.)

Note that, since the calculated growth rate is based only upon the initial and final observations, it could be unreliable if either of these two values is an outlier.

---

### The power of compound growth

The *Economist* magazine provided some amusing and interesting examples of how a $1 investment can grow over time. They assumed that an investor (they named her Felicity Foresight, for reasons that become obvious) started with $1 in 1900 and had the foresight or luck to invest, each year, in the best performing asset of the year. Sometimes she invested in equities, some years in gold, and so on. By the end of the century she had amassed $9.6 quintillion ($9.6 \times 10^{18}$, more than world GDP, so highly unrealistic). This is equivalent to an average annual growth rate of 55%. In contrast, Henry Hindsight did the same, but invested in the *previous year's* best asset. This might be thought more realistic. Unfortunately, his $1 turned into only $783, a still respectable annual growth rate of 6.9%. This, however, is beaten by the strategy of investing in the previous year's *worst* performing asset (what goes down must come up . . . ). This turned $1 into $1730, a return of 7.7%. Food for thought!

*Source: The Economist*, 12th February 2000, p. 111.

---

**The geometric mean**

In calculating the average growth rate of investment we have implicitly calculated the geometric mean of a series. If we have a series of $n$ values, then their geometric mean is calculated as the $n$th root of the *product* of the values, i.e.[7]

---

[7] The symbol Π (Greek capital 'pi') means 'the product of' in the same way as Σ means the sum.

**Table 1.15** Calculation of the geometric mean – annual growth factors

| Year | Investment | Growth factors |
|---|---|---|
| 1970 | 10 036 | |
| 1971 | 11 243 | 1.1203 (=11 243/10 036) |
| 1972 | 12 347 | 1.0982 (=12 347/11 243) |
| 1973 | 15 227 | 1.2333 etc. |
| ⋮ | ⋮ | ⋮ |
| 1997 | 133 776 | 1.0593 |
| 1998 | 150 540 | 1.1253 |
| 1999 | 154 647 | 1.0273 |
| 2000 | 161 210 | 1.0424 |
| 2001 | 166 691 | 1.0340 |
| 2002 | 169 972 | 1.0197 |

*Note*: Each growth factor simply shows the ratio of that year's investment to the previous year's.

$$(1.30) \qquad geometric\ mean = \sqrt[n]{\prod_{i=1}^{n} x_i}$$

The $x$ values in this case are the growth factors in each year, as in Table 1.15 (the values in the intermediate years are omitted).

The product of the 32 growth factors is 16.936 (the same as is obtained by dividing the final observation by the initial one – why?) and the 32nd root of this is 1.092. This latter figure, 1.092, is the geometric mean of the growth factors and from it we can derive the growth rate of 9.2% p.a. by subtracting 1.

Whenever one is dealing with growth data (or any series that is based on a multiplicative process) one should use the geometric mean rather than the arithmetic mean to get the answer. However, using the arithmetic mean in this case generally gives only a small error, as is indicated below.

**An approximate way of obtaining the average growth rate**

We have seen that when calculating rates of growth one should use the geometric mean, but if the growth rate is reasonably small then taking the arithmetic mean will give approximately the right answer. The arithmetic mean of the growth factors is

$$\frac{1.1203 + 1.0982 + \ldots + 1.0340 + 1.0197}{32} = 1.095$$

giving an estimate of the growth rate of 9.5% p.a. – close to the correct value. Note also that one could equivalently take the average of the annual growth rates (0.1203, 0.0982, etc.), giving 0.095, to get the same result. Use of the arithmetic mean is justified in this context if one needs only an approximation to the right answer and annual growth rates are reasonably small.

**The variance of a time series**

How should we describe the variance of a time series? The variance of the investment data can be calculated, but it would be uninformative in the same way as the mean. Since the series is trended, and this is likely to continue in the longer run, the variance is in principle equal to infinity. The calculated variance would be closely tied to the sample size: the larger it is, the larger the variance. Again it makes more sense to calculate the variance of the growth rate, which has little trend in the long run.

## Compound interest

The calculations we have performed relating to growth rates are analogous to computing **compound interest**. If we invest £100 at a rate of interest of 10% per annum, then the investment will grow at 10% p.a. (assuming all the interest is reinvested). Thus after one year the total will have grown to £100 × 1.1 (£110), after two years to £100 × 1.1$^2$ (£121) and after $t$ years to £100 × 1.1$^t$. The general formula for the terminal value $S_t$ of a sum $S_0$ invested for $t$ years at a rate of interest $r$ is

**(1.31)**    $S_t = S_0(1 + r)^t$

where $r$ is expressed as a decimal. Rearranging (1.31) to make $r$ the subject yields

**(1.32)**    $r = \sqrt[t]{S_t / S_0} - 1$

which is precisely the formula for the average growth rate. To give a further example: suppose an investment fund turns an initial deposit of £8000 into £13 500 over 12 years. What is the average rate of return on the investment? Setting $S_0 = 8$, $S_t = 13.5$, $t = 12$ and using (1.32) we obtain

$r = \sqrt[12]{13.5 / 8} - 1 = 0.045$

or 4.5% per annum.

Formula (1.32) can also be used to calculate the **depreciation rate** and the amount of annual depreciation on a firm's assets. In this case, $S_0$ represents the initial value of the asset, $S_t$ represents the final or scrap value, and the annual rate of depreciation is given by $r$ from equation (1.32).

---

This variance can be calculated from the formula:

**(1.33)**    $s^2 = \dfrac{\Sigma(x - \bar{x})^2}{n - 1} = \dfrac{\Sigma x^2 - n\bar{x}^2}{n - 1}$

where $\bar{x}$ is the (arithmetic) average rate of growth. The calculation is set out in Table 1.16 using the right-hand formula in (1.33).

The variance is therefore

$s^2 = \dfrac{0.4635 - 32 \times 0.092^2}{31} = 0.0056$

and the standard deviation is 0.075, the square root of the variance. The coefficient of variation is

$cv = \dfrac{0.075}{0.092} = 0.815$

that is the standard deviation of the growth rate is about 80% of the mean.

Note three things about this calculation: first, we have used the arithmetic mean (using the geometric mean makes very little difference); second, we have used the formula for the sample variance since the period 1970–2002 constitutes a sample of all the possible data we could collect; and third, we could have equally used the growth factors for the calculation of the variance (why?).

Table 1.16 **Calculation of the variance of the growth rate**

| Year | Investment | Growth rate | |
|---|---|---|---|
| | | $x$ | $x^2$ |
| 1971 | 11 243 | 0.1203 | 0.0145 |
| 1972 | 12 347 | 0.0982 | 0.0096 |
| 1973 | 15 227 | 0.2333 | 0.0544 |
| 1997 | ⋮ | ⋮ | ⋮ |
| 1998 | 150 540 | 0.1253 | 0.0157 |
| 1999 | 154 647 | 0.0273 | 0.0007 |
| 2000 | 161 210 | 0.0424 | 0.0018 |
| 2001 | 166 691 | 0.0340 | 0.0012 |
| 2002 | 169 972 | 0.0197 | 0.0004 |
| Totals | | 3.0392 | 0.4635 |

Worked example 1.6

Given the following data:

| Year | 1999 | 2000 | 2001 | 2002 | 2003 |
|---|---|---|---|---|---|
| Price of a laptop PC | 1100 | 900 | 800 | 750 | 700 |

we can work out the average rate of price growth per annum as follows. The overall growth factor is $\frac{700}{1100}$ = 0.6363. The fact that this number is less than 1 simply reflects the fact that the price has fallen over time. It has fallen to 64% of its original value. To find the annual rate, we take the fourth root of 0.6363 (four years of growth). Hence we get $\sqrt[4]{0.6363}$ = 0.893 , i.e. each year the price falls to 89% of its value the previous year. This implies price is falling at 0.893 – 1 = –0.107, or approximately an 11% fall each year.

We can see if the fall is more or less the same each year, by calculating each year's growth factor. These are:

| Year | 1999 | 2000 | 2001 | 2002 | 2003 |
|---|---|---|---|---|---|
| Laptop price | 1100 | 900 | 800 | 750 | 700 |
| Growth factor | | 0.818 | 0.889 | 0.9375 | 0.933 |
| Price fall | | –19% | –11% | –6% | –7% |

The price fall was larger in the earlier years, in percentage as well as absolute terms. Calculating the standard deviation of the values in the final row provides a measure of the variability from year to year. The variance is given by

$$s^2 = \frac{(19 - 11)^2 + (11 - 11)^2 + (6 - 11)^2 + (7 - 11)^2}{3} = 30.7$$

and the standard deviation is then 5.54%. (The calculations are shown rounded but the answer is accurate.)

(a) Using the data in Exercise 1.5, calculate the average level of profit over the time period and the average growth rate of profit over the period. Which appears more useful?

(b) Calculate the variance of profit and compare it to the variance of sales.


## Graphing bivariate data: the scatter diagram

The analysis of investment is an example of the use of univariate methods: only a single variable is involved. However, we often wish to examine the relationship between two (or sometimes more) variables and we have to use bivariate (or multivariate) methods. To illustrate the methods involved we shall examine the relationship between investment expenditures and Gross Domestic Product (GDP). Economics tells us to expect a positive relationship between these variables, higher GDP is usually associated with higher investment. Table 1.17 provides data on GDP for the UK.

A scatter diagram (also called an XY chart) plots one variable (in this case investment) on the *y* axis, the other (GDP) on the *x* axis, and therefore shows the relationship between them. For example, one can see whether high values of one variable tend to be associated with high values of the other. Figure 1.24 shows the relationship for investment and GDP.

The chart shows a strong linear relationship between the two variables, apart from a curious dip in the middle. This reflects the sharp fall in investment after 1990 which is *not* matched by a fall in GDP (if it were, the XY chart would show a linear relationship without the dip). It is important to recognise the difference between the time-series plot and the XY chart. Because of inflation later observations tend to be towards the top right of the XY chart (both investment and GDP are increasing over time) but this does not *have* to happen; if both variables fluctuated up and down, later observations could be at the bottom-left (or centre, or anywhere). By contrast, in a time-series plot, later observations are always further to the right.

Note that both variables are in nominal terms, i.e. they make no correction for inflation over the time period. This may be seen algebraically: investment

**Table 1.17** GDP data

| Year | GDP | Year | GDP | Year | GDP |
|------|------|------|------|------|------|
| 1970 | 51 515 | 1981 | 253 000 | 1992 | 610 854 |
| 1971 | 57 449 | 1982 | 277 090 | 1993 | 642 327 |
| 1972 | 64 317 | 1983 | 302 774 | 1994 | 681 327 |
| 1973 | 73 979 | 1984 | 324 407 | 1995 | 719 176 |
| 1974 | 83 742 | 1985 | 354 952 | 1996 | 763 290 |
| 1975 | 105 773 | 1986 | 381 317 | 1997 | 810 944 |
| 1976 | 125 098 | 1987 | 419 631 | 1998 | 859 436 |
| 1977 | 145 528 | 1988 | 468 386 | 1999 | 903 865 |
| 1978 | 167 806 | 1989 | 514 168 | 2000 | 951 265 |
| 1979 | 197 355 | 1990 | 557 300 | 2001 | 994 037 |
| 1980 | 230 695 | 1991 | 586 149 | 2002 | 1 043 306 |

Figure 1.24
Scatter diagram of
investment (vertical
axis) against GDP
(horizontal axis)
(nominal values)

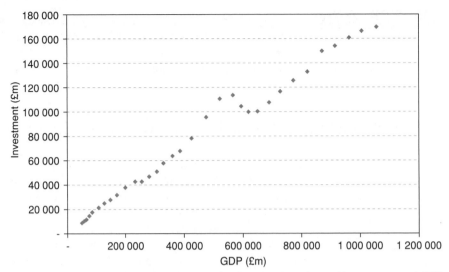

*Note*: The (x, y) coordinates of each point are given by the values of investment and GDP respectively. Thus the first (1970) data point is drawn 10 036 units above the horizontal axis and 51 515 units from the vertical one.

expenditure is made up of the *volume* of investment ($I$) times its *price* ($P_I$). Similarly, nominal GDP is real GDP ($Y$) times its price ($P_Y$). Thus the scatter diagram actually charts $P_I \times I$ against $P_Y \times Y$. It is likely that the two prices follow a similar trend over time and that this dominates the movements in real investment and GDP. The chart then shows the relationship between a mixture of prices and quantities, when the more interesting relationship is between the *quantities* of investment and output.

Figure 1.25 shows the relationship between the quantities of investment and output, i.e. after the price effects have been removed. It is not so straightforward as the nominal graph. There is now a 'knot' of points in centre where perhaps both (real) investment and GDP fluctuated. It is clear that something 'interesting' happened around 1990 that merits additional investigation.

Figure 1.25
The relationship
between real
investment and real
output

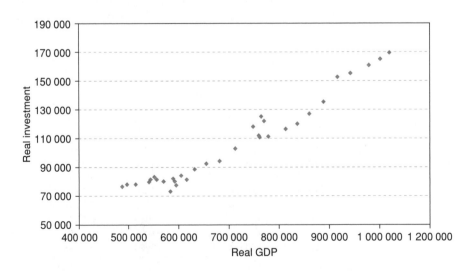

Chapter 10, on index numbers, explains in detail how to derive real variables from nominal ones, as we have done here, and generally describes how to correct for the effects of inflation on economic magnitudes.

Exercise 1.7

(a)  Once again using the data from Exercise 1.5, draw an *XY* chart with profits on the vertical axis, sales on the horizontal axis. Choose the scale of the axes appropriately.

(b)  (If using Excel to produce graphs) right click on the graph, choose 'Add trendline' and choose a linear trend. This gives the 'line of best fit' (covered in detail in Chapter 7). What does this appear to show?

# Data transformations

In analysing employment and investment data in the examples above we have often changed the variables in some way in order to bring out the important characteristics. In statistics one usually works with data that have been transformed in some way rather than using the original numbers. It is therefore worth summarising the main data transformations available, providing justifications for their use and exploring the implications of such adjustments to the original data. We briefly deal with the following transformations:

- rounding;
- grouping;
- dividing or multiplying by a constant;
- differencing;
- taking logarithms;
- taking the reciprocal;
- deflating.

**Rounding**

Rounding improves readability. Too much detail can hide the message, so rounding the answer makes it more memorable. To give an example, the average wealth holding calculated earlier in this chapter is actually £133 442.893 (to three decimal places). It would be absurd to present it in this form however. We do not know for certain that this figure is accurate (in fact, it almost certainly is not). There is a spurious degree of precision which might mislead the reader. How much should this be rounded for presentational purposes therefore? Remember that the figures have already been effectively rounded by allocation to classes of width 10 000 or more (all observations have been rounded to the mid-point of the interval). However, much of this rounding is offsetting, i.e. numbers rounded up offset those rounded down, so the mean is reasonably accurate. Rounding to £133 000 makes the figure much easier to remember, and is only a change of 0.3% (133 000/133 443 = 0.9967), so is a reasonable compromise. In the text above, the answer was not rounded to such an extent since the purpose was to highlight the methods of calculation.

Rounding is a 'trap door' function: you cannot obtain the original value from the transformed (rounded) value. Therefore, if you are going to need the original value in further calculations you should not round your answer. Furthermore, small rounding errors can cumulate, leading to a large error in the final answer. Therefore, you should *never* round an intermediate answer, only the final one. Even if you only round the intermediate answer by a small amount, the final answer could be grossly inaccurate. Try the following: calculate $60.29 \times 30.37 - 1831$ both before and after rounding the first two numbers to integers. In the first case you get 0.0073, in the second −31.

**Grouping**

When there is too much data to present easily, grouping solves the problem, although at the cost of hiding some of the information. The examples relating to education and unemployment and to wealth used grouped data. Using the raw data would have given us far too much information, so grouping is a first stage in data analysis. Grouping is another trap door transformation: once it's done you cannot recover the original information.

**Dividing/ multiplying by a constant**

This transformation is carried out to make numbers more readable or to make calculation simpler by removing trailing zeros. The data on wealth were divided by 1000 to ease calculation; otherwise the $fx^2$ column would have contained extremely large values. Some summary statistics (e.g. the mean) will be affected by the transformation, but not all (e.g. the coefficient of variation). Try to remember which are affected! E and V operators (see Appendix 1B, p. **72**) can help. The transformation is easy to reverse.

**Differencing**

In time-series data there may be a trend, and it is better to describe the features of the data relative to the trend. The result may also be more economically meaningful, e.g. governments are often more concerned about the growth of output than about its level. Differencing is one way of eliminating the trend. Differencing was used for the investment data for both of these reasons. One of the implications of differencing is that information about the *level* of the variable is lost and cannot be recovered.

**Taking logarithms**

Taking logarithms is used to linearise a non-linear series, in particular one that is growing at a constant rate. It is often easier to see the important features of such a series if the logarithm is graphed rather than the raw data. The logarithmic transformation is also useful in regression (see Chapter 9) because it yields estimates of elasticities (e.g. of demand). Taking the logarithm of the investment data linearised the series and tended to smooth it. The inverses of the logarithmic transformations are $10^x$ (for common logarithms) and $e^x$ (for natural logarithms) so one can recover the original data.

**Taking the reciprocal**

The reciprocal of a variable might have a useful interpretation and provide a more intuitive explanation of a phenomenon. The reciprocal transformation will also turn a linear series into a non-linear one. The reciprocal of turnover in the labour market (i.e. the number leaving unemployment divided by the number unemployed) gives an idea of the duration of unemployment. If a half of those unemployed find work each year (turnover = 0.5) then the average duration of unemployment is 2 years (= 1/0.5). If a graph of turnover shows a linear decline over time, then the average duration of unemployment will be rising, at a faster and faster rate. Repeating the reciprocal transformation recovers the original data.

**Deflating**

Deflating turns a nominal series into a real one, i.e. one that reflects changes in quantities without the contamination of price changes. This is dealt with in more detail in Chapter 10. It is often more meaningful in economic terms to talk about a real variable than a nominal one. Consumers are more concerned about their real income than about their money income, for example.

Confusing real and nominal variables is dangerous! For example, someone's nominal (money) income may be rising yet their real income falling (if prices are rising faster than money income). It is important to know which series you are dealing with (this is a common failing among students new to statistics and economics). An income series that is growing at 2–3% per annum is probably a real series; one that is growing at 10% per annum or more is likely to be nominal.

## Guidance to the student: how to measure your progress

Now you have reached the end of the chapter your work is not yet over! It is very unlikely that you have fully understood everything after one read through. What you should do now is:

- Check back over the learning intentions at the start of the chapter. Do you feel you have achieved them? For example, can you list the various different data types you should be able to recognise (the first learning outcome)?
- Read the chapter summary below to help put things in context. You should recognise each topic and be aware of the main issues, techniques, etc. within them. There should be no surprises or gaps!
- Read the list of key terms. You should be able to give a brief and precise definition or description of each one. Do not worry if you cannot remember all the formulae (though you should try to memorise simple ones such as that for the mean).
- Try out the problems (most important!). Answers to odd-numbered problems are at the back of the book, so you can check your answers.

From all of this you should be able to work out whether you have really mastered the chapter. Do not be surprised if you have not – it will take more than one reading. Go back over those parts where you feel unsure of your knowledge. Use these same learning techniques for each chapter of the book.

## Summary

- Descriptive statistics are useful for summarising large amounts of information, highlighting the main features but omitting the detail.
- Different techniques are suited to different types of data, e.g. bar charts for cross-section data and rates of growth for time series.
- Graphical methods, such as the bar chart, provide a picture of the data. These give an informal summary but they are unsuitable as a basis for further analysis.

- Important graphical techniques include the bar chart, frequency distribution, relative and cumulative frequency distributions, histogram and pie chart. For time-series data a time-series chart of the data is informative.

- Numerical techniques are more precise as summaries. Measures of location (such as the mean), of dispersion (the variance) and of skewness form the basis of these techniques.

- Important numerical summary statistics include the mean, median and mode; variance, standard deviation and coefficient of variation; coefficient of skewness.

- For bivariate data the scatter diagram (or *XY* graph) is a useful way of illustrating the data.

- Data are often transformed in some way before analysis, e.g. by taking logs. Transformations often make it easier to see key features of the data in graphs and sometimes make summary statistics easier to interpret. For example, with time-series data the average rate of growth may be more appropriate than the mean of the series.

**Key terms and concepts**

| | | |
|---|---|---|
| cross-section data | pie chart | frequency table |
| bar chart | relative and | mean |
| histogram |   cumulative | quantiles |
| median |   frequencies | coefficient of |
| variance | mode |   variation |
| z score | standard deviation | outliers |
| data transformation | skewness | scatter diagram |
| box and whiskers plot | compound growth |   (*XY* chart) |
| time-series data | cross-tabulation | |

# Problems

Some of the more challenging problems are indicated by highlighting the **problem number** in colour.

**Problem 1.1**    The following data show the education and employment status of women aged 20–29 (from the 1991 *General Household Survey*):

| | Higher education | A levels | Other qualification | No qualification | Total |
|---|---|---|---|---|---|
| In work | 209 | 182 | 577 | 92 | 1060 |
| Unemployed | 12 | 9 | 68 | 32 | 121 |
| Inactive | 17 | 34 | 235 | 136 | 422 |
| Sample size | 238 | 225 | 880 | 260 | 1603 |

(a) Draw a bar chart of the numbers in work in each education category. Can this be easily compared with the similar diagram for 2003 (Figure 1.1)?

(b) Draw a stacked bar chart using all the employment states, similar to Figure 1.3. Comment upon any similarities and differences from the diagram in the text.

(c)  Convert the table into (column) percentages and produce a stacked bar chart similar to Figure 1.4. Comment upon any similarities and differences.

(d)  Draw a pie chart showing the distribution of educational qualifications of those in work and compare it to Figure 1.5 in the text.

**Problem 1.2**  The data below show the median weekly earnings (in £s) of those in full-time employment in Great Britain in 1992, by category of education.

|  | Degree | Other higher education | A level | GCSE A–C | GCSE D–G | None |
|---|---|---|---|---|---|---|
| Males | 433 | 310 | 277 | 242 | 226 | 220 |
| Females | 346 | 278 | 201 | 183 | 173 | 146 |

(a)  In what fundamental way do the data in this table differ from those in Problem 1.1?

(b)  Construct a bar chart showing male and female earnings by education category. What does it show?

(c)  Why would it be inappropriate to construct a stacked bar chart of the data? How should one graphically present the combined data for males and females? What extra information is necessary for you to do this?

**Problem 1.3**  Using the data from Problem 1.1:

(a)  Which education category has the highest proportion of people in work? What is the proportion?

(b)  Which category of employment status has the highest proportion of people with a degree? What is the proportion?

**Problem 1.4**  Using the data from Problem 1.2:

(a)  What is the premium, in terms of median earnings, of a degree over A levels? Does this differ between men and women?

(b)  Would you expect *mean* earnings to show a similar picture? What differences, if any, might you expect?

**Problem 1.5**  The distribution of marketable wealth in 1979 in the UK is shown in the table below (taken from *Inland Revenue Statistics 1981*, p. 105):

| Range | Number 000s | Amount £m |
|---|---|---|
| 0– | 1606 | 148 |
| 1 000– | 2927 | 5 985 |
| 3 000– | 2562 | 10 090 |
| 5 000– | 3483 | 25 464 |
| 10 000– | 2876 | 35 656 |
| 15 000– | 1916 | 33 134 |
| 20 000– | 3425 | 104 829 |
| 50 000– | 621 | 46 483 |
| 100 000– | 170 | 25 763 |
| 200 000– | 59 | 30 581 |

Draw a bar chart and histogram of the data (assume the final class interval has a width of 200 000). Comment on the differences between the two. Comment on any differences between this histogram and the one for 2001 given in the text.

**Problem 1.6** The data below show the number of manufacturing plants in the UK in 1991/92 arranged according to employment:

| Number of employees | Number of firms |
|---|---|
| 1– | 95 409 |
| 10– | 15 961 |
| 20– | 16 688 |
| 50– | 7 229 |
| 100– | 4 504 |
| 200– | 2 949 |
| 500– | 790 |
| 1000– | 332 |

Draw a bar chart and histogram of the data (assume the mid-point of the last class interval is 2000). What are the major features apparent in each and what are the differences?

**Problem 1.7** Using the data from Problem 1.5:

(a) Calculate the mean, median and mode of the distribution. Why do they differ?

(b) Calculate the inter-quartile range, variance, standard deviation and coefficient of variation of the data.

(c) Calculate the skewness of the distribution.

(d) From what you have calculated, and the data in the chapter, can you draw any conclusions about the degree of inequality in wealth holdings, and how this has changed?

(e) What would be the effect upon the mean of assuming the final class width to be £10m? What would be the effects upon the median and mode?

**Problem 1.8** Using the data from Problem 1.6:

(a) Calculate the mean, median and mode of the distribution. Why do they differ?

(b) Calculate the inter-quartile range, variance, standard deviation and coefficient of variation of the data.

(c) Calculate the coefficient of skewness of the distribution.

**Problem 1.9** A motorist keeps a record of petrol purchases on a long journey, as follows:

| Petrol station | 1 | 2 | 3 |
|---|---|---|---|
| Litres purchased | 33 | 40 | 25 |
| Price per litre | 55.7 | 59.6 | 57.0 |

Calculate the average petrol price for the journey.

**Problem 1.10** Demonstrate that the weighted average calculation given in equation (1.9) in the text is equivalent to finding the total expenditure on education divided by the total number of pupils.

**Problem 1.11**   On a test taken by 100 students, the average mark is 65, with variance 144. Student A scores 83, student B scores 47.

(a)   Calculate the $z$ scores for these two students.

(b)   What is the maximum number of students with a score either better than A's or worse than B's?

(c)   What is the maximum number of students with a score better than A's?

**Problem 1.12**   The average income of a group of people is £8000. 80% of the group have incomes within the range £6000–10 000. What is the minimum value of the standard deviation of the distribution?

**Problem 1.13**   The following data show car registrations in the UK during 1970–91 (source: *ETAS 1993*, p. 57):

| Year | Registrations | Year | Registrations | Year | Registrations |
|------|---------------|------|---------------|------|---------------|
| 1970 | 91.4 | 1978 | 131.6 | 1986 | 156.9 |
| 1971 | 108.5 | 1979 | 142.1 | 1987 | 168.0 |
| 1972 | 177.6 | 1980 | 126.6 | 1988 | 184.2 |
| 1973 | 137.3 | 1981 | 124.5 | 1989 | 192.1 |
| 1974 | 102.8 | 1982 | 132.1 | 1990 | 167.1 |
| 1975 | 98.6 | 1983 | 150.5 | 1991 | 133.3 |
| 1976 | 106.5 | 1984 | 146.6 | | |
| 1977 | 109.4 | 1985 | 153.5 | | |

(a)   Draw a time-series graph of car registrations. Comment upon the main features of the series.

(b)   Draw time-series graphs of the change in registrations, the (natural) log of registrations, and the change in the ln. Comment upon the results.

**Problem 1.14**   The table below shows the different categories of investment, 1983–2002.

| Year | Dwellings | Transport | Machinery | Intangible fixed assets | Other buildings |
|------|-----------|-----------|-----------|-------------------------|-----------------|
| 1983 | 10 447 | 4 781 | 18 377 | 1 728 | 16 157 |
| 1984 | 11 932 | 5 938 | 20 782 | 2 229 | 17 708 |
| 1985 | 12 219 | 6 726 | 24 349 | 2 458 | 18 648 |
| 1986 | 14 140 | 6 527 | 25 218 | 2 184 | 20 477 |
| 1987 | 16 548 | 7 872 | 28 225 | 2 082 | 24 269 |
| 1988 | 21 097 | 9 227 | 32 614 | 2 592 | 30 713 |
| 1989 | 22 771 | 10 624 | 38 417 | 2 823 | 36 689 |
| 1990 | 21 048 | 10 571 | 37 776 | 3 571 | 41 334 |
| 1991 | 18 339 | 9 051 | 35 094 | 4 063 | 38 632 |
| 1992 | 18 825 | 8 420 | 35 071 | 3 782 | 34 485 |
| 1993 | 19 892 | 9 315 | 35 316 | 3 648 | 32 856 |
| 1994 | 21 233 | 11 395 | 38 226 | 3 613 | 33 847 |
| 1995 | 21 664 | 11 295 | 45 012 | 3 939 | 35 538 |
| 1996 | 22 516 | 12 222 | 50 197 | 4 136 | 37 220 |
| 1997 | 23 928 | 12 972 | 51 533 | 4 249 | 41 094 |
| 1998 | 25 222 | 16 143 | 59 512 | 4 547 | 45 116 |
| 1999 | 25 700 | 15 067 | 59 766 | 4 645 | 49 469 |
| 2000 | 27 394 | 13 444 | 62 698 | 4 966 | 52 708 |
| 2001 | 29 311 | 15 168 | 61 461 | 5 016 | 55 735 |
| 2002 | 35 597 | 15 825 | 54 624 | 5 542 | 58 384 |

Use appropriate graphical techniques to analyse the properties of any one of the investment series. Comment upon the results.

**Problem 1.15**  Using the data from Problem 1.13:

(a)  Calculate the average rate of growth of the series.

(b)  Calculate the standard deviation around the average growth rate.

(c)  Does the series appear to be more or less volatile than the investment figures used in the chapter? Suggest reasons.

**Problem 1.16**  Using the data from Problem 1.14:

(a)  Calculate the average rate of growth of the series for dwellings.

(b)  Calculate the standard deviation around the average growth rate.

(c)  Does the series appear to be more or less volatile than the investment figures used in the chapter? Suggest reasons.

**Problem 1.17**  How would you *expect* the following time-series variables to look when graphed? (e.g. Trended? Linear trend? Trended up or down? Stationary? Autocorrelated? Cyclical? Anything else?)

(a)  Nominal national income.

(b)  Real national income.

(c)  The nominal interest rate.

**Problem 1.18**  How would you expect the following time-series variables to look when graphed?

(a)  The price level.

(b)  The inflation rate.

(c)  The £/$ exchange rate.

**Problem 1.19**  (a)  A government bond is issued, promising to pay the bearer £1000 in five years' time. The prevailing market rate of interest is 7%. What price would you expect to pay now for the bond? What would its price be after two years? If, after two years, the market interest rate jumped to 10%, what would the price of the bond be?

(b)  A bond is issued which promises to pay £200 per annum over the next five years. If the prevailing market interest rate is 7%, how much would you be prepared to pay for the bond? Why does the answer differ from the previous question? (Assume interest is paid at the end of each year.)

**Problem 1.20**  A firm purchases for £30 000 a machine which is expected to last for 10 years, after which it will be sold for its scrap value of £3000. Calculate the average rate of depreciation per annum, and calculate the written-down value of the machine after one, two and five years.

**Problem 1.21**  Depreciation of BMW and Mercedes cars is given in the following table:

| Age | BMW 525i | Mercedes 200E |
| --- | --- | --- |
| Current | 22 275 | 21 900 |
| 1 year | 18 600 | 19 700 |
| 2 years | 15 200 | 16 625 |
| 3 years | 12 600 | 13 950 |
| 4 years | 9 750 | 11 600 |
| 5 years | 8 300 | 10 300 |

(a) Calculate the average rate of depreciation of each type of car.

(b) Use the calculated depreciation rates to estimate the value of the car after 1, 2, etc. years of age. How does this match the actual values?

(c) Graph the values and estimated values for each car.

**Problem 1.22** A bond is issued which promises to pay £400 per annum in perpetuity. How much is the bond worth now, if the interest rate is 5%? (Hint: the sum of an infinite series of the form

$$\frac{1}{1 + r} + \frac{1}{(1 + r)^2} + \frac{1}{(1 + r)^3} + \dots$$

is $1/r$, as long as $r > 0$.)

**Problem 1.23** Demonstrate, using $\Sigma$ notation, that $E(x + k) = E(x) + k$.

**Problem 1.24** Demonstrate, using $\Sigma$ notation, that $V(kx) = k^2 V(x)$.

**Problem 1.25** Criticise the following statistical reasoning. The average price of a dwelling is £54 150. The average mortgage advance is £32 760. So purchasers have to find £21 390, that is, about 40% of the purchase price. On any basis that is an enormous outlay which young couples, in particular, who are buying a house for the first time would find incredibly difficult, if not impossible, to raise.

**Problem 1.26** Criticise the following statistical reasoning. Amongst arts graduates 10% fail to find employment. Amongst science graduates only 8% remain out of work. Therefore, science graduates are better than arts graduates. (*Hint*: Imagine there are two types of job: popular and unpopular. Arts graduates tend to apply for the former, scientists for the latter.)

**Problem 1.27 (Project 1)** It has been claimed that, in spite of the UK government's desire to see lower taxation, the level of taxation in 2000 was higher than in 1979. Is this claim correct?

You should gather data which you think appropriate to the task, summarise it as necessary and write a brief report of your findings. You might like to consider the following points:

■ Should one consider tax revenue, or revenue as a proportion of GNP?

■ Should one distinguish between tax rates and the tax base (i.e. what is taxed)?

■ Has the balance between direct and indirect taxation changed?

■ Have different sections of the population fared differently?

You might like to consider other points, and do the Problem for a different country. Suitable data sources for the UK are: *Inland Revenue Statistics*, *UK National Accounts*, *Annual Abstract of Statistics* or *Financial Statistics*.

**Problem 1.28 (Project 2)** Is the employment and unemployment experience of the UK economy worse than that of its competitors? Write a report on this topic in a similar manner to the project above. You might consider rates of unemployment in the UK and other countries; trends in unemployment in each of the countries; the growth in employment in each country; the structure of employment (e.g. full-time/part-time) and unemployment (e.g. long-term/short-term).

You might use data for a number of countries, or concentrate on two in more depth. Suitable data sources are: *OECD Main Economic Indicators*; *European Economy* (published by the European Commission); *Employment Gazette*.

**Reference**    A.B. Atkinson, *The Economics of Inequality*, 2nd edn, Oxford University Press, 1983.

# Answers to exercises

**Exercise 1.1**    (a)

(b)

(c)

**English tourists**

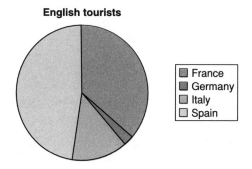

It is clear the English are more likely to visit Spain than are other nationalities.

Exercise 1.2   (a)   Bar chart

Histogram

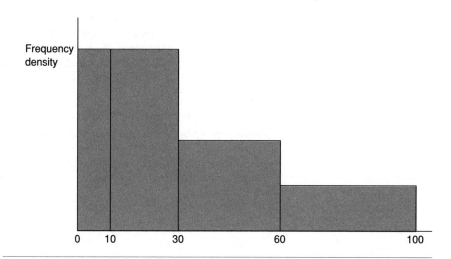

**Exercise 1.3** (a)

| | Midpoint, $x$ | Frequency, $f$ | $fx$ |
|---|---|---|---|
| 0–10 | 5 | 20 | 100 |
| 11–30 | 20 | 40 | 800 |
| 31–60 | 45 | 30 | 1350 |
| 60–100 | 80 | 20 | 1600 |
| | | 110 | 3850 |

Hence the mean = 3850/110 = 35.

The median is contained in the 11–30 group and is 35/40 of the way through the interval (20 + 35 gets us to observation 55). Hence the median is $11 + 35/40 \times 19 = 27.625$.

The mode is anywhere in the 0–30 range, the frequency density is the same throughout this range.

(b)

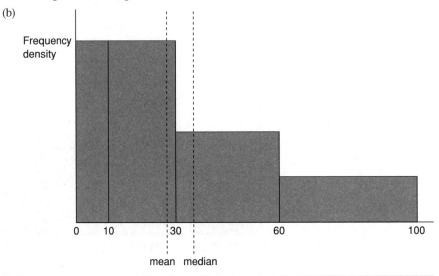

**Exercise 1.4** (a) Q1 relates to observation 27.5 (=110/4). This observation lies in the 11–30 range. There are 20 observations in the first class interval, so Q1 will relate to observation 7.5 in the second interval. Hence we need to go 7.5/40 of the way through the interval. This gives $11 + (7.5/40) \times 19 = 14.6$. Similarly, Q3 is 22.5/30 of the way through the third interval, yielding Q3 = $31 + 22.5/30 \times 29 = 52.8$. The IQR is therefore 38, approximately. For the variance we obtain $\Sigma fx = 3850$ and $\Sigma fx^2 = 205\,250$. The variance is therefore $\sigma^2 = 205\,250/110 - 35^2 = 640.9$ and the standard deviation 25.3.

(b) CV = 25.3/35 = 0.72.

(c) $1.3 \times 25.3 = 32.9$, not far from the IQR value of 38.

(d) 1 standard deviation either side of the mean takes us from 9.7 up to 60.3. This contains all 70 observations in the second and third intervals plus perhaps one from the first interval. Thus we get approximately 71 observations within this range. Chebyshev's inequality does not help us here as it is not defined for $k \leq 1$.

**Exercise 1.5**    (a)

(b)

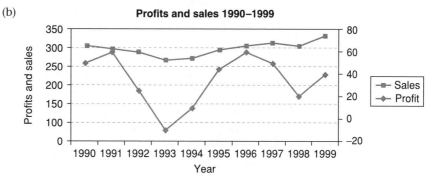

Using the second axis brings out the variability of profits relative to sales.

**Exercise 1.6**    (a)    The average profit is 35. The average rate of growth is calculated by comparing the end values 50 and 40, over the ten-year period. The ratio is 0.8. Taking the ninth root of this (nine years of growth) gives $\sqrt[9]{0.8} = 0.926$ so the annual rate of growth is $0.976 - 1 = -2.4\%$.

(b)    The variances are (using the sample variance formula): for profits, $\Sigma(x - \mu)^2 = 4800$ and dividing by 9 gives 533.3. For sales, the mean is 291 and $\Sigma(x - \mu)^2 = 4540$. The variance is therefore $4540/9 = 504.4$. This is similar in absolute size to the variance of profits, but relative to the mean it is much smaller.

**Exercise 1.7**    (a/b)

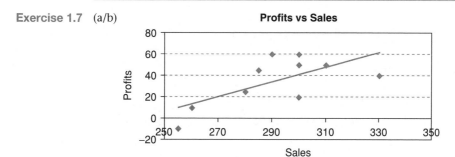

The trend line seems to show a positive relationship between the variables: higher profits are associated with higher sales.

## Appendix 1A    Σ notation

The Greek symbol $\Sigma$ (capital sigma) means 'add up' and is a shorthand way of writing what would otherwise be long algebraic expressions. For example, given the following observations on $x$:

| $x_1$ | $x_2$ | $x_3$ | $x_4$ | $x_5$ |
|---|---|---|---|---|
| 3 | 5 | 6 | 4 | 8 |

then

$$\sum_{i=1}^{5} x_i = x_1 + x_2 + x_3 + x_4 + x_5 = 3 + 5 + 6 + 4 + 8 = 26$$

To expand the sigma expression, the subscript $i$ is replaced by successive integers, beginning with the one below the $\Sigma$ sign and ending with the one above it. Similarly

$$\sum_{i=2}^{4} x_i = x_2 + x_3 + x_4 = 5 + 6 + 4 = 15$$

When it is clear what range of values $i$ takes, the formula can be simplified to $\Sigma_i x_i$ or $\Sigma x_i$ or even $\Sigma x$.

When frequencies are associated with each of the observations, as in the data below:

| $i$ | 1 | 2 | 3 | 4 | 5 |
|---|---|---|---|---|---|
| $x_i$ | 3 | 5 | 6 | 4 | 8 |
| $f_i$ | 2 | 2 | 4 | 3 | 1 |

then

$$\sum_{i=1}^{i=5} f_i x_i = f_1 x_1 + \ldots + f_5 x_5 = 2 \times 3 + \ldots + 1 \times 8 = 60$$

and

$$\Sigma f_i = 2 + 2 + 4 + 3 + 1 = 12$$

Thus the sum of the 12 observations is 60 and the mean is

$$\frac{\Sigma fx}{\Sigma f} = \frac{60}{12} = 5$$

Further examples are:

$$\Sigma x^2 = x_1^2 + x_2^2 + \ldots + x_5^2 = 150$$

$$(\Sigma x)^2 = (x_1 + x_2 + \ldots + x_5)^2 = 676$$

$$\Sigma fx^2 = f_1 x_1^2 + f_2 x_2^2 + \ldots + f_5 x_5^2 = 2 \times 3^2 + 2 \times 5^2 + \ldots + 1 \times 8^2 = 324$$

Using $\Sigma$ notation we can see the effect of transforming $x$ by dividing by 1000, as was done in calculating the average level of wealth. Instead of working with $x$ we used $kx$, where $k = 1/1000$. In finding the mean we calculated

(1.34) $\quad \dfrac{\Sigma kx}{N} = \dfrac{kx_1 + kx_2 + \ldots}{N} = \dfrac{k(x_1 + x_2 + \ldots)}{N} = k\dfrac{\Sigma x}{N}$

so to find the mean of the original variable $x$ we had to divide by $k$ again, i.e. multiply by 1000. In general, whenever each observation in a sum is multiplied by a constant, the constant can be taken outside the summation operator, as in (1.34) above.

## Problems on Σ notation

**Problem 1A.1**  Given the following data on $x_i$: {4, 6, 3, 2, 5}, evaluate:

$\Sigma x_i, \Sigma x_i^2, (\Sigma x_i)^2, \Sigma(x_i - 3), \Sigma x_i - 3, \displaystyle\sum_{i=2}^{4} x_i$

**Problem 1A.2**  Given the following data on $x_i$: {8, 12, 6, 4, 10}, evaluate:

$\Sigma x_i, \Sigma x_i^2, (\Sigma x_i)^2, \Sigma(x_i - 3), \Sigma x_i - 3, \displaystyle\sum_{i=2}^{4} x_i$

**Problem 1A.3**  Given the following frequencies, $f_i$, associated with the $x$ values in Problem A1: {5, 3, 3, 8, 5}, evaluate:

$\Sigma fx, \Sigma fx^2, \Sigma f(x - 3), \Sigma fx - 3$

**Problem 1A.4**  Given the following frequencies, $f_i$, associated with the $x$ values in Problem 1.A2: {10, 6, 6, 16, 10}, evaluate:

$\Sigma fx, \Sigma fx^2, \Sigma f(x - 3), \Sigma fx - 3$

**Problem 1A.5**  Given the pairs of observations on $x$ and $y$,

| $x$ | 4 | 3 | 6 | 8 | 12 |
|---|---|---|---|---|---|
| $y$ | 3 | 9 | 1 | 4 | 3 |

evaluate:

$\Sigma xy, \Sigma x(y - 3), \Sigma(x + 2)(y - 1)$

**Problem 1A.6**  Given the pairs of observations on $x$ and $y$,

| $x$ | 3 | 7 | 4 | 1 | 9 |
|---|---|---|---|---|---|
| $y$ | 1 | 2 | 5 | 1 | 2 |

evaluate:

$\Sigma xy, \Sigma x(y - 2), \Sigma(x - 2)(y + 1).$

**Problem 1A.7**  Demonstrate that

$$\frac{\Sigma f(x - k)}{\Sigma f} = \frac{\Sigma fx}{\Sigma f} - k$$

where $k$ is a constant.

**Problem 1A.8**  Demonstrate that

$$\frac{\Sigma f(x - \mu)^2}{\Sigma f} = \frac{\Sigma fx^2}{\Sigma f} - \mu^2$$

## Appendix 1B  E and V operators

These operators are an extremely useful form of notation that we shall make use of later in the book. It is quite easy to keep track of the effects of data transformations using them. There are a few simple rules for manipulating them that allow some problems to be solved quickly and elegantly.

$E(x)$ is the mean of a distribution and $V(x)$ is its variance. We showed above in (1.34) that multiplying each observation by a constant $k$ multiplies the mean by $k$. We can express this as:

**(1.35)**     $E(kx) = kE(x)$

If a constant is added to every observation the effect is to add that constant to the mean (see Problem 1.23):

**(1.36)**     $E(x + a) = E(x) + a$

(Graphically, the whole distribution is shifted $a$ units to the right and hence so is the mean.) Combining (1.35) and (1.36):

**(1.37)**     $E(kx + a) = kE(x) + a$

Similarly for the variance operator it can be shown that:

**(1.38)**     $V(x + k) = V(x)$

Proof:

$$V(x + k) = \frac{\Sigma((x + k) - (\mu + k))^2}{N} = \frac{\Sigma((x - \mu) + (k - k))^2}{N} = \frac{\Sigma(x - \mu)^2}{N} = V(x)$$

(A shift of the whole distribution leaves the variance unchanged.) Also:

**(1.39)**     $V(kx) = k^2V(x)$

(See Problem 1.24 above.) This is why, when the wealth figures were divided by 1000, the variance became divided by $1000^2$. Applying (1.38) and (1.39):

**(1.40)**     $V(kx + a) = k^2V(x)$

Finally, we should note that V itself can be expressed in terms of E:

**(1.41)**     $V(x) = E(x - E(x))^2$

## Appendix 1C    Using logarithms

Logarithms are less often used now that cheap electronic calculators are available. Formerly logarithms were an indispensable aid to calculation. However, the logarithmic transformation is useful in other contexts in statistics and economics so its use is briefly set out here.

The logarithm (to the base 10) of a number $x$ is defined as the power to which 10 must be raised to give $x$. For example, $10^2 = 100$, so the log of 100 is 2 and we write $\log_{10} 100 = 2$ or simply $\log 100 = 2$.

Similarly, the log of 1000 is 3 ($1000 = 10^3$), of 10 000 it is 4, etc. We are not restricted to integer (whole number) powers of 10, so for example $10^{2.5} = 316.227766$ (try this if you have a scientific calculator), so the log of 316.227766 is 2.5. Every number $x$ can therefore be represented by its logarithm.

**Multiplication of two numbers**

We can use logarithms to multiply two numbers $x$ and $y$, based on the property

$$\log xy = \log x + \log y$$

For example, to multiply 316.227766 by 10:

$$\begin{aligned} \log(316.227766 \times 10) &= \log 316.227766 + \log 10 \\ &= 2.5 + 1 \\ &= 3.5 \end{aligned}$$

The *anti-log* of 3.5 is given by $10^{3.5} = 3162.27766$ which is the answer.

Taking the anti-log (i.e. 10 raised to a power) is the inverse of the log transformation. Schematically we have:

$$x \rightarrow \text{take logarithms} \rightarrow a \ (= \log x) \rightarrow \text{raise 10 to the power } a \rightarrow x$$

**Division**

To divide one number by another we subtract the logs. For example, to divide 316.227766 by 100:

$$\begin{aligned} \log(316.227766/100) &= \log 316.227766 - \log 100 \\ &= 2.5 - 2 \\ &= 0.5 \end{aligned}$$

and

$$10^{0.5} = 3.16227766$$

**Powers and roots**

Logarithms simplify the process of raising a number to a power. To find the square of a number, multiply the logarithm by 2, e.g. to find $316.227766^2$:

$$\log(316.227766^2) = 2 \log(316.227766) = 5$$

and

$$10^5 = 100\ 000$$

To find the square root of a number (equivalent to raising it to the power $\frac{1}{2}$) divide the log by 2. To find the $n$th root, divide the log by $n$. For example, in the text we have to find the $32^{nd}$ root of 16.936:

$$\frac{\log(16.936)}{32} = 0.0384$$

and

$$10^{0.0384} = 1.092$$

**Common and natural logarithms**

Logarithms to the base 10 are known as common logarithms but one can use any number as the base. *Natural* logarithms are based on the number e (= 2.71828 . . . ) and we write ln $x$ instead of log $x$ to distinguish them from common logarithms. So, for example,

ln 316.227766 = 5.756462732

since

$$e^{5.756462732} = 316.227766$$

Natural logarithms can be used in the same way as common logarithms and have similar properties. Use the 'ln' key on your calculator just as you would the 'log' key, but remember that the inverse transformation is $e^x$ rather than $10^x$.

## Problems on logarithms

**Problem 1C.1**    Find the common logarithms of: 0.15, 1.5, 15, 150, 1500, 83.7225, 9.15, –12.

**Problem 1C.2**    Find the log of the following values: 0.8, 8, 80, 4, 16, –37.

**Problem 1C.3**    Find the natural logarithms of: 0.15, 1.5, 15, 225, –4.

**Problem 1C.4**    Find the ln of the following values: 0.3, e, 3, 33, –1.

**Problem 1C.5**    Find the anti-log of the following values: –0.823909, 1.1, 2.1, 3.1, 12.

**Problem 1C.6**    Find the anti-log of the following values: –0.09691, 2.3, 3.3, 6.3.

**Problem 1C.7**    Find the anti-ln of the following values: 2.70805, 3.70805, 1, 10.

**Problem 1C.8**    Find the anti-ln of the following values: 3.496508, 14, 15, –1.

**Problem 1C.9**    Evaluate: $\sqrt[2]{10}$, $\sqrt[4]{3.7}$, $4^{1/4}$, $12^{-3}$, $25^{-3/2}$.

**Problem 1C.10**   Evaluate: $\sqrt[3]{30}$, $\sqrt[6]{17}$, $8^{1/4}$, $15^{0}$, $12^{0}$, $3^{-1/3}$.

# 2 Probability

**Learning outcomes**

By the end of this chapter you should be able to:

- understand the essential concept of the probability of an event occurring

- appreciate that the probability of a combination of events occurring can be calculated using simple arithmetic rules (the addition and multiplication rules)

- understand that a probability can depend upon the outcome of other events (conditional probability)

- know how to make use of probability theory to help make decisions in situations of uncertainty

## Probability theory and statistical inference

In October 1985 Mrs Evelyn Adams of New Jersey, USA, won $3.9 million in the State lottery at odds of 1 in 3 200 000. In February 1986 she again won, though this time only (!) $1.4 million at odds of 1 in 5 200 000. The odds against both these wins were calculated at about 1 in 17 300 billion. Mrs Adams is quoted as saying 'They say good things come in threes, so . . .'.

The above story illustrates the principles of probability at work. The same principles underlie the theory of statistical inference. Statistical inference is the task of drawing conclusions (inferences) about a population from a sample of data drawn from that population. For example, we might have a survey which shows that 30% of a sample of 100 families intend to take a holiday abroad next year. What can we conclude from this about *all* families? The techniques set out in this and subsequent chapters show how to accomplish this.

Why is knowledge of probability necessary for the study of statistical inference? In order to be able to say something about a population on the basis of some sample evidence we must first examine how the sample data are collected. In many cases, the sample is a random one, i.e. the observations making up the sample are chosen at random from the population. If a second sample were selected it would almost certainly be different from the first. Each member of the population has a particular probability of being in the sample (in simple random sampling the probability is the same for all members of the population). To understand sampling procedures, and the implications for statistical inference, we must therefore first examine the theory of probability.

As an illustration of this, suppose we wish to know if a coin is fair, i.e. equally likely to fall heads or tails. The coin is tossed ten times and ten heads are recorded. This constitutes a random sample of tosses of the coin. What can we infer about the coin? *If* it is fair, the probability of getting ten heads is 1 in 1024, so a fairly unlikely event seems to have happened. We might reasonably infer therefore that the coin is biased towards heads.

## The definition of probability

The first task is to define precisely what is meant by probability. This is not as easy as one might imagine and there are a number of different schools of thought on the subject. Consider the following questions:

- What is the probability of 'heads' occurring on the toss of a coin?
- What is the probability of a driver having an accident in a year of driving?
- What is the probability of a country such as Peru defaulting on its international loan repayments (as Mexico did in the 1980s)?

We shall use these questions as examples when examining the different schools of thought on probability.

**The frequentist view**

Considering the first question above, the frequentist view would be that the probability is equal to the proportion of heads obtained from a coin in the

**Figure 2.1**
**Proportion of heads in**
**250 tosses of a coin**

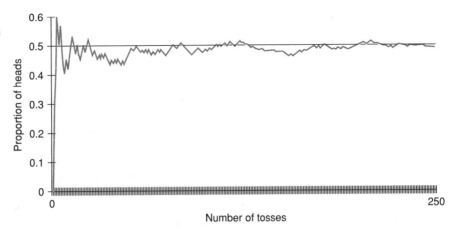

long run, i.e. if the coin were tossed many times. The first few results of such an experiment might be:

H, T, T, H, H, H, T, H, T, . . .

After a while, the proportion of heads settles down at some particular fraction and subsequent tosses will individually have an insignificant effect upon the value. Figure 2.1 shows the result of tossing a coin 250 times and recording the proportion of heads (actually, this was simulated on a computer: life is too short to do it for real).

This shows the proportion settling down at a value of about 0.50, which indicates an unbiased coin (or rather, an unbiased computer in this case!). This value is the probability, according to the frequentist view. To be more precise, the probability is the proportion of heads obtained as the number of tosses *approaches infinity*. In general we can define Pr(*H*), the probability of event *H* (in this case heads) occurring, as

$$\Pr(H) = \frac{\text{number of occurrences of } H}{\text{number of trials}} \quad \textit{as the number of trials approaches infinity}$$

In this case, each toss of the coin constitutes a trial.

This definition gets round the obvious question of how many trials are needed before the probability emerges, but means that the probability of an event cannot strictly be obtained in finite time.

Although this approach appears attractive in theory, it does have its problems. One couldn't actually toss the coin an infinite number of times. Or, what if one took a different coin, would the results from the first coin necessarily apply to the second?

Perhaps more seriously, the definition is of less use for the second and third questions posed above. Calculating the probability of an accident is not too problematic: it may be defined as the proportion of all drivers having an accident during the year. However, this may not be relevant for a *particular* driver, since drivers vary so much in their accident records. And how would you answer the third question? There is no long run that we can appeal to. We cannot re-run history over and over again to see in what proportion of cases the country defaults. Yet this is what lenders want to know and credit-rating agencies have to assess. Maybe another approach is needed.

**The subjective view**

According to the subjective view, probability is a degree of belief that someone holds about the likelihood of an event occurring. It is inevitably subjective and therefore some argue that it should be the degree of belief that it is *rational* to hold, but this just shifts the argument to what is meant by 'rational'. Some progress can be made by distinguishing between prior and posterior beliefs. The former are those held before any evidence is considered; the latter are the modified probabilities in the light of the evidence. For example, one might initially believe a coin to be fair (the prior probability of heads is one-half), but not after seeing only five heads in fifty tosses (the posterior probability would be less than a half).

Although it has its attractions, this approach (which is the basis of Bayesian statistics) also has its drawbacks. It is not always clear how one should arrive at the prior beliefs, particularly when one really has no prior information. Also, these methods often require the use of sophisticated mathematics, which may account for the limited use made of them. The development of more powerful computers and user-friendly software may increase the popularity of the Bayesian approach.

There is not universal agreement therefore as to the precise definition of probability. We do not have space here to explore the issue further, so we will ignore the problem! The probability of an event occurring will be defined as a certain value and we won't worry about the precise origin or meaning of that value. This is an axiomatic approach: we simply state what the probability is, without justifying it, and then examine the consequences.

**Exercise 2.1**

(a)  Define the probability of an event according to the frequentist view.

(b)  Define the probability of an event according to the subjective view.

**Exercise 2.2**

For the following events, suggest how their probability might be calculated. In each case, consider whether you have used the frequentist or subjective view of probability (or possibly some mixture).

(a)  The Republican party winning the next US election.

(b)  The number 5 being drawn in next week's lottery.

(c)  A repetition of the 2004 Asian tsunami.

(d)  Your train home being late.

## Probability theory: the building blocks

We start with a few definitions, to establish a vocabulary that we will subsequently use:

- An experiment is an action such as flipping a coin, which has a number of possible outcomes or events, such as heads or tails.
- A trial is a single performance of the experiment, with a single outcome.

**Figure 2.2**
**The sample space for drawing from a pack of cards**

| | A | K | Q | J | 10 | 9 | 8 | 7 | 6 | 5 | 4 | 3 | 2 |
|---|---|---|---|---|---|---|---|---|---|---|---|---|---|
| ♠ | • | • | • | • | • | • | • | • | • | • | • | • | • |
| ♥ | • | • | • | • | • | • | • | • | • | • | • | • | • |
| ♦ | • | • | • | • | • | • | • | • | • | • | • | • | • |
| ♣ | • | • | • | • | • | • | • | • | • | • | • | • | • |

- The sample space consists of all the possible outcomes of the experiment. The outcomes for a single toss of a coin are {heads, tails}, for example, and these constitute the sample space for a toss of a coin. The outcomes in the sample space are mutually exclusive, which means that the occurrence of one rules out all the others. One cannot have both heads and tails in a single toss of a coin. As a further example, if a single card is drawn at random from a pack, then the sample space may be drawn as in Figure 2.2. Each point represents one card in the pack and there are 52 points altogether. (The sample space could be set out in alternative ways. For instance, one could write a list of all the cards: ace of spades, king of spades, . . . , two of clubs. One can choose the representation most suitable for the problem at hand.)
- With each outcome in the sample space we can associate a probability, which is the chance of that outcome occurring. The probability of heads is one-half; the probability of drawing the ace of spades from a pack of cards is one in 52, etc.

There are restrictions upon the probabilities we can associate with the outcomes in the sample space. These are needed to ensure that we do not come up with self-contradictory results; for example, it would be odd to arrive at the conclusion that we could expect heads more than half the time *and* tails more than half the time. To ensure our results are always consistent, the following rules apply to probabilities:

- The probability of an event must lie between 0 and 1, i.e.

**(2.1)**    $0 \leq \Pr(A) \leq 1$, for any event $A$

The explanation is straightforward. If $A$ is certain to occur it occurs in 100% of all trials and so its probability is 1. If $A$ is certain not to occur then its probability is 0, since it never happens however many trials there are. Since one cannot be more certain than certain, probabilities of less than 0 or more than 1 can never occur, and (2.1) follows.

- The sum of the probabilities associated with all the outcomes in the sample space is 1. Formally

**(2.2)**    $\sum P_i = 1$

where $P_i$ is the probability of event $i$ occurring. This follows from the fact that one, and only one, of the outcomes *must* occur, since they are mutually exclusive and also exhaustive, i.e. they define all the possibilities.

- Following on from (2.2) we may define the complement of an event as everything in the sample space apart from that event. The complement of heads is tails, for example. If we write the complement of $A$ as not-$A$ then it follows that $\text{Pr}(A) + \text{Pr}(\text{not-}A) = 1$ and hence

(2.3)     $\text{Pr}(\text{not-}A) = 1 - \text{Pr}(A)$

## Compound events

Most practical problems require the calculation of the probability of a set of outcomes rather than just a single one, or the probability of a series of outcomes in separate trials. For example, the probability of drawing a spade at random from a pack of cards encompasses 13 points in the sample space (one for each spade). This probability is 13 out of 52, or one-quarter, which is fairly obvious; but for more complex problems the answer is not immediately evident. We refer to such sets of outcomes as compound events. Some examples are getting a five *or* a six on a throw of a die or drawing an ace *and* a queen to complete a 'straight' in a game of poker.

It is sometimes possible to calculate the probability of a compound event by examining the sample space, as in the case of drawing a spade above. However, in many cases this is not so, for the sample space is too complex or even impossible to write down. For example, the sample space for three draws of a card from a pack consists of over 140 000 points! (A typical point might be, for example, the ten of spades, eight of hearts and three of diamonds.) An alternative method is needed. Fortunately there are a few simple rules for manipulating probabilities which help us to calculate the probabilities of compound events.

If the previous examples are examined closely it can be seen that outcomes are being compounded using the words 'or' and 'and': '. . . five *or* six on a single throw . . .'; '. . . an ace *and* a queen . . .'. 'And' and 'or' act as *operators*, and compound events are made up of simple events compounded by these two operators. The following rules for manipulating probabilities show how to handle these operators and thus how to calculate the probability of a compound event.

## The addition rule

This rule is associated with 'or'. When we want the probability of one outcome *or* another occurring, we add the probabilities of each. More formally, the probability of $A$ or $B$ occurring is given by

(2.4)     $\text{Pr}(A \text{ or } B) = \text{Pr}(A) + \text{Pr}(B)$

So, for example, the probability of a five or a six on a roll of a die is

(2.5)     $\text{Pr}(5 \text{ or } 6) = 1/6 + 1/6 = 1/3$

This answer can be verified from the sample space, as shown in Figure 2.3. Each dot represents a simple event (one to six). The compound event is made up of two of the six points, shaded in Figure 2.3, so the probability is 2/6 or 1/3.

However, (2.4) is not a general solution to this type of problem, i.e. it does not *always* work, as can be seen from the following example. What is the probability of a queen or a spade in a single draw from a pack of cards? $\text{Pr}(Q) = 4/52$ (four queens in the pack) and $\text{Pr}(S) = 13/52$ (13 spades), so applying (2.4) gives

(2.6)     $\text{Pr}(Q \text{ or } S) = \text{Pr}(Q) + \text{Pr}(S) = 4/52 + 13/52 = 17/52$

**Figure 2.3**
**The sample space for rolling a die**

**Figure 2.4**
**The sample space for drawing a queen or a spade**

However, if the sample space is examined the correct answer is found to be 16/52, as in Figure 2.4. The problem is that one point in the sample space (the one representing the queen of spades) is double-counted, once as a queen and again as a spade. The event 'drawing a queen *and* a spade' is possible, and gets double-counted. Equation (2.4) has to be modified by subtracting the probability of getting a queen *and* a spade, to eliminate the double counting. The correct answer is obtained from

(2.7)　　$\Pr(Q \text{ or } S) = \Pr(Q) + \Pr(S) - \Pr(Q \text{ and } S)$
　　　　　　　$= 4/52 + 13/52 - 1/52$
　　　　　　　$= 16/52$

The general rule is therefore

(2.8)　　$\Pr(A \text{ or } B) = \Pr(A) + \Pr(B) - \Pr(A \text{ and } B)$

Rule (2.4) worked for the die example because $\Pr(5 \text{ and } 6) = 0$ since a five and a six cannot simultaneously occur. The double counting did not affect the calculation of the probability.

In general, therefore, one should use (2.8), but when two events are mutually exclusive the rule simplifies to (2.4).

**The multiplication rule**

The multiplication rule is associated with use of the word 'and' to combine events. Consider a mother with two children. What is the probability that they are both boys? This is really a compound event: a boy on the first birth *and* a boy on the second. Assume that in a single birth a boy or girl is equally likely, so $\Pr(\text{boy}) = \Pr(\text{girl}) = 0.5$. Denote by $\Pr(B1)$ the probability of a boy on the first birth and by $\Pr(B2)$ the probability of a boy on the second. Thus the question asks for $\Pr(B1 \text{ and } B2)$ and this is given by:

(2.9)　　$\Pr(B1 \text{ and } B2) = \Pr(B1) \times \Pr(B2) = 0.5 \times 0.5$
　　　　　　　$= 0.25$

Intuitively, the multiplication rule can be understood as follows. One-half of mothers have a boy on their first birth and of these, one-half will again have a boy on the second. Therefore a quarter of mothers have two boys.

Like the addition rule, the multiplication rule requires slight modification before it can be applied generally and give the right answer in all circumstances. The example assumes first and second births to be independent events, i.e. that having a boy on the first birth does not affect the probability of a boy on the second. This assumption is not always valid.

Write $\Pr(B2|B1)$ to indicate the probability of the event *B2 given* that the event *B1* has occurred. (This is known as the conditional probability, more precisely the probability of $B2$ conditional upon $B1$.) Let us drop the independence assumption and suppose the following:

(2.10)    $\Pr(B1) = \Pr(G1) = 0.5$

i.e. boys and girls are equally likely on the first birth, and

(2.11)    $\Pr(B2|B1) = \Pr(G2|G1) = 0.6$

i.e. a boy is more likely to be followed by another boy, and a girl by another girl. (It is easy to work out $\Pr(B2|G1)$ and $\Pr(G2|B1)$. What are they?)

Now what is the probability of two boys? Half of all mothers have a boy first, and of these, 60% have another boy. Thus 30% (60% of 50%) of mothers have two boys. This is obtained from the rule:

(2.12)    $$\begin{aligned} \Pr(B1 \text{ and } B2) &= \Pr(B1) \times \Pr(B2|B1) \\ &= 0.5 \times 0.6 \\ &= 0.3 \end{aligned}$$

Thus in general we have:

(2.13)    $\Pr(A \text{ and } B) = \Pr(A) \times \Pr(B|A)$

which simplifies to

(2.14)    $\Pr(A \text{ and } B) = \Pr(A) \times \Pr(B)$

if $A$ and $B$ are independent.

Independence may therefore be defined as follows: two events, $A$ and $B$, are independent if the probability of one occurring is not influenced by the fact of the other having occurred. Formally, if $A$ and $B$ are independent then

(2.15)    $\Pr(B|A) = \Pr(B|\text{not } A) = \Pr(B)$

and

(2.16)    $\Pr(A|B) = \Pr(A|\text{not } B) = \Pr(A)$

The concept of independence is an important one in statistics, as it usually simplifies problems considerably. If two variables are known to be independent then we can analyse the behaviour of one without worrying about what is happening to the other variable. For example, sales of computers are independent of temperature, so if one is trying to predict sales next month one does not need to worry about the weather. In contrast, ice cream sales do depend on the weather, so predicting sales accurately requires one to forecast the weather first.

---

### Intuition does not always work with probabilities!

Counter-intuitive results frequently arise in probability, which is why it is wise to use the rules to calculate probabilities in tricky situations, rather than rely on intuition. Take the following questions:

■ What is the probability of obtaining two heads (HH) in two tosses of a coin?
■ What is the probability of obtaining tails followed by heads (TH)?
■ If a coin is tossed until either HH or TH occurs, what are the probabilities of each sequence occurring first?

The answers to the first two are easy: $^1/_2 \times {}^1/_2 = {}^1/_4$ in each case. You might therefore conclude that each sequence is equally likely to be the first observed, but you would be wrong!

Unless HH occurs on the first two tosses, then TH *must* occur first. HH is therefore the first sequence *only* if it occurs on the first two tosses, which has a probability of $^1/_4$. The probability that TH is first is therefore $^3/_4$. The probabilities are unequal, a strange result. Now try the same thing with HHH and THH and three tosses of a coin.

**Combining the addition and multiplication rules**

More complex problems can be solved by suitable combinations of the addition and multiplication formulae. For example, what is the probability of a mother having one child of each sex? This could occur in one of two ways: a girl followed by a boy or a boy followed by a girl. It is important to note that these are two different routes to the same outcome. Therefore we have (assuming non-independence according to (2.11))

$$\Pr(1 \text{ girl, } 1 \text{ boy}) = \Pr((G1 \text{ and } B2) \text{ or } (B1 \text{ and } G2))$$
$$= \Pr(G1) \times \Pr(B2|G1) + \Pr(B1) \times \Pr(G2|B1)$$
$$= (0.5 \times 0.4) + (0.5 \times 0.4)$$
$$= 0.4$$

The answer can be checked if we remember (2.2) stating that probabilities must sum to 1. We have calculated the probability of two boys (0.3) and of a child of each sex (0.4). The only other possibility is of two girls. This probability must be 0.3, the same as two boys, since boys and girls are treated symmetrically in this problem (even with the non-independence assumption). The sum of the three possibilities (two boys, one of each or two girls) is therefore $0.3 + 0.4 + 0.3 = 1$, as it should be.

Note that the problem would have been different if we had asked for the probability of the mother having one girl with a younger brother.

**Tree diagrams**

The preceding problem can be illustrated using a tree diagram, which often helps to clarify a problem. A tree diagram is an alternative way of enumerating all possible outcomes in the sample space, with the associated probabilities. The diagram for two children is shown in Figure 2.5.

The diagram begins at the left and the first node shows the possible alternatives (boy, girl) at that point and the associated probabilities (0.5, 0.5). The next two nodes show the alternatives and probabilities for the second birth, given the sex of the first child. The final four nodes show the possible results: boy, boy; boy, girl; girl, boy; and girl, girl.

To find the probability of two girls, using the tree diagram, follow the lowest path, multiplying the probabilities along it to give $0.5 \times 0.6 = 0.3$. To find the probability of one child of each sex it is necessary to follow all the routes which lead to such an outcome. There are two in this case: leading to boy, girl and to girl, boy. Each of these has a probability of 0.2, obtained by multiplying the probabilities along that branch of the tree. Adding these together (since either one *or* the other leads to the desired outcome) yields the answer, giving $0.2 + 0.2 = 0.4$. This provides a graphical alternative to the formulae used above and may help comprehension.

**Figure 2.5**
**Tree diagram for a family with two children**

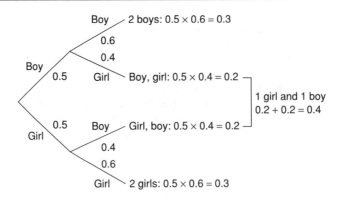

The tree diagram can obviously be extended to cover third and subsequent children although the number of branches rapidly increases (in geometric progression). The difficulty then becomes not just the calculation of the probability attached to each outcome, but sorting out which branches should be taken into account in the calculation. Suppose we consider a family of five children of whom three are girls. To simplify matters we again assume independence of probabilities. The appropriate tree diagram has $2^5 = 32$ end-points, each with probability 1/32. How many of these relate to families with three girls and two boys, for example? One can draw the diagram and count them, yielding the answer 10, but it takes considerable time and is prone to error. Far better would be to use a formula. To develop this, we use the ideas of **combinations** and **permutations**.

**Combinations and permutations**

How can we establish the number of ways of having three girls and two boys in a family of five children? One way would be to write down all the possible orderings:

GGGBB   GGBGB   GGBBG   GBGGB   GBGBG
GBBGG   BGGGB   BGGBG   BGBGG   BBGGG

This shows that there are ten such orderings, so the probability of three girls and two boys in a family of five children is 10/32. In more complex problems this soon becomes difficult or impossible. The record number of children born to a British mother is 39 (!) of whom 32 were girls. The appropriate tree diagram has over five thousand billion 'routes' through it, and drawing one line (i.e. for one child) per second would imply 17 433 years to complete the task! Rather than do this, we use the **combinatorial** formula. Suppose there are $n$ children, $r$ of them girls, then the number of orderings, denoted $nCr$, is obtained from[1]

(2.17)    $$nCr = \frac{n!}{r!(n-r)!} = \frac{n \times (n-1) \times \ldots \times 1}{\{r \times (r-1) \times \ldots \times 1\} \times \{(n-r) \times (n-r-1) \times \ldots \times 1\}}$$

[1] $n!$ is read '$n$ factorial' and is defined as the product of all the integers up to and including $n$. Thus, for example, $3! = 3 \times 2 \times 1 = 6$.

In the above example $n = 5$, $r = 3$ so the number of orderings is

(2.18)    $5C3 = \dfrac{5 \times 4 \times 3 \times 2 \times 1}{\{3 \times 2 \times 1\} \times \{2 \times 1\}} = 10$

If there were four girls out of five children then the number of orderings or combinations would be

(2.19)    $5C4 = \dfrac{5 \times 4 \times 3 \times 2 \times 1}{\{4 \times 3 \times 2 \times 1\} \times 1} = 5$

This gives five possible orderings, i.e. the single boy could be the first, second, third, fourth or fifth born.

Why does this formula work? Consider five empty places to fill, corresponding to the five births in chronological order. Take the case of three girls (call them Amanda, Bridget and Caroline for convenience) who have to fill three of the five places. For Amanda there is a choice of five empty places. Having 'chosen' one, there remain four for Bridget, so there are $5 \times 4 = 20$ possibilities (i.e. ways in which these two could choose their places). Three remain for Caroline, so there are 60 (= $5 \times 4 \times 3$) possible orderings in all (the two boys take the two remaining places). Sixty is the number of *permutations* of three *named* girls in five births. This is written $5P3$ or in general $nPr$. Hence

$5P3 = 5 \times 4 \times 3$

or in general

(2.20)    $nPr = n \times (n - 1) \times \ldots \times (n - r + 1)$

A simpler formula is obtained by multiplying and dividing by $(n - r)!$

(2.21)    $nPr = \dfrac{n \times (n - r) \times \ldots \times (n - r + 1) \times (n - r)!}{(n - r)!}$

$= \dfrac{n!}{(n - r)!}$

What is the difference between $nPr$ and $nCr$? The latter does not distinguish between the girls; the two cases Amanda, Bridget, Caroline, boy, boy and Bridget, Amanda, Caroline, boy, boy are effectively the same (three girls followed by two boys). So $nPr$ is larger by a factor representing the number of ways of ordering the three girls. This factor is given by $r! = 3 \times 2 \times 1 = 6$ (any of the three girls could be first, either of the other two second, and then the final one). Thus to obtain $nCr$ one must divide $nPr$ by $r!$, giving (2.17).

**Exercise 2.3**

(a)  A dart is thrown at a dartboard. What is the sample space for this experiment?

(b)  An archer has a 30% chance of hitting the bull's eye on the target. What is the complement to this event and what is its probability?

(c)  What is the probability of two mutually exclusive events both occurring?

(d)  A spectator reckons there is a 70% probability of Lance Armstrong winning the Tour de France and a 40% probability of Jan Ullrich winning. Comment.

| | |
|---|---|
| **Exercise 2.4** | (a) For the archer in Exercise 2.3(b) what is the probability that she hits the target with one (and only one) of two arrows? |
| | (b) What is the probability that she hits the target with both arrows? |
| | (c) Explain the importance of the assumption of independence for the answers to both parts (a) and (b) of this exercise. |
| | (d) If the archer becomes more confident after a successful shot (i.e. her probability of a shot on target rises to 50%) and less confident (probability falls to 20%) after a miss, how would this affect the answers to parts (a) and (b)? |

| | |
|---|---|
| **Exercise 2.5** | (a) Draw the tree diagrams associated with Exercise 2.4. You will need one for the case of independence of events, one for non-independence. |
| | (b) Extend the diagram (assuming independence) to a third arrow. Use this to mark out the paths with two successful shots out of three. Calculate the probability of two hits out of three shots. |
| | (c) Repeat part (b) for the case of non-independence. For this you may assume that a hit raises the problem of success with the next arrow to 50%. A miss lowers it to 20%. |

| | |
|---|---|
| **Exercise 2.6** | (a) Show how the answer to Exercise 2.5(b) may be arrived at using algebra, including the use of the combinatorial formula. |
| | (b) Repeat part (a) for the non-independence case. |

# Bayes' theorem

Bayes' theorem is a factual statement about probabilities which in itself is uncontroversial. However, the use and interpretation of the result is at the heart of the difference between classical and Bayesian statistics. The theorem itself is easily derived from first principles. Equation (2.22) is similar to equation (2.13) covered earlier when discussing the multiplication rule:

**(2.22)**    $\Pr(A \text{ and } B) = \Pr(A \mid B) \times \Pr(B)$

hence,

**(2.23)**    $\Pr(A \mid B) = \dfrac{\Pr(A \text{ and } B)}{\Pr(B)}$

Expanding both top and bottom of the right-hand side,

**(2.24)**    $\Pr(A \mid B) = \dfrac{\Pr(B \mid A) \times \Pr(A)}{\Pr(B \mid A) \times \Pr(A) + \Pr(B \mid \text{not } A) \times \Pr(\text{not } A)}$

Equation (2.24) is known as Bayes' theorem and is a statement about the probability of the event $A$, conditional upon $B$ having occurred. The following example demonstrates its use.

Two bags contain red and yellow balls. Bag $A$ contains six red and four yellow balls, bag $B$ has three red and seven yellow balls. A ball is drawn at random from one bag and turns out to be red. What is the probability that it came from bag $A$? Since bag $A$ has relatively more red balls to yellow balls than does bag $B$, it seems bag $A$ ought to be favoured. The probability should be more than 0.5. We can check if this is correct.

Denoting:

Pr($A$) = 0.5      (the probability of choosing bag $A$ at random) = Pr($B$)
Pr($R|A$) = 0.6   (the probability of selecting a red ball from bag $A$), etc.

we have

$$(2.25) \qquad \Pr(A|R) = \frac{\Pr(R|A) \times \Pr(A)}{\Pr(R|A) \times \Pr(A) + \Pr(R|B) \times \Pr(B)}$$

using Bayes' theorem. Evaluating this gives

$$(2.26) \qquad \Pr(A|R) = \frac{0.6 \times 0.5}{0.6 \times 0.5 + 0.3 \times 0.5}$$

$$= {}^2/_3$$

(You can check that Pr($B|R$) = 1/3 so that the sum of the probabilities is 1.) As expected, this result is greater than 0.5.

Bayes' theorem can be extended to cover more than two bags: if there are five bags, for example, labelled $A$ to $E$, then

$$(2.27) \qquad \Pr(A|R) = \frac{\Pr(R|A) \times \Pr(A)}{\Pr(R|A) \times \Pr(A) + \Pr(R|B) \times \Pr(B) + \ldots + \Pr(R|E) \times \Pr(E)}$$

In Bayesian language, Pr($A$), Pr($B$), etc. are known as the prior (to the drawing of the ball) probabilities, Pr($R|A$), Pr($R|B$), etc. are the likelihoods and Pr($A|R$), Pr($B|R$), etc. are the posterior probabilities. Bayes' theorem can alternatively be expressed as

$$(2.28) \qquad \text{posterior probability} = \frac{\text{likelihood} \times \text{prior probability}}{\Sigma(\text{likelihoods} \times \text{prior probabilities})}$$

This is illustrated below, by reworking the above example.

| | Prior probabilities | Likelihoods | Prior × likelihood | Posterior probabilities |
|---|---|---|---|---|
| $A$ | 0.5 | 0.6 | 0.30 | 0.30/0.45 = 2/3 |
| $B$ | 0.5 | 0.3 | 0.15 | 0.15/0.45 = 1/3 |
| Total | | | 0.45 | |

The general version of Bayes' theorem may be stated as follows. If there are $n$ events labelled $E_1, \ldots, E_n$ then the probability of the event $E_i$ occurring, given the sample evidence $S$, is

$$(2.29) \qquad \Pr(E_i|S) = \frac{\Pr(S|E_i) \times \Pr(E_i)}{\Sigma(\Pr(S|E_i) \times \Pr(E_i))}$$

As stated earlier, dispute arises over the interpretation of Bayes' theorem. In the above example there is no difficulty because the probability statements can be interpreted as relative frequencies. If the experiment of selecting a bag at random and choosing a ball from it were repeated many times, then of those occasions when a red ball is selected, in two-thirds of them bag $A$ will have been chosen. However, consider an alternative interpretation of the symbols:

$A$: a coin is fair
$B$: a coin is unfair
$R$: the result of a toss is a head

Then, given a toss (or series of tosses) of a coin, this evidence can be used to calculate the probability of the coin being fair. But this makes no sense according to the frequentist school: either the coin is fair or not; it is not a question of probability. The calculated value must be interpreted as a degree of belief and be given a subjective interpretation.

**Exercise 2.7**

(a) Repeat the 'balls in the bag' exercise from the text, but with bag A containing five red and three yellow balls, bag B containing one red and two yellow ball. The single ball drawn is red. Before doing the calculation, predict which bag is more likely to be the source of the drawn ball. Explain why.

(b) Bag A now contains 10 red and six yellow balls (i.e. twice as many as before, but in the same proportion). Does this alter the answer you obtained in part (a)?

(c) Set out your answer to part (b) in the form of prior probabilities and likelihoods, in order to obtain the posterior probability.

# Decision analysis

The study of probability naturally leads on to the analysis of decision making where risk is involved. This is the realistic situation facing most firms and the use of probability can help to illuminate the problem. To illustrate the topic, we use the example of a firm facing a choice of three different investment projects. The uncertainty which the firm faces concerns the interest rate at which to discount the future flows of income. If the interest/discount rate is high then projects which have income far in the future become less attractive relative to projects with more immediate returns. A low rate reverses this conclusion. The question is: which project should the firm select? As we shall see, there is no unique, right answer to the question but, using probability theory we can see why the answer might vary.

Table 2.1 provides the data required for the problem. The three projects are imaginatively labelled *A*, *B* and *C*. There are four possible states of the world, i.e. future scenarios, each with a different interest rate, as shown across the top of the table. This is the only source of uncertainty, otherwise the states of the world are identical. The figures in the body of the table show the present value of each income stream at the given discount rate.

**Table 2.1 Data for decision analysis: present values of three investment projects at different interest rates (£000)**

| Project | Future interest rate | | | |
|---|---|---|---|---|
| | 4% | 5% | 6% | 7% |
| *A* | 1475 | 1363 | 1200 | 1115 |
| *B* | 1500 | 1380 | 1148 | 1048 |
| *C* | 1650 | 1440 | 1200 | 810 |
| Probability | 0.1 | 0.4 | 0.4 | 0.1 |

> ## Present value
>
> The present value of future income is its value today and is obtained using the interest rate. For example, if the interest rate is 10%, the present value (i.e. today) of £110 received in one year's time is £100. In other words, one could invest £100 today at 10% and have £110 in one year's time. £100 today and £110 next year are equivalent.
>
> The present value of £110 received in two years' time is smaller since one has to wait longer to receive it. It is calculated as $£110/1.1^2 = 90.91$. Again, £90.91 invested at 10% per annum will yield £110 in two years' time. After one year it is worth $£90.91 \times 1.1 = 100$ and after a second year that £100 becomes £110. Notice that, if the interest rate rises, the present value falls. For example, if the interest rate is 20%, £110 next year is worth only $£110/1.2 = 91.67$ today.
>
> The present value of £110 in one year's time and another £110 in two years' time is $£110/1.1 + £110/1.1^2 = £190.91$. The present value of more complicated streams of income can be calculated by extension of this principle. In the example used in the text you do not need to worry about how the present value is arrived at. Before reading on you may wish to do Exercise 2.8 to practise calculation of present value.

Thus, for example, if the interest rate turns out to be 4% then project *A* has a present value of £1 475 000 while *B*'s is £1 500 000. If the discount rate turns out to be 5% the *PV* for *A* is £1 363 000 while for *B* it has changed to £1 380 000. Obviously, as the discount rate rises, the present value of the return falls. (Alternatively, we could assume that a higher interest rate increases the cost of borrowing to finance the project, which reduces its profitability.) We assume that each project requires a (certain) initial outlay of £1 100 000 with which the *PV* should be compared.

The final row of the table shows the probabilities which the firm attaches to each interest rate. These are obviously someone's subjective probabilities and are symmetric around a central value of 5.5%.

**Exercise 2.8**

(a) At an interest or discount rate of 10%, what is the present value of £1200 received in one year's time?

(b) If the interest rate rises to 15%, how is the present value altered? The interest rate has risen by 50% (from 10% to 15%): how has the present value changed?

(c) At an interest rate of 10% what is the present value of £1200 received in (i) two years' time and (ii) five years' time?

(d) An income of £500 is received at the end of years one, two and three (i.e. £1500 in total). What is its present value?

(e) Project A provides an income of £300 after one year and another £600 after two years. Project B provides £400 and £488 at the same times. At a discount rate of 10% which project has the higher present value? What happens if the discount rate rises to 20%?

**Decision criteria: maximising the expected value**

We need to decide how a decision is to be made on the basis of these data. The first criterion involves the expected value of each project. Because of the uncertainty about the interest rate there is no single present value for each project. We therefore calculate the expected value, using the E operator which was

Table 2.2 **Expected values of the three projects**

| Project | Expected value |
|---|---|
| A | 1284.2 |
| B | 1266.0 |
| C | 1302.0 |

*Note*: 1284.2 is calculated as $1475 \times 0.1 + 1363 \times 0.4 + 1200 \times 0.4 + 1115 \times 0.1$. This is the weighted average of the four *PV* values. A similar calculation is performed for the other projects.

introduced in Chapter 1. In other words, we find the expected present value of each project, by taking a weighted average of the *PV* figures, the weights being the probabilities. The project with the highest expected return is chosen.

The expected values are calculated in Table 2.2. The highest expected present value is £1 302 000, associated with project *C*. On this criterion therefore, *C* is chosen. Is this a wise choice? You may notice that if the interest rate turns out to be 7% then *C* would be the *worst* project to choose and the firm would make a substantial loss in such circumstances. Project *C* is the most sensitive to the discount rate (it has the greatest *variance* of *PV* values of the three projects) and therefore the firm faces more risk by opting for *C*. Perhaps some alternative criteria should be looked at. These we look at next, in particular the maximin, maximax and minimax regret strategies.

**Maximin, maximax and minimax regret**

The maximin criterion looks at the worst-case scenario for each project and then selects the project which does best in these circumstances. It is inevitably a pessimistic or cautious view therefore. Table 2.3 illustrates the calculation. This time we observe that project *A* is preferred. In the worst case (which occurs when *r* = 7% for all projects) then *A* does best, with a *PV* of £1 115 000 and therefore a slight profit. The maximin criterion may be a good one in business where managers tend to over-optimism. Calculating the maximin may be a salutary exercise, even if it is not the ultimate deciding factor.

The opposite criterion is the optimistic one where the maximax criterion is used. In this case one looks at the *best* circumstances for each project and chooses the best-performing project. Each project does best when the interest rate is at its lowest level, 3%. Examining the first column of Table 2.1 shows that project *C* (*PV* = 1650) performs best and is therefore chosen. Given the earlier warning about over-optimism, this may not be suitable as the sole criterion for making investment decisions.

A final criterion is that of minimax regret. If project *B* were chosen but the interest rate turns out to be 7% then we would regret not having chosen *A*, the

Table 2.3 **The maximin criterion**

| Project | Minimum |
|---|---|
| A | 1115 |
| B | 1048 |
| C | 810 |
| Maximum | 1115 |

Table 2.4 **The costs of taking the wrong decision**

| Project | 4% | 5% | 6% | 7% | Maximum |
|---|---|---|---|---|---|
| A | 175 | 77 | 0 | 0 | 175 |
| B | 150 | 60 | 52 | 67 | 150 |
| C | 0 | 0 | 0 | 305 | 305 |
| Minimum | | | | | 150 |

best project under these circumstances. Our *regret* would be the extent of the difference between the two, a matter of 1115 − 1048 = 67. Similarly, the regret if we had chosen C would be 1115 − 810 = 305. We can calculate these regrets at the other interest rates too, always comparing the *PV* of a project with the best *PV* given that interest rate. This gives us Table 2.4.

The final column of the table shows the maximum regret for each project. The minimax regret criterion is to choose the minimum of these figures. This is given at the bottom of the final column; it is 150 which is associated with project B. A justification for using this criterion might be that you don't want to fall too far behind your competitors. If other firms are facing similar investment decisions, then the regret table shows the difference in *PV* (and hence profits) if they choose the best project while you do not. Choosing the minimax regret solution ensures that you won't fall too far behind. During the internet bubble of the 1990s it was important to gain market share and keep up with, or surpass, your competitors. The minimax regret strategy might be a useful tool during such times.

You will probably have noticed that we have managed to find a justification for choosing all three projects! No one project comes out best on all criteria. Nevertheless, the analysis might be of some help: if the investment project is one of many small, independent investments the firm is making, then this would justify use of the expected value criterion. On the other hand, if this is a big, one-off project which could possibly bankrupt the firm if it goes wrong, then the maximin criterion would be appropriate.

**The expected value of perfect information**

Often a firm can improve its knowledge about future possibilities via research, which costs money. This effectively means buying information about the future state of the world. The question arises: how much should a firm pay for such information? **Perfect information** would reveal the future state of the world with certainty – in this case, the future interest rate. In that case you could be sure of choosing the right project given each state of the world. If interest rates turn out to be 4%, the firm would invest in C, if 7% in A, and so on.

In such circumstances, the firm would expect to earn:

$$(0.1 \times 1650) + (0.4 \times 1440) + (0.4 \times 1200) + (0.1 \times 1115) = 1332.5$$

i.e. the probability of each state of the world is multiplied by the *PV* of the *best* project for that state. This gives a figure which is greater than the expected value calculated earlier, without perfect information, 1302. The **expected value of perfect information** is therefore the difference between these two, 30.5. This sets a *maximum* to the value of information, for it is unlikely in the real world that any information about the future is going to be perfect.

**Exercise 2.9**    (a)  Evaluate the three projects detailed in the table below, using the criteria of expected value, maximin, maximax and minimax regret. The probability of a 4% interest rate is 0.3, of 6% 0.4 and of 8% 0.3.

| Project | 4% | 6% | 8% |
|---------|-----|-----|-----|
| A | 100 | 80 | 70 |
| B | 90 | 85 | 75 |
| C | 120 | 60 | 40 |

(b)  What would be the value of perfect information about the interest rate?

## Summary

- The theory of probability forms the basis of statistical inference, the drawing of inferences on the basis of a random sample of data. It is the probability basis of random sampling that is the reason for this.

- A convenient definition of the probability of an event is the number of times the event occurs divided by the number of trials (occasions when the event could occur).

- For more complex events, their probabilities can be calculated by combining probabilities, using the addition and multiplication rules.

- The probability of events A or B occurring is calculated according to the addition rule.

- The probability of A and B occurring is given by the multiplication rule.

- If A and B are not independent, then $\Pr(A \text{ and } B) = \Pr(A) \times \Pr(B|A)$, where $\Pr(B|A)$ is the probability of B occurring given that A has occurred (the conditional probability).

- Tree diagrams are a useful technique for enumerating all the possible paths in series of probability trials, but for large numbers of trials the huge number of possibilities makes the technique impractical.

- For experiments with a large number of trials (e.g. obtaining 20 heads in 50 tosses of a coin) the formulae for combinations and permutations can be used.

- The combinatorial formula $nCr$ gives the number of ways of combining $r$ similar objects among $n$ objects, e.g. the number of orderings of three girls (and hence implicitly two boys also) in five children.

- The permutation formula $nPr$ gives the number of orderings of $r$ distinct objects among $n$, e.g. three named girls among five children.

- Bayes' theorem provides a formula for calculating a conditional probability, e.g. the probability of someone being a smoker, given they have been diagnosed with cancer. It forms the basis of Bayesian statistics, allowing us to calculate the probability of a hypothesis being true, based on the sample evidence and prior beliefs. Classical statistics disputes this approach.

- Probabilities can also be used as the basis for decision making in conditions of uncertainty, using as decision criteria expected value maximisation, maximin, maximax or minimax regret.

**Key terms and concepts**

| | | |
|---|---|---|
| probability of an event | expected value of perfect information | subjective approach |
| probability experiment | frequentist approach | sample space |
| mutually exclusive | outcome or event | complement |
| compound event | exhaustive | multiplication rule |
| independent events | addition rule | combinations |
| permutations | tree diagram | conditional probability |
| maximin | Bayes' theorem | minimax regret |
| | minimax | |

# Problems

Some of the more challenging problems are indicated by highlighting the problem number in colour.

**Problem 2.1**   Given a standard pack of cards, calculate the following probabilities:

(a)   drawing an ace;

(b)   drawing a court card (i.e. jack, queen or king);

(c)   drawing a red card;

(d)   drawing three aces without replacement;

(e)   drawing three aces with replacement.

**Problem 2.2**   The following data give duration of unemployment by age, in July 1986.

| Age | Duration of unemployment (weeks) | | | | Total | Economically active |
|---|---|---|---|---|---|---|
| | ≤8 | 8–26 | 26–52 | >52 | (000s) | (000s) |
| | | (Percentage figures) | | | | |
| 16–19 | 27.2 | 29.8 | 24.0 | 19.0 | 273.4 | 1270 |
| 20–24 | 24.2 | 20.7 | 18.3 | 36.8 | 442.5 | 2000 |
| 25–34 | 14.8 | 18.8 | 17.2 | 49.2 | 531.4 | 3600 |
| 35–49 | 12.2 | 16.6 | 15.1 | 56.2 | 521.2 | 4900 |
| 50–59 | 8.9 | 14.4 | 15.6 | 61.2 | 388.1 | 2560 |
| ≥60 | 18.5 | 29.7 | 30.7 | 21.4 | 74.8 | 1110 |

The 'economically active' column gives the total of employed (not shown) plus unemployed in each age category.

(a)   In what sense may these figures be regarded as probabilities? What does the figure 27.2 (top-left cell) mean following this interpretation?

(b)   Assuming the validity of the probability interpretation, which of the following statements are true?

(i)   The probability of an economically active adult aged 25–34, drawn at random, being unemployed is 531.4/3600.

(ii)   If someone who has been unemployed for over one year is drawn at random, the probability that they are aged 16–19 is 19%.

(iii)   For those aged 35–49 who became unemployed before July 1985, the probability of their still being unemployed is 56.2%.

(iv)  If someone aged 50–59 is drawn at random from the economically active population, the probability of their being unemployed for eight weeks or less is 8.9%.

(v)  The probability of someone aged 35–49 drawn at random from the economically active population being unemployed for between 8 and 26 weeks is $0.166 \times 521.2/4900$.

(c)  A person is drawn at random from the population and found to have been unemployed for over one year. What is the probability that they are aged between 16 and 19?

**Problem 2.3**  'Odds' in horserace betting are defined as follows: 3/1 (three-to-one against) means a horse is expected to win once for every three times it loses; 3/2 means two wins out of five races; 4/5 (five to four *on*) means five wins for every four defeats, etc.

(a)  Translate the above odds into 'probabilities' of victory.

(b)  In a three-horse race, the odds quoted are 2/1, 6/4, and 1/1. What makes the odds different from probabilities? Why are they different?

(c)  Discuss how much the bookmaker would expect to win in the long run at such odds, assuming each horse is backed equally.

**Problem 2.4**  (a)  Translate the following odds to 'probabilities': 13/8, 2/1 *on*, 100/30.

(b)  In the 2.45 race at Plumpton on 18/10/94 the odds for the five runners were:

| | |
|---|---|
| Philips Woody | 1/1 |
| Gallant Effort | 5/2 |
| Satin Noir | 11/2 |
| Victory Anthem | 9/1 |
| Common Rambler | 16/1 |

Calculate the 'probabilities' and their sum.

(c)  Should the bookmaker base his odds on the true probabilities of each horse winning, or on the amount bet on each horse?

**Problem 2.5**  How might you estimate the probability of Peru defaulting on its debt repayments next year?

**Problem 2.6**  How might you estimate the probability of a corporation reneging on its bond payments?

**Problem 2.7**  Judy is 33, unmarried and assertive. She is a graduate in political science, and involved in union activities and anti-discrimination movements. Which of the following statements do you think is more probable?

(a)  Judy is a bank clerk.

(b)  Judy is a bank clerk, active in the feminist movement.

**Problem 2.8**  In March 1994 a news item revealed that a London 'gender' clinic (which reportedly enables you to choose the sex of your child) had just set up in business. Of its first six births, two were of the 'wrong' sex. Assess this from a probability point of view.

**Problem 2.9**  A newspaper advertisement reads 'The sex of your child predicted, or your money back!' Discuss this advertisement from the point of view of (a) the advertiser and (b) the client.

**Problem 2.10**   'Roll six sixes to win a Mercedes!' is the announcement at a fair. You have to roll six dice. If you get six sixes you win the car, valued at £20 000. The entry ticket costs £1. What is your expected gain or loss on this game? The organisers of the fair have to take out insurance against the car being won. This costs £250 for the day. Does this seem a fair premium? If not, why not?

**Problem 2.11**   At another stall, you have to toss a coin numerous times. If a head does not appear in 20 tosses you win £1 billion. The entry fee for the game is £100.
(a)   What are your expected winnings?
(b)   Would you play?

**Problem 2.12**   A four-engine plane can fly as long as at least two of its engines work. A two-engine plane flies as long as at least one engine works. The probability of an individual engine failure is 1 in 1000.
(a)   Would you feel safer in a four- or two-engine plane, and why? Calculate the probabilities of an accident for each type.
(b)   How much safer is one type than the other?
(c)   What crucial assumption are you making in your calculation? Do you think it is valid?

**Problem 2.13**   Which of the following events are independent?
(a)   Two flips of a fair coin.
(b)   Two flips of a biased coin.
(c)   Rainfall on two successive days.
(d)   Rainfall on St Swithin's day and rain one month later.

**Problem 2.14**   Which of the following events are independent?
(a)   A student getting the first two questions correct in a multiple-choice exam.
(b)   A driver having an accident in successive years.
(c)   IBM and Dell earning positive profits next year.
(d)   Arsenal Football Club winning on successive weekends.
How is the answer to (b) reflected in car insurance premiums?

**Problem 2.15**   Manchester United beat Liverpool 4–2 at soccer, but you do not know the order in which the goals were scored. Draw a tree diagram to display all the possibilities and use it to find (a) the probability that the goals were scored in the order L, MU, MU, MU, L, MU, and (b) the probability that the score was 2–2 at some stage.

**Problem 2.16**   An important numerical calculation on a spacecraft is carried out independently by three computers. If all arrive at the same answer it is deemed correct. If one disagrees it is overruled. If there is no agreement then a fourth computer does the calculation and, if its answer agrees with any of the others, it is deemed correct. The probability of an individual computer getting the answer right is 99%. Use a tree diagram to find:
(a)   the probability that the first three computers get the right answer;
(b)   the probability of getting the right answer;
(c)   the probability of getting no answer;
(d)   the probability of getting the wrong answer.

**Problem 2.17** The French national lottery works as follows. Six numbers from the range 0 to 49 are chosen at random. If you have correctly guessed all six you win the first prize. What are your chances of winning if you are only allowed to choose six numbers? A single entry like this costs one euro. For 210 euros you can choose ten numbers and you win if the six selected numbers are among them. Is this better value than the single entry?

**Problem 2.18** The UK national lottery works as follows. You choose six (different) numbers in the range 1 to 49. If all six come up in the draw (in any order) you win the first prize, expected to be around £2m (which could be shared if someone else chooses the six winning numbers).

(a) What is your chance of winning with a single ticket?

(b) You win a second prize if you get five out of six right, *and* your final chosen number matches the 'bonus' number in the draw (also in the range 1 to 49). What is the probability of winning a second prize?

(c) Calculate the probabilities of winning a third, fourth or fifth prize, where a third prize is won by matching five out of the six numbers, a fourth prize by matching four out of six and a fifth prize by matching three out of six.

(d) What is the probability of winning a prize?

(e) The prizes are as follows:

| Prize | Value | |
|---|---|---|
| First | £2 million | (expected, possibly shared) |
| Second | £100 000 | (expected, for each winner) |
| Third | £1500 | (expected, for each winner) |
| Fourth | £65 | (expected, for each winner) |
| Fifth | £10 | (guaranteed, for each winner) |

Comment upon the distribution of the fund between first, second, etc. prizes.

(f) Why is the fifth prize guaranteed whereas the others are not?

(g) In the first week of the lottery, 49 million tickets were sold. There were 1 150 000 winners, of which 7 won (a share of) the jackpot, 39 won a second prize, 2139 won a third prize and 76 731 a fourth prize. Are you surprised by these results or are they as you would expect?

**Problem 2.19** A coin is either fair or has two heads. You initially assign probabilities of 0.5 to each possibility. The coin is then tossed twice, with two heads appearing. Use Bayes' theorem to work out the posterior probabilities of each possible outcome.

**Problem 2.20** A test for AIDS is 99% successful, i.e. if you are HIV+ it will detect it in 99% of all tests, and if you are not, it will again be right 99% of the time. Assume that about 1% of the population are HIV+. You take part in a random testing procedure, which gives a positive result. What is the probability that you are HIV+? What implications does your result have for AIDS testing?

**Problem 2.21** (a) Your initial belief is that a defendant in a court case is guilty with probability 0.5. A witness comes forward claiming he saw the defendant commit the crime. You know the witness is not totally reliable and tells the truth with probability $p$. Use Bayes' theorem to calculate the posterior probability that the defendant is guilty, based on the witness's evidence.

(b) A second witness, equally unreliable, comes forward and claims she saw the defendant commit the crime. Assuming the witnesses are not colluding, what is your posterior probability of guilt?

(c) If $p < 0.5$, compare the answers to (a) and (b). How do you account for this curious result?

**Problem 2.22** A man is mugged and claims that the mugger had red hair. In police investigations of such cases, the victim was able correctly to identify the assailant's hair colour 80% of the time. Assuming that 10% of the population have red hair, what is the probability that the assailant in this case did, in fact, have red hair? Guess the answer first, then find the right answer using Bayes' theorem. What are the implications of your results for juries' interpretation of evidence in court, particularly in relation to racial minorities?

**Problem 2.23** A firm has a choice of three projects, with profits as indicated below, dependent upon the state of demand.

| Project | Demand | | |
|---|---|---|---|
| | Low | Middle | High |
| A | 100 | 140 | 180 |
| B | 130 | 145 | 170 |
| C | 110 | 130 | 200 |
| Probability | 0.25 | 0.45 | 0.3 |

(a) Which project should be chosen on the expected value criterion?

(b) Which project should be chosen on the maximin and maximax criteria?

(c) Which project should be chosen on the minimax regret criterion?

(d) What is the expected value of perfect information to the firm?

**Problem 2.24** A firm can build a small, medium or large factory, with anticipated profits from each dependent upon the state of demand, as in the table below.

| Factory | Demand | | |
|---|---|---|---|
| | Low | Middle | High |
| Small | 300 | 320 | 330 |
| Medium | 270 | 400 | 420 |
| Large | 50 | 250 | 600 |
| Probability | 0.3 | 0.5 | 0.2 |

(a) Which project should be chosen on the expected value criterion?

(b) Which project should be chosen on the maximin and maximax criteria?

(c) Which project should be chosen on the minimax regret criterion?

(d) What is the expected value of perfect information to the firm?

Problem 2.25   There are 25 people at a party. What is the probability that there are at least two with a birthday in common? (Hint: the *complement* is (much) easier to calculate.)

Problem 2.26   This problem is tricky, but amusing. Three gunmen, A, B and C, are shooting at each other. The probabilities that each will hit what they aim at are respectively 1, 0.75, 0.5. They take it in turns to shoot (in alphabetical order) and continue until only one is left alive. Calculate the probabilities of each winning the contest. (Assume they draw lots for the right to shoot first.)

Hint 1: Start with one-on-one gunfights, e.g. the probability of A beating B, or of B beating C.

Hint 2: You'll need the formula for the sum of an infinite series, given in Chapter 1.

## Answers to exercises

Exercise 2.1   Answer in text.

Exercise 2.2   (a)   A subjective view would have to be taken, informed by such things as opinion polls.

(b)   1/49, a frequentist view. Some people do add their own subjective evaluations (e.g. that 5 must come up as it has not been drawn for several weeks) but these are often unwarranted according to the frequentist approach.

(c)   A mixture of objective and subjective criteria might be used here. Historical data on the occurrence of tsunamis might give a (frequentist) baseline figure, to which might be added subjective considerations such as the amount of recent seismic activity.

(d)   A mixture again. Historical data gives a benchmark (possibly of little relevance) while immediate factors such as the weather might alter one's subjective judgement. (As I write it is snowing outside, which seems to have a huge impact on British trains!)

Exercise 2.3   (a)   1, 2, 3, . . . , 20, 21 (a triple seven), 22 (double eleven), 24, 25 (outer bull), 26, 27, 28, 30, 32, 33, 34, 36, 38, 39, 40, 42, 44, 45, 46, 48, 50. Or it could miss altogether!

(b)   The complement is missing the target, with probability $1 - 0.3 = 70\%$.

(c)   Zero, it is impossible.

(d)   Impossible, the probabilities sum to more than one.

Exercise 2.4   (a)   $0.3 \times 0.7 + 0.7 \times 0.3 = 0.42$. This is a hit followed by a miss or a miss followed by a hit.

(b)   $0.3 \times 0.3 = 0.09$.

(c)   It is assumed that the probability of the second arrow hitting the target is the same as the first. Altering this assumption would affect both answers.

(d)   Part (a) becomes $0.3 \times (1 - 0.5) + 0.7 \times 0.2 = 0.29$. Part (b) becomes $0.3 \times 0.5 = 0.15$.

Exercise 2.5    (a)

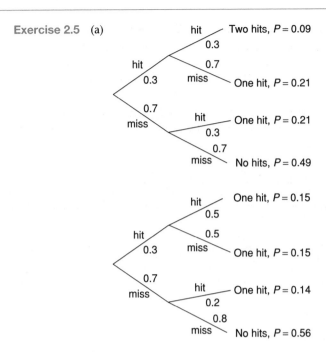

hit 0.3 → hit 0.3 → Two hits, $P = 0.09$
hit 0.3 → miss 0.7 → One hit, $P = 0.21$
miss 0.7 → hit 0.3 → One hit, $P = 0.21$
miss 0.7 → miss 0.7 → No hits, $P = 0.49$

hit 0.3 → hit 0.5 → One hit, $P = 0.15$
hit 0.3 → miss 0.5 → One hit, $P = 0.15$
miss 0.7 → hit 0.2 → One hit, $P = 0.14$
miss 0.7 → miss 0.8 → No hits, $P = 0.56$

(b)

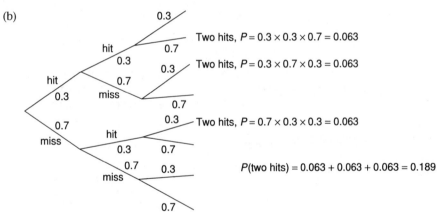

Two hits, $P = 0.3 \times 0.3 \times 0.7 = 0.063$
Two hits, $P = 0.3 \times 0.7 \times 0.3 = 0.063$
Two hits, $P = 0.7 \times 0.3 \times 0.3 = 0.063$

$P(\text{two hits}) = 0.063 + 0.063 + 0.063 = 0.189$

(c)

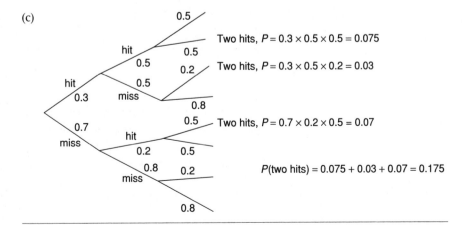

Two hits, $P = 0.3 \times 0.5 \times 0.5 = 0.075$
Two hits, $P = 0.3 \times 0.5 \times 0.2 = 0.03$
Two hits, $P = 0.7 \times 0.2 \times 0.5 = 0.07$

$P(\text{two hits}) = 0.075 + 0.03 + 0.07 = 0.175$

**Exercise 2.6** (a) Pr(2 hits) = Pr(H and H and M) × 3C2 = $0.3 \times 0.3 \times 0.7 \times 3 = 0.189$.

(b) This cannot be done using the combinatorial formula, because of the non-independence of probabilities. Instead one has to calculate Pr(H and H and M) + Pr(H and M and H) + Pr(M and H and H), yielding the answer 0.175.

**Exercise 2.7** (a) Bag A has proportionately more red balls than bag B, hence should be the favoured bag from which the single red ball was drawn. Performing the calculation:

$$Pr(A|R) = \frac{Pr(R|A) \times Pr(A)}{Pr(R|A) \times Pr(A) + Pr(R|B) \times Pr(B)} = \frac{0.625 \times 0.5}{0.625 \times 0.5 + 0.5 \times 0.5} = 0.556$$

(b) The result is the same as $Pr(R|A) = 0.625$ as before. The number of balls does not enter the calculation.

(c)

|  | Prior probabilities | Likelihoods | Prior × likelihood | Posterior probabilities |
|---|---|---|---|---|
| A | 0.5 | 0.625 | 0.3125 | 0.3125/0.5625 = 0.556 |
| B | 0.5 | 0.5 | 0.25 | 0.25/0.5625 = 0.444 |
| Total |  |  | 0.5625 |  |

**Exercise 2.8** (a) $1200/1.1 = 1090.91$.

(b) $1200/1.15 = 1043.48$. The PV has only changed by 4.3%. This is calculated as $1.1/1.15 - 1 = -0.043$.

(c) $1200/1.1^2 = 991.74$; $1200/1.1^5 = 745.11$.

(d) $PV = 500/1.1 + 500/1.1^2 + 500/1.1^3 = 1243.43$.

(e) At 10%: project A yields a PV of $300/1.1 + 600/1.1^2 = 768.6$. Project B yields $400/1.1 + 488/1.1^2 = 766.9$. At 20% the PVs are 666.7 and 672.2, reversing the rankings. A's large benefits in year 2 are penalised by the higher discount rate.

**Exercise 2.9** (a)

| Project | Expected value | Minimum | Maximum |
|---|---|---|---|
| A | $0.3 \times 100 + 0.4 \times 80 + 0.3 \times 70 = 83$ | 70 | 100 |
| B | $0.3 \times 90 + 0.4 \times 85 + 0.3 \times 75 = 83.5$ | 75 | 90 |
| C | $0.3 \times 120 + 0.4 \times 60 + 0.3 \times 40 = 72$ | 40 | 120 |

The maximin is 75, associated with project B and the maximax is 120, associated with project C. The regret values are given by

|  | 4% | 6% | 8% | Max |
|---|---|---|---|---|
| A | 20 | 5 | 5 | 20 |
| B | 30 | 0 | 0 | 30 |
| C | 0 | 25 | 35 | 35 |
|  |  |  | Min | 20 |

The minimax regret is 20, associated with project A.

(b) With perfect information the firm could earn $0.3 \times 120 + 0.4 \times 85 + 0.3 \times 75 = 92.5$. The highest expected value is 83.5, so the value of perfect information is $92.5 - 83.5 = 9$.

# 3 Probability distributions

**Learning outcomes**

By the end of this chapter you should be able to:

■ recognise that the result of most probability experiments (e.g. the score on a die) can be described as a random variable

■ appreciate how the behaviour of a random variable can often be summarised by a probability distribution (a mathematical formula)

■ recognise the most common probability distributions and be aware of their uses

■ solve a range of probability problems using the appropriate probability distribution

## Introduction

In this chapter the probability concepts introduced in the last chapter are generalised by using the idea of a **probability distribution**. A probability distribution lists, in some form, all the possible outcomes of a probability experiment and the probability associated with each one. For example, the simplest experiment is tossing a coin, for which the possible outcomes are heads or tails, each with probability one-half. The probability distribution can be expressed in a

**Figure 3.1**

**The probability distribution for the toss of a coin**

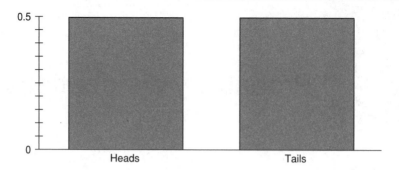

variety of ways: in words, or in a graphical or mathematical form. For tossing a coin, the graphical form is shown in Figure 3.1, and the mathematical form is:

$$\Pr(H) = \tfrac{1}{2}$$

$$\Pr(T) = \tfrac{1}{2}$$

The different forms of presentation are equivalent but one might be more suited to a particular purpose.

Some probability distributions occur often and so are well known. Because of this they have names so we can refer to them easily; for example, the **Binomial distribution** or the **Normal distribution**. In fact, these are *families* of distributions. A single toss of a coin gives rise to one member of the Binomial distribution; two tosses would give rise to another member of that family. These two distributions differ only in the number of tosses. If a biased coin were tossed, this would lead to another Binomial distribution, but it would differ from the previous two because of the different probability of heads.

In order to understand fully the idea of a probability distribution a new concept is first introduced, that of a **random variable**. As will be seen later in the chapter, an important random variable is the sample mean, and to understand how to draw inferences from the sample mean it is important to recognise it as a random variable.

## Random variables

Examples of random variables have already been encountered in the previous chapter, for example, the result of the toss of a coin, or the number of boys in a family of five children. A random variable is one whose outcome or value is the result of chance and is therefore unpredictable, although the range of possible outcomes and the probability of each outcome may be known. It is impossible to know in advance the outcome of a toss of a coin for example, but it must be either heads or tails, each with probability one-half. The number of heads in 250 tosses is another random variable, which can take any value between zero and 250, although values near 125 are the most likely. You are very unlikely to get 250 heads from tossing a fair coin!

The time of departure of a train is a random variable. It may be timetabled to depart at 11.15, but it probably (almost certainly!) won't leave at exactly that time. If a sample of ten basketball players were taken, and their average height calculated, this would be a random variable. In this latter case, it is the process of taking a sample that introduces the variability which makes the resulting average a random variable. If the experiment were repeated, a different sample and a different value of the random variable would be obtained.

The above examples can be contrasted with some things which are *not* random variables. If one were to take *all* basketball players and calculate their average height, the result would not be a random variable. This time there is no sampling procedure to introduce variability into the result. If the experiment were repeated the same result would be obtained, since the same people would be measured the second time (this assumes that the population does not change, of course). Just because the value of something is unknown does not mean it qualifies as a random variable. This is an important distinction to bear in mind, since it is legitimate to make probability statements about random variables ('the probability that the average height of a sample of basketball players is over 195 cm is 60%') but not about parameters ('the probability that the Pope is over six feet is 60%'). Here again there is a difference of opinion between frequentist and subjective schools of thought. The latter group would argue that it is possible to make probability statements about the Pope's height. It is a way of expressing lack of knowledge about the true value. The frequentists would say the Pope's height is a fact that we do not happen to know; that does not make it a random variable.

# The Binomial distribution

One of the simplest distributions which a random variable can have is the Binomial. The Binomial distribution arises whenever the underlying probability experiment has just two possible outcomes, e.g. heads or tails from the toss of a coin. Even if the coin is tossed many times (so one could end up with one, two, three . . . etc. heads in total) the *underlying* experiment has only two outcomes, so the Binomial distribution should be used. A counter-example would be the rolling of die, which has six possible outcomes (in this case the Multinomial distribution, not covered in this book, would be used). Note, however, that if we were interested only in rolling a six or not, we *could* use the Binomial by defining the two possible outcomes as 'six' and 'not-six'. It is often the case in statistics that by suitable transformation of the data we can use different distributions to tackle the same problem. We will see more of this later in the chapter.

The Binomial distribution can therefore be applied to the type of problem encountered in the previous chapter, concerning the sex of children. It provides a general formula for calculating the probability of $r$ boys in $n$ births or, in more general terms, the probability of $r$ 'successes' in $n$ trials.[1] We shall use it to calculate the probabilities of $0, 1, \ldots, 5$ boys in five births.

[1] The identification of a boy with 'success' is a purely formal one and is not meant to be pejorative!

For the Binomial distribution to apply we first need to assume independence of successive events and we shall assume that, for any birth:

$$\Pr(\text{boy}) = P = \tfrac{1}{2}$$

It follows that

$$\Pr(\text{girl}) = 1 - \Pr(\text{boy}) = 1 - P = \tfrac{1}{2}$$

Although we have $P = \tfrac{1}{2}$ in this example, the Binomial distribution can be applied for any value of $P$ between 0 and 1.

First we consider the case of $r = 5$, $n = 5$, i.e. five boys in five births. This probability is found using the multiplication rule:

$$\Pr(r = 5) = P \times P \times P \times P \times P = P^5 = (\tfrac{1}{2})^5 = 1/32$$

The probability of four boys (and then implicitly one girl) is

$$\Pr(r = 4) = P \times P \times P \times P \times (1 - P) = 1/32$$

But this gives only one possible ordering of the four boys and one girl. Our original statement of the problem did not specify a particular ordering of the children. There are five possible orderings (the single girl could be in any of five positions in rank order). Recall that we can use the combinatorial formula $nCr$ to calculate the number of orderings, giving $5C4 = 5$. Hence the probability of four boys and one girl in any order is $5/32$. Summarising, the formula for four boys and one girl is

$$\Pr(r = 4) = 5C4 \times P^4 \times (1 - P)$$

For three boys (and two girls) we obtain

$$\Pr(r = 3) = 5C3 \times P^3 \times (1 - P)^2 = 10 \times 1/8 \times 1/4 = 10/32$$

In a similar manner

$$\Pr(r = 2) = 5C2 \times P^2 \times (1 - P)^3 = 10/32$$

$$\Pr(r = 1) = 5C1 \times P^1 \times (1 - P)^4 = 5/32$$

$$\Pr(r = 0) = 5C0 \times P^0 \times (1 - P)^5 = 1/32$$

As a check on our calculations we may note that the sum of the probabilities equals 1, as they should do, since we have enumerated all possibilities.

A fairly clear pattern emerges. The probability of $r$ boys in $n$ births is given by

$$\Pr(r) = nCr \times P^r \times (1 - P)^{n-r}$$

and this is known as the Binomial formula or distribution. The Binomial distribution is appropriate for analysing problems with the following characteristics:

- There is a number ($n$) of trials.
- Each trial has only two possible outcomes, 'success' (with probability $P$) and 'failure' (probability $1 - P$) and the outcomes are independent between trials.
- The probability $P$ does not change between trials.

The probabilities calculated by the Binomial formula may be illustrated in a diagram, as shown in Figure 3.2. This is very similar to the relative frequency distribution which was introduced in Chapter 1. That distribution was based

Figure 3.2
Probability
distribution of the
number of boys in five
children

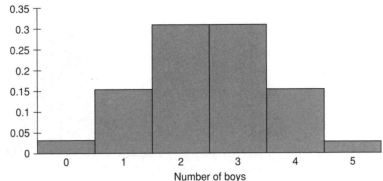

on empirical data (to do with wealth) while the Binomial probability distribution is a theoretical construction, built up from the basic principles of probability theory.

As stated earlier, the Binomial is, in fact, a family of distributions and each member of this family is distinguished by two parameters, $n$ and $P$. The Binomial is thus a distribution with two parameters, and once their values are known the distribution is completely determined (i.e. $\Pr(r)$ can be calculated for all values of $r$). To illustrate the difference between members of the family of the Binomial distribution, Figure 3.3 presents three other Binomial distributions, for different values of $P$ and $n$. It can be seen that for the value of $P = \frac{1}{2}$ the distribution is symmetric, while for all other values it is skewed to either the left or the right. Part (b) of the figure illustrates the distribution relating to the worked example of rolling a die, described below.

Since the Binomial distribution depends only upon the two values $n$ and $P$, a shorthand notation can be used, rather than using the formula itself. A random variable $r$, which has a Binomial distribution with the parameters $n$ and $P$, can be written in general terms as

**(3.1)**     $r \sim B(n, P)$

Thus for the previous example of children, where $r$ represents the number of boys,

$r \sim B(5, \frac{1}{2})$

This is simply a brief and convenient way of writing down the information available; it involves no new problems of a conceptual nature. Writing

$r \sim B(n, P)$

is just a shorthand for

$\Pr(r) = nCr \times P^r \times (1 - P)^{n-r}$

**The mean and variance of the Binomial distribution**

In Chapter 1 we calculated the mean and variance of a set of data, of the distribution of wealth. The picture of that distribution (Figure 1.9) looks not too dissimilar to one of the Binomial distributions shown in Figure 3.3 above. This suggests that we can calculate the mean and variance of a Binomial distribution,

**Figure 3.3**
**Binomial distributions with different parameter values**

just as we did for the empirical distribution of wealth. Calculating the mean would provide the answer to a question such as 'If we have a family with five children, how many do we expect to be boys?'. Intuitively the answer seems clear, 2.5 (even though such a family could not exist!). The Binomial formula allows us to confirm this intuition.

The mean and variance are most easily calculated by drawing up a relative frequency table based on the Binomial frequencies. This is shown in Table 3.1

**Table 3.1** Calculating the mean and variance of the Binomial distribution

| $r$ | $\Pr(r)$ | $r \times \Pr(r)$ | $r^2 \times \Pr(r)$ |
|---|---|---|---|
| 0 | 1/32 | 0 | 0 |
| 1 | 5/32 | 5/32 | 5/32 |
| 2 | 10/32 | 20/32 | 40/32 |
| 3 | 10/32 | 30/32 | 90/32 |
| 4 | 5/32 | 20/32 | 80/32 |
| 5 | 1/32 | 5/32 | 25/32 |
| Totals | 32/32 | 80/32 | 240/32 |

for the values $n = 5$ and $P = \frac{1}{2}$. Note that $r$ is equivalent to $x$ in our usual notation and $\Pr(r)$, the relative frequency, to $f(x)/\Sigma f(x)$. The mean of this distribution is given by

$$(3.2) \qquad E(r) = \frac{\Sigma r \times \Pr(r)}{\Sigma \Pr(r)} = \frac{80/32}{32/32} = 2.5$$

and the variance is given by

$$(3.3) \qquad V(r) = \frac{\Sigma r^2 \times \Pr(r)}{\Sigma \Pr(r)} - \mu^2 = \frac{240/32}{32/32} - 2.5^2 = 1.25$$

The mean value tells us that in a family of five children we would expect, on average, two and a half boys. Obviously no single family can be like this; it is the average over all such families. The variance is more difficult to interpret intuitively, but it tells us something about how the number of boys will be spread around the average of 2.5.

There is a quicker way to calculate the mean and variance of the Binomial distribution. It can be shown that the mean can be calculated as $nP$, i.e. the number of trials times the probability of success. For example, in a family with five children and an equal probability that each child is a boy or a girl, then we expect $nP = 5 \times \frac{1}{2} = 2.5$ to be boys.

The variance can be calculated as $nP(1 - P)$. This gives $5 \times \frac{1}{2} \times \frac{1}{2} = 1.25$, as found above by extensive calculation.

---

**Worked example 3.1**

### Rolling a die

If a die is thrown four times, what is the probability of getting two or more sixes? This is a problem involving repeated experiments (rolling the die) with but two types of outcome for each roll: success (a six) or failure (anything but a six). Note that we combine several possibilities (scores of 1, 2, 3, 4, or 5) together and represent them all as failure. The probability of success (one-sixth) does not vary from one experiment to another, and so use of the Binomial distribution is appropriate. The values of the parameters are $n = 4$ and $P = 1/6$. Denoting by $r$ the random variable 'the number of sixes in four rolls of the die' then

$$(3.4) \qquad r \sim B(4, \tfrac{1}{6})$$

Hence

$$\Pr(r) = nCr \times P^r(1 - P)^{(n-r)}$$

where $P = \frac{1}{6}$ and $n = 4$. The probabilities of two, three and four sixes are then given by

$$\Pr(r = 2) = 4C2(\tfrac{1}{6})^2(\tfrac{5}{6})^2 = 0.116$$

$$\Pr(r = 3) = 4C3(\tfrac{1}{6})^3(\tfrac{5}{6})^1 = 0.015$$

$$\Pr(r = 4) = 4C4(\tfrac{1}{6})^4(\tfrac{5}{6})^0 = 0.00077$$

Since these events are mutually exclusive, the probabilities can simply be added together to get the desired result, which is 0.132, or 13.2%. This is the probability of two or more sixes in four rolls of a die.

This result can be illustrated diagrammatically as part of the area under the appropriate Binomial distribution, shown in Figure 3.4.

The shaded areas represent the probabilities of two or more sixes and together their area represents 13.2% of the whole distribution. This illustrates an important principle: that probabilities can be represented by areas under an appropriate probability distribution. We shall see more of this later.

**Figure 3.4**
**Probability of two or more sixes in four rolls of a die**

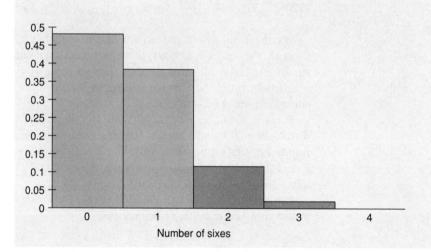

Number of sixes

**Exercise 3.1**

(a) The probability of a randomly drawn individual having blue eyes is 0.6. What is the probability that four people drawn at random all have blue eyes?

(b) What is the probability that two of the sample of four have blue eyes?

(c) For this particular example, write down the Binomial formula for the probability of $r$ blue eyed individuals, for $r = 0 \ldots 4$. Confirm that the probabilities sum to one.

**Exercise 3.2**

(a) Calculate the mean and variance of the number of blue eyed individuals in the previous exercise.

(b) Draw a graph of this Binomial distribution and on it mark the mean value and the mean value +/− one standard deviation.

Having introduced the concept of probability distributions using the Binomial, we now move on to the most important of all probability distributions, the Normal.

# The Normal distribution

The Binomial distribution applies when there are two possible outcomes to an experiment, but not all problems fall into this category. For instance, the (random) arrival time of a train is a continuous variable and cannot be analysed using the Binomial. There are many probability distributions in statistics, developed to analyse different types of problem. Several of them are covered in this book and the most important of them is the Normal distribution, which we now turn to. It was discovered by the German mathematician Gauss in the nineteenth century (hence it is also known as the Gaussian distribution), in the course of his work on regression (see Chapter 7).

Many random variables turn out to be Normally distributed. Men's (or women's) heights are Normally distributed. IQ (the measure of intelligence) is also Normally distributed. Another example is of a machine producing (say) bolts with a nominal length of 5 cm which will actually produce bolts of slightly varying length (these differences would probably be extremely small) due to factors such as wear in the machinery, slight variations in the pressure of the lubricant, etc. These would result in bolts whose length varies, in accordance with the Normal distribution. This sort of process is extremely common, with the result that the Normal distribution often occurs in everyday situations.

The Normal distribution tends to arise when a random variable is the result of many independent, random influences added together, none of which dominates the others. A man's height is the result of many genetic influences, plus environmental factors such as diet, etc. As a result, height is Normally distributed. If one takes the height of men and women together, the result is not a Normal distribution, however. This is because there is one influence which dominates the others: gender. Many variables familiar in economics are not Normal – incomes, for example (though the logarithm of income is approximately Normal). We shall learn techniques to deal with such circumstances in due course.

Having introduced the idea of the Normal distribution, what does it look like? It is presented below in graphical and then mathematical forms. Unlike the Binomial, the Normal distribution applies to continuous random variables such as height and a typical Normal distribution is illustrated in Figure 3.5. Since the Normal distribution is a continuous one it can be evaluated for all values of $x$, not just for integers. The figure illustrates the main features of the distribution:

- It is unimodal, having a central peak. If this were men's heights it would illustrate the fact that most men are clustered around the average height, with a few very tall and a few very short people.
- It is symmetric, the left and right halves being mirror images of each other.
- It is bell-shaped.

**Figure 3.5**
**The Normal**
**distribution**

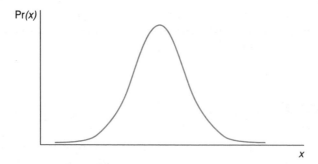

- It extends continuously over all the values of $x$ from minus infinity to plus infinity, though the value of $Pr(x)$ becomes extremely small as these values are approached (the pages of this book being of only finite width, this last characteristic is not faithfully reproduced!). This also demonstrates that most empirical distributions (such as men's heights) can only be an approximation to the theoretical ideal, though the approximation is close and good enough for practical purposes.

In mathematical terms the formula for the Normal distribution is ($x$ is the random variable)

(3.5)     $$Pr(x) = \frac{1}{\sigma\sqrt{2\pi}} e^{-\frac{1}{2}\left(\frac{x-\mu}{\sigma}\right)^2}$$

The mathematical formulation is not so formidable as it appears. $\mu$ and $\sigma$ are the parameters of the distribution, like $n$ and $P$ for the Binomial (though they have different meanings); $\pi$ is 3.1416 and $e$ is 2.7183. If the formula is evaluated using different values of $x$ the values of $Pr(x)$ obtained will map out a Normal distribution. Fortunately, as we shall see, we do not need to use the mathematical formula in most practical problems.

Like the Binomial, the Normal is a family of distributions differing from one another only in the values of the parameters $\mu$ and $\sigma$. Several Normal distributions are drawn in Figure 3.6 for different values of the parameters.

Whatever value of $\mu$ is chosen turns out to be the centre of the distribution. Since the distribution is symmetric, $\mu$ is its mean. The effect of varying $\sigma$ is to narrow (small $\sigma$) or widen (large $\sigma$) the distribution. $\sigma$ turns out to be the standard deviation of the distribution. The Normal is another two-parameter family of distributions like the Binomial, and once the mean $\mu$ and the standard deviation $\sigma$ (or equivalently the variance, $\sigma^2$) are known the whole of the distribution can be drawn. The shorthand notation for a Normal distribution is

(3.6)     $x \sim N(\mu, \sigma^2)$

meaning 'the variable $x$ is Normally distributed with mean $\mu$ and variance $\sigma^2$'. This is similar in form to the expression for the Binomial distribution, though the meanings of the parameters are different.

Use of the Normal distribution can be illustrated using a simple example. The height of adult males is Normally distributed with mean height $\mu = 174$ cm and standard deviation $\sigma = 9.6$ cm. Let $x$ represent the height of adult males;

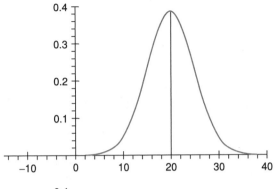

Figure 3.6(a)
The Normal
distribution,
$\mu = 20$, $\sigma = 5$

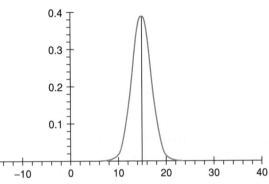

Figure 3.6(b)
The Normal
distribution,
$\mu = 15$, $\sigma = 2$

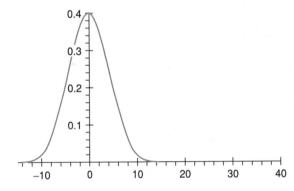

Figure 3.6(c)
The Normal
distribution,
$\mu = 0$, $\sigma = 4$

then

**(3.7)**    $x \sim N(174, 92.16)$

and this is illustrated in Figure 3.7. Note that (3.7) contains the variance rather than the standard deviation.

What is the probability that a randomly selected man is taller than 180 cm? If all men are equally likely to be selected, this is equivalent to asking what proportion of men are over 180 cm in height. This is given by the area under the Normal distribution, to the right of $x = 180$, i.e. the shaded area in Figure 3.7. The further from the mean of 174, the smaller the area in the tail of the distribution. One way to find this area would be to make use of equation (3.5), but this requires the use of sophisticated mathematics.

**Figure 3.7**
**Illustration of men's height distribution**

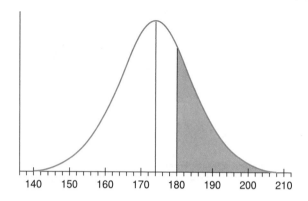

Since this is a frequently encountered problem, the answers have been set out in the tables of the standard Normal distribution. We can simply look up the solution. However, since there is an infinite number of Normal distributions (for every combination of $\mu$ and $\sigma^2$) it would be an impossible task to tabulate them all. The standard Normal distribution, which has a mean of zero and variance of one, is therefore used to represent all Normal distributions. Before the table can be consulted, therefore, the data have to be transformed so that they accord with the standard Normal distribution.

The required transformation is the $z$ score, which was introduced in Chapter 1. This measures the distance between the value of interest (180) and the mean, measured in terms of standard deviations. Therefore we calculate

$$(3.8) \qquad z = \frac{x - \mu}{\sigma}$$

and $z$ is a Normally distributed random variable with mean 0 and variance 1, i.e. $z \sim N(0, 1)$. This transformation shifts the original distribution $\mu$ units to the left and then adjusts the dispersion by dividing through by $\sigma$, resulting in a mean of 0 and variance 1. $z$ is Normally distributed because $x$ is Normally distributed. The transformation in (3.8) retains the Normal distribution shape, despite the changes to mean and variance. If $x$ had some other distribution then $z$ would not be Normal either.

It is easy to verify the mean and variance of $z$ using the rules for E and V operators encountered in Chapter 1:

$$E(z) = E\left(\frac{x - \mu}{\sigma}\right) = \frac{1}{\sigma}(E(x) - \mu) = 0 \quad \text{(since } E(x) = \mu\text{)}$$

$$V(z) = V\left(\frac{x - \mu}{\sigma}\right) = \frac{1}{\sigma^2}V(x) = \frac{\sigma^2}{\sigma^2} = 1$$

Evaluating the $z$ score from our data we obtain

$$(3.9) \qquad z = \frac{180 - 174}{9.6} = 0.63$$

Table 3.2 Areas of the standard Normal distribution (excerpt from Table A2)

| z | 0.00 | 0.01 | 0.02 | 0.03 | ... | 0.09 |
|---|------|------|------|------|-----|------|
| 0.0 | .5000 | .4960 | .4920 | .4880 | ... | .4641 |
| 0.1 | .4602 | .4562 | .4522 | .4483 | ... | .4247 |
| ⋮ | ⋮ | ⋮ | ⋮ | ⋮ | ... | ⋮ |
| 0.5 | .3085 | .3050 | .3015 | .2981 | ... | .2776 |
| 0.6 | .2743 | .2709 | .2676 | .2643 | ... | .2451 |
| 0.7 | .2420 | .2389 | .2358 | .2327 | ... | .2148 |

This shows that 180 is 0.63 standard deviations above the mean, 174, of the distribution. This is a measure of how far 180 is from 174 and allows us to look up the answer in tables. The task now is to find the area under the standard Normal distribution to the right of 0.63 standard deviations above the mean. This answer can be read off directly from the table of the standard Normal distribution, included as Table A2 in the appendix to this book. An excerpt from Table A2 (see page **366**) is presented in Table 3.2.

The left-hand column gives the z score to one place of decimals. The appropriate row of the table to consult is the one for $z = 0.6$, which is shaded. For the second place of decimals (0.03) we consult the appropriate column, also shaded. At their intersection we find the value 0.2643, which is the desired area and therefore probability. In other words, 26.43% of the distribution lies to the right of 0.63 standard deviations above the mean. Therefore 26.43% of men are over 180 cm in height.

Use of the standard Normal table is possible because, although there is an infinite number of Normal distributions, they are all fundamentally the same, so that the area to the right of 0.63 standard deviations above the mean is the same for all of them. As long as we measure the distance in terms of standard deviations then we can use the standard Normal table. The process of standardisation turns all Normal distributions into a standard Normal distribution with a mean of zero and a variance of one. This process is illustrated in Figure 3.8.

The area in the right-hand tail is the same for both distributions. It is the standard Normal distribution in Figure 3.8(b) which is tabulated in Table A2. To demonstrate how standardisation turns all Normal distributions into the standard Normal, the earlier problem is repeated but taking all measurements in inches. The answer should obviously be the same. Taking 1 inch = 2.54 cm the figures are

$$x = 70.87 \quad \sigma = 3.78 \quad \mu = 68.50$$

What proportion of men are over 70.87 inches in height? The appropriate Normal distribution is now

**(3.10)** $\quad x \sim N(68.50, 3.78^2)$

The z score is

**(3.11)** $\quad z = \dfrac{70.87 - 68.50}{3.78} = 0.63$

which is the same z score as before and therefore gives the same probability.

**Figure 3.8(a)**
**The Normal distribution**

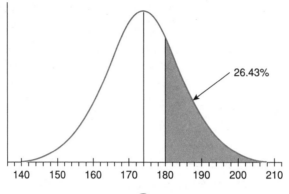

**Figure 3.8(b)**
**The standard Normal distribution corresponding to Figure 3.8(a)**

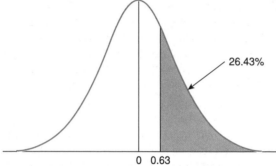

---

**Worked example 3.2**

Packets of cereal have a nominal weight of 750 grams, but there is some variation around this as the machines filling the packets are imperfect. Let us assume that the weights follow a Normal distribution. Suppose that the standard deviation around the mean of 750 is 5 grams. What proportion of packets weigh more than 760 grams?

Summarising our information, we have $x \sim N(750, 25)$, where $x$ represents the weight. We wish to find $\Pr(x > 760)$. To be able to look up the answer, we need to measure the distance between 760 and 750 in terms of standard deviations. This is

$$z = \frac{760 - 750}{5} = 2.0$$

Looking up $z = 2.0$ in Table A2 reveals an area of 0.0228 in the tail of the distribution. Thus 2.28% of packets weigh more than 760 grams.

---

Since a great deal of use is made of the standard Normal tables, it is worth working through a couple more examples to reinforce the method. We have so far calculated that $\Pr(z > 0.63) = 0.2643$. Since the total area under the graph equals one (i.e. the sum of probabilities must be one), the area to the left of $z = 0.63$ must equal 0.7357, i.e. 73.57% of men are under 180 cm. It is fairly easy to manipulate areas under the graph to arrive at any required area. For example, what proportion of men are between 174 and 180 cm in height? It is helpful to refer to Figure 3.9 at this point.

Figure 3.9
The proportion of men
between 174 cm and
180 cm in height

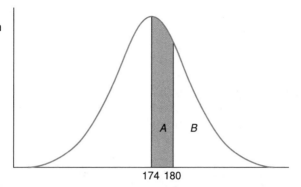

The size of area A is required. Area B has already been calculated as 0.2643. Since the distribution is symmetric the area A + B must equal 0.5, since 174 is at the centre (mean) of the distribution. Area A is therefore 0.5 − 0.2643 = 0.2357. 23.57% is the desired result.

> ## Using software to find areas under the standard Normal distribution
>
> If you use a spreadsheet program you can look up the z-distribution directly and hence dispense with tables. In *Excel*, for example, the function '=NORMS-DIST(0.63)' gives the answer 0.7357, i.e. the area to the *left* of the z score. The area in the right-hand tail is then obtained by subtracting this value from 1, i.e. 1 − 0.7357 = 0.2643. Entering the formula '=1 − NORMSDIST(0.63)' in a cell will give the area in the right-hand tail directly.

As a final exercise consider the question of what proportion of men are between 166 and 178 cm tall. As shown in Figure 3.10 area C + D is wanted. The only way to find this is to calculate the two areas separately and then add them together. For area D the z score associated with 178 is:

**(3.12)** $$z_D = \frac{178 - 174}{9.6} = 0.42$$

Figure 3.10
The proportion of men
between 166 cm and
178 cm in height

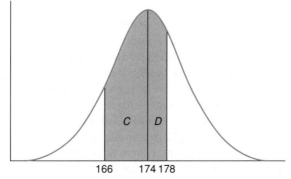

Table A2 (see page **366**) indicates that the area in the right-hand tail, beyond $z = 0.42$, is 0.3372, so area D = 0.5 − 0.3372 = 0.1628. For C, the $z$ score is

$$(3.13) \qquad z_C = \frac{166 - 174}{9.6} = -0.83$$

The minus sign indicates that it is the left-hand tail of the distribution, below the mean, which is being considered. Since the distribution is symmetric, it is the same as if it were the right-hand tail, so the minus sign may be ignored when consulting the table. Looking up $z = 0.83$ in Table A2 gives an area of 0.2033 in the tail, so area C is therefore 0.5 − 0.2033 = 0.2967. Adding areas C and D gives 0.1628 + 0.2967 = 0.4595. So nearly half of all men are between 166 and 178 cm in height.

An alternative interpretation of the results obtained above is that if a man is drawn at random from the adult population, the probability that he is over 180 cm tall is 26.43%. This is in line with the frequentist school of thought. Since 26.43% of the population is over 180 cm in height, that is the probability of a man over 180 cm being drawn at random.

**Exercise 3.3**

(a) The random variable $x$ is distributed Normally, with $x \sim N(40, 36)$. Find the probability that $x > 50$.

(b) Find $\Pr(x < 45)$.

(c) Find $\Pr(36 < x < 44)$.

**Exercise 3.4**

The mean +/− 0.67 standard deviations cuts off 25% in each tail of the Normal distribution. Hence the middle 50% of the distribution lies within +/− 0.67 standard deviations of the mean. Use this fact to calculate the inter-quartile range for the distribution $x \sim N(200, 256)$.

**Exercise 3.5**

As suggested in the text, the logarithm of income is approximately Normally distributed. Suppose the log (to the base 10) of income has the distribution $x \sim N(4.18, 2.56)$. Calculate the inter-quartile range for $x$ and then take anti-logs to find the inter-quartile range of income.

# The sample mean as a Normally distributed variable

One of the most important concepts in statistical inference is the probability distribution of the mean of a random sample, since we often use the sample mean to tell us something about an associated population. Suppose that, from the population of adult males, a random sample of size $n = 36$ is taken, their heights measured, and the mean height of the sample calculated. What can we infer from this about the true average height of the population? To do this, we need to know about the statistical properties of the sample mean. The sample mean is a random variable because of the chance element of random sampling (different samples would yield different values of the sample mean). Since the sample mean is a random variable it must have associated with it a probability distribution.

We therefore need to know, first, what is the appropriate distribution and, second, what are its parameters. From the definition of the sample mean we have

(3.14)    $\bar{x} = \dfrac{1}{n}(x_1 + x_2 + \ldots + x_n)$

where each observation, $x_i$, is itself a Normally distributed random variable, with $x_i \sim N(\mu, \sigma^2)$, because each comes from the parent distribution with such characteristics. (We stated earlier that men's heights are Normally distributed.) We now make use of the following theorem to demonstrate that $x$ is Normally distributed:

> **Theorem**   Any linear combination of independent, Normally distributed random variables is itself Normally distributed.

A linear combination of two variables $x_1$ and $x_2$ is of the form $w_1x_1 + w_2x_2$ where $w_1$ and $w_2$ are constants. This can be generalised to any number of $x$ values. As long as the observations are independently drawn, therefore, the sample mean is Normally distributed. In this case, the weight $w$ on each observation is $1/n$.

We now need the parameters (mean and variance) of the distribution. For this we use the E and V operators once again:

(3.15)    $E(\bar{x}) = \dfrac{1}{n}(E(x_1) + E(x_2) + \ldots + E(x_n)) = \dfrac{1}{n}(\mu + \mu + \ldots + \mu) = \dfrac{1}{n}n\mu = \mu$

(3.16)    $V(\bar{x}) = V\left(\dfrac{1}{n}[x_1 + x_2 + \ldots + x_n]\right)$

$\qquad\qquad = \dfrac{1}{n^2}(V(x_1) + V(x_2) + \ldots + V(x_n))$

$\qquad\qquad = \dfrac{1}{n^2}(\sigma^2 + \sigma^2 + \ldots + \sigma^2)$

$\qquad\qquad = \dfrac{1}{n^2}n\sigma^2 = \dfrac{\sigma^2}{n}$

Putting all this together, we have[2]

(3.17)    $\bar{x} \sim N\left(\mu, \dfrac{\sigma^2}{n}\right)$

This we may summarise in the following theorem:

> **Theorem** The sample mean, $\bar{x}$, drawn from a population which has a Normal distribution with mean $\mu$ and variance $\sigma^2$, has a sampling distribution which is Normal, with mean $\mu$ and variance $\sigma^2/n$, where $n$ is the sample size.

The meaning of this theorem is as follows. First of all it is assumed that the population from which the samples are to be drawn is itself Normally distributed (this assumption will be relaxed in a moment), with mean $\mu$ and variance $\sigma^2$. From this population many samples are drawn, each of sample size $n$,

---

[2] Don't worry if you didn't follow the derivation of this formula, just accept that it is correct.

**Figure 3.11**
**The parent distribution and the distribution of sample means**

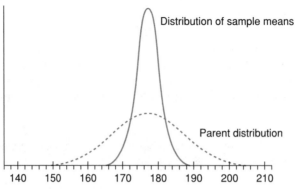

*Note*: The distribution of $\bar{x}$ is drawn for a sample size of $n = 9$. A larger sample size would narrow the $\bar{x}$ distribution; a smaller sample size would widen it.

and the mean of each sample is calculated. The samples are independent, meaning that the observations selected for one sample do not influence the selection of observations in the other samples. This gives many sample means, $\bar{x}_1$, $\bar{x}_2$, etc. If these sample means are treated as a new set of observations, then the probability distribution of these observations can be derived. The theorem states that this distribution is Normal, with the sample means centred around $\mu$, the population mean, and with variance $\sigma^2/n$. The argument is set out diagrammatically in Figure 3.11.

Intuitively this theorem can be understood as follows. If the height of adult males is a Normally distributed random variable with mean $\mu = 174$ cm and variance $\sigma^2 = 92.16$, then it would be expected that a random sample of (say) nine males would yield a sample mean height of around 174 cm, perhaps a little more, perhaps a little less. In other words, the sample mean is centred around 174 cm, or the mean of the distribution of sample means is 174 cm.

The larger is the size of the individual samples (i.e. the larger $n$), the closer the sample mean would tend to be to 174 cm. For example, if the sample size is only two, a sample of two very tall people is quite possible, with a high sample mean as a result, well over 174 cm, e.g. 182 cm. But if the sample size were 20, it is very unlikely the 20 very tall males would be selected and the sample mean is likely to be much closer to 174. This is why the sample size $n$ appears in the formula for the variance of the distribution of the sample mean, $\sigma^2/n$.

Note that, once again, we have transformed one (or more) random variables, the $x_i$'s, with a particular probability distribution into another random variable, $\bar{x}$, with a (slightly) different distribution. This is common practice in statistics: transforming a variable will often put it into a more useful form, e.g. one whose probability distribution is well known.

The above theorem can be used to solve a range of statistical problems. For example, what is the probability that a random sample of nine adult males will have a mean height greater than 180 cm? The height of all adult males is known to be Normally distributed with mean $\mu = 174$ cm and variance $\sigma^2 = 92.16$. The theorem can be used to derive the probability distribution of the sample mean. For the population we have:

$x \sim N(\mu, \sigma^2)$, i.e. $x \sim N(174, 92.16)$

Figure 3.12
The proportion of
sample means greater
than $\bar{x} = 180$

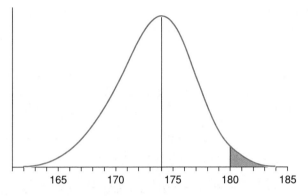

Hence for the sample mean:

$\bar{x} \sim N(\mu, \sigma^2/n)$, i.e. $\bar{x} \sim N(174, 92.16/9)$

This is shown diagrammatically in Figure 3.12.

To answer the question posed, the area to the right of 180, shaded in Figure 3.12, has to be found. This should by now be a familiar procedure. First the $z$ score is calculated:

(3.18)   $$z = \frac{\bar{x} - \mu}{\sqrt{\sigma^2/n}} = \frac{180 - 174}{\sqrt{92.16/9}} = 1.88$$

Note that the $z$ score formula is subtly different because we are dealing with the sample mean $\bar{x}$ rather than $x$ itself. In the numerator we use $\bar{x}$ rather than $x$ and in the denominator we use $\sigma^2/n$, not $\sigma^2$. This is because $\bar{x}$ has a variance $\sigma^2/n$, not $\sigma^2$, which is the population variance. $\sqrt{\sigma^2/n}$ is known as the **standard error**, to distinguish it from $\sigma$, the standard deviation of the population. The principle behind the $z$ score is the same however: it measures how far is a sample mean of 180 from the population mean of 174, measured in terms of standard deviations.

Looking up the value of $z = 1.88$ in Table A2 (see page **366**) gives an area of 0.0311 in the right-hand tail of the Normal distribution. Thus 3.11% of sample means will be greater than or equal to 180 cm when the sample size is nine. The desired probability is therefore 3.11%.

Since this probability is quite small, we might consider the reasons for this. There are two possibilities:

1 through bad luck, the sample collected is not very representative of the population as a whole, or
2 the sample is representative of the population, but the population mean is not 174 cm after all.

Only one of these two possibilities can be correct. How to decide between them will be taken up later on, in Chapter 5 on hypothesis testing.

It is interesting to examine the difference between the answer for a sample size of nine (3.11%) and the one obtained earlier for a single individual (26.43%). The latter may be considered as a sample of size one from the population. The examples illustrate the fact that the larger the sample size, the closer the sample mean is likely to be to the population mean. Thus larger samples tend to give better estimates of the population mean.

**Sampling from a non-Normal population**

The previous theorem and examples relied upon the fact that the population followed a Normal distribution. But what happens if it is not Normal? After all, it is not known for certain that the heights of all adult males are exactly Normally distributed, and there are many populations which are not Normal (e.g. wealth, as shown in Chapter 1). What can be done in these circumstances? The answer is to use another theorem about the distribution of sample means (presented without proof). This is known as the **Central Limit Theorem**:

> **Central Limit Theorem** The sample mean $\bar{x}$, drawn from a population with mean $\mu$ and variance $\sigma^2$, has a sampling distribution which approaches a Normal distribution with mean $\mu$ and variance $\sigma^2/n$, as the sample size approaches infinity.

This is very useful, since it drops the assumption that the population is Normally distributed. Note that the distribution of sample means is only Normal as long as the sample size is infinite; for any finite sample size the distribution is only approximately Normal. However, the approximation is close enough for practical purposes if the sample size is larger than 25 or so observations. If the population distribution is itself nearly Normal then a smaller sample size would suffice. If the population distribution is particularly skewed then more than 25 observations would be desirable. Twenty-five observations constitutes a rule of thumb that is adequate in most circumstances. This is another illustration of statistics as an inexact science. It does not provide absolutely clear-cut answers to questions but, used carefully, helps us to arrive at sensible conclusions.

As an example of the use of the Central Limit Theorem, we return to the wealth data of Chapter 1. Recall that the mean level of wealth was 133.443 (measured in £000) and the variance 52 880. Suppose that a sample of $n = 50$ people were drawn from this population. What is the probability that the sample mean is greater than 150 (i.e. £150 000)?

On this occasion we know that the parent distribution is highly skewed so it is fortunate that we have 50 observations. This should be ample for us to justify applying the Central Limit Theorem. The distribution of $\bar{x}$ is therefore

$$(3.19) \quad \bar{x} \sim N(\mu, \sigma^2/n)$$

and, inserting the parameter values, this gives[3]

$$(3.20) \quad \bar{x} \sim N(133.443, 52\,880/50)$$

To find the area beyond a sample mean of 150, the $z$ score is first calculated:

$$(3.21) \quad z = \frac{150 - 133.433}{\sqrt{52\,880/50}} = 0.51$$

[3] Note that if we used 133 443 for the mean we would have 52 880 000 000 as the variance. Using £000 keeps the numbers more manageable. The $z$ score is the same in both cases.

**Figure 3.13**
**The probability of $\bar{x}$ lying within £64 000 either side of £133 443**

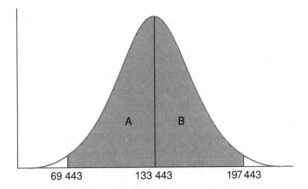

Referring to the standard Normal tables, the area in the tail is then found to be 30.5%. This is the desired probability. So there is a probability of 30.5% of finding a mean of £150 000 or greater with a sample of size 50. This demonstrates that there is quite a high probability of getting a sample mean which is a relatively long way from £133 443. This is a consequence of the high degree of dispersion in the distribution of wealth.

Extending this example, we can ask what is the probability of the sample mean lying within, say, £64 000 either side of the mean value of £133 443 (i.e. between 69 443 and 197 443)? Figure 3.13 illustrates the situation, with the desired area shaded. By symmetry, areas A and B must be equal, so we only need find one of them. For B, we calculate the z score:

$$(3.22) \qquad z = \frac{197.443 - 133.433}{\sqrt{52\ 880/50}} = 1.968$$

From the standard Normal table, this cuts off approximately 2.5% in the upper tail, so area B = 0.475. Areas A and B together make up 95% of the distribution, therefore. There is thus a 95% probability of the sample mean falling within the range [69 443, 197 443] and we call this the 95% **probability interval** for the sample mean. We write this:

$$(3.23) \qquad \Pr(69\ 443 \leq \bar{x} \leq 197\ 443) = 0.95$$

or, in terms of the formulae we have used:[4]

$$(3.24) \qquad \Pr(\mu - 1.96\sqrt{\sigma^2/n} \leq \bar{x} \leq \mu + 1.96\sqrt{\sigma^2/n}) = 0.95$$

The 95% probability interval and the related concept of the 95% confidence interval (introduced in Chapter 4) play important roles in statistical inference. We deliberately designed the example above to arrive at an answer of 95% for this reason.

**Exercise 3.6**

(a)  If x is distributed as $x \sim N(50, 64)$ and samples of size $n = 25$ are drawn, what is the distribution of the sample mean $\bar{x}$?

(b)  If the sample size doubles to 50, how is the standard error of $\bar{x}$ altered?

(c)  Using the sample size of 25, (i) what is the probability of $\bar{x} > 51$? (ii) What is $\Pr(\bar{x} < 48)$? (iii) What is $\Pr(49 < \bar{x} < 50.5)$?

---

[4]  1.96 is the precise value cutting off 2.5% in each tail.

# The relationship between the Binomial and Normal distributions

Many statistical distributions are related to one another in some way. This means that many problems can be solved by a variety of different methods (using different distributions), though usually one is more convenient than the others. This point may be illustrated by looking at the relationship between the Binomial and Normal distributions.

Recall the experiment of tossing a coin repeatedly and noting the number of heads. We said earlier that this can be analysed via the Binomial distribution. But note that the number of heads, a random variable, is influenced by many independent random events (the individual tosses) added together. Furthermore, each toss counts equally, none dominates. These are just the conditions under which a Normal distribution arises, so it looks like there is a connection between the two distributions.

This idea is correct. Recall that if a random variable $r$ follows a Binomial distribution then

**(3.1)**   $r \sim B(n, P)$

and the mean of the distribution is $nP$ and the variance $nP(1 - P)$. It turns out that as $n$ gets larger, the Binomial distribution becomes approximately the same as a Normal distribution with mean $nP$ and variance $nP(1 - P)$. This approximation is sufficiently accurate as long as $nP > 5$ and $n(1 - P) > 5$, so the approximation may not be very good (even for large values of $n$) if $P$ is very close to zero or one. For the coin tossing experiment, where $P = 0.5$, 10 tosses should be sufficient. Note that this approximation is good enough with only 10 observations even though the underlying probability distribution is nothing like a Normal distribution.

To demonstrate, the following problem is solved using both the Binomial and Normal distributions. Forty students take an exam in statistics which is simply graded pass/fail. If the probability, $P$, of any individual student passing is 60%, what is the probability of at least 30 students passing the exam?

The sample data are:

$$P = 0.6$$
$$1 - P = 0.4$$
$$n = 40$$

**Binomial distribution method**

To solve the problem using the Binomial distribution it is necessary to find the probability of exactly 30 students passing, plus the probability of 31 passing, plus the probability of 32 passing, etc., up to the probability of 40 passing (the fact that the events are mutually exclusive allows this). The probability of 30 passing is

$$\Pr(r = 30) = nCr \times P^r(1 - P)^{n-r}$$
$$= 40C^{30} \times 0.6^{30} \times 0.4^{10}$$
$$= 0.020$$

(N.B. This calculation assumes that the probabilities are independent, i.e. no copying!) This by itself is quite a tedious calculation, but $\Pr(31)$, $\Pr(32)$, etc. still have to be calculated. Calculating these and summing them gives the result of 3.52% as the probability of at least 30 passing. (It would be a useful exercise for you to do, if only to appreciate how long it takes.)

**Normal distribution method**

As stated above, the Binomial distribution can be approximated by a Normal distribution with mean $nP$ and variance $nP(1 - P)$. $nP$ in this case is 24 ($40 \times 0.6$) and $n(1 - P)$ is 16, both greater than 5, so the approximation can be safely used. Thus

$$r \sim N(nP, nP(1 - P))$$

and inserting the parameter values gives

$$r \sim N(24, 9.6)$$

The usual methods are then used to find the appropriate area under the distribution. However, before doing so, there is one adjustment to be made (this only applies when approximating the Binomial distribution by the Normal). The Normal distribution is a continuous one while the Binomial is discrete. Thus 30 in the Binomial distribution is represented by the area under the Normal distribution between 29.5 and 30.5. 31 is represented by 30.5 to 31.5, etc. Thus it is the area under the Normal distribution to the right of 29.5, not 30, which must be calculated. This is known as the continuity correction. Calculating the $z$ score gives

$$(3.25) \qquad z = \frac{29.5 - 24}{\sqrt{9.6}} = 1.78$$

This gives an area of 3.75%, not far off the correct answer as calculated by the Binomial distribution. The time saved and ease of calculation would seem to be worth the slight loss in accuracy.

Other examples can be constructed to test this method, using different values of $P$ and $n$. Small values of $n$, or values of $nP$ or $n(1 - P)$ less than 5, will give poor results, i.e. the Normal approximation to the Binomial will not be very good.

**Exercise 3.7**

(a) A coin is tossed 20 times. What is the probability of more than 14 heads? Perform the calculation using both the Binomial and Normal distributions, and compare results.

(b) A biased coin, for which $\Pr(H) = 0.7$ is tossed 6 times. What is the probability of more than 4 heads? Compare Binomial and Normal methods in this case. How accurate is the Normal approximation?

(c) Repeat part (b) but for more than 5 heads.

## The Poisson distribution

The section above showed how the Binomial distribution could be approximated by a Normal distribution under certain circumstances. The approximation does not work particularly well for very small values of $P$, when $nP$ is less than 5. In these circumstances the Binomial may be approximated instead by the Poisson distribution, which is given by the formula

$$(3.26) \qquad \Pr(x) = \frac{\mu^x e^{-\mu}}{x!}$$

where $\mu$ is the mean of the distribution (like $\mu$ for the Normal distribution and $nP$ for the Binomial). Like the Binomial, but unlike the Normal, the Poisson is a discrete probability distribution, so that equation (3.26) is only defined for integer values of $x$. Furthermore, it is applicable to a series of trials which are independent, as in the Binomial case.

The use of the Poisson distribution is appropriate when the probability of 'success' is very small and the number of trials large. Its use is illustrated by the following example. A manufacturer gives a two-year guarantee on the TV screens it makes. From past experience it knows that 0.5% of its tubes will be faulty and fail within the guarantee period. What is the probability that of a consignment of 500 tubes (a) none will be faulty, (b) more than three are faulty?

The mean of the Poisson distribution in this case is $\mu = 2.5$ (0.5% of 500). Therefore

$$(3.27) \qquad \Pr(x = 0) = \frac{2.5^0 e^{-2.5}}{0!} = 0.082$$

giving a probability of 8.2% of no failures. The answer to this problem via the Binomial method is

$$\Pr(r = 0) = 0.995^{500} = 0.0816$$

Thus the Poisson method gives a reasonably accurate answer. The Poisson approximation to the Binomial is satisfactory if $nP$ is less than about 7.

The probability of more than three tubes expiring is calculated as

$$\Pr(x > 3) = 1 - \Pr(x = 0) - \Pr(x = 1) - \Pr(x = 2) - \Pr(x = 3)$$

$$\Pr(x = 1) = \frac{2.5^1 e^{-2.5}}{1!} = 0.205$$

$$\Pr(x = 2) = \frac{2.5^2 e^{-2.5}}{2!} = 0.256$$

$$\Pr(x = 3) = \frac{2.5^3 e^{-2.5}}{3!} = 0.214$$

$$\text{So } \Pr(x > 3) = 1 - 0.082 - 0.205 - 0.256 - 0.214$$
$$= 0.242$$

Thus there is a probability of about 24% of more than three failures. The Binomial calculation is much more tedious, but gives an answer of 24.2% also.

The Poisson distribution is also used in problems where events occur over time, such as goals scored in a football match (see Problem 3.25) or queuing-type problems (e.g. arrivals at a bank cash machine). In these problems, there is no natural 'number' of trials but it is clear that, if we take a short interval of time, the probability of an event occurring is small. We can then consider the number of trials to be the number of time intervals. This is illustrated by the following example. A football team scores, on average, two goals every game (you can vary the example by using your own favourite team plus their scoring record!). What is the probability of the team scoring zero or one goal during a game?

The mean of the distribution is 2, so we have, using the Poisson distribution:

$$\Pr(x = 0) = \frac{2^0 e^{-2}}{0!} = 0.135$$

$$\Pr(x = 1) = \frac{2^1 e^{-2}}{1!} = 0.271$$

You should continue to calculate the probabilities of 2 or more goals and verify that the probabilities sum to 1.

A queuing-type problem is the following. If a shop receives, on average, 20 customers per hour, what is the probability of no customers within a five-minute period while the owner takes a coffee break?

The average number of customers per five-minute period is $20 \times 5/60 = 1.67$. The probability of a free five-minute spell is therefore

$$\Pr(x = 0) = \frac{1.67^0 e^{-1.67}}{0!} = 0.189$$

a probability of about 19%. Note that this problem cannot be solved by the Binomial method since $n$ and $P$ are not known separately, only their product.

**Exercise 3.8**

(a) The probability of winning a prize in a lottery is 1 in 50. If you buy 50 tickets, what is the probability that (i) 0 tickets win, (ii) 1 ticket wins, (iii) 2 tickets win. (iv) What is the probability of winning at least one prize?

(b) On average, a person buys a lottery ticket in a supermarket every 5 minutes. What is the probability that 10 minutes will pass with no buyers?

---

### Railway accidents

Andrew Evans of University College, London, used the Poisson distribution to examine the numbers of fatal railway accidents in Britain between 1967 and 1997. Since railway accidents are, fortunately, rare, the probability of an accident in any time period is very small and so use of the Poisson distribution is appropriate. He found that the average number of accidents has been falling over time and by 1997 had reached 1.25 per annum. This figure is therefore used as the mean $\mu$ of the Poisson distribution, and we can calculate the probabilities of 0, 1, 2, etc. accidents each year. Using $\mu = 1.25$ and inserting this into equation 3.26 we obtain the following table:

| Number of accidents | 0 | 1 | 2 | 3 | 4 | 5 | 6 |
|---|---|---|---|---|---|---|---|
| Probability | | 0.287 | 0.358 | 0.224 | 0.093 | 0.029 | 0.007 | 0.002 |

and this distribution can be graphed:

Poisson distribution of railway accidents

Thus the most likely outcome is one fatal accident per year and anything over four is extremely unlikely. In fact, Evans found that the Poisson was not a perfect fit to the data: the actual variation was less than that predicted by the model.

*Source*: A. W. Evans, Fatal train accidents on Britain's mainline railways, *J. Royal Statistical Society*, Series A, vol. 163 (1), 2000.

## Summary

- The behaviour of many random variables (e.g. the result of the toss of a coin) can be described by a probability distribution (in this case, the Binomial distribution).

- The Binomial distribution is appropriate for problems where there are only two possible outcomes of a chance event (e.g. heads/tails, success/failure) and the probability of success is the same each time the experiment is conducted.

- The Normal distribution is appropriate for problems where the random variable has the familiar bell-shaped distribution. This often occurs when the variable is influenced by many, independent factors, none of which dominates the others. An example is men's heights, which are Normally distributed.

- The Poisson distribution is used in circumstances where there is a very low probability of 'success' and a high number of trials.

- Each of these distributions is actually a family of distributions, differing in the parameters of the distribution. Both the Binomial and Normal distributions have two parameters: $n$ and $P$ in the former case, $\mu$ and $\sigma^2$ in the latter. The Poisson distribution has one parameter, its mean $\mu$.

- The mean of a random sample follows a Normal distribution, because it is influenced by many independent factors (the sample observations), none of which dominates in the calculation of the mean. This statement is always true if the population from which the sample is drawn follows a Normal distribution.

- If the population is not Normally distributed then the Central Limit Theorem states that the sample mean is Normally distributed in large samples. In this case 'large' means a sample of about 25 or more.

**Key terms and concepts**

| | | |
|---|---|---|
| probability distribution | random variable | standard Normal distribution |
| parameters of a distribution | Normal distribution | Poisson distribution |
| standard error | Central Limit Theorem | |
| | Binomial distribution | |

## Problems

Some of the more challenging problems are indicated by highlighting the problem number in colour.

**Problem 3.1** Two dice are thrown and the sum of the two scores is recorded. Draw a graph of the resulting probability distribution of the sum and calculate its mean and variance. What is the probability that the sum is 9 or greater?

**Problem 3.2**   Two dice are thrown and the absolute difference of the two scores recorded. Graph the resulting probability distribution and calculate its mean and variance. What is the probability that the absolute difference is 4 or more?

**Problem 3.3**   Sketch the probability distribution for the likely time of departure of a train. Locate the timetabled departure time on your chart.

**Problem 3.4**   A train departs every half hour. You arrive at the station at a completely random moment. Sketch the probability distribution of your waiting time. What is your expected waiting time?

**Problem 3.5**   Sketch the probability distribution for the number of accidents on a stretch of road in one day.

**Problem 3.6**   Sketch the probability distribution for the number of accidents on the same stretch of road in one year. How and why does this differ from your previous answer?

**Problem 3.7**   Six dice are rolled and the number of sixes is noted. Calculate the probabilities of 0, 1, . . . , 6 sixes and graph the probability distribution.

**Problem 3.8**   If the probability of a boy in a single birth is $\frac{1}{2}$ and is independent of the sex of previous babies then the number of boys in a family of 10 children follows a Binomial distribution with mean 5 and variance 2.5. In each of the following instances, describe how the distribution of the number of boys differs from the Binomial described above.

(a)   The probability of a boy is 6/10.

(b)   The probability of a boy is $\frac{1}{2}$ but births are not independent. The birth of a boy makes it more than an even chance that the next child is a boy.

(c)   As (b) above, except that the birth of a boy makes it less than an even chance that the next child will be a boy.

(d)   The probability of a boy is 6/10 on the first birth. The birth of a boy makes it a more than even chance that the next baby will be a boy.

**Problem 3.9**   A firm receives components from a supplier in large batches, for use in its production process. Production is uneconomic if a batch containing 10% or more defective components is used. The firm checks the quality of each incoming batch by taking a sample of 15 and rejecting the whole batch if more than one defective component is found.

(a)   If a batch containing 10% defectives is delivered, what is the probability of its being accepted?

(b)   How could the firm reduce this probability of erroneously accepting bad batches?

(c)   If the supplier produces a batch with 3% defective, what is the probability of the firm sending back the batch?

(d)   What role does the assumption of a 'large' batch play in the calculation?

**Problem 3.10**   The UK record for the number of children born to a mother is 39, 32 of them girls. Assuming the probability of a girl in a single birth is 0.5 and that this probability is independent of previous births:

(a)   Find the probability of 32 girls in 39 births (you'll need a scientific calculator or a computer to help with this!).

(b)   Does this result cast doubt on the assumptions?

**Problem 3.11**   Using equation (3.5) describing the Normal distribution and setting $\mu = 0$ and $\sigma^2 = 1$, graph the distribution for the values $x = -2, -1.5, -1, -0.5, 0, 0.5, 1, 1.5, 2$.

**Problem 3.12**   Repeat the previous Problem for the values $\mu = 2$ and $\sigma^2 = 3$. Use values of $x$ from $-2$ to $+6$ in increments of 1.

**Problem 3.13**   For the standard Normal variable $z$, find

(a)   $\Pr(z > 1.64)$

(b)   $\Pr(z > 0.5)$

(c)   $\Pr(z > -1.5)$

(d)   $\Pr(-2 < z < 1.5)$

(e)   $\Pr(z = -0.75)$.

For (a) and (d), shade in the relevant areas on the graph you drew for Problem 3.11.

**Problem 3.14**   Find the values of $z$ which cut off

(a)   the top 10%

(b)   the bottom 15%

(c)   the middle 50%

of the standard Normal distribution.

**Problem 3.15**   If $x \sim N(10, 9)$ find

(a)   $\Pr(x > 12)$

(b)   $\Pr(x < 7)$

(c)   $\Pr(8 < x < 15)$

(d)   $\Pr(x = 10)$.

**Problem 3.16**   IQ (the intelligence quotient) is Normally distributed with mean 100 and standard deviation 16.

(a)   What proportion of the population has an IQ above 120?

(b)   What proportion of the population has IQ between 90 and 110?

(c)   In the past, about 10% of the population went to university. Now the proportion is about 30%. What was the IQ of the 'marginal' student in the past? What is it now?

**Problem 3.17**   Ten adults are selected at random from the population and their IQ measured.

(a)   What is the probability distribution of the sample average IQ?

(b)   What is the probability that the average IQ of the sample is over 110?

(c)   If many such samples were taken, in what proportion would you expect the average IQ to be over 110?

(d)  What is the probability that the average IQ lies within the range 90 to 110? How does this answer compare to the answer to part (b) of Problem 16? Account for the difference.

(e)  What is the probability that a random sample of ten university students has an average IQ greater than 110?

(f)  The first adult sampled has an IQ of 150. What do you expect the average IQ of the sample to be?

**Problem 3.18**  The average income of a country is known to be £10 000 with standard deviation £2500. A sample of 40 individuals is taken and their average income calculated.

(a)  What is the probability distribution of this sample mean?

(b)  What is the probability of the sample mean being over £10 500?

(c)  What is the probability of the sample mean being below £8000?

(d)  If the sample size were 10, why could you not use the same methods to find the answers to (a)–(c)?

**Problem 3.19**  A coin is tossed ten times. Write down the distribution of the number of heads,

(a)  exactly, using the Binomial distribution,

(b)  approximately, using the Normal distribution.

(c)  Find the probability of four or more heads, using both methods. How accurate is the Normal method, with and without the continuity correction?

**Problem 3.20**  A machine producing electronic circuits has an average failure rate of 15% (they're difficult to make). The cost of making a batch of 500 circuits is £8400 and the good ones sell for £20 each. What is the probability of the firm making a loss on any one batch?

**Problem 3.21**  An experienced invoice clerk makes an error once in every 100 invoices, on average.

(a)  What is the probability of finding a batch of 100 invoices without error?

(b)  What is the probability of finding such a batch with more than two errors?

Calculate the answers using both the Binomial and Poisson distributions. If you try to solve the problem using the Normal method, how accurate is your answer?

**Problem 3.22**  A firm employing 100 workers has an average absenteeism rate of 4%. On a given day, what is the probability of (a) no workers, (b) one worker, (c) more than six workers being absent?

**Problem 3.23**
**(Computer project)**  This problem demonstrates the Central Limit Theorem at work. In your spreadsheet, use the =RAND() function to generate a random sample of 25 observations (I suggest entering this function in cells A4:A28, for example). Copy these cells across 100 columns, to generate 100 samples. In row 29, calculate the mean of each sample. Now examine the distribution of these sample means. (Hint: you will find the RAND() function recalculates automatically every time you perform an operation in the spreadsheet. This makes it difficult to complete the analysis. The solution is to copy and then use 'Edit, Paste Special, Values' to create a copy of the values of the sample means. These will remain stable.)

(a) What distribution would you expect them to have?

(b) What is the parent distribution from which the samples are drawn?

(c) What are the parameters of the parent distribution and of the sample means?

(d) Do your results accord with what you would expect?

(e) Draw up a frequency table of the sample means and graph it. Does it look as you expected?

(f) Experiment with different sample sizes and with different parent distributions to see the effect that these have.

**Problem 3.24 (Project)** An extremely numerate newsagent (with a spreadsheet program, as you will need) is trying to work out how many copies of a newspaper he should order. The cost to him per copy is 15 pence, which he then sells at 45 pence. Sales are distributed Normally with an average daily sale of 250 and variance 625. Unsold copies cannot be returned for credit or refund; he has to throw them away, losing 15p per copy.

(a) What do you think the seller's objective should be?

(b) How many copies should he order?

(c) What happens to the *variance* of profit as he orders more copies?

(d) Calculate the probability of selling *more than X* copies. (Create an extra column in the spreadsheet for this.) What is the value of this probability at the optimum number of copies ordered?

(e) What would the price–cost ratio have to be to justify the seller ordering X copies?

(f) The wholesaler offers a sale or return deal, but the cost per copy is 16p. Should the seller take up this new offer?

(g) Are there other considerations which might influence the seller's decision?

*Hints*:
Set up your spreadsheet as follows:

col. A: (cells A10:A160) 175, 176, . . . up to 325 in unit increments (to represent sales levels).

col. B: (cells B10:B160) the probability of sales falling between 175 and 176, between 176 and 177, etc. up to 325–326. (*Excel* has the '=NORMDIST()' function to do this – see the help facility.)

col. C: (cells C10:C160) total cost (= 0.15 × number ordered. Put the latter in cell F3 so you can reference it and change its value).

col. D: (cells D10:D160) total revenue ('=MIN(sales, number ordered) × 0.45').

col. E: profit (revenue – cost).

col. F: profit × probability (i.e. col. E × col. B).

cell F161: the sum of F10:F160 (this is the expected profit).

Now vary the number ordered (cell F3) to find the maximum value in F161. You can also calculate the variance of profit fairly simply, using an extra column.

**Problem 3.25 (Project)** Using a weekend's football results from the Premier (or other) league, see if the number of goals per game can be adequately modelled by a Poisson process. First calculate the average number of goals per game for the whole league, then derive the distribution of goals per game using the Poisson distribution. Do the actual numbers of goals per game follow this distribution? You might want to take several weeks' results to obtain more reliable results.

## Answers to exercises

**Exercise 3.1** (a) $0.6^4 = 0.1296$ or 12.96%.

(b) $0.6^2 \times 0.4^2 \times 4C2 = 0.3456$.

(c) $\Pr(r) = 0.6^r \times 0.4^{4-r}\ 4Cr$. The probabilities of $r = 0 \ldots 4$ are respectively 0.0256, 0.1536, 0.3456, 0.3456, 0.1296, which sum to one.

**Exercise 3.2** (a)

| $r$ | $P(r)$ | $r \times P(r)$ | $r^2 \times P(r)$ |
|---|---|---|---|
| 0 | 0.0256 | 0 | 0 |
| 1 | 0.1536 | 0.1536 | 0.1536 |
| 2 | 0.3456 | 0.6912 | 1.3824 |
| 3 | 0.3456 | 1.0368 | 3.1104 |
| 4 | 0.1296 | 0.5184 | 2.0736 |
| Totals | 1 | 2.4 | 6.72 |

The mean = 2.4/1 = 2.4 and the variance = $6.72/1 - 2.4^2 = 0.96$. Note that these are equal to $nP$ and $nP(1 - P)$.

(b)

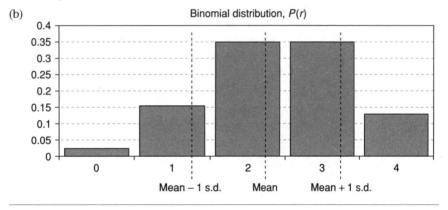

**Exercise 3.3** (a) $z = (50 - 40)/\sqrt{36} = 1.67$ and the area beyond $z = 1.67$ is 4.75%.

(b) $z = -0.83$ so area is 20.33%.

(c) This is symmetric around the mean, $z = \pm 0.67$ and the area within these two bounds is 49.72%.

**Exercise 3.4** To obtain the IQR we need to go 0.67 s.d.s above and below the mean, giving $200 \pm 0.67 \times 16 = [189.28, 210.72]$.

**Exercise 3.5** The IQR (in logs) is within $4.18 \pm 0.67 \times \sqrt{2.56} = [3.11, 5.25]$. Translated out of logs (using $10^x$) yields [1288.2, 177 827.9].

**Exercise 3.6** (a) $\bar{x} \sim N(50, 64/25)$.

(b) The s.e. gets smaller. It is $1/\sqrt{2}$ times its previous value.

(c) (i) $z = (51 - 50)/\sqrt{(64/25)} = 0.625$. Hence area in tail = 26.5%. (ii) $z = -1.25$, hence area = 10.56%. (iii) $z$ values are $-0.625$ and $+0.3125$, giving tail areas of 26.5% and 37.8%, totalling 64.3%. The area between the limits is therefore 35.7%.

**Exercise 3.7**   (a)  Binomial method: $\Pr(r) = 0.5^r \times 0.5^{(20-r)} \times 20Cr$. This gives probabilities of 15, 16, etc. heads of 0.0148, 0.0046, etc., which total 0.0207 or 2.1%. By the Normal approximation, $r \sim N(10,5)$ and $z = (14.5 - 10)/\sqrt{5} = 2.01$. The area in the tail is then 2.22%, not far off the correct value (a 10% error). Note that $nP = 10 = n(1 - P)$.

         (b)  Binomial method: $\Pr(5$ or $6$ heads$) = 0.302 + 0.118 = 0.420$ or 42%. By the Normal, $r \sim N(4.2, 1.26)$, $z = 0.267$ and the area is 39.36%, still reasonably close to the correct answer despite the fact that $n(1 - P) = 1.8$.

         (c)  By similar methods the answers are 11.8% (Binomial) and 12.3% (Normal).

---

**Exercise 3.8**   (a)  (i) $\mu = 1$ in this case $(1/50 \times 50)$ so $\Pr(x = 0) = 1^0 e^{-1}/0! = 0.368$. (ii) $\Pr(x = 1) = 1^1 e^{-1}/1! = 0.368$. (iii) $1^2 e^{-1}/2! = 0.184$. (iv) $1 - 0.368 = 0.632$.

         (b)  The average number of customer per 10 minutes is 2 (= 10/5). Hence $\Pr(x = 0) = 2^0 e^{-2}/0! = 0.135$.

---

# 4 Estimation and confidence intervals

**Learning outcomes**

By the end of this chapter you should be able to:

- recognise the importance of probability theory in drawing valid inferences (or deriving estimates) from a sample of data
- understand the criteria for constructing a good estimate
- construct estimates of parameters of interest from sample data, in a variety of different circumstances
- appreciate that there is uncertainty about the accuracy of any such estimate
- provide measures of the uncertainty associated with an estimate
- recognise the relationship between the size of a sample and the precision of an estimate derived from it

## Introduction

We now come to the heart of the subject of statistical inference. Up until now the following type of question has been examined: given the population parameters $\mu$ and $\sigma^2$, what is the probability of the sample mean $\bar{x}$, from a sample of size $n$, being greater than some specified value or within some range of values? The parameters $\mu$ and $\sigma^2$ are assumed to be known and the objective is to try to form some conclusions about possible values of $\bar{x}$. However, in practice it is usually the sample values $\bar{x}$ and $s^2$ that are known, while the population parameters $\mu$ and $\sigma^2$ are not. Thus a more interesting question to ask is: given the values of $\bar{x}$ and $s^2$, what can be said about $\mu$ and $\sigma^2$? Sometimes the population variance is known, and inferences have to be made about $\mu$ alone. For example, if a sample of 50 British families finds an average weekly expenditure on food ($\bar{x}$) of £37.50 with a standard deviation ($s$) of £6.00, what can be said about the average expenditure ($\mu$) of *all* British families?

Schematically this type of problem is shown as follows:

| Sample information | | Population parameters |
|---|---|---|
| $\bar{x}, s^2$ | inferences about $\longrightarrow$ | $\mu, \sigma^2$ |

This chapter covers the estimation of population parameters such as $\mu$ and $\sigma^2$ while Chapter 5 describes testing hypotheses about these parameters. The two procedures are very closely related.

## Point and interval estimation

There are basically two ways in which an estimate of a parameter can be presented. The first of these is a point estimate, i.e. a single value which is the best estimate of the parameter of interest. The point estimate is the one which is most prevalent in everyday usage; for example, the average Briton surfs the internet for 30 minutes per day. Although this is presented as a fact, it is actually an estimate, obtained from a survey of people's use of personal computers. Since it is obtained from a sample there must be some doubt about its accuracy – the sample will probably not exactly represent the whole population. For this reason interval estimates are also used, which give some idea of the likely accuracy of the estimate. If the sample size is small, for example, then it is quite possible that the estimate is not very close to the true value and this would be reflected in a wide interval estimate, for example, that the average Briton spends between 5 and 55 minutes surfing the net per day. A larger sample, or a better method of estimation, would allow a narrower interval to be derived and thus a more precise estimate of the parameter to be obtained, such as an average surfing time of between 20 and 40 minutes. Interval estimates are better for the consumer of the statistics, since they not only show the estimate of the parameter but also give an idea of the confidence which the researcher has in that estimate. The following sections describe how to construct both types of estimate.

# Rules and criteria for finding estimates

In order to estimate a parameter such as the population mean, a rule (or set of rules) is required which describes how to derive the estimate of the parameter from the sample data. Such a rule is known as an **estimator**. An example of an estimator for the population mean is 'use the sample mean'. It is important to distinguish between an estimator, a rule, and an estimate, which is the value derived as a result of applying the rule to the data.

There are many possible estimators for any parameter, so it is important to be able to distinguish between good and bad estimators. The following examples provide some possible estimators of the population mean:

1  the sample mean;
2  the smallest sample observation;
3  the first sample observation.

A set of criteria is needed for discriminating between good and bad estimators. Which of the above three estimators is 'best'? Two important criteria by which to judge estimators are **bias** and **precision**.

**Bias**

It is impossible to know if a single estimate of a parameter, derived by applying a particular estimator to the sample data, gives a correct estimate of the parameter or not. The estimate might be too low or too high and, since the parameter is unknown, it is impossible to check this. What *is* possible, however, is to say whether an estimator gives the correct answer *on average*. An estimator which gives the correct answer on average is said to be unbiased. Another way of expressing this is to say that an unbiased estimator does not *systematically* mislead the researcher away from the correct value of the parameter. It is important to remember, though, that even using an unbiased estimator does not guarantee that a single use of the estimator will yield a correct estimate of the parameter. Bias (or the lack of it) is a theoretical property.

Formally, an estimator is unbiased if its expected value is equal to the parameter being estimated. Consider trying to estimate the population mean using the three estimators suggested above. Taking the sample mean first, we have already learned (see equation (3.15)) that its expected value is $\mu$, i.e.

$$E(\bar{x}) = \mu$$

which immediately shows that the sample mean is an unbiased estimator.

The second estimator (the smallest observation in the sample) can easily be shown to be biased, using the result derived above. Since the smallest sample observation must be less than the sample mean, its expected value must be less than $\mu$. Denote the smallest observation by $x_s$, then

$$E(x_s) < \mu$$

so this estimator is biased downwards. It underestimates the population mean. The size of the bias is simply the difference between the expected value of the estimator and the value of the parameter, so the bias in this case is

**(4.1)**    $\text{Bias} = E(x_s) - \mu$

For the sample mean $\bar{x}$ the bias is obviously zero.

Turning to the third rule (the first sample observation) this can be shown to be another unbiased estimator. Choosing the first observation from the sample is equivalent to taking a random sample of size one from the population in the first place. Thus the single observation may be considered as the sample mean from a random sample of size one. Since it is a sample mean it is unbiased, as demonstrated earlier.

**Precision**

Two of the estimators above were found to be unbiased, and, in fact, there are many unbiased estimators (the sample median is another). Some way of choosing between the set of all unbiased estimators is therefore required, which is where the criterion of precision helps. Unlike bias, precision is a relative concept, comparing one estimator to another. Given two estimators A and B, A is more precise than B if the estimates it yields (from all possible samples) are less spread out than those of estimator B. A precise estimator will tend to give similar estimates for all possible samples.

Consider the two unbiased estimators found above: how do they compare on the criteria of precision? It turns out that the sample mean is the more precise of the two, and it is not difficult to understand why. Taking just a single sample observation means that it is quite likely to be unrepresentative of the population as a whole, and thus leads to a poor estimate of the population mean. The sample mean on the other hand is based on all the sample observations and it is unlikely that all of them are unrepresentative of the population. The sample mean is therefore a good estimator of the population mean, being more precise than the single observation estimator.

Just as bias was related to the expected value of the estimator, so precision can be defined in terms of the variance. One estimator is more precise than another if it has a smaller variance. Recall that the probability distribution of the sample mean is

**(4.2)**     $\bar{x} \sim N(\mu, \sigma^2/n)$

in large samples, so the variance of the sample mean is

$V(\bar{x}) = \sigma^2/n$

As the sample size $n$ gets larger the variance of the sample mean becomes smaller, so the estimator becomes more precise. For this reason large samples give better estimates than small samples, and so the sample mean is a better estimator than taking just one observation from the sample. The two estimators can be compared in a diagram (see Figure 4.1) which draws the probability distributions of the two estimators.

It is easily seen that the sample mean yields estimates which are *on average* closer to the population mean.

A related concept is that of **efficiency**. The efficiency of one unbiased estimator, relative to another, is given by the ratio of their sampling variances. Thus the efficiency of the first observation estimator, relative to the sample mean, is given by

**(4.3)**     $\text{Efficiency} = \dfrac{\text{var}(\bar{x})}{\text{var}(x_1)} = \dfrac{\sigma^2/n}{\sigma^2} = \dfrac{1}{n}$

Thus the efficiency is determined by the relative sample sizes in this case.

Figure 4.1
The sampling
distribution of two
estimators

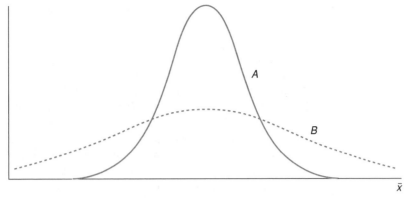

*Note:* Curve *A* shows the distribution of sample means, which is the more precise estimator. *B* shows the distribution of estimates using a single observation.

**The trade-off between bias and precision: the Bill Gates effect**

It should be noted that just because an estimator is biased does not necessarily mean that it is imprecise. Sometimes there is a trade-off between an unbiased, but imprecise, estimator and a biased, but precise, one. Figure 4.2 illustrates this.

Although estimator *A* is biased it will nearly always yield an estimate which is fairly close to the true value; even though the estimate is expected to be wrong, it is not likely to be far wrong. Estimator *B*, though unbiased, can give estimates which are far away from the true value, so that *A* might be the preferred estimator.

As an example of this, suppose we are trying to estimate the average wealth of the US population. Consider the following two estimators:

1  Use the mean wealth of a random sample of Americans.
2  Use the mean wealth of a random sample of Americans but, if Bill Gates is in the sample, omit him from the calculation.

Bill Gates is the Chairman of Microsoft and the world's richest man. Because of this, he is a dollar billionaire (about $50bn according to recent reports). His presence in a sample of, say, 30 observations would swamp the sample and give a highly misleading result. Assuming Bill Gates has $50bn and the others each have $200 000 of wealth, the average wealth would be estimated at about $1.6bn, which is surely wrong.

Figure 4.2
The trade-off between
bias and precision

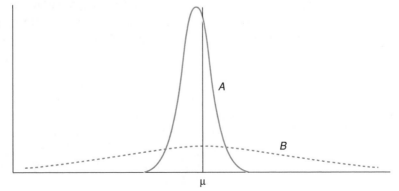

The first rule could therefore give us a wildly incorrect answer, although the rule is unbiased. The second rule is clearly biased but does rule out the possibility of such an unlucky sample. We can work out the approximate bias. It is the difference between the average wealth of all Americans and the average wealth of all Americans except Bill Gates. If the true average of all 250 million Americans is $200 000, then total wealth is $50 000bn. Subtracting Bill's $50bn leaves $49 950bn shared amongst the rest, giving $199 800 each, a difference of 0.1%. This is what we would expect the bias to be.

It might seem worthwhile therefore to accept this degree of bias in order to improve the precision of the estimate. Furthermore, if we did use the biased rule, we could always adjust the sample mean upwards by 0.1% to get an approximately unbiased estimate.

Of course, this point applies to any exceptionally rich person, not just Bill Gates. It points to the need to ensure that the rich are not over- (nor under-) represented in the sample. Chapter 9 on sampling methods investigates this point in more detail. In the rest of this book only unbiased estimators are considered, the most important being the sample mean.

## Estimation with large samples

For the type of problem encountered in this chapter the method of estimation differs according to the size of the sample. 'Large' samples, by which is meant sample sizes of 25 or more, are dealt with first, using the Normal distribution. Small samples are considered in a later section, where the $t$ distribution is used instead of the Normal. The differences are relatively minor in practical terms and there is a close theoretical relationship between the $t$ and Normal distributions.

With large samples there are several types of estimation problem to consider. First, we look at the estimation of a mean from a sample of data. Second, we look at the estimation of a proportion on the basis of sample evidence. This would consider a problem such as estimating the proportion of the population intending to vote for the Conservative Party in an election, based upon evidence from a sample of voters. Each voter in the sample would simply indicate a preference for one or other parties. The principles of estimation are the same in both cases but the formulae used for calculation are slightly different. The final case is where we deal with estimating the difference of two means (or proportions), for example a problem such as estimating the difference between men and women's expenditure on clothes. Once again, the principles are the same, the formulae different.

**Estimating a mean**   To demonstrate the principles and practice of estimating the population mean, we shall take the example of estimating the average wealth of the UK population, the full data for which were given in Chapter 1. Suppose that we did not have this information but were required to estimate the average wealth from a sample of data. In particular, let us suppose that the sample size is $n = 100$, the sample mean is $\bar{x} = 130$ (in £000) and the sample variance is $s^2 = 50\,000$. Obviously, this sample has got fairly close to the true values (see Chapter 1) but we could not know that from the sample alone. What can we infer about the population mean $\mu$ from the sample data alone?

For the point estimate of $\mu$ the sample mean is a good candidate since it is unbiased, and it is more precise than other sample statistics such as the median. The point estimate of $\mu$ is simply £130 000, therefore.

The point estimate does not give an idea of the uncertainty associated with the estimate. We are not *absolutely* sure that the mean is £130 000 (in fact, it isn't – it is £133 443). The interval estimate gives some idea of the uncertainty. It is centred on the sample mean, but gives a range of values to express the uncertainty.

To obtain the interval estimate we first require the probability distribution of $\bar{x}$, first established in Chapter 3 (equation 3.17):

**(4.4)**    $\bar{x} \sim N(\mu, \sigma^2/n)$

From this, it was calculated that there is a 95% probability of the sample mean lying within 1.96 standard errors of $\mu$[1], i.e.

$$\Pr(\mu - 1.96\sqrt{\sigma^2/n} \leq \bar{x} \leq \mu + 1.96\sqrt{\sigma^2/n}) = 0.95$$

We can manipulate each of the inequalities within the brackets to make $\mu$ the subject of the expression:

$$\mu - 1.96\sqrt{\sigma^2/n} \leq \bar{x} \quad \text{implies} \quad \mu \leq \bar{x} + 1.96\sqrt{\sigma^2/n}$$

Similarly

$$\bar{x} \leq \mu + 1.96\sqrt{\sigma^2/n} \quad \text{implies} \quad \bar{x} - 1.96\sqrt{\sigma^2/n} \leq \mu$$

Combining these two new expressions we obtain

**(4.5)**    $[\bar{x} - 1.96\sqrt{\sigma^2/n} \leq \mu \leq \bar{x} + 1.96\sqrt{\sigma^2/n}]$

We have transformed the probability interval. Instead of saying $\bar{x}$ lies within 1.96 standard errors of $\mu$, we now say $\mu$ lies within 1.96 standard errors of $\bar{x}$. Figure 4.3 illustrates this manipulation. Figure 4.3(a) shows $\mu$ at the centre of a probability interval for $\bar{x}$. Figure 4.3(b) shows a sample mean $\bar{x}$ at the centre of an interval relating to the possible positions of $\mu$.

The interval shown in equation (4.5) is called the 95% confidence interval and this is the interval estimate for $\mu$. In this example the value of $\sigma^2$ is unknown, but in large ($n \geq 25$) samples it can be replaced by $s^2$ from the sample. $s^2$ is here used as an estimate of $\sigma^2$ which is unbiased and sufficiently precise in large ($n \geq 25$ or so) samples. The 95% confidence interval is therefore

**(4.6)**    $[\bar{x} - 1.96\sqrt{s^2/n} \leq \mu \leq \bar{x} + 1.96\sqrt{s^2/n}]$

$$= [130 - 1.96\sqrt{50\ 000/100}, 130 + 1.96\sqrt{50\ 000/100}\,]$$

$$= [86.2, 173.8]$$

---

[1] See equation (3.24) in Chapter 3 to remind yourself of this. Remember that ±1.96 is the $z$ score which cuts off 2.5% in each tail of the Normal distribution.

**Figure 4.3(a)**
**The 95% probability**
**interval for $\bar{x}$ around**
**the population mean $\mu$**

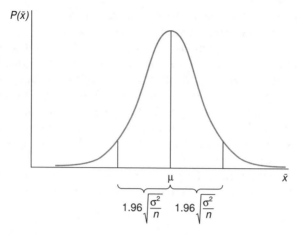

**Figure 4.3(b)**
**The 95% confidence**
**interval for $\mu$ around**
**the sample mean $\bar{x}$**

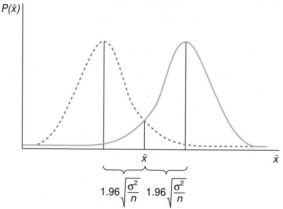

Thus we are 95% confident that the true average level of wealth lies between
£86 200 and £173 800. It should be noted that £130 000 lies exactly at the centre of the interval[2] (because of the symmetry of the Normal distribution).

By examining equation (4.6) one can see that the confidence interval is
wider

1  the smaller the sample size,
2  the greater the standard deviation of the sample.

The greater uncertainty which is associated with smaller sample sizes is man-
ifested in a wider confidence interval estimate of the population mean. This
occurs because a smaller sample has more chance of being unrepresentative
(just because of an unlucky sample).

Greater variation in the sample data also leads to greater uncertainty about
the population mean and a wider confidence interval. Greater sample variation
suggests greater variation in the population so, again, a given sample could
include observations which are a long way off the mean.

[2] The two values are the lower and upper limits of the interval, separated by a comma.
This is the standard way of writing a confidence interval.

Note that the width of the confidence interval does *not* depend upon the population size – a sample of 100 observations reveals as much about a population of 10 000 as it does about a population of 10 000 000. This point will be discussed in more detail in Chapter 9 on sampling methods. This is a result that often surprises people, who generally believe that a larger sample is required if the population is larger.

**Worked example 4.1**

A sample of 50 school students found that they spent 45 minutes doing homework each evening, with a standard deviation of 15 minutes. Estimate the average time spent on homework by all students.

The sample data are $\bar{x} = 45$, $s = 15$ and $n = 50$. If we can assume the sample is representative we may use $\bar{x}$ as an unbiased estimate of $\mu$, the population mean. The point estimate is therefore 45 minutes.

The 95% confidence interval is given by equation (4.6):

$$[\bar{x} - 1.96\sqrt{s^2/n} \leq \mu \leq \bar{x} + 1.96\sqrt{s^2/n}]$$

$$= [45 - 1.96\sqrt{15^2/50} \leq \mu \leq 45 + 1.96\sqrt{15^2/50}]$$

$$= [40.8, 49.2]$$

We are 95% confident the true answer lies between 40.8 and 49.2.

**Exercise 4.1**

(a) A sample of 100 is drawn from a population. The sample mean is 25 and the sample standard deviation is 50. Calculate the point and 95% confidence interval estimates for the population mean.

(b) If the sample size were 64, how would this alter the point and interval estimates?

**Exercise 4.2**

A sample of size 40 is drawn with sample mean 50 and standard deviation 30. Is it likely that the true population mean is 60?

## Precisely what is a confidence interval?

There is often confusion over what a confidence interval actually means. This is not really surprising since the obvious interpretation turns out to be wrong. It does *not* mean that there is a 95% chance that the true mean lies within the interval. We cannot make such a probability statement, because of our definition of probability (based on the frequentist view of a probability). That view states that one can make a probability statement about a random variable (such as $\bar{x}$) but not about a parameter (such as $\mu$). $\mu$ either lies within the interval or it does not – it cannot lie 95% within it. Unfortunately, we just do not know what the truth is.

It is for this reason that we use the term 'confidence interval' rather than 'probability interval'. Unfortunately, words are not as precise as numbers or algebra, and so most people fail to recognise the distinction. A precise explanation of the 95% confidence interval runs as follows. If we took many samples (all the same size) from a population with mean $\mu$ and calculated a confidence

**Figure 4.4**

**Confidence intervals calculated from 20 samples**

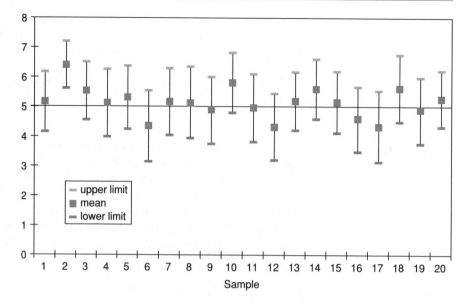

interval from each, we would find that $\mu$ lies within 95% of the calculated intervals. Of course, in practice we do not take many samples, usually just one. We do not know (and cannot know) if our one sample is one of the 95% or one of the 5% that miss the mean.

Figure 4.4 illustrates the point. It shows 95% confidence intervals calculated from 20 samples drawn from a population with a mean of 5. As expected, we see that 19 of these intervals contain the true mean, while the interval calculated from the second sample does not contain the true value. This is the expected result, but is not guaranteed. You might obtain all 20 intervals containing the true mean, or fewer than 19. In the long run (with lots of estimates) we would expect 95% of the calculated intervals to contain the true mean.

A second question is why use a probability (and hence a confidence level) of 95%? In fact, one can choose any confidence level, and thus confidence interval. The 90% confidence interval can be obtained by finding the $z$ score which cuts off 10% of the Normal distribution (5% in each tail). From Table A2 (see page **366**) this is $z = 1.64$, so the 90% confidence interval is

**(4.7)**  $[\bar{x} - 1.64\sqrt{s^2/n}, \bar{x} + 1.64\sqrt{s^2/n}\,]$

$= [130 - 1.64\sqrt{50\,000/100}, 130 + 1.64\sqrt{50\,000/100}\,]$

$= [93.3, 166.7]$

Notice that this is narrower than the 95% confidence level. The greater the degree of confidence required, the wider the interval has to be. Any confidence level may be chosen, and by careful choice of this level the confidence interval can be made as wide or as narrow as wished. This would seem to undermine the purpose of calculating the confidence interval, which is to obtain some idea of the uncertainty attached to the estimate. This is not the case, however, because the reader of the results can interpret them appropriately, as long as the confidence level is made clear. To simplify matters, the 95% and 99% confidence levels are the most commonly used and serve as conventions. Beware of the researcher who calculates the 76% confidence interval – this may have been chosen in order to obtain the desired answer rather than in the spirit of scientific enquiry! The general formula for the $(100 - \alpha)$% confidence interval is

**(4.8)** $\quad [\bar{x} - z_\alpha\sqrt{s^2/n}, \ \bar{x} + z_\alpha\sqrt{s^2/n}]$

where $z_\alpha$ is the $z$ score which cuts off the extreme $\alpha$% of the Normal distribution.

**Estimating a proportion**

It is often the case that we wish to estimate the proportion of the population that has a particular characteristic (e.g. is unemployed), rather than wanting an average. Given what we have already learned this is fairly straightforward and is based on similar principles. Suppose that, following Chapter 1, we wish to estimate the proportion of educated men who are unemployed. We have a random sample of 200 men, of whom 15 are unemployed. What can we infer?

The sample data are:

$n = 200$, and
$p = 0.075 \ (= 15/200)$

where $p$ is the (sample) proportion unemployed. We denote the population proportion by the Greek letter $\pi$ and it is this that we are trying to estimate using data from the sample.

The key to solving this problem is recognising $p$ as a random variable just like the sample mean. This is because its value depends upon the sample drawn and will vary from sample to sample. Once the probability distribution of this random variable is established the problem is quite easy to solve, using the same methods as were used for the mean. The sampling distribution of $p$ is[3]

**(4.9)** $\quad p \sim N\left(\pi, \dfrac{\pi(1 - \pi)}{n}\right)$

This tells us that the sample proportion is centred around the true value but will vary around it, varying from sample to sample. This variation is expressed by the variance of $p$, whose formula is $\pi(1 - \pi)/n$. Having derived the probability distribution of $p$ the same methods of estimation can be used as for the sample mean. Since the expected value of $p$ is $\pi$, the sample proportion is an unbiased estimate of the population parameter. The point estimate of $\pi$ is simply $p$, therefore. Thus it is estimated that 7.5% of all educated men are unemployed.

Given the sampling distribution for $p$ in equation (4.9) above, the formula for the 95% confidence interval[4] for $\pi$ can immediately be written down as:

**(4.10)** $\quad \left[p - 1.96\sqrt{\dfrac{\pi(1 - \pi)}{n}}, \ p + 1.96\sqrt{\dfrac{\pi(1 - \pi)}{n}}\right]$

Since the value of $\pi$ is unknown the confidence interval cannot yet be calculated, so the sample value of 0.075 has to be used instead of the unknown $\pi$. Like the substitution of $s^2$ for $\sigma^2$ in the case of the sample mean above, this is acceptable in large samples. Thus the 95% confidence interval becomes

[3] See the Appendix to this chapter (page **158**) for the derivation of this formula.
[4] As usual, the 95% confidence interval limits are given by the point estimate plus and minus 1.96 standard errors.

$$(4.11) \quad \left[ p - 1.96 \sqrt{\frac{0.075(1 - 0.075)}{200}},\ p + 1.96 \sqrt{\frac{0.075(1 - 0.075)}{200}} \right]$$

$$= [0.075 - 0.037,\ 0.075 + 0.037]$$

$$= [0.038, 0.112]$$

We say that we are 95% confident that the true proportion of unemployed, educated men lies between 3.8% and 11.2%.

It can be seen that these two cases apply a common method. The 95% confidence interval is given by the point estimate plus or minus 1.96 standard errors. For a different confidence level, 1.96 would be replaced by the appropriate value from the standard Normal distribution.

With this knowledge two further cases can be swiftly dealt with.

---

**Worked example 4.2**

### Music down the phone

Do you get angry when you try to phone an organisation and you get an automated reply followed by music while you hang on? Well, you are not alone. Mintel (a consumer survey company) asked 1946 adults what they thought of music played to them while they were trying to get through on the phone. 36% reported feeling angered by the music played to them and more than one in four were annoyed by the automated voice response.

With these data we can calculate a confidence interval for the true proportion of people who dislike the music. First, we assume that the sample is a truly random one. This is probably not strictly true, so our calculated confidence interval will only be an approximate one. With $p = 0.36$ and $n = 1946$ we obtain the following 95% interval:

$$p \pm 1.96 \times \sqrt{\frac{p(1 - p)}{n}} = 0.36 \pm 1.96 \times \sqrt{\frac{0.36(1 - 0.36)}{1946}}$$

$$= 0.36 \pm 0.021 = [0.339, 0.381]$$

Mintel further estimated that 2800 million calls were made by customers to call centres per year, so we can be (approximately) 95% confident that between 949 million and 1067 million of those calls have an unhappy customer on the line!

*Source: The Times,* 10 July 2000.

---

**Estimating the difference between two means**

We now move on to estimating differences. In this case we have two samples and want to know whether there is a difference between their respective populations. One sample might be of men, the other of women, or we could be comparing two different countries, etc. A point estimate of the difference is easy to obtain but once again there is some uncertainty around this figure, because it is based on samples. Hence we measure that uncertainty via a confidence interval. All we require are the appropriate formulae. Consider the following example.

Sixty pupils from school 1 scored an average mark of 62% in an exam, with a standard deviation of 18%; 35 pupils from school 2 scored an average of 70% with standard deviation 12%. Estimate the true difference between the two schools in the average mark obtained.

This is a more complicated problem than those previously treated since it involves two samples rather than one. An estimate has to be found for $\mu_1 - \mu_2$ (the true difference in the mean marks of the schools), in the form of both point and interval estimates. The pupils taking the exams may be thought of as samples of all pupils in the schools who could potentially take the exams.

Notice that this is a problem about sample means, not proportions, even though the question deals in percentages. The point is that each observation in the sample (i.e. each student's mark) can take a value between 0 and 100, and one can calculate the standard deviation of the marks. For this to be a problem of sample proportions the mark for each pupil would each have to be of the pass/fail type, so that one could only calculate the proportion who passed.

It might be thought that the way to approach this problem is to derive one confidence interval for each sample (along the lines set out above), and then to somehow combine them; for example, the degree of overlap of the two confidence intervals could be assessed. This is not the best approach, however. It is sometimes a good strategy, when faced with an unfamiliar problem to solve, to translate it into a more familiar problem and then solve it using known methods. This is the procedure which will be followed here. The essential point is to keep in mind the concept of a random variable and its probability distribution.

Problems involving a single random variable have already been dealt with above. The current problem deals with two samples and therefore there are two random variables to consider, i.e. the two sample means $\bar{x}_1$ and $\bar{x}_2$. Since the aim is to estimate $\mu_1 - \mu_2$, an obvious candidate for an estimator is the difference between the two sample means, $\bar{x}_1 - \bar{x}_2$. We can think of this as a single random variable (even though two means are involved) and use the methods we have already learned. We therefore need to establish the sampling distribution of $\bar{x}_1 - \bar{x}_2$. This is derived in the Appendix to this chapter (see page 158) and results in equation (4.12):

$$\textbf{(4.12)} \qquad \bar{x}_1 - \bar{x}_2 \sim N\left( \mu_1 - \mu_2, \frac{\sigma_1^2}{n_1} + \frac{\sigma_2^2}{n_2} \right)$$

This equation states that the difference in sample means will be centred on the difference in the two population means, with some variation around this as measured by the variance. One assumption behind the derivation of (4.12) is that the two samples are independently drawn. This is likely in this example; it is difficult to see how the samples from the two schools could be connected. However, one must always bear this possibility in mind when comparing samples. For example, if one were comparing men's and women's heights, it would be dangerous to take samples of men and their wives as they are unlikely to be independent. People tend to marry partners of a similar height to themselves, so this might bias the results.

The distribution of $\bar{x}_1 - \bar{x}_2$ is illustrated in Figure 4.5. Equation (4.12) shows that $\bar{x}_1 - \bar{x}_2$ is an unbiased estimator of $\mu_1 - \mu_2$. The difference between the sample means will therefore be used as the point estimate of $\mu_1 - \mu_2$. Thus the point estimate of the true difference between the schools is

$$\bar{x}_1 - \bar{x}_2 = 62 - 70 = -8\%$$

**Figure 4.5**
**The distribution of**
$\bar{x}_1 - \bar{x}_2$

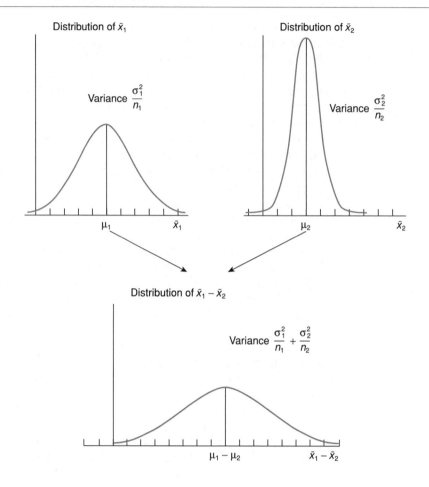

Distribution of $\bar{x}_1$

Variance $\dfrac{\sigma_1^2}{n_1}$

$\mu_1$     $\bar{x}_1$

Distribution of $\bar{x}_2$

Variance $\dfrac{\sigma_2^2}{n_2}$

$\mu_2$     $\bar{x}_2$

Distribution of $\bar{x}_1 - \bar{x}_2$

Variance $\dfrac{\sigma_1^2}{n_1} + \dfrac{\sigma_2^2}{n_2}$

$\mu_1 - \mu_2$     $\bar{x}_1 - \bar{x}_2$

The 95% confidence interval estimate is derived in the same manner as before, making use of the standard error of the random variable. The formula is[5]

**(4.13)**
$$\left[ (\bar{x}_1 - \bar{x}_2) - 1.96\sqrt{\frac{s_1^2}{n_1} + \frac{s_2^2}{n_2}}, \ (\bar{x}_1 - \bar{x}_2) + 1.96\sqrt{\frac{s_1^2}{n_1} + \frac{s_2^2}{n_2}} \right]$$

Since the values of $\sigma^2$ are unknown they have been replaced in equation (4.13) by their sample values. As in the single sample case, this is acceptable in large samples. The 95% confidence interval for $\mu_1 - \mu_2$ is therefore

$$\left[ (62 - 70) - 1.96\sqrt{\frac{18^2}{60} + \frac{12^2}{35}}, \ (62 - 70) + 1.96\sqrt{\frac{18^2}{60} + \frac{12^2}{35}} \right]$$

$$= [-14.05, -1.95]$$

The estimate is that school 2's average mark is between 1.95 and 14.05 percentage points above that of school 1. Notice that the confidence interval does not

---

[5] The term under the square root sign is the standard error for $\bar{x}_1 - \bar{x}_2$.

include the value zero, which would imply equality of the two schools' marks. Equality of the two schools can thus be ruled out with 95% confidence.

**Worked example 4.3**

A survey of holidaymakers found that on average women spent 3 hours per day sunbathing, men spent 2 hours. The sample sizes were 36 in each case and the standard deviations were 1.1 hours and 1.2 hours respectively. Estimate the true difference between men and women in sunbathing habits. Use the 99% confidence level.

The point estimate is simply one hour, the difference of sample means. For the confidence interval we have:

$$\left[(\bar{x}_1 - \bar{x}_2) - 2.57\sqrt{\frac{s_1^2}{n_1} + \frac{s_2^2}{n_2}} \le \mu \le (\bar{x}_1 - \bar{x}_2) + 2.57\sqrt{\frac{s_1^2}{n_1} + \frac{s_2^2}{n_2}}\right]$$

$$= \left[(3 - 2) - 2.57\sqrt{\frac{1.1^2}{36} + \frac{1.2^2}{36}} \le \mu \le (3 - 2) + 2.57\sqrt{\frac{1.1^2}{36} + \frac{1.2^2}{36}}\right]$$

$$= [0.30, 1.70]$$

This evidence suggests women do spend more time sunbathing than men (zero is not in the confidence interval). Note that we might worry the samples might not be independent here – it could represent 36 couples. If so, the evidence is likely to underestimate the true difference, if anything, as couples are likely to spend time sunbathing together.

**Estimating the difference between two proportions**

We move again from means to proportions. We use a simple example to illustrate the analysis of this type of problem. Suppose that a survey of 80 Britons showed that 60 owned personal computers. A similar survey of 50 Swedes showed 30 with computers. Are personal computers more widespread in Britain than Sweden?

Here the aim is to estimate $\pi_1 - \pi_2$, the difference between the two population proportions, so the probability distribution of $p_1 - p_2$ is needed, the difference of the sample proportions. The derivation of this follows similar lines to those set out above for the difference of two sample means, so is not repeated. The probability distribution is

$$(4.14) \quad p_1 - p_2 \sim N\left(\pi_1 - \pi_2, \frac{\pi_1(1 - \pi_1)}{n_1} + \frac{\pi_2(1 - \pi_2)}{n_2}\right)$$

Again, the two samples must be independently drawn for this to be correct (it is difficult to see how they could not be in this case).

Since the difference between the sample proportions is an unbiased estimate of the true difference, this will be used for the point estimate. The point estimate is therefore

$$p_1 - p_2 = 60/80 - 30/50$$
$$= 0.15$$

or 15%. The 95% confidence interval is given by

**(4.15)** $$\left[ p_1 - p_2 - 1.96\sqrt{\frac{\pi_1(1 - \pi_1)}{n_1} + \frac{\pi_2(1 - \pi_2)}{n_2}},\right.$$

$$\left. p_1 - p_2 + 1.96\sqrt{\frac{\pi_1(1 - \pi_1)}{n_1} + \frac{\pi_2(1 - \pi_2)}{n_2}}\right]$$

$\pi_1$ and $\pi_2$ are unknown so have to be replaced by $p_1$ and $p_2$ for purposes of calculation, so the interval becomes

**(4.16)** $$\left[ 0.75 - 0.60 - 1.96\sqrt{\frac{0.75 \times 0.25}{80} + \frac{0.60 \times 0.40}{50}},\right.$$

$$\left. 0.75 - 0.60 + 1.96\sqrt{\frac{0.75 \times 0.25}{80} + \frac{0.60 \times 0.40}{50}}\right]$$

$$= [0.016, 0.316]$$

The result is a fairly wide confidence interval due to the relatively small sample sizes. The interval does not include zero however, so we can be 95% confident there is a difference between the two countries.

**Exercise 4.3**

(a) Seven people out of a sample of 50 are left-handed. Estimate the true proportion of left-handed people in the population, finding both point and interval estimates.

(b) Repeat part (a) but find the 90% confidence interval. How does the 90% interval compare with the 95% interval?

(c) Calculate the 99% interval and compare to the others.

**Exercise 4.4**

Given the following data from two samples, calculate the true difference between the means. Use the 95% confidence level.

$\bar{x}_1 = 25$     $\bar{x}_2 = 30$
$s_1 = 18$     $s_2 = 25$
$n_1 = 36$     $n_2 = 49$

**Exercise 4.5**

A survey of 50 16-year old girls revealed that 40% had a boyfriend. A survey of 100 16-year old boys revealed 20% with a girlfriend. Estimate the true difference in proportions between the sexes.

## Estimation with small samples: the *t* distribution

So far only large samples (defined as sample sizes in excess of 25) have been dealt with, which means that (by the Central Limit Theorem) the sampling distribution of $\bar{x}$ follows a Normal distribution, whatever the distribution of the parent population. Remember, from the two theorems of Chapter 3, that

■ if the population follows a Normal distribution, $\bar{x}$ is also Normally distributed, and

■ if the population is not Normally distributed, $\bar{x}$ is approximately Normally distributed in large samples ($n \geq 25$).

In both cases, confidence intervals can be constructed based on the fact that

(4.17)     $$\frac{\bar{x} - \mu}{\sqrt{\sigma^2/n}} \sim N(0, 1)$$

and so the standard Normal distribution is used to find the values which cut off the extreme 5% of the distribution ($z = \pm 1.96$). In practical examples, we had to replace $\sigma$ by its estimate, $s$. Thus the confidence interval was based on the fact that

(4.18)     $$\frac{\bar{x} - \mu}{\sqrt{s^2/n}} \sim N(0, 1)$$

in large samples. For small sample sizes, equation (4.18) is no longer true. Instead, the relevant distribution is the $t$ distribution and we have[6]

(4.19)     $$\frac{\bar{x} - \mu}{\sqrt{s^2/n}} \sim t_{n-1}$$

The random variable defined in equation (4.19) has a $t$ distribution with $n - 1$ degrees of freedom. As the sample size gets larger, the $t$ distribution approaches the standard Normal, so the latter can be used for large samples.

The $t$ distribution was derived by W.S. Gossett in 1908 while conducting tests on the average strength of Guinness beer (who says statistics has no impact on the real world?). He published his work under the pseudonym 'Student', since the company did not allow its employees to publish under their own names, so the distribution is sometimes also known as the Student distribution.

The $t$ distribution is in many ways similar to the standard Normal, insofar as it is

■ unimodal;
■ symmetric;
■ centred on zero;
■ bell-shaped;
■ extends from minus infinity to plus infinity.

The differences are that it is more spread out (has a larger variance) than the standard Normal distribution, and has only one parameter rather than two: the **degrees of freedom**, denoted by the Greek letter $v$ (pronounced 'nu'[7]). In problems involving the estimation of a sample mean the degrees of freedom are given by the sample size minus one, i.e. $v = n - 1$.

The $t$ distribution is drawn in Figure 4.6 for various values of the parameter $v$. Note that the fewer the degrees of freedom (smaller sample size) the more dispersed is the distribution.

---

[6] We also require the assumption that the parent population is Normally distributed for (4.19) to be true.
[7] Actually, the Greeks pronounce this 'ni'. They also pronounce $\pi$ 'pee' rather than 'pie' as in English. This makes statistics lectures in English hard for Greeks to understand!

**Figure 4.6**
**The *t* distribution drawn for different degrees of freedom**

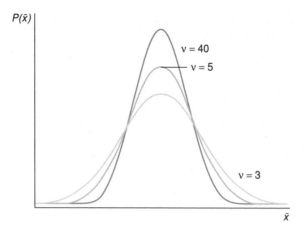

To summarise the argument so far, when

- the sample size is small, *and*
- the sample variance is used to estimate the population variance,

then the *t* distribution should be used for constructing confidence intervals, not the standard Normal. This results in a slightly wider interval than would be obtained using the standard Normal distribution, which reflects the slightly greater uncertainty involved when $s^2$ is used as an estimate of $\sigma^2$ if the sample size is small.

Apart from this, the methods are exactly as before and are illustrated by the examples below. We look first at estimating a single mean, then at estimating the difference of two means. The *t* distribution cannot be used for small sample proportions (explained below) so these cases are not considered.

**Estimating a mean**    The following would seem to be an appropriate example. A sample of 15 bottles of beer showed an average specific gravity of 1035.6, with standard deviation 2.7. Estimate the true specific gravity of the brew.

The sample information may be summarised as

$\bar{x} = 1035.6$
$s = 2.7$
$n = 15$

The sample mean is still an unbiased estimator of $\mu$ (this is true regardless of the distribution of the population) and serves as point estimate of $\mu$. The point estimate of $\mu$ is therefore 1035.6.

Since $\sigma$ is unknown, the sample size is small and it can be assumed that the specific gravity of all bottles of beer is Normally distributed (numerous small random factors affect the specific gravity) we should use the *t* distribution. Thus:

**(4.20)**    $\dfrac{\bar{x} - \mu}{\sqrt{s^2/n}} \sim t_{n-1}$

The 95% confidence interval estimate is given by

**(4.21)**    $[\bar{x} - t_{n-1}\sqrt{s^2/n}, \bar{x} + t_{n-1}\sqrt{s^2/n}]$

Table 4.1 **Percentage points of the *t* distribution (excerpt from Table A3)**

| | \multicolumn{7}{c}{Area ($\alpha$) in each tail} |
|---|---|---|---|---|---|---|---|
| $v$ | 0.4 | 0.25 | 0.10 | 0.05 | 0.025 | 0.01 | 0.005 |
| 1 | 0.325 | 1.000 | 3.078 | 6.314 | 12.706 | 31.821 | 63.656 |
| 2 | 0.289 | 0.816 | 1.886 | 2.920 | 4.303 | 6.965 | 9.925 |
| ⋮ | ⋮ | ⋮ | ⋮ | ⋮ | ⋮ | ⋮ | ⋮ |
| 13 | 0.259 | 0.694 | 1.350 | 1.771 | 2.160 | 2.650 | 3.012 |
| 14 | 0.258 | 0.692 | 1.345 | 1.761 | 2.145 | 2.624 | 2.977 |
| 15 | 0.258 | 0.691 | 1.341 | 1.753 | 2.131 | 2.602 | 2.947 |

*Note*: The appropriate *t* value for constructing the confidence interval is found at the intersection of the shaded row and column.

where $t_{n-1}$ is the value of the *t* distribution which cuts off the extreme 5% (2.5% in each tail) of the *t* distribution with *v* degrees of freedom. Table A3 (see page **367**) gives percentage points of the *t* distribution and part of it is reproduced in Table 4.1.

The structure of the *t* distribution table is different from that of the standard Normal table. The first column of the table gives the degrees of freedom. In this example we want the row corresponding to $v = n - 1 = 14$. The appropriate column of the table is the one headed '0.025' which indicates the area cut off in *each* tail. At the intersection of this row and column we find the appropriate value, $t_{14} = 2.145$. Therefore the confidence interval is given by

$$[1035.6 - 2.145\sqrt{2.7^2/15}, \ 1035.6 + 2.145\sqrt{2.7^2/15}]$$

which when evaluated gives

[1034.10, 1037.10]

We can be 95% confident that the true specific gravity lies within this range. If the Normal distribution had (incorrectly) been used for this problem then the *t* value of 2.145 would have been replaced by a *z* score of 1.96, giving a confidence interval of

[1034.23, 1036.97]

This underestimates the true confidence interval and gives the impression of a more precise estimate than is actually the case. Use of the Normal distribution leads to a confidence interval which is 8.7% too narrow in this case.

**Estimating the difference between two means**

As in the case of a single mean the *t*-distribution needs to be used in small samples when the population variances are unknown. Again, both parent populations must be Normally distributed and in addition it must be assumed that the population variances are equal, i.e. $\sigma_1^2 = \sigma_2^2$ (this is required in the mathematical derivation of the *t* distribution). This latter assumption was not required in the large-sample case using the Normal distribution. Consider the following example as an illustration of the method.

A sample of 20 Labour-controlled local authorities shows that they spend an average of £175 per taxpayer on administration with a standard deviation of £25. A similar survey of 15 Conservative-controlled authorities finds an average figure of £158 with standard deviation of £30. Estimate the true difference in expenditure between Labour and Conservative authorities.

The sample information available is

$\bar{x}_1 = 175$        $\bar{x}_2 = 158$
$s_1 = 25$          $s_2 = 30$
$n_1 = 20$          $n_2 = 15$

We wish to estimate $\mu_1 - \mu_2$. The point estimate of this is $\bar{x}_1 - \bar{x}_2$ which is an unbiased estimate. This gives $175 - 158 = 17$ as the expected difference between the two sets of authorities.

For the confidence interval, the $t$ distribution has to be used since the sample sizes are small and the population variances unknown. It is assumed that the populations are Normally distributed and that the samples have been independently drawn. We also assume that the population variances are equal, which seems justified since $s_1$ and $s_2$ do not differ by much (this kind of assumption is tested in Chapter 6). The confidence interval is given by the formula:

$$(4.22) \quad \left[ (\bar{x}_1 - \bar{x}_2) - t_v\sqrt{\frac{S^2}{n_1} + \frac{S^2}{n_2}}, \le \mu \le (\bar{x}_1 - \bar{x}_2) + t_v\sqrt{\frac{S^2}{n_1} + \frac{S^2}{n_2}} \right]$$

where

$$(4.23) \quad S^2 = \frac{(n_1 - 1)s_1^2 + (n_2 - 1)s_2^2}{n_1 + n_2 - 2}$$

is known as the **pooled variance** and

$$v = n_1 + n_2 - 2$$

gives the degrees of freedom associated with the $t$ distribution.

$S^2$ is an estimate of the (common value of) the population variances. It would be inappropriate to have the differing values $s_1^2$ and $s_2^2$ in the formula for the $t$ distribution, for this would be contrary to the assumption that $\sigma_1^2 = \sigma_2^2$, which is essential for the use of the $t$ distribution. The estimate of the common population variance is just the weighted average of the sample variances, using degrees of freedom as weights. Each sample has $n - 1$ degrees of freedom, and the total number of degrees of freedom for the problem is the sum of the degrees of freedom in each sample. The degrees of freedom is thus $20 + 15 - 2 = 33$ and hence the value $t = 2.042$ cuts off the extreme 5% of the distribution. The $t$ table in the appendix does not give the value for $v = 33$ so we have used $v = 30$ instead, which will give a close approximation.

To evaluate the 95% confidence interval we first calculate $S^2$:

$$S^2 = \frac{(20 - 1) \times 25^2 + (15 - 1) \times 30^2}{20 + 15 - 2} = 741.6$$

Inserting this into equation (4.22) gives

$$\left[ 17 - 2.042\sqrt{\frac{741.6}{20} + \frac{741.6}{15}}, 17 + 2.042\sqrt{\frac{741.6}{20} + \frac{741.6}{15}} \right] = [-1.99, 35.99]$$

Thus the true difference is quite uncertain and the evidence is even consistent with Conservative authorities spending more than Labour authorities. The large degree of uncertainty arises because of the small sample sizes and the quite wide variation within each sample.

One should be careful about the conclusions drawn from this test. The greater expenditure on administration could be either because of inefficiency or because of a higher level of services provided. To find out which is the case would require further investigation. The statistical test carried out here examines the levels of expenditure, but not whether they are productive or not.

## Estimating proportions

Estimating proportions when the sample size is small cannot be done with the $t$ distribution. Recall that the distribution of the sample proportion $p$ was derived from the distribution of $r$ (the number of successes in $n$ trials), which followed a Binomial distribution (see the Appendix to this chapter (page **158**)). In large samples the distribution of $r$ is approximately Normal, thus giving a Normally distributed sample proportion. In small samples it is inappropriate to approximate the Binomial distribution with the $t$ distribution, and indeed is unnecessary, since the Binomial itself can be used. Small-sample methods for the sample proportion should be based on the Binomial distribution, therefore, as set out in Chapter 3. These methods are not discussed further here, therefore.

**Exercise 4.6**

A sample of size $n = 16$ is drawn from a population which is known to be Normally distributed. The sample mean and variance are calculated as 74 and 121. Find the 99% confidence interval estimate for the true mean.

**Exercise 4.7**

Samples are drawn from two populations to see if they share a common mean. The sample data are:

$$\bar{x}_1 = 45 \quad \bar{x}_2 = 55$$
$$s_1 = 18 \quad s_2 = 21$$
$$n_1 = 15 \quad n_2 = 20$$

Find the 95% confidence interval estimate of the difference between the two population means.

## Summary

- Estimation is the process of using sample information to make good estimates of the value of population parameters, e.g. using the sample mean to estimate the mean of a population.

- There are several criteria for finding a good estimate. Two important ones are the (lack of) bias and precision of the estimator. Sometimes there is a trade-off between these two criteria – one estimator might have a smaller bias but be less precise than another.

- An estimator is unbiased if it gives a correct estimate of the true value on average. Its expected value is equal to the true value.

- The precision of an estimator can be measured by its sampling variance (e.g. $s^2/n$ for the mean of a sample).

- Estimates can be in the form of a single value (point estimate) or a range of values (confidence interval estimate). A confidence interval estimate gives some idea of how reliable the estimate is likely to be.
- For unbiased estimators, the value of the sample statistic (e.g. $\bar{x}$) is used as the point estimate.
- In large samples the 95% confidence interval is given by the point estimate plus or minus 1.96 standard errors (e.g. $\bar{x} \pm 1.96\sqrt{s^2/n}$ for the mean).
- For small samples the $t$ distribution should be used instead of the Normal (i.e. replace 1.96 by the critical value of the $t$ distribution) to construct confidence intervals of the mean.

**Key terms and concepts**

| | | |
|---|---|---|
| inference | bias | confidence level and |
| estimator | maximum likelihood | interval |
| efficiency | interval estimate | |
| point estimate | precision | |

# Problems

Some of the more challenging problems are indicated by highlighting the problem number in colour.

**Problem 4.1** (a) Why is an interval estimate better than a point estimate?

(b) What factors determine the width of a confidence interval?

**Problem 4.2** Is the 95% confidence interval (a) twice as wide, (b) more than twice as wide, (c) less than twice as wide, as the 47.5% interval? Explain your reasoning.

**Problem 4.3** Explain the difference between an estimate and an estimator. Is it true that a good estimator always leads to a good estimate?

**Problem 4.4** Explain why an unbiased estimator is not always to be preferred to a biased one.

**Problem 4.5** A random sample of two observations, $x_1$ and $x_2$, is drawn from a population. Prove that $w_1 x_1 + w_2 x_2$ gives an unbiased estimate of the population mean as long as $w_1 + w_2 = 1$. (Hint: Prove that $E(w_1 x_1 + w_2 x_2) = \mu$.)

**Problem 4.6** Following the previous question, prove that the most precise unbiased estimate is obtained by setting $w_1 = w_2 = \frac{1}{2}$. (Hint: Minimise $V(w_1 x_1 + w_2 x_2)$ with respect to $w_1$ after substituting $w_2 = 1 - w_1$. You will need a knowledge of calculus to solve this.)

**Problem 4.7** Given the sample data

$\bar{x} = 40 \qquad s = 10 \qquad n = 36$

calculate the 99% confidence interval estimate of the true mean. If the sample size were 20, how would the method of calculation and width of the interval be altered?

**Problem 4.8**  A random sample of 100 record shops found that the average weekly sale of a particular record was 260 copies, with standard deviation of 96. Find the 95% confidence interval to estimate the true average sale for all shops. To compile the record chart it is necessary to know the correct average weekly sale to within 5% of its true value. How large a sample size is required?

**Problem 4.9**  Given the sample data $p = 0.4$, $n = 50$, calculate the 99% confidence interval estimate of the true proportion.

**Problem 4.10**  A political opinion poll questions 1000 people. Some 464 declare they will vote Conservative. Find the 95% confidence interval estimate for the Conservative share of the vote.

**Problem 4.11**  Given the sample data

$$\bar{x}_1 = 25 \qquad \bar{x}_2 = 22$$
$$s_1 = 12 \qquad s_2 = 18$$
$$n_1 = 80 \qquad n_2 = 100$$

estimate the true difference between the means with 95% confidence.

**Problem 4.12**  (a)  A sample of 200 women from the labour force found an average wage of £6000 p.a. with standard deviation £2500. A sample of 100 men found an average wage of £8000 with standard deviation £1500. Estimate the true difference in wages between men and women.

(b)  A different survey, of men and women doing similar jobs, obtained the following results:

$$\bar{x}_W = £7200 \qquad \bar{x}_M = £7600$$
$$s_W = £1225 \qquad s_M = £750$$
$$n_W = 75 \qquad n_M = 50$$

Estimate the difference between male and female wages using these new data. What can be concluded from the results of the two surveys?

**Problem 4.13**  67% out of 150 pupils from school A passed an exam; 62% of 120 pupils at school B passed. Estimate the 99% confidence interval for the true difference between the proportions passing the exam.

**Problem 4.14**  (a)  A sample of 954 adults in early 1987 found that 23% of them held shares. Given a UK adult population of 41 million and assuming a proper random sample was taken, find the 95% confidence interval estimate for the number of shareholders in the UK.

(b)  A 'similar' survey the previous year had found a total of 7 million shareholders. Assuming 'similar' means the same sample size, find the 95% confidence interval estimate of the increase in shareholders between the two years.

**Problem 4.15**  A sample of 16 observations from a Normally distributed population yields a sample mean of 30 with standard deviation 5. Find the 95% confidence interval estimate of the population mean.

**Problem 4.16** A sample of 12 families in a town reveals an average income of £15 000 with standard deviation £6000. Why might you be hesitant about constructing a 95% confidence interval for the average income in the town?

**Problem 4.17** Two samples were drawn, each from a Normally distributed population, with the following results:

$$\bar{x}_1 = 45 \quad s_1 = 8 \quad n_1 = 12$$
$$\bar{x}_2 = 52 \quad s_2 = 5 \quad n_2 = 18$$

Estimate the difference between the population means, using the 95% confidence level.

**Problem 4.18** The heights of 10 men and 15 women were recorded, with the following results:

|       | Mean  | Variance |
|-------|-------|----------|
| Men   | 173.5 | 80       |
| Women | 162   | 65       |

Estimate the true difference between men's and women's heights. Use the 95% confidence level.

**Problem 4.19 (Project)** Estimate the average weekly expenditure upon alcohol by students. Ask a (reasonably) random sample of your fellow students for their weekly expenditure on alcohol. From this, calculate the 95% confidence interval estimate of such spending by all students.

## Answers to exercises

**Exercise 4.1** (a) The point estimate is 25 and the 95% confidence interval is $25 \pm 1.96 \times 50/\sqrt{100} = 25 \pm 9.8 = [15.2, 34.8]$.

(b) The CI becomes larger as the sample size reduces. In this case we would have $25 \pm 1.96 \times 50/\sqrt{64} = 25 \pm 12.25 = [12.75, 37.25]$. Note that the width of the CI is inversely proportional to the square root of the sample size.

**Exercise 4.2** The 95% CI is $50 \pm 1.96 \times 30/\sqrt{40} = 50 \pm 9.30 = [40.70, 59.30]$. The value of 60 lies (just) outside this CI so is unlikely to be the true mean.

**Exercise 4.3** (a) The point estimate is 14% (7/50). The 95% CI is given by

$$0.14 \pm 1.96 \times \sqrt{\frac{0.14 \times (1 - 0.14)}{50}} = 0.14 \pm 0.096.$$

(b) Use 1.64 instead of 1.96, giving $0.14 \pm 0.080$.

(c) $0.14 \pm 0.126$.

**Exercise 4.4** $\bar{x}_1 - \bar{x}_2 = 25 - 30 = -5$ is the point estimate. The interval estimate is given by

$$(\bar{x}_1 - \bar{x}_2) \pm 1.96\sqrt{\frac{s_1^2}{n_1} + \frac{s_2^2}{n_2}} = -5 \pm 1.96\sqrt{\frac{18^2}{36} + \frac{25^2}{49}} = -5 \pm 9.14 = [-14.14, 4.14]$$

**Exercise 4.5** The point estimate is 20%. The interval estimate is

$$0.2 \pm 1.96 \times \sqrt{\frac{0.4 \times 0.6}{50} + \frac{0.2 \times 0.8}{100}} = 0.2 \pm 0.157 = [0.043, 0.357]$$

**Exercise 4.6** The 99% CI is given by $74 \pm t^* \times \sqrt{121/16} = 74 \pm 2.947 \times 2.75 = 74 \pm 8.10 = [65.90, 82.10]$.

**Exercise 4.7** The pooled variance is given by

$$S^2 = \frac{(15-1) \times 18^2 + (20-1) \times 21^2}{15 + 20 - 2} = 391.36$$

The 95% CI is therefore

$$(45 - 55) \pm 2.042 \times \sqrt{\frac{391.36}{15} + \frac{391.36}{20}} = -10 \pm 13.80 = [-3.8, 23.8]$$

| Appendix | Derivations of sampling distributions |
| --- | --- |

**Derivation of the sampling distribution of $p$**

The sampling distribution of $p$ is fairly straightforward to derive, given what we have already learned. The sampling distribution of $p$ can be easily derived from the distribution of $r$, the number of successes in $n$ trials of an experiment, since $p = r/n$. The distribution of $r$ for large $n$ is approximately Normal (from Chapter 3):

**(4.24)**    $r \sim N(nP, nP(1 - P))$

Knowing the distribution of $r$, is it possible to find that of $p$? Since $p$ is simply $r$ multiplied by a constant, $1/n$, it is also Normally distributed. The mean and variance of the distribution can be derived using the E and V operators. The expected value of $p$ is

**(4.25)**    $E(p) = E(r/n) = \dfrac{1}{n}E(r) = \dfrac{1}{n}nP = P = \pi$

The expected value of the sample proportion is equal to the population proportion (note that the probability $P$ and the population proportion $\pi$ are the same thing and may be used interchangeably). The sample proportion therefore gives an unbiased estimate of the population proportion.

For the variance:

**(4.26)**    $V(p) = V\left(\dfrac{r}{n}\right) = \dfrac{1}{n^2}V(r) = \dfrac{1}{n^2}nP(1 - P) = \dfrac{\pi(1 - \pi)}{n}$

Hence the distribution of $p$ is given by

**(4.27)**    $p \sim N\left(\pi, \dfrac{\pi(1 - \pi)}{n}\right)$

**Derivation of the sampling distribution of $\bar{x}_1 - \bar{x}_2$**

This is the difference between two random variables so is itself a random variable. Since any linear combination of Normally distributed, independent random variables is itself Normally distributed, the difference of sample means follows a Normal distribution. The mean and variance of the distribution can be found using the E and V operators. Letting

$E(\bar{x}_1) = \mu_1$, $V(\bar{x}_1) = \sigma_1^2/n_1$ and
$E(\bar{x}_2) = \mu_2$, $V(\bar{x}_2) = \sigma_2^2/n_2$

then

**(4.28)**    $E(\bar{x}_1 - \bar{x}_2) = E(\bar{x}_1) - E(\bar{x}_2) = \mu_1 - \mu_2$

and

**(4.29)**    $V(\bar{x}_1 - \bar{x}_2) = V(\bar{x}_1) + V(\bar{x}_2) = \dfrac{\sigma_1^2}{n_1} + \dfrac{\sigma_2^2}{n_2}$

Equation (4.29) assumes $\bar{x}_1$ and $\bar{x}_2$ are independent random variables. The probability distribution of $\bar{x}_1 - \bar{x}_2$ can therefore be summarised as:

**(4.30)**    $\bar{x}_1 - \bar{x}_2 \sim N\left(\mu_1 - \mu_2, \dfrac{\sigma_1^2}{n_1} + \dfrac{\sigma_2^2}{n_2}\right)$

This is equation (4.12) in the text.

# 5 Hypothesis testing

**Learning outcomes**

By the end of this chapter you should be able to:

- understand the philosophy and scientific principles underlying hypothesis testing
- appreciate that hypothesis testing is about deciding whether a hypothesis is true or false on the basis of a sample of data
- recognise the type of evidence which leads to a decision that the hypothesis is false
- carry out hypothesis tests for a variety of statistical problems
- recognise the relationship between hypothesis testing and a confidence interval
- recognise the shortcomings of hypothesis testing

# Introduction

This chapter deals with issues very similar to those of the previous chapter on estimation, but examines them in a different way. The estimation of population parameters and the testing of hypotheses about those parameters are similar techniques (indeed they are formally equivalent in a number of respects), but there are important differences in the interpretation of the results arising from each method. The process of estimation is appropriate when measurement is involved, such as measuring the true average expenditure on food; hypothesis testing is better when decision making is involved, such as whether to accept that a supplier's products are up to a specified standard. Hypothesis testing is also used to make decisions about the truth or otherwise of different theories, such as whether rising prices are caused by rising wages; and it is here that the issues become contentious. It is sometimes difficult to interpret correctly the results of hypothesis tests in these circumstances. This is discussed further later in this chapter.

# The concepts of hypothesis testing

In many ways hypothesis testing is analogous to a criminal trial. In a trial there is a defendant who is *initially presumed innocent*. The *evidence* against the defendant is then presented and, if the jury finds this convincing *beyond all reasonable doubt*, he is found guilty; the presumption of innocence is overturned. Of course, mistakes are sometimes made: an innocent person is convicted or a guilty person set free. Both of these errors involve costs (not only in the monetary sense), either to the defendant or to society in general, and the errors should be avoided if at all possible. The laws under which the trial is held may help avoid such errors. The rule that the jury must be convinced 'beyond all reasonable doubt' helps to avoid convicting the innocent, for instance.

The situation in hypothesis testing is similar. First there is a **maintained** or **null hypothesis** which is initially *presumed* to be true. The empirical evidence, usually data from a random sample, is then gathered and assessed. If the evidence seems inconsistent with the null hypothesis, i.e. it has a low probability of occurring *if* the hypothesis were true, then the null hypothesis is *rejected* in favour of an alternative. Once again there are two types of error one can make, either rejecting the null hypothesis when it is really true, or not rejecting it when in fact it is false. Ideally one would like to avoid both types of error.

An example helps to clarify the issues and the analogy. Suppose that you are thinking of taking over a small business franchise. The current owner claims the weekly turnover of each existing franchise is £5000 and at this level you are willing to take on a franchise. You would be more cautious if the turnover is less than this figure. You examine the books of 26 franchises chosen at random and find that the average turnover was £4900 with standard deviation £280. What do you do?

The null hypothesis in this case is that average weekly turnover is £5000 (or more; that would be even more to your advantage). The **alternative hypothesis** is that turnover is strictly less than £5000 per week. We may write these more succinctly as follows:

$H_0$: $\mu = 5000$
$H_1$: $\mu < 5000$

$H_0$ is conventionally used to denote the null hypothesis, $H_1$ the alternative. Initially, $H_0$ is presumed to be true and this presumption will be tested using the sample evidence. Note that the sample evidence is *not* used as part of the hypothesis.

You have to decide whether the owner is telling the truth ($H_0$) or not ($H_1$). The two types of error you could make are as follows:

- **Type I error** – reject $H_0$ when it is in fact true. This would mean missing a good business opportunity.
- **Type II error** – not rejecting $H_0$ when it is in fact false. You would go ahead and buy the business and then find out that it is not as attractive as claimed. You would have overpaid for the business.

The situation is set out in Figure 5.1.

Obviously a good decision rule would give a good chance of making a correct decision and rule out errors as far as possible. Unfortunately it is impossible to completely eliminate the possibility of errors. As the decision rule is changed to reduce the probability of a Type I error, the probability of making a Type II error inevitably increases. The skill comes in balancing these two types of error.

Again a diagram is useful in illustrating this. Assuming that the null hypothesis is true, then the sample observations are drawn from a population with mean 5000 and some variance, which we shall assume is accurately measured by the sample variance. The distribution of $\bar{x}$ is then given by

(5.1)    $\bar{x} \sim N(\mu, \sigma^2/n)$ or
         $\bar{x} \sim N(5000, 280^2/26)$

Under the alternative hypothesis the distribution of $\bar{x}$ would be the same except that it would be centred on a value less than 5000. These two situations are illustrated in Figure 5.2. The distribution of $\bar{x}$ under $H_1$ is shown by a dashed curve to signify that its exact position is unknown, only that it lies to the left of the distribution under $H_0$.

A **decision rule** amounts to choosing a point or dividing line on the horizontal axis in Figure 5.2. If the sample mean lies to the left of this point then $H_0$ is rejected (the sample mean is too far away from $H_0$ for it to be credible) in favour of $H_1$ and you do not buy the firm. If $\bar{x}$ lies above this decision point then $H_0$ is not rejected and you go ahead with the purchase. Such a decision

**Figure 5.1**
**The two different types of error**

| | | True situation | |
|---|---|---|---|
| | | $H_0$ true | $H_0$ false |
| Decision | Accept $H_0$ | Correct decision | Type II error |
| | Reject $H_0$ | Type I error | Correct decision |

**Figure 5.2**
**The sampling distributions of $\bar{x}$ under $H_0$ and $H_1$**

point is shown in Figure 5.2, denoted by $\bar{x}_D$. To the left of $\bar{x}_D$ lies the rejection (of $H_0$) region; to the right lies the non-rejection region.

Based on this point, we can see the probabilities of Type I and Type II errors. The area under the $H_0$ distribution to the left of $\bar{x}_D$, labelled I, shows the probability of rejecting $H_0$ given that it is in fact true: a Type I error. The area under the $H_1$ distribution to the right of $\bar{x}_D$, labelled II, shows the probability of a Type II error: not rejecting $H_0$ when it is in fact false (and $H_1$ is true).

Shifting the decision line to the right or left alters the balance of these probabilities. Moving the line to the right increases the probability of a Type I error but reduces the probability of a Type II error. Moving the line to the left has the opposite effect.

The Type I error probability can be calculated for any value of $\bar{x}_D$. Suppose we set $\bar{x}_D$ to a value of 4950. Using the distribution of $\bar{x}$ given in equation (5.1) above, the area under the distribution to the left of 4950 is obtained using the $z$ score:

$$(5.2) \qquad z = \frac{\bar{x}_D - \mu}{\sqrt{s^2/n}} = \frac{4950 - 5000}{\sqrt{280^2/26}} = -0.91$$

From the tables of the standard Normal distribution we find that the probability of a Type I error is 18.1%. Unfortunately, the Type II error probability cannot be established because the exact position of the distribution under $H_1$ is unknown. Therefore we cannot decide on the appropriate position of $\bar{x}_D$ by some balance of the two error probabilities.

The convention therefore is to set the position of $\bar{x}_D$ by using a Type I error probability of 5%, known as the significance level[1] of the test. In other words, we are prepared to accept a 5% probability of rejecting $H_0$ when it is, in fact, true. This allows us to establish the position of $\bar{x}_D$. From Table A2 (see page 366) we find that $z = -1.64$ cuts off the bottom 5% of the distribution, so the decision line should be 1.64 standard errors below 5000. The value $-1.64$ is known as the critical value of the test. We therefore obtain

$$(5.3) \qquad \bar{x}_D = 5000 - 1.64\sqrt{280^2/26} = 4910$$

---

[1] The term size of the test is also used, not to be confused with the sample size. We use the term 'significance' level in this text.

Since the sample mean of 4900 lies below 4910 we reject $H_0$ *at the 5% significance level* or equivalently we reject *with 95% confidence*. The significance level is generally denoted by the symbol $\alpha$ and the complement of this, given by $1 - \alpha$, is known as the confidence level (as used in the confidence interval).

An equivalent procedure would be to calculate the $z$ score associated with the sample mean, known as the **test statistic**, and then compare this to the critical value of the test. This allows the hypothesis testing procedure to be broken down into five neat steps:

1 Write down the null and alternative hypotheses:

   $H_0: \mu = 5000$
   $H_1: \mu < 5000$

2 Choose the significance level of the test, conventionally $\alpha = 0.05$ or 5%.
3 Look up the critical value of the test from statistical tables, based on the chosen significance level. $z^* = 1.64$ is the critical value in this case.
4 Calculate the test statistic:

$$(5.4) \qquad z = \frac{\bar{x} - \mu}{\sqrt{s^2/n}} = \frac{-100}{\sqrt{280^2/26}} = -1.82$$

5 Decision rule. Compare the test statistic with the critical value: if $z < -z^*$ reject $H_0$ in favour of $H_1$. Since $-1.82 < -1.64$ $H_0$ is rejected with 95% confidence. Note that we use $-z^*$ here because we are dealing with the left-hand tail of the distribution.

| Worked example 5.1 | A sample of 100 workers found the average overtime hours worked in the previous week was 7.8, with standard deviation 4.1 hours. Test the hypothesis that the average for all workers is 5 hours or less. |
|---|---|

A sample of 100 workers found the average overtime hours worked in the previous week was 7.8, with standard deviation 4.1 hours. Test the hypothesis that the average for all workers is 5 hours or less.

We can set out the five steps of the answer as follows:

1 $H_0: \mu = 5$
   $H_1: \mu > 5$
2 Significance level, $\alpha = 5\%$.
3 Critical value $z^* = 1.64$.
4 Test statistic:

$$z = \frac{\bar{x} - \mu}{\sqrt{s^2/n}} = \frac{7.8 - 5}{\sqrt{4.1^2/100}} = 6.8$$

5 Decision rule: $6.8 > 1.64$ so we reject $H_0$ in favour of $H_1$. Note that in this case we are dealing with the right-hand tail of the distribution. Only high values of $\bar{x}$ reject $H_0$.

**One-tail and two-tail tests**

In the above example the rejection region for the test consisted of one tail of the distribution of $\bar{x}$, since the buyer was only concerned about turnover being less than claimed. For this reason it is known as a one-tail test. Suppose now that an accountant is engaged to sell the franchise and wants to check the claim about turnover before advertising the business for sale. In this case she would be concerned about turnover being either below *or* above 5000.

**Figure 5.3**
**A two-tail hypothesis test**

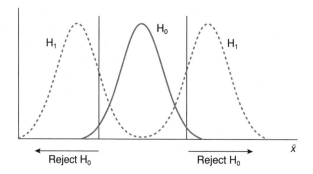

This would now become a **two-tail test** with the null and alternative hypotheses being

$H_0$: $\mu = 5000$
$H_1$: $\mu \neq 5000$

Now there are two rejection regions for the test. Either a very low sample mean *or* a very high one will serve to reject the null hypothesis. The situation is presented graphically in Figure 5.3.

The distribution of $\bar{x}$ under $H_0$ is the same as before, but under the alternative hypothesis the distribution could be shifted either to the left or to the right, as depicted. If the significance level is still chosen to be 5%, then the complete rejection region consist of the *two* extremes of the distribution under $H_0$, containing 2.5% in each tail (hence 5% in total). This gives a Type I error probability of 5% as before.

The critical value of the test therefore becomes $z^* = 1.96$, the value which cuts off 2.5% in each tail of the standard Normal distribution. Only if the test statistic falls into one of the rejection regions beyond 1.96 standard errors from the mean is $H_0$ rejected.

Using data from the previous example, the test statistic remains $z = -1.82$ so that the null hypothesis cannot be rejected in this case, as $-1.82$ does not fall beyond $-1.96$. To recap, the five steps of the test are:

1  $H_0$: $\mu = 5000$
   $H_1$: $\mu \neq 5000$
2  Choose the significance level: $\alpha = 0.05$.
3  Look up the critical value: $z^* = 1.96$.
4  Evaluate the test statistic:

$$z = \frac{-100}{\sqrt{280^2/26}} = -1.82$$

5  Compare test statistic and critical values: if $z < -z^*$ or $z > z^*$ reject $H_0$ in favour of $H_1$. In this case $-1.82 > -1.96$ so $H_0$ cannot be rejected with 95% confidence.

One- and two-tail tests therefore differ only at steps 1 and 3. Note that we have come to different conclusions according to whether a one- or two-tail test was used, with the same sample evidence. There is nothing wrong with this, however, for there are different interpretations of the two results. If the investor always uses his rule, he will miss out on 5% of good investment opportunities, when sales are (by chance) low. He will never miss out on a good opportunity because the investment appears too good (i.e. sales by chance are very high). For the accountant, 5% of the firms with sales averaging £5000 will not be advertised as such, *either* because sales appear too low *or* because they appear too high.

It is tempting on occasion to use a one-tail test because of the sample evidence. For example, the accountant might look at the sample evidence above and decide that the franchise operation can only have true sales less than or equal to 5000. Therefore she uses a one-tail test. This is a dangerous practice, since the sample evidence is being used to help formulate the hypothesis, which is then tested on that same evidence. This is going round in circles; the hypothesis should be chosen *independently* of the evidence which is then used to test it. Presumably the accountant would also use a one-tail test (with $H_1$: $\mu > 5000$ as the alternative hypothesis) if she noticed that the sample mean were *above* the hypothesised value. In effect therefore she would be using the 10% significance level, not the 5% level, since there would be 5% in each tail of the distribution. She would make a Type I error on 10% of all occasions rather than 5%.

It is acceptable to use a one-tail test when you have *independent* information about what the alternative hypothesis should be, or you are not concerned about one side of the distribution (like the investor) and can effectively add that in to the null hypothesis. Otherwise, it is safer to use a two-tail test.

**Exercise 5.1**

(a) Two political parties are debating crime figures. One party says that crime has increased compared to the previous year. The other party says it has not. Write down the null and alternative hypotheses.

(b) Explain the two types of error that could be made in this example and the possible costs of each type of error.

**Exercise 5.2**

(a) We test the hypothesis $H_0$: $\mu = 100$ against $H_1$: $\mu > 100$ by rejecting $H_0$ if our sample mean is greater than 108. If in fact $\bar{x} \sim N(100, 900/25)$, what is the probability of making a Type I error?

(b) If we wanted a 5% Type I error probability, what decision rule should we adopt?

(c) If we knew that $\mu$ could only take on the values 100 (under $H_0$) or 112 (under $H_1$) what would be the Type II error probability using the decision rule in part (a)?

**Exercise 5.3**

Test the hypothesis $H_0$: $\mu = 500$ versus $H_1$: $\mu \neq 500$ using the evidence $\bar{x} = 530$, $s = 90$ from a sample of size $n = 30$.

**The choice of significance level**

We justified the choice of the 5% significance level by reference to convention. This is usually a poor argument for anything, but it does have some justification. In an ideal world we would have precisely specified null *and* alternative hypotheses (e.g. we would test $H_0$: $\mu = 5000$ against $H_1$: $\mu = 4500$, these being the only possibilities). Then we could calculate the probabilities of both Type I *and* Type II errors, for any given decision rule. We could then choose the optimal decision rule, which gives the best compromise between the two types of error. This is reflected in a court of law. In criminal cases, the jury must be convinced of the prosecution's case beyond reasonable doubt, because of the cost of committing a Type I error. In a civil case (libel, for example) the jury need only be convinced *on the balance of probabilities*. In a civil case, the costs of Type I and Type II error are more evenly balanced and so the burden of proof is lessened.

However, in practice we usually do not have the luxury of two well-specified hypotheses. As in the example, the null hypothesis is precisely specified (it has to be or the test could not be carried out) but the alternative hypothesis is imprecise (sometimes called a composite hypothesis because it encompasses a range of values). Statistical inference is often used not so much as an aid to decision making but to provide evidence for or against a particular theory, to alter one's degree of belief in the truth of the theory. For example, an economic theory might assert that rising prices are caused by rising wages (the cost–push theory of inflation). The null and alternative hypotheses would be:

$H_0$: there is no connection between rising wages and rising prices
$H_1$: there is some connection between rising wages and rising prices

(Note that the null has 'no connection', since this is a precise statement. 'Some connection' is too vague to be the null hypothesis.) Data could be gathered to test this hypothesis (the appropriate methods will be discussed in the chapters on correlation and regression). But what decision rests upon the result of this test? It could be thought that government might make a decision to impose a prices and incomes policy, but if every academic study of inflation led to the imposition or abandonment of a prices and incomes policy there would have been an awful lot of policies! (In fact, there *were* a lot of such policies, but not as many as the number of studies of inflation.) No single study is decisive ('more research is needed' is a very common phrase) but each does influence the climate of opinion which may eventually lead to a policy decision. But if a hypothesis test is designed to influence opinion, how is the significance level to be chosen?

It is difficult to trade-off the costs of Type I and Type II errors and the probability of making those errors. A Type I error in this case means concluding that rising wages do cause rising prices when, in fact, they do not. So what would be the cost of this error, i.e. imposing a prices and incomes policy when, in fact, it is not needed? It is extremely difficult, if not impossible, to put a figure on it. It would depend on what type of prices and incomes policy were imposed – would wages be frozen or allowed to rise with productivity, how fast would prices be allowed to rise, would company dividends be frozen? The costs of the Type II error would also be problematic (not imposing a needed prices and incomes policy), for they would depend, amongst other things, on what alternative policies might be adopted.

The 5% significance level really does depend upon convention therefore, it cannot be justified by reference to the relative costs of Type I and Type II errors (it is too much to believe that everyone does consider these costs and independently arrives at the conclusion that 5% is the appropriate significance level!). However, the 5% convention does impose some sort of discipline upon research; it sets some kind of standard which all theories (hypotheses) should be measured against. Beware the researcher who reports that a particular hypothesis is rejected at the 8% significance level; it is likely that the significance level was chosen so that the hypothesis could be rejected, which is what the researcher was hoping for in the first place!

# The Prob-value approach

Suppose a result is significant at the 4.95% level (i.e. it just meets the 5% convention and the null hypothesis is rejected). A *very* slight change in the sample data could have meant the result being significant at only the 5.05% level, and the null hypothesis not being rejected. Would we really be happy to alter our belief completely on such fragile results? Most researchers (but not all!) would be cautious if their results were only just significant (or fell just short of significance).

This suggests an alternative approach: the significance level of the test statistic could be reported and the reader could make his own judgements about it. This is known as the Prob-value approach, the Prob-value being the significance level of the calculated test statistic. For example, the calculated test statistic for the investor problem was $z = -1.82$ and the associated Prob-value is obtained from Table A2 (see page **366**) as 3.44%, i.e. $-1.82$ cuts off 3.44% in one tail of the standard Normal distribution. This means that the null hypothesis can be rejected at the 3.44% significance level or, alternatively expressed, with 96.56% confidence.

Notice that Table A2 gives the Prob-value for a one-tail test; for a two-tail test the Prob-value should be doubled. Thus for the accountant, using the two-tail test, the significance level is 6.88% and this is the level at which the null hypothesis can be rejected. Alternatively we could say we reject the null with 93.12% confidence. This does not meet the standard 5% criterion (for the significance level) which is most often used, so would result in non-rejection of the null.

An advantage of using the Prob-value approach is that many statistical software programs routinely provide the Prob-value of a calculated test statistic. If one understands the use of Prob-values then one does not have to look up tables (this applies to any distribution, not just the Normal), which can save a lot of time.

To summarise, one rejects the null hypothesis if either:

■ (Method 1) – the test statistic is greater than the critical value, i.e. $z > z^*$, or
■ (Method 2) – the Prob-value associated with the test statistic is less than the significance level, i.e. $P < 0.05$ (if the 5% significance level is used).

I have found that many students initially find this confusing, because of the opposing inequality in the two versions (greater than and less than). For example, a program might calculate a hypothesis test and report the result as '$z = 1.4$ ($P$ value $= 0.162$)'. The first point to note is that most software programmes report the Prob-value for a two-tail test by default. Hence, assuming a 5% significance level, in this case we cannot reject $H_0$ because $z = 1.4 < 1.96$ or equivalently because $0.162 > 0.05$, against a two-tailed alternative (i.e. $H_1$ contains $\neq$).

If you wish to conduct a one-tailed test you have to halve the reported Prob-value, becoming 0.081 in this example. This is again greater than 5%, so the hypothesis is still accepted, even against a one-sided alternative ($H_1$ contains $>$ or $<$). Equivalently, one could compare 1.4 with the one-tail critical value, 1.64, showing non-rejection of the null, but one has to look up the standard Normal table with this method. Computers cannot guess whether a one- or two-sided test is wanted, so take the conservative option and report the two-sided value. The correction for a one-sided test has to be done manually.

## Significance, effect size and power

Researchers usually look for 'significant' results. Academic papers report that 'the results are significant' or that 'the coefficient is significantly different from zero at the 5% significance level'. It is vital to realise that the word 'significant' is used here in the *statistical* sense and not in its everyday sense of being *important*. Something can be statistically significant yet still unimportant.

Suppose that we have some more data about the business examined earlier. Data for 100 franchises have been uncovered, revealing an average weekly turnover of £4975 with standard deviation £143. Can we reject the hypothesis that the average weekly turnover is £5000? The test statistic is

$$z = \frac{4975 - 5000}{\sqrt{143^2/100}} = -1.75$$

Since this is less than $-z^* = -1.64$ the null is rejected with 95% confidence. True average weekly turnover is less than £5000. However, the difference is only £25 per week, which is 0.5% of £5000. Common sense would suggest that the difference may be unimportant, even if it is significant in the statistical sense. One should not interpret statistical results in terms of significance alone, therefore; one should also look at the size of the difference (sometimes known as the **effect size**) and ask whether it is important or not. This is a mistake made by even experienced researchers; a review of articles in the prestigious *American Economic Review* reported that 82% of them confused statistical significance for economics significance in some way (McCloskey and Ziliak, 2004).

This problem with hypothesis testing paradoxically gets worse as the sample size increases. For example, if 250 observations reveal average sales of 4985 with standard deviation 143, the null would (just) be rejected at 5% significance. In fact, given a large enough sample size we can virtually guarantee to reject the null hypothesis even before we have gathered the data. This can be seen from equation (5.4) for the $z$ score test statistic: as $n$ gets larger, the test statistic also inevitably gets larger.

A related way of considering the effect of increasing sample size is via the concept of the **power** of a test. This is defined as

(5.5)    Power of a test = $1 - \Pr(\text{Type II error}) = 1 - \beta$

where $\beta$ is the symbol conventionally used to indicate the probability of a Type II error. Since a Type II error is defined as not rejecting $H_0$ when false (equivalent to rejecting $H_1$ when true), power is the probability of rejecting $H_0$ when false (if $H_0$ is false, it must be *either* accepted *or* rejected; hence these probabilities sum to one). This is one of the correct decisions identified earlier, associated with the lower right-hand box in Figure 5.1, that of correctly rejecting a false null hypothesis. The power of a test is therefore given by the area under the $H_1$ distribution, to the left of the decision line, as illustrated (shaded) in Figure 5.4 (for a one-tail test).

**Figure 5.4**
**The power of a test**

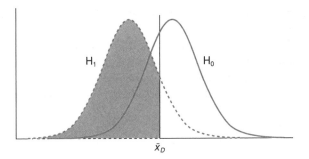

It is generally desirable to maximise the power of a test, as long as the probability of a Type I error is not raised in the process. There are essentially three ways of doing this:

- Avoid situations where the null and alternative hypotheses are very similar, i.e. the hypothesised means are not far apart (a small effect size).
- Use a large sample size. This reduces the sampling variance of $\bar{x}$ (under both $H_0$ and $H_1$) so the two distributions become more distinct.
- Use good sampling methods which have small sampling variances. This has a similar effect to increasing the sample size.

Unfortunately, in economics and business the data are very often given in advance and there is little or no control possible over the sampling procedures. This leads to a neglect of consideration of power, unlike in psychology, for example, where the experiment can often be designed by the researcher. The gathering of sample data will be covered in detail in Chapter 9.

**Exercise 5.4**

If a researcher believes the cost of making a Type I error is much greater than the cost of a Type II error, should they choose a 5% or 1% significance level? Explain why.

**Exercise 5.5**

(a) A researcher uses Excel to analyse data and test a hypothesis. The program reports a test statistic of $z = 1.77$ ($P$ value = 0.077). Would you reject the null hypothesis if carrying out (i) a one-tailed test (ii) a two-tailed test? Use the 5% significance level.

(b) Repeat part (a) using a 1% significance level.

## Further hypothesis tests

We now proceed to consider a number of different types of hypothesis test, all involving the same principles but differing in detail. This is similar to the exposition in the last chapter covering, in turn, tests of a proportion, tests of the difference of two means and proportions, and finally problems involving small sample sizes.

**Testing a proportion**

A car manufacturer claims that no more than 10% of its cars should need repairs in the first three years of their life, the warranty period. A random sample of 50 three-year-old cars found that 8 had required attention. Does this contradict the maker's claim?

This problem can be handled in a very similar way to the methods used for a mean. The key, once again, is to recognise the sample proportion as a random variable with an associated probability distribution. From Chapter 4 (equation (4.9)), the sampling distribution of the sample proportion in large samples is given by

$$(5.6) \qquad p \sim N\left(\pi, \frac{\pi(1 - \pi)}{n}\right)$$

In this case $\pi = 0.10$ (under the null hypothesis, the maker's claim). The sample data are

$p = 8/50 = 0.16$
$n = 50$

Thus 16% of the sample required attention within the warranty period. This is substantially higher than the claimed 10%, but is this just because of a bad sample or does it reflect the reality that the cars are badly built? The hypothesis test is set out along the same lines as for a sample mean:

1 $H_0: \pi = 0.10$
  $H_1: \pi > 0.10$
  (The only concern is the manufacturer not matching its claim.)
2 Significance level: $\alpha = 0.05$.
3 The critical value of the one-tail test at the 5% significance level is $z^* = 1.64$, obtained from the standard Normal table.
4 The test statistic is

$$z = \frac{p - \pi}{\sqrt{\dfrac{\pi(1 - \pi)}{n}}} = \frac{0.16 - 0.10}{\sqrt{\dfrac{0.1 \times 0.9}{50}}} = 1.41$$

5 Since the test statistic is less than the critical value, it falls into the non-rejection region. The null hypothesis is not rejected by the data. The manufacturer's claim is not unreasonable.

Note that for this problem, the rejection region lies in the *upper* tail of the distribution because of the 'greater than' inequality in the alternative hypothesis. The null hypothesis is therefore rejected in this case if $z > z^*$.

**Testing the difference of two means**

Suppose a car company wishes to compare the performance of its two factories producing an identical model of car. The factories are equipped with the same machinery but their outputs might differ due to managerial ability, labour relations, etc. Senior management wishes to know if there is any difference between the two factories. Output is monitored for 30 days, chosen at random, with the following results:

|  | Factory 1 | Factory 2 |
|---|---|---|
| Average daily output | 420 | 408 |
| Standard deviation of daily output | 25 | 20 |

Does this produce sufficient evidence of a real difference between the factories, or does the difference between the samples simply reflect random differences such as minor breakdowns of machinery? The information at our disposal may be summarised as

$$\bar{x}_1 = 420 \qquad \bar{x}_2 = 408$$
$$s_1 = 25 \qquad s_2 = 20$$
$$n_1 = 30 \qquad n_2 = 30$$

The hypothesis test to be conducted concerns the difference between the factories' outputs, so the appropriate random variable to examine is $\bar{x}_1 - \bar{x}_2$. From Chapter 4 (equation (4.12)), this has the following distribution, in large samples:

$$(5.7) \qquad \bar{x}_1 - \bar{x}_2 \sim N\left(\mu_1 - \mu_2, \frac{\sigma_1^2}{n_1} + \frac{\sigma_2^2}{n_2}\right)$$

The population variances, $\sigma_1^2$ and $\sigma_2^2$, may be replaced by their sample estimates, $s_1^2$ and $s_2^2$, if the former are unknown, as here. The hypothesis test is therefore as follows.

1  $H_0$: $\mu_1 - \mu_2 = 0$
   $H_1$: $\mu_1 - \mu_2 \neq 0$
   The null hypothesis posits no real difference between the factories. This is a two-tail test since there is no *a priori* reason to believe one factory is better than the other, apart from the sample evidence.
2  Significance level: $\alpha = 1\%$. This is chosen since the management does not want to interfere unless it is really confident of some difference between the factories. In order to favour the null hypothesis, a lower significance level than the conventional 5% is set.
3  The critical value of the test is $z^* = 2.57$. This cuts off 0.5% in each tail of the standard Normal distribution.
4  The test statistic is

$$z = \frac{(\bar{x}_1 - \bar{x}_2) - (\mu_1 - \mu_2)}{\sqrt{\dfrac{s_1^2}{n_1} + \dfrac{s_2^2}{n_2}}} = \frac{(420 - 408) - 0}{\sqrt{\dfrac{25^2}{30} + \dfrac{20^2}{30}}} = 2.05$$

Note that this is of the same form as in the single-sample cases. The hypothesised value of the difference (zero in this case) is subtracted from the sample difference and this is divided by the standard error of the random variable.
5  Decision rule: $z < z^*$ so the test statistic falls into the non-rejection region. There does not appear to be a significant difference between the two factories.

A number of remarks about this example should be made. First, it should be noted that it is not necessary for the two sample sizes to be equal (although they are in the example). 45 days' output from factory 1 and 35 days' from factory 2, for example, could have been sampled. Second, the values of $s_1^2$ and $s_2^2$ do not have to be equal. They are respectively estimates of $\sigma_1^2$ and $\sigma_2^2$ and although the null hypothesis asserts that $\mu_1 = \mu_2$ it does not assert that the variances are equal. Management wants to know if the *average* levels of output are the same; it is not concerned about daily fluctuations in output. A test of the hypothesis of equal variances is set out in Chapter 6.

The final point to consider is whether all the necessary conditions for the correct application of this test have been met. The example noted that the 30 days were chosen at random. If the 30 days sampled were consecutive we might doubt whether the observations were truly independent. Low output on one day (due to a mechanical breakdown, for example) might influence the following day's output (if a special effort were made to catch up on lost production, for example).

## Testing the difference of two proportions

The general method should by now be familiar, so we will proceed by example for this case. Suppose that, in a comparison of two holiday companies' customers, of the 75 who went with Happy Days Tours, 45 said they were satisfied, while 48 of the 90 who went with Fly by Night Holidays were satisfied. Is there a significant difference between the companies?

This problem can be handled by a hypothesis test on the difference of two sample proportions. The procedure is as follows. The sample evidence is

$$p_1 = 45/75 = 0.6 \qquad n_1 = 75$$
$$p_2 = 48/90 = 0.533 \qquad n_2 = 90$$

The hypothesis test is carried out as follows

1  $H_0: \pi_1 - \pi_2 = 0$
   $H_1: \pi_1 - \pi_2 \neq 0$
2  Significance level: $\alpha = 5\%$.
3  Critical value: $z^* = 1.96$.
4  Test statistic: The distribution of $p_1 - p_2$ is

$$p_1 - p_2 \sim N\left(\pi_1 - \pi_2, \frac{\pi_1(1 - \pi_1)}{n_1} + \frac{\pi_2(1 - \pi_2)}{n_2}\right)$$

so the test statistic is

(5.8)  $$z = \frac{(p_1 - p_2) - (\pi_1 - \pi_2)}{\sqrt{\dfrac{\pi_1(1 - \pi_1)}{n_1} + \dfrac{\pi_2(1 - \pi_2)}{n_2}}}$$

However, $\pi_1$ and $\pi_2$ in the denominator of equation (5.8) have to be replaced by estimates from the samples. They cannot simply be replaced by $p_1$ and $p_2$ because these are unequal; to do so would contradict the null hypothesis that they *are* equal. Since the null hypothesis is assumed to be true (for the moment), it doesn't make sense to use a test statistic which explicitly supposes the null hypothesis to be false. Therefore $\pi_1$ and $\pi_2$ are replaced by an estimate of their common value which is denoted $\hat{\pi}$ and whose formula is

(5.9)  $$\hat{\pi} = \frac{n_1 p_1 + n_2 p_2}{n_1 + n_2}$$

i.e. a weighted average of the two sample proportions. This yields

$$\hat{\pi} = \frac{75 \times 0.6 + 90 \times 0.533}{75 + 90} = 0.564$$

This, in fact, is just the proportion of all customers who were satisfied, 93 out of 165. The test statistic therefore becomes

$$z = \frac{0.6 - 0.533 - 0}{\sqrt{\dfrac{0.564 \times (1 - 0.564)}{75} + \dfrac{0.564 \times (1 - 0.564)}{90}}} = 0.86$$

5 The test statistic is less than the critical value so the null hypothesis cannot be rejected with 95% confidence. There is not sufficient evidence to demonstrate a difference between the two companies' performance.

## Do boys or girls do better at school?

At an infant school (for pupils of 5–7 years of age) where I was a governor, girls appeared to be doing better than boys. In maths, 78% achieved level 2 or better, compared to 75% of boys. In reading, the scores were 82% and 72%, a bigger difference. (Level 2 is the grade that the government expects 7-year-old children to achieve.) 55 girls and 61 boys took the tests.

Are these results significant, however? We can compare the two sample proportions to test the hypothesis $H_0$: $\pi_B - \pi_G = 0$, i.e. that girls and boys are really equally able and that what we observe here is just sampling error. The *Excel* worksheet provides details of the calculations.

Microsoft Excel - Book1

File Edit View Insert Format Tools Data Window Help

F12    =    =D7*(1-D7)/D6+E7*(1-E7)/E6

|  | A | B | C | D | E | F | G |
|---|---|---|---|---|---|---|---|
| 1 |  |  | School SATS test results |  |  |  |  |
| 2 |  |  |  |  |  |  |  |
| 3 |  |  |  | Maths |  | Reading |  |
| 4 |  |  |  | Boys | Girls | Boys | Girls |
| 5 | Number achieving level 2 or better |  |  | 46 | 43 | 44 | 45 |
| 6 | Total number of pupils |  |  | 61 | 55 | 61 | 55 |
| 7 |  |  |  | 75.4% | 78.2% | 72.1% | 81.8% |
| 8 |  |  |  |  |  |  |  |
| 9 | Testing whether the boys' and girls' scores are significantly different: |  |  |  |  |  |  |
| 10 |  |  |  |  |  |  |  |
| 11 | Maths: | Difference of means | 0.754 - 0.782 = |  |  | -0.028 |  |
| 12 |  | Variance of difference | 0.0030 + 0.0031 = |  |  | 0.0061 |  |
| 13 |  | Standard error |  |  |  | 0.0784 |  |
| 14 |  | z score | -0.028/0.0784 = |  |  | -0.354 |  |
| 15 |  |  |  |  |  |  |  |
| 16 | Reading | Difference of means | 0.721 - 0.818 = |  |  | -0.097 |  |
| 17 |  | Variance of difference | 0.0033 + 0.0027 = |  |  | 0.0060 |  |
| 18 |  | Standard error |  |  |  | 0.0775 |  |
| 19 |  | z score | -0.097/0.0775 = |  |  | -1.251 |  |
| 20 |  |  |  |  |  |  |  |

Sheet1 / Sheet2 / Sheet3 /

Ready                                                    NUM

The calculations should be self-explanatory by now. The 'Variance of difference' line gives the variance of $p_B - p_G$, as in the denominator of equation (5.8). You can see how it is calculated in *Excel* near the top of the screenshot. The z scores in both maths and reading are fairly low – certainly less than the critical value 1.96. We cannot, on the basis of this evidence, conclude that girls do better than boys in this school.

**Exercise 5.6**  A survey of 80 voters finds that 65% are in favour of a particular policy. Test the hypothesis that the true proportion is 50%, against the alternative that a majority is in favour.

**Exercise 5.7**  A survey of 50 teenage girls found that on average they spent 3.6 hours per week chatting with friends over the internet. The standard deviation was 1.2 hours. A similar survey of 90 teenage boys found an average of 3.9 hours, with standard deviation 2.1 hours. Test if there is any difference between boys' and girls' behaviour.

**Exercise 5.8**  One gambler on horse racing won on 23 of his 75 bets. Another won on 34 out of 95. Is the second person a better judge of horses, or just luckier?

## Hypothesis tests with small samples

As with estimation, slightly different methods have to be employed when the sample size is small ($n < 25$) and the population variance is unknown. When both of these conditions are satisfied the $t$ distribution must be used rather than the Normal, so a $t$ test is conducted rather than a $z$ test. This means consulting tables of the $t$ distribution to obtain the critical value of a test, but otherwise the methods are similar. These methods will be applied to hypotheses about sample means only, since they are inappropriate for tests of a sample proportion, as was the case in estimation.

**Testing the sample mean**

A large chain of supermarkets sells 5000 packets of cereal in each of its stores each month. It decides to test-market a different brand of cereal in 15 of its stores. After a month the 15 stores have sold an average of 5200 packets each, with a standard deviation of 500 packets. Should all supermarkets switch to selling the new brand?

The sample information is

$\bar{x} = 5200$, $s = 500$, $n = 15$

From Chapter 4 the distribution of the sample mean from a small sample when the population variance is unknown is based upon

(5.10)   $$\frac{\bar{x} - \mu}{\sqrt{s^2/n}} \sim t_v$$

with $v = n - 1$ degrees of freedom. The hypothesis test is based on this formula and is conducted as follows:

1  $H_0$: $\mu = 5000$
   $H_1$: $\mu > 5000$
   (Only an improvement in sales is relevant.)
2  Significance level: $\alpha = 1\%$ (chosen because the cost of changing brands is high).
3  The critical value of the $t$ distribution for a one-tail test at the 1% significance level with $v = n - 1 = 14$ degrees of freedom is $t^* = 2.62$.
4  The test statistic is

$$t = \frac{\bar{x} - \mu}{\sqrt{s^2/n}} = \frac{5200 - 5000}{\sqrt{500^2/15}} = 1.55$$

5  The null hypothesis is not rejected since the test statistic, 1.55, is less than the critical value, 2.62. It would probably be unwise to switch over to the new brand of cereals.

**Testing the difference of two means**

A survey of 20 British companies found an average annual expenditure on research and development of £3.7m with a standard deviation of £0.6m. A survey of 15 similar German companies found an average expenditure on research and development of £4.2m with standard deviation £0.9m. Does this evidence lend support to the view often expressed that Britain does not invest enough in research and development?

This is a hypothesis about the difference of two means, based on small sample sizes. The test statistic is again based on the $t$ distribution, i.e.

(5.11)    $$\frac{\bar{x}_1 - \bar{x}_2 - (\mu_1 - \mu_2)}{\sqrt{\dfrac{S^2}{n_1} + \dfrac{S^2}{n_2}}} \sim t_v$$

where $S^2$ is the pooled variance (as given in equation (4.23)) and the degrees of freedom are given by $v = n_1 + n_2 - 2$.

The hypothesis test procedure is as follows:

1  $H_0$: $\mu_1 - \mu_2 = 0$
   $H_1$: $\mu_1 - \mu_2 < 0$
2  Significance level: $\alpha = 5\%$.
3  The critical value of the $t$ distribution at the 5% significance level for a one-tail test with $v = n_1 + n_2 - 2 = 33$ degrees of freedom is approximately $t^* = 1.70$.
4  The test statistic is based on equation (5.11):

$$t = \frac{\bar{x}_1 - \bar{x}_2 - (\mu_1 - \mu_2)}{\sqrt{\dfrac{S^2}{n_1} + \dfrac{S^2}{n_2}}} = \frac{3.7 - 4.2 - 0}{\sqrt{\dfrac{0.55}{20} + \dfrac{0.55}{15}}} = -1.97$$

where $S^2$ is the pooled variance, calculated by

$$S^2 = \frac{(n_1 - 1)s_1^2 + (n_2 - 1)s_2^2}{n_1 + n_2 - 2} = \frac{19 \times 0.6^2 + 14 \times 0.9^2}{33} = 0.55$$

5  The test statistic falls in the rejection region, $t < -t^*$, so the null hypothesis is rejected. The data do support the view that Britain spends less on R&D than Germany.

**Exercise 5.9**

It is asserted that parents spend, on average, £540 per annum, on toys for each child. A survey of 24 parents finds expenditure of £490, with standard deviation £150. Does this evidence contradict the assertion?

**Exercise 5.10**

A sample of 15 final-year students were found to spend on average 15 hours per week in the university library, with standard deviation 3 hours. A sample of 20 freshers found they spend on average 9 hours per week in the library, standard deviation 5 hours. Is this sufficient evidence to conclude that finalists spend more time in the library?

## Are the test procedures valid?

A variety of assumptions underlie each of the tests which we have applied above and it is worth considering in a little more detail whether these assumptions are justified. This will demonstrate that one should not rely upon the statistical tests alone; it is important to retain one's sense of judgement.

The first test concerned the weekly turnover of a series of franchise operations. To justify the use of the Normal distribution underlying the test, the sample observations must be independently drawn. The random errors around the true mean turnover figure should be independent of each other. This might not be the case if, for example, similar events could affect the turnover figures of all franchises.

If one were using time-series data, as in the car factory comparison, similar issues arise. Do the 30 days represent independent observations or might there be an autocorrelation problem (e.g. if the sample days were close together in time)? Suppose that factory 2 suffered a breakdown of some kind which took three days to fix. Output would be reduced on three successive days and factory 2 would almost inevitably appear less efficient than factory 1. The fact that the standard deviation for factory 2 is higher than that for factory 1 suggests this could have occurred. A look at the individual sample observations might be worthwhile, therefore. It would have been altogether better if the samples had been collected on randomly chosen days over a longer time period to reduce the danger of this type of problem.

If the two factories both obtain their supplies from a common, but limited, source then the output of one factory might not be independent of the output of the other. A high output of one factory would tend to be associated with a low output from the other, which has little to do with their relative efficiencies. This might leave the average difference in output unchanged but might increase the variance substantially (either a very high positive value of $\bar{x}_1 - \bar{x}_2$ or a very high negative value is obtained). This would lead to a low value of the test statistic and the conclusion of no difference in output. Any real difference in efficiency is masked by the common supplier problem. If the two samples are not independent then the distribution of $\bar{x}_1 - \bar{x}_2$ may not be Normal.

## Hypothesis tests and confidence intervals

Formally, two-tail hypothesis tests and confidence intervals are equivalent. Any value which lies within the 95% confidence interval around the sample mean cannot be rejected as the 'true' value using the 5% significance level in a hypothesis test using the same sample data. For example, our by now familiar accountant could construct a confidence interval for the firm's sales. This yields the 95% confidence interval

**(5.12)**    [4792, 5008]

Notice that the hypothesised value of 5000 is within this interval and that it was not rejected by the hypothesis test carried out earlier. As long as the same confidence level is used for both procedures, they are equivalent.

Having said this, their interpretation is different. The hypothesis test forces us into the reject/do not reject dichotomy, which is rather a stark choice. We have seen how it becomes more likely that the null hypothesis is rejected as the sample size increases. This problem does not occur with estimation. As the sample size increases the confidence interval gets narrower (around the un-biased point estimate) which is entirely beneficial. The estimation approach also tends to emphasise importance over significance in most people's minds. With a hypothesis test one might know that turnover is significantly different from 5000 without knowing how far from 5000 it actually is.

On some occasions a confidence interval is inferior to a hypothesis test, however. Consider the following case. In the UK only 17 out of 465 judges are women (3.7%).[2] The Equal Opportunities Commission commented that since the appointment system is so secretive it is impossible to tell if there is discrim-ination or not. What can the statistician say about this? No discrimination (in its broadest sense) would mean half of all judges would be women. Thus the hypotheses are

$H_0$: $\pi = 0.5$ (no discrimination)
$H_1$: $\pi < 0.5$ (discrimination against women)

The sample data are $p = 0.037$, $n = 465$. The $z$ score is

$$z = \frac{p - \pi}{\sqrt{\dfrac{\pi(1 - \pi)}{n}}} = \frac{0.037 - 0.5}{\sqrt{\dfrac{0.5 \times 0.5}{465}}} = -19.97$$

This is clearly significant (*and* 3.7% is a long way from 50%!) so the null hypothesis is rejected. There is some form of discrimination somewhere against women (unless women choose not to be judges). But a confidence interval esti-mate of the 'true' proportion of female judges would be meaningless. To what population is this 'true' proportion related?

The lesson from all this is that there exist differences between confidence intervals and hypothesis tests, despite their formal similarity. Which technique is more appropriate is a matter of judgement for the researcher. With hypothe-sis testing, the rejection of the null hypothesis at some significance level might actually mean a small (and unimportant) deviation from the hypothesised value. It should be remembered that the rejection of the null hypothesis based on a large sample of data is also consistent with the true value and hypothesised value possibly being quite close together.

## Independent and dependent samples

The following example illustrates the differences between independent samples (as encountered so far) and dependent samples where slightly different methods of analysis are required. The example also illustrates how a particular problem can often be analysed by a variety of statistical methods.

---

[2] This figure is somewhat out of date now, but it is still a useful example.

A company introduces a training programme to raise the productivity of its clerical workers, which is measured by the number of invoices processed per day. The company wants to know if the training programme is effective. How should it evaluate the programme? There is a variety of ways of going about the task, as follows:

- Take two (random) samples of workers, one trained and one not trained, and compare their productivity.
- Take a sample of workers and compare their productivity before and after training.
- Take two samples of workers, one to be trained and the other not. Compare the improvement of the trained workers with any change in the other group's performance over the same time period.

We shall go through each method in turn, pointing out any possible difficulties.

**Two independent samples**

Suppose a group of ten workers is trained and compared to a group of ten non-trained workers, with the following data being relevant:

$\bar{x}_T = 25.5$   $\bar{x}_N = 21.00$
$s_T = 2.55$   $s_N = 2.91$
$n_T = 10$   $n_N = 10$

Thus, trained workers process 25.5 invoices per day compared to only 21 by non-trained workers. The question is whether this is significant, given that the sample sizes are quite small.

The appropriate test here is a $t$ test of the difference of two sample means, as follows:

$H_0: \mu_T - \mu_N = 0$
$H_1: \mu_T - \mu_N > 0$

$$t = \frac{25.5 - 21.0}{\sqrt{\dfrac{7.49}{10} + \dfrac{7.49}{10}}} = 3.68$$

(7.49 is $S^2$, the pooled variance). The $t$ statistic leads to rejection of the null hypothesis; the training programme does seem to be effective.

One problem with this test is that the two samples might not be truly random and thus not properly reflect the effect of the training programme. Poor workers might have been reluctant (and thus refused) to take part in training, departmental managers might have selected better workers for training as some kind of reward, or simply better workers may have volunteered. In a well-designed experiment this should not be allowed to happen, of course, but we do not rule out the possibility. There is also the 5% (significance level) chance of unrepresentative samples being selected and a Type I error occurring.

**Paired samples**

This is the situation where a sample of workers is tested before and after training. The sample data are as follows:

| Worker | 1 | 2 | 3 | 4 | 5 | 6 | 7 | 8 | 9 | 10 |
|---|---|---|---|---|---|---|---|---|---|---|
| Before | 21 | 24 | 23 | 25 | 28 | 17 | 24 | 22 | 24 | 27 |
| After | 23 | 27 | 24 | 28 | 29 | 21 | 24 | 25 | 26 | 28 |

In this case, the observations in the two samples are paired and this has implications for the method of analysis. One *could* proceed by assuming these are two independent samples and conduct a *t* test. The summary data and results are:

$$\bar{x}_B = 23.50 \qquad \bar{x}_A = 25.5$$
$$s_B = 3.10 \qquad s_A = 2.55$$
$$n_B = 10 \qquad n_A = 10$$

The resulting test statistic is $t_{18} = 1.58$ which is not significant at the 5% level.

There are two problems with this test and its result. First, the two samples are not truly independent, since the before and after measurements refer to the same group of workers. Second, nine out of ten workers in the sample have shown an improvement, which is odd in view of the result found above, of no significant improvement. If the training programme really has no effect, then the probability of a single worker showing an improvement is $\frac{1}{2}$. The probability of nine or more workers showing an improvement is, by the Binomial method, $(\frac{1}{2})^{10} \times 10C9 + (\frac{1}{2})^{10}$, which is about one in a hundred. A very unlikely event seems to have occurred.

The *t* test used above is inappropriate because it does not make full use of the information in the sample. It does not reflect the fact, for example, that the before and after scores, 21 and 23, relate to the same worker. The Binomial calculation above does reflect this fact. A re-ordering of the data would not affect the *t* test result, but would affect the Binomial, since a different number of workers would now show an improvement. Of course, the Binomial does not use all the sample information either – it dispenses with the actual productivity data for each worker and replaces it with 'improvement' or 'no improvement'. It disregards the amount of improvement for each worker.

The best use of the sample data comes by measuring the improvement for each worker, as follows (if a worker had deteriorated, this would be reflected by a negative number):

| Worker | 1 | 2 | 3 | 4 | 5 | 6 | 7 | 8 | 9 | 10 |
|---|---|---|---|---|---|---|---|---|---|---|
| Improvement | 2 | 3 | 1 | 3 | 1 | 4 | 0 | 3 | 2 | 1 |

These new data can be treated by single sample methods, and account is taken both of the actual data values and of the fact that the original samples were dependent (re-ordering of the data would produce different improvement figures). The summary statistics of the new data are as follows:

$$\bar{x} = 2.00, \; s = 1.247, \; n = 10$$

The null hypothesis of no improvement can now be tested as follows:

$H_0: \mu = 0$
$H_1: \mu > 0$

$$t = \frac{2.0 - 0}{\sqrt{\dfrac{1.247^2}{10}}} = 5.07$$

This is significant at the 5% level so the null hypothesis of no improvement is rejected. The correct analysis of the sample data has thus reversed the previous conclusion.

Matters do not end here, however. Although we have discovered an improvement, this might be due to other factors apart from the training programme. For example, if the before and after measurements were taken on different days of the week (that Monday morning feeling . . . ), or if one of the days were sunnier, making people feel happier and therefore be more productive, this would bias the results. These may seem trivial examples but these effects do exist, for example the 'Friday afternoon car', which has more faults than the average.

The way to solve this problem is to use a control group, so called because extraneous factors are controlled for, in order to isolate the effects of the factor under investigation. In this case, the productivity of the control group would be measured (twice) at the same times as that of the training group, though no training would be given to them. Suppose that the average improvement of the control group were 0.5 invoices per day with standard deviation 1.0 (again for a group of ten). This can be compared with the improvement of the training group via the two-sample $t$ test, giving

$$t = \frac{2.0 - 0.5}{\sqrt{\dfrac{1.13^2}{10} + \dfrac{1.13^2}{10}}} = 2.97$$

($1.13^2$ is the pooled variance). This confirms the finding that the training programme is of value.

**Exercise 5.11**

A group of students' marks on two tests, before and after instruction, were as follows:

| Student | 1 | 2 | 3 | 4 | 5 | 6 | 7 | 8 | 9 | 10 | 11 | 12 |
|---|---|---|---|---|---|---|---|---|---|---|---|---|
| Before | 14 | 16 | 11 | 8 | 20 | 19 | 6 | 11 | 13 | 16 | 9 | 13 |
| After | 15 | 18 | 15 | 11 | 19 | 18 | 9 | 12 | 16 | 16 | 12 | 13 |

Test the hypothesis that the instruction had no effect, using both the independent sample and paired sample methods. Compare the two results.

# Discussion of hypothesis testing

The above exposition has served to illustrate how to carry out a hypothesis test and the rationale behind it. However, the methodology has been subject to criticism and it is important to understand this since it gives a greater insight into the meaning of the results of a hypothesis test.

In the previous examples the problem has often been posed as a decision-making one, yet we noted that in many instances no decision is actually taken and therefore it is difficult to justify a particular significance level. Bayesian statisticians would argue that their methods do not suffer from this problem, since the result of their analysis (termed a posterior probability) gives the degree of belief which the researcher has in the truth of the null hypothesis. However, this posterior probability does in part depend upon the prior probability (i.e. before the statistical analysis) that the researcher attaches to the null hypothesis. As noted in Chapter 2, the derivation of the prior probabilities can be difficult.

In practice, most people do not regard the results of a hypothesis test as all-or-nothing proof, but interpret the result on the basis of the quality of the data, the care the researcher has taken in analysing the data, personal experience, and a multitude of other factors. Both schools of thought, classical and Bayesian, introduce subjectivity into the analysis and interpretation of data: classical statisticians in the choice of the significance level (and choice of one- or two-tail test), Bayesians in their choice of prior probabilities. It is not clear which method is superior, but classical methods have the advantage of being simpler.

Another criticism of hypothesis testing is that it is based on weak methodological foundations. The philosopher Karl Popper argued that theories should be rigorously tested against the evidence, and that strenuous efforts should be made to try to falsify the theory or hypothesis. This methodology is not strictly followed in hypothesis testing, where the researcher's favoured hypothesis is usually the alternative. A conclusion in favour of the alternative hypothesis is arrived at by default, because of the failure of the null hypothesis to survive the evidence.

Consider the researcher who believes that health standards have changed in the last decade. This may be tested by gathering data on health and testing the null hypothesis of no change in health standards against the alternative hypothesis of some change. The researcher's theory thus becomes the alternative hypothesis and is never actually tested against the data. No attempt is made to falsify the (alternative) hypothesis; it gets accepted by default if the null hypothesis falls. *Only* the null hypothesis ever gets tested.

A further problem is the asymmetry between the null and alternative hypotheses. The null hypothesis is that there is *exactly* no change in health standards whereas the alternative hypothesis contains all other possibilities, from a large deterioration to a large improvement. The dice seem loaded against the null hypothesis. Indeed, as noted earlier, if a large enough sample is taken the null hypothesis is almost certain to be rejected, because there is bound to have been *some* change, however small. The large sample size leads to a small standard error ($\sigma^2/n$) and thus a large z score. This suggests that the significance level of a test should decrease as the sample size increases.

These particular problems are avoided by the technique of estimation, which measures the size of the change and focuses attention upon that, rather than upon some accept/reject decision. As the sample size gets larger, the confidence interval narrows and an improved measure of the true change in health standards is obtained. Zero (i.e. no change in health standards) might be in the confidence interval or it might not; it is not the central issue. We might say that an estimate tells us what the value of a population parameter *is*, while a hypothesis test tells us what it is *not*. Thus the techniques of estimation and hypothesis testing put different emphasis upon interpretation of the results, even though they are formally identical.

## Summary

- Hypothesis testing is the set of procedures for deciding whether a hypothesis is true or false. When conducting the test we presume the hypothesis, termed the null hypothesis, is true until it is proved false on the basis of some sample evidence.

- If the null is proved false, it is rejected in favour of the alternative hypothesis. The procedure is conceptually similar to a court case, where the defendant is presumed innocent until the evidence proves otherwise.

- Not all decisions turn out to be correct and there are two types of error that can be made. A Type I error is to reject the null hypothesis when it is in fact true. A Type II error is not to reject the null when it is false.

- Choosing the appropriate decision rule (for rejecting the null hypothesis) is a question of trading off Type I and Type II errors. Because the alternative hypothesis is imprecisely specified, the probability of a Type II error usually cannot be specified.

- The rejection region for a test is therefore chosen to give a 5% probability of making a Type I error (sometimes a 1% probability is chosen). The critical value of the test statistic (sometimes referred to as the critical value of the test) is the value which separates the acceptance and rejection regions.

- The decision is based upon the value of a test statistic, which is calculated from the sample evidence and from information in the null hypothesis

$$\left( \text{e.g. } z = \frac{\bar{x} - \mu}{s/\sqrt{n}} \right)$$

- The null hypothesis is rejected if the test statistic falls into the rejection region for the test (i.e. it exceeds the critical value).

- For a two-tail test there are two rejection regions, corresponding to very high and very low values of the test statistic.

- Instead of comparing the test statistic to the critical value, an equivalent procedure is to compare the Prob-value of the test statistic with the significance level. The null is rejected if the Prob-value is less than the significance level.

- The power of a test is the probability of a test correctly rejecting the null hypothesis. Some tests have low power (e.g. when the sample size is small) and therefore are not very useful.

| Key terms and concepts | | |
|---|---|---|
| null or maintained hypothesis | alternative hypothesis | Type I and Type II errors |
| rejection region | significance level | critical value |
| one- and two-tail tests | Prob-value | effect size |
| power | independent samples | paired samples |

# Problems

Some of the more challenging problems are indicated by highlighting the problem number in colour.

**Problem 5.1**  Answer true or false, with reasons if necessary.

(a) There is no way of reducing the probability of a Type I error without simultaneously increasing the probability of a Type II error.

(b) The probability of a Type I error is associated with an area under the distribution of $\bar{x}$ assuming the null hypothesis to be true.

(c) It is always desirable to minimise the probability of a Type I error.

(d) A larger sample, *ceteris paribus*, will increase the power of a test.

(e) The significance level is the probability of a Type II error.

(f) The confidence level is the probability of a Type II error.

**Problem 5.2**  Consider the investor in the text, seeking out companies with weekly turnover of at least £5000. He applies a one-tail hypothesis test to each firm, using the 5% significance level. State whether each of the following statements is true or false (or not known) and explain why.

(a) 5% of his investments are in companies with less than £5000 turnover.

(b) 5% of the companies he *fails* to invest in have turnover greater than £5000 per week.

(c) He invests in 95% of all companies with turnover of £5000 or over.

**Problem 5.3**  A coin which is either fair or has two heads is to be tossed twice. You decide on the following decision rule: if two heads occur you will conclude it is a two-headed coin, otherwise you will presume it is fair. Write down the null and alternative hypotheses and calculate the probabilities of Type I and Type II errors.

**Problem 5.4**  In comparing two medical treatments for a disease, the null hypothesis is that the two treatments are equally effective. Why does making a Type I error not matter? What significance level for the test should be set as a result?

**Problem 5.5**  A firm receives components from a supplier, which it uses in its own production. The components are delivered in batches of 2000. The supplier claims that there are only 1% defective components on average from its production. However, production occasionally gets out of control and a batch is produced with 10% defective components. The firm wishes to intercept these low-quality batches, so a sample of size 50 is taken from each batch and tested. If two or more defectives are found in the sample then the batch is rejected.

(a) Describe the two types of error the firm might make in assessing batches of components.

(b) Calculate the probability of each type of error given the data above.

(c) If instead, samples of size 30 were taken and the batch rejected if one or more rejects were found, how would the error probabilities be altered?

(d) The firm can alter the two error probabilities by choice of sample size and rejection criteria. How should it set the relative sizes of the error probabilities

      (i)    if the product might affect consumer safety?

      (ii)   if there are many competitive suppliers of components?

      (iii)  if the costs of replacement under guarantee are high?

**Problem 5.6**  Computer diskettes which do not meet the quality required for high-density (1.44 Mb) diskettes are sold as double-density diskettes (720 kb) for 80 pence each. High-density diskettes are sold for £1.20 each. A firm samples 30 diskettes from each batch of 1000 and if any fail the quality test the whole batch is sold as double-density diskettes. What are the types of error possible and what is the cost to the firm of a Type I error?

**Problem 5.7**  Testing the null hypothesis that $\mu = 10$ against $\mu > 10$, a researcher obtains a sample mean of 12 with standard deviation 6 from a sample of 30 observations. Calculate the $z$ score and the associated Prob-value for this test.

**Problem 5.8**  Given the sample data $\bar{x} = 45$, $s = 16$, $n = 50$, at what level of confidence can you reject $H_0$: $\mu = 40$ against a two-sided alternative?

**Problem 5.9**  What is the power of the test carried out in Problem 3?

**Problem 5.10**  Given the two hypotheses

$H_0$: $\mu = 400$
$H_1$: $\mu = 415$
and $\sigma^2 = 1000$ (for both hypotheses):

(a)   Draw the distribution of $\bar{x}$ under both hypotheses.

(b)   If the decision rule is chosen to be: reject $H_0$ if $\bar{x} \geq 410$ from a sample of size 40, find the probability of a Type II error and the power of the test.

(c)   What happens to these answers as the sample size is increased? Draw a diagram to illustrate.

**Problem 5.11**  Given the following sample data:

$\bar{x} = 15$    $s^2 = 270$    $n = 30$

test the null hypothesis that the true mean is equal to 12, against a two-sided alternative hypothesis. Draw the distribution of $\bar{x}$ under the null hypothesis and indicate the rejection regions for this test.

**Problem 5.12**  From experience it is known that a certain brand of tyre lasts, on average, 15 000 miles with standard deviation 1250. A new compound is tried and a sample of 120 tyres yields an average life of 15 150 miles. Are the new tyres an improvement? Use the 5% significance level.

**Problem 5.13**  Test $H_0$: $\pi = 0.5$ against $H_0$: $\pi \neq 0.5$ using $p = 0.45$ from a sample of size $n = 35$.

**Problem 5.14**  Test the hypothesis that 10% of your class or lecture group are left-handed.

**Problem 5.15** Given the following data from two independent samples:

$$\bar{x}_1 = 115 \quad \bar{x}_2 = 105$$
$$s_1 = 21 \quad s_2 = 23$$
$$n_1 = 49 \quad n_2 = 63$$

test the hypothesis of no difference between the population means against the alternative that the mean of population 1 is greater than the mean of population 2.

**Problem 5.16** A transport company wants to compare the fuel efficiencies of the two types of lorry it operates. It obtains data from samples of the two types of lorry, with the following results:

| Type | Average mpg | Std devn | Sample size |
|------|-------------|----------|-------------|
| A | 31.0 | 7.6 | 33 |
| B | 32.2 | 5.8 | 40 |

Test the hypothesis that there is no difference in fuel efficiency, using the 99% confidence level.

**Problem 5.17** A random sample of 180 men who took the driving test found that 103 passed. A similar sample of 225 women found that 105 passed. Test whether pass rates are the same for men and women.

**Problem 5.18** (a) A pharmaceutical company testing a new type of pain reliever administered the drug to 30 volunteers experiencing pain. Sixteen of them said that it eased their pain. Does this evidence support the claim that the drug is effective in combating pain?

(b) A second group of 40 volunteers were given a placebo instead of the drug. Thirteen of them reported a reduction in pain. Does this new evidence cast doubt upon your previous conclusion?

**Problem 5.19** (a) A random sample of 20 observations yielded a mean of 40 and standard deviation 10. Test the hypothesis that $\mu = 45$ against the alternative that it is not. Use the 5% significance level.

(b) What assumption are you implicitly making in carrying out this test?

**Problem 5.20** A photo processing company sets a quality standard of no more than 10 complaints per week on average. A random sample of 8 weeks showed an average of 13.6 complaints, with standard deviation 5.3. Is the firm achieving its quality objective?

**Problem 5.21** Two samples are drawn. The first has a mean of 150, variance 50 and sample size 12. The second has mean 130, variance 30 and sample size 15. Test the hypothesis that they are drawn from populations with the same mean.

**Problem 5.22** (a) A consumer organisation is testing two different brands of battery. A sample of 15 of brand A shows an average useful life of 410 hours with a standard deviation of 20 hours. For brand B, a sample of 20 gave an average useful life of 391 hours with standard deviation 26 hours. Test whether there is any significant difference in battery life.

(b) What assumptions are being made about the populations in carrying out this test?

**Problem 5.23**  The output of a group of 11 workers before and after an improvement in the lighting in their factory is as follows:

| Before | 52 | 60 | 58 | 58 | 53 | 51 | 52 | 59 | 60 | 53 | 55 |
|--------|----|----|----|----|----|----|----|----|----|----|----|
| After  | 56 | 62 | 63 | 50 | 55 | 56 | 55 | 59 | 61 | 58 | 56 |

Test whether there is a significant improvement in performance

(a)  assuming these are independent samples,

(b)  assuming they are dependent.

**Problem 5.24**  Another group of workers were tested at the same times as those in Problem 5.23, although their department *also* introduced rest breaks into the working day.

| Before | 51 | 59 | 51 | 53 | 58 | 58 | 52 | 55 | 61 | 54 | 55 |
|--------|----|----|----|----|----|----|----|----|----|----|----|
| After  | 54 | 63 | 55 | 57 | 63 | 63 | 58 | 60 | 66 | 57 | 59 |

Does the introduction of rest days alone appear to improve performance?

**Problem 5.25**  Discuss in general terms how you might 'test' the following:

(a)  astrology,

(b)  extra-sensory perception,

(c)  the proposition that company takeovers increase profits.

**Problem 5.26 (Project)**  Can your class tell the difference between tap water and bottled water? Set up an experiment as follows: fill $r$ glasses with tap water and $n - r$ glasses with bottled water. The subject has to guess which is which. If she gets more than $p$ correct, you conclude she can tell the difference. Write up a report of the experiment including:

(a)  a description of the experimental procedure,

(b)  your choice of $n$, $r$ and $p$, with reasons,

(c)  the power of your test,

(d)  your conclusions.

**Problem 5.27 (Computer project)**  Use the $= RAND( )$ function in your spreadsheet to create 100 samples of size 25 (which are effectively all from the same population). Compute the mean and standard deviation of each sample. Calculate the $z$ score for each sample, using a hypothesised mean of 0.5 (since the $= RAND( )$ function chooses a random number in the range 0 to 1).

(a)  How many of the $z$ scores would you expect to exceed 1.96 in absolute value? Explain why.

(b)  How many do exceed this? Is this in line with your prediction?

(c)  Graph the sample means and comment upon the shape of the distribution. Shade in the area of the graph beyond $z = \pm1.96$.

**Reference**  McCloskey, D. and S. Ziliak (2004) Size Matters: the Standard Error of Regressions in the *American Economic Review*, *Journal of Socio-Economics*, 33, 527–546.

## Answers to exercises

Exercise 5.1  (a) $H_0$: crime is the same as last year, $H_1$: crime has increased.

(b) Type I error – concluding crime has risen, when in fact it has not. Type II – concluding it has not risen, when, in fact, it has. The cost of the former might be employing more police officers which are not in fact warranted; of the latter, not employing more police to counter the rising crime level. (The *Economist* magazine (19 July 2003) reported that 33% of respondents to a survey in the UK felt that crime had risen in the previous two years, only 4% thought that it had fallen. In fact, crime had fallen slightly, by about 2%. A lot of people were making a Type I error, therefore.)

Exercise 5.2  (a) $z = (108 - 100)/\sqrt{36} = 1.33$. The area in the tail beyond 1.33 is 9.18%, which is the probability of a Type I error.

(b) $z = 1.64$ cuts off 5% in the upper tail of the distribution, hence we need the decision rule to be at $\bar{x} + 1.64 \times s/\sqrt{n} = 100 + 1.64 \times \sqrt{36} = 109.84$.

(c) Under $H_1$: $\mu = 112$, we can write $\bar{x} \sim N(112, 900/25)$. (We assume the same variance under both $H_0$ and $H_1$ in this case.) Hence $z = (108 - 112)/\sqrt{36} = -0.67$. This gives an area in the tail of 25.14%, which is the Type II error probability. Usually, however, we do not have a precise statement of the value of $\mu$ under $H_1$ so cannot do this kind of calculation.

Exercise 5.3  $\alpha = 0.05$ (significance level chosen), hence the critical value is $z^* = 1.96$. The test statistic is $z = (530 - 500)/(90/\sqrt{30}) = 1.83 < 1.96$ so $H_0$ is not rejected at the 5% significance level.

Exercise 5.4  One wants to avoid making a Type I error if possible, i.e. rejecting $H_0$ when true. Hence set a low significance level (1%) so that $H_0$ is only rejected by very strong evidence.

Exercise 5.5  (a) (i) Reject. The Prob-value should be halved, to 0.0385, which is less than 5%. Alternatively, 1.77 > 1.64. (ii) Do not reject, the Prob-value is greater than 5%; equivalently 1.77 < 1.96.

(b) In this case, the null is not rejected in both cases. In the one-tailed case, 0.0385 > 1%, so the null is not rejected.

Exercise 5.6  $z = \dfrac{0.65 - 0.5}{\sqrt{\dfrac{0.5 \times 0.5}{80}}} = 2.68$  hence the null is decisively rejected.

Exercise 5.7  We have the data: $\bar{x}_1 = 3.6$, $s_1 = 1.2$, $n_1 = 50$; $\bar{x}_2 = 3.9$, $s_2 = 2.1$, $n_2 = 90$. The null hypothesis is $H_0$: $\mu_1 = \mu_2$ versus $H_1$: $\mu_1 \neq \mu_2$. The test statistic is

$$z = \frac{(\bar{x}_1 - \bar{x}_2) - (\mu_1 - \mu_2)}{\sqrt{\dfrac{s_1^2}{n_1} + \dfrac{s_2^2}{n_2}}} = \frac{(3.6 - 3.9) - 0}{\sqrt{\dfrac{1.2^2}{50} + \dfrac{2.1^2}{90}}} = -1.08 < 1.96$$

(absolute value) so the null is not rejected at the 5% significance level.

**Exercise 5.8** The evidence is $p_1 = 23/75$, $n_1 = 75$, $p_2 = 34/95$, $n_2 = 95$. The hypothesis to be tested is $H_0: \pi_1 - \pi_2 = 0$ vs $H_1: \pi_1 - \pi_2 < 0$. Before calculating the test statistic we must calculate the pooled variance as

$$\hat{\pi} = \frac{n_1 p_1 + n_2 p_2}{n_1 + n_2} = \hat{\pi} = \frac{75 \times 0.3067 + 95 \times 0.3579}{75 + 95} = 0.3353$$

The test statistic is then

$$z = \frac{0.3067 - 0.3579 - 0}{\sqrt{\dfrac{0.3353 \times (1 - 0.3353)}{75} + \dfrac{0.3353 \times (1 - 0.3353)}{95}}} = -0.70$$

This is less in absolute magnitude than 1.64, the critical value of a one tailed test, so the null is not rejected. The second gambler is just luckier than the first, we conclude. We have to be careful about our interpretation however: one of the gamblers might prefer longer-odds bets, so wins less often but gets more money each time. Hence this may not be a fair comparison.

---

**Exercise 5.9** We shall treat this as a two-tailed test, though a one-tailed test might be justified if there were other evidence that spending had fallen. The hypothesis is $H_0: \mu = 540$ vs $H_1: \mu \neq 540$. Given the sample evidence, the test statistic is

$$t = \frac{\bar{x} - \mu}{\sqrt{s^2/n}} = \frac{490 - 540}{\sqrt{150^2/24}} = -1.63$$

The critical value of the $t$ distribution for 23 degrees of freedom is 2.069, so the null is not rejected.

---

**Exercise 5.10** The hypothesis to test is $H_0: \mu_F - \mu_N = 0$ vs $H_1: \mu_F - \mu_N > 0$ ($F$ indexes finalists, $N$ the new students). The pooled variance is calculated as

$$S^2 = \frac{(n_1 - 1)s_1^2 + (n_2 - 1)s_2^2}{n_1 + n_2 - 2} = \frac{15 \times 3^2 + 20 \times 5^2}{35} = 18.14$$

The test statistic is

$$t = \frac{\bar{x}_1 - \bar{x}_2 - (\mu_1 - \mu_2)}{\sqrt{\dfrac{S^2}{n_1} + \dfrac{S^2}{n_2}}} = \frac{15 - 9 - 0}{\sqrt{\dfrac{18.14}{15} + \dfrac{18.14}{20}}} = 4.12$$

The critical value of the $t$ distribution with $15 + 20 - 2 = 33$ degrees of freedom is approximately 1.69 (5% significance level, for a one-tailed test). Thus the null is decisively rejected and we conclude finalists do spend more time in the library.

---

**Exercise 5.11** By the method of independent samples we obtain $\bar{x}_1 = 13$, $\bar{x}_2 = 14.5$, $s_1 = 4.29$, $s_2 = 3.12$, with $n = 12$ in both cases. The test statistic is therefore

$$t = \frac{\bar{x}_1 - \bar{x}_2 - (\mu_1 - \mu_2)}{\sqrt{\dfrac{S^2}{n_1} + \dfrac{S^2}{n_2}}} = \frac{13 - 14.5 - 0}{\sqrt{\dfrac{14.05}{12} + \dfrac{14.05}{12}}} = -0.98$$

with pooled variance

$$S^2 = \frac{(n_1 - 1)s_1^2 + (n_2 - 1)s_2^2}{n_1 + n_2 - 2} = \frac{11 \times 4.29^2 + 11 \times 3.12^2}{22} = 14.05$$

The null of no effect is therefore accepted. By the method of paired samples, we have a set of improvements as follows:

| Student | 1 | 2 | 3 | 4 | 5 | 6 | 7 | 8 | 9 | 10 | 11 | 12 |
|---|---|---|---|---|---|---|---|---|---|---|---|---|
| Improvement | 1 | 2 | 4 | 3 | −1 | −1 | 3 | 1 | 3 | 0 | 3 | 0 |

The mean of these is 1.5 and the variance is 3. The $t$ statistic is therefore

$$t = \frac{1.5 - 0}{\sqrt{3/12}} = 3$$

This now conclusively rejects the null hypothesis (critical value 1.8), in stark contrast to the former method. The difference arises because 10 out of 12 students have improved or done as well as before, only two have fallen back (slightly). The gain in marks is modest but applies consistently to nearly all candidates.

# 6

# The $\chi^2$ and $F$ distributions

**Learning outcomes**

By the end of this chapter you should be able to:

- understand the uses of two new probability distributions: $\chi^2$ and $F$
- construct confidence interval estimates for a variance
- perform hypothesis tests concerning variances
- analyse and draw inferences from data contained in contingency tables
- construct a simple analysis of variance table and interpret the results

## Introduction

The final two distributions to be studied are the $\chi^2$ (pronounced 'kye-squared') and $F$ distributions. Both of these distributions have a variety of uses, the most common of which are illustrated in this chapter. These distributions allow us to extend some of the estimation and testing procedures covered in Chapters 4 and 5. The $\chi^2$ distribution allows us to establish confidence interval estimates for a variance, just as the Normal and $t$ distributions were used in the case of a mean. Further, just as the Binomial distribution was used to examine situations where the result of an experiment could be either 'success' or 'failure', the $\chi^2$ distribution allows us to analyse situations where there are more than two categories of outcome. The $F$ distribution enables us to conduct hypotheses tests regarding the equality of two variances and also to make comparisons between the means of multiple samples, not just two. The $F$ distribution is also used in Chapters 7 and 8 on regression analysis.

# The $\chi^2$ distribution

The $\chi^2$ distribution has a number of uses. In this chapter we make use of it in three ways:

■ To calculate a confidence interval estimate of the population variance.
■ To compare actual observations on a variable with the (theoretically) expected values.
■ To test for association between two variables in a contingency table.

The use of the distribution is in many ways similar to the Normal and $t$ distributions already encountered. Once again, it is actually a family of distributions depending upon one parameter, the degrees of freedom, similar to the $t$ distribution. The number of degrees of freedom can have slightly different interpretations, depending upon the particular problem, but is often related to sample size. Some typical $\chi^2$ distributions are drawn in Figure 6.1 for different values of the parameter. Note the distribution has the following characteristics:

■ It is always non-negative.
■ It is skewed to the right.
■ It becomes more symmetric as the number of degrees of freedom increases.

Confidence intervals are constructed in the usual way, by using the critical values of the distribution (given in Table A4 (see page **368**)) which cut off an area $\alpha/2$ in each tail of the distribution. For hypothesis tests, a rejection region is defined which cuts off an area $\alpha$ in either one or both tails of the distribution, whichever is appropriate. These principles should be familiar from previous chapters, so are not repeated in detail. The following examples show how this works for the $\chi^2$ distribution.

**Figure 6.1**
**The $\chi^2$ distribution with different degrees of freedom**

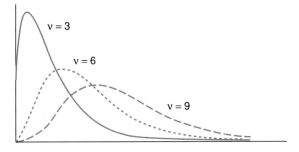

**Estimating a variance**

The sample variance is also a random variable like the mean; it takes on different values from sample to sample. We can therefore ask the usual question: given a sample variance, what can we infer about the true value?

To give an example, we use the data on spending by Labour boroughs in the example in Chapter 4 (see page **151**). In that sample of 20 boroughs, the average spending on administration was £175 (per taxpayer), with standard deviation 25 (and hence variance of 625). What can we say about the true variance and standard deviation?

We work in terms of variances (this is more convenient when using the $\chi^2$ distribution), taking the square root when we need to refer to the standard deviation. First of all, the sample variance is an unbiased estimator of the population variance,[1] $E(s^2) = \sigma^2$, so we may use this as our point estimate, which is therefore 625. To construct the confidence interval around this we need to know about the distribution of $s^2$. Unfortunately, this does not have a convenient probability distribution, so we transform it to

(6.1) $$\frac{(n-1)s^2}{\sigma^2}$$

which does have a $\chi^2$ distribution, with $v = n - 1$ degrees of freedom.

To construct the 95% confidence interval around the point estimate we proceed in a similar fashion to the Normal or $t$ distribution. First, we find the critical values of the $\chi^2$ distribution which cut off 2.5% in each tail. These are no longer symmetric around zero as was the case with the standard Normal and $t$ distributions. Table 6.1 shows an excerpt from the $\chi^2$ table which is given in full in Table A4 in the Appendix at the end of the book (see page **368**).

Like the $t$ distribution, the first column gives the degrees of freedom, so we require the row corresponding to $v = n - 1 = 19$.

- For the *left-hand* critical value (cutting off 2.5% in the left-hand tail) we look at the column headed '0.975', representing 97.5% in the right-hand tail. This critical value is 8.91.
- For the *right-hand* critical value we look up the column headed '0.025' (2.5% in the right-hand tail), giving 32.85.

**Table 6.1 Excerpt from Table A4 – the $\chi^2$ distribution**

| $v$ | 0.99 | 0.975 | . . . | 0.10 | 0.05 | 0.025 | 0.01 |
|---|---|---|---|---|---|---|---|
| 1 | 0.0002 | 0.0010 | . . . | 2.7055 | 3.8415 | 5.0239 | 6.6349 |
| 2 | 0.0201 | 0.0506 | . . . | 4.6052 | 5.9915 | 7.3778 | 9.2104 |
| ⋮ | ⋮ | ⋮ | . . . | | ⋮ | ⋮ | ⋮ |
| 18 | 7.0149 | 8.2307 | . . . | 25.9894 | 28.8693 | 31.5264 | 34.8052 |
| 19 | 7.6327 | 8.9065 | . . . | 27.2036 | 30.1435 | 32.8523 | 36.1908 |
| 20 | 8.2604 | 9.5908 | . . . | 28.4120 | 31.4104 | 34.1696 | 37.5663 |

*Note*: The two critical values are found at the intersections of the shaded row and columns. Alternatively you can use *Excel*. The formula =*CHIINV* (0.975, 19) gives the left-hand critical value, 8.91; similarly, =*CHIINV* (0.025, 19) gives the answer 32.85, the right-hand critical value.

---

[1] This was stated, without proof, in Chapter 1, see page **35**.

We can therefore be 95% confident that $(n - 1)s^2/\sigma^2$ lies between these two values, i.e.

(6.2)   $$\left[ 8.91 \leq \frac{(n - 1)s^2}{\sigma^2} \leq 32.85 \right]$$

We actually want an interval estimate for $\sigma^2$ so we need to rearrange equation (6.2) so that $\sigma^2$ lies between the two inequality signs. Rearranging yields

(6.3)   $$\left[ \frac{(n - 1)s^2}{32.85} \leq \sigma^2 \leq \frac{(n - 1)s^2}{8.91} \right]$$

and evaluating this expression leads to the 95% confidence interval for $\sigma^2$ which is

$$\left[ \frac{19 \times 625}{32.85} \leq \sigma^2 \leq \frac{19 \times 625}{8.91} \right] = [361.5, 1332.8]$$

Note that the point estimate, 625, is no longer at the centre of the interval but is closer to the lower limit. This is a consequence of the skewness of the $\chi^2$ distribution.

---

**Worked example 6.1**

Given a sample of size $n = 51$ yielding a sample variance $s^2 = 81$, we may calculate the 95% confidence interval for the population variance as follows.

Since we are using the 95% confidence level the critical values cutting off the extreme 5% of the distribution are 32.36 and 71.42, from Table A4 (see page **368**). We can therefore use equation (6.3) to find the interval:

$$\left[ \frac{(n - 1) \times s^2}{71.42} \leq \sigma^2 \frac{(n - 1) \times s^2}{32.36} \right]$$

Substituting in the values gives

$$\left[ \frac{(51 - 1) \times 81}{71.42} \leq \sigma^2 \frac{(51 - 1) \times 81}{32.36} \right]$$

yielding a confidence interval of [56.71, 125.15].

Note that if we wished to find a 95% confidence interval for the standard deviation we can simply take the square root of the result to obtain [7.53, 11.19].

The 99% CI for the variance can be obtained by altering the critical values. The values cutting off 0.5% in each tail of the distribution are (again from Table A4) 27.99 and 79.49. Using these critical values results in an interval [50.95, 144.69]. Note that, as expected, the 99% CI is wider than the 95% interval.

---

**Exercise 6.1**

(a) Given a sample variance of 65 from a sample of size $n = 30$, calculate the 95% confidence interval for the variance of the population from which the sample was drawn.

(b) Calculate the 95% CI for the standard deviation.

(c) Calculate the 99% interval estimate of the variance.

Table 6.2 Calculation of the $\chi^2$ statistic for the die problem

| Score | Observed frequency (O) | Expected frequency (E) | O − E | (O − E)² | $\dfrac{(O - E)^2}{E}$ |
|---|---|---|---|---|---|
| 1 | 6 | 12 | −6 | 36 | 3.00 |
| 2 | 15 | 12 | 3 | 9 | 0.75 |
| 3 | 15 | 12 | 3 | 9 | 0.75 |
| 4 | 7 | 12 | −5 | 25 | 2.08 |
| 5 | 15 | 12 | 3 | 9 | 0.75 |
| 6 | 14 | 12 | 2 | 4 | 0.33 |
| Totals | 72 | 72 | 0 | | 7.66 |

**Comparing actual and expected values of a variable**

A second use of the $\chi^2$ distribution provides a hypothesis test, allowing us to compare a set of observed values to expected values, the latter calculated on the basis of some null hypothesis to be tested. If the observed and expected values differ significantly, as judged by the $\chi^2$ test (the test statistic falls into the rejection region of the $\chi^2$ distribution), then the null hypothesis is rejected. Again, this is similar in principle to hypothesis testing using the Normal or $t$ distributions, but allows a slightly different type of problem to be handled.

This can be illustrated with a very simple example. Suppose that throwing a die 72 times yields the following data:

| Score on die | 1 | 2 | 3 | 4 | 5 | 6 |
|---|---|---|---|---|---|---|
| Frequency | 6 | 15 | 15 | 7 | 15 | 14 |

Are these data consistent with the die being unbiased? A crude examination of the data suggests a slight bias against 1 and 4, but is this truly bias or just a random fluctuation quite common in this type of experiment? First the null and alternative hypotheses are set up:

$H_0$: the die is unbiased
$H_1$: the die is biased

Note that the null hypothesis should be constructed in such a way as to permit the calculation of the expected outcomes of the experiment. Thus the null and alternative hypotheses could not be reversed in this case, since 'the die is biased' is a vague statement (exactly how biased, for example?) and would not permit the calculation of the expected outcomes of the experiment.

On the basis of the null hypothesis, the expected values are based on the uniform distribution, i.e. each number should come up an equal number of times. The expected values are therefore 12 (= 72/6) for each number on the die.

This gives the data shown in Table 6.2 with observed and expected frequencies in columns two and three respectively (ignore columns 4–6 for the moment). The $\chi^2$ test statistic is now constructed using the formula

(6.4) $\qquad \chi^2 = \sum \dfrac{(O - E)^2}{E}$

which has a $\chi^2$ distribution with $v = k - 1$ degrees of freedom ($k$ is the number of different outcomes, here 6).[2] $O$ represents the observed frequencies and $E$ the

[2] Note that, on this occasion, the degrees of freedom are not based on the sample size.

expected. If the value of this test statistic falls into the rejection region, i.e. the tail of the $\chi^2$ distribution, then we conclude the die is biased, rejecting the null. The calculation of the test statistic is shown in columns 4–6 of Table 6.2, and is straightforward, yielding a value of the test statistic of $\chi^2 = 7.66$, to be compared to the critical value of the distribution, for $6 - 1 = 5$ degrees of freedom.

> **Trap!**
>
> In my experience many students misinterpret formula (6.4) and use
>
> $$\chi^2 = \frac{\Sigma(O - E)^2}{\Sigma E}$$
>
> instead. This is not the same as the correct formula and gives the wrong answer! Check that you recognise the difference between the two and that you always use the correct version.

Looking up the critical value for this test takes a little care as one needs first to consider if it is a one- or two-tailed test. Looking at the alternative hypothesis *suggests* a two-sided test, since the error could be in either direction. However, this intuition is wrong, for the following reason. Looking closely at equation (6.4) reveals that large discrepancies between observed and expected values (however occurring) can *only* lead to large values of the test statistic. Conversely, small values of the test statistic must mean that differences between $O$ and $E$ are small, so the die must be unbiased. Thus the null is only rejected by large values of the $\chi^2$ statistic or, in other words, the rejection region is in the right-hand tail only of the $\chi^2$ distribution. It is a one-tailed test. This is illustrated in Figure 6.2.

The critical value of the $\chi^2$ distribution in this case ($v = 5$, 5% significance level) is 11.1, found from Table A4 (see page **368**). Note that we require 5% of the distribution in the right-hand tail to establish the rejection region. Since the test statistic is less than the critical value ($7.66 < 11.1$) the null hypothesis is not rejected. The differences between scores are due to sampling error rather than to bias in the die.

An important point to note is that the value of the test statistic is sensitive to the total frequency (72 in this case). Therefore the test should not be carried out on the *proportion* of occasions on which each number comes up (the

**Figure 6.2**
**The rejection region for the $\chi^2$ test**

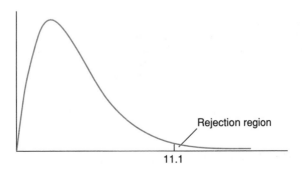

Rejection region

11.1

expected values would all be $12/72 = 0.167$, and the observed values $8/72$, $13/72$, etc.), since information about the 'sample size' (number of rolls of the die) would be lost. As with all sampling experiments, the inferences that can be drawn depend upon the sample size, with larger sample sizes giving more reliable results, so care must be taken to retain information about sample size in the calculations. If the test had been incorrectly conducted in terms of proportions, all $O$ and $E$ values would have been divided by 72, and this would have reduced the test statistic by a factor of 72 (check the formula to confirm this), reducing it to 0.14, nowhere near significance. It would be surprising if any data would yield significance given this degree of mistreatment!

A second, more realistic, example will now be examined to reinforce the message about the use of the $\chi^2$ distribution and to show how the expected values might be generated in different ways. This example looks at road accident figures to see if there is any variation through the year. One might reasonably expect more accidents in the winter months due to weather conditions, poorer light, etc. Quarterly data on the number of people killed on British roads are used, and the null hypothesis is that the number does not vary seasonally.

$H_0$: there is no difference in fatal accidents between quarters
$H_1$: there is some difference in fatal accidents between quarters

Such a study might be carried out by government, for example, to try to find the best means of reducing road accidents.

Table 6.3 shows data on road fatalities in 2002 by quarter in Great Britain, adapted from data taken from the UK government's *StatBase* website. There does appear some evidence of more accidents in the final two quarters of the year but is this convincing evidence or just random variation? Under the null hypothesis the total number of deaths (3431) would be evenly split between the four quarters, yielding Table 6.4 and the $\chi^2$ calculation that follows.

The calculated value of the test statistic is 31.24, given at the foot of the final column. The number of degrees of freedom is $v = k - 1 = 3$, so the critical value at the 5% significance level is 7.82. Since the test statistic exceeds this the null hypothesis is rejected; there is a difference between seasons in the accident rate.

The reason for this difference might be the increased hours of darkness during winter months, leading to more accidents. This particular hypothesis can

**Table 6.3 Road casualties in Great Britain, 2002**

| Quarter | I | II | III | IV | Total |
|---|---|---|---|---|---|
| Casualties | 770 | 784 | 921 | 956 | 3431 |

**Table 6.4 Calculation of the $\chi^2$ statistic for road deaths**

| Quarter | Observed deaths | Expected deaths | $O - E$ | $(O - E)^2$ | $\dfrac{(O - E)^2}{E}$ |
|---|---|---|---|---|---|
| I | 770 | 857.75 | −87.75 | 7700.063 | 8.98 |
| II | 784 | 857.75 | −73.75 | 5439.063 | 6.34 |
| III | 921 | 857.75 | 63.25 | 4000.563 | 4.66 |
| IV | 956 | 857.75 | 98.25 | 9653.063 | 11.25 |
| Totals | 3431 | 3431 | | | 31.24 |

**Table 6.5 Seasonal variation in road deaths**

| Season | Observed deaths | Expected deaths | $O - E$ | $(O - E)^2$ | $\dfrac{(O - E)^2}{E}$ |
|---|---|---|---|---|---|
| Summer | 1705 | 1715.5 | −10.5 | 110.25 | 0.064 |
| Winter | 1726 | 1715.5 | 10.5 | 110.25 | 0.064 |
| Totals | 3431 | 3431 | 0 | | 0.129 |

be tested using the same data, but combining quarters I and IV (to represent winter) and quarters II and III (summer). The null hypothesis is of no difference between summer and winter, and the calculation is set out in Table 6.5. The $\chi^2$ test statistic is much reduced, and now falls below the new critical value ($v = 1$, 5% significance level) of 3.84, so the null hypothesis is not rejected. Thus the variation between quarters does not appear to be a straightforward summer/winter effect (providing, of course, that combining quarters I and IV to represent winter and II and III to represent summer is a valid way of combining the quarters).[3]

Another point which the example brings out is that the data can be examined in a number of ways using the $\chi^2$ technique. Some of the classes were combined to test a slightly different hypothesis from the original one. This is a quite acceptable technique but should be used with caution. In any set of data (even totally random data) there is bound to be *some* way of dividing it up such that there are significant differences between the divisions. The point, however, is whether there is any meaning to the division. In the above example the amalgamation of the quarters into summer and winter has some intuitive meaning and we have good reason to believe that there might be differences between them. Driving during the hours of darkness might be more dangerous and might have had some relevance to accident prevention policy (e.g. an advertising campaign to persuade people to check that their lights work correctly). The hypothesis is led by some prior theorising and is worth testing.

### Road accidents and darkness

The question of the effect of darkness on road accidents has been extensively studied, particularly in relation to putting the clocks forward and back in spring and autumn. A study by H. Green in 1980 reported the following numbers of accidents (involving death or serious injury) on the five weekday evenings before and after the clocks changed:

| Year | Spring | | Autumn | |
|---|---|---|---|---|
| | Before | After | Before | After |
| 1975 | 19 | 11 | 20 | 31 |
| 1976 | 14 | 9 | 23 | 36 |
| 1977 | 22 | 8 | 12 | 29 |

[3] The previous edition of this book, using data from 1993, *did* find a significant difference between summer and winter, so either things have changed or there are still some puzzles to resolve.

It is noticeable that accidents fell in spring after the hour change (when it becomes lighter) but increased in autumn (when it becomes darker). This is a better test than simply combining quarterly figures as in our example, so casts doubt upon our result. Evidence from other countries also supports the view that the light level has an important influence on accidents.

*Source*: H. Green, Some effects on accidents of changes in light conditions at the beginning and end of British Summer Time, *Supplementary Report 587*, Transport and Road Research Laboratory, 1980. For an update on research, see J. Boughton *et al.*, Influence of light level on the incidence of road casualties, *J. Royal Statistical Society*, Series A, 162 (2), 1999.

It is dangerous, however, to look at the data and then formulate a hypothesis. From Table 6.4 there appears to be a large difference between the first and second halves of the year. If quarters I and II were combined, and III and IV combined, the $\chi^2$ test statistic might be significant (in fact it is, $\chi^2 = 30.4$) but does this signify anything? It is extremely easy to look for a big difference *somewhere* in any set of data and then pronounce it 'significant' according to some test. The probability of making a Type I error (rejecting a correct null) is much greater than 5% in such a case. The point, as usual, is that it is no good looking at data in a vacuum and simply hoping that they will 'tell you something'.

A related warning is that we should be wary of testing one hypothesis and, on the basis of that result, formulating another hypothesis and testing it (as we have done by going on to compare summer and winter). Once again we are (indirectly) using the data to help formulate the hypothesis and the true significance level of the test is likely to be different from 5% (even though we use the 5% critical value). We have therefore sinned, but is difficult to do research without sometimes resorting to this kind of behaviour. There are formal methods for dealing with such situations but they are beyond the scope of this book.

There is one further point to make about carrying out a $\chi^2$ test, and this involves circumstances where classes *must* be combined. The theoretical $\chi^2$ distribution from which the critical value is obtained is a continuous distribution, yet the calculation of the test statistic comes from data which are divided up into a discrete number of classes. The calculated test statistic is therefore only an approximation to a true $\chi^2$ variable, but this approximation is good enough as long as each expected (not observed) value is greater than or equal to five. It does not matter what the observed values are. In other circumstances, the class (or classes) with expected values less than five must be combined with other classes until all expected values are at least five. An example of this will be given below.

In all cases of $\chi^2$ testing the most important part of the analysis is the calculation of the expected values (the rest of the analysis is mechanical). Therefore it is always worth devoting most of the time to this part of the problem. The expected values are, of course, calculated on the basis of the null hypothesis being true, so different null hypotheses will give different expected values. Consider again the case of road fatalities. Although the null hypothesis ('no differences in fatal accidents between quarters') seems clear enough, it could mean different things. Here it was taken to mean an equal number of deaths in each quarter; but another interpretation is an equal number of deaths per

**Table 6.6 Index of road traffic, 1998–2002**

|        | Q1 | Q2 | Q3 | Q4 | Total |
|--------|----|----|----|----|-------|
| Index  | 93 | 101 | 105 | 100 | 399 |

**Table 6.7**

| Quarter | Observed deaths | Expected deaths | $O - E$ | $(O - E)^2$ | $\dfrac{(O - E)^2}{E}$ |
|---------|-----------------|-----------------|---------|-------------|------------------------|
| I       | 770  | 799.7 | −29.7 | 882.49  | 1.1  |
| II      | 784  | 868.5 | −84.5 | 7140.04 | 8.2  |
| III     | 921  | 902.9 | 18.1  | 327.80  | 0.4  |
| IV      | 956  | 859.9 | 96.1  | 9235.26 | 10.7 |
| Totals  | 3431 | 3431  |       |         | 20.4 |

*Note*: The first expected value is calculated as $3431 \times 93 \div 399 = 799.7$, the second as $3431 \times 101 \div 399 = 868.5$ and so on.

car-kilometre travelled in each quarter; in other words accidents might be higher in a given quarter simply because there are more journeys in that quarter (during holiday periods, for example). Table 6.6 gives an index of average daily traffic flows on British roads in each quarter of the year.

The pattern of fatalities might follow the pattern of road usage – the first quarter of the year has the fewest fatalities and also the least travel. This may be tested by basing the expected values on the average traffic flow: the 3431 total casualties are allocated to the four quarters in the ratios 93:101:105:100. This is shown in Table 6.7, along with the calculation of the $\chi^2$ statistic.

The $\chi^2$ test statistic is 20.4, well in excess of the critical value, 7.82. This indicates that there are significant differences between the quarters, even after accounting for different amounts of traffic. In fact, the statistic is little changed from before, suggesting either that traffic flows do not affect accident probabilities or that the flows do not actually vary very much. It is evident that the variation in traffic flows is much less than the variation in casualties.

| **Worked example 6.2** | One hundred volunteers each toss a coin twice and note the numbers of heads. The results of the experiment are as follows: |
|---|---|

| Heads     | 0  | 1  | 2  | Total |
|-----------|----|----|----|-------|
| Frequency | 15 | 55 | 30 | 100   |

Can we reject the hypothesis that a fair coin (or strictly, coins) was used for the experiment?

On the basis of the Binomial distribution the probability of no heads is 0.25 ($= \frac{1}{2} \times \frac{1}{2}$), of one head is 0.5 and of two heads is again 0.25, as explained in Chapter 2. The expected frequencies are therefore 25, 50 and 25. The calculation of the test statistic is set out below:

| Number of heads | $O$ | $E$ | $O-E$ | $(O-E)^2$ | $\dfrac{(O-E)^2}{E}$ |
|---|---|---|---|---|---|
| 0 | 15 | 25 | −10 | 100 | 4 |
| 1 | 55 | 50 | 5 | 25 | 0.5 |
| 2 | 30 | 25 | 5 | 25 | 1 |
| Totals | 100 | 100 | | | 5.5 |

The test statistic of 5.5 compares to a critical value of 5.99 ($v = 2$) so we cannot reject the null hypothesis of a fair coin being used.

Note that we could test the hypothesis using a $z$ test using the methods of Chapter 5. There have been a total of 200 tosses, of which 115 (= 55 + 2 × 30) were heads, i.e. a ratio of 0.575 against the expected 0.5. We can therefore test $H_0$: $\pi = 0.5$ against $H_1$: $\pi \neq 0.5$ using the evidence $n = 200$ and $p = 0.575$. This yields the test statistic

$$z = \frac{0.575 - 0.5}{\sqrt{\dfrac{0.5 \times 0.5}{200}}} = 2.12$$

Interestingly (!) we now *reject* the null as the test statistic is greater than the critical value of 1.96. How can we reconcile these conflicting results?

Note that both results are close to the critical values, so narrowly reject or accept the null. The $\chi^2$ and $t$ distributions are both continuous ones and in this case are approximations to the underlying Binomial experiment. This is the cause of the problem. If we alter the data very slightly, to 16, 55, 29 observed frequencies of no heads, one head and two heads, then both methods accept the null hypothesis. Similarly, for frequencies 14, 55, 31 both methods reject the null.

The lesson of this example is to be cautious when the test statistic is close to the critical value. We cannot say decisively that the null has been accepted or rejected.

**Exercise 6.2**

The following data show the observed and expected frequencies of an experiment with four possible outcomes, A–D.

| Outcome | A | B | C | D |
|---|---|---|---|---|
| Observed | 40 | 60 | 75 | 90 |
| Expected | 35 | 55 | 75 | 100 |

Test the hypothesis that the results are in line with expectations using the 5% significance level.

**Exercise 6.3**

(a) Verify the claim in the worked example above, that both $\chi^2$ and $z$ statistic methods give the same qualitative (accept or reject) result when the observed frequencies are 16, 55, 29 and when they are 14, 55, 31.

(b) In each case, look up or calculate (using Excel) the Prob-values for the $\chi^2$ and $z$ test statistics and compare.

**Contingency tables**

Data are often presented in the form of a two-way classification as shown in Table 6.8, known as a **contingency table** and this is another situation where

Table 6.8 Data on voting intentions by social class

| Social class | Labour | Conservative | Liberal Democrat | Total |
|---|---|---|---|---|
| A | 10 | 15 | 15 | 40 |
| B | 40 | 35 | 25 | 100 |
| C | 30 | 20 | 10 | 60 |
| Totals | 80 | 70 | 50 | 200 |

the $\chi^2$ distribution is useful. It provides a test of whether or not there is an association between the two variables represented in the table.

The table shows the voting intentions of a sample of 200 voters, cross-classified by social class. The interesting question that arises from these data is whether there is any association between people's voting behaviour and their social class. Are manual workers (social class C in the table) more likely to vote for the Labour party than for the Conservative party? The table would appear to indicate support for this view, but is this truly the case for the whole population or is the evidence insufficient to draw this conclusion?

This sort of problem is amenable to analysis by a $\chi^2$ test. The data presented in the table represent the observed values, so expected values need to be calculated and then compared to them using a $\chi^2$ test statistic. The first task is to formulate a null hypothesis, on which to base the calculation of the expected values, and an alternative hypothesis. These are

$H_0$: there is no association between social class and voting behaviour
$H_1$: there is some association between social class and voting behaviour

As always, the null hypothesis has to be precise, so that expected values can be calculated. In this case it is the precise statement that there is no association between the two variables, they are independent.

**Constructing the expected values**

If $H_0$ is true and there is no association, we would expect the proportions voting Labour, Conservative and Liberal Democrat to be the same in each social class. Further, the parties would be identical in the proportions of their support coming from social classes A, B and C. This means that, since the whole sample of 200 splits 80:70:50 for the Labour, Conservative and Liberal Democrat parties (see the bottom row of the table), each social class should split the same way. Thus of the 40 people of class A, 80/200 of them should vote Labour, 70/200 Conservative and 50/200 Liberal Democrat. This yields:

*Split of social class A*:
Labour                $40 \times 80/200 = 16$
Conservative          $40 \times 70/200 = 14$
Liberal Democrat      $40 \times 50/200 = 10$

*For class B*:
Labour                $100 \times 80/200 = 40$
Conservative          $100 \times 70/200 = 35$
Liberal Democrat      $100 \times 50/200 = 25$

And for C the 60 votes are split Labour 24, Conservative 21 and Liberal Democrat 15.

Both observed and expected values are presented in Table 6.9 (expected values are in brackets). Notice that both the observed and expected values sum

**Table 6.9 Observed and expected values (latter in brackets)**

| Social class | Labour | Conservative | Liberal Democrat | Total |
|---|---|---|---|---|
| A | 10 (16) | 15 (14) | 15 (10) | 40 |
| B | 40 (40) | 35 (35) | 25 (25) | 100 |
| C | 30 (24) | 20 (21) | 10 (15) | 60 |
| Totals | 80 | 70 | 50 | 200 |

to the appropriate row and column totals. It can be seen that, compared with the 'no association' position, Labour gets too few votes from Class A and the Liberal Democrats too many. However, Labour gets disproportionately many class C votes, the Liberal Democrats too few. The Conservatives' observed and expected values are identical, indicating that the propensities to vote Conservative are the same in all social classes.

A quick way to calculate the expected value in any cell is to multiply the appropriate row total by column total and divide through by the grand total (200). For example, to get the expected value for the class A/Labour cell:

$$expected\ value = \frac{row\ total \times column\ total}{grand\ total} = \frac{40 \times 80}{200} = 16$$

In carrying out the analysis care should again be taken to ensure that information is retained about the sample size, i.e. the numbers in the table should be actual numbers and not percentages or proportions. This can be checked by ensuring that the grand total is always the same as the sample size.

As was the case before, the $\chi^2$ test is only valid if the expected value in each cell is not less than five. In the event of one of the expected values being less than five, some of the rows or columns have to be combined. How to do this is a matter of choice and depends upon the aims of the research. Suppose for example that the expected number of class C voting Liberal Democrat were less than five. There are four options open:

1 Combine the Liberal Democrat column with the Labour column.
2 Combine the Liberal Democrat column with the Conservative column.
3 Combine the class C row with the class A row.
4 Combine the class C row with the class B row.

Whether rows or columns are combined depends upon whether interest centres more upon differences between parties or differences between classes. If the main interest is the difference between class A and the others, option 4 should be chosen. If it is felt that the Liberal Democrat and Conservative parties are similar, option 2 would be preferred, and so on. If there are several expected values less than five, rows and columns must be combined until all are eliminated.

The $\chi^2$ test on a contingency table is similar to the one carried out before, the formula being the same:

$$(6.5) \qquad \chi^2 = \sum \frac{(O - E)^2}{E}$$

with the number of degrees of freedom given by $v = (r - 1) \times (c - 1)$ where $r$ is the number of rows in the table and $c$ is the number of columns. In this case $r = 3$ and $c = 3$, so

$$v = (3 - 1) \times (3 - 1) = 4$$

The reason why there are only four degrees of freedom is that once any four cells of the contingency table have been filled, the other five are constrained by the row and column totals. The number of 'free' cells can always be calculated as the number of rows less one, times the number of columns less one, as given above.

**Calculation of the test statistic**

The evaluation of the test statistic then proceeds as follows, cell by cell:

$$\frac{(10 - 16)^2}{16} + \frac{(15 - 14)^2}{14} + \frac{(15 - 10)^2}{10}$$

$$+ \frac{(40 - 40)^2}{40} + \frac{(35 - 35)^2}{35} + \frac{(25 - 25)^2}{25}$$

$$+ \frac{(30 - 24)^2}{24} + \frac{(20 - 21)^2}{21} + \frac{(10 - 15)^2}{15}$$

$$= 2.25 + 0.07 + 2.50$$
$$+ 0 + 0 + 0$$
$$+ 1.5 + 0.05 + 1.67$$
$$= 8.04$$

This must be compared with the critical value from the $\chi^2$ distribution with four degrees of freedom. At the 5% significance level this is 9.50 (from Table A4, see page **368**).

Since $8.04 < 9.50$ the test statistic is smaller than the critical value, so the null hypothesis cannot be rejected. The evidence is not strong enough to support an association between social class and voting intention. We cannot reject the null of the lack of any association with 95% confidence. Note, however, that the test statistic is fairly close to the critical value, so there is some weak evidence of an association, but not enough to satisfy conventional statistical criteria.

---

## Oops!

A leading firm of chartered accountants produced a report for the UK government on education funding. One question it asked of schools was: Is the school budget sufficient to provide help to pupils with special needs? This produced the following table:

|  | Primary schools | Secondary schools |
| --- | --- | --- |
| Yes | 34% | 45% |
| No | 63% | 50% |
| No response | 3% | 5% |
| Totals | 100% | 100% |
| $n =$ | 137 | 159 |
| $\chi^2 = 3.50$ n.s. |  |  |

Their analysis produces the conclusion that there is no significant difference between primary and secondary schools. But the $\chi^2$ statistic is based on the percentage figures! Using frequencies (which can be calculated from the sample size figures) gives a correct $\chi^2$ figure of 5.05. Fortunately for the accountants, this is still not significant.

## Cohabitation

J. Ermisch and M. Francesconi examined the rise in cohabitation in the UK and asked whether it led on to marriage or not. One of their tables shows the relation between employment status and the outcome of living together. Their results, including the calculation of the $\chi^2$ statistic for association between the variables, are shown in the figure.

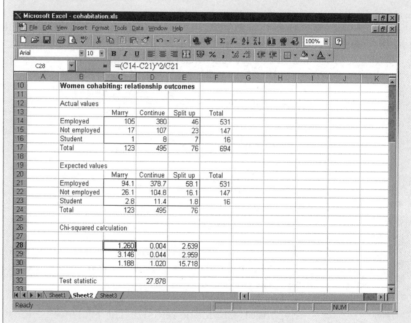

There were 694 cohabiting women in the sample. Of the 531 who were employed, 105 of them went on to marry their partner, 46 split up and 380 continued living together. Similar figures are shown for unemployed women and for students. The expected values for the contingency table then appear (based on the null hypothesis of no association), followed by the calculation of the $\chi^2$ test statistic. You can see the formula for one of the elements of the calculation in the formula bar.

The test statistic is significant at the 5% level (critical value 9.49 for four degrees of freedom), so there is an association. The biggest contribution to the test statistic comes from the bottom right hand cell, where the actual value is much higher than the expected. It appears that, unfortunately, those student romances often do not turn out to be permanent.

*Source*: J. Ermisch and M. Francesconi, Cohabitation: not for long but here to stay, *J. Royal Statistical Society*, Series A, 163 (2), 2000.

---

**Exercise 6.4**

Suppose that the data on educational achievement and employment status in Chapter 1 were obtained from a sample of 1002 people, as follows:

|  | Higher education | A-levels | Other qualification | No qualification | Total |
|---|---|---|---|---|---|
| In work | 222 | 153 | 302 | 70 | 747 |
| Unemployed | 6 | 6 | 19 | 8 | 39 |
| Inactive | 26 | 37 | 84 | 69 | 216 |
| Total | 254 | 196 | 405 | 147 | 1002 |

Test whether there is an association between education and employment status, using the 5% significance level for the test.

# The *F* distribution

The second distribution we encounter in this chapter is the *F* distribution. It has a variety of uses in statistics; in this section we look at two of these: testing for the equality of two variances and conducting an **analysis of variance** (ANOVA) test. Both of these are variants on the hypothesis test procedures which should by now be familiar. The *F* distribution will also be encountered in later chapters on regression analysis.

The *F* family of distributions resembles the $\chi^2$ distribution in shape: it is always non-negative and is skewed to the right. It has two sets of degrees of freedom (these are its parameters, labelled $v_1$ and $v_2$) and these determine its precise shape. Typical *F* distributions are shown in Figure 6.3. As usual, for a hypothesis test we define an area in one or both tails of the distribution to be the rejection region. If a test statistic falls into the rejection region then the null hypothesis upon which the test statistic was based is rejected. Once again, examples will clarify the principles.

**Testing the equality of two variances**

Just as one can conduct a hypothesis test on a mean, so it is possible to test the variance. It is unusual to want to conduct a test of a specific value of a variance, since we usually have little intuitive idea what the variance should be in most circumstances. A more likely circumstance is a test of the equality of two variances (across two samples). In Chapter 5 two car factories were tested for the equality of average daily output *levels*. One can also test whether the *variance* of output differs or not. A more consistent output (lower variance) from a factory might be beneficial to the firm, e.g. dealers can be reassured that they are more likely to be able to obtain models when they require them. In the example in Chapter 5, one factory had a standard deviation of daily output of 25, the second of 20, both from samples of size 30 (i.e. 30 days' output was sampled at each factory). We can now test whether the difference between these figures is significant or not.

Such a test is set up as follows. It is known as a **variance ratio test** for reasons which will become apparent.

The null and alternative hypotheses are

$H_0: \sigma_1^2 = \sigma_2^2$
$H_1: \sigma_1^2 \neq \sigma_2^2$

**Figure 6.3**
**The *F* distribution, for different $v_1(v_2 = 25)$**

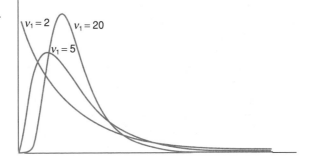

or, equivalently

(6.6)     $H_0: \sigma_1^2/\sigma_2^2 = 1$
          $H_1: \sigma_1^2/\sigma_2^2 \neq 1$

It is appropriate to write the hypotheses in the form shown in (6.6) since the random variable we shall use is in the form of the ratio of sample variances, $s_1^2/s_2^2$. This is a random variable which follows an $F$ distribution with $v_1 = n_1 - 1$, $v_2 = n_2 - 1$ degrees of freedom. We require the assumption that the two samples are independent for the variance ratio to follow an $F$ distribution. Thus we write:

(6.7)     $\dfrac{s_1^2}{s_2^2} \sim F_{n_1-1, n_2-1}$

The $F$ distribution thus has two parameters, the two sets of degrees of freedom, one ($v_1$) associated with the numerator, the other ($v_2$) associated with the denominator of the formula. In each case, the degrees of freedom are given by the sample size minus one.

Note that $s_2^2/s_1^2$ is also an $F$ distribution (i.e. it doesn't matter which variance goes into the numerator) but with the degrees of freedom reversed, $v_1 = n_2 - 1$, $v_2 = n_1 - 1$.

The sample data are:

$s_1 = 25, s_2 = 20$
$n_1 = 30, n_2 = 30$

The test statistic is simply the ratio of sample variances. In testing it is less confusing if the larger of the two variances is made the numerator of the test statistic (you will see why soon). Therefore we have the following test statistic:

(6.8)     $F = \dfrac{25^2}{20^2} = 1.5625$

This must be compared to the critical value of the $F$ distribution with $v_1 = 29$, $v_2 = 29$ degrees of freedom.

The rejection regions for the test are the two tails of the distribution, cutting off 2.5% in each tail. Since we have placed the larger variance in the denominator, only large values of $F$ reject the null hypothesis so we need only consult the upper critical value of the $F$ distribution, i.e. that value which cuts off the top 2.5% of the distribution. (This is the advantage of putting the larger variance in the numerator of the test statistic.)

Table 6.10 shows an excerpt from the $F$ distribution. The degrees of freedom for the test are given along the top row ($v_1$) and down the first column ($v_2$). The numbers in the table give the critical values cutting off the top 2.5% of the distribution. The critical value in this case is 2.09, at the intersection of the row corresponding to $v_2 = 29$ and the column corresponding to $v_1 = 30$ ($v_1 = 29$ is not given so 30 is used instead; this gives a very close approximation to the correct critical value). Since the test statistic does not exceed the critical value, the null hypothesis of equal variances cannot be rejected with 95% confidence.

**Table 6.10 Excerpt from the _F_ distribution: upper 2.5% points**

| $v_1$ | 1 | 2 | 3 | ... | 20 | 24 | 30 | 40 |
|---|---|---|---|---|---|---|---|---|
| $v_2$ | | | | | | | | |
| 1 | 647.7931 | 799.4822 | 864.1509 | ... | 993.0809 | 997.2719 | 1001.4046 | 1005.5955 |
| 2 | 38.5062 | 39.0000 | 39.1656 | ... | 39.4475 | 39.4566 | 39.4648 | 39.4730 |
| 3 | 17.4434 | 16.0442 | 15.4391 | ... | 14.1674 | 14.1242 | 14.0806 | 14.0365 |
| ⋮ | ⋮ | ⋮ | ⋮ | ... | ⋮ | ⋮ | ⋮ | ⋮ |
| 28 | 5.6096 | 4.2205 | 3.6264 | ... | 2.2324 | 2.1735 | 2.1121 | 2.0477 |
| 29 | 5.5878 | 4.2006 | 3.6072 | ... | 2.2131 | 2.1540 | 2.0923 | 2.0276 |
| 30 | 5.5675 | 4.1821 | 3.5893 | ... | 2.1952 | 2.1359 | 2.0739 | 2.0089 |
| 40 | 5.4239 | 4.0510 | 3.4633 | ... | 2.0677 | 2.0069 | 1.9429 | 1.8752 |

_Note_: The critical value lies at the intersection of the shaded row and column. Alternatively, use _Excel_ or another computer package to give the answer. In _Excel_, the formula $=FINV(0.025, 29, 29)$ will give the answer 2.09, the upper 2.5% critical value of the _F_ distribution with $v_1 = 29$, $v_2 = 29$ degrees of freedom.

**Exercise 6.5**

Samples of 3-volt batteries from two manufacturers yielded the following outputs, measured in volts:

| Brand A | 3.1 | 3.2 | 2.9 | 3.3 | 2.8 | 3.1 | 3.2 |
|---|---|---|---|---|---|---|---|
| Brand B | 3.0 | 3.0 | 3.2 | 3.4 | 2.7 | 2.8 | |

Test whether there is any difference in the variance of output voltage of batteries from the two companies. Why might the variance be an important consideration for the manufacturer or for customers?

# Analysis of variance

In Chapter 5 we learned how to test the hypothesis that the means of two samples are the same, using a $z$ or $t$ test, depending upon the sample size. This type of hypothesis test can be generalised to more than two samples using a technique called analysis of variance (ANOVA), based on the _F_ distribution. Although it is called analysis of variance, it actually tests differences in means. The reason for this will be given below. Using this technique we can test the hypothesis that the means of _all_ the samples are equal, versus the alternative hypothesis that at least one of them is different from the others. To illustrate the technique we shall extend the example in Chapter 5 where two different car factories' outputs were compared.

The assumptions underlying the analysis of variance technique are essentially the same as those used in the $t$ test when comparing two different means. We assume that the samples are randomly and independently drawn from Normally distributed populations which have equal variances.

Suppose there are three factories, whose outputs have been sampled, with the results shown in Table 6.11. We wish to answer the question whether this is evidence of different outputs from the three factories, or simply random variations around a (common) average output level. The null and alternative hypotheses are therefore:

**Table 6.11 Samples of output from three factories**

| Observation | Factory 1 | Factory 2 | Factory 3 |
| --- | --- | --- | --- |
| 1 | 415 | 385 | 408 |
| 2 | 430 | 410 | 415 |
| 3 | 395 | 409 | 418 |
| 4 | 399 | 403 | 440 |
| 5 | 408 | 405 | 425 |
| 6 | 418 | 400 | |
| 7 | | 399 | |

$H_0$: $\mu_1 = \mu_2 = \mu_3$
$H_1$: at least one mean is different from the others

This is the simplest type of ANOVA, known as one-way analysis of variance. In this case there is only one factor which affects output – the factory. The factor which may affect output is also known as the independent variable. In more complex designs, there can be two or more factors which influence output. The output from the factories is the dependent or response variable in this case.

Figure 6.4 presents a chart of the output from the three factories, which shows the greatest apparent difference between factories 2 and 3. Their ranges scarcely overlap, which does suggest some genuine difference between them but as yet we cannot be sure that this is not just due to sampling variation. Factory 1 appears to be mid-way between the other two and this must also be included in the analysis.

To decide whether or not to reject $H_0$ we compare the variance of output *within* factories to the variance of output *between* (the means of) the factories. Both methods provide estimates of the overall true variance of output and, under the null hypothesis that factories make no difference, should provide similar estimates. The ratio of the variances should be approximately unity. If the null is false however, the between-samples estimate will tend to be larger than the within-samples estimate and their ratio will exceed unity. This ratio

**Figure 6.4**
**Chart of factory output on sample days**

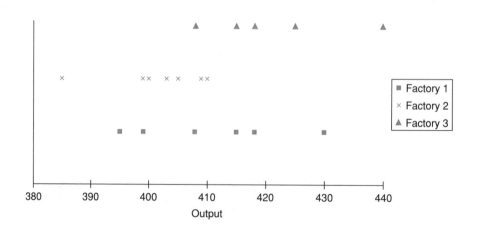

has an $F$ distribution and so if it is sufficiently large that it falls into the upper tail of the distribution then $H_0$ is rejected.

To summarise: if there appears little variation between different days' outputs, but they differed substantially between factories, then we would reject $H_0$; at the other extreme, if each factory's output varied substantially from one day to another, but the average levels of output were similar, it would be clear that there is no difference between them. In this case we would conclude that the variations were due to other random factors, not the factories.

To formalise this we break down the total variance of all the observations into

1 the variance due to differences between factories, and
2 the variance due to differences within factories (also known as the error variance).

Initially we work with sums of squares rather than variances. Recall from Chapter 1 that the sample variance is given by

**(6.9)**  $$s^2 = \frac{\Sigma(x - \bar{x})^2}{n - 1}$$

The numerator of the right-hand side of this expression gives the sum of squares, i.e. the sum of squared deviations from the mean.

Accordingly we have to work with three sums of squares:

- The total sum of squares measures (squared) deviations from the overall or grand average using all the observations. It ignores the existence of the different factors.
- The between sum of squares is based upon the averages for each factor and measures how they deviate from the grand average.
- The within sum of squares is based on squared deviations of observations from their own factor mean.

It can be shown that there is a relationship between these sums of squares, i.e.

**(6.10)**  $$\frac{\text{Total sum}}{\text{of squares}} = \frac{\text{Between sum}}{\text{of squares}} + \frac{\text{Within sum}}{\text{of squares}}$$

which is often helpful for calculation. The larger is the between sum of squares relative to the within sum of squares, the more likely it is that the null is false.

Because we have to sum over factors and over observations within those factors, the formulae look somewhat complicated, involving double summation signs. It is therefore important to follow the example showing how the calculations are actually done.

The total sum of squares is given by the formula:

**(6.11)**  $$\text{Total sum of squares} = \sum_{j=1}^{n_i} \sum_{i=1}^{k} (x_{ij} - \bar{x})^2$$

where $x_{ij}$ is the output from factory $i$ on day $j$ and $\bar{x}$ is the grand average. The index $i$ runs from 1 to 3 in this case (there are three classes or groups for this factor) and the index $j$ (indexing the observations) goes from 1 to 6, 7, or 5 (for factories 1, 2 and 3 respectively).

Although this looks complex, it simply means that you calculate the sum of squared deviations from the overall mean. The overall mean of the 18 values is

410.11 and the total sum of squares may be calculated as:

Total sum of squares $= (415 - 410.11)^2 + (430 - 410.11)^2 + \ldots + (440 - 410.11)^2$
$$+ (425 - 410.11)^2 = 2977.778$$

An alternative formula for the total sum of squares is

**(6.12)**      Total sum of squares $= \displaystyle\sum_{j=1}^{n_i} \sum_{i=1}^{k} x_{ij}^2 - n\bar{x}^2$

where $n$ is the total number of observations. The sum of the squares of all the observations $(\Sigma x^2)$ is $415^2 + 430^2 + \ldots + 425^2 = 3\,030\,418$ and the total sum of squares is given by

**(6.13)**      $\displaystyle\sum_{j=1}^{n_i} \sum_{i=1}^{k} x_{ij}^2 - n\bar{x}^2 = 3\,030\,418 - 18 \times 410.11^2 = 2977.778$

as before.

The between sum of squares is calculated using the formula

**(6.14)**      Between sum of squares $= \displaystyle\sum_{j} \sum_{i} (\bar{x}_i - \bar{x})^2$

where $\bar{x}_i$ denotes the mean output of factor $i$. This part of the calculation effectively ignores the differences that exist within factors and compares the differences between them. It does this by replacing the observations within each factor by the mean for that factor. Hence all the factor 1 observations are replaced by 410.83, for factor 2 they are replaced by the mean 401.57 and for factor 3 by 421.2. We then calculate the sum of squared deviations of these values from the grand mean. Hence we get

Between sum of squares $= 6 \times (410.83 - 410.11)^2 + 7 \times (401.57 - 410.11)^2$
$$+ 5 \times (421.2 - 410.11)^2 = 1128.43$$

Note that we take account of the number of observations within each factor in this calculation.

Once again there is an alternative formula which may be simpler for calculation purposes:

**(6.15)**      Between sum of squares $= \displaystyle\sum_{i} n_i \bar{x}_i^2 - n\bar{x}^2$

Evaluating this results in the same answer as above:

**(6.16)**      $\displaystyle\sum_{i} n_i \bar{x}_i^2 - n\bar{x}^2 = 6 \times 410.83^2 + 7 \times 401.57^2 + 5 \times 421.2^2 - 18 \times 410.10^2$

$$= 1128.43$$

We have arrived at the result that 37% ($= 1128.43/2977.78$) of the total variation (sum of squared deviations) is due to differences between factories and the remaining 63% is therefore due to variation (day to day) within factories. We can therefore immediately calculate the within sum of squares as:

Within sum of squares $= 2977.778 - 1128.430 = 1849.348$

For completeness, the formula for the within sum of squares is

**(6.17)**      Within sum of squares $= \displaystyle\sum_{j} \sum_{i} (x_{ij} - \bar{x}_i)^2$

The term $x_{ij} - \bar{x}_i$ measures the deviations of the observations from the factor mean and so the within sum of squares gives a measure of dispersion within the classes. Hence it can be calculated as:

$$\begin{aligned}
\text{Within sum of squares} &= (415 - 410.83)^2 + \ldots + (418 - 410.83)^2 \\
&+ (385 - 401.57)^2 + \ldots + (399 - 401.57)^2 \\
&+ (408 - 421.2)^2 + \ldots + (425 - 421.2)^2 \\
&= 1849.348
\end{aligned}$$

### The result of the hypothesis test

The $F$ statistic is based upon comparison between and within sums of squares ($BSS$ and $WSS$) but we must also take account of the degrees of freedom for the test. The degrees of freedom adjust for the number of observations and for the number of factors. Formally, the test statistic is

$$F = \frac{BSS/(k-1)}{WSS/(n-k)}$$

which has $k - 1$ and $n - k$ degrees of freedom. $k$ is the number of factors, 3 in this case, and $n$ the overall number of observations, 18. We thus have

$$F = \frac{1128.43/(3-1)}{1849.348/(18-3)} = 4.576$$

The critical value of $F$ for 2 and 15 degrees of freedom at the 5% significance level is 3.682. As the test statistic exceeds the critical value we reject the null hypothesis of no difference between factories.

**The analysis of variance table**

ANOVA calculations are conventionally summarised in an analysis of variance table. Figure 6.5 shows such a table, as produced by *Excel*. *Excel* can produce

**Figure 6.5**
**One-way analysis of variance: *Excel* output**

| K28 | | 4.57633064942054 | | | | |
|---|---|---|---|---|---|---|

| | G | H | I | J | K | L | M |
|---|---|---|---|---|---|---|---|
| 13 | | | | | | | |
| 14 | Anova: Single-Factor | | | | | | |
| 15 | | | | | | | |
| 16 | Summary | | | | | | |
| 17 | | | | | | | |
| 18 | Groups | Count | Sum | Average | Variance | | |
| 19 | | | | | | | |
| 20 | factory 1 | 6 | 2465 | 410.833 | 166.967 | | |
| 21 | factory 2 | 7 | 2811 | 401.571 | 70.619 | | |
| 22 | factory 3 | 5 | 2106 | 421.200 | 147.700 | | |
| 23 | | | | | | | |
| 24 | ANOVA | | | | | | |
| 25 | | | | | | | |
| 26 | Source of Variation | | | | | | |
| 27 | | SS | df | MS | F | P value | F crit |
| 28 | Between Groups | 1128.430 | 2 | 564.215 | 4.576 | 0.028 | 3.682 |
| 29 | Within Groups | 1849.348 | 15 | 123.290 | | | |
| 30 | | | | | | | |
| 31 | Total | 2977.7778 | 17 | | | | |

*Note: Excel*, like many other statistical packages, performs all the ANOVA calculations automatically, based on the data in the spreadsheet. There is no need to evaluate any formulae, so you can concentrate on the interpretation of the results.

the table automatically from data presented in the form shown in Table 6.11 and there is no need to do any of the calculations by hand. (In *Excel* you need to install the Analysis ToolPak in order to perform ANOVA. Other software packages, such as *SPSS*, also have routines to perform ANOVA.)

The first part of the table summarises the information for each factory, in the form of means and variances. Note that the means were used in the calculation of the *between sum of squares*. The ANOVA section of the output then follows, giving sums of squares and other information.

The column of the ANOVA table headed '*SS*' gives the sums of squares, which we calculated above. It can be seen that the between-group sum of squares makes up about 37% of the total, suggesting that the differences between factories (referred to as 'groups' by *Excel*) do make a substantial contribution to the total variation in output.

The '*df*' column gives the degrees of freedom associated with each sum of squares. These degrees of freedom are given by

| | |
|---|---|
| Between sum of squares | $k - 1$ |
| Within sum of squares | $n - k$ |
| Total sum of squares | $n - 1$ |

The '*MS*' ('mean square') column divides the sums of squares by their degrees of freedom and the $F$ column gives the $F$ statistic, which is the ratio of the two values in the *MS* column, i.e. $4.576 = 564.215/123.290$. This is the test statistic for the hypothesis test, which we calculated above. *Excel* helpfully gives the critical value of the test (at the 5% significance level) in the final column, 3.68. The Prob-value (labelled '*P value*') is given in the penultimate column and reveals that only 2.8% of the $F$ distribution lies beyond the test statistic value of 4.576.

The test has found that the between sum of squares is 'large' relative to the within sum of squares, too large to be due simply to random variation, and this is why the null hypothesis of equal outputs is rejected. The rejection region for the test consists of the *upper* tail only of the $F$ distribution; small values of the test statistic would indicate small differences between factories and hence non-rejection of $H_0$.

This simple example involves only three groups, but the extension to four or more follows the same principles, with different values of $k$ in the formulae, and is fairly straightforward. Also, we have covered only the simplest type of ANOVA, with a one-way classification. More complex experimental designs are possible, with a two-way classification, for example, where there are two independent factors affecting the dependent variable. This is not covered in this book, although Chapter 8 on the subject of multiple regression does examine a method of modelling situations where two or more explanatory variables influence a dependent variable.

**Worked example 6.3**

ANOVA calculations are quite complex and are easiest handled by software which calculates all the results directly from the initial data. However, this is a kind of 'black box' approach to learning, so this example shows all the calculations mechanically.

Suppose we have six observations on each of three factors, as follows:

| A | B | C |
|---|---|---|
| 44 | 41 | 48 |
| 35 | 36 | 37 |
| 60 | 58 | 61 |
| 28 | 32 | 37 |
| 43 | 40 | 44 |
| 55 | 59 | 61 |

(These might be, for example, scores of different groups of pupils in a test.) We wish to examine whether there is a significant difference between the different groups. We need to see how the differences between the groups compare to those within groups.

First we calculate the total sum of squares by ignoring the groupings and treating all 18 observations together. The overall mean is 45.5 so the squared deviations are $(44 - 45.5)^2$, $(41 - 45.5)^2$, etc. Summing these gives 2020.5 as the TSS.

For the between sum of squares we first calculate the means of each factor. These are 44.17, 44.33 and 48. We compare these to the grand average. The squared deviations are therefore $(44.17 - 45.5)^2$, $(44.33 - 45.5)^2$ and $(48 - 45.5)^2$. Rather than sum these, we must take account of the number of observations in each group which in this case is 6. Hence we obtain

$$\text{Between sum of squares} = 6 \times (44.17 - 45.5)^2 + 6 \times (44.33 - 45.5)^2 + 6 \times (48 - 45.5)^2 = 56.33$$

The within sum of squares can be explicitly calculated as follows. For group A, the squared deviations from the group mean are $(44 - 44.17)^2$, $(35 - 44.17)^2$, etc. Summing these for group A gives 714.8. Similar calculations give 653.3 and 596 for groups B and C. These sum to 1964.2, which is the within sum of squares. As a check, we note:

$$2020.5 = 56.3 + 1964.2$$

The degrees of freedom are $k - 1 = 3 - 1 = 2$ for the between sum of squares, $n - k = 18 - 3 = 15$ for the within sum of squares and $n - 1 = 18 - 1 = 17$. The test statistic is therefore

$$F = \frac{56.33/2}{1964.2/15} = 0.22$$

The critical value at the 5% significance level is 3.68, so we cannot reject the null of no difference between the factors.

**Exercise 6.6**

The reaction times of three groups of sportsmen were measured on a particular task, with the following results (time in milliseconds):

| Racing drivers | 31 | 28 | 39 | 42 | 36 | 30 | |
|---|---|---|---|---|---|---|---|
| Tennis players | 41 | 35 | 41 | 48 | 44 | 39 | 38 |
| Boxers | 44 | 47 | 35 | 38 | 51 | | |

Test whether there is a difference in reaction times between the three groups.

## Summary

■ The $\chi^2$ and $F$ distributions play important roles in statistics, particularly in problems relating to the goodness of fit of the data to that predicted by a null hypothesis.

■ A random variable based on the sample variance, $(n-1)s^2/\sigma^2$, has a $\chi^2$ distribution with $n-1$ degrees of freedom. Based on this fact, the $\chi^2$ distribution may be used to construct confidence interval estimates for the variance $\sigma^2$. Since the $\chi^2$ is not a symmetric distribution, the confidence interval is not symmetric around the (unbiased) point estimate $s^2$.

■ The $\chi^2$ distribution may also be used to compare actual and expected values of a variable and hence to test the hypothesis upon which the expected values were constructed.

■ A two-way classification of observations is known as a contingency table. The independence or otherwise of the two variables may be tested using the $\chi^2$ distribution, by comparing observed values with those expected under the null hypothesis of independence.

■ The $F$ distribution is used to test a hypothesis of the equality of two variances. The test statistic is the ratio of two sample variances which, under the null hypothesis, has an $F$ distribution with $n_1 - 1$, $n_2 - 1$ degrees of freedom.

■ The $F$ distribution may also be used in an analysis of variance, which tests for the equality of means across several samples. The results are set out in an analysis of variance table, which compares the variation of the observations *within* each sample to the variation *between* samples.

**Key terms and concepts**

| | | |
|---|---|---|
| actual and expected values | contingency table | analysis of variance |
| variance ratio test | independent variable | dependent or response variable |
| total sum of squares | between sum of squares | within sum of squares |
| classes or groups | grand average | ANOVA table |

## Problems

Some of the more challenging problems are indicated by highlighting the problem number in colour.

**Problem 6.1** A sample of 40 observations has a standard deviation of 20. Estimate the 95% confidence interval for the standard deviation of the population.

**Problem 6.2** Using the data $n = 70$, $s = 15$, construct a 99% confidence interval for the true standard deviation.

**Problem 6.3** Use the data in Table 6.3 to see if there is a significant difference between road casualties in quarters I and III on the one hand and quarters II and IV on the other.

**Problem 6.4** A survey of 64 families with five children found the following gender distribution:

| Number of boys | 0 | 1 | 2 | 3 | 4 | 5 |
|---|---|---|---|---|---|---|
| Number of families | 1 | 8 | 28 | 19 | 4 | 4 |

Test whether the distribution can be adequately modelled by the Binomial distribution.

**Problem 6.5** Four different holiday firms which all carried equal numbers of holidaymakers reported the following numbers who expressed satisfaction with their holiday:

| Firm | A | B | C | D |
|---|---|---|---|---|
| Number satisfied | 576 | 558 | 580 | 546 |

Is there any significant difference between the firms? If told that the four firms carried 600 holidaymakers each, would you modify your conclusion? What do you conclude about your first answer?

**Problem 6.6** A company wishes to see whether there are any differences between its departments in staff turnover. Looking at their records for the past year the company finds the following data:

| Department | Personnel | Marketing | Admin. | Accounts |
|---|---|---|---|---|
| Number in post at start of year | 23 | 16 | 108 | 57 |
| Number leaving | 3 | 4 | 20 | 13 |

Do the data provide evidence of a difference in staff turnover between the various departments?

**Problem 6.7** A survey of 100 firms found the following evidence regarding profitability and market share:

| Profitability | Market share | | |
|---|---|---|---|
| | <15% | 15–30% | >30% |
| Low | 18 | 7 | 8 |
| Medium | 13 | 11 | 8 |
| High | 8 | 12 | 15 |

Is there evidence that market share and profitability are associated?

**Problem 6.8** The following data show the percentages of firms using computers in different aspects of their business:

| Firm size | Computers used in | | | Total numbers |
|---|---|---|---|---|
| | Admin. | Design | Manufacture | of firms |
| Small | 60% | 24% | 20% | 450 |
| Medium | 65% | 30% | 28% | 140 |
| Large | 90% | 44% | 50% | 45 |

Is there an association between the size of firm and its use of computers?

**Problem 6.9**   (a)  Do the accountants' job properly for them (see the *Oops!* box in the text (page **203**)).

          (b)  It might be justifiable to omit the 'no responses' entirely from the calculation. What happens if you do this?

---

**Problem 6.10**   A roadside survey of the roadworthiness of vehicles obtained the following results:

|  | Roadworthy | Not roadworthy |
|---|---|---|
| Private cars | 114 | 30 |
| Company cars | 84 | 24 |
| Vans | 36 | 12 |
| Lorries | 44 | 20 |
| Buses | 36 | 12 |

Is there any association between the type of vehicle and the likelihood of it being unfit for the road?

---

**Problem 6.11**   Given the following data on two sample variances, test whether there is any significant difference. Use the 1% significance level.

$$s_1^2 = 55 \qquad s_2^2 = 48$$
$$n_1 = 25 \qquad n_2 = 30$$

---

**Problem 6.12**   An example in Chapter 4 compared R&D expenditure in Britain and Germany. The sample data were:

$$\bar{x}_1 = 3.7 \qquad \bar{x}_2 = 4.2$$
$$s_1 = 0.6 \qquad s_2 = 0.9$$
$$n_1 = 20 \qquad n_2 = 15$$

Is there evidence, at the 5% significance level, of difference in the variances of R&D expenditure between the two countries? What are the implications, if any, for the test carried out on the difference of the two means, in Chapter 4?

---

**Problem 6.13**   Groups of children from four different classes in a school were randomly selected and sat a test, with the following test scores:

| Class | Pupil | | | | | | |
|---|---|---|---|---|---|---|---|
|  | 1 | 2 | 3 | 4 | 5 | 6 | 7 |
| A | 42 | 63 | 73 | 55 | 66 | 48 | 59 |
| B | 39 | 47 | 47 | 61 | 44 | 50 | 52 |
| C | 71 | 65 | 33 | 49 | 61 |  |  |
| D | 49 | 51 | 62 | 48 | 63 | 54 |  |

  (a)  Test whether there is any difference between the classes, using the 95% confidence level for the test.

  (b)  How would you interpret a 'significant' result from such a test?

**Problem 6.14** Lottery tickets are sold in different outlets: supermarkets, smaller shops and out-door kiosks. Sales were sampled from several of each of these, with the following results:

| | | | | |
|---|---|---|---|---|
| Supermarkets | 355 | 251 | 408 | 302 |
| Small shops | 288 | 257 | 225 | 299 |
| Kiosks | 155 | 352 | 240 | |

Does the evidence indicate a significant difference in sales? Use the 5% significance level.

**Problem 6.15**
**(Project)**
Conduct a survey among fellow students to examine whether there is any association between:

(a) gender and political preference, or

(b) subject studied and political preference, or

(c) star sign and personality (introvert/extrovert – self-assessed: I am told that Aries, Cancer, Capricorn, Gemini, Leo and Scorpio are associated with an extrovert personality), or

(d) any other two categories of interest.

**Problem 6.16**
**(Computer project)**
Use your spreadsheet or other computer program to generate 100 random integers in the range 0 to 9. Draw up a frequency table and use a $\chi^2$ test to examine whether there is any bias towards any particular integer. Compare your results with those of others in your class.

## Answers to exercises

**Exercise 6.1**
$$\left[ \frac{(30-1) \times 65}{45.72} \le \sigma^2 \le \frac{(30-1) \times 65}{16.05} \right]$$

yields the interval [41.2, 117.4] (b) [6.4, 10.8] (c) [36.0, 143.7].

**Exercise 6.2** The calculation of the test statistic is

| Outcome | Observed | Expected | $O - E$ | $(O - E)^2$ | $(O - E)^2/E$ |
|---|---|---|---|---|---|
| A | 40 | 35 | 5 | 25 | 0.714286 |
| B | 60 | 55 | 5 | 25 | 0.454545 |
| C | 75 | 75 | 0 | 0 | 0 |
| D | 90 | 100 | −10 | 100 | 1 |
| Total | | | | | 2.168831 |

This is smaller than the critical value of 7.81 so the null is not rejected.

**Exercise 6.3** The test statistics are for (16, 55, 29) $\chi^2 = 4.38$ (Prob-value = 0.112) and $z = 1.84$ (Prob-value = 0.066) and for (14, 55, 31) $\chi^2 = 6.78$ (Prob-value = 0.038) and $z = 2.40$ (Prob-value = 0.016). The two methods agree on the results, though the Prob-values are quite different.

**Exercise 6.4** The expected values are:

| | Higher education | A levels | Other qualifications | No qualifications | Total |
|---|---|---|---|---|---|
| In work | 189 | 146 | 302 | 110 | 747 |
| Unemployed | 10 | 8 | 16 | 6 | 39 |
| Inactive | 55 | 42 | 87 | 32 | 216 |
| Totals | 254 | 196 | 405 | 147 | 1002 |

(These are calculated by multiplying row and column totals and dividing by the grand total, e.g. $189 = 747 \times 254/1002$.)

The test statistic is

$$5.6 + 0.3 + 0.0 + 14.3 + 1.5 + 0.3 + 0.7 + 0.9 + 15.1 + 0.7 + 0.1 + 43.9 = 83.5$$

This should be compared to a critical value of 12.59 ($v = (3-1) \times (4-1) = 6$) so the null is rejected.

**Exercise 6.5** The two variances are $s_A^2 = 0.031$ and $s_B^2 = 0.066$. We therefore form the ratio $F = 0.066/0.031 = 2.09$, which has an $F$ distribution with 6 and 7 degrees of freedom. The 5% critical value is therefore 3.87 and the null is not rejected. There appears no differences between manufacturers. The variance is important because consumers want a reliable product – they would not be happy if one battery lasted a long time but the next only a few days, even if the average were quite respectable.

**Exercise 6.6** The answer is summarised in this Excel table:

SUMMARY

| Groups | Count | Sum | Average | Variance |
|---|---|---|---|---|
| Racing drivers | 6 | 206 | 34.333 | 30.667 |
| Tennis players | 7 | 286 | 40.857 | 17.810 |
| Boxers | 5 | 215 | 43 | 42.5 |

ANOVA

| Source of variation | SS | df | MS | F | P-value | F crit |
|---|---|---|---|---|---|---|
| Between groups | 233.421 | 2 | 116.710 | 4.069 | 0.039 | 3.682 |
| Within groups | 430.190 | 15 | 28.679 | | | |
| Totals | 663.611 | 17 | | | | |

The result shows that there is a difference between the three groups, with an $F$ statistic of 4.069 ($P$ value 3.9%). The difference appears to be largely between racing drivers and the other two types.

| | |
|---|---|
| **Appendix** | # Use of $\chi^2$ and $F$ distribution tables |

**Tables of the $\chi^2$ distribution**

Table A4 (see page **368**) presents critical values of the $\chi^2$ distribution for a selection of significance levels and for different degrees of freedom. As an example, to find the critical value of the $\chi^2$ distribution at the 5% significance level, for $v = 20$ degrees of freedom, the cell entry in the column labelled '0.05' and the row labelled '20' are consulted. The critical value is 31.4. A test statistic greater than this value implies rejection of the null hypothesis at the 5% significance level.

**Tables of the $F$ distribution**

Table A5 (see page **370**) presents critical values of the $F$ distribution. Since there are two sets of degrees of freedom to be taken into account, a separate table is required for each significance level. Four sets of tables are provided, giving critical values cutting off the top 5%, 2.5%, 1% and 0.5% of the distribution (Tables A5(a), A5(b), A5(c) and A5(d) respectively). These allow both one- and two-tail tests at the 5% and 1% significance levels to be conducted. Its use is illustrated by example.

### Two-tail test

To find the critical values of the $F$ distribution at the 5% significance level for degrees of freedom $v_1$ (numerator) = 10, $v_2 = 20$. The critical values in this case cut off the extreme 2.5% of the distribution in each tail, and are found in Table A5(b):

- Right-hand critical value: this is found from the cell of the table corresponding to the column $v_1 = 10$ and row $v_2 = 20$. Its value is 2.77.
- Left-hand critical value: this cannot be obtained directly from the tables, which only give right-hand values. However, it is obtained indirectly as follows:
  (a) Find the right-hand critical value for $v_1 = 20$, $v_2 = 10$ (note reversal of degrees of freedom). This gives 3.42.
  (b) Take the reciprocal to obtain the desired left-hand critical value. This gives $1/3.42 = 0.29$.

The rejection region thus consists of values of the test statistic less than 0.29 and greater than 2.77.

### One-tail test

To find the critical value at the 5% significance level for $v_1 = 15$, $v_2 = 25$. As long as the test statistic has been calculated with the larger variance in the numerator, the critical value is in the right-hand tail of the distribution and can be obtained directly from Table A5(a). For $v_1 = 15$, $v_2 = 25$ the value is 2.09. The null hypothesis is rejected, therefore, if the test statistic is greater than 2.09.

# 7

# Correlation and regression

| Learning outcomes | By the end of this chapter you should be able to: |
| --- | --- |
| | ■ understand the principles underlying correlation and regression |
| | ■ calculate and interpret a correlation coefficient and relate it to an *XY* graph of the two variables |
| | ■ calculate the line of best fit (regression line) and interpret the result |
| | ■ recognise the statistical significance of the results, using confidence intervals and hypothesis tests |
| | ■ recognise the importance of the units in which the variables are measured and of transformations to the data |
| | ■ use computer software (*Excel*) to derive the regression line and interpret the computer output |

# Introduction

Correlation and regression are techniques for investigating the statistical relationship between two, or more, variables. In Chapter 1 we examined the relationship between investment and GDP using graphical methods (the $XY$ chart). Although visually helpful, this did not provide any precise measurement of the strength of the relationship. In Chapter 6 the $\chi^2$ test did provide a test of the significance of the association between two category-based variables, but this test cannot be applied to variables measured on a ratio scale. Correlation and regression fill in these gaps: the strength of the relationship between two (or more) ratio scale variables can be measured and the significance tested.

Correlation and regression are the techniques most often used by economists and forecasters. They can be used to answer such questions as

- Is there a link between the money supply and the price level?
- Do bigger firms produce at lower cost than smaller firms?
- Does instability in a country's export performance hinder its growth?

Each of these questions is about economics or business as much as about statistics. The statistical analysis is part of a wider investigation into the problem; it cannot provide a complete answer to the problem but, used sensibly, is a vital input. Correlation and regression techniques may be applied to time-series or cross-section data. The methods of analysis are similar in each case, though there are differences of approach and interpretation which are highlighted in this chapter and the next.

This chapter begins with the topic of correlation and simple (i.e. two variable) regression, using as an example the determinants of the birth rate in developing countries. In Chapter 8, multiple regression is examined, where a single dependent variable is explained by more than one explanatory variable. This is illustrated using time-series data pertaining to imports into the UK. This shows how a small research project can be undertaken, avoiding the many possible pitfalls along the way. Finally, a variety of useful additional techniques, tips and traps is set out, to help you understand and overcome a number of problems that can arise in regression analysis.

# What determines the birth rate in developing countries?

This example follows the analysis in Michael Todaro's book, *Economic Development in the Third World* (3rd edn, pp. 197–200) where he tries to establish which of three variables (GNP per capita, the growth rate per capita, or income inequality) is most important in determining a country's birth rate. (This analysis has been dropped from later editions of Todaro's book.) The analysis is instructive as an example of correlation and regression techniques in a number of ways. First, the question is an important one; it was discussed at the UN International Conference on Population and Development in Cairo in 1995. It is felt by many that reducing the birth rate is a vital factor in economic development (birth rates in developed countries average around 12 per 1000 population, in developing countries around 30). Second, Todaro uses the

**Table 7.1** Todaro's data on birth rate, GNP, growth and inequality

| Country | Birth rate | 1981 GNP p.c. | GNP growth | Income ratio |
|---|---|---|---|---|
| Brazil | 30 | 2200 | 5.1 | 9.5 |
| Colombia | 29 | 1380 | 3.2 | 6.8 |
| Costa Rica | 30 | 1430 | 3.0 | 4.6 |
| India | 35 | 260 | 1.4 | 3.1 |
| Mexico | 36 | 2250 | 3.8 | 5.0 |
| Peru | 36 | 1170 | 1.0 | 8.7 |
| Philippines | 34 | 790 | 2.8 | 3.8 |
| Senegal | 48 | 430 | −0.3 | 6.4 |
| South Korea | 24 | 1700 | 6.9 | 2.7 |
| Sri Lanka | 27 | 300 | 2.5 | 2.3 |
| Taiwan | 21 | 1170 | 6.2 | 3.8 |
| Thailand | 30 | 770 | 4.6 | 3.3 |

statistical analysis to arrive at an unjustified conclusion (it's always best to learn from other's mistakes).

The data used by Todaro are shown in Table 7.1 for a sample of 12 developing countries. Two points need to be made initially. First, the sample only includes developing countries, so the results will not give an all-embracing explanation of the birth rate. Different factors might be relevant to developed countries, for example. Second, there is the important question of why these particular countries were chosen as the sample and others ignored. The choice of country was, in fact, limited by data availability, and one should ask whether countries with data available are likely to be representative of all countries. Data were, in fact, available for more than 12 countries, so Todaro was selective. You are asked to explore the implications of this in some of the problems at the end of the chapter.

The variables are defined as follows:

*Birth rate*: the number of births per 1000 population in 1981.
*GNP per capita*: 1981 gross national product p.c., in US dollars.
*Growth rate*: the growth rate of GNP p.c. per annum, 1961–81.
*Income ratio*: the ratio of the income share of the richest 20% to that of the poorest 40%. A higher value of this ratio indicates greater inequality.

We leave aside the concerns about the sample until later and concentrate now on analysing the figures. The first thing it is useful to do is to graph the variables to see if anything useful is revealed. *XY* graphs are the most suitable in this case and they are shown in Figure 7.1. From these we see a reasonably tidy relationship between the birth rate and the growth rate, with a negative slope; there is a looser relationship with the income ratio, with a positive slope; and there is little discernible pattern (apart from a flat line) in the graph of birth rate against GNP. Todaro asserts that the best relationship is between the birth rate and income inequality. He rejects the growth rate as an important determinant of the birth rate because of the four countries at the top of the chart, which have very different growth rates, yet similar birth rates. In the following sections we shall see whether Todaro's conclusions are justified.

**Figure 7.1**
Graphs of the birth
rate against (a) GNP,
(b) growth, and
(c) income ratio

(a)

(b)

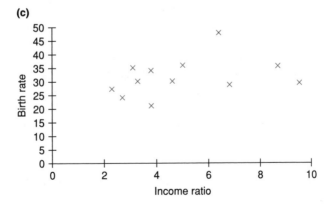

(c)

## Correlation

The relationships graphed in Figure 7.1 can first be summarised numerically by measuring the correlation coefficient between any pair of variables. We illustrate this by calculating the correlation coefficient between the birth rate ($B$) and growth ($G$), though we also present the results for the other cases. Just as the mean is a number that summarises information about a single variable, so the correlation coefficient is a number which summarises the relationship between two variables.

**Figure 7.2**
**Perfect positive**
**correlation**

The different types of possible relationship between any two variables, $X$ and $Y$, may be summarised as follows:

- High values of $X$ tend to be associated with low values of $Y$ and vice versa. This is termed **negative correlation**, and appears to be the case for $B$ and $G$.
- High (low) values of $X$ tend to be associated with high (low) values of $Y$. This is **positive correlation** and reflects (rather weakly) the relationship between $B$ and the income ratio ($IR$).
- No relationship between $X$ and $Y$ exists. High (low) values of $X$ are associated about equally with high and low values of $Y$. This is **zero**, or the absence of, **correlation**. There appears to be little correlation between the birth rate and per capita GNP.

It should be noted that positive correlation does not mean that high values of $X$ are *always* associated with high values of $Y$, but usually they are. It is also the case that correlation only represents a *linear* relationship between the two variables. As a counter-example, consider the backward-bending labour supply curve, as suggested by economic theory (higher wages initially encourage extra work effort, but above a certain point the benefit of higher wage rates is taken in the form of more leisure). The relationship is non-linear and the measured degree of correlation between wages and hours of work is likely to be low, even though the former obviously influences the latter.

The sample correlation coefficient, $r$, is a numerical statistic which distinguishes between the types of cases shown in Figure 7.1. It has the following properties:

- It always lies between $-1$ and $+1$.
- A positive value of $r$ indicates positive correlation, a higher value indicating a stronger correlation between $X$ and $Y$ (i.e. the observations lie closer to a straight line). $r = 1$ indicates perfect positive correlation and means that all the observations lie precisely on a straight line with positive slope, as Figure 7.2 illustrates.
- A negative value of $r$ indicates negative correlation. Similar to the above, a larger negative value indicates stronger negative correlation and $r = -1$ signifies perfect negative correlation.
- A value of $r = 0$ (or close to it) indicates a lack of correlation between $X$ and $Y$.
- The relationship is symmetric, i.e. the correlation between $X$ and $Y$ is the same as between $Y$ and $X$. It does not matter which variable is labelled $Y$ and which is labelled $X$.

Table 7.2 Calculation of the correlation coefficient, $r$

| Country | Birth rate $Y$ | GNP growth $X$ | $Y^2$ | $X^2$ | $XY$ |
|---|---|---|---|---|---|
| Brazil | 30 | 5.1 | 900 | 26.01 | 153.0 |
| Colombia | 29 | 3.2 | 841 | 10.24 | 92.8 |
| Costa Rica | 30 | 3.0 | 900 | 9.00 | 90.0 |
| India | 35 | 1.4 | 1 225 | 1.96 | 49.0 |
| Mexico | 36 | 3.8 | 1 296 | 14.44 | 136.8 |
| Peru | 36 | 1.0 | 1 296 | 1.00 | 36.0 |
| Philippines | 34 | 2.8 | 1,156 | 7.84 | 95.2 |
| Senegal | 48 | −0.3 | 2 304 | 0.09 | −14.4 |
| South Korea | 24 | 6.9 | 576 | 47.61 | 165.6 |
| Sri Lanka | 27 | 2.5 | 729 | 6.25 | 67.5 |
| Taiwan | 21 | 6.2 | 441 | 38.44 | 130.2 |
| Thailand | 30 | 4.6 | 900 | 21.16 | 138.0 |
| Totals | 380 | 40.2 | 12 564 | 184.04 | 1139.7 |

*Note*: In addition to the $X$ and $Y$ variables in the first two columns, three other columns are needed, for $X^2$, $Y^2$ and $XY$ values.

The formula[1] for calculating the correlation coefficient is given in equation (7.1):

$$(7.1) \qquad r = \frac{n\Sigma XY - \Sigma X \Sigma Y}{\sqrt{(n\Sigma X^2 - (\Sigma X)^2)(n\Sigma Y^2 - (\Sigma Y)^2)}}$$

The calculation of $r$ for the relationship between birth rate ($Y$) and growth ($X$) is shown in Table 7.2 and equation (7.2). From the totals in Table 7.2 we calculate:

$$(7.2) \qquad r = \frac{12 \times 1139.7 - 40.2 \times 380}{\sqrt{(12 \times 184.04 - 40.2^2)(12 \times 12\ 564 - 380^2)}} = -0.824$$

This result indicates a fairly strong negative correlation between the birth rate and growth. Countries which have higher economic growth rates also tend to have lower birth rates. The result of calculating the correlation coefficient for the case of the birth rate and the income ratio is $r = 0.35$, which is positive as expected. Greater inequality (higher IR) is associated with a higher birth rate, though the degree of correlation is not particularly strong and less than the correlation with the growth rate. Between the birth rate and GNP per capita the value of $r$ is only −0.26 indicating only a modest degree of correlation. All of this begins to cast doubt upon Todaro's interpretation of the data.

**Exercise 7.1**

(a) Perform the required calculations to confirm that the correlation between the birth rate and the income ratio is 0.35.

(b) In *Excel*, use the = CORREL() function to confirm your calculations in the previous two exercises. (For example, the function = CORREL(A1:A12,B1:B12) would calculate the correlation between a variable $X$ in cells A1:A12 and $Y$ in cells B1:B12.)

(c) Calculate the correlation coefficient between the birth rate and the growth rate again, but expressing the birth rate per 100 population and the growth rate as a decimal. (In other words, divide $Y$ by 10 and $X$ by 100.) Your calculation should confirm that changing the units of measurement leaves the correlation coefficient unchanged.

[1] The formula for $r$ can be written in a variety of different ways. The one given here is the most convenient for calculation.

### Are the results significant?

These results come from a (small) sample, one of many that could have been collected. Once again we can ask the question, what can we infer about the population (of all developing countries) from the sample? *Assuming* the sample was drawn at random (which may not be justified) we can use the principles of hypothesis testing introduced in Chapter 5. As usual, there are two possibilities:

1 The truth is that there is no correlation (in the population) and that our sample exhibits such a large (absolute) value by chance.
2 There really is a correlation between the birth rate and the growth rate and the sample correctly reflects this.

Denoting the true but unknown population correlation coefficient by $\rho$ (the Greek letter 'rho') the possibilities can be expressed in terms of a hypothesis test:

$H_0: \rho = 0$
$H_1: \rho \neq 0$

The test statistic in this case is not $r$ itself but a transformation of it:

$$(7.3) \qquad t = \frac{r\sqrt{n-2}}{\sqrt{1-r^2}}$$

which has a $t$ distribution with $n - 2$ degrees of freedom. The five steps of the test procedure are therefore:

1 Write down the null and alternative hypotheses (shown above).
2 Choose the significance level of the test: 5% by convention.
3 Look up the critical value of the test for $n - 2 = 10$ degrees of freedom: $t_{10}^* = 2.228$ for a two-tail test.
4 Calculate the test statistic using equation (7.3):

$$t = \frac{-0.824\sqrt{12-2}}{\sqrt{1-(-0.824)^2}} = -4.59$$

5 Compare the test statistic with the critical value. In this case $t < -t_{10}^*$ so $H_0$ is rejected. There is a less than 5% chance of the sample evidence occurring if the null hypothesis were true, so the latter is rejected. There does appear to be a genuine association between the birth rate and the growth rate.

Performing similar calculations (see Exercise 7.2 below) for the income ratio and for GNP reveals that in both cases the null hypothesis cannot be rejected at the 5% significance level. These observed associations could well have arisen by chance.

### Are significant results important?

Following the discussion in Chapter 5, we might ask if a certain value of the correlation coefficient is economically important as well as being significant. We saw earlier that 'significant' results need not be important. The difficulty in this case is that we have little intuitive understanding of the correlation coefficient. Is $\rho = 0.5$ important, for example? Would it make much difference if it were only 0.4?

Our understanding may be helped if we look at some graphs of variables with different correlation coefficients. Three are shown in Figure 7.3. Panel (a)

**Figure 7.3**
**Variables with different correlations**

of the figure graphs two variables with a correlation coefficient of 0.2. Visually there seems little relationship between the variables, yet the correlation coefficient is (just) significant: $t = 2.06$ ($n = 100$ and the Prob-value is 0.042). This is a significant result which does not impress.

In panel (b) the correlation coefficient is 0.5 and there is a clear positive slope, though there is a substantial scatter of the observations around a straight line. The relationship between $X$ and $Y$ does not appear particularly strong. Yet the $t$ statistic in this case is a massive 65.3, hugely significant.

Finally, panel (c) shows an example where $n = 1000$. To the eye this looks like a random scatter, with no discernable pattern. Yet the correlation coefficient is 0.1 and the $t$ statistic is 100.8, again hugely significant.

The lesson is obvious. One should not always be impressed by large $t$ statistics, especially if the sample size is large. Looking at a graph of the data is a useful, even vital, supplement.

**Exercise 7.2**

(a) Test the hypothesis that there is no association between the birth rate and the income ratio.

(b) Look up the Prob-value associated with the test statistic and confirm that it does not reject the null hypothesis.

**Correlation and causality**

It is important to test the significance of any result because almost every pair of variables will have a non-zero correlation coefficient, even if they are totally unconnected (the chance of the sample correlation coefficient being *exactly* zero is very, very small). Therefore it is important to distinguish between correlation coefficients which are significant and those which are not, using the $t$ test just outlined. But even when the result is significant one should beware of the danger of 'spurious' correlation. Many variables which clearly cannot be related turn out to be 'significantly' correlated with each other. One now famous example is between the price level and cumulative rainfall. Since they both rise year after year it is easy to see why they are correlated, yet it is hard to think of a plausible reason why they should be causally related to each other.

Apart from spurious correlation there are four possible reasons for a non-zero value of $r$:

1 $X$ influences $Y$.
2 $Y$ influences $X$.
3 $X$ and $Y$ jointly influence each other.
4 Another variable, $Z$, influences both $X$ and $Y$.

Correlation alone does not allow us to distinguish between these alternatives. For example, wages ($X$) and prices ($Y$) are highly correlated. Some people believe this is due to cost–push inflation, i.e. that wage rises lead to price rises. This is case (1) above. Others believe that wages rise to keep up with the cost of living (i.e. rising prices), which is (2). Perhaps a more convincing explanation is (3), a wage–price spiral where each feeds upon the other. Others would suggest that it is the growth of the money supply, $Z$, which allows both wages and prices to rise. To distinguish between these alternatives is important for the control of inflation, but correlation alone does not allow that distinction to be made.

Correlation is best used therefore as a suggestive and descriptive piece of analysis, rather than a technique which gives definitive answers. It is often a preparatory piece of analysis, which gives some clues to what the data might yield, to be followed by more sophisticated techniques such as regression.

**The coefficient of rank correlation**

Sometimes the original data are unavailable but the ranks are. For example, schools may be ranked in terms of their exam results, but the actual pass rates are not available. Similarly, they may be ranked in terms of spending per pupil, with actual spending levels unavailable. Although the original data are missing, one can still test for an association between spending and exam success by calculating the correlation between the ranks. If extra spending improves exam performance, schools ranked higher on spending should also be ranked higher on exam success, leading to a positive correlation. In this case, Spearman's coefficient of rank correlation is calculated.

In some circumstances it may be preferable to use the ranks rather than the original data, even though one is effectively throwing away information (e.g. by *how much* do countries' growth rates differ). If there are extreme values to one or both variables, this may distort the results and using the ranks will avoid this danger. This is similar to the situation where the median can prove superior to the mean as a measure of central tendency.

We will calculate the rank correlation coefficient for the data on birth and growth rates, to provide a comparison with the ordinary correlation coefficient calculated earlier. Table 7.3 presents the data for birth and growth rates in the form of ranks. Calculating the ranks is straightforward, though there are a couple of points to note.

The country with the highest birth rate has the rank of 1, the next highest 2, and so on. Similarly, the country with the highest growth rate ranks 1, etc. One could reverse a ranking, so the lowest birth rate ranks 1, for example; the direction of ranking is somewhat arbitrary. This would leave the rank correlation

**Table 7.3** Calculation of Spearman's rank correlation coefficient

| Country | Birth rate Y | Growth rate X | Rank Y | Rank X | Difference d | $d^2$ |
|---|---|---|---|---|---|---|
| Brazil | 30 | 5.1 | 7 | 3 | 4 | 16 |
| Colombia | 29 | 3.2 | 9 | 6 | 3 | 9 |
| Costa Rica | 30 | 3.0 | 7 | 7 | 0 | 0 |
| India | 35 | 1.4 | 4 | 10 | −6 | 36 |
| Mexico | 36 | 3.8 | 2.5 | 5 | −2.5 | 6.25 |
| Peru | 36 | 1.0 | 2.5 | 11 | −8.5 | 72.25 |
| Philippines | 34 | 2.8 | 5 | 8 | −3 | 9 |
| Senegal | 48 | −0.3 | 1 | 12 | −11 | 121 |
| South Korea | 24 | 6.9 | 11 | 1 | 10 | 100 |
| Sri Lanka | 27 | 2.5 | 10 | 9 | 1 | 1 |
| Taiwan | 21 | 6.2 | 12 | 2 | 10 | 100 |
| Thailand | 30 | 4.6 | 7 | 4 | 3 | 9 |
| Totals | 380 | 40.2 | | | | 479.5 |

*Note*: The country with the highest growth rate (South Korea) is ranked 1 for variable *X*; Taiwan, the next fastest growth nation, is ranked 2, etc. For the birth rate, Senegal is ranked 1, having the highest birth rate, 48. Taiwan has the lowest birth rate and so is ranked 12 for variable *Y*. The difference between ranks *d* is calculated as 4 for Brazil, which is 7 − 3, its rank values for the birth rate and growth rate respectively.

coefficient unchanged in value, but the sign would change, e.g. 0.5 would become –0.5. This could be confusing as we would now have a 'negative' correlation rather than a positive one (though the birth rate variable would now have to be redefined). It is better to use the 'natural' order of ranking for each variable.

Where two or more observations are the same, as are the birth rates of Mexico and Peru, then they are given the same rank, which is the average of the relevant ranking values. For example, both countries are given the rank of 2.5, which is the average of 2 and 3. Similarly, Brazil, Costa Rica and Thailand are all given the rank of 7, which is the average of 6, 7 and 8. The next country, Colombia, is then given the rank of 9.

*Spearman's rank correlation coefficient*, $r_s$, is calculated using formula (7.4):[2]

$$(7.4) \quad r_s = 1 - \frac{6 \times \Sigma d^2}{n(n^2 - 1)}$$

where $d$ is the difference in the ranks. The differences and their squared values are shown in the final columns of Table 7.3 and from these we obtain

$$(7.5) \quad r_s = 1 - \frac{6 \times 479.5}{12 \times (12^2 - 1)} = -0.676$$

This indicates a negative rank correlation between the two variables, as with the standard correlation coefficient ($r = -0.824$), but with a slightly smaller absolute value.

To test the significance of the result a hypothesis test can be performed on the value of $\rho_s$, the corresponding population parameter.

$H_0: \rho_s = 0$
$H_1: \rho_s \neq 0$

This time the $t$ distribution cannot be used, but prepared tables of the critical values for $\rho_s$ itself may be consulted; these are given in Table A6 (see page **378**), and an excerpt is given in Table 7.4.

The critical value at the 5% significance level, for $n = 12$, is 0.591. Hence the null hypothesis is rejected if the test statistic falls outside the range [–0.591, 0.591], which it does in this case. Thus the null can be rejected with 95% confidence; the data do support the hypothesis of a relationship between the birth rate and growth. This critical value shown in the table is for a two-tail

**Table 7.4 Excerpt from Table A6: Critical values of the rank correlation coefficient**

| n | 10% | 5% | 2% | 1% |
|---|---|---|---|---|
| 5 | 0.900 | | | |
| 6 | 0.829 | 0.886 | 0.943 | |
| ⋮ | ⋮ | ⋮ | ⋮ | ⋮ |
| 11 | 0.523 | 0.623 | 0.763 | 0.794 |
| 12 | 0.497 | 0.591 | 0.703 | 0.780 |
| 13 | 0.475 | 0.566 | 0.673 | 0.746 |

*Note*: The critical value is given at the intersection of the shaded row and column.

[2] You can also use formula (7.1) on the ranks, but (7.4) is easier.

test. For a one-tail test, the significance level given in the top row of the table should be halved.

**Exercise 7.3**

(a) Rank the observations for the income ratio across countries (highest = 1) and calculate the coefficient of rank correlation with the birth rate.

(b) Test the hypothesis that $\rho_s = 0$.

(c) Reverse the rankings for both variables and confirm that this does not affect the calculated test statistic.

**Worked example 7.1**

To illustrate all the calculations and bring them together without distracting explanation, we work through a simple example with the following data on $X$ and $Y$:

| Y | 17 | 18 | 19 | 20 | 27 | 18 |
|---|----|----|----|----|----|----|
| X | 3  | 4  | 7  | 6  | 8  | 5  |

An $XY$ graph of the data reveals the following picture, which suggests positive correlation:

Note that one point appears to be something of an outlier. All the calculations for correlation may be based on the following table:

| | Y | X | Y² | X² | XY | rank Y | rank X | d | d² |
|---|---|---|----|----|----|--------|--------|---|----|
| | 17 | 3 | 289 | 9 | 51 | 6 | 6 | 0 | 0 |
| | 18 | 4 | 324 | 16 | 72 | 4.5 | 5 | −0.5 | 0.25 |
| | 19 | 7 | 361 | 49 | 133 | 3 | 2 | 1 | 1 |
| | 20 | 6 | 400 | 36 | 120 | 2 | 3 | −1 | 1 |
| | 27 | 8 | 729 | 64 | 216 | 1 | 1 | 0 | 0 |
| | 18 | 5 | 324 | 25 | 90 | 4.5 | 4 | 0.5 | 0.25 |
| Totals | 119 | 33 | 2427 | 199 | 682 | | | | 2.5 |

The correlation coefficient $r$ is therefore:

$$r = \frac{n\Sigma XY - \Sigma X \Sigma Y}{\sqrt{(n\Sigma X^2 - (\Sigma X)^2)(n\Sigma Y^2 - (\Sigma Y)^2)}} = \frac{6 \times 682 - 33 \times 119}{\sqrt{(6 \times 199 - 33^2)(6 \times 2427 - 119^2)}}$$

$$= 0.804$$

The hypothesis $H_0$: $\rho = 0$ vs $H_1$: $\rho \neq 0$ can be tested using the $t$ test statistic:

$$t = \frac{r\sqrt{n-2}}{\sqrt{1-r^2}} = \frac{0.804 \times \sqrt{6-2}}{\sqrt{1-0.804^2}} = 2.7$$

which is compared to a critical value of 2.776, so the null hypothesis is not rejected, narrowly. This is largely due to the small number of observations. The rank correlation coefficient is calculated as

$$r_s = 1 - \frac{6 \times \sum d^2}{n(n^2 - 1)} = 1 - \frac{6 \times 2.5}{6 \times (6^2 - 1)} = 0.928$$

The critical value at the 5% significance level is 0.886, so the rank correlation coefficient *is* significant, in contrast to the previous result. Not too much should be read into this, however; with few observations the ranking process can easily alter the result substantially.

## Regression analysis

Regression analysis is a more sophisticated way of examining the relationship between two (or more) variables than is correlation. The major differences between correlation and regression are the following:

- Regression can investigate the relationships between two *or more* variables.
- A *direction* of causality is asserted, from the explanatory variable (or variables) to the dependent variable.
- The *influence* of each explanatory variable upon the dependent variable is measured.
- The *significance* of each explanatory variable can be ascertained.

Thus regression permits answers to such questions as:

- Does the growth rate influence a country's birth rate?
- If the growth rate increases, by how much might a country's birth rate be expected to fall?
- Are other variables important in determining the birth rate?

In this example we assert that the direction of causality is from the growth rate ($X$) to the birth rate ($Y$) and not vice versa. The growth rate is therefore the **explanatory** variable (also referred to as the **independent** or **exogenous** variable) and the birth rate is the **dependent** variable (also called the **explained** or **endogenous** variable).

Regression analysis describes this causal relationship by fitting a straight line drawn through the data, which best summarises them. It is sometimes called 'the line of best fit' for this reason. This is illustrated in Figure 7.4 for the birth rate and growth rate data. Note that (by convention) the explanatory variable is placed on the horizontal axis, the explained on the vertical. This regression line is downward sloping (its derivation will be explained shortly) for the same reason that the correlation coefficient is negative, i.e. high values of $Y$ are generally associated with low values of $X$ and vice versa.

Since the regression line summarises knowledge of the relationship between $X$ and $Y$, it can be used to predict the value of $Y$ given any particular value of $X$. In Figure 7.4 the value of $X = 3$ (the observation for Costa Rica) is related via the regression line to a value of $Y$ (denoted by $\hat{Y}$) of 32.6. This predicted value

**Figure 7.4**
**The line of best fit**

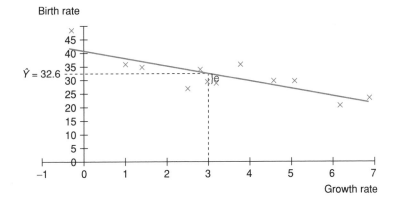

is close (but not identical) to the actual birth rate of 30. The difference reflects the absence of perfect correlation between the two variables.

The difference between the actual value, $Y$, and the predicted value, $\hat{Y}$, is called the **error** or **residual**. It is labelled $e$ in Figure 7.4. Why should such errors occur? The relationship is never going to be an exact one for a variety of reasons. There are bound to be other factors besides growth which affect the birth rate (e.g. the education of women) and these effects are all subsumed into the error term. There might additionally be simple measurement error (of $Y$) and, of course, people do act in a somewhat random fashion rather than follow rigid rules of behaviour.

All of these factors fall into the error term and this means that the observations lie around the regression line rather than on it. If there are many of these factors, none of which is predominant, and they are independent of each other, then these errors may be assumed to be Normally distributed about the regression line.

Why not include these factors explicitly? On the face of it this would seem to be an improvement, making the model more realistic. However, the costs of doing this are that the model becomes more complex, calculation becomes more difficult (not so important now with computers) and it is generally more difficult for the reader (or researcher) to interpret what is going on. If the main interest is the relationship between the birth rate and growth, why complicate the model unduly? There is a virtue in simplicity, as long as the simplified model still gives an undistorted view of the relationship. In Chapter 10 on multiple regression the trade-off between simplicity and realism will be further discussed, particularly with reference to the problems which can arise if relevant explanatory variables are omitted from the analysis.

**Calculation of the regression line**

The equation of the sample regression line may be written

(7.6)     $\hat{Y}_i = a + bX_i$

where

$\hat{Y}_i$ is the predicted value of $Y$ for observation (country) $i$
$X_i$ is the value of the explanatory variable for observation $i$, and
$a$, $b$ are fixed coefficients to be estimated; $a$ measures the intercept of the regression line on the $Y$ axis, $b$ measures its slope.

This is illustrated in Figure 7.5.

**Figure 7.5**

**Intercept and slope of the regression line**

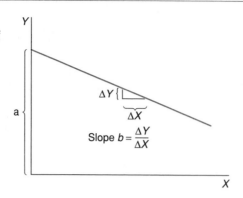

The first task of regression analysis is to find the values of $a$ and $b$ so that the regression line may be drawn. To do this we proceed as follows. The difference between the actual value, $Y_i$, and its predicted value, $\hat{Y}_i$, is $e_i$, the error. (*Note:* The italic $e$ denoting the error term should not be confused with the roman letter e, used as the base for natural logarithms (see the Appendix to Chapter 1, page **74**). Thus

**(7.7)**    $Y_i = \hat{Y}_i + e_i$

Substituting equation (7.6) into equation (7.7) the regression equation can be written

**(7.8)**    $Y_i = a + bX_i + e_i$

Equation (7.8) shows that observed birth rates are made up of two components:

1  that part explained by the growth rate, $a + bX_i$, and
2  an error component, $e_i$.

In a good model, part (1) should be large relative to part (2) and the regression line is based upon this principle. The line of best fit is therefore found by finding the values of $a$ and $b$ which *minimise the sum of squared errors* $(\Sigma e_i^2)$ from the regression line. For this reason, this method is known as 'the method of least squares' or simply 'ordinary least squares' (OLS). The use of this criterion will be justified later on, but it can be said in passing that the sum of the errors is not minimised because that would not lead to a unique answer for the values $a$ and $b$. In fact, there is an infinite number of possible regression lines which all yield a sum of errors equal to zero. Minimising the sum of *squared* errors does yield a unique answer.

The task is therefore to

**(7.9)**    minimise $\Sigma e_i^2$

by choice of $a$ and $b$.

Rearranging equation (7.8) the error is given by

**(7.10)**    $e_i = Y_i - a - bX_i$

so equation (7.9) becomes

**(7.11)**    minimise $\Sigma(Y_i - a - bX_i)^2$

by choice of $a$ and $b$.

Finding the solution to (7.11) requires the use of differential calculus, and is not presented here. The resulting formulae for $a$ and $b$ are

(7.12)    $b = \dfrac{n\Sigma XY - \Sigma X \Sigma Y}{n\Sigma X^2 - (\Sigma X)^2}$

and

(7.13)    $a = \bar{Y} - b\bar{X}$

where $\bar{X}$ and $\bar{Y}$ are the mean values of $X$ and $Y$ respectively. The values necessary to evaluate equations (7.12) and (7.13) can be obtained from Table 7.2 which was used to calculate the correlation coefficient. These values are repeated for convenience:

$$\Sigma Y = 380 \qquad \Sigma Y^2 = 12\ 564$$
$$\Sigma X = 40.2 \qquad \Sigma X^2 = 184.04$$
$$\Sigma XY = 1139.70 \qquad n = 12$$

Using these values we obtain

$$b = \frac{12 \times 1139.70 - 40.2 \times 380}{12 \times 184.04 - 40.2^2} = -2.700$$

and

$$a = \frac{380}{12} - (-2.700) \times \frac{40.2}{12} = 40.711$$

Thus the regression equation can be written, to two decimal places for clarity, as

$$Y_i = 40.71 - 2.70X_i + e_i$$

**Interpretation of the slope and intercept**

The most important part of the result is the slope coefficient $b = -2.7$ since it measures the effect of $X$ upon $Y$. This result implies that a unit increase in the growth rate (e.g. from 2% to 3% p.a.) would lower the birth rate by 2.7, e.g. from 30 births per 1000 population to 27.3. Given that the growth data refer to a 20-year period (1961 to 1981), this increase in the growth rate would have to be sustained over such a time, not an easy task. How big is the effect upon the birth rate? The average birth rate in the sample is 31.67, so a reduction of 2.7 for an average country would be a fall of 8.5% ($2.7/31.67 \times 100$). This is reasonably substantial (though not enough to bring the birth rate down to developed country levels) but would need a considerable, sustained increase in the growth rate to bring it about.

The value of $a$, the intercept, may be interpreted as the predicted birth rate of a country with zero growth (since $\hat{Y}_i = a$ at $X = 0$). This value of 40.71 is fairly close to that of Senegal, which actually had negative growth over the period and whose birth rate was 48, a little higher than the intercept value. Although $a$ has a sensible interpretation in this case, this is not always so. For example, in a regression of the demand for a good on its price, $a$ would represent demand at zero price, which is unlikely ever to be observed.

**Exercise 7.4**

(a)  Calculate the regression line relating the birth rate to the growth rate.

(b)  Interpret the coefficients of this equation.

**Measuring the goodness of fit of the regression line**

Having calculated the regression line we now ask whether it provides a good fit for the data, i.e. do the observations tend to lie close to, or far away from, the line? If the fit is poor, perhaps the effect of $X$ upon $Y$ is not so strong after all. Note that even if $X$ has *no* effect upon $Y$ we can still calculate a regression line and its slope coefficient $b$. Although $b$ is likely to be small, it is unlikely to be exactly zero. Measuring the goodness of fit of the data to the line helps us to distinguish between good and bad regressions.

We proceed by comparing the competing models explaining the birth rate. Which of them fits the data best? Using the income ratio and the GNP variable gives the following regressions (calculations not shown) to compare with our original model:

for the income ratio (IR): $B = 26.44 + 1.045 IR + e$
for GNP: $B = 34.72 - 0.003 GNP + e$
for growth: $B = 40.71 - 2.70 GROWTH + e$

How can we decide which of these three is 'best' on the basis of the regression equations alone? From Figure 7.1 it is evident that some relationships appear stronger than others, yet this is not revealed by examining the regression equation alone. More information is needed. (You cannot choose the best equation simply by looking at the size of the coefficients. Try to think why.)

The goodness of fit is calculated by comparing two lines: the regression line and the 'mean line' (i.e. a horizontal line drawn at the mean value of $Y$). The regression line *must* fit the data better (if the mean line were the best fit, that is also where the regression line would be) but the question is how much better. This is illustrated in Figure 7.6, which demonstrates the principle behind the calculation of the **coefficient of determination**, denoted by $R^2$ and usually more simply referred to as 'R squared'.

The figure shows the mean value of $Y$, the calculated sample regression line and an arbitrarily chosen sample observation ($X_i$, $Y_i$). The difference between $Y_i$ and $\bar{Y}$ (length $Y_i - \bar{Y}$) can be divided up into:

1 That part 'explained' by the regression line, $\hat{Y}_i - \bar{Y}$ (i.e. explained by the value of $X_i$).
2 The error term $e_i = Y_i - \hat{Y}_i$.

**Figure 7.6**
**The calculation of $R^2$**

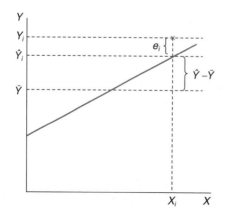

In algebraic terms,

**(7.14)**     $Y_i - \bar{Y} = (Y_i - \hat{Y}_i) + (\hat{Y}_i - \bar{Y})$

A good regression model should 'explain' a large part of the differences between the $Y_i$ values and $\bar{Y}$, i.e. the length $\hat{Y}_i - \bar{Y}$ should be large relative to $Y_i - \bar{Y}$. A measure of fit would therefore be $(\hat{Y}_i - \bar{Y})/(Y_i - \bar{Y})$. We need to apply this to all observations, not just a single one. Hence we need to sum this expression over all the sample observations. A problem is that some of the terms would take a negative value and offset the positive terms. To get round this problem we square each of the terms in equation (7.14) to make them all positive, and then sum over the observations. This gives

$\sum(Y_i - \bar{Y})^2$, known as the total sum of squares (TSS)
$\sum(\hat{Y}_i - \bar{Y})^2$, the regression sum of squares (RSS), and
$\sum(Y_i - \hat{Y}_i)^2$, the error sum of squares (ESS)

The measure of goodness of fit, $R^2$, is then defined as the ratio of the regression sum of squares to the total sum of squares, i.e.

**(7.15)**     $R^2 = \dfrac{\text{RSS}}{\text{TSS}}$

The better the divergences between $Y_i$ and $\bar{Y}$ are explained by the regression line, the better the goodness of fit, and the higher the calculated value of $R^2$. Further, it is true that

**(7.16)**     $\text{TSS} = \text{RSS} + \text{ESS}$

From equations (7.15) and (7.16) we can see that $R^2$ must lie between 0 and 1 (note that since each term in equation (7.16) is a sum of squares, none of them can be negative). Thus

$0 \leq R^2 \leq 1$

A value of $R^2 = 1$ indicates that all the sample observations lie exactly on the regression line (equivalent to perfect correlation). If $R^2 = 0$ then the regression line is of no use at all – $X$ does not influence $Y$ (linearly) at all, and to try to predict a value of $Y_i$ one might as well use the mean $\bar{Y}$ rather than the value $X_i$ inserted into the sample regression equation.

To calculate $R^2$, alternative formulae to those above make the task easier. Instead we use:

$\text{TSS} = \sum(Y_i - \bar{Y})^2 = \sum Y_i^2 - n\bar{Y}^2 = 12\,564 - 12 \times 31.67^2 = 530.667$

$\text{ESS} = \sum(Y_i - \hat{Y})^2 = \sum Y_i^2 - a\sum Y_i - b\sum X_i Y_i$
$\qquad = 12\,564 - 40.711 \times 380 - (-2.7) \times 1139.70 = 170.754$

$\text{RSS} = \text{TSS} - \text{ESS} = 530.667 - 170.754 = 359.913$

This gives the result

$R^2 = \dfrac{\text{RSS}}{\text{TSS}} = \dfrac{359.913}{530.667} = 0.678$

This is interpreted as follows. Countries' birth rates vary around the overall mean value of 31.67. 67.8% of this variation is explained by variation in countries' growth rates. This is quite a respectable figure to obtain, leaving only 32.8% of the variation in $Y$ left to be explained by other factors (or pure random variation). The regression seems to make a worthwhile contribution to explaining why birth rates differ.

It turns out that in simple regression (i.e. where there is only one explanatory variable), $R^2$ is simply the square of the correlation coefficient between $X$ and $Y$. Thus for the income ratio and for GNP we have:

for IR: $\quad R^2 = 0.35^2 = 0.13$
for GNP: $\quad R^2 = -0.26^2 = 0.07$

This shows, once again, that these other variables are not terribly useful in explaining why birth rates differ. Each of them only explains a small proportion of the variation in $Y$.

It should be emphasised at this point that $R^2$ is not the only criterion (or even an adequate one in all cases) for judging the quality of a regression equation and that other statistical measures, set out below, are also required.

| Exercise 7.5 | (a) Calculate the $R^2$ value for the regression of the birth rate on the income ratio, calculated in Exercise 7.4. |
|---|---|
|  | (b) Confirm that this result is the same as the square of the correlation coefficient between these two variables, calculated in Exercise 7.1. |

## Inference in the regression model

So far, regression has been used as a descriptive technique, to measure the relationship between the two variables. We now go on to draw inferences from the analysis about what the *true* regression line might look like. As with correlation, the estimated relationship is in fact a *sample* regression line, based upon data for 12 countries. The estimated coefficients $a$ and $b$ are random variables, since they would differ from sample to sample. What can be inferred about the true (but unknown) regression equation?

The question is best approached by first writing down a true or population regression equation, in a form similar to the sample regression equation:

(7.17) $\quad Y_i = \alpha + \beta X_i + \varepsilon_i$

As usual, Greek letters denote true, or population, values. $\alpha$ and $\beta$ are thus the population *parameters*, of which $a$ and $b$ are (point) estimates, using the method of least squares. $\varepsilon$ is the population error term. If we could observe the individual error terms $\varepsilon_i$ then we would be able to get exact values of $\alpha$ and $\beta$ (even from a sample), rather than just estimates.

Given that $a$ and $b$ are estimates, we can ask about their properties: whether they are unbiased and how precise they are, compared to alternative estimators. Under reasonable assumptions (see Thomas (1993), Chapter 1; Maddala (1992), Chapter 3) it can be shown that the OLS estimates of the coefficients are unbiased. Thus OLS provides useful point estimates of the parameters (the true values $\alpha$ and $\beta$). This is one reason for using the least squares method. It can also be shown that, among the class of linear unbiased

**Table 7.5 Calculation of residuals**

|  | Actual birth rate | Fitted values | Residuals |
|---|---|---|---|
| Brazil | 30 | 26.9 | 3.1 |
| Colombia | 29 | 32.1 | −3.1 |
| Costa Rica | 30 | 32.6 | −2.6 |
| ⋮ | ⋮ | ⋮ | ⋮ |
| Sri Lanka | 27 | 34.0 | −7.0 |
| Taiwan | 21 | 24.0 | −3.0 |
| Thailand | 30 | 28.3 | 1.7 |

estimators, OLS has the minimum variance, i.e. the method provides the most precise estimates. This is another, powerful justification for the use of OLS. So, just as the sample mean provides a more precise estimate of the population mean than does a single observation, the least squares estimates of $\alpha$ and $\beta$ are the most precise.

**Analysis of the errors**

To find confidence intervals for $\alpha$ and $\beta$ we need to know which statistical distribution we should be using, i.e. the distributions of $a$ and $b$. These can be derived, based on the assumptions that the error term $\varepsilon$ in equation (7.17) above is Normally distributed and that the errors are statistically independent of each other. Since we are using cross-section data from countries which are different geographically, politically and socially it seems reasonable to assume the errors are independent.

To check the Normality assumption we can graph the residuals calculated from the sample regression line. If the true errors are Normal it seems likely that these residuals should be approximately Normal also. The residuals are calculated according to equation (7.10) above. For example, to calculate the residual for Brazil we subtract the fitted value from the actual value. The fitted value is calculated by substituting the growth rate into the estimated regression equation, yielding $\hat{Y} = 40.712 - 2.7 \times 5.1 = 26.9$. Subtracting this from the actual value gives $Y_i - \hat{Y} = 30 - 26.9 = 3.1$. Other countries' residuals are calculated in similar manner, yielding the results shown in Table 7.5.

These residuals may then be gathered together in a frequency table (as in Chapter 1) and graphed. This is shown in Figure 7.7.

Although the number of observations is small (and therefore the graph is not a smooth curve) the chart does have the greater weight of frequencies in the centre as one would expect, with less weight as one moves into the tails of the distribution. The assumption that the true error term is Normally distributed does not seem unreasonable.

If the residuals from the sample regression equation appeared distinctly non-Normal (heavily skewed, for example) then one should be wary of constructing confidence intervals using the formulae below. Instead, one might consider transforming the data (see below) before continuing. There are more formal tests for Normality of the residuals but they are beyond the scope of this book. Drawing a graph is an informal alternative which can be useful, but remember that graphical methods can be misinterpreted.

If one were using time-series data one should also check the residuals for autocorrelation at this point. This occurs when the error in period $t$ is dependent

**Figure 7.7**
**Bar chart of residuals from the regression equation**

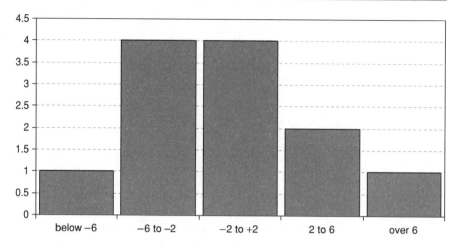

in some way on the error in the previous period(s) and implies that the method of least squares may not be the best way of estimating the relationship. In this example we have cross-section data, so it is not appropriate to check for auto-correlation, since the ordering of the data does not matter. The next chapter, on multiple regression, covers this topic.

**Confidence interval estimates of $\alpha$ and $\beta$**

Having checked that the residuals appear reasonably Normal we can proceed with inference. This means finding interval estimates of the parameters $\alpha$ and $\beta$ and, later on, conducting hypothesis tests. As usual, the 95% confidence interval is obtained by adding and subtracting approximately two standard errors from the point estimate. We therefore need to calculate the standard error of $a$ and of $b$ and we also need to look up tables to find the precise number of standard errors to add and subtract. The principle is just the same as for the confidence interval estimate of the sample mean, covered in Chapter 4.

The estimated sampling variance of $b$, the slope coefficient, is given by

$$(7.18) \qquad s_b^2 = \frac{s_e^2}{\Sigma(X_i - \bar{X})^2}$$

where

$$(7.19) \qquad s_e^2 = \frac{\Sigma e_i^2}{n-2} = \frac{ESS}{n-2}$$

is the estimated variance of the error term, $\varepsilon$.

The sampling variance of $b$ measures the uncertainty associated with the estimate. Note that the uncertainty is greater (a) the larger the error variance $s_e^2$ (i.e. the more scattered the points around the regression line) and (b) the lower the dispersion of the $X$ observations. When $X$ does not vary much it is then more difficult to measure the effect of changes in $X$ upon $Y$, and this is reflected in the formula.

First we need to calculate $s_e^2$. The value of this is

$$(7.20) \qquad s_e^2 = \frac{170.754}{10} = 17.0754$$

and so the estimated variance of $b$ is

**(7.21)**     $s_b^2 = \dfrac{17.0754}{49.37} = 0.346$

(Use $\Sigma(X_i - \bar{X})^2 = \Sigma X^2 - n\bar{X}^2$ in calculating (7.21) – it makes the calculation easier.) The estimated standard error of $b$ is the square root of (7.21),

**(7.22)**     $s_b = \sqrt{0.346} = 0.588$

To construct the confidence interval around the point estimate, $b = -2.7$, the $t$ distribution is used (in regression this applies to all sample sizes, not just small ones). The 95% confidence interval is thus given by

**(7.23)**     $[b - t_v s_b, \ b + t_v s_b]$

where $t_v$ is the (two-tail) critical value of the $t$ distribution at the appropriate significance level (5% in this case), with $v = n - 2$ degrees of freedom. The critical value is 2.228. Thus the confidence interval evaluates to:

$[-2.7 - 2.228 \times 0.588, -2.7 + 2.228 \times 0.588] = [-4.01, -1.39]$

Thus we can be 95% confident that the true value of $\beta$ lies within this range. Note that the interval only includes negative values: we can rule out an upward-sloping regression line.

For the intercept $a$, the estimate of the variance is given by

**(7.24)**     $s_a^2 = s_e^2 \times \left( \dfrac{1}{n} + \dfrac{\bar{X}^2}{\Sigma(X_i - \bar{X})^2} \right) = 17.0754 \times \left( \dfrac{1}{12} + \dfrac{3.35^2}{49.37} \right) = 5.304$

and the estimated standard error of $a$ is the square root of this, 2.303. The 95% confidence interval for $\alpha$, again using the $t$ distribution, is

$[40.71 - 2.228 \times 2.303, 40.71 + 2.228 \times 2.303] = [35.57, 45.84]$

The results so far can be summarised as follows:

$Y_i = 40.711 - 2.70X_i + e_i$
s.e.  (2.30)     (0.59)

$R^2 = 0.678$     $n = 12$

This conveys, at a glance, all the necessary information to the reader, who can then draw the inferences deemed appropriate. Any desired confidence interval (not just the 95% one) can be quickly calculated with the aid of a set of $t$ tables.

**Testing hypotheses about the coefficients**

As well as calculating confidence intervals, one can use hypothesis tests as the basis for statistical inference in the regression model. These tests are quickly and easily explained given the information already assembled. Consider the following hypothesis:

$H_0$: $\beta = 0$
$H_1$: $\beta \neq 0$

This null hypothesis is interesting because it implies no influence of $X$ upon $Y$ at all (i.e. the slope of the true regression line is flat and $Y_i$ can be equally well predicted by $\bar{Y}$). The alternative hypothesis asserts that $X$ does in fact influence $Y$.

The procedure is in principle the same as in Chapter 5 on hypothesis testing. We measure how many standard deviations separate the observed value of $b$ from the hypothesised value. If this is greater than an appropriate critical value we reject the hypothesis. The test statistic is calculated using the formula:

$$(7.25) \quad t = \frac{b - \beta}{s_b} = \frac{-2.7 - 0}{0.588} = -4.59$$

Thus the sample coefficient $b$ differs by 4.59 standard errors from its hypothesised value $\beta = 0$. This is compared to the critical value of the $t$ distribution, using $n - 2$ degrees of freedom. Since $t < -t_{10}^*$ ($= -2.228$), in this case the null hypothesis is rejected with 95% confidence. $X$ does have some influence on $Y$. Similar tests using the income ratio and GDP to attempt to explain the birth rate show that in neither case is the slope coefficient significantly different from zero, i.e. neither of these variables appears to influence the birth rate.

---

### Rule of thumb for hypothesis tests

A quick and reasonably accurate method for establishing whether a coefficient is significantly different from zero is to see if it is at least twice its standard error. If so, it is significant. This works because the critical value (at 95%) of the $t$ distribution for reasonable sample sizes is about 2.

---

Sometimes regression results are presented with the $t$ statistic (as calculated above), rather than the standard error, below each coefficient. This implicitly assumes that the hypothesis of interest is that the coefficient is zero. This is not always appropriate: in the consumption function a test for the marginal propensity to consume being equal to 1 might be of greater relevance, for example. In a demand equation, one might want to test for unit elasticity. For this reason, it is better to present the standard errors rather than the $t$ statistics.

Note that the test statistic $t = -4.59$ is exactly the same result as in the case of testing the correlation coefficient. This is no accident, for the two tests are equivalent. A non-zero slope coefficient means there is a relationship between $X$ and $Y$ which also means the correlation coefficient is non-zero. Both null hypotheses are rejected.

**Testing the significance of $R^2$: the $F$ test**

Another check of the quality of the regression equation is to test whether the $R^2$ value, calculated earlier, is significantly greater than zero. This is a test using the $F$ distribution and turns out once again to be equivalent to the two previous tests $H_0: \beta = 0$ and $H_0: \rho = 0$, conducted in previous sections, using the $t$ distribution.

The null hypothesis for the test is $H_0: R^2 = 0$, implying once again that $X$ does not influence $Y$ (hence equivalent to $\beta = 0$). The test statistic is

$$(7.26) \quad F = \frac{R^2/1}{(1 - R^2)/(n - 2)}$$

or equivalently

$$(7.27) \quad F = \frac{RSS/1}{ESS/(n - 2)}$$

The $F$ statistic is therefore the ratio of the regression sum of squares to the error sum of squares, each divided by their degrees of freedom (for the RSS there is one degree of freedom because of the one explanatory variable, for the ESS there are $n - 2$ degrees of freedom). A high value of the $F$ statistic rejects $H_0$ in favour of the alternative hypothesis, $H_1$: $R^2 > 0$. Evaluating (7.26) gives

$$(7.28) \qquad F = \frac{0.678/1}{(1 - 0.678)/10} = 21.078$$

The critical value of the $F$ distribution at the 5% significance level, with $v_1 = 1$ and $v_2 = 10$, is $F^*_{1,10} = 4.96$. The test statistic exceeds this, so the regression as a whole is significant. It is better to use the regression model to explain the birth rate than to use the simpler model which assumes all countries have the same birth rate (the sample average).

As stated before, this test is equivalent to those carried out before using the $t$ distribution. The $F$ statistic is, in fact, the square of the $t$ statistic calculated earlier ($-4.59^2 = 21.078$) and reflects the fact that, in general,

$$F_{1,n-2} = t^2_{n-2}$$

The Prob-value associated with both statistics is the same (approximately 0.001 in this case) so both tests reject the null at the same level of significance. However, in multiple regression with more than one explanatory variable, the relationship no longer holds and the tests do fulfil different roles, as we shall see in the next chapter.

**Exercise 7.6**

(a) For the regression of the birth rate on the income ratio, calculate the standard errors of the coefficients and hence construct 95% confidence intervals for both.

(b) Test the hypothesis that the slope coefficient is zero against the alternative that it is not zero.

(c) Test the hypothesis $H_0$: $R^2 = 0$.

**Interpreting computer output**

Having shown how to use the appropriate formulae to derive estimates of the parameters, their standard errors and test hypotheses, we now present all these results as they would be generated by a computer software package, in this case *Excel*. This removes all the effort of calculation and allows us to concentrate on more important issues such as the interpretation of the results. Table 7.6 shows the computer output.

The table presents all the results we have already derived, plus a few more.

- The regression coefficients, standard errors and $t$ ratios are given at the bottom of the table, suitably labelled. The column headed '*P value*' (this is how *Excel* refers to the *Prob-value*, discussed in Chapter 5) gives some additional information – it shows the significance level of the $t$ statistic. For example, the slope coefficient is significant at the level of 0.1%,[3] i.e. there is this probability of getting such a sample estimate by chance. This is much less than our usual 5% criterion, so we conclude that the sample evidence did not arise by chance.
- The program helpfully calculates the 95% confidence interval for the coefficients also, which were derived above in equation (7.23).

[3] This is the area in *both* tails, so it is for a two-tail test.

**Table 7.6 Regression analysis output using *Excel***

| | A | B | C | D | E | F | G |
|---|---|---|---|---|---|---|---|
| 2 | *Regression Statistics* | | | | | | |
| 3 | | | | | | | |
| 4 | Multiple R | 0.824 | | | | | |
| 5 | R Square | 0.678 | | | | | |
| 6 | Adj. R Square | 0.646 | | | | | |
| 7 | Standard Error | 4.132 | | | | | |
| 8 | Observations | 12 | | | | | |
| 9 | | | | | | | |
| 10 | *Analysis of Variance* | | | | | | |
| 11 | | *df* | *SS* | *MS* | *F* | *Significance F* | |
| 12 | Regression | 1 | 359.913 | 359.913 | 21.078 | 0.001 | |
| 13 | Residual | 10 | 170.754 | 17.075 | | | |
| 14 | Total | 11 | 530.667 | | | | |
| 15 | | | | | | | |
| 16 | | *Coefficients* | *Std Err* | *t Statistic* | *P value* | *Lower 95%* | *Upper 95%* |
| 17 | | | | | | | |
| 18 | Intercept | 40.712 | 2.303 | 17.677 | 0.000 | 35.580 | 45.843 |
| 19 | growth | −2.700 | 0.588 | −4.591 | 0.001 | −4.010 | −1.390 |
| 20 | | | | | | | |

- Moving up the table, there is a section headed '*Analysis of Variance*'. This is similar to the ANOVA covered in Chapter 6. This table provides the sums of squares values (RSS, ESS and TSS, in that order) and their associated degrees of freedom in the '*df*' column. The '*MS*' ('mean square') column calculates the sums of squares each divided by their degrees of freedom, whose ratio gives the *F* statistic in the next column. This is the value calculated in equation (7.28). The '*Significance F*' value is similar to the *P value* discussed previously: it shows the level at which the *F* statistic is significant (0.1% in this case) and saves us looking up the *F* tables.
- At the top of the table is given the $R^2$ value and the standard error of the error term, $s_e$, labelled 'Standard Error', which we have already come across. 'Multiple R' is simply the square root of $R^2$; 'Adjusted $R^2$' (sometimes called 'R-bar squared' and written $\bar{R}^2$) adjusts the $R^2$ value for the degrees of freedom. This is an alternative measure of fit, which is not affected by the number of explanatory variables, unlike $R^2$. See Thomas (1993) Chapter 2 for a more detailed explanation.

**Prediction**

Earlier we showed that the regression line could be used for prediction, using the figures for Costa Rica. The point estimate of Costa Rica's birth rate is calculated simply by putting its growth rate into the regression equation and assuming a zero value for the error, i.e.

$$\hat{Y} = 40.711 - 2.7 \times 3 + 0 = 32.6$$

This is a point estimate, which is unbiased, around which we can build a confidence interval. There are, in fact, two confidence intervals we can construct, the first for the position of the *regression line* at $X = 3$, the second for an *individual observation* (on $Y$) at $X = 3$. Using the 95% confidence level, the first interval is given by the formula

(7.29)   $$\left[ \hat{Y} - t_{n-2} \times s_e \sqrt{\frac{1}{n} + \frac{(X_P - \bar{X})^2}{\Sigma(X - \bar{X})^2}}, \hat{Y} + t_{n-2} \times s_e \sqrt{\frac{1}{n} + \frac{(X_P - \bar{X})^2}{\Sigma(X - \bar{X})^2}} \right]$$

where $X_P$ is the value of $X$ for which the prediction is made. $t_{n-2}$ denotes the critical value of the $t$ distribution at the 5% significance level (for a two-tail test) with $n - 2$ degrees of freedom. This evaluates to

$$\left[ 32.6 - 2.228 \times 4.132 \sqrt{\frac{1}{12} + \frac{(3 - 3.35)^2}{49.37}}, 32.6 + 2.228 \times 4.132 \sqrt{\frac{1}{12} + \frac{(3 - 3.35)^2}{49.37}} \right]$$

$= [29.90, 35.30]$

This means that we predict with 95% confidence that the *average* birth rate of all countries growing at 3% p.a. is between 29.9 and 35.3.

The second type of interval, for the value of $Y$ itself at $X_P = 3$, is somewhat wider, because there is an additional element of uncertainty: individual countries do not lie on the regression line, but around it. This is referred to as the 95% **prediction interval**. The formula for this interval is

(7.30)   $$\left[ \hat{Y} - t_{n-2} \times s_e \sqrt{1 + \frac{1}{n} + \frac{(X_P - \bar{X})^2}{\Sigma(X - \bar{X})^2}}, \right.$$
$$\left. \hat{Y} + t_{n-2} \times s_e \sqrt{1 + \frac{1}{n} + \frac{(X_P - \bar{X})^2}{\Sigma(X - \bar{X})^2}} \right]$$

Note the extra '1' inside the square root sign. When evaluated, this gives a 95% prediction interval of [23.01, 42.19]. Thus we are 95% confident that an individual country growing at 3% p.a. will have a birth rate within this range.

The two intervals are illustrated in Figure 7.8. Note that the prediction is more precise (the interval is smaller):

- the closer the sample observations lie to the regression line (smaller $s_e$),
- the greater the spread of sample $X$ values (larger $\Sigma(X - \bar{X})^2$),
- the closer to the mean of $X$ the prediction is made (smaller $X_P - \bar{X}$),
- the larger the sample size.

**Figure 7.8**
Confidence and prediction intervals: *a* = confidence interval, *b* = prediction interval

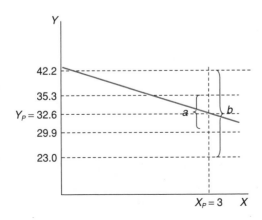

**Figure 7.9**
**The danger of prediction outside the range of sample data**

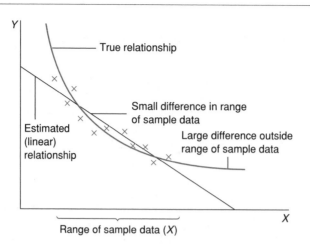

There is an additional danger of predicting far outside the range of sample $X$ values, if the true regression line is not linear as we have assumed. The linear sample regression line might be close to the true line within the range of sample $X$ values but diverge substantially outside. Figure 7.9 illustrates this point.

In the birth rate sample, we have a fairly wide range of $X$ values; few countries grow more slowly than Senegal or faster than Korea.

**Exercise 7.7**

Use Excel's regression tool to confirm your answers to exercises 7.4 to 7.6.

**Exercise 7.8**

(a)  Predict (point estimate) the birth rate for a country with an income ratio of 10.

(b)  Find the 95% confidence interval prediction for a typical country with IR = 10.

(c)  Find the 95% confidence interval prediction for an individual country with IR = 10.

**Worked example 7.2**

We continue the previous worked example, completing the calculations needed for regression. The previous table contains most of the preliminary calculations. To find the regression line we use:

$$b = \frac{n \sum XY - \sum X \sum Y}{n \sum X^2 - (\sum X)^2} = \frac{6 \times 682 - 33 \times 119}{6 \times 199 - 33^2} = 1.57$$

and

$$a = 19.83 - 1.57 \times 5.5 = 11.19$$

Hence we obtain the equation:

$$Y_i = 11.19 + 1.57 X_i + e_i$$

For inference, we start with the sums of squares:

$$\text{TSS} = \sum (Y - \bar{Y})^2 = \sum Y^2 - n\bar{Y}^2 = 2427 - 6 \times 19.83^2 = 66.83$$

$$\begin{aligned}\text{ESS} &= \sum (Y - \hat{Y})^2 = \sum Y^2 - a\sum Y - b\sum XY \\ &= 2427 - 11.19 \times 119 - 1.57 \times 682 = 23.62\end{aligned}$$

$$\text{RSS} = \text{TSS} - \text{ESS} = 66.83 - 23.62 = 43.21$$

We then get $R^2 = RSS/TSS = 43.21/66.83 = 0.647$ or 64.7% of the variation in $Y$ explained by variation in $X$.

To obtain the standard errors of the coefficients, we first calculate the error variance as $s_e^2 = ESS/(n-2) = 23.62/4 = 5.905$ and the estimated variance of the slope coefficient is:

$$s_b^2 = \frac{s_e^2}{\Sigma(X-\bar{X})^2} = \frac{5.905}{17.50} = 0.338$$

and the standard error of $b$ is therefore $\sqrt{0.338} = 0.581$.

Similarly for $a$ we obtain:

$$s_a^2 = s_e^2 \times \left(\frac{1}{n} + \frac{\bar{X}^2}{\Sigma(X-\bar{X})^2}\right) = 5.905 \times \left(\frac{1}{6} + \frac{5.5^2}{17.50}\right) = 11.19$$

and the standard error of $a$ is therefore 3.34.

Confidence intervals for $a$ and $b$ can be constructed using the critical value of the $t$ distribution, 2.776 (5%, $v = 4$), yielding $1.57 \pm 2.776 \times 0.581 = [-0.04, 3.16]$ for $b$ and [1.90, 20.47] for $a$. Note that zero is inside the confidence interval for $b$. This is also reflected in the test of $H_0: \beta = 0$ which is

$$t = \frac{1.57 - 0}{0.581} = 2.71$$

which falls short of the two-tailed critical value, 2.776. Hence $H_0$ cannot be rejected.

The $F$ statistic, to test $H_0: R^2 = 0$ is:

$$F = \frac{RSS/1}{ESS/(n-2)} = \frac{43.21/1}{23.62/(6-2)} = 7.32$$

which compares to a critical value of $F(1,4)$ of 7.71 so, again, the null cannot be rejected (remember that this and the $t$ test on the slope coefficient are equivalent in simple regression).

We shall predict the value of $Y$ for a value of $X = 10$, yielding $\hat{Y} = 11.19 + 1.57 \times 10 = 26.90$. The 95% confidence interval for this prediction is calculated using (7.29), which gives

$$\left[ \begin{array}{l} 26.90 - 2.776 \times 2.43\sqrt{\dfrac{1}{6} + \dfrac{(10-5.5)^2}{17.50}}, \\[3mm] 26.90 + 2.776 \times 2.43\sqrt{\dfrac{1}{6} + \dfrac{(10-5.5)^2}{17.50}} \end{array} \right] = [19.14, 34.66].$$

The 95% prediction interval for an actual observation at $X = 10$ is given by (7.30), resulting in

$$\left[ \begin{array}{l} 26.90 - 2.776 \times 2.43\sqrt{1 + \dfrac{1}{6} + \dfrac{(10-5.5)^2}{17.50}}, \\[3mm] 26.90 + 2.776 \times 2.43\sqrt{1 + \dfrac{1}{6} + \dfrac{(10-5.5)^2}{17.50}} \end{array} \right] = [16.62, 37.18].$$

Table 7.7 The effects of data transformations

| Factor (k) multiplying . . . | | Effect upon | | | |
|---|---|---|---|---|---|
| Y | X | a | $s_a$ | b | $s_b$ |
| k | 1 | – all multiplied by k – | | | |
| 1 | k | unchanged | | divided by k | |
| k | k | multiplied by k | | unchanged | |

## Units of measurement

The measurement and interpretation of the regression coefficients depends upon the units in which the variables are measured. For example, suppose we had measured the birth rate in births per *hundred* (not *thousand*) of population; what would be the implications? Obviously nothing fundamental is changed; we ought to get the same qualitative result, with the same interpretation. However, the regression coefficients cannot remain the same: if the slope coefficient remained $b = -2.7$, this would mean that an increase in the growth rate of one percentage point reduces the birth rate by 2.7 births *per hundred*, which is clearly wrong. The right answer should be 0.27 births per hundred (equivalent to 2.7 per thousand) so the coefficient should change to $b = -0.27$. Thus, in general, the sizes of the coefficients depend upon the units in which the variables are measured. This is why one cannot judge the importance of a regression equation from the size of the coefficients alone.

It is easiest to understand this in graphical terms. A graph of the data will look exactly the same, except that the scale on the Y-axis will change; it will be divided by 10. The intercept of the regression line will therefore change to $a = 4.0711$ and the slope to $b = -0.27$. Thus the regression equation becomes

$$Y_i = 4.0711 - 0.27X_i + e'_i$$
$$(e'_i = e_i/10)$$

Since nothing fundamental has altered, any hypothesis test must yield the same test statistic. Thus t and F statistics are unaltered by changes in the units of measurement; nor is $R^2$ altered. However, standard errors will be divided by 10 (they have to be to preserve the t statistics; see equation (7.25) for example). Table 7.7 sets out the effects of changes in the units of measurement upon the coefficients and standard errors. In the table it is assumed that the variables have been multiplied by a constant k; in the above case $k = 1/10$ was used.

It is important to be aware of the units in which the variables are measured. If not, it is impossible to know how large is the effect of X upon Y. It may be statistically significant but you have no idea of how important it is. This may occur if, for instance, one of the variables is presented as an index number (see Chapter 10) rather than in the original units.

## How to avoid measurement problems: calculating the elasticity

A neat way of avoiding the problems of measurement is to calculate the elasticity, i.e. the *proportionate* change in Y divided by the *proportionate* change in X. The proportionate changes are the same whatever units the variables are measured in. The proportionate change in X is given by $\Delta X/X$, where $\Delta X$ indicates the *change* in X. Thus if X changes from 100 to 110, the proportionate change is $\Delta X/X = 10/100 = 0.1$ or 10%. The elasticity, $\eta$, is therefore given by

$$(7.31) \qquad \eta = \frac{\Delta Y/Y}{\Delta X/X} = \frac{\Delta Y}{\Delta X} \times \frac{X}{Y}$$

The second form of the equation is more useful, since $\Delta Y/\Delta X$ is simply the slope coefficient $b$. We simply need to multiply this by the ratio $X/Y$, therefore. But what values should be used for $X$ and $Y$? The convention is to use the means, so we obtain the following formula for the elasticity, from a linear regression equation:

$$(7.32) \qquad \eta = b \times \frac{\bar{X}}{\bar{Y}}$$

This evaluates to $-2.7 \times 3.35/31.67 = -0.29$. This is interpreted as follows: a 1% increase in the growth rate would lead to a 0.29% decrease in the birth rate. Equivalently, and perhaps a little more usefully, a 10% rise in growth (from say 3% to 3.3% p.a.) would lead to a 2.9% decline in the birth rate (e.g. from 30 to 29.13). This result is the same whatever units the variables $X$ and $Y$ are measured in.

Note that this elasticity is measured at the means; it would have a different value at different points along the regression line. Later on we show an alternative method for estimating the elasticity, in this case the elasticity of demand which is familiar in economics.

**Non-linear transformations**

So far only *linear* regression has been dealt with, that is fitting a straight line to the data. This can sometimes be restrictive, especially when there is good reason to believe that the true relationship is non-linear (e.g. the labour supply curve). Poor results would be obtained by fitting a straight line through the data in Figure 7.10, yet the shape of the relationship seems clear at a glance.

Fortunately this problem can be solved by transforming the data, so that when graphed a linear relationship between the two variables appears. Then a straight line can be fitted to these transformed data. This is equivalent to fitting a curved line to the original data. All that is needed is to find a suitable transformation to 'straighten out' the data. Given the data represented in Figure 7.10, if $Y$ were graphed against $1/X$ the relationship shown in Figure 7.11 would appear.

Thus, if the regression line

$$(7.33) \qquad Y_i = a + b\frac{1}{X_i} + e_i$$

**Figure 7.10**
**Graph of $Y$ against $X$**

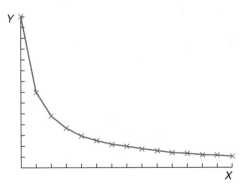

Figure 7.11
Figure 7.10
transformed: Y
against 1/X

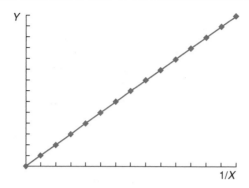

were fitted, this would provide a good representation of the data in Figure 7.10. The procedure is straightforward. First, calculate the reciprocal of each of the $X$ values and then use these (together with the original data for $Y$), using exactly the same methods as before. This transformation appears inappropriate for the birth rate data (see Figure 7.1) but serves as an illustration. The transformed $X$ values are 0.196 (= 1/5.1) for Brazil, 0.3125 (= 1/3.2) for Colombia, etc. The resulting regression equation is

$$(7.34) \qquad Y_i = 31.92 - 3.96\frac{1}{X_i} + e_i$$

$$\text{s.e. } (1.64) \quad (1.56)$$

$R^2 = 0.39, F = 6.44, n = 12$

This appears worse than the original specification (the $R^2$ is low and the slope coefficient is not significantly different from zero) so the transformation does not appear to be a good one. Note also that it is difficult to calculate the effect of $X$ upon $Y$ in this equation. We can see that a unit increase in $1/X$ reduces the birth rate by 3.96, but we do not have an intuitive feel for the inverse of the growth rate. This latest result also implies that a *fall* in the growth rate (hence $1/X$ rises) lowers the birth rate – the converse of our previous result. In the next chapter, we deal with a different example where a non-linear transformation does improve matters.

Table 7.8 presents a number of possible shapes for data, with suggested data transformations which will allow the relationship to be estimated using linear regression. In each case, once the data have been transformed, the methods and formulae used above can be applied.

It is sometimes difficult to know which transformation (if any) to apply. A graph of the data is unlikely to be as tidy as the diagrams in Table 7.8. Economic theory rarely suggests the form which a relationship should follow, and there are no simple statistical tests for choosing alternative formulations. The choice can sometimes be made after visual inspection of the data, or on the basis of convenience. The double log transformation is often used in economics as it has some very convenient properties. Unfortunately it cannot be used with the growth rate data here because Senegal's growth rate was negative. It is impossible to take the logarithm of a negative number. We therefore postpone the use of the log transformation in regression until the next chapter.

**Table 7.8 Data transformations**

| Name | Graph of relationship | Original relationship | Transformed relationship | Regression |
|---|---|---|---|---|
| Double log | $b > 1$, $0 < b < 1$, $b < 0$ | $Y = aX^b e$ | $\ln Y = \ln a + b \ln X + \ln e$ | $\ln Y$ on $\ln X$ |
| Reciprocal | $a$, $b > 0$, $b < 0$ | $Y = a + b/X + e$ | $Y = a + b\dfrac{1}{X} + e$ | $Y$ on $\dfrac{1}{X}$ |
| Semi-log | | $e^Y = aX^b e$ | $Y = \ln a + b \ln X + \ln e$ | $Y$ on $\ln X$ |
| Exponential | $b > 0$, $b < 0$ | $Y = e^{a+bX+e}$ | $\ln Y = a + bX + e$ | $\ln Y$ on $X$ |

**Exercise 7.9**

(a) Calculate the elasticity of the birth rate with respect to the income ratio, using the results of previous exercises.

(b) Give a brief interpretation of the meaning of this figure.

**Exercise 7.10**

Calculate a regression relating the birth rate to the inverse of the income ratio $1/IR$.

# Summary

- Correlation refers to the extent of association between two variables. The (sample) correlation coefficient is a measure of this association, extending from $r = -1$ to $r = +1$.

- Positive correlation ($r > 0$) exists when high values of $X$ tend to be associated with high values of $Y$ and low $X$ values with low $Y$ values.

- Negative correlation ($r < 0$) exists when high values of $X$ tend to be associated with low values of $Y$ and vice versa.

- Values of $r$ around 0 indicate an absence of correlation.

- As the sample correlation coefficient is a random variable we can test for its significance, i.e. test whether the true value is zero or not. This test is based upon the $t$ distribution.

- The existence of correlation (even if 'significant') does not necessarily imply causality. There can be other reasons for the observed association.

- Regression analysis extends correlation by asserting a causality from $X$ to $Y$ and then measuring the relationship between the variables via the regression line, the 'line of best fit'.

- The regression line $Y = a + bX$ is defined by the intercept $a$ and slope coefficient $b$. Their values are found by minimising the sum of squared errors around the regression line.

- The slope coefficient $b$ measures the responsiveness of $Y$ to changes in $X$.

- A measure of how well the regression line fits the data is given by the coefficient of determination, $R^2$, varying between 0 (very poor fit) and 1 (perfect fit).

- The coefficients $a$ and $b$ are unbiased point estimates of the true values of the parameters. Confidence interval estimates can be obtained, based on the $t$ distribution. Hypothesis tests on the parameters can also be carried out using the $t$ distribution.

- A test of the hypothesis $R^2 = 0$ (implying the regression is no better at predicting $Y$ than simply using the mean of $Y$) can be carried out using the $F$ distribution.

- The regression line may be used to predict $Y$ for any value of $X$ by assuming the residual to be zero for that observation.

- The measured response of $Y$ to $X$ (given by $b$) depends upon the units of measurement of $X$ and $Y$. A better measure is often the elasticity, which is the proportionate response of $Y$ to a proportionate change in $X$.

- Data are often transformed prior to regression (e.g. by taking logs) for a variety of reasons (e.g. to fit a curve to the original data).

**Key terms and concepts**

| | | |
|---|---|---|
| correlation coefficient | coefficient of rank correlation | standard error |
| independent (exogenous) variable | dependent (endogenous) variable | elasticity |
| | | regression line or equation |
| intercept | coefficient of determination ($R^2$) | error term (or residual) |
| total sum of squares | | slope |
| autocorrelation | regression sum of squares | error sum of squares |
| prediction | | $t$ ratio |

# Problems

Some of the more challenging problems are indicated by highlighting the **problem number** in colour.

**Problem 7.1** The other data which Todaro might have used to analyse the birth rate were:

| Country | Birth rate | GNP | Growth | Income ratio |
|---|---|---|---|---|
| Bangladesh | 47 | 140 | 0.3 | 2.3 |
| Tanzania | 47 | 280 | 1.9 | 3.2 |
| Sierra Leone | 46 | 320 | 0.4 | 3.3 |
| Sudan | 47 | 380 | −0.3 | 3.9 |
| Kenya | 55 | 420 | 2.9 | 6.8 |
| Indonesia | 35 | 530 | 4.1 | 3.4 |
| Panama | 30 | 1910 | 3.1 | 8.6 |
| Chile | 25 | 2560 | 0.7 | 3.8 |
| Venezuela | 35 | 4220 | 2.4 | 5.2 |
| Turkey | 33 | 1540 | 3.5 | 4.9 |
| Malaysia | 31 | 1840 | 4.3 | 5.0 |
| Nepal | 44 | 150 | 0.0 | 4.7 |
| Malawi | 56 | 200 | 2.7 | 2.4 |
| Argentina | 20 | 2560 | 1.9 | 3.6 |

For *one* of the three possible explanatory variables (in class, different groups could examine each of the variables):

(a) Draw an *XY* chart of the data and comment upon the result.

(b) Would you expect a line of best fit to have a positive or negative slope? Roughly, what would you expect the slope to be?

(c) What would you expect the correlation coefficient to be?

(d) Calculate the correlation coefficient, and comment.

(e) Test to see if the correlation coefficient is different from zero. Use the 95% confidence level.

(Analysis of this problem continues in Problem 7.5.)

**Problem 7.2** The data below show consumption of margarine (in ounces per person per week) and its real price, for the UK.

| Year | Consumption | Price | Year | Consumption | Price |
|---|---|---|---|---|---|
| 1970 | 2.86 | 125.6 | 1980 | 3.83 | 104.2 |
| 1971 | 3.15 | 132.9 | 1981 | 4.11 | 95.5 |
| 1972 | 3.52 | 126.0 | 1982 | 4.33 | 88.1 |
| 1973 | 3.03 | 119.6 | 1983 | 4.08 | 88.9 |
| 1974 | 2.60 | 138.8 | 1984 | 4.08 | 97.3 |
| 1975 | 2.60 | 141.0 | 1985 | 3.76 | 100.0 |
| 1976 | 3.06 | 122.3 | 1986 | 4.10 | 86.7 |
| 1977 | 3.48 | 132.7 | 1987 | 3.98 | 79.8 |
| 1978 | 3.54 | 126.7 | 1988 | 3.78 | 79.9 |
| 1979 | 3.63 | 115.7 | | | |

(a) Draw an *XY* plot of the data and comment.

(b) From the chart, would you expect the line of best fit to slope up or down? *In theory*, which way should it slope?

(c) What would you expect the correlation coefficient to be, approximately?

(d) Calculate the correlation coefficient between margarine consumption and its price.

(e) Is the coefficient significantly different from zero? What is the implication of the result?

(The following totals will reduce the burden of calculation: $\Sigma Y = 67.52$; $\Sigma X = 2101.70$; $\Sigma Y^2 = 245.055$; $\Sigma X^2 = 240\ 149.27$; $\Sigma XY = 7299.638$; $Y$ is consumption, $X$ is price. If you wish, you could calculate a logarithmic correlation. The relevant totals are: $\Sigma y = 23.88$; $\Sigma x = 89.09$; $\Sigma y^2 = 30.45$; $\Sigma x^2 = 418.40$; $\Sigma xy = 111.50$, where $y = \ln Y$ and $x = \ln X$.)

(Analysis of this problem continues in Problem 7.6.)

**Problem 7.3**   What would you expect to be the correlation coefficient between the following variables? Should the variables be measured contemporaneously or might there be a lag in the effect of one upon the other?

(a)   Nominal consumption and nominal income.

(b)   GDP and the imports/GDP ratio.

(c)   Investment and the interest rate.

**Problem 7.4**   As Problem 7.3, for

(a)   real consumption and real income;

(b)   individuals' alcohol and cigarette consumption;

(c)   UK and US interest rates.

**Problem 7.5**   Using the data from Problem 7.1, calculate the rank correlation coefficient between the variables and test its significance. How does it compare with the ordinary correlation coefficient?

**Problem 7.6**   Calculate the rank correlation coefficient between price and quantity for the data in Problem 7.2. How does it compare with the ordinary correlation coefficient?

**Problem 7.7**   (a)   For the data in Problem 7.1, find the estimated regression line and calculate the $R^2$ statistic. Comment upon the result. How does it compare with Todaro's findings?

(b)   Calculate the standard error of the estimate and the standard errors of the coefficients. Is the slope coefficient significantly different from zero? Comment upon the result.

(c)   Test the overall significance of the regression equation and comment.

(d)   Taking your own results and Todaro's, how confident do you feel that you understand the determinants of the birth rate?

(e)   What do you think will be the result of estimating your equation using all 26 countries' data? Try it! What do you conclude?

**Problem 7.8**   (a)   For the data given in Problem 7.2, estimate the sample regression line and calculate the $R^2$ statistic. Comment upon the results.

(b)   Calculate the standard error of the estimate and the standard errors of the coefficients. Is the slope coefficient significantly different from zero? Is demand inelastic?

(c)   Test the overall significance of the regression and comment upon your result.

**Problem 7.9**   From your results for the birth rate model, predict the birth rate for a country with *either* (a) GNP equal to $3000, (b) a growth rate of 3% p.a., *or* (c) an income ratio of 7. How does your prediction compare with one using Todaro's results? Comment.

**Problem 7.10**   Predict margarine consumption given a price of 70. Use the 99% confidence level.

**Problem 7.11 (Project)**   Update Todaro's study using more recent data.

**Problem 7.12**   Try to build a model of the determinants of infant mortality. You should use cross-section data for 20 countries or more and should include both developing and developed countries in the sample.

Write up your findings in a report which includes the following sections: discussion of the problem; data gathering and transformations; estimation of the model; interpretation of results. Useful data may be found in the Human Development Report (use Google to find it online).

**References**   Maddala, G.S. (1992) *Introduction to Econometrics*, 2nd edition, Macmillan.

Thomas, R.L. (1993) *Introductory Econometrics*, 2nd edition, Longman.

Todaro, M.P. (1985) *Economic Development in the Third World*, 3rd edition, Longman.

## Answers to exercises

**Exercise 7.1**   (a)   The calculation is:

| | Birth rate Y | Income ratio X | $Y^2$ | $X^2$ | XY |
|---|---|---|---|---|---|
| Brazil | 30 | 9.5 | 900 | 90.25 | 285 |
| Colombia | 29 | 6.8 | 841 | 46.24 | 197.2 |
| Costa Rica | 30 | 4.6 | 900 | 21.16 | 138 |
| India | 35 | 3.1 | 1 225 | 9.61 | 108.5 |
| Mexico | 36 | 5 | 1 296 | 25 | 180 |
| Peru | 36 | 8.7 | 1 296 | 75.69 | 313.2 |
| Philippines | 34 | 3.8 | 1 156 | 14.44 | 129.2 |
| Senegal | 48 | 6.4 | 2 304 | 40.96 | 307.2 |
| South Korea | 24 | 2.7 | 576 | 7.29 | 64.8 |
| Sri Lanka | 27 | 2.3 | 729 | 5.29 | 62.1 |
| Taiwan | 21 | 3.8 | 441 | 14.44 | 79.8 |
| Thailand | 30 | 3.3 | 900 | 10.89 | 99 |
| Totals | 380 | 60 | 12 564 | 361.26 | 1964 |

$$r = \frac{12 \times 1964 - 60 \times 380}{\sqrt{(12 \times 361.26 - 60^2)(12 \times 12\ 564 - 380^2)}} = 0.355$$

(c)   As for (a) except $\Sigma X = 0.6$, $\Sigma Y = 38$, $\Sigma X^2 = 0.036126$, $\Sigma Y^2 = 125.64$, $\Sigma XY = 1.964$. Hence

$$r = \frac{12 \times 1.964 - 0.6 \times 38}{\sqrt{(12 \times 0.036126 - 0.6^2)(12 \times 125.64 - 38^2)}} = 0.355$$

**Exercise 7.2** (a) $t = \dfrac{0.355\sqrt{12-2}}{\sqrt{1-(0.355)^2}} = 1.20$

(b) The Prob-value, for a two-tailed test is 0.257 or 25%, so we do not reject the null of no correlation.

**Exercise 7.3** (a) The calculation is:

|  | BR | IR | Rank of BR | Rank of IR | d | d² |
|---|---|---|---|---|---|---|
| Brazil | 30 | 9.5 | 7 | 1 | 6 | 36 |
| Colombia | 29 | 6.8 | 9 | 3 | 6 | 36 |
| Costa Rica | 30 | 4.6 | 7 | 6 | 1 | 1 |
| India | 35 | 3.1 | 4 | 10 | −6 | 36 |
| Mexico | 36 | 5 | 2.5 | 5 | −2.5 | 6.25 |
| Peru | 36 | 8.7 | 2.5 | 2 | 0.5 | 0.25 |
| Philippines | 34 | 3.8 | 5 | 7.5 | −2.5 | 6.25 |
| Senegal | 48 | 6.4 | 1 | 4 | −3 | 9 |
| South Korea | 24 | 2.7 | 11 | 11 | 0 | 0 |
| Sri Lanka | 27 | 2.3 | 10 | 12 | −2 | 4 |
| Taiwan | 21 | 3.8 | 12 | 7.5 | 4.5 | 20.25 |
| Thailand | 30 | 3.3 | 7 | 9 | −2 | 4 |
| Totals |  |  | 78 | 78 |  | 159 |

$r_s = 1 - \dfrac{6 \times 159}{12 \times (12^2 - 1)} = 0.444$

(b) This is less than the critical value of 0.591 so the null of no rank correlation cannot be rejected.

(c) The differences $d$ should change in sign, but this is eliminated when $d^2$ is calculated, so the result is the same with the rankings reversed.

**Exercise 7.4** (a) Using the data and calculations in the answer to Exercise 7.1 we obtain:

$b = \dfrac{12 \times 1964 - 60 \times 380}{12 \times 361.26 - 60^2} = 1.045$

$a = \dfrac{380}{12} - (1.045) \times \dfrac{60}{12} = 26.443$

(b) A unit increase in the measure of inequality leads to approximately one additional birth per 1000 mothers. The constant has no useful interpretation. The income ratio cannot be zero (in fact, it cannot be less than 0.5).

**Exercise 7.5** (a) $\text{TSS} = \Sigma(Y_i - \bar{Y})^2 = \Sigma Y_i^2 - n\bar{Y}^2 = 12\,564 - 12 \times 31.66^2 = 530.667$

$\text{ESS} = \Sigma(\hat{Y}_i - \bar{Y})^2 = \Sigma \hat{Y}_i^2 - a\Sigma Y_i - b\Sigma X_i Y_i$
$= 12\,564 - 26.443 \times 380 - 1.045 \times 1139.70 = 463.804$

$\text{RSS} = \text{TSS} - \text{ESS} = 530.667 - 463.804 = 66.863$

$R^2 = 0.126.$

(b) This is the square of the correlation coefficient, calculated earlier as 0.355.

**Exercise 7.6** (a) $s_e^2 = \dfrac{463.804}{10} = 46.3804$

and so

$s_b^2 = \dfrac{46.3804}{61.26} = 0.757$

and

$s_b = \sqrt{0.757} = 0.870$

For $a$ the estimated variance is

$s_a^2 = s_e^2 \times \left(\dfrac{1}{n} + \dfrac{\bar{X}^2}{\Sigma(X_i - \bar{X})^2}\right) = 46.3804 \times \left(\dfrac{1}{12} + \dfrac{5^2}{61.26}\right) = 22.793$

and hence $s_a = 4.774$. The 95% CIs are therefore $1.045 \pm 2.228 \times 0.87 = [-0.894, 2.983]$ for $b$ and $26.443 \pm 2.228 \times 4.774 = [15.806, 37.081]$.

(b) $t = \dfrac{1.045 - 0}{0.870} = 1.201$

Not significant.

(c) $F = \dfrac{RSS/1}{ESS/(n-2)} = \dfrac{66.863/1}{463.804/(12-2)} = 1.44$

---

**Exercise 7.7** Excel should give the same answers.

---

**Exercise 7.8** (a) $\bar{BR} = 26.44 + 1.045 \times 10 = 36.9$.

(b) $\left[36.9 - 2.228 \times 6.81\sqrt{\dfrac{1}{12} + \dfrac{(10-5)^2}{61.26}}, \ 36.9 + 2.228 \times 6.81\sqrt{\dfrac{1}{12} + \dfrac{(10-5)^2}{61.26}}\right]$

$= [26.3, 47.5]$

(c) $\left[36.9 - 2.228 \times 6.81\sqrt{1 + \dfrac{1}{12} + \dfrac{(10-5)^2}{61.26}}, \ 36.9 + 2.228 \times 6.81\sqrt{1 + \dfrac{1}{12} + \dfrac{(10-5)^2}{61.26}}\right]$

$= [18.4, 55.4]$

---

**Exercise 7.9** (a) $e = 1.045 \times \dfrac{5}{31.67} = 0.165$

(b) A 10% rise in the inequality measure (e.g. from 4 to 4.4) raises the birth rate by 1.65% (e.g. from 30 to 30.49).

---

**Exercise 7.10** $BR = 38.82 - 29.61 \times \dfrac{1}{IR} + e$

s.e.                    (19.0)
$R^2 = 0.19$, $F(1,10) = 2.43$.

The regression is rather poor and the $F$ statistic is not significant.

---

# 8 Multiple regression

**Learning outcomes**

By the end of this chapter you should be able to:

- understand the extension of simple regression to multiple regression, with more than one explanatory variable

- use computer software to calculate a multiple regression equation and interpret its output

- recognise the role of (economic) theory in deriving an appropriate regression equation

- interpret the effect of each explanatory variable on the dependent variable

- understand the statistical significance of the results

- judge the adequacy of the model and know how to improve it

# Introduction

Simple regression is rather restrictive, as it assumes that there is only one explanatory factor affecting the dependent variable, which is unlikely to be true in most situations. Price *and* income affect demand, for example. Multiple regression, the subject of this chapter, overcomes this problem by allowing there to be several explanatory variables (though still only one dependent variable) in a model. The techniques are an extension of those used in simple, or bivariate, regression. Multivariate regression allows more general and more helpful models to be estimated, although this does involve new problems as well as advantages.

The regression relationship now becomes

(8.1)     $Y = b_0 + b_1X_1 + b_2X_2 + \ldots + b_kX_k + e$

where there are now $k$ explanatory variables. The principles used in multiple regression are basically the same as in the two-variable case: the coefficients $b_0$, $\ldots$, $b_k$ are found by minimising the sum of squared errors; a standard error can be calculated for each coefficient; $R^2$, $t$ ratios, etc. can be calculated and hypothesis tests performed. However, there are a number of additional issues which arise and these are dealt with in this chapter.

The formulae for calculating coefficients, standard errors, etc. become very complicated in multiple regression and are time-consuming (and error-prone) when done by hand. For this reason, these calculations are invariably done by computer nowadays. Therefore the formulae are not given in this book: instead we present the results of computer calculations (which you can replicate) and concentrate on understanding and interpretting the results. This is as it should be; the calculations themselves are the means to an end, not the end in itself.

---

## Using spreadsheet packages

Standard spreadsheet packages such as *Excel* can perform multiple regression analysis and are sufficient for most routine tasks. A regression equation can be calculated via menus and dialogue boxes and no knowledge of the formulae is required. However, when problems such as autocorrelation (see below) are present, specialised packages such as *TSP*, *Microfit* or *Stata* are much easier to use and provide more comprehensive results.

---

We also introduce a new example in this section, estimating a demand equation for imports into the UK over the period 1973–2003. There are a number of reasons for this switch, for we could have continued with the birth rate example (you are asked to do this in the exercises). First, it allows us to work through a small 'research project' from beginning to end, including the gathering of data, data transformations, interpretation of results, etc. Second, the example uses time-series data and this allows us to bring out some of the particular issues that arise in such cases. Time-series data do not generally constitute a random sample of observations such as we have dealt with in the rest of this book. This is because the observations are constrained to follow one another in time rather than being randomly chosen. The proper analysis of time-series data goes far beyond the scope of this book; however, students often want or need to analyse such data using elementary techniques. This chapter therefore also emphasises the checking of the adequacy of the regression equation for such data. For a fuller treatment of the issues, the reader should consult a more advanced text such as Maddala (1992) or Thomas (1993).

## Principles of multiple regression

We illustrate some of the principles involved in multiple regression using two explanatory variables, $X_1$ and $X_2$. Since we are using time-series data we replace the subscript $i$ with a subscript $t$ to denote the individual observations.

The sample regression equation now becomes

(8.2)     $Y_t = b_0 + b_1 X_{1t} + b_2 X_{2t} + e_t$     $t = 1, \ldots, T$

with three coefficients, $b_0$, $b_1$ and $b_2$, to be estimated. Note that $b_0$ now signifies the constant. Rather than fitting a line through the data, the task is now to fit a *plane* to the data, in three dimensions, as shown in Figure 8.1.

The plane is drawn sloping down in the direction of $X_1$ and up in the direction of $X_2$. The observations are now points dotted about in three-dimensional space (with coordinates $X_{1t}$, $X_{2t}$ and $Y_t$) and the task of regression analysis is to find the equation of the plane so as to minimise the sum of squares of vertical distances from each point to the plane. The principle is the same as in simple regression and the regression plane is the one that best summarises the data.

The coefficient $b_0$ gives the intercept on the $Y$ axis, $b_1$ is the slope of the plane in the direction of the $X_1$ axis and $b_2$ is the slope in the direction of the $X_2$ axis. Thus $b_1$ gives the effect upon $Y$ of a unit change in $X_1$ *assuming $X_2$*

**Figure 8.1**
**The regression plane in three dimensions**

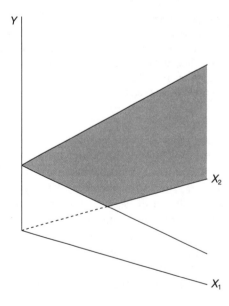

*remains constant.* Similarly, $b_2$ gives the response of $Y$ to a unit change in $X_2$, given no change in $X_1$. If $X_1$ and $X_2$ both change by 1, then the effect on $Y$ is $b_1 + b_2$. $b_1$ and $b_2$ are both estimates of the true parameters $\beta_1$ and $\beta_2$ and so standard errors and confidence intervals can be calculated, implying that we are not absolutely certain about the true position of the plane. In general, the smaller these standard errors, the better, since it implies less uncertainty about the true relationship between $Y$ and the $X$ variables.

When there are more than two explanatory variables, more than three dimensions are needed to draw a picture of the data. The reader will understand that this is a difficult (if not impossible) task; however, it is possible to estimate such a model and interpret the results in a similar manner to the more simple model.

# What determines imports into the UK?

To illustrate multiple regression we suppose that we have the job of finding out what determines the volume of imports into the United Kingdom and whether there are any policy implications of the result. We are given this very open-ended task, which we have to carry through from start to finish. We end up by estimating a demand equation, so the analysis serves as a model for any demand estimation, for example, a firm trying to find out about the demand for its product.

How should we set about this task? The project can be broken down into the following steps:

1 Theoretical considerations: what can economic theory tell us about the problem and how will this affect our estimation procedures?
2 Data gathering: what data do we need? Are there any definitional problems, for example?
3 Data transformation: are the data suitable for the task? We might want to transform one or more variables before estimation.
4 Estimation: this is mainly done automatically, by the computer.
5 Interpretation of the results: what do the results tell us? Do they appear satisfactory? Do we need to improve the model? Are there any policy conclusions?

Although this appears reasonably clear-cut, in practice these steps are often mixed up. A researcher might gather the data, estimate a model and then not be happy with the results. He therefore goes back and gets some different data, perhaps some new variables, or maybe tries a different method of investigation until 'satisfactory' results are obtained. There is usually some element of data 'mining' or 'fishing' involved. These methodological issues are examined in more detail later on.

**Theoretical issues**    What does economic theory tell us about imports? Like any market, the quantity transacted depends upon supply and demand. Strictly, therefore, we should estimate a **simultaneous equation model** of both the demand and supply equations. Since this is beyond the scope of this book (see Thomas, Chapter 8 or Maddala, Chapter 9 for analyses of such models) we simplify by assuming that, as the UK is a small economy in the world market, we can buy any quantity of imports that we demand (at the prevailing price). In other words, supply is never a constraint, and the UK's demand never influences the world price. This assumption, which seems reasonable, means that we can concentrate on estimating the demand equation alone.

Second, economic theory suggests that demand depends upon income and relative prices, particularly the prices of close substitutes and complements. Furthermore, rational consumers do not suffer from money illusion, so real variables should be used throughout.

Economic theory does *not* tell us some things, however. It does not tell us whether the relationship is linear or not. Nor does it tell us whether demand responds *immediately* to price or income changes, or whether there is a lag. For these questions, the data are more likely to give us the answer.

**Data**

The raw data are presented in Table 8.1, obtained from official UK statistics. Note that there is some slight rounding of the figures: imports are measured to

**Table 8.1** Original data for study of imports

| Year | Imports | GDP | GDP deflator | Price of imports | RPI all items |
|------|---------|--------|--------------|------------------|---------------|
| 1973 | 18.8 | 74.0 | 24.8 | 21.5 | 25.1 |
| 1974 | 27.0 | 83.7 | 28.9 | 31.3 | 29.1 |
| 1975 | 28.7 | 105.8 | 35.8 | 35.6 | 36.1 |
| 1976 | 36.5 | 125.1 | 41.5 | 43.7 | 42.1 |
| 1977 | 42.3 | 145.5 | 47.1 | 50.5 | 48.8 |
| 1978 | 45.2 | 167.8 | 52.6 | 52.5 | 52.8 |
| 1979 | 54.2 | 197.4 | 60.8 | 55.8 | 59.9 |
| 1980 | 57.4 | 230.7 | 76.9 | 65.5 | 70.7 |
| 1981 | 60.2 | 253.0 | 81.6 | 71.2 | 79.1 |
| 1982 | 67.6 | 277.1 | 85.9 | 77.3 | 85.9 |
| 1983 | 77.4 | 302.8 | 90.3 | 84.2 | 89.8 |
| 1984 | 92.6 | 324.4 | 94.9 | 91.9 | 94.3 |
| 1985 | 98.7 | 355.0 | 100.0 | 96.3 | 100.0 |
| 1986 | 100.9 | 381.3 | 103.7 | 91.9 | 103.4 |
| 1987 | 111.4 | 419.6 | 108.9 | 94.7 | 107.7 |
| 1988 | 124.7 | 468.4 | 116.1 | 93.8 | 113.0 |
| 1989 | 142.7 | 514.2 | 124.3 | 97.7 | 121.8 |
| 1990 | 148.3 | 557.3 | 133.9 | 100.0 | 133.3 |
| 1991 | 142.1 | 586.1 | 142.6 | 101.2 | 141.1 |
| 1992 | 151.7 | 610.9 | 148.2 | 102.1 | 146.4 |
| 1993 | 170.1 | 642.3 | 152.4 | 112.3 | 148.7 |
| 1994 | 185.3 | 681.3 | 155.1 | 116.1 | 152.4 |
| 1995 | 207.1 | 719.2 | 159.1 | 123.6 | 157.6 |
| 1996 | 227.4 | 763.3 | 164.4 | 123.4 | 161.4 |
| 1997 | 232.0 | 810.9 | 168.9 | 115.1 | 166.5 |
| 1998 | 238.8 | 859.4 | 173.7 | 108.2 | 172.2 |
| 1999 | 254.7 | 903.9 | 177.8 | 107.7 | 174.8 |
| 2000 | 286.6 | 951.3 | 180.5 | 111.2 | 180.0 |
| 2001 | 299.3 | 994.0 | 184.6 | 110.2 | 183.2 |
| 2002 | 304.7 | 1043.3 | 190.5 | 107.2 | 186.3 |
| 2003 | 308.4 | 1099.4 | 196.1 | 106.6 | 191.7 |

the nearest £0.1bn (£100m) so there is a possible (rounding) error of up to about 0.1%. This is unlikely to substantially affect our estimates.

The variables are defined as follows:

- *Imports* (variable *M*): imports of goods and services into the UK, at current prices, in £bn.
- *Income* (*GDP*): UK gross domestic product at factor cost, at current prices, in £bn.
- *The GDP deflator* ($P_{GDP}$): an index of the ratio of nominal to real GDP. 1985 = 100. This is an index of general price increases and may be used to transform nominal GDP to real GDP.
- *The price of imports* ($P_M$): the unit value index of imports, 1990 = 100.
- *The price of competing products* (*P*): the retail price index (RPI), 1985 = 100.

These variables were chosen from a wide range of possibilities. To take income as an example, we could use personal disposable income or GDP. Since firms as well as consumers import goods, the wider measure is used. Then there is the question of whether to use GDP or GNP, and whether to measure them at factor cost or market prices. Because there is little difference between these different magnitudes, this is not an important decision in this case. However, in a research project one might have to consider such issues in more detail.

**Data transformations**

Before calculating the regression equation we must transform the data in Table 8.1. This is because they measure expenditures on imports and GDP which have not been adjusted for price changes (inflation). Part of the observed increase in the imports series is due to prices increasing over time, not increased consumption of imported goods. It is the latter we are trying to explain.

Since expenditure on any good (including imports) can be expressed as the quantity purchased multiplied by the price, to obtain the quantity of imports ('real' imports) we must divide the expenditure by the price of imports. In algebraic terms:

expenditure = price × quantity, hence

$$\text{quantity} = \frac{\text{expenditure}}{\text{price}}$$

We therefore adjust both imports and GDP for the effect of price changes in this way. This process is covered in more detail in Chapter 10 on index numbers (you may wish to read that before proceeding with this chapter, though it is not essential).

We also need to adjust the import price series, which influences the demand for imports. People make their spending decisions by looking at the price of an imported good *relative to* prices generally. Hence we divide the price of imports by the retail price index to give the relative, or real, price of imports.

In summary, the transformed variables are derived as follows:

- *Real imports* ($M/P_M$): this series is obtained by dividing the nominal series for imports by the unit value index (i.e. the import price index). The series gives imports at 1990 prices (in £bn). (Note that the nominal and real series are identical in 1990.)

**Table 8.2 Transformed data**

| Year | Real imports | Real GDP | Real import prices |
|------|--------------|----------|--------------------|
| 1973 | 87.4 | 399.5 | 114.2 |
| 1974 | 86.3 | 387.8 | 143.4 |
| 1975 | 80.6 | 395.7 | 131.5 |
| 1976 | 83.5 | 403.6 | 138.4 |
| 1977 | 83.8 | 413.6 | 137.9 |
| 1978 | 86.1 | 427.2 | 132.5 |
| 1979 | 97.1 | 434.7 | 124.2 |
| 1980 | 87.6 | 401.7 | 123.5 |
| 1981 | 84.6 | 415.2 | 120.0 |
| 1982 | 87.5 | 431.9 | 120.0 |
| 1983 | 91.9 | 449.0 | 125.0 |
| 1984 | 100.8 | 457.7 | 129.9 |
| 1985 | 102.5 | 475.3 | 128.4 |
| 1986 | 109.8 | 492.3 | 118.5 |
| 1987 | 117.6 | 515.9 | 117.2 |
| 1988 | 132.9 | 540.2 | 110.7 |
| 1989 | 146.1 | 553.9 | 106.9 |
| 1990 | 148.3 | 557.3 | 100.0 |
| 1991 | 140.4 | 550.3 | 95.6 |
| 1992 | 148.6 | 552.0 | 93.0 |
| 1993 | 151.5 | 564.3 | 100.7 |
| 1994 | 159.6 | 588.2 | 101.5 |
| 1995 | 167.6 | 605.3 | 104.5 |
| 1996 | 184.3 | 621.7 | 101.9 |
| 1997 | 201.6 | 642.9 | 92.1 |
| 1998 | 220.7 | 662.5 | 83.8 |
| 1999 | 236.5 | 680.7 | 82.1 |
| 2000 | 257.7 | 705.7 | 82.3 |
| 2001 | 271.6 | 721.0 | 80.2 |
| 2002 | 284.2 | 733.3 | 76.7 |
| 2003 | 289.3 | 750.7 | 74.1 |

- *Real income* ($GDP/P_{GDP}$): this is the nominal GDP series divided by the GDP deflator to give GDP at 1990 prices (in £bn).
- *Real import prices* ($P_M/P$): the unit value index is divided by the RPI to give this series. It is an index number series. It shows the price of imports relative to the price of all goods. The higher this price ratio the less attractive imports would be relative to domestically produced goods.

The transformed variables are shown in Table 8.2. Do not worry if you have not fully understood the process of transforming to real terms. You can simply begin with the data in Table 8.2, recognising them as the quantity of imports demanded, the level of real income or output and the price of imports relative to all goods.

We should now 'eyeball' the data using appropriate graphical techniques. This will give a broad overview of the characteristics of the data and any unusual or erroneous observations may be spotted. This is an important step in the analysis.

Figure 8.2 shows a time-series plot of the three variables. The graph shows that both imports and GDP increase smoothly over the period, and that there

**Figure 8.2**
**A time-series plot of imports, GDP and import prices (real terms)**

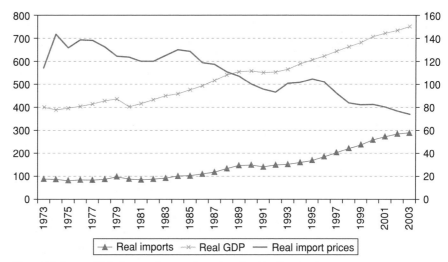

*Note*: This is a multiple time-series graph as described in Chapter 1.

**Figure 8.3**
*XY* **graph of imports against GDP**

appears to be a fairly close relationship between them. This is confirmed by the *XY* plot of imports and GDP in Figure 8.3, which shows an approximately linear relationship. Care should be taken in interpreting this however, since it shows only the *partial* relationship between two of the three variables. However, it does appear to be fairly strong.

The price of imports has declined by about 35% over the period (this is relative to all goods generally) so this might also have contributed to the rise in imports. Figure 8.4 provides an *XY* chart of these two variables. There appears to be a clear negative relationship between imports and their price. On the basis of the graphs we might expect a positive relation between imports and GDP, and a negative one between imports and their price. Both of these expectations are in line with what economic theory would predict.

**Figure 8.4**
*XY* graph of imports
against import prices

For the exercises in this chapter we will be looking at the determinants of travel by car in the UK, which has obviously been increasing steadily and causes concern because of issues such as pollution and congestion. Data for these exercises are as follows:

| Year | Car travel (billions of passenger-kilometres) | Real price of car travel | Real price of rail travel | Real price of bus travel | Real personal disposable income |
|---|---|---|---|---|---|
| 1980 | 388 | 107.0 | 76.2 | 78.9 | 54.2 |
| 1981 | 394 | 107.1 | 77.8 | 79.3 | 54.0 |
| 1982 | 406 | 104.2 | 82.3 | 84.6 | 53.8 |
| 1983 | 411 | 106.4 | 83.4 | 85.5 | 54.9 |
| 1984 | 432 | 103.8 | 79.8 | 83.3 | 57.0 |
| 1985 | 441 | 101.7 | 80.4 | 81.6 | 58.9 |
| 1986 | 465 | 97.4 | 82.7 | 87.1 | 61.3 |
| 1987 | 500 | 99.5 | 84.1 | 88.4 | 63.6 |
| 1988 | 536 | 98.4 | 85.4 | 88.4 | 67.0 |
| 1989 | 581 | 95.9 | 85.7 | 88.6 | 70.2 |
| 1990 | 588 | 93.3 | 86.3 | 88.9 | 72.6 |
| 1991 | 582 | 96.4 | 89.9 | 92.4 | 74.1 |
| 1992 | 583 | 98.3 | 93.5 | 94.7 | 76.2 |
| 1993 | 584 | 101.6 | 97.6 | 97.3 | 78.3 |
| 1994 | 591 | 101.3 | 99.2 | 99.2 | 79.4 |
| 1995 | 596 | 99.7 | 100.4 | 100.5 | 81.3 |
| 1996 | 606 | 101.4 | 101.1 | 103.1 | 83.3 |
| 1997 | 614 | 102.7 | 100.6 | 105.1 | 86.6 |
| 1998 | 618 | 102.1 | 101.5 | 106.6 | 86.9 |
| 1999 | 613 | 103.9 | 103.2 | 109.3 | 89.8 |
| 2000 | 618 | 103.7 | 102.2 | 110.0 | 95.3 |
| 2001 | 624 | 101.2 | 102.9 | 112.0 | 100.0 |

(a)  Draw time-series graphs of car travel and its price and comment on the main features.

(b)  Draw *XY* plots of car travel against (i) price and (ii) income. Comment upon the major features of the graphs.

(c)  In a multiple regression of car travel on its price and on income, what would you expect the signs of the two slope coefficients to be? Explain your answer.

(d)  If the prices of bus and rail travel are added, what would expect the signs on their coefficients to be? Justify your answer.

**Estimation**

The model to be estimated is therefore

$$(8.3) \qquad \left(\frac{M}{P_M}\right)_t = b_0 + b_1\left(\frac{GDP}{P_{GDP}}\right)_t + b_2\left(\frac{P_M}{P}\right)_t + e_t$$

To simplify notation we rewrite this as

$$(8.4) \qquad m_t = b_0 + b_1 gdp_t + b_2 pm_t + e_t$$

The results of estimating this equation are shown in Table 8.3, which shows the output using Excel. We have used the data in years 1973–2001 for estimation purposes, ignoring the observations for 2002 and 2003. Later on we will use the results to predict imports in 2002 and 2003.

The print-out gives all the results we need, which may be summarised as

$$(8.5) \qquad m_t = -103.2 + 0.50 gdp_t - 0.19 pm_t + e_t$$
$$\qquad\qquad\qquad (0.06) \qquad (0.34)$$

$$R^2 = 0.95, \ F_{2,26} = 264.6, \ n = 29$$

How do we judge and interpret these results? As expected, we obtain a positive coefficient on income and a negative one on price. Note that it is difficult to give a sensible interpretation to the constant. The coefficients should be judged in two ways: in terms of their *size* and their *significance*.

### Size

As noted earlier, the size of a coefficient depends upon the units of measurement. How 'big' is the coefficient 0.50, for income? This tells us that a rise in GDP, measured in 1990 prices, of £1bn would raise imports, also measured in 1990 prices, by £0.50bn. This is a bit cumbersome. It is better to interpret everything in *proportionate* terms, and calculate the *elasticity* of imports with

**Table 8.3 Regression results using Excel**

**SUMMARY OUTPUT**

|  | Regression statistics |
|---|---|
| Multiple R | 0.98 |
| R Square | 0.95 |
| Adjusted R Square | 0.95 |
| Standard Error | 12.69 |
| Observations | 29 |

**ANOVA**

|  | df | SS | MS | F | Significance F |
|---|---|---|---|---|---|
| Regression | 2 | 85 209.41 | 42 604.70 | 264.64 | 5.2E-18 |
| Residual | 26 | 4 185.82 | 160.99 |  |  |
| Totals | 28 | 89 395.23 |  |  |  |

|  | Coefficients | Standard error | t Stat | P value | Lower 95% | Upper 95% |
|---|---|---|---|---|---|---|
| Intercept | −103.22 | 67.96 | −1.52 | 0.14 | −242.92 | 36.48 |
| Real GDP | 0.50 | 0.06 | 8.30 | 0.00 | 0.38 | 0.63 |
| Real import prices | −0.19 | 0.34 | −0.57 | 0.58 | −0.89 | 0.50 |

respect to income. This is the proportionate change in imports divided by the proportionate change in price:

$$(8.6) \qquad \eta_{gdp} = \frac{\Delta m/m}{\Delta gdp/gdp}$$

which can be evaluated (see equation (7.32)) as:

$$(8.7) \qquad \eta_{gdp} = b_1 \times \frac{\overline{gdp}}{\bar{m}} = 0.5 \times \frac{518.9}{136.4} = 1.90$$

which shows that imports are highly responsive to income. A 3% rise in real GDP (a fairly typical annual figure) leads to an approximate 6% rise in imports, as long as prices do not change at the same time. Thus as income rises, imports rise substantially faster. More generally we would interpret the result as showing that a 1% rise in GDP leads to a 1.9% rise in imports.

A similar calculation for the price variable yields

$$(8.8) \qquad \eta_{pm} = -0.19 \times \frac{111.7}{136.4} = -0.16$$

which suggests that imports are inelastic with respect to price. A 10% price rise (relative to domestic prices) would lower import demand by only 1.6%.

### Significance

We can test whether each coefficient is significantly different from zero, i.e. whether the variable truly affects imports or not, using a conventional hypothesis test. For income we have the test statistic

$$t = \frac{0.50 - 0}{0.06} = 8.30$$

which has a $t$ distribution with $n - k - 1 = 29 - 2 - 1 = 26$ degrees of freedom ($k$ is the number of explanatory variables excluding the constant, 2). The critical value for a one-tail test at the 95% confidence level is 1.706. Since the test statistic comfortably exceeds this we reject $H_0: \beta_1 = 0$ in favour of $H_1: \beta_1 > 0$. Hence income does indeed affect imports; the sample data are unlikely to have arisen purely by chance. Note that this $t$ ratio is given on the *Excel* print-out.

For price, the test statistic is

$$t = \frac{-0.19 - 0}{0.34} = -0.57$$

which is greater (nearer to zero) than −1.706, so does not fall into the rejection region. $H_0: \beta_2 = 0$ cannot be rejected, therefore. So not only is the coefficient on price quantitatively small, it is insignificantly different from zero, i.e. there is a reasonable probability of this result arising simply by chance. This result arises despite the fact that the graph of imports against price seemed to show a strong negative relationship. That graph was in fact somewhat misleading. The regression tells us that the more important relationship is with income and, once that is accounted for, price provides little additional explanation of imports.

**The significance of the regression as a whole**

We can test the overall significance via an $F$ test as we did for simple regression. This is a test of the hypothesis that *all* the slope coefficients are simultaneously zero (equivalent to the hypothesis that $R^2 = 0$):

$H_0: \beta_1 = \beta_2 = 0$
$H_1: \beta_1 \neq \beta_2 \neq 0$

This tests whether *either* income *or* price affects demand. Since we have already found that income is a significant explanatory variable, via the *t* test, it would be surprising if this null hypothesis were not rejected. The test statistic is similar to equation (7.27):

(8.9) $\quad F = \dfrac{\text{RSS}/k}{\text{ESS}/(n - k - 1)}$

which has an *F* distribution with *k* and $n - k - 1$ degrees of freedom. Substituting in the appropriate values gives

$$F = \frac{85\,209.41/2}{4185.82/(29 - 2 - 1)} = 264.6$$

which is in excess of the critical value for the *F* distribution of 3.37 (at 5% significance), so the null hypothesis is rejected, as expected. The actual significance level is given by *Excel* as '5.2E–18', i.e. $5.2 \times 10^{-18}$, effectively zero and certainly less than 5%.

---

## Does corruption harm investment?

The World Bank examined this question in its 1997 World Development Report, using regression methods. There is a concern that levels of corruption in many countries harm investment and hence also economic growth.

The study looked at the relationship between investment (measured as a percentage of GDP) and the following variables: the level of corruption, the predictability of corruption, the level of secondary school enrolment, GDP per capita and a measure of 'policy distortion'. Both the level and predictability of corruption were based upon replies to surveys of businesses in the 39 countries studied, which asked questions such as 'Do you have to make additional payments to get things done?' The policy distortion variable measures how badly economic policy is run, based on openness to trade, the exchange rate, etc. Higher values of the index indicate poorer economic management.

The regression obtained was

$$\frac{Inv}{GDP} = 19.5 - 5.8\,CORR + 6.3\,PRED\_CORR + 2.0\,SCHOOL$$
$$\text{(s.e.)} \quad (13.5)\ (2.2) \qquad (2.6) \qquad\qquad (2.2)$$

$$- 1.1\,GDP - 2.0\,DISTORT$$
$$(1.9) \qquad (1.5)$$

$\bar{R}^2 = 0.24$

Thus only the corruption variables prove significant at the 5% level. A rise in the level of corruption lowers investment (note the negative coefficient, –5.8) as expected, but a rise in the *predictability* of corruption raises it. This is presumably because people learn how to live with corruption. Unfortunately, units of measurement are not given, so it is impossible to tell just how important are the sizes of the coefficients and, in particular, to find the trade-off between corruption and its predictability.

Adapted from: *World Development Report*, 1997.

**Exercise 8.2**

(a) Using the data from Exercise 8.1, calculate a regression explaining the level of car travel, using price and income as explanatory variables. Use only the observations from 1980 to 1999. As well as calculating the coefficients you should calculate standard errors and $t$ ratios, $R^2$ and the $F$ statistic.

(b) Interpret the results. You should evaluate the size of the effect of the explanatory variables as well as their significance and evaluate the goodness of fit of the model.

## Are the results satisfactory?

The results so far *appear* satisfactory: we have found one significant coefficient, the $R^2$ value is quite high at 95% (although $R^2$ values tend to be high in time-series regressions) and the result of the $F$ test proves the regression is worthwhile. Nevertheless, it is perhaps surprising to find no effect from the price variable; we might as well drop it from the equation and just regress imports on GDP.

A more stringent test is to use the equation for forecasting, since this uses out-of-sample information for the test. So far, the diagnostic tests such as the $F$ test are based on the same data that were used for estimation. A more suitable test might be to see if the equation can forecast imports to within (say) 3% of the correct value. Since real imports increased by about 4.1% p.a. on average between 1973 and 2001, a simple forecasting rule would be to increase the current year's figure by 4.1%. The regression model might be compared to this standard.

Forecasts for 2002 and 2003[1] are obtained by inserting the values of the explanatory variables for these years into the regression equation, giving

2002: $\hat{m} = -103.2 + 0.50 \times 733.3 - 0.19 \times 76.7 = 250.9$
2003: $\hat{m} = -103.2 + 0.50 \times 750.7 - 0.19 \times 74.1 = 260.2$

Table 8.4 summarises the actual and forecast values, with the error between them. The percentage error is about 12% in each year. This is not very good! Both years are under-predicted by a large amount. The simple growth rule would have given predictions of $271.6 \times 1.041 = 282.8$ and $271.6 \times 1.041^2 = 294.5$ which are much closer. More work needs to be done.

## Improving the model – using logarithms

There are various ways in which we might improve our model. We might try to find additional variables to improve the fit (though since we already have $R^2 = 0.95$ this might be difficult), or we might try lagged variables (e.g. the previous year's price) as explanatory variables, on the grounds that the effects do not work through instantaneously. Alternatively, we might try a different functional form for the equation. We have presumed that the regression should be a straight line, although we made no justification for this. Indeed, the graph of

**Table 8.4** Actual, forecast and error values

| Year | Actual | Forecast | Error |
|------|--------|----------|-------|
| 2002 | 284.2  | 250.9    | 33.3  |
| 2003 | 289.3  | 260.2    | 29.1  |

[1] Remember that data from 2002 and 2003 were not used to estimate the regression equation.

imports against income showed some degree of curvature (see Figure 8.3 above). Hence we might try a non-linear transformation of the data, as briefly discussed at the end of Chapter 7.

We shall re-estimate the regression equation, having transformed all the data using (natural) logarithms. Not only does this method fit a curve to the data but has the additional advantage of giving more direct estimates of the elasticities, as we shall see. Because of such advantages, estimating a regression equation in logs is extremely common in economics and analysts often start with the logarithmic form in preference to the linear form.

We will therefore estimate the equation

$$\ln m_t = b_0 + b_1 \ln gdp_t + b_2 \ln pm_t + e_t$$

where $\ln m_t$ indicates the logarithm of imports in period $t$, etc. We therefore need to transform our three variables into logarithms, as shown in Table 8.6 (selected years only).

We now use the new data for the regression, with $\ln m$ as the dependent variable, $\ln gdp$ and $\ln pm$ as the explanatory variables. We also use exactly the same formulae as before, applied to this new data. This gives the following results:

SUMMARY OUTPUT

|  | Regression statistics |
| --- | --- |
| Multiple R | 0.99 |
| R Square | 0.98 |
| Adjusted R Square | 0.98 |
| Standard Error | 0.06 |
| Observations | 29 |

ANOVA

|  | df | SS | MS | F | Significance F |
| --- | --- | --- | --- | --- | --- |
| Regression | 2 | 4.02 | 2.01 | 638.10 | 8.01E-23 |
| Residual | 26 | 0.08 | 0.00 |  |  |
| Totals | 28 | 4.10 |  |  |  |

|  | Coefficients | Standard error | t Stat | P value | Lower 95% | Upper 95% |
| --- | --- | --- | --- | --- | --- | --- |
| Intercept | -2.52 | 1.61 | -1.57 | 0.13 | -5.83 | 0.79 |
| ln GDP | 1.54 | 0.14 | 10.92 | 0.00 | 1.25 | 1.83 |
| ln import prices | -0.48 | 0.16 | -2.95 | 0.01 | -0.81 | -0.15 |

The regression equation we have is therefore

$$\operatorname{lm} m_t = -2.52 + 1.54 \ln gdp_t - 0.48 \ln pm_t$$

Because we have transformed the variables the slope coefficients are very different from the values we had before, from the linear equation. However, the interpretation of the log regression equation is different. A big advantage of this formulation is that the coefficients give direct estimates of the elasticities;

**Table 8.6 Data in natural logarithm form**

| Year | Real imports | ln $m$ | Real GDP | ln $gdp$ | Real import prices | ln $pm$ |
|------|------|------|------|------|------|------|
| 1973 | 87.4 | 4.47 | 399.5 | 5.99 | 114.2 | 4.74 |
| 1974 | 86.3 | 4.46 | 387.8 | 5.96 | 143.4 | 4.97 |
| 1975 | 80.6 | 4.39 | 395.7 | 5.98 | 131.5 | 4.88 |
| 1976 | 83.5 | 4.42 | 403.6 | 6.00 | 138.4 | 4.93 |
| 1977 | 83.8 | 4.43 | 413.6 | 6.02 | 137.9 | 4.93 |
| ⋮ | ⋮ | ⋮ | ⋮ | ⋮ | ⋮ | ⋮ |
| 2000 | 257.7 | 5.55 | 705.7 | 6.56 | 82.3 | 4.41 |
| 2001 | 271.6 | 5.60 | 721 | 6.58 | 80.2 | 4.38 |
| 2002 | 284.2 | 5.65 | 733.3 | 6.60 | 76.7 | 4.34 |
| 2003 | 289.3 | 5.67 | 750.7 | 6.62 | 74.1 | 4.31 |

*Note*: You can obtain the natural logarithm by using the 'ln' key on your calculator or the 'ln' function in Excel (or other software). Thus we have ln (87.4) = 4.47, etc.

there is no need to multiply by the ratio of the means, as with the linear form (see equation 8.7).

Hence the income elasticity of demand is estimated as 1.54 and the price elasticity is –0.48. These contrast with the values calculated from the linear equation, of 1.90 and –0.16 respectively. It is difficult to say which is the 'right' answer, both are estimates of the unknown, true values. One advantage of the log model is that the elasticity does not vary along the demand curve, as it does with the linear model. With the latter we had to calculate the elasticity at the means of the variables, but the value inevitably varies along the curve. For example, taking 2001 values for imports and income we obtain an elasticity of

$$\eta_{gdp} = 0.50 \times \frac{721.0}{271.6} = 1.33$$

This is quite different from the value at the mean, 1.90. A convenient mathematical property of the log formulation is that the elasticity does not change along the curve.

We can compare the linear and log models further to judge which is preferable. The log model has a higher price elasticity and is 'significant' ($t = -2.95$) so we can now reject the hypothesis that price has no effect upon import demand. The $R^2$ value is also higher (0.98 versus 0.95) but this is a misleading comparison. $R^2$ tells us how much of the variation in the dependent variable is explained by the explanatory variables. However, we have a different dependent variable now: the log of imports rather than imports. Although they are both measuring imports, they are different variables, making direct comparison of $R^2$ invalid.

We can also compare the predictive abilities of the two models. For the log model we have the following predictions:

2002: ln $\hat{m}$ = –2.52 + 1.54 × 6.60 – 0.48 × 4.34 = 5.58
2003: ln $\hat{m}$ = –2.52 + 1.54 × 6.62 – 0.48 × 4.31 = 5.63

These are log values, so we need to take anti-logs to get back to the original units:

$e^{5.58} = 264.1$ and $e^{5.63} = 278.4$

These predictions are substantially better than from the linear equation, as we see below:

| Year | Actual | Fitted | Error | % error |
|---|---|---|---|---|
| 2002 | 284.2 | 264.1 | 20.1 | 7.6 |
| 2003 | 289.3 | 278.4 | 10.9 | 3.9 |

The errors are less than half the size they were in the linear formulation and, overall, the log regression is beginning to look much better.

We have so far succeeded in estimating a reasonably good model explaining the levels of imports. The fit of the model, measured by $R^2$, is good, the coefficients have the anticipated signs and are both significant. The forecasting performance is adequate but could be improved. The rest of this chapter goes on to look at more advanced topics relating to the regression model. These are not essential as far as estimation of the regression model goes but are useful 'diagnostic tools' which allow us to check the quality of the estimates in more depth.

**Testing the accuracy of the forecasts: the Chow test**

There is a formal test for the accuracy of the forecasts (which can be applied to both linear and log forms of the equation), based on the $F$ distribution. This is the Chow test (named after its inventor). The null hypothesis is that the true prediction errors are all equal to zero, so the errors we do observe are just random variation from the regression line. Alternatively, we can interpret the hypothesis as asserting that the same regression line applies to both estimation and prediction periods. If the predictions lie too far from the estimated regression line then the null is rejected. The alternative hypothesis is that the model has changed in some way and that a different regression line should be applied to the prediction period.

The test procedure is as follows:

1 Use the first $n_1$ observations for estimation, the last $n_2$ observations for the forecast. In this case we have $n_1 = 29$, $n_2 = 2$.
2 Estimate the regression equation using the first $n_1$ observations, as above, and obtain the error sum of squares, $ESS_1$.
3 Re-estimate the equation using all $n_1 + n_2$ observations, and obtain the pooled error sum of squares, $ESS_p$.
4 Calculate the $F$ statistic:

$$F = \frac{(ESS_p - ESS_1)/n_2}{ESS_1/(n_1 - k - 1)}$$

We then compare this test statistic with the critical value of the $F$ distribution with $n_2$, $n_1 - k - 1$ degrees of freedom. If the test statistic exceeds the critical value, the model fails the prediction test. A large value of the test statistic indicates a large divergence between $ESS_p$ and $ESS_1$ (adjusted for the different sample sizes), suggesting that the model does not fit the two periods equally well. The bigger the prediction errors, the more $ESS_p$ will exceed $ESS_1$, leading to a large $F$ statistic.

Evaluating the test (for the log regression), we have $ESS_1 = 0.08193$ (which can be obtained directly from the results above). Estimating over the whole sample, 1973–2003, gives:

$$\ln m_t = -2.22 + 1.53 \ln gdp_t - 0.53 \ln pm_{t-1}$$
$$R^2 = 0.98, F_{2,26} = 848.02, \text{ESS}_p = 0.08696$$

so the test statistic is

$$F = \frac{(0.08696 - 0.08193)/2}{0.08193/26} = 0.80$$

The critical value of the $F$ distribution for 2, 26 degrees of freedom is 3.37, so the equation passes the test for parameter stability, i.e. the same regression line may be considered valid for both sub-periods.

It is noticeable that the predictions are always too low (for all the models); the errors in both years are positive. This suggests a slight 'boom' in imports relative to what one might expect (despite the result of the Chow test). Perhaps we have omitted an explanatory variable which has changed markedly in 2002–03 or perhaps the errors are not truly random. Alternatively, we still could have the wrong functional form for the model. Since we already have an $R^2$ value of 0.98 we are unlikely to find another variable which adds significantly to the explanatory power of the model. We have already tried two functional forms. Therefore we shall examine the errors in the model.

**Exercise 8.3**

(a) Use the regression equation from Exercise 8.2 to forecast the level of car travel in 2000 and 2001. How accurate are your forecasts? Is this a satisfactory result?

(b) Convert the variables to (natural) logarithms and repeat the regression calculation. Interpret your result and compare to the linear equation.

(c) Calculate price and income elasticities from the linear model and compare to those obtained from the log model.

(d) Forecast car travel in 2000 and 2001 using the log model and compare the results to those from the linear model. (Use the function $e^x$ to convert the forecasts in logs back to the original units.)

(e) Use a Chow test to test whether the forecasts are accurate. Is there any difference between linear and log models?

**Analysis of the errors**

This is another important part of the checking procedure, to see if the model is adequate or whether it is mis-specified (e.g. has the wrong functional form, or a missing explanatory variable). If the model is a good one then the error term should be random and ideally should be unpredictable. If there are any predictable elements to it, then we could use this information to improve our model and forecasts. Unlike forecasting, this is a within-sample procedure. Second, we expect the observed errors to be approximately Normally distributed, since this assumption underlies the $t$ and $F$ distributions used for inference. If the errors are not Normal, this would cast doubt on our use of $t$ and $F$ statistics for inference purposes.

A complete, formal, treatment of these issues is beyond the scope of this book (see, for example, Thomas, Chapter 5, or Maddala, Chapters 5, 6 and 12). Instead, we give an outline of how to detect the problems and some simple procedures which might overcome them. At least, if you are aware of the problem you will know that you should consult a more advanced text.

First, we can check the errors for Normality by constructing their frequency distribution, as was done in the previous chapter. This is left as an exercise for the reader. (The histogram of residuals does not look much like a Normal distribution, but formal tests (beyond the scope of this book) do not reject Normality.) Second, we can examine the error term for evidence of autocorrelation. This was introduced briefly in Chapter 1. To recapitulate: autocorrelation occurs when one error observation is correlated with an earlier (often the previous) one. It only occurs with time-series data (in cross-section, the ordering of the observations does not matter, so there is not a natural 'preceding' observation). Autocorrelation could occur in the import equation because of the 'stickiness' of imports, i.e. if imports are higher than predicted in period $t$, then they are likely to be high in $t+1$ also. This could explain the two negative forecasting errors. Alternatively, it could be a sign of the wrong functional form of the equation having been estimated.

### Checking for autocorrelation

The errors are obtained by subtracting the fitted values from the actual observations. Using time-series data we have:

$$(8.10) \qquad e_t = Y_t - \hat{Y}_t = Y_t - b_0 - b_1 X_{1t} - b_2 X_{2t}$$

The errors obtained from the import demand equation (for the logarithmic model of import demand) are shown in Table 8.7 and are graphed in Figure 8.5. The graph suggests a definite pattern, that of *positive* errors initially, followed by a series of negative errors, followed in turn by more positive errors. This is definitely not a random pattern: a positive error is likely to be followed by a positive error, a negative error by another negative error. From this graph we might confidently predict that the two errors for 2002–03 are positive (as in fact they are). This means our regression equation is inadequate in some way – we are expecting it to under-predict. If so, we ought to be able to improve it.

The phenomenon we have uncovered (positive errors following positive, negative following negative) is known as positive autocorrelation. In other

Table 8.7 **Calculation of residuals**

| Year | Actual | Predicted | Residuals |
|------|--------|-----------|-----------|
| 1973 | 4.47 | 4.45 | 0.02 |
| 1974 | 4.46 | 4.30 | 0.16 |
| 1975 | 4.39 | 4.37 | 0.02 |
| 1976 | 4.42 | 4.37 | 0.05 |
| ⋮ | ⋮ | ⋮ | ⋮ |
| 1997 | 5.31 | 5.29 | 0.02 |
| 1998 | 5.40 | 5.38 | 0.02 |
| 1999 | 5.47 | 5.43 | 0.04 |
| 2000 | 5.55 | 5.48 | 0.07 |
| 2001 | 5.60 | 5.53 | 0.08 |

*Note*: in logs, the residual is approximately the percentage error. So, for example, the first residual 0.02 indicates the error is of the order of 2%.

**Figure 8.5**
**Time-series graph of the errors from the import demand equation**

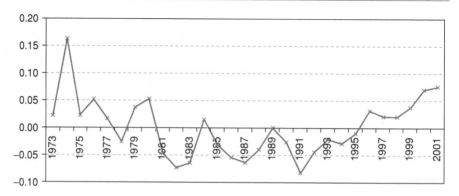

words, there appears to be a positive correlation between successive errors $e_t$ and $e_{t-1}$. A truly random series would have a low or zero correlation. Less common in economic models is **negative autocorrelation**, where positive errors tend to follow negative ones, negative follow positive. We will concentrate on positive autocorrelation.

This non-randomness can be summarised and tested numerically by the **Durbin–Watson** (DW) statistic (named after its two inventors). This is routinely printed out by specialist software packages but, unfortunately, not by spreadsheet programs. The statistic is a one-tail test of the null hypothesis of no autocorrelation against the alternative of positive, or of negative, autocorrelation. The test statistic always lies in the range 0–4 and is compared to critical values $d_L$ and $d_U$ (given in Appendix Table A7, see page **379**). The decision rule is best presented graphically, as in Figure 8.6.

**Figure 8.6**
**The Durbin–Watson test statistic**

Low values of DW (below $d_L$) suggest positive autocorrelation, high values (above $4 - d_L$) suggest negative autocorrelation, and a value near 2 (between $d_U$ and $4 - d_U$) suggests the problem is absent. There are also two regions where the test is, unfortunately, inconclusive, between the $d_L$ and $d_U$ values).

The test statistic can be calculated by the formula[2]

$$(8.11) \qquad DW = \frac{\sum_{t=2}^{n}(e_t - e_{t-1})^2}{\sum_{t=1}^{n} e_t^2}$$

[2] The DW statistic can also be approximated using the correlation coefficient $r$ between $e_t$ and $e_{t-1}$, and then $DW \approx 2 \times (1 - r)$. The approximation gets closer, the larger the sample size. It should be reasonably accurate if you have 20 observations or more.

Table 8.8 Calculation of the DW statistic

| Year | $e_t$ | $e_{t-1}$ | $e_t - e_{t-1}$ | $(e_t - e_{t-1})^2$ | $e_t^2$ |
|------|-------|-----------|-----------------|---------------------|---------|
| 1973 | 0.0208 | | | | |
| 1974 | 0.1628 | 0.0208 | 0.1420 | 0.02016 | 0.02650 |
| 1975 | 0.0220 | 0.1628 | −0.1408 | 0.01983 | 0.00048 |
| 1976 | 0.0513 | 0.0220 | 0.0293 | 0.00086 | 0.00263 |
| ⋮ | ⋮ | ⋮ | ⋮ | ⋮ | ⋮ |
| 1998 | 0.0193 | 0.0202 | −0.0009 | 0.00000 | 0.00037 |
| 1999 | 0.0369 | 0.0193 | 0.0176 | 0.00031 | 0.00136 |
| 2000 | 0.0683 | 0.0369 | 0.0314 | 0.00099 | 0.00466 |
| 2001 | 0.0754 | 0.0683 | 0.0071 | 0.00005 | 0.00568 |
| Totals | | | | 0.07994 | 0.08150 |

This is relatively straightforward to calculate using a spreadsheet program. Table 8.8 shows part of the calculation. Hence:

$$DW = \frac{0.07994}{0.08150} = 0.98$$

The result suggests positive autocorrelation[3] of the errors. For $n = 30$ (close enough to $n = 29$) the critical values are $d_L = 1.284$ and $d_U = 1.567$ (using the 95% confidence level, see Table A7, page **379**) so we clearly reject the null of no autocorrelation.

### Consequences of autocorrelation

The presence of autocorrelation in this example causes our forecasts to be too low. If we took account of the pattern of errors over time we could improve the forecasting performance of the model. A second general consequence of auto-correlation is that the standard errors are often under-estimated, resulting in excessive $t$ and $F$ statistics. This leads us to think the estimates are 'significant' when they might not, in fact, be so. We may have what is sometimes known as a 'spurious' regression – it looks good but is misleading. The bias in the stan-dard errors and $t$ statistics can be large and this is potentially a serious problem.

This danger occurs particularly when the variables used in the analysis are trended (as many economic variables are) over time. Variables trending over time *appear* to be correlated with each other but there may be no true under-lying relationship. One now-famous study[4] noted a strong correlation between cumulative rainfall and the price level (both increase over time but are unlikely to be related). It has been suggested that a low value of the DW statistic (typic-ally, less than the $R^2$ value) can be a symptom of such a problem. The fact that economic theory supports the idea of a causal relationship between demand, prices and income should make us a little more confident that we have found a valid economic relationship rather than a spurious one in this case.

---

[3] The correlation between $e_t$ and $e_{t-1}$ is, in fact, 0.494.

[4] Hendry, D.F. (1980), Econometrics – Alchemy or Science? *Economica*, vol 47, 387–406.

This topic goes well beyond the scope of this book but it is raised because it is important to be aware of the potential shortcomings of simple models. If you estimate a time-series regression equation, check the DW statistic to test for autocorrelation. If present, you may want to seek further advice rather than accept the results as they are, even if they appear to be good. The cause of the autocorrelation is often (though not always) the omission of lagged variables in the model, i.e. a failure to recognise that it may take time for the effect of the independent variables to work through to the dependent variable.

**Exercise 8.4**

(a) Using the log model, calculate the residuals from the regression equation and draw a line graph of them. Do they appear to be random or is some time-dependence apparent?

(b) Calculate the Durbin–Watson statistic and interpret the result.

(c) If autocorrelation is present, what are the implications for your estimates?

## Finding the right model

How do you know that you have found the 'right' model for the data? Can you be confident that another researcher, using the same data, would arrive at the same results? How can you be sure there isn't a relevant explanatory variable out there that you have omitted from your model? Without trying them all it is difficult to be sure. Good modelling is based on theoretical considerations (e.g. models that are consistent with economic or business principles) and statistical ones (e.g. significant $t$ ratios). One can identify two different approaches to modelling:

- *General to specific*: this starts off with a comprehensive model, including all the likely explanatory variables, then simplifies it.
- *Specific to general*: this begins with a simple model that is easy to understand, then explanatory variables are added to improve the model's explanatory power.

There is something to be said for both approaches, but it is not guaranteed that the two will end up with the same model. The former approach is usually favoured nowadays; it suffers less from the problem of omitted variable bias (discussed below) and the simplifying procedure is usually less ad hoc than that of generalising a simple model. A very general model will almost certainly initially contain a number of irrelevant explanatory variables. However, this is not much of a problem (and less serious than omitted variable bias): standard errors on the coefficients tend to be higher than otherwise, but this is remedied once the irrelevant variables are excluded.

It is rare for either of these approaches to be adopted in its pure, ideal form. For example, in the import demand equation we should have started out with several lags on the price variable, since we cannot be sure how long imports take to adjust to price changes. Therefore we might have started with (assuming a maximum lag of one year is 'reasonable'):

(8.12)    $m_t = b_0 + b_1 gdp_t + b_2 gdp_{t-1} + b_3 pm_t + b_4 pm_{t-1} + b_5 m_{t-1} + e_t$

If $b_4$ proved to be insignificantly different from zero we would then re-estimate the equation without $pm_{t-1}$ and obtain new coefficient estimates. If the new $b_2$ proved insignificant we would omit $gdp_{t-1}$ and re-estimate. This process would continue until all the remaining coefficients had significant $t$ ratios. We would then have the final, simplified model. At each stage we would omit the variable with the least significant coefficient. Having found the right model we could then test it on new data, to see if it can explain the new observations.

---

### Uncertainty regarding the correct model

The remarks about finding the right model apply to many of the other techniques used in this book. For example, we might employ the Poisson distribution to model manufacturing faults in televisions but we are *assuming* this is the correct distribution to use. In the example of railway accidents recounted in Chapter 4, it was found that the Poisson distribution did not fit the data precisely – the real world betrayed less variation than predicted by the model.

Our estimates of parameters, and the associated confidence intervals, are based on the assumption that we are using the correct model. To our uncertainty about the estimates we should ideally add the uncertainty about the correct model, but unfortunately this is difficult to measure. It may be that if we used a different model we would obtain a different conclusion. If possible therefore, it is a good idea to try out different models to see if the results are robust, and also to inform the reader about alternative methods that have been tried but not reported.

---

In practice the procedure is not as mechanical (nor as pure) as this, and more judgement should be exercised. You may not want to exclude all the price variables from a demand equation even though the $t$ ratios are small. A coefficient may be large in *size* even though it is not *significant*. 'Not significant' does not mean the same as 'insignificant', rather that there is a lot of uncertainty about its true value. In modelling imports, we used the 2002 and 2003 observations to test the model's forecasts. When it failed, we revised the model and applied the forecast test again. But this is no longer a strictly independent test, since we used the 2002–03 observations to decide upon revision to the model.

To briefly sum up a complex and contentious debate, a good model should be:

- *consistent with theory*: an estimated demand curve should not slope upwards, for example;
- *statistically satisfactory*: there should be good explanatory power (e.g. $R^2$, $F$ statistics), the coefficients should be statistically significant ($t$ ratios) and the errors should be random. It should also predict well, using new data (i.e. data not used in the estimation procedure);
- *simple*: although a very complicated model predicts better, it might be difficult for the reader to understand and interpret.

Sometimes these criteria conflict and then the researcher must use her judgement and experience to decide between them.

## Testing compound hypotheses

Simplifying a general model is largely based on hypothesis testing. Usually this means a hypothesis of the form $H_0$: $\beta = 0$ using a $t$ test. Sometimes, however, the hypothesis is more complex, as in the following examples:

■ You want to test the equality of two coefficients, $H_0$: $\beta_1 = \beta_2$.
■ You want to test if a *group* of coefficients are all zero, $H_0$: $\beta_1 = \beta_2 = 0$.

A general method for testing these compound hypotheses is to use an $F$ test. We illustrate this by examining whether consumers suffer from money illusion in the import demand equation. We assumed, in line with economic theory, that only relative prices matter and used $P_M/P$ as an explanatory variable. But suppose consumers actually respond differently to changes in $P_M$ and in $P$? In that case we should enter $P_M$ and $P$ as separate explanatory variables and they would have different coefficients. In other words, we should estimate (using the log form[5]):

(8.13)     $\ln m_t = c_0 + c_1 \ln gdp_t + c_2 \ln P_{Mt} + c_3 \ln P_t + e_t$

rather than

(8.14)     $\ln m_t = b_0 + b_1 \ln gdp_t + b_2 \ln pm_t + e_t$

where $P_M$ is the nominal price of imports and $P$ is the nominal price level. We would expect $c_2 < 0$ and $c_3 > 0$. Note that (8.14) is a *restricted* form of (8.13), with the restriction $c_2 = -c_3$ imposed. A lack of money illusion implies that this restriction should be valid and that (8.14) is the correct form of model. The hypothesis to test is therefore $H_0$: $c_2 = -c_3$ (or alternatively $H_0$: $c_2 + c_3 = 0$).

How can we test this? If the restriction is valid, (8.13) and (8.14) should fit equally well and thus have similar error sums of squares. Conversely, if they have very different ESS values, then we would reject the validity of the restriction. To carry out the test, we therefore do the following:

■ Estimate the *unrestricted* model (8.13) and obtain the *unrestricted* ESS from it ($ESS_U$).
■ Estimate the *restricted* model (8.14) and obtain the *restricted* ESS ($ESS_R$).
■ Form the test statistic

(8.15)     $F = \dfrac{(ESS_R - ESS_U)/q}{ESS_U/(n - k - 1)}$

where $q$ is the number of restrictions (1 in this case) and $k$ is the number of explanatory variables in the *unrestricted* model.
■ Compare the test statistic with the critical value of the $F$ distribution with $q$ and $n - k - 1$ degrees of freedom. If the test statistic exceeds the critical value, reject the restricted model in favour of the unrestricted one.

We have already estimated the restricted model (equation (8.14)) and from that we obtain $ESS_R = 0.08193$ (see Table 8.6). Estimating the unrestricted model gives

(8.16)     $\ln m_t = -7.05 + 2.00 \ln gdp_t - 0.39 \ln P_{Mt-1} + 0.24 \ln P_{t-1+e_t}$

[5] Note that it is much easier to test the restriction in log form, since $p_m$ and $p$ are entered additively. It would be much harder to do this in levels form.

with $ESS_U = 0.04546$. The test statistic is therefore

(8.17)     $$F = \frac{(0.08193 - 0.04546)/1}{0.04546/(29 - 3 - 1)} = 20.05$$

The critical value at the 95% confidence level is 4.24, so the restriction is rejected. Consumers do not use relative prices alone in making decisions, but are somehow influenced by the general rate of inflation as well. This is contrary to what one would expect from economic theory. Interestingly, the equation using nominal prices does not suffer from autocorrelation, so imposing the restriction (estimating with the real price of imports) induces autocorrelation, another indication that the restriction is inappropriate.

To our earlier finding we might therefore add that consumers appear to take account of nominal prices. We do not have space to investigate this issue in more detail but further analysis of these nominal effects would be worthwhile. There may be a theoretical reason for nominal prices to have an influence. Alternatively, there could be measurement problems with the data or inadequacies in the model which mask the truth that it is, after all, relative prices that matter.

Whatever the results, this method of hypothesis testing is quite general: it is possible to test any number of (linear) restrictions by estimating the restricted and unrestricted forms of the equation and comparing how well they fit the data. If the restricted model fits almost as well as the unrestricted model, it is preferred on the grounds of simplicity. The $F$ test is the criterion by which we compare the fit of the two models, using error sums of squares.

## Omitted variable bias

Omitting a relevant explanatory variable from a regression equation can lead to serious problems. Not only is the model inadequate because there is no information about the effect of the omitted variable but, in addition, the coefficients on the variables which *are* included are usually biased. This is called omitted variable bias (OVB).

We encountered an example of this in the model of import demand. Notice how the coefficient on income changed from 1.54 to 2.00 when nominal prices were included. This is a substantial change and shows that the original equation with only the real price of imports included may be misleading with respect to the effect of income upon imports. The coefficient on income was biased downwards.

The direction of OVB depends upon two things: the correlation between the omitted and included explanatory variables and the sign of the coefficient on the omitted variable. Thus, if you have to omit what you believe is a relevant explanatory variable (because the observations are unavailable, for example) you might be able to infer the direction of bias on the included variable(s). Table 8.9 summarises the possibilities, where the true model is $Y = b_0 + b_1X_1 + b_2X_2 + e$ but the estimated model omits the $X_2$ variable. Table 8.9 only applies to a single omitted variable; when there are several, matters are more complicated (see Maddala, Chapter 4).

In addition to coefficients being biased, their standard errors are biased upwards as well, so that inferences and confidence intervals will be incorrect. The best advice therefore is to ensure you don't omit a relevant variable!

Table 8.9 **The effects of omitted variable bias**

| Sign of omitted coefficient, $b_2$ | Correlation between $X_1$ and $X_2$ | Direction of bias of $b_1$ | Example values of $b_1$ | |
|---|---|---|---|---|
| | | | True | Estimated |
| $> 0$ | $> 0$ | upwards | 0.5 | 0.9 |
| | | | −0.5 | −0.1 |
| $> 0$ | $< 0$ | downwards | 0.5 | 0.1 |
| | | | −0.5 | −0.9 |
| $< 0$ | $> 0$ | downwards | 0.5 | 0.1 |
| | | | −0.5 | −0.9 |
| $< 0$ | $< 0$ | upwards | 0.5 | 0.9 |
| | | | −0.5 | −0.1 |

**Exercise 8.5**

(a) Calculate the simple correlation coefficients between price, income, the price of rail travel and the price of bus travel.

(b) The prices of rail and bus travel may well influence the demand for car travel. If so, the models calculated in previous exercises are mis-specified. What are the possible consequences of this? How might the correlations calculated in part (a) help?

(c) Extend the regression equation to include these two extra prices. (Estimate in logs, using 1980–1999. For simplicity, do not include lags.) Does this change any of your conclusions?

(d) One might expect the bus and rail price variables to have similar coefficients, as they are both substitutes for car travel. Test the hypothesis $H_0: \beta_{rail} - \beta_{bus} = 0$ by comparing error sums of squares from restricted and unrestricted regressions.

**Dummy variables, trends and seasonals**

A *dummy variable* is one that takes on a restricted range of values, usually just 0 and 1. Despite this simplicity, it can be useful in a number of situations. For example, suppose we suspect that the UK's import demand function shifted after the rise in the oil price in 1979. Ideally, we might include oil prices in our model, but suppose these data are unavailable. How could we then explore this possibility empirically?

One answer is to construct a variable, $D_t$, which takes the value 0 for the years 1973–79, and 1 thereafter (i.e. 0, 0, . . . , 0, 1, 1, . . . , 1, the switch occurring after 1979). We then estimate:

(8.18)     $\ln m_t = b_0 + b_1 \ln gdp_t + b_2 \ln pm_t + b_3 D_t + e_t$

The coefficient $b_3$ gives the size of the shift in 1979. The constant for the equation is equal to $b_0$ for 1973–79, when $D_t = 0$, and equal to $b_0 + b_3$ thereafter, when $D_t = 1$. The sign of $b_3$ shows the direction of any shift, and one can also test its significance, via the $t$ ratio. If it turns out not to be significant, then there was probably no shift in the relationship.

Note that we do not use the log of $D$ – this would be impossible as ln 0 is not defined. In any case, a dummy variable only needs to have two different values, it does not matter what they are (though 0, 1 is convenient for interpretation). Note also that $b_3$ will give the change in ln $m$, which is approximately the percentage change in $m$.

Estimating equation (8.21) yields the following result:

Figure 8.7
**The dummy variable effect**

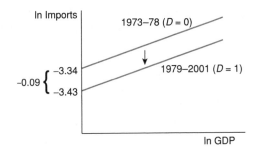

**(8.19)**     $\ln m_t = -3.34 + 1.68 \ln gdp_t - 0.47 \ln pm_t - 0.09\,D_t + e_t$

s.e.                                   (0.13)              (0.14)              (0.03)

$$R^2 = 0.99 \quad F(3, 25) = 598.6 \quad n = 29$$

We note that the dummy variable has a significant coefficient and that after 1979 imports were 9% lower than before, after taking account of any price and income effects. We presume it is the oil shock that has caused this, but in fact it could be due to anything that changed in 1979. Figure 8.7 shows the effect of introducing such a dummy variable and from the figure we can see that the effect of the dummy variable is to shift the regression line downwards for the years from 1979 onwards.

---

**Trap!**

There were, in fact, two oil shocks – in 1973 and 1979. With a longer series of data you might therefore be tempted to use a dummy variable {0, 0, . . . , 0, 1, . . . , 1, 2, . . . , 2}, with the first switch in 1973, the second in 1979 (this assumes you have some pre-1973 observations). This is wrong! It implicitly assumes that the two shocks had the same effect upon the dependent variable. The correct technique is to use two dummies, both using only zeros and ones. The first dummy would switch from 0 to 1 in 1973, the second would switch in 1979. Their individual coefficients would then measure the size of each shock.

---

A **time trend** is another useful type of dummy variable used with time-series data. It takes the values {1, 2, 3, 4, . . . , $T$} where there are $T$ observations. It is used as a proxy for a variable which we cannot measure and which we believe increases in a linear fashion. For example, suppose we are trying to model petrol consumption of cars. Price and income would obviously be relevant explanatory variables; but in addition, technical progress has made cars more fuel-efficient over time. It is impossible to measure this accurately, so we use a time trend as an additional regressor. In this case it should have a negative coefficient which would measure the annual reduction in consumption due to more fuel-efficient cars. Remember also, that if the dependent variable is in logs, the coefficient on the time trend shows the percentage change per annum (or per time period), e.g. a coefficient of –0.05 would indicate a 5% per annum fall in the dependent variable, independent of movements in other explanatory variables.

**Exercise 8.6**

(a) The graph of car travel suggests a break in 1990 – the rise is slower after this point than before. Test whether this break is significant or not using a dummy variable with a value of 0 up to (and including) 1990, 1 thereafter. (Estimate in logs using all three prices and income, 1980–1999.)

(b) The quality of cars has improved steadily over time, perhaps leading to increased travel by car. Add a time trend to the regression equation in part (a) and re-estimate. Is there evidence to support this idea?

## Multicollinearity

Sometimes some or all of the explanatory variables are highly correlated (in the sample data) which means that it is difficult to tell *which* of them is influencing the dependent variable. This is known as multicollinearity. Since all variables are correlated to some degree, multicollinearity is a problem of degree also. For example, if GDP and import prices both rise over time, it may be difficult to tell which of them influences imports. There has to be some independent movement of the explanatory variables for us to be able to disentangle their separate influences.

The symptoms of multicollinearity are:

- high correlation between two or more of the explanatory variables
- high standard errors of the coefficients leading to low $t$ ratios
- a high value of $R^2$ (and significant $F$ statistic) in spite of the insignificance of the individual coefficients.

In this situation, one might make the mistake of concluding that a variable is insignificant because of a large standard error, when, in fact, multicollinearity is to blame. It may be useful therefore, to examine the correlations between all the explanatory variables to see if such a problem is apparent. For example, the correlation between nominal import prices and the retail price index is 0.95. Hence it may be difficult to disentangle their individual effects.

The best cure is to obtain more data which might exhibit more independent variation of the explanatory variables. This is not always possible, however, for example if a sample survey has already been completed. An alternative is to drop one of the correlated variables from the regression equation, though the choice of which to exclude is somewhat arbitrary. Another procedure is to obtain extraneous estimates of the effects of one of the collinear variables (for example from another study). These effects can then be allowed for when estimates of the remaining coefficients are made.

## Measurement error

It is not always possible to measure the variables in a regression equation precisely, so the problem of measurement error arises. Either or both the endogenous or exogenous variables could be affected. This is more of a problem for estimation when the measurement error is systematic rather than random (in which case it may disappear into the error term) and can result in biased estimates. If transport costs are left out of the measured price of imported goods, and these costs have declined over time, then there is systematic measurement error in the price variable and possible bias in the coefficient.

**Exercise 8.7**

We noted in Exercise 8.5 that rail and bus prices were highly correlated. This may be why they both appear to be 'insignificant' in the regression equation. It could be the case that either of them could be influencing demand, but we cannot tell which. We can examine this by testing the hypothesis $H_0$: $\beta_{RAIL} = \beta_{BUS} = 0$. The restricted regression therefore excludes these two variables, the unrestricted regression includes them. One can then use equation (8.15) with $q = 2$ restrictions to test the hypothesis. What is the result? (Do not include dummy or trend in the equation.)

**Some final advice on regression**

- As always, large samples are better than small. Reasonable results were obtained above with only 29 observations, but this is rather a small sample size on which to base solid conclusions.
- Check the data carefully before calculation. This is especially true if a computer is used to analyse the data. If the data are typed in incorrectly, *every* subsequent result will be wrong. A substantial part of any research project should be devoted to verifying the data, checking the definitions of variables, etc. The work is tedious, but important.
- Don't go fishing. Otherwise known as data-mining, this is searching through the data hoping something will turn up. Some idea of what the data is expected to reveal, and why, allows the search to be conducted more effectively. It is easy to see imaginary patterns in data if an aimless search is being conducted. Try looking at the table of random numbers (Table A1, see page **364**), which will probably soon reveal something 'significant', like your telephone number or your credit card number.
- Don't be afraid to start with fairly simple techniques. Draw a graph of demand against price to see what it looks like, if it looks linear or log linear, if there are any outliers (a data error?), etc. This will give an overview of the problem which can be kept in mind when more refined techniques are used.

## Summary

- Multiple regression extends the principles of simple regression to models using several explanatory variables to explain variation in $Y$.
- The multiple regression equation is derived by minimising the sum of squared residuals, as in simple regression. This principle leads to the formulae for slope coefficients, standard errors, etc.
- The significance of the individual slope coefficients can be tested using the $t$ distribution and the overall significance of the model is based on the $F$ distribution.
- It is important to check the adequacy of the model. This can be done in various ways, including examining the accuracy of predictions and checking that the residuals appear random.
- One important form of non-randomness is termed autocorrelation, where the error in one period is correlated with earlier errors (this can occur in time-series data). This can lead to incorrect inferences being drawn.

■ The Durbin–Watson statistic is one diagnostic test for autocorrelation. If there is a problem of autocorrelation it can often be eliminated by including lagged regressors.

■ A good model should be (i) consistent with economic (or some other) theory, (ii) statistically satisfactory and (iii) simple. Sometimes there is a trade-off between these different criteria.

■ Complex hypothesis tests can often be performed by comparing restricted and unrestricted forms of the model. If the former fits the data almost as well as the latter then the (simplifying) restrictions specified in the null hypothesis are accepted.

■ Omitting relevant explanatory variables from the model is likely to cause bias to the estimated coefficients. This suggests it is often best to start off with a fairly general model and simplify it.

■ Regression analysis can become very complicated (well beyond the scope of this book), involving issues such as multicollinearity and simultaneous equations. However, the methods given in this chapter can provide helpful insights into a range of problems, especially if the potential shortcomings of the model are appreciated.

| Key terms and concepts | regression coefficients | autocorrelation | spurious regression |
| --- | --- | --- | --- |
| | omitted variable bias | dummy variables | multicollinearity |
| | simultaneity | measurement error | |

## Problems

Some of the more challenging problems are indicated by highlighting the problem number in colour.

**Problem 8.1**   (a)   Using the data in Problem 7.1 (page **253**), estimate a multiple regression model of the birth rate explained by GNP, the growth rate and the income ratio. Comment upon:
  (i)   the sizes and signs of the coefficients,
  (ii)  the significance of the coefficients,
  (iii) the overall significance of the regression.

(b)   How would you simplify the model?

(c)   Test for the *joint* significance of the coefficients on growth and the income ratio.

(d)   Repeat the above steps for all 26 observations. Comment.

(e)   Do you feel your understanding of the birth rate is improved after estimating the multiple regression equation?

(f)   What other possible explanatory variables do you think it might be worth investigating?

**Problem 8.2** The following data show the real price of butter and real incomes, to supplement the data in Problem 7.2 (see page **253**).

| Year | Price of butter | Real income | Year | Price of butter | Real income |
|------|-----------------|-------------|------|-----------------|-------------|
| 1970 | 105.5 | 70.3 | 1980 | 119.2 | 92.1 |
| 1971 | 130.9 | 71.1 | 1981 | 114.2 | 91.4 |
| 1972 | 131.9 | 77.1 | 1982 | 114.5 | 90.9 |
| 1973 | 99.5 | 82.1 | 1983 | 110.0 | 93.3 |
| 1974 | 89.6 | 81.5 | 1984 | 107.9 | 96.8 |
| 1975 | 92.1 | 81.9 | 1985 | 100.0 | 100.0 |
| 1976 | 109.1 | 81.7 | 1986 | 104.2 | 104.5 |
| 1977 | 118.2 | 79.9 | 1987 | 99.8 | 108.1 |
| 1978 | 123.4 | 85.8 | 1988 | 100.2 | 114.6 |
| 1979 | 130.6 | 90.7 | | | |

(a) Estimate a multiple regression model of the demand for margarine. Do the coefficients have the expected signs?

(b) Test the significance of the individual coefficients and of the regression as a whole.

(c) Should the model be simplified?

(d) Calculate the elasticity of demand. How does it differ from your earlier answer?

(e) Estimate the cross-price demand elasticity.

(f) Should other variables be added to improve the model, in your view?

**Problem 8.3** Using the results from Problem 8.1 forecast the birth rate of a country with the characteristics given in Problem 7.9 (see page **254**) (point estimate only).

**Problem 8.4** Given the following data for 1989 and 1990:

| Year | Price of margarine | Price of butter | Real income |
|------|--------------------|-----------------|-------------|
| 1989 | 79.3 | 104.3 | 120.2 |
| 1990 | 79.3 | 97.0 | 122.7 |

(a) Predict the levels of margarine consumption in the two years.

(b) The actual values of consumption for the two years were 3.47 and 3.19. How accurate are your forecasts?

(c) Test for the stability of the coefficients between sample and forecast periods.

**Problem 8.5** How would you most appropriately measure the following variables:

(a) social class in a model of alcohol consumption,

(b) crime,

(c) central bank independence from political interference.

**Problem 8.6** As Problem 8.5, for

(a) the output of a car firm, in a production function equation,

(b) potential trade union influence in wage bargaining,

(c) the performance of a school.

**Problem 8.7**   Would it be better to use time-series or cross-section data in the following models?
(a)   the relationship between the exchange rate and the money supply,
(b)   the determinants of divorce,
(c)   the determinants of hospital costs.
Explain your reasoning.

**Problem 8.8**   As Problem 8.7, for
(a)   measurement of economies of scale in the production of books,
(b)   the determinants of cinema attendances,
(c)   the determinants of the consumption of perfume.

**Problem 8.9**   How would you estimate a model explaining the following variables?
(a)   airline efficiency,
(b)   infant mortality,
(c)   bank profits.
You should consider such issues as whether to use time-series or cross-section data; the explanatory variables to use and any measurement problems; any relevant data transformations; the expected results.

**Problem 8.10**   As Problem 8.9, for
(a)   investment,
(b)   the pattern of UK exports (i.e. which countries they go to),
(c)   attendance at football matches.

**Problem 8.11**   R. Dornbusch and S. Fischer (in R.E. Caves and L.B. Krause, *Britain's Economic Performance*, Brookings, 1980) report the following equation for predicting the UK balance of payments:

$$B = 0.29 + 0.24U + 0.17 \ln Y - 0.004t - 0.10 \ln P - 0.24 \ln C$$
$$t \quad (.56) \quad (5.9) \quad (2.5) \quad (3.8) \quad (3.2) \quad (3.9)$$

$R^2 = 0.76$, $s_e = 0.01$, $n = 36$ (quarterly data 1970:1–1978:1)

where

$B$:   the current account of the balance of payments as a percentage of gross domestic product (a balance of payments deficit of 3% of GDP would be recorded as –3.0, for example)
$U$:   the rate of unemployment
$Y$:   the OECD index of industrial production
$t$:   a time trend
$P$:   the price of materials relative to the GDP deflator (price index)
$C$:   an index of UK competitiveness (a lower value of the index implies greater competitiveness)

(ln indicates the natural logarithm of a variable)
(a)   Explain why each variable is included in the regression. Do they all have the expected sign for the coefficient?
(b)   Which of the following lead to a higher BOP deficit (relative to GDP): (i) higher unemployment; (ii) higher OECD industrial production; (iii) higher material prices; (iv) greater competitiveness?

(c)  What is the implied shape of the relationship between $B$ and (i) $U$, (ii) $Y$?

(d)  Why cannot a double log equation be estimated for this data? What implications does this have for obtaining elasticity estimates? Why are elasticity estimates not very useful in this context?

(e)  Given the following values of the explanatory variables, estimate the state of the current account (point estimate): unemployment rate = 10%, OECD index = 110, time trend = 37, materials price index = 100, competitiveness index = 90.

**Problem 8.12**  In a cross-section study of the determinants of economic growth (National Bureau of Economic Research, *Macroeconomic Annual*, 1991), Stanley Fischer obtained the following regression equation:

$$GY = 1.38 - 0.52RGDP70 + 2.51PRIM70 + 11.16INV - 4.75INF + 0.17SUR$$
$$\quad\quad\quad\quad (-5.9) \quad\quad\quad (2.69) \quad\quad\quad (3.91) \quad\quad (2.7) \quad\quad (4.34)$$

$$\quad - 0.33DEBT80 - 2.02SSA - 1.98LAC$$
$$\quad\quad (-0.79) \quad\quad\quad (-3.71) \quad\quad (-3.76)$$

$$R^2 = 0.60, n = 73$$

where

| | |
|---|---|
| *GY*: | growth per capita, 1970–85 |
| *RGDP*: | real GDP per capita, 1970 |
| *PRIM70*: | primary school enrolment rate, 1970 |
| *INV*: | investment/GNP ratio |
| *INF*: | inflation rate |
| *SUR*: | budget surplus/GNP ratio |
| *DEBT80*: | foreign debt/GNP ratio |
| *SSA*: | dummy for sub-Saharan Africa |
| *LAC*: | dummy for Latin America and the Caribbean |

(a)  Explain why each variable is included. Does each have the expected sign on its coefficient? Are there any variables which are left out, in your view?

(b)  If a country were to increase its investment ratio by 0.05, by how much would its estimated growth rate increase?

(c)  Interpret the coefficient on the inflation variable.

(d)  Calculate the $F$ statistic for the overall significance of the regression equation. Is it significant?

(e)  What do the *SSA* and *LAC* dummy variables tell us?

**Problem 8.13 (Project)**  Build a suitable model to predict car sales in the UK. You should use time-series data (at least 20 annual observations). You should write a report in a similar manner to Problem 7.12 (see page **255**).

**References**  Maddala, G.S. (1992) *Introduction to Econometrics*, 2nd edition, Macmillan.

Thomas, R.L. (1993) *Introductory Econometrics*, 2nd edition, Longman.

## Answers to exercises

Exercise 8.1 (a) Demand rises rapidly until around 1990, then rises more slowly

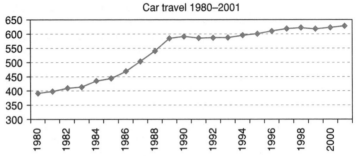

Car travel 1980–2001

Price falls quite quickly until 1990, then rises. This may relate to the pattern of travel demand, above

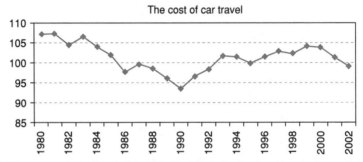

The cost of car travel

(b) The cross-plot of travel (vertical axis) against price is not clear-cut. There may be a slight negative relationship

Car travel vs price

Again, there is not an obvious bivariate relationship between travel and income

Car travel vs income

(c) Economic theory would suggest a negative price coefficient and a positive income coefficient.

(d) If bus and rail are substitutes for car travel, one would expect positive coefficients on their prices. However, they might be complements – commuters may drive to the station to catch the train.

Exercise 8.2 (a) The regression is:[6]

```
      Source |       SS    df          MS        Number of obs =       20
-------------+------------------------------      F( 2,  17)    = 483.10
       Model | 138 136.463   2  69 068.2316       Prob > F      = 0.0000
    Residual | 2430.48675   17  142.969809        R-squared     = 0.9827
-------------+------------------------------      Adj R-squared = 0.9807
       Total | 140 566.95   19  7 398.26053        Root MSE      = 11.957


------------------------------------------------------------------------------
         car |      Coef.   Std. Err.      t    P>|t|     [95% Conf. Interval]
-------------+----------------------------------------------------------------
       rpcar |  -6.390429   .7639393   -8.37   0.000    -8.0022    -4.778658
        rpdi |   6.048783   .2340236   25.85   0.000    5.555037    6.54253
       _cons |   748.1112     83.857    8.92   0.000    571.1884    925.034
------------------------------------------------------------------------------
```

(b) The signs of the coefficients are as expected. A unit increase in price lowers demand by 6.4 units; a unit rise in income raises demand by about 6 units. Without knowledge of the units of measurement it is hard to give a more precise interpretation. Both coefficients are highly significant, as is the $F$ statistic. 98% of the variation of car travel demand is explained by these two variables, a high figure.

Exercise 8.3 (a) The forecast values are 661.9 and 706.3 in 2000 and 2001. These compare with actual values of 618 and 624, so the errors are −6.6% and −11.7%. Assuming 2000 and 2001 would be the same as 1999 would actually give better results.

(b) In logs the results are:

```
      Source |       SS    df          MS        Number of obs =       20
-------------+------------------------------      F( 2,  17)    = 599.39
       Model | .557417045    2  .278708523        Prob > F      = 0.0000
    Residual | .007904751   17  .000464985        R-squared     = 0.9860
-------------+------------------------------      Adj R-squared = 0.9844
       Total | .565321796   19  .029753779        Root MSE      = .02156


------------------------------------------------------------------------------
        lcar |      Coef.   Std. Err.      t    P>|t|     [95% Conf. Interval]
-------------+----------------------------------------------------------------
      lrpcar |  -1.192195   .1410668   -8.45   0.000    -1.48982    -.8945699
       lrpdi |   .8408944   .0296594   28.35   0.000    .7783184    .9034704
       _cons |   8.193106   .7057587   11.61   0.000    6.704085    9.682127
------------------------------------------------------------------------------
```

Demand is elastic with respect to price ($e = -1.19$) and slightly less than elastic for income ($e = 0.84$). The coefficients are again highly significant.

(c) Price and income elasticities from the linear model are $-6.4 \times 101.1/526.5 = -1.23$ and $6.0 \times 70.2/526.5 = 0.8$. These are very similar to the log coefficients.

(d) The forecasts in logs are 6.492 and 6.561 which translate into 659.8 and 706.8. The predictions (and errors) are similar to the linear model.

[6] These results were produced using *Stata*. The layout is similar to that of Excel. Prob-values are indicated by 'Prob > F' and 'P > |t|'. 'rpcar' indicates the real price of car travel, 'rpdi' indicates real personal disposable income. Later on, an 'l' in front of a variable name indicates it is in log form.

(e)  For the linear model the Chow test is

$$F = \frac{(ESS_P - ESS_1)/n_2}{ESS_1/(n_1 - k - 1)} = \frac{(7672.6 - 2430.5)/2}{2430.5/(20 - 2 - 1)} = 18.3$$

The critical value is $F(2, 17) = 3.59$, so there appears to be a change between estimation and forecast periods. A similar calculation for the log model yields an $F$ statistic of 13.9 ($ESS_P = 0.0208$), also significant.

---

**Exercise 8.4**   (a)   The residuals from the log regression are as follows:

There is some evidence of positive autocorrelation and, in particular, the last two residuals (from the forecast period) are substantially larger than the rest

(b)  The Durbin–Watson statistic is DW = 1.52, against an upper critical value of $d_U$ = 1.54. The test statistic (just) falls into the uncertainty region, but the evidence for autocorrelation is very mild.

(c)  Autocorrelation would imply biased standard errors so inference would be dubious, but the coefficients themselves are still unbiased.

---

**Exercise 8.5**   (a)   The correlations are:

```
        |    rpcar     rpdi    rprail    rpbus
--------+---------------------------------------
 rpcar  |   1.0000
  rpdi  |  -0.3112   1.0000
rprail  |  -0.1468   0.9593   1.0000
 rpbus  |  -0.1421   0.9632   0.9827   1.0000
```

The price of car travel has a low correlation with the other variables, which are all highly correlated with each other ($r > 0.95$).

(b)  There may be omitted variable bias. Since the omitted variables are correlated with income, the income coefficient we have observed may be misleading. The car price variable is unlikely to be affected much, as it has a low correlation with the omitted variables.

(c)  The results are:

```
     Source |       SS   df       MS              Number of obs =      20
------------+----------------------------         F( 4, 15)     = 285.36
      Model | .557989155    4  .139497289         Prob > F      = 0.0000
   Residual | .007332641   15  .000488843         R-squared     = 0.9870
------------+----------------------------         Adj R-squared = 0.9836
      Total | .565321796   19  .029753779         Root MSE      = .02211
-----------------------------------------------------------------------------

       lcar |      Coef.  Std. Err.       t   P>|t|    [95% Conf. Interval]
------------+----------------------------------------------------------------
     lrpcar | -1.195793   .1918915   -6.23   0.000   -1.6048   -.786786
      lrpdi |  .8379483   .1372577    6.10   0.000   .5453904   1.130506
    lrprail |  .3104458   .3019337    1.03   0.320  -.3331106   .9540023
     lrpbus | -.3085937   .3166891   -0.97   0.345  -.9836004   .3664131
      _cons |   8.22269   .7318088   11.24   0.000   6.662877   9.782503
-----------------------------------------------------------------------------
```

The new price variables are not significant so there is unlikely to have been a serious OVB problem. Neither car price nor income coefficients have changed. The simpler model seems to be preferred.

(d)  The restricted equation is $y = \beta_1 + \beta_2 P_{CAR} + \beta_3 RPDI + \beta_4 (P_{RAIL} + P_{BUS}) + u$ (in logs) and estimating this yields $ESS_R = 0.007901$. The test statistic is therefore

$$F = \frac{(0.007901 - 0.007333)/1}{0.007333/(20 - 4 - 1)} = 1.16$$

This is not significant so the hypothesis of equal coefficients is accepted.

**Exercise 8.6**  (a)  The result is:

```
     Source |       SS   df       MS              Number of obs =      20
------------+----------------------------         F( 5, 14)     = 232.28
      Model | .558588344    5  .111717669         Prob > F      = 0.0000
   Residual | .006733452   14  .000480961         R-squared     = 0.9881
------------+----------------------------         Adj R-squared = 0.9838
      Total | .565321796   19  .029753779         Root MSE      = .02193
-----------------------------------------------------------------------------

       lcar |      Coef.  Std. Err.       t   P>|t|    [95% Conf. Interval]
------------+----------------------------------------------------------------
     lrpcar | -1.107049   .2062769   -5.37   0.000  -1.549469   -.6646293
      lrpdi |  .8898566   .1438706    6.19   0.000    .581285    1.198428
    lrprail |  .5466294   .3667016    1.49   0.158  -.2398673   1.333126
     lrpbus | -.4867887   .3523676   -1.38   0.189  -1.242542   .2689648
      d1990 | -.0314327   .0281614   -1.12   0.283   -.091833   .0289676
      _cons |  7.352081   1.065511    6.90   0.000   5.066787   9.637375
-----------------------------------------------------------------------------
```

The new coefficient, −0.03, suggests car travel is 3% lower after 1990 than before, *ceteris paribus*. However, the coefficient is not significantly different from zero, so there is little evidence of structural break. The change in car usage appears due to changes in prices and income.

(b)  The result is:

```
      Source |       SS   df            MS          Number of obs =       20
-------------+-------------------------------        F( 6,  13)    = 191.34
       Model | .558991816    6    .093165303         Prob > F      = 0.0000
    Residual |  .00632998   13    .000486922         R-squared     = 0.9888
-------------+-------------------------------        Adj R-squared = 0.9836
       Total | .565321796   19    .029753779         Root MSE      = .02207
-----------------------------------------------------------------------------

        lcar |      Coef.  Std. Err.      t    P>|t|   [95% Conf. Interval]
-------------+---------------------------------------------------------------
      lrpcar |  -1.116536   .2078126   -5.37   0.000  -1.565488    -.6675841
       lrpdi |   1.107112   .2791366    3.97   0.002   .5040736     1.71015
     lrprail |    .558322   .3691905    1.51   0.154  -.2392655    1.355909
      lrpbus |  -.2707759   .4266312   -0.63   0.537  -1.192457    .6509048
       d1990 |   -.036812   .0289451   -1.27   0.226   -.099344     .02572
       trend | -.0099434   .0109234   -0.91   0.379   -.033542    .0136552
       _cons |   5.553859   2.247619    2.47   0.028   .6981737    10.40954
-----------------------------------------------------------------------------
```

The trend is not significant. Note that the income coefficient has changed substantially. This is due to the high correlation between income and the trend ($r = 0.99$). It seems preferable to keep income and exclude the trend.

**Exercise 8.7**  The $F$ statistic is

$$F = \frac{(0.007905 - 0.007333)/2}{0.007333/(20 - 4 - 1)} = 0.59$$

This is less than the critical value of $F(2, 15) = 3.68$ so the hypothesis that both coefficients are zero is accepted.

# 9 Data collection and sampling methods

**Learning outcomes**

By the end of this chapter you should be able to:

- recognise the distinction between primary and secondary data sources
- avoid a variety of common pitfalls when using secondary data
- make use of electronic sources to gather data
- recognise the main types of random sample and understand their relative merits
- appreciate how such data are collected
- conduct a small sample survey yourself

## Introduction

It may seem a little odd to look at data collection now, after several chapters covering the analysis of data. Collection of data logically comes first, but the fact is that most people's experience is as a user of data, which determines their priorities. Also, it is difficult to have the motivation for learning about data collection when one does not know what it is subsequently used for. Having spent considerable time learning how to analyse data, it is now time to look at its collection and preparation.

There are two reasons why you might find this chapter useful. First, it will help if you have to carry out some kind of survey yourself. Second, it will help you in your data analysis, even if you are using someone else's data. Knowing the issues involved in data collection can help your judgement about the quality of the data you are using.

When conducting statistical research, there are two ways of obtaining data:

1 use **secondary data sources**, such as the UN Yearbook, or
2 collect sample data personally, a **primary data source**.

The first category should nowadays be divided into two sub-sections: printed and electronic sources. The latter is obviously becoming more important as time progresses, but printed documentation still has its uses. Using secondary data sources sounds simple, but it is easy to waste valuable time by making elementary errors. The first part of this chapter provides some simple advice to help you avoid such mistakes.

Much of this text has been concerned with the analysis of sample evidence and the inferences that can be drawn from it. It has been stressed that this evidence must come from randomly drawn samples and, although the notion of randomness was discussed in Chapter 2, the precise details of random sampling have not been set out.

The second part of this chapter is therefore concerned with the problems of collecting sample survey data prior to its analysis. The decision to collect the data personally depends upon the type of problem faced, the current availability of data relating to the problem and the time and cost needed to conduct a survey. It should not be forgotten that the first question that needs answering is whether the answer obtained is worth the cost of finding it. It is probably not worthwhile for the government to spend £50 000 to find out how many biscuits people eat, on average (though it may be worth biscuit manufacturers doing this). The sampling procedure is always subject to some limit on cost, therefore, and the researcher is trying to obtain the best value for money.

## Using secondary data sources

Much of the research in economics is based on secondary data sources, i.e. data which the researcher did not collect herself. The data may be in the form of official statistics such as those published in *Economic Trends* or they may come from unofficial surveys. In either case one has to use the data as presented; there is no control over sampling procedures.

It may seem easy enough to look up some figures in a publication, but there are a number of pitfalls for the unwary. The following advice comes from experience, some of it painful, and it may help you to avoid wasting time and effort. I have also learned much from the experiences of my students, whom I have also watched suffer.

A lot of data is now available online, so the advice given here covers both printed and electronic sources, with a separate section for the latter.

**Make sure you collect the right data**

This may seem obvious, but most variables can be measured in a variety of different ways. Suppose you want to measure the cost of labour (over time) to firms. Should you use the wage rate or earnings? The latter includes payment for extra hours such as overtime payments and reflects general changes in the length of the working week. Is the wage measured per hour or per week? Does it include part-time workers? If so, a trend in the proportion of part-timers will bias the wage series. Does the series cover all workers, men only, or women only? Again, changes in the composition will influence the wage series. What about tax and social security costs? Are they included? There are many questions one could ask.

One needs to have a clear idea therefore of the precise variable one needs to collect. This will presumably depend upon the issue in question. Economic theory might provide some guidance: for instance, theory suggests that firms care about *real* wage rates (i.e. after taking account of inflation, so related to the price of the goods the firm sells) so this is what one should measure. Check the definition of any series you collect (this is often at the back of the printed publication, or in a separate supplement giving explanatory notes and definitions). Make sure that the definition has not changed over the time period you require: the definition of unemployment used in the UK changed about twenty times in the 1980s, generally with the effect of reducing *measured* unemployment, even if actual unemployment was unaffected. In the UK the geographical coverage of data may vary: one series may relate to the UK, another to Great Britain and yet another to England and Wales. Care should obviously be taken if one is trying to compare such series.

**Try to get the most up-to-date figures**

Many macroeconomic series are revised as more information becomes available. The balance of payments serves as a good example. The first edition of this book showed the balance of payments (current balance, in £m for the UK) for 1970, as published in successive years, as follows:

| 1971 | 1972 | 1973 | 1974 | 1975 | 1976 | 1977 | 1978 | ... | 1986 |
|------|------|------|------|------|------|------|------|-----|------|
| 579 | 681 | 692 | 707 | 735 | 733 | 695 | 731 | ... | 795 |

The difference between the largest and smallest figures is of the order of 37%, a wide range. In the third edition of this book the figure was (from the 1999 edition of *Economic Trends Annual Supplement*) £911m which is 57% higher than the initial estimate. The latest figure at the time of writing is £819m. Most series are better than this. The balance of payments is hard to measure because it is the small difference between two large numbers, exports and imports. A

5% increase in measured exports and a 5% decrease in measured imports could thus change the measured balance by 100% or more.

One should always try to get the most up-to-date figures, therefore, which often means working *backwards* through data publications, i.e. use the current issue first and get data back as far as is available, then get the previous issue to go back a little further, etc. This can be tedious but it will also give some idea of the reliability of the data from the size of data revisions.

**Keep a record of your data sources**

You should always keep *precise* details of where you obtained each item of data. If you need to go back to the original publication (to check on the definition of a series, for example) you will then be able to find it easily. It is easy to spend hours (if not *days*) trying to find the source of some interesting numbers that you wish to update. 'Precise details' means the name of the publication, issue number or date, and table or page number. It also helps to keep the library reference number of the publication if it is obscure. It is best to take a photocopy of the data (but check copyright restrictions) rather than just copy it down, if possible.

> **Keeping data in *Excel* or another spreadsheet**
>
> Spreadsheets are ideal for keeping your data. It is often a good idea to keep the data all together in one worksheet and extract portions of them as necessary and analyse them in another worksheet. Alternatively, it is usually quite easy to transfer data from the spreadsheet to another program (e.g. *Minitab* or *SPSS*) for more sophisticated analysis. In most spreadsheets you can attach a comment to any cell, so you can use this to keep a record of the source of each observation, changes of definition, etc. Thus you can retain all the information about your data together in one place.

**Check your data**

Once you have collected your data you must check it. Once you have done this, it is probably worth checking it again. Better, get someone else to do the second check. Note that if your data are wrong then all your subsequent calculations could be incorrect and you will have wasted much time.

A useful way to check the data is first to graph it (e.g. a time-series plot). Obvious outliers will show up and you can investigate them for possible errors. Do not just rely on the graphs, however, look through your data and check it against the original source. Don't forget that the original source could be wrong too, so be wary of 'unusual' observations.

## Using electronic sources of data

A vast amount of data is now available electronically, usually online, and this is becoming increasingly the norm. Sometimes the data are available free but sometimes they have to be paid for, especially if they have a commercial value. My experience suggests that many students nowadays only consider online resources, which I feel is a mistake. Not everything is online and sometimes, even if it is, it is extremely hard to find. It can sometimes take less time to go to the library, find the appropriate journal and type in the numbers. As an estimate, one hundred observations should take no longer than about ten minutes to type into a computer, which is probably quicker than finding them electronically, converting to the right format, etc. Hence the advantage of online data lies principally with large datasets.

Obtaining data electronically should avoid input errors and provide consistent, up-to-date figures. However, this is not always guaranteed. For example, the UK Office for National Statistics (ONS) online databank provides plenty of information, but some of the series clearly have breaks in them and there is little warning of this in the on-screen documentation. The series for revenue per admission to cinemas (roughly the price of admission) goes:

| 1963 | 1964 | 1965 | 1966 | 1967 |
|---|---|---|---|---|
| 37.00 | 40.30 | 45.30 | 20.60 | 21.80 |

which strongly suggests a break in the series in 1966 (especially as admissions *fell* by 12% between 1965 and 1966!). Later in the series, the observations appear to be divided by 100. The lesson is that even with electronic data you should check the numbers to ensure they are correct.

You need to follow the same advice with electronic sources as with printed ones: make sure you collect the right variables and keep a note of your source. Online sources seem to be less good than many printed sources about providing definitions of the variables. It is often unclear if the data are in real terms, seasonally adjusted, etc. Sometimes you may need to go to the printed document to find the definitions, even if the data themselves come from the internet. Keeping a note of your source means taking down the URL of the site you visit. Remember that some sites generate the page 'on demand' so the web address is not a permanent one and typing it in later on will not take you back to the same source. In these circumstances is may be better to note the 'root' part of the address (e.g. www.imf.org/data/) rather than the complete detail. You should also take a note of the date you accessed the site, this may be needed if you put the source into a bibliography.

## Tips on downloading data

- If you are downloading a spreadsheet, save it to your hard disk then include the URL of the source within the spreadsheet itself. You will always know where it came from. You can do the same with Word documents.
- You cannot do this with PDF files, which are read-only. You could save the file to your disk, including the URL within the file name (but avoid putting extra full stops in the file name, that confuses the operating system. Replace them with hyphens.)
- You can use the 'Text select tool' within Acrobat to copy items of data from a PDF file and then paste them into a spreadsheet.
- Often, when pasting several columns of data into Excel, all the numbers go into a single column. You can fix this using the Data, Text to Columns menu. Experimentation is required, but it works well.

Since there are now so many online sources (and they are constantly changing) a list of useful data sites rapidly becomes out of date. The following sites seem to have withstood the test of time so far and have a good chance of surviving throughout the life of this edition.

■ The UK Office for National Statistics is at http://www.statistics.gov.uk/ and their Statbase service supplies over 1000 datasets online for free. This is tied to information on 13 'themes', such as education, agriculture, etc.

■ The Data and Story Library at http://lib.stat.cmu.edu/DASL/ is just that: datasets with accompanying statistical analyses which are useful for learning.

■ The IMF's World Economic Database is at http://www.imf.org/ (follow the links to publications, World Economic Outlook, then the database). It has macroeconomic series for most countries for several years. It is easy to download in csv (text) format, for use in spreadsheets.

■ The Biz/Ed site at http://www.bized.ac.uk/ contains useful material on business (including financial case studies of companies) as well as economic data. There is a link from here to the Penn World Tables, which contain national accounts data for many countries (on a useful, comparable basis) from 1960 onwards. Alternatively, visit the Penn home page at http://pwt.econ.upenn.edu/.

■ The World Bank provides a lot of information, particularly relating to developing countries, at http://www.worldbank.org/data/. Much of the data appears to be in .pdf format so, although it is easy to view on-screen, it cannot be easily transferred into a spreadsheet or similar software.

■ Bill Goffe's Resources for Economists site (www.rfe.wustl.edu/EconFAQ) contains a data section which is a good starting-off point for data sources.

■ Google. Possibly the most useful website of all. Intelligent use of this search tool is often the best way to find what you want.

■ http://davidmlane.com/hyperstat/index.html has an online textbook and glossary. This is useful if you have a computer handy but not a textbook.

## Collecting primary data

**Primary data** are data that you have collected yourself from original sources, often by means of a sample survey. This has the advantage that you can design the questionnaire to include the questions of interest to you and you have total control over all aspects of data collection. You can also choose the size of the sample (as long as you have sufficient funds available) so as to achieve the desired width of any confidence intervals.

Almost all surveys rely upon some method of sampling, whether random or not. The probability distributions which have been used in previous chapters as the basis of the techniques of estimation and hypothesis testing rely upon the samples having been drawn at random from the population. If this is not the case, then the formulae for confidence intervals, hypothesis tests, etc. are incorrect and not strictly applicable (they may be reasonable approximations but it is difficult to know how reasonable). In addition, the results about the bias and precision of estimators will be incorrect. For example, suppose an estimate of the average expenditure on repairs and maintenance by car owners is obtained from a sample survey. A poor estimate would arise if only Rolls-Royce owners were sampled, since they are not representative of the population as a whole. The precision of the estimator (the sample mean, $\bar{x}$) is likely to be poor because the mean of the sample could either be very low (Rolls-Royce cars are very reliable so rarely need repairs) or very high (if they do break down the high quality of the car necessitates a costly repair). This means the confidence interval estimate will be very wide and thus imprecise. It is not immediately obvious if the estimator would be biased upwards or downwards.

Thus some form of random sampling method is needed to be able to use the theory of the probability distributions of random variables. Nor should it be believed that the theory of random sampling can be ignored if a very large sample is taken, as the following cautionary tale shows. In 1936 the *Literary Digest* tried to predict the result of the forthcoming US election by sending out 10 million mail questionnaires. Two million were returned, but even with this enormous sample size Roosevelt's vote was incorrectly estimated by a margin of 19 percentage points. The problem is that those who respond to questionnaires are not a random sample of those who receive them.

## The meaning of random sampling

The definition of random sampling is that every element of the population should have a known, non-zero probability of being included in the sample. The problem with the sample of cars used above was that Ford cars (for example) had a zero probability of being included. Many sampling procedures give an equal probability of being selected to each member of the population but this is not an essential requirement. It is possible to adjust the sample data to take account of unequal probabilities of selection. If, for example, Rolls-Royce had a much greater chance of being included than Ford, then the estimate of the population mean would be calculated as a weighted average of the sample observations, with greater weight being given to the few 'Ford' observations than to relatively abundant 'Rolls-Royce' observations. A very simple illustration of this is given below. Suppose that for the population we have the following data:

|  | Rolls-Royce | Ford |
| --- | --- | --- |
| Number in population | 20 000 | 2 000 000 |
| Annual repair bill | £1000 | £200 |

Then the average repair bill is

$$\mu = \frac{20\ 000 \times 1000 + 2\ 000\ 000 \times 200}{2\ 020\ 000} = 207.92$$

Suppose the sample data are as follows:

|  | Rolls-Royce | Ford |
| --- | --- | --- |
| Number in sample | 20 | 40 |
| Probability of selection | 1/1000 | 1/50 000 |
| Repair bill | £990 | £205 |

To calculate the average repair bill from the sample data we use a weighted average, using the relative population sizes as weights, not the sample sizes:

$$\bar{x} = \frac{20\ 000 \times 990 + 2\ 000\ 000 \times 205}{2\ 020\ 000} = 212.77$$

If the sample sizes were used as weights the average would come out at £466.67, which is substantially incorrect.

As long as the probability of being in the sample is known (and hence the relative population sizes known), the weight can be derived; but if the probability is zero this procedure breaks down.

Other theoretical assumptions necessary for deriving the probability distribution of the sample mean or proportion are that the population is of infinite size and that each observation is independently drawn. In practice the former condition is never satisfied since no population is of infinite size, but most populations are large enough that it does not matter. For each observation to be independently drawn (i.e. the fact of one observation being drawn does not alter the probability of others in the sample being drawn) strictly requires that sampling be done with replacement, i.e. each observation drawn is returned to the population before the next observation is drawn. Again in practice this is often not the case, sampling being done without replacement, but again this is of negligible practical importance.

On occasion the population is quite small and the sample constitutes a substantial fraction of it. In these circumstances the finite population correction (fpc) should be applied to the formula for the variance of $\bar{x}$, the fpc being given by

(9.1)     $\text{fpc} = (1 - n/N)$

where $N$ is the population size and $n$ the sample size. The table below illustrates its usage:

| Variance of $\bar{x}$ from infinite population | Variance of $\bar{x}$ from finite population | Example values of fpc | | | |
|---|---|---|---|---|---|
| | | $n = 20$ | 25 | 50 | 100 |
| | | $N = 50$ | 100 | 1000 | 10 000 |
| $\sigma^2/n$ | $\sigma^2/n \times (1 - n/N)$ | 0.60 | 0.75 | 0.95 | 0.99 |

The finite population correction serves to narrow the confidence interval because a sample size of (say) 25 reveals more about a population of 100 than about a population of 100 000, so there is less uncertainty about population parameters. When the sample size constitutes only a small fraction of the population (e.g. 5% or less) the finite population correction can be ignored in practice. If the whole population is sampled ($n = N$) then the variance becomes zero and there is no uncertainty about the population mean.

A further important aspect of random sampling occurs when there are two samples to be analysed, when it is important that the two samples are independently drawn. This means that the drawing of the first sample does not influence the drawing of the second sample. This is a necessary condition for the derivation of the probability distribution of the difference between the sample means (or proportions).

**Types of random sample**

The meaning and importance of randomness in the context of sampling has been explained. However, there are various different types of sampling, all of them random, but which have different statistical properties. Some methods lead to greater precision of the estimates, while others can lead to considerable cost savings in the collection of the sample data, but at the cost of lower precision. The aim of sampling is usually to obtain the most precise estimates of the parameter in question, but the best method of sampling will depend on the circumstances of each case. If it is costly to sample individuals, a sampling method which lowers cost may allow a much larger sample size to be drawn and thus good (precise) estimates to be obtained, even if the method is inherently not very precise. These issues are investigated in more detail below, as a number of different sampling methods are examined.

**Simple random sampling**

This type of sampling has the property that every possible sample that could be obtained from the population has an equal chance of being selected. This implies that each element of the population has an equal probability of being included in the sample, but this is not the defining characteristic of simple random sampling. As will be shown below, there are sampling methods where every member of the population has an equal chance of being selected, but some samples (i.e. certain combinations of population members) can never be selected.

The statistical methods in this book are based upon the assumption of simple random sampling from the population. It leads to the most straightforward formulae for estimation of the population parameters. Although many statistical surveys are not based upon simple random sampling, the use of statistical tests based on simple random sampling is justified since the sampling process is often hypothetical. For example, if one were to compare annual growth rates of two countries over a 30-year period, a z test on the difference of two sample means (i.e. the average annual growth rate in each country) would be conducted. In a sense the data are not a sample since they are the only possible data for those two countries over that time period. Why not just regard the data as constituting the whole population, therefore? Then it would just be a case of finding which country had the higher growth rate; there would be no uncertainty about it.

The alternative way of looking at the data would be to suppose that there exists some hypothetical population of annual growth rates and that the data for the two countries were drawn by (simple) random sampling from this population. Is this story consistent with the data available? In other words, could the data we have simply arise by chance? If the answer to this is no (i.e. the z score exceeds the critical value) then there is something causing a difference between the two countries (it may not be clear what that something is). In this case it is reasonable to assume that all possible samples have an equal chance of selection, i.e. that simple random sampling takes place. Since the population is hypothetical one might as well suppose it to have an infinite number of members, again required by sampling theory.

**Stratified sampling**

Returning to the practical business of sampling, one problem with simple random sampling is that it is possible to collect 'bad' samples, i.e. those which are unrepresentative of the population. An example of this is the 'basketball player' problem, i.e. in trying to estimate the average height of the population, the sample (by sheer bad luck) contains a lot of basketball players. One way round this problem is to ensure that the proportion of basketball players in the sample accurately reflects the proportion of basketball players in the population (i.e. very small!). The way to do this is to divide up the population into 'strata' and then to ensure that each stratum is properly represented in the sample. This is best illustrated by means of an example.

A survey of newspaper readership, which is thought to be associated with social class, is to be carried out. People higher up the social scale are more likely to read a newspaper and to read different newspapers from those at the bottom of the social scale. Suppose the population is made up of three social classes, $A$ (highest), $B$ and $C$ as follows:

| Percentage of population in social class | | |
|---|---|---|
| *A* | *B* | *C* |
| 20% | 50% | 30% |

Suppose a sample of size 100 is taken. With luck it would contain 20 people from class $A$, 50 from $B$ and 30 from $C$ and thus would be representative of the population as a whole. But if, by bad luck (or bad sample design), all 100 people in the sample were from class $A$, poor results would be obtained since newspaper readership differs between social classes.

To avoid this type of problem a stratified sample is taken, which ensures that all social classes are represented in the sample. This means that the survey would have to ask people about their social class as well as their reading habits. The simplest form of stratified sampling is equiproportionate sampling, whereby a stratum which constitutes (say) 20% of the population also makes up 20% of the sample. For the example above the sample would be made up as follows:

| Class | *A* | *B* | *C* | Total |
|---|---|---|---|---|
| Number in sample | 20 | 50 | 30 | 100 |

It should be clear why stratified sampling constitutes an improvement over simple random sampling, since it rules out 'bad' samples, i.e. those not representative of the population. It is simply impossible to get a sample consisting completely of social class $A$, or $B$, or $C$. In fact, it is impossible to get a sample in anything but the proportions 20:50:30, as in the population; this is ensured by the method of collecting the sample.

It is easy to see when stratification leads to large improvements over simple random sampling. If there were no difference between strata (social classes) in reading habits then there would be no gain from stratification. If reading habits were the same regardless of social class there would be no point in dividing up the population by social class. On the other hand, if there were large differences between strata, but within strata reading habits were similar, then the gains from stratification would be large.

Stratification is beneficial therefore when

- the between-strata differences are large and
- the within-strata differences are small.

These benefits take the form of greater precision of the estimates, i.e. narrower confidence intervals.[1] The greater precision arises because stratified sampling makes use of supplementary information – i.e. the proportion of the population in each social class. Simple random sampling does not make use of this. Obviously, therefore, if those proportions of the population are unknown, stratified sampling cannot be carried out. However, even if the proportions are only known approximately there could be a gain in precision.

In this example social class is a stratification factor, i.e. a variable which is used to divide the population into strata. Other factors could, of course, be used, such as income or even height. A good stratification factor is one which is related to the subject of investigation. Income would probably be a good stratification factor, therefore, since it is related to reading habits, but height is not since there is probably little difference between tall and short people in the newspaper they read. What is a good stratification factor obviously depends upon the subject of study. A bed manufacturer might well find height to be a good stratification factor if conducting an enquiry into preferences about the size of beds. Although good stratification factors improve the precision of estimates, bad factors do not make them worse; there will simply be no gain over simple random sampling. It would be as if there were no differences between the social classes in reading habits, so that ensuring the right proportions in the sample is irrelevant, but it has no detrimental effects.

Proportional allocation of sample observations to the different strata (as done above) is the simplest method but is not necessarily the best. For the optimal allocation there should generally be a divergence from proportional allocation, and the sample should have more observations in a particular stratum (relative to proportional allocation):

- the more diverse the stratum, and
- the cheaper it is to sample the stratum.

Starting from the 20:50:30 proportional allocation derived earlier, suppose that members of class $A$ all read the same newspaper, but those of class $C$ read a variety of titles. Then the representation of class $C$ in the sample should be increased, and that of $A$ reduced. If it really were true that everyone in class $A$ read the same paper then one observation from that class would be sufficient to yield all there is to know about it. Furthermore, if it is cheaper to sample class $C$, perhaps because they are geographically more concentrated than class $A$, then again the representation of class $C$ in the sample should be increased. This is because, for a given budget, it will allow a larger total sample size.

---

[1] The formulae for calculating confidence intervals with stratified sampling are not given here, since they merit a whole book to themselves. The interested reader should consult C.A. Moser and G. Kalton, *Survey Methods in Social Investigation*, Heinemann, 1971.

### Surveying concert-goers

A colleague and I carried out a survey of people attending a concert in Brighton (by Jamiroquai – hope they're still popular by the time you read this) to find out who they were, how much they spent in the town and how they got to the concert. The spreadsheet gives some of the results.

Note that the data are kept on one sheet and results on another, which are named appropriately.

The data were collected by face-to-face interviews before the concert. We did not have a sampling frame, so the (student) interviewers simply had to choose the sample themselves on the night. The one important instruction about sampling we gave them was that they should not interview more than one person in any group. People in the same group are likely to be influenced by each other (e.g. travel together) so we would not get independent observations, reducing the effective sample size.

From the results you can see that 41.1% either worked or studied in Brighton and that only one person in the sample was neither working nor studying. The second half of the table shows that 64.4% travelled to the show in a car (obviously adding to congestion in the town), about half of whom shared a car ride. Perhaps surprisingly, Brighton residents were just as likely to use their car to travel as were those from out of town.

The average level of spending was £24.20, predominantly on food (£7.38), drink (£5.97) and shopping (£5.37). The last category had a high variance associated with it – many people spent nothing, one person spent £200 in the local shops.

**Cluster sampling**   A third form of sampling is cluster sampling which, although intrinsically inefficient, can be much cheaper than other forms of sampling, allowing a larger sample size to be collected. Drawing a simple, or stratified, random sample of size 100 from the whole of Britain would be very expensive to collect since the sample observations would be geographically very spread out. Interviewers would have to make many long and expensive journeys simply to collect one or two observations. To avoid this, the population can be divided into 'clusters' (for example, regions or local authorities) and one or more of these clusters are then randomly chosen. Sampling takes place only within the selected clusters, and is therefore geographically concentrated, and the cost of sampling falls, allowing a larger sample to be collected.

Within each cluster one can have either a 100% sample or a lower sampling fraction, which is called multi-stage sampling (this is explained further below). Cluster sampling gives unbiased estimates of population parameters but, for a given sample size, these are less precise than the results from simple or stratified sampling. This arises in particular when the clusters are very different from each other, but fairly homogeneous within themselves. In this case, once a cluster is chosen, if it is unrepresentative of the population, a poor (inaccurate) estimate of the population parameter is inevitable. The ideal circumstances for cluster sampling are when all clusters are identical, since in that case examining one cluster is as good as examining the whole population.

Dividing up the population into clusters and dividing it into strata are similar procedures, but the difference is that sampling is from one or at most a few clusters, but from all strata. This is reflected in the characteristics which make for good sampling. In the case of stratified sampling, it is beneficial if the between-strata differences are large and the within-strata differences small. For cluster sampling this is reversed: it is desirable to have small between-cluster differences but heterogeneity within clusters. Cluster sampling is less efficient (precise) for a given sample size, but is cheaper and so can offset this disadvantage with a larger sample size. In general, cluster sampling needs a much larger sample to be effective, so is only worthwhile where there are significant gains in cost.

**Multi-stage sampling**

Multi-stage sampling was briefly referred to in the previous section and is commonly found in practice. It may consist of a mixture of simple, stratified and cluster sampling at the various stages of sampling. Consider the problem of selecting a random sample of 1000 people from a population of 25 million to find out about voting intentions. A simple random sample would be extremely expensive to collect, for the reasons given above, so an alternative method must be found. Suppose further that it is suspected that voting intentions differ according to whether one lives in the north or south of the country and whether one is a home owner or renter. How is the sample to be selected? The following would be one appropriate method.

First the country is divided up into clusters of counties or regions, and a random sample of these taken, say one in five. This would be the first way of reducing the cost of selection, since only one-fifth of all counties now need to be visited. This one-in-five sample would be stratified to ensure that north and south were both appropriately represented. To ensure that each voter has an equal chance of being in the sample, the probability of a county being drawn should be proportional to its adult population. Thus a county with twice the population of another should have twice the probability of being in the sample.

Having selected the counties, the second stage would be to select a random sample of local authorities within each selected county. This might be a one-in-ten sample from each county and would be a simple random sample within each cluster. Finally a selection of voters from within each local authority would be taken, stratified according to tenure. This might be a one in 500 sample. The sampling fractions would therefore be

$$\frac{1}{5} \times \frac{1}{10} \times \frac{1}{500} = \frac{1}{25\,000}$$

So from the population of 25 million voters a sample of 1000 would be collected. For different population sizes the sampling fractions could be adjusted so as to achieve the goal of a sample size of 1000.

The sampling procedure is a mixture of simple, stratified and cluster sampling. The two stages of cluster sampling allow the selection of 50 local authorities for study and so costs are reduced. The north and south of the country are both adequately represented and housing tenures are also correctly represented in the sample by the stratification at the final stage. The resulting confidence intervals will be difficult to calculate but should give an improvement over the method of simple random sampling.

## Quota sampling

Quota sampling is a non-random method of sampling and therefore it is impossible to use sampling theory to calculate confidence intervals from the sample data, or to find whether or not the sample will give biased results. Quota sampling simply means obtaining the sample information as best one can, for example, by asking people in the street. However, it is by far the cheapest method of sampling and so allows much larger sample sizes. As shown above, large sample sizes can still give biased results if sampling is non-random; but in some cases the budget is too small to afford even the smallest properly conducted random sample, so a quota sample is the only alternative.

Even with quota sampling, where the interviewer is simply told to go out and obtain (say) 1000 observations, it is worth making some crude attempt at stratification. The problem with human interviewers is that they are notoriously non-random, so that when they are instructed to interview every tenth person they see (a reasonably random method), if that person turns out to be a shabbily dressed tramp slightly the worse for drink, they are quite likely to select the eleventh person instead. Shabbily dressed tramps, slightly the worse for drink, are therefore under-represented in the sample. To combat this sort of problem the interviewers are given quotas to fulfil, for example, 20 men and 20 women, ten old-age pensioners, one shabbily dressed tramp, etc., so that the sample will at least broadly reflect the population under study and give reasonable results.

It is difficult to know how accurate quota samples are, since it is rare for their results to be checked against proper random samples or against the population itself. Probably the most common quota samples relate to voting intentions and so can be checked against actual election results. The 1992 UK general election provides an interesting illustration. The opinion polls predicted a fairly substantial Labour victory but the outcome was a narrow Conservative majority. An enquiry concluded that the erroneous forecast occurred because a substantial number of voters changed their minds at the last moment and that there was 'differential turn-out', i.e. Conservative supporters were more likely to vote than Labour ones. Presumably, future opinion polls will try to take this into account.

## Calculating the required sample size

Before collecting sample data it is obviously necessary to know how large the sample size has to be. The required sample size will depend upon two factors:

■ the desired level of precision of the estimate, and
■ the funds available to carry out the survey.

The greater the precision required the larger the sample size needs to be, other things being equal. But a larger sample will obviously cost more to collect and this might conflict with a limited amount of funds being available. There is a trade-off therefore between the two desirable objectives of high precision and low cost. The following example shows how these two objectives conflict.

A firm producing sweets wishes to find out the average amount of pocket money children receive per week. It wants to be 99% confident that the estimate is within 20 pence of the correct value. How large a sample is needed?

The problem is one of estimating a confidence interval, turned on its head. Instead of having the sample information $\bar{x}$, $s$ and $n$, and calculating the confidence interval for $\mu$, the desired width of the confidence interval is given and it is necessary to find the sample size $n$ which will ensure this. The formula for the 99% confidence interval, assuming a Normal rather than $t$ distribution (i.e. it is assumed that the required sample size will be large), is

**(9.2)**     $[\bar{x} - 2.58 \times \sqrt{s^2/n}, \bar{x} + 2.58 \times \sqrt{s^2/n}]$

Diagrammatically this can be represented as in Figure 9.1.

The firm wants the distance between $\bar{x}$ and $\mu$ to be no more than 20 pence in either direction, which means that the confidence interval must be 40 pence wide. The value of $n$ which makes the confidence interval 40 pence wide has to be found. This can be done by solving the equation

$$20 = 2.58 \times \sqrt{s^2/n}$$

and hence by rearranging:

**(9.3)**     $n = \dfrac{2.58^2 \times s^2}{20^2}$

**Figure 9.1**
**The desired width of the confidence interval**

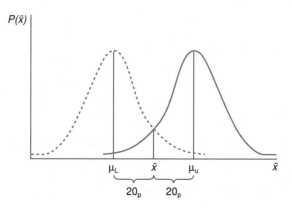

All that is now required to solve the problem is the value of $s^2$, the sample variance; but since the sample hasn't yet been taken this is not available. There are a number of ways of trying to get round this problem:

■ using the results of existing surveys if available,
■ conducting a small, preliminary, survey,
■ guessing.

These may not seem very satisfactory (particularly the last), but something has to be done and some intelligent guesswork should give a reasonable estimate of $s^2$. Suppose, for example, that a survey of children's *spending* taken five years previously showed a standard deviation of 30p. It might be reasonable to expect that the standard deviation of spending would be similar to the standard deviation of income, so 30p (updated for inflation) can be used as an estimate of the standard deviation. Suppose that five years' inflation turns the 30p into 50p. Using $s = 50$ we obtain

$$n = \frac{2.58^2 \times 50^2}{20^2} = 41.6$$

giving a required sample size of 42 (the sample size has to be an integer). This is a large ($n \geq 25$) sample size so the use of the Normal distribution was justified.

Is the firm willing to pay for such a large sample? Suppose it was willing to pay out £1000 in total for the survey, which costs £600 to set up and then £6 per person sampled. The total cost would be £600 + 42 × 6 = £852 which is within the firm's budget. If the firm wished to spend less than this, it would have to accept a smaller sample size and thus a lower precision or a lower level of confidence. For example, if only a 95% confidence level were required, the appropriate $z$ score would be 1.96, yielding

$$n = \frac{1.96^2 \times 50^2}{20^2} = 24.01$$

A sample size of 24 would only cost £600 + 6 × 24 = £804. (At this sample size the assumption that $\bar{x}$ follows a Normal distribution becomes less tenable, so the results should be treated with caution. Use of the $t$ distribution is tricky, because the appropriate $t$ value depends upon the number of degrees of freedom which in turn depends on sample size, which is what is being looked for!)

The general formula for finding the required sample size is

(9.4)     $$n = \frac{z_\alpha^2 \times s^2}{p^2}$$

where $z_\alpha$ is the $z$ score appropriate for the $(100 - \alpha)$% confidence level and $p$ is the desired accuracy (20 pence in this case).

## Collecting the sample

**The sampling frame**

We now move on to the fine detail of how to select the individual observations which make up the sample. In order to do this it is necessary to have some sort of sampling frame, i.e. a list of all the members of the population from which the sample is to be drawn. This can be a problem if the population is extremely large, for example the population of a country, since it is difficult to manipulate so much information (cutting up 50 million pieces of paper to put into a hat for a random draw is a tedious business). Alternatively the list might not even exist or, if it does, not be in one place convenient for consultation and use. In this case there is often an advantage to multi-stage sampling, for the selection of regions or even local authorities is fairly straightforward and not too time-consuming. Once at this lower level the sampling frame is more manageable (each local authority has an electoral register, for example) and individual observations can be relatively easily chosen. Thus it is not always necessary to have a complete sampling frame for the entire population in one place.

**Choosing from the sampling frame**

There is a variety of methods available for selecting a sample of (say) 1000 observations from a sampling frame of (say) 25 000 names, varying from the manual to the electronic. The oldest method is to cut up 25 000 pieces of paper, put them in a (large) hat, shake it (to randomise) and pick out 1000. This is fairly time-consuming, however, and has some pitfalls – if the pieces are not all cut to the same size is the probability of selection the same? It is much better if the population in the sampling frame is numbered in some way, for then one only has to select random numbers. This can be done by using a table of random numbers (see Table A1 on page **364**, for example), or a computer. The use of random number tables for such purposes is an important feature of statistics and in 1955 the Rand Corporation produced a book entitled *A Million Random Digits with 100 000 Normal Deviates*. This book, as the title suggests, contained nothing but pages of random numbers which allowed researchers to collect random samples. Interestingly, the authors did not bother to fully proofread the text, since a few (random) errors here and there wouldn't matter! These numbers were calculated electronically and nowadays every computer has a facility for rapidly choosing a set of random numbers. (It is an interesting question how a computer, which follows rigid rules of behaviour, can select random numbers which, by definition, are unpredictable by any rule.)

A further alternative, if a 1 in 25 sample is required, is to select a random starting point between 1 and 25 and then select every subsequent 25th observation (e.g. the 3rd, 28th, 53rd, etc.). This is a satisfactory procedure if the sampling frame is randomly sorted to start with, but otherwise there can be problems. For example, if the list is sorted by income (poorest first), a low starting value will almost certainly give an underestimate of the population mean. If all the numbers were randomly selected, this 'error' in the starting value will not be important.

**Interviewing techniques**

Good training of interviewers is vitally important to the results of a survey. It is very easy to lead an interviewee into a particular answer to a question. Consider the following two sets of questions:

*A*
1 Do you know how many people were killed by the atomic bomb at Hiroshima?
2 Do you think nuclear weapons should be banned?

*B*
1 Do you believe in nuclear deterrence?
2 Do you think nuclear weapons should be banned?

*A*2 is almost certain to get a higher 'yes' response than *B*2. Even a different ordering of the questions can have an effect upon the answers (consider asking *A*2 before *A*1). The construction of the questionnaire has to be done with care, therefore. The manner in which the questions are asked is also important, since it can often suggest the answer. Good interviewers are trained to avoid these problems by sticking precisely to the wording of the question and not to suggest an expected answer.

---

### Telephone surveys

An article by M. Collins in the *Journal of the Royal Statistical Society* reveals some of the difficulties in conducting surveys by telephone. First, the sampling frame is incomplete since, although most people have a telephone, some are not listed in the directory. In the late 1980s this was believed to be around 12% of all numbers, but it has been growing since, to around 40%. (Part of this trend, of course, may be due to people getting fed up with being pestered by salespersons and 'market researchers'.) Researchers have responded with 'random digit dialling' which is presumably made easier by modern computerised equipment.

Matters are unlikely to improve for researchers in the future. The answering machine is often used as a barrier to unwanted calls and many residential lines connect to fax machines. Increasing deregulation and mobile phone use mean it will probably become more and more difficult to obtain a decent sampling frame for a proper survey.

*Source*: M. Collins, Sampling for UK telephone surveys, *J. Royal Statistical Society*, Series A, 162 (1), 1999.

---

Even when these procedures are adhered to there can be various types of response bias. The first problem is of non-response, due to the subject not being at home when the interviewer calls. There might be a temptation to remove that person from the sample and call on someone else, but this should be resisted. There could well be important differences between those who are at home all day and those who are not, especially if the survey concerns employment or spending patterns, for example. Continued efforts should be made to contact the subject. One should be wary of surveys which have low response rates, particularly where it is suspected that the non-response is in some way systematic and related to the goal of the survey.

A second problem is that subjects may not answer the question truthfully for one reason or another, sometimes inadvertently. An interesting example of this occurred in the survey into sexual behaviour carried out in Britain in 1992 (see *Nature*, 3 December 1992). Amongst other things, this found the following:

- The average number of heterosexual partners during a woman's lifetime is 3.4.
- The average number of heterosexual partners during a man's lifetime is 9.9.

This may be in line with one's beliefs about behaviour, but, in fact, the figures must be wrong. The *total* number of partners of all women must by definition equal the *total* number for all men. Since there are approximately equal numbers of males and females in the UK the averages must therefore be about the same. So how do the above figures come about?

It is too much to believe that international trade holds the answer. It seems unlikely that British men are so much more attractive to foreign women than British women are to foreign men. Nor is an unrepresentative sample likely. It was carefully chosen and quite large (around 20 000). The answer would appear to be that some people are lying. Either women are being excessively modest or (more likely?) men are boasting. Perhaps the answer is to divide by three whenever a man talks about his sexual exploits!

For an update on this story, see the article by J. Wadsworth *et al.*, What is a mean? An examination of the inconsistency between men and women in reporting sexual partnerships, *J. Royal Statistical Society*, 1996, Series A. 159 (1).

## Case study: the UK Expenditure and Food Survey

**Introduction**

The Expenditure and Food Survey (EFS) is an example of a large government survey which examines households' expenditure patterns (with a particular focus on food expenditures) and income receipts. It is worth having a brief look at it, therefore, to see how the principles of sampling techniques outlined in this chapter are put into practice. The EFS succeeded the Family Expenditure in 2001 and uses a similar design. The EFS is used for many different purposes, including the calculation of weights to be used in the UK Retail Price Index, and the assessment of the effects of changes in taxes and state benefits upon different households.

**Choosing the sample**

The sample design is known as a **three-stage, rotating, stratified, random sample**. This is obviously quite complex so will be examined stage by stage.

### Stage 1

The country is first divided into 168 strata, each stratum made up of a number of local authorities sharing similar characteristics. The characteristics used as stratification factors are

- geographic area,
- urban or rural character (based on a measure of population density),
- prosperity (based on a measure of property values).

A stratum might therefore be made up of local authorities in the South West region, of medium population density and high prosperity.

In each quarter of the year, one local authority from each stratum is chosen at random, the probability of selection being proportional to population. Once an authority has been chosen, it remains in the sample for one year (four quarters) before being replaced. Only a quarter of the authorities in the sample are replaced in any quarter, which gives the sample its 'rotating' characteristic. Each quarter some authorities are discarded, some kept and some new ones brought in.

### Stage 2

From each local authority selected, four wards (smaller administrative units) are selected, one to be used in each of the four quarters for which the local authority appears in the sample.

**Stage 3**

Finally, within each ward, 16 addresses are chosen at random, and these constitute the sample.

Altogether this means that 10 752 ($168 \times 4 \times 16$) households are chosen each year to make up the sample.

**The sampling frame**

The Postcode Address File, a list of all postal delivery addresses, is used as the sampling frame. Previously the register of electors in each ward was used but had some drawbacks: it was under-representative of those who have no permanent home or who move frequently (e.g. tramps, students, etc.). The fact that many people took themselves off the register in the early 1990s in order to avoid paying the Community Charge could also have affected the sample. The addresses are chosen from the register by interval sampling from a random starting point.

About 12 000 addresses are targeted each year, but around 11% prove to be business addresses, leaving approximately the 10 752 households mentioned above. The response rate is about 63% (from the 12 000), meaning that the actual sample consists of about 7500 households each year. Given the complexity of the information gathered, this is a remarkably good figure.

**Collection of information**

The data are collected by interview, and by asking participants to keep a diary in which they record everything they purchase over a two-week period. Highly skilled interviewers are required to ensure accuracy and compliance with the survey, and each participating family is visited serveral times. As a small inducement to cooperate, each member of the family is paid a small sum of money (it is to be hoped that the anticipation of this does not distort their expenditure patterns!).

**Sampling errors**

Given the complicated survey design it is difficult to calculate sampling errors exactly. The multi-stage design of the sample actually tends to increase the sampling error relative to a simple random sample, but, of course, this is offset by cost savings which allow a greatly increased sample size. Overall, the results of the survey are of good quality, and can be verified by comparison with other statistics, such as retail sales, for example.

## Summary

- A primary data source is one where you obtain the data yourself or have access to all the original observations.
- A secondary data source contains a summary of the original data, usually in the form of tables.
- When collecting data always keep detailed notes of the sources of all information, how it was collected, precise definitions of the variables, etc.
- Some data can be obtained electronically, which saves having to type it into a computer, but the data still need to be checked for errors.

■ There are various types of random sample, including simple, stratified and clustered random samples. The methods are sometimes combined in multi-stage samples.

■ The type of sampling affects the size of the standard errors of the sample statistics. The most precise sampling method is not necessarily the best if it costs more to collect (since the overall sample size that can be afforded will be smaller).

■ Quota sampling is a non-random method of sampling which has the advantage of being extremely cheap. It is often used for opinion polls and surveys.

■ The sampling frame is the list (or lists) from which the sample is drawn. If it omits important elements of the population its use could lead to biased results.

■ Careful interviewing techniques are needed to ensure reliable answers are obtained from participants in a survey.

**Key terms and concepts**

| | | |
|---|---|---|
| primary and secondary data | quota sampling | spreadsheet |
| online data sources | sampling methods | finite population correction |
| simple random sampling | random sample | cluster sampling |
| | stratified sampling | sampling frame |
| | multi-stage sampling | |

## Problems

Some of the more challenging problems are indicated by highlighting the problem number in colour.

**Problem 9.1** What issues of definition arise in trying to measure 'output'?

**Problem 9.2** What issues of definition arise in trying to measure 'unemployment'?

**Problem 9.3** Find the gross domestic product for both the UK and the US for the period 1995–2003. Obtain both series in constant prices.

**Problem 9.4** Find figures for the monetary aggregate M0 for the years 1995–2003 in the UK, in nominal terms.

**Problem 9.5** A firm wishes to know the average weekly expenditure on food by households to within £2, with 95% confidence. If the variance of food expenditure is thought to be about 400, what sample size does the firm need to achieve its aim?

**Problem 9.6** A firm has £10 000 to spend on a survey. It wishes to know the average expenditure on gas by businesses to within £30 with 99% confidence. The variance of expenditure is believed to be about 40 000. The survey costs £7000 to set up and then £15 to survey each firm. Can the firm achieve its aim with the budget available?

**Problem 9.7**
**(Project)**

Visit your college library to collect data to answer the following question. Has females' remuneration risen relative to men's over the past ten years? You should write a short report on your findings. This should include a section describing the data collection process, including any problems encountered and decisions you had to make. Compare your results with those of other students.

**Problem 9.8**
**(Project)**

Do a survey to find the average age of cars parked on your college campus. (A letter or digit denoting the registration year can be found on the number plate – precise details can be obtained in various guides to used-car prices.) You might need stratified sampling (e.g. if administrators have newer cars than faculty and students, for example). You could extend the analysis by comparing the results with a public car park. You should write a brief report outlining your survey methods and the results you obtain. If several students do such a survey you could compare results.

**References**

C.A. Moset and G. Kalton, *Survey Methods in Social Investigations*, Heinemann, 1971.

Rand Corporation, *A Million Random Digits with 100 000 Normal Deviates*, The Glencoe Press, 1955.

# 10

# Index numbers

By the end of this chapter you should be able to:

- represent a set of data in index number form

- understand the role of index numbers in summarising or presenting data

- recognise the relationship between price, quantity and expenditure index numbers

- turn a series measured at current prices into one at constant prices (or in volume terms)

- splice separate index number series together

- measure inequality using index numbers

# Introduction

'The Retail Price Index in June 2004 was 197.5, up 3.1% on its value a year earlier.'

The retail price index (RPI) referred to above is an example of an index number, which summarises a whole mass of information about the prices of different goods and services. Index numbers can also summarise information about quantities as well as prices. An index number is similar in purpose to other summary statistics such as the mean, and shares their advantages and disadvantages: it provides a useful overview of the data but misses out the finer detail.

We have used index numbers earlier in the book (for example, in the chapters on regression), without fully explaining their derivation or use. This will now be remedied.

Index numbers are most commonly used for following trends in data over time, such as the RPI measuring the price level or the index of industrial production (IIP) measuring the output of industry. The RPI also allows calculation of the rate of inflation, which is simply the rate of change of the price index; and from the IIP it is easy to measure the rate of growth of output. Index numbers are also used with cross-section data, for example, an index of regional house prices would summarise information about the different levels of house prices in different regions of the country at a particular point in time. There are many other examples of index numbers in use, common ones being the Financial Times All Share index, the trade weighted exchange rate index, and the index of the value of retail sales.

This chapter will explain how index numbers are constructed from original data and the problems which arise in doing this. There is also a brief discussion of the RPI to illustrate some of these problems and to show how they are resolved in practice. Finally, a different set of index numbers is examined, which are used to measure inequality, such as inequality in the distribution of income, or in the market shares held by different firms competing in a market.

# A simple index number

We begin with the simplest case, where we wish to construct an index number series for a single commodity. In this case, we shall construct an index number

Table 10.1 The price of coal, 1999–2003

| Price (£/tonne) | 1999 | 2000 | 2001 | 2002 | 2003 |
|---|---|---|---|---|---|
| | 34.77 | 35.12 | 38.07 | 34.56 | 34.50 |

Table 10.2 The price index for coal, 1999 = 100

| Year | Price | Index | |
|---|---|---|---|
| 1999 | 34.77 | 100.0 | (= 34.77/34.77 × 100) |
| 2000 | 35.12 | 101.0 | (= 35.12/34.77 × 100) |
| 2001 | 38.07 | 109.5 | (= 38.07/34.77 × 100) |
| 2002 | 34.56 | 99.4 | etc. |
| 2003 | 34.50 | 99.2 | |

Table 10.3 The price index for coal, 2001 = 100

| Year | Price | Index | |
|---|---|---|---|
| 1999 | 34.77 | 91.3 | (= 34.77/38.07 × 100) |
| 2000 | 35.12 | 92.3 | (= 35.12/38.07 × 100) |
| 2001 | 38.07 | 100.0 | (= 38.07/38.07 × 100) |
| 2002 | 34.56 | 90.8 | etc. |
| 2003 | 34.50 | 90.6 | |

series representing the price of coal to industrial users, for the years 1999–2003. The raw data are given in Table 10.1 (adapted from the Digest of UK Energy Statistics, 2003, available on the internet). The index will show how the price of coal changes over the period. We assume that the product itself has not changed from year to year, so that the index provides a fair representation of costs. This means, for example, that the quality of coal has not changed during the period.

To construct a price index from these data we choose one year as the reference year (1999 in this case) and set the price index in that year equal to 100. The prices in the other years are then measured *relative* to the reference year figure of 100. The index, and its construction, are presented in Table 10.2.

The price index in Table 10.2 presents the same information as Table 10.1 but in a slightly different form. We have (perhaps) gained some degree of clarity, but we have lost the original information about the actual level of prices. Since it is usually *relative* prices that are of interest, this loss of information about the actual price level is not too serious, and information about relative prices is retained by the price index. For example, using either the index or actual prices, we can see that the price of coal was 0.8% lower in 2003 than in 1999.

The choice of reference year is arbitrary and we can easily change it for a different year. If we choose 2001 to be the reference year, then we set the price in that year equal to 100 and again measure all other prices relative to it. This is shown in Table 10.3 which can be derived from Table 10.2 or directly from the original data on prices. You should choose whichever reference year is most convenient for your purposes. Whichever year is chosen, the informational content is the same.

(a) Average house prices in the UK for the past five years have been as follows:

| Year | 2000 | 2001 | 2002 | 2003 | 2004 |
|---|---|---|---|---|---|
| Price (£) | 86 095 | 96 337 | 121 137 | 140 687 | 161 940 |

Turn this into an index with a reference year of 2000.

(b) Recalculate the index with reference year 2003.

(c) Check that the ratio of house prices in 2004 relative to 2000 is the same for both indexes.

# A price index with more than one commodity

In practice, of course, industry uses other sources of energy as well as coal, such as gas, petroleum and electricity. Suppose that an index of the cost of all fuels used by industry is wanted, rather than just for coal (in the late 1980s, for example, industrialists were complaining about the high cost of *energy* in the UK). This is a more common requirement in reality, rather than the simple index number series calculated above. If the price of each fuel were rising at the same rate, say at 5% per year, then it is straightforward to say that the price of energy to industry is also rising at 5% per year. But supposing, as is likely, that the prices are all rising at different rates, as shown in Table 10.4. Is it now possible to say how fast the price of energy is increasing? Several different prices now have to be combined in order to construct an index number, a more complex process than the simple index number calculated above.

From the data presented in Table 10.4 we can calculate that the price of coal has fallen by 0.8% over the four-year period, petrol has risen by 33%, electricity has fallen by 22% and gas has risen by 48%. It is difficult to decide whether the overall price of energy is rising or falling, given these figures.

**Using base-year weights: the Laspeyres index**

We tackle the problem by taking a weighted average of the price changes of the individual fuels, the weights being derived from the quantities of each fuel used by the industry. Thus, if industry uses relatively more coal than petrol, more weight is given to the rise in the price of coal in the calculation.

We put this principle into effect by constructing a hypothetical 'shopping basket' of the fuels used by industry, and measure how the cost of this basket has risen (or fallen) over time. Table 10.5 gives the quantities of each fuel consumed by industry in 1999 (again from the Digest of UK Energy Statistics,

Table 10.4 **Fuel prices to industry, 1999–2003**

| Year | Coal (£/tonne) | Petroleum (£/tonne) | Electricity (£/MWh) | Gas (£/therm) |
|---|---|---|---|---|
| 1999 | 34.77 | 104.93 | 36.23 | 0.546 |
| 2000 | 35.12 | 137.90 | 34.69 | 0.606 |
| 2001 | 38.07 | 148.10 | 31.35 | 0.816 |
| 2002 | 34.56 | 150.16 | 29.83 | 0.780 |
| 2003 | 34.50 | 140.00 | 28.44 | 0.807 |

Table 10.5 **Quantities of fuel used by industry, 1999**

| | |
|---|---|
| Coal (m tonnes) | 2.04 |
| Petroleum (m tonnes) | 5.33 |
| Electricity (m MWh) | 110.98 |
| Gas (m therms) | 6039 |

Table 10.6 **Cost of the energy basket, 1999**

| | Price | Quantity | Price × quantity |
|---|---|---|---|
| Coal (£/tonne) | 34.77 | 2.04 | 70.931 |
| Petroleum (£/tonne) | 104.93 | 5.33 | 559.277 |
| Electricity (£/MWh) | 36.23 | 110.98 | 4020.805 |
| Gas (£/m therms) | 0.546 | 6039 | 3297.294 |
| Total | | | 7948.307 |

Table 10.7 **The cost of the 1999 energy basket at 2000 prices**

| | 2000 price | 1999 quantity | Price × quantity |
|---|---|---|---|
| Coal (£/tonne) | 35.12 | 2.04 | 71.645 |
| Petroleum (£/tonne) | 137.90 | 5.33 | 735.007 |
| Electricity (£/MWh) | 34.69 | 110.98 | 3849.896 |
| Gas (£/m therms) | 0.606 | 6039 | 3659.634 |
| Total | | | 8316.182 |

2003) and it is this which forms the shopping basket. 1999 is referred to as the base year since it is the quantities consumed in this year which are used to make up the shopping basket.

The cost of the basket in 1999 prices therefore works out as shown in Table 10.6 (using information from Tables 10.4 and 10.5). The final column of the table shows the expenditure on each of the four energy inputs and the total cost of the basket is 7948.3 (this is in £m, so altogether about £7.96bn was spent on energy by industry). This sum may be written as:

$$\sum_i p_{0i}q_{0i} = 7948.307$$

where the summation is calculated over all the four fuels. Here, $p$ refers to prices, $q$ to quantities. The first subscript (0) refers to the year, the second ($i$) to each energy source in turn. We refer to 1999 as year 0, 2000 as year 1, etc., for brevity of notation. Thus, for example, $p_{01}$ means the price of coal in 1999, $q_{12}$ the consumption of petroleum by industry in 2000.

We now need to find what the 1999 basket of energy would cost in each of the subsequent years, using the prices pertaining to those years. For example, for 2000 we value the 1999 basket using the 2000 prices. This is shown in Table 10.7.

Firms would therefore have to spend an extra £368m (8316–7948) in 2000 to buy the same quantities of energy as in 1999. The sum of £8316m may be expressed as $\sum p_{1i}q_{0i}$, since it is obtained by multiplying the prices in year 1 (2000) by quantities in year 0 (1999).

Table 10.8 **The cost of the energy basket, 1999–2003**

|  | Formula | Cost |
|---|---|---|
| 1999 | $\Sigma p_0 q_0$ | 7948.31 |
| 2000 | $\Sigma p_1 q_0$ | 8316.18 |
| 2001 | $\Sigma p_2 q_0$ | 9274.08 |
| 2002 | $\Sigma p_3 q_0$ | 8891.81 |
| 2003 | $\Sigma p_4 q_0$ | 8846.32 |

*Note*: For brevity, we have dropped the *i* subscript in the formula.

Similar calculations for subsequent years produce the costs of the basket as shown in Table 10.8.

It can be seen that *if* firms had purchased the same quantities of each energy source in the following years, they would have had to pay more in each subsequent year up to 2001, after which there was a decrease in the cost.

To obtain the energy price index from these numbers we measure the cost of the basket in each year relative to its 1999 cost, i.e. we divide the cost of the basket in each successive year by $\Sigma p_{0i} q_{0i}$ and multiply by 100.

This index is given in Table 10.9 and is called the Laspeyres price index after its inventor. We say that it uses base-year weights (i.e. quantities in the base year 1999 form the weights in the basket).

We have set the value of the index to 100 in 1999, i.e. the reference year and the base year coincide, though this is not essential.

The Laspeyres index for year *n* with the base year as year 0 is given by the following formula:

**(10.1)**   $$P_L^n = \frac{\Sigma p_{ni} q_{0i}}{\Sigma p_{0i} q_{0i}} \times 100$$

(Henceforth we shall omit the *i* subscript on prices and quantities in the formulae for index numbers, for brevity.) The index shows that energy prices increased by 11.3% over the period – obviously the rise in the prices of petroleum and gas outweighed the fall in the electricity price. The rise amounts to an average increase of 2.7% p.a. in the cost of energy. During the same period, prices in general rose by 9.7% so in relative terms energy became relatively more expensive, by a small margin.

Table 10.9 **The Laspeyres price index**

| Year | Formula | Index | |
|---|---|---|---|
| 1999 | $\frac{\Sigma p_0 q_0}{\Sigma p_0 q_0} \times 100$ | 100 | $(= 7948.31/7948.31 \times 100)$ |
| 2000 | $\frac{\Sigma p_1 q_0}{\Sigma p_0 q_0} \times 100$ | 104.63 | $(= 8316.18/7948.31 \times 100)$ |
| 2001 | $\frac{\Sigma p_2 q_0}{\Sigma p_0 q_0} \times 100$ | 116.68 | etc. |
| 2002 | $\frac{\Sigma p_3 q_0}{\Sigma p_0 q_0} \times 100$ | 111.87 | |
| 2003 | $\frac{\Sigma p_4 q_0}{\Sigma p_0 q_0} \times 100$ | 111.30 | |

Table 10.10 The Laspeyres price index using the 2000 basket

|  | Cost of basket | Laspeyres index 2000 = 100 | Laspeyres index 1999 = 100 | Laspeyres index using 1999 basket |
|---|---|---|---|---|
| 1999 | 8159.14 | 95.52 | 100 | 100 |
| 2000 | 8541.56 | 100 | 104.69 | 104.63 |
| 2001 | 9534.51 | 111.62 | 116.86 | 116.68 |
| 2002 | 9144.37 | 107.06 | 112.08 | 111.87 |
| 2003 | 9098.78 | 106.52 | 111.52 | 111.30 |

The choice of 1999 as the base year for the index was an arbitrary one; any year will do. If we choose 2000 as the base year then the cost of the 2000 basket is evaluated in each year (including 1999), and this will result in a slightly different Laspeyres index. The calculations are in Table 10.10. The final two columns of the table compare the Laspeyres index constructed using the 2000 and 1999 baskets respectively (the former adjusted to 1999 = 100). A slight difference can be seen, due to the different consumption patterns (electricity and gas are more important in the 2000 basket). The difference is numerically quite small, however, amounting to about 0.1% of the value of the index.

The Laspeyres price index shows the increase in the price of energy for the 'average' firm, i.e. one which consumes energy in the same proportions as the 1999 basket overall. There are probably very few such firms: most would use perhaps only one or two energy sources. Individual firms may therefore experience price rises quite different from those shown here. For example, a firm depending upon electricity alone would face a 22% decline over the four years, significantly different from the figure of +11% suggested by the Laspeyres index.

**Exercise 10.2**

(a) The prices of fuels used by industry 1995–1999 were:

|  | Coal (£/tonne) | Petroleum (£/tonne) | Electricity (£/MWh) | Gas (£/therm) |
|---|---|---|---|---|
| 1995 | 37.27 | 92.93 | 40.07 | 0.677 |
| 1996 | 35.41 | 98.33 | 39.16 | 0.464 |
| 1997 | 34.42 | 90.86 | 36.87 | 0.509 |
| 1998 | 35.16 | 87.23 | 36.67 | 0.560 |
| 1999 | 34.77 | 104.93 | 36.23 | 0.546 |

and quantities consumed by industry were:

|  | Coal (m tonnes) | Petroleum (m tonnes) | Electricity (m MWh) | Gas (m therms) |
|---|---|---|---|---|
| 1995 | 2.91 | 6.37 | 102.88 | 4938 |

Calculate the Laspeyres price index of energy based on these data. Use 1995 as the reference year.

(b) Recalculate the index making 1997 the reference year.

(c) The quantities consumed in 1996 were:

|  | Coal (m tonnes) | Petroleum (m tonnes) | Electricity (m MWh) | Gas (m therms) |
|---|---|---|---|---|
| 1996 | 2.22 | 6.21 | 105.45 | 5406 |

Calculate the Laspeyres index using this basket and compare to the answer to part (a).

**Table 10.11 Quantities of energy used, 2000–2003**

|  | Coal (m tonnes) | Petroleum (m tonnes) | Electricity (m MWh) | Gas (m therms) |
|---|---|---|---|---|
| 2000 | 0.72 | 5.52 | 114.11 | 6265 |
| 2001 | 1.69 | 6.60 | 111.34 | 6142 |
| 2002 | 1.10 | 5.81 | 112.37 | 5650 |
| 2003 | 0.69 | 6.69 | 113.93 | 5880 |

**Using current-year weights: the Paasche index**

Firms do not of course consume the same basket of energy every year. One would expect them to respond to changes in the relative prices of fuels and to other factors. Technological progress means that the efficiency with which the fuels can be used changes, causing fluctuations in demand. Table 10.11 shows the quantities consumed in the years after 1999 and indicates that firms did indeed alter their pattern of consumption.

Each of these patterns of consumption could be used as the 'shopping basket' for the purpose of constructing the Laspeyres index and each would give a slightly different price index, as we saw with the usage of the 1999 and 2000 baskets. One cannot say that one of these is more correct than the others. One further problem is that whichever basket is chosen remains the same over time and eventually becomes unrepresentative of the current pattern of consumption.

The **Paasche index** (denoted $P_P^n$ to distinguish it from the Laspeyres index) overcomes these problems by using **current-year weights** to construct the index, in other words the basket is continually changing. Suppose 1999 is to be the reference year, so $P_P^0 = 100$. To construct the Paasche index for 2000 we use the 2000 weights (or basket), for the 2001 value of the index we use the 2001 weights, and so on. An example will clarify matters.

The Paasche index for 2000 will be the cost of the 2000 basket at 2000 prices relative to its cost at 1999 prices, i.e.

$$P_P^1 = \frac{\sum p_1 q_1}{\sum p_0 q_1} \times 100$$

This gives:

$$P_P^1 = \frac{8541.56}{8159.14} \times 100 = 104.69$$

The general formula for the Paasche index in year $n$ is given in equation (10.2).

(10.2)    $$P_P^n = \frac{\sum p_n q_n}{\sum p_0 q_n} \times 100$$

Table 10.12 shows the calculation of this index for the later years.

The Paasche formula gives a slightly different result than does the Laspeyres, as is usually the case. The Paasche should generally give a slower rate of increase than does the Laspeyres index. This is because one would expect profit-maximising firms to respond to changing relative prices by switching their consumption in the direction of the inputs which are becoming relatively cheaper. The Paasche index, by using the current weights, captures this change, but the Laspeyres, assuming fixed weights, does not. This may happen slowly,

**Table 10.12** The Paasche price index

|      | Cost of basket at current prices | Cost at 1999 prices | Index |
|------|----------------------------------|---------------------|-------|
| 1999 | 7948.31                          | 7948.31             | 100   |
| 2000 | 8541.56                          | 8159.14             | 104.69|
| 2001 | 9544.18                          | 8138.68             | 117.27|
| 2002 | 8669.44                          | 7803.96             | 111.09|
| 2003 | 8945.73                          | 8064.14             | 110.93|

as it takes time for firms to switch to different fuels, even if technically possible. This is why the Paasche can increase faster than the Laspeyres in some years (e.g. 2001) though in the long run it should increase more slowly.

Is one of the indices more 'correct' than the other? The answer is that neither is definitively correct. It can be shown that the 'true' value lies somewhere between the two, but it is difficult to say exactly where. If all the items which make up the index increase in price at the same rate then the Laspeyres and Paasche indices would give the same answer, so it is the change in *relative* prices and the resultant change in consumption patterns which causes problems.

**Units of measurement**

It is important that the units of measurement in the price and quantity tables be consistent. Note that in the example, the price of coal was measured in £/tonne and the consumption was measured in millions of tonnes. The other fuels were similarly treated (in the case of electricity, one MWh equals one million watt-hours). But suppose we had measured electricity consumption in kWh instead of MWh (1 MWh = 1000 kWh), but still measured its price in £ per MWh? We would then have 1999 data of 36.23 for price as before, but 110 980 for quantity. It is as if electricity consumption has been boosted 1000-fold, and this would seriously distort the results. The (Laspeyres) energy price index would be (by a similar calculation to the one above):

| 1999 | 2000 | 2001 | 2002 | 2003 |
|------|------|------|------|------|
| 100  | 95.8 | 86.6 | 82.4 | 78.6 |

### The Human Development Index

One of the more interesting indices to appear in recent years is the Human Development Index (HDI), produced by the United Nations Development Programme (UNDP). The HDI aims to provide a more comprehensive socio-economic measure of a country's progress than GDP (national output). Output is a measure of how well-off we are in material terms, but makes no allowance for the quality of life and other factors.

The HDI combines a measure of well-being (GDP per capita) with longevity (life expectancy) and knowledge (based on literacy and years of schooling). As a result, each country obtains a score, from 0 (poor) to 1 (good). Some selected values are given in the table.

| Country | HDI 1970 | HDI 1980 | HDI 2003 | Rank (HDI 92) | Rank (GDP) |
|---------|----------|----------|----------|---------------|------------|
| Canada | 0.887 | 0.911 | 0.932 | 1 | 11 |
| UK | 0.873 | 0.892 | 0.919 | 10 | 19 |
| Hong Kong | 0.737 | 0.830 | 0.875 | 24 | 22 |
| Gabon | 0.378 | 0.468 | 0.525 | 114 | 42 |
| Senegal | 0.176 | 0.233 | 0.322 | 143 | 114 |

One can see that there is an association between the HDI and GDP, but not a perfect one. Canada has the world's 11th highest GDP per capita but comes top of the HDI rankings. In contrast, Gabon, some way up the GDP rankings, is much lower when the HDI is calculated.

So how is the HDI calculated from the initial data? How can we combine life expectancy (which can stretch from 0 to 80 years or more) with literacy (the proportion of the population who can read and write)? The answer is to score all of the variables on a scale from 0 to 100.

The HDI sets a range for (national average) life expectancy between 25 and 85 years. A country with a life expectancy of 52.9 (the case of Gabon) therefore scores 0.465, i.e. 52.9 is 46.5% of the way between 25 and 85.

Adult literacy can vary between 0% and 100% of the population, so needs no adjustment. Gabon's figure is 0.625. The scale used for years of schooling is 0 to 15, so Gabon's very low average of 2.6 yields a score of 0.173. Literacy and schooling are then combined in a weighted average (with a $2/3$ weight on literacy) to give a score for knowledge of $2/3 \times 0.625 + 1/3 \times 0.173 = 0.473$.

For income, Gabon's average of $3498 is compared to the global average of $5185 to give a score of 0.636. (Incomes above $5185 are manipulated to avoid scores above 1.)

A simple average of 0.465, 0.473 and 0.636 then gives Gabon's final figure of 0.525. One can see that its average income is brought down by the poorer scores in the two other categories, resulting in a poorer HDI ranking.

The construction of this index number shows how disparate information can be brought together into a single index number for comparative purposes. Further work by UNDP adjusts the HDI on the basis of gender and reveals the stark result that no country treats its women as well as it does its men.

Adapted from: Human Development Report, 1994 and other years. More on the HDI can be found at http://www.undp.org/

This is incorrect, and shows a much lower value than the correct Laspeyres index (because electricity is now given too much weight in the calculation, and electricity prices were falling both in absolute and relative terms).

It is possible to make some manipulations of the units of measurement (usually to make calculation easier) as long as all items are treated alike. If, for example, all prices were measured in pence rather than pounds (so all prices in Table 10.4 were multiplied by 100) then this would have no effect on the resultant index, as you would expect. Similarly, if all quantity figures were measured in thousands of tonnes, thousands of therms and thousands of MWh there would be no effects on the index, even if prices remained in £/tonne, etc. But if electricity were measured in pence per MWh, while all other fuels were in £/tonne, a wrong answer would again be obtained. Quantities consumed should also be measured over the same time period, e.g. millions of therms *per annum*. It does not matter what the time period is (days, weeks, months or years) as long as all the items are treated similarly.

**Exercise 10.3**

The quantities of energy used in subsequent years were:

|  | Coal (m tonnes) | Petroleum (m tonnes) | Electricity (m MWh) | Gas (m therms) |
|---|---|---|---|---|
| 1997 | 2.14 | 5.64 | 107.31 | 5565 |
| 1998 | 1.81 | 5.37 | 107.97 | 5639 |
| 1999 | 2.04 | 5.33 | 110.98 | 6039 |

Calculate the Paasche index for 1995–1999 with 1995 as reference year. Compare this to the Laspeyres index result.

## Using expenditures as weights

On occasion the quantities of each commodity consumed are not available, but expenditures are, and a price index can still be constructed using slightly modified formulae. It is often easier to find the expenditure on a good than to know the actual quantity consumed (think of housing as an example). We shall illustrate the method with a simplified example, using the data on energy prices and consumption for the years 1999 and 2000 only. The data are repeated in Table 10.13.

The data for consumption are assumed to be no longer available, but only the expenditure on each energy source as a percentage of total expenditure. Expenditure is derived as the product of price and quantity consumed.

The formula for the Laspeyres index can be easily manipulated to accord with the data as presented in Table 10.13.

The Laspeyres index formula based on expenditure shares is given in equation (10.3):[1]

$$(10.3) \qquad P_L^n = \sum \frac{p_n}{p_0} \times s_0 \times 100$$

Equation (10.3) is made up of two component parts. The first, $p_n/p_0$, is simply the price in year $n$ relative to the base-year price for each energy source. The

Table 10.13 **Expenditure shares, 1999**

|  | Price | Quantity | Expenditure | Share |
|---|---|---|---|---|
| Coal (£/tonne) | 34.77 | 2.04 | 70.93 | 0.9% |
| Petroleum (£/tonne) | 104.93 | 5.33 | 559.28 | 7.0% |
| Electricity (£/MWh) | 36.23 | 110.98 | 4020.81 | 50.6% |
| Gas (£/m therms) | 0.546 | 6039.00 | 3297.29 | 41.5% |
| Totals |  |  | 7948.31 | 100.0% |

*Note*: The 0.9% share of coal is calculated as (70.93/7948.31) × 100. Other shares are calculated similarly.

[1] See the appendix to this chapter (page **357**) for the derivation of this formula.

second component, $s_0 = p_0q_0/\Sigma p_0q_0$, is the share or proportion of total expenditure spent on each energy source in the base year, the data for which are in Table 10.13. It should be easy to see that the sum of the $s_0$ values is 1, so that equation (10.3) calculates a weighted average of the individual price increases, the weights being the expenditure shares.

The calculation of the Laspeyres index for 2000 using 1999 as the base year is therefore:

$$P_1^n = \frac{35.12}{34.77} \times 0.009 + \frac{137.90}{104.93} \times 0.07 + \frac{34.69}{36.23} \times 0.506 + \frac{0.606}{0.546} \times 0.415 = 1.0463$$

giving the value of the index as 104.63, the same value as derived earlier using the more usual methods. Values of the index for subsequent years are calculated by appropriate application of equation (10.3) above. This is left as an exercise for the reader, who may use Table 10.9 to verify the answers.

The Paasche index may similarly be calculated from data on prices and expenditure shares, as long as these are available for each year for which the index is required. The formula for the Paasche index is

$$(10.4) \qquad P_P^n = \frac{1}{\Sigma \dfrac{p_0}{p_n} s_n} \times 100$$

The calculation of the Paasche index is also left as an exercise.

**Comparison of the Laspeyres and Paasche indices**

The advantages of the Laspeyres index are that it is easy to calculate and that it has a fairly clear intuitive meaning, i.e. the cost each year of a particular basket of goods. The Paasche index involves more computation, and it is less easy to envisage what it refers to. As an example of this point, consider the following simple case. The Laspeyres index values for 2001 and 2002 are 116.68 and 111.87. The ratio of these two numbers, 0.959, would suggest that prices fell by 4.1% between these years. What does this figure actually represent? The 2002 Laspeyres index has been divided by the same index for 2001, i.e.

$$\frac{P_L^3}{P_L^2} = \frac{\Sigma p_3 q_0}{\Sigma p_0 q_0} \Big/ \frac{\Sigma p_2 q_0}{\Sigma p_0 q_0} = \frac{\Sigma p_3 q_0}{\Sigma p_2 q_0}$$

which is the ratio of the cost of the 1999 basket at 2002 prices to its cost at 2001 prices. This makes some intuitive sense. Note that it is not the same as the Laspeyres index for 2002 with 2001 as base year, which would require using $q_2$ in the calculation.

If the same is done with the Paasche index numbers a fall of 5.3% is obtained between 2001 and 2002. But the meaning of this is not so clear, for

$$\frac{P_P^3}{P_P^2} = \frac{\Sigma p_3 q_3}{\Sigma p_0 q_3} \Big/ \frac{\Sigma p_2 q_2}{\Sigma p_0 q_2}$$

which does not simplify further. This is a curious mixture of 2001 and 2002 quantities, and 1999, 2001 and 2002 prices!

The major advantage of the Paasche index is that the weights are continuously updated, so that the basket of goods never becomes out of date. In the case of the Laspeyres index the basket remains unchanged over a period, becoming less and less representative of what is being bought by consumers.

When revision is finally made there may therefore be a large change in the weighting scheme. The extra complexity of calculation involved in the Paasche index is less important now that computers do most of the work.

**Exercise 10.4**
(a) Calculate the share of expenditure going to each of the four fuel types in the previous exercises and use this result to re-calculate the Laspeyres and Paasche indexes using equations (10.3) and (10.4).

(b) Check that the results are the same as calculated in previous exercises.

## Quantity and expenditure indices

Just as one can calculate price indices, it is also possible to calculate **quantity** and **value indices**. We first concentrate on quantity indices, which provide a measure of the total quantity of energy consumed by industry each year. The problem again is that we cannot easily aggregate the different sources of energy. It makes no sense to add together tonnes of coal and petroleum, therms of gas and megawatts of electricity. Some means has to be found to put these different fuels on a comparable basis. To do this, we now reverse the roles of prices and quantities: the quantities of the different fuels are weighted by their different prices (prices represent the value to the firm, at the margin, of each different fuel). As with price indices, one can construct both Laspeyres and Paasche quantity indices.

**The Laspeyres quantity index**

The Laspeyres quantity index for year $n$ is given by

$$(10.5) \quad Q_L^n = \frac{\sum q_n p_0}{\sum q_0 p_0} \times 100$$

i.e. it is the ratio of the cost of the year $n$ basket to the cost of the year 0 basket, both valued at year 0 prices. Note that it is the same as equation (10.1) but with prices and quantities reversed.

Using 1999 as the base year, the cost of the 2000 basket at 1999 prices is:

$$\sum q_1 p_0 = 0.72 \times 34.77 + 5.52 \times 104.93 + 114.11 \times 36.23 + 6265 \times 0.546 = 8159.14$$

and the cost of the 1999 basket at 1999 prices is 7948.31 (calculated earlier). The value of the quantity index for 2000 is therefore

$$Q_L^1 = \frac{8159.14}{7948.31} \times 100 = 102.65$$

In other words, if prices had remained constant between 1999 and 2000, industry would have consumed 2.65% more energy (and spent 2.65% more also). The value of the index for subsequent years is shown in Table 10.14, using the formula given in equation (10.5).

**The Paasche quantity index**

Just as there are Laspeyres and Paasche versions of the price index, the same is true for the quantity index. The Paasche quantity index is given by

$$(10.6) \quad Q_P^n = \frac{\sum q_n p_n}{\sum q_0 p_n} \times 100$$

Table 10.14 Calculation of the Laspeyres quantity index

|  | $\Sigma p_0 q_n$ | Index |  |
|---|---|---|---|
| 1999 | 7948.31 | 100 |  |
| 2000 | 8159.14 | 102.65 | (= 8159.14/7948.31 × 100) |
| 2001 | 8138.68 | 102.40 | (= 8138.68/7948.31 × 100) |
| 2002 | 7803.96 | 98.18 | etc. |
| 2003 | 8064.14 | 101.46 |  |

Table 10.15 Calculation of the Paasche quantity index

|  | $\Sigma p_n q_n$ | $\Sigma p_n q_0$ | Index |
|---|---|---|---|
| 1999 | 7948.31 | 7948.31 | 100 |
| 2000 | 8541.56 | 8316.18 | 102.71 |
| 2001 | 9544.18 | 9274.08 | 102.91 |
| 2002 | 8669.44 | 8891.81 | 97.50 |
| 2003 | 8945.73 | 8846.32 | 101.12 |

*Note*: The final column is calculated as the ratio of the previous two columns.

Table 10.16 The expenditure index

|  | $\Sigma p_n q_n$ | Index |
|---|---|---|
| 1999 | 7948.31 | 100 |
| 2000 | 8541.56 | 107.46 |
| 2001 | 9544.18 | 120.08 |
| 2002 | 8669.44 | 109.07 |
| 2003 | 8945.73 | 112.55 |

*Note*: The expenditure index is a simple index of the expenditures in the previous column.

and is the analogue of equation (10.2) with prices and quantities reversed. The calculation of this index is shown in Table 10.15, which shows a similar trend to the Laspeyres index in Table 10.14. Normally one would expect the Paasche to show a slower increase than the Laspeyres quantity index: firms should switch to inputs whose relative prices fall; the Paasche gives lesser weight (current prices) to these quantities than does the Laspeyres (base-year prices) and thus shows a slower rate of increase.

**Expenditure indices**

The expenditure or value index is simply an index of the cost of the year $n$ basket at year $n$ prices and so it measures how expenditure changes over time. The formula for the index in year $n$ is

$$(10.7) \qquad E^n = \frac{\Sigma p_n q_n}{\Sigma p_0 q_0}$$

There is obviously only one value index and one does not distinguish between Laspeyres and Paasche formulations. The index can be easily derived from Table 10.16. The expenditure index shows how industry's expenditure on energy is changing over time. Thus expenditure in 2003 was 12.55% higher than in 1999. What the value index does not show is how that increased expenditure may be divided up into price and quantity changes. This decomposition is shown in the next section.

**Relationships between price, quantity and expenditure indices**

Just as multiplying a price by a quantity gives total value, or expenditure, the same is true of index numbers. The value index can be decomposed as the product of a price index and a quantity index. In particular, it is the product of a Paasche quantity index and a Laspeyres price index, *or* the product of a Paasche price index and a Laspeyres quantity index. This can be very simply demonstrated using $\Sigma$ notation:

$$(10.8) \qquad E^n = \frac{\Sigma p_n q_n}{\Sigma p_0 q_0} = \frac{\Sigma p_n q_n}{\Sigma p_n q_0} \times \frac{\Sigma p_n q_0}{\Sigma p_0 q_0} = Q_P^n \times P_L^n$$

or

$$(10.9) \qquad E^n = \frac{\Sigma p_n q_n}{\Sigma p_0 q_0} = \frac{\Sigma p_n q_n}{\Sigma p_0 q_n} \times \frac{\Sigma p_0 q_n}{\Sigma p_0 q_0} = P_P^n \times Q_L^n$$

Thus increases in value or expenditure can be decomposed into price and quantity effects. Two decompositions are possible and give slightly different answers.

It is also evident that a quantity index can be constructed by dividing a value index by a price index, since by simple manipulation of (10.8) and (10.9) we obtain

$$(10.10) \qquad Q_P^n = E^n / P_L^n$$

and

$$(10.11) \qquad Q_L^n = E^n / P_P^n$$

Note that dividing the expenditure index by a Laspeyres price index gives a Paasche quantity index, and dividing by a Paasche price index gives a Laspeyres quantity index. This is known as **deflating** a series and is a widely used and very useful technique. We shall reconsider our earlier data in the light of this. Table 10.17 provides the detail. Column 2 of the table shows the expenditure on fuel at **current prices** or in **cash terms**. Column 3 contains the Laspeyres price index repeated from Table 10.9 above. Deflating (dividing) column 2 by column 3 and multiplying by 100 yields column 4 which shows expenditure on fuel in **quantity** or **volume terms**. The final column gives an index of energy expenditure in volume terms.

This final index is equivalent to a Paasche quantity index, as illustrated by equation (10.7) and in Table 10.15 above.

**Trap!**

A common mistake is to believe that once a series has been turned into an index, it is inevitably in real terms. This is *not* the case. One can have an index of a nominal series (e.g. in Table 10.16 above) *or* of a real series (the final column of Table 10.17). An index number is really just a change of the units of measurement to something more useful for presentation purposes; it is not the same as deflating the series.

In the example above we used the price index for energy to deflate the expenditure series. However, it is also possible to use a *general* price index (such as the retail price index or the GDP deflator) to deflate. This gives a slightly different result, both in numerical terms and in its interpretation. Deflating by a

Table 10.17 Deflating the expenditure series

|  | Expenditure at current prices | Laspeyres price index | Expenditure in volume terms | Index |
|---|---|---|---|---|
| 1999 | 7948.31 | 100 | 7948.31 | 100 |
| 2000 | 8541.56 | 104.63 | 8163.72 | 102.71 |
| 2001 | 9544.18 | 116.68 | 8179.79 | 102.91 |
| 2002 | 8669.44 | 111.87 | 7749.54 | 97.50 |
| 2003 | 8945.73 | 111.30 | 8037.63 | 101.12 |

general price index yields a series of expenditures in constant prices or in real terms. Deflating by a specific price index (e.g. of energy) results in a quantity or volume series.

An example should clarify this (see Problem 10.11 for data). The government spends billions of pounds each year on the health service. If this cash expenditure series is deflated by a general price index (e.g. the GDP deflator) then we obtain expenditure on health services at constant prices, or real expenditure on the health service. If the NHS pay and prices index is used as a deflator, then the result is an index of the quantity or volume of health services provided. Since the NHS index tends to rise more rapidly than the GDP deflator, the volume series rises more slowly than the series of expenditure at constant prices. This can lead to an interesting, if pointless, political debate. The government claims it is spending more on the health service, in real terms, while the opposition claims that the health service is getting fewer resources. As we have seen, both can be right.

**Exercise 10.5**

(a) Use the data from earlier exercises to calculate the Laspeyres quantity index.

(b) Calculate the Paasche quantity index.

(c) Calculate the expenditure index.

(d) Check that dividing the expenditure index by the price index gives the quantity index (remember that there are two ways of doing this).

---

### The real rate of interest

Another example of 'deflating' is the real rate of interest. This adjusts the actual rate of interest for changes in the value of money, i.e. inflation. If you earn a 7% rate of interest on your money over a year, but the price level rises by 5% at the same time, you are clearly not 7% better off. The real rate of interest in this case would be given by

(10.12)    $\text{real interest rate} = \dfrac{1 + 0.07}{1 + 0.05} - 1 = 0.019 = 1.9\%$

In general, if $r$ is the interest rate and $i$ is the inflation rate, the real rate of interest is given by

(10.13)    $\text{real interest rate} = \dfrac{1 + r}{1 + i} - 1$

A simpler method is often used in practice, which gives virtually identical results for small values of $r$ and $i$. This is to subtract the inflation rate from the interest rate, giving 7% − 5% = 2% in this case.

**Chain indices**

Whenever an index number series over a long period of time is wanted, it is usually necessary to link together a number of separate, shorter indices, resulting in a **chain index**. Without access to the original raw data it is impossible to construct a proper Laspeyres or Paasche index, so the result will be a mixture of different types of index number but it is the best that can be done in the circumstances.

Suppose that the following two index number series are available. Access to the original data is assumed to be impossible.

**Laspeyres price index for energy, 1999–2003 (from Table 10.9)**

| 1999 | 2000 | 2001 | 2002 | 2003 |
|------|------|------|------|------|
| 100 | 104.63 | 116.68 | 111.87 | 111.30 |

**Laspeyres price index for energy, 1995–99**

| 1995 | 1996 | 1997 | 1998 | 1999 |
|------|------|------|------|------|
| 100 | 96.3 | 95.6 | 92.1 | 88.1 |

The two series have different reference years and use different shopping baskets of consumption. The first index measures the cost of the 1999 basket in each of the subsequent years. The second measures the price of the 1995 basket in subsequent years. There is an 'overlap' year which is 1999. How do we combine these into one continuous index covering the whole period?

The obvious method is to use the ratio of the costs of the two baskets in 1999, 88.1/100 = 0.881, to alter one of the series. To base the continuous series on 1995 = 100 requires multiplying each of the post-1999 figures by 0.881, as is demonstrated in Table 10.18. The continuous series could just as easily be based on 1999 = 100 by a simple rescaling, which would be equivalent to dividing the 'old' series by 0.881 and leaving the 'new' series unchanged.

The continuous series is not a proper Laspeyres index number as can be seen if we examine the formulae used. We shall examine the 2003 figure, 98.1, by

**Table 10.18 A chain index of energy prices, 1995–2003**

| | 'Old' index | 'New' index | Chain index |
|------|------|------|------|
| 1995 | 100 | | 100 |
| 1996 | 96.3 | | 96.3 |
| 1997 | 95.6 | | 95.6 |
| 1998 | 92.1 | | 92.1 |
| 1999 | 88.1 | 100 | 88.1 |
| 2000 | | 104.63 | 92.2 |
| 2001 | | 116.68 | 102.8 |
| 2002 | | 111.87 | 98.6 |
| 2003 | | 111.30 | 98.1 |

*Note*: After 1999, the chain index values are calculated by multiplying the 'new' index by 0.881; e.g. 92.2 = 104.63 × 0.881 for 2000.

way of example. This figure is calculated as $98.1 = 111.30 \times 88.1/100$ which in terms of our formulae is

(10.14) $\quad \dfrac{\Sigma p_{03} q_{99}}{\Sigma p_{99} q_{99}} \times \dfrac{\Sigma p_{99} q_{95}}{\Sigma p_{95} q_{95}} \Big/ 100$

The proper Laspeyres index for 2003 using 1995 weights is

(10.15) $\quad \dfrac{\Sigma p_{03} q_{95}}{\Sigma p_{95} q_{95}} \times 100$

There is no way that this latter equation can be derived from equation (10.14), proving that the former is not a properly constructed Laspeyres index number. Although it is not a proper index number series it does have the advantage of the weights being revised and therefore more up-to-date.

Similar problems arise when deriving a chain index from two Paasche index number series. Investigation of this is left to the reader; the method follows that outlined above for the Laspeyres case.

## The Retail Price Index

The UK Retail Price Index is one of the more sophisticated of index numbers, involving the recording of the prices of 650 items each month, and weighting them on the basis of households' expenditure patterns as revealed by the Expenditure and Food Survey (the EFS was explained in more detail in Chapter 9 on sampling methods). The principles involved in the calculation are similar to those set out above, with slight differences due to a variety of reasons.

The RPI is something of a compromise between a Laspeyres and a Paasche index. It is calculated monthly, and within each calendar year the weights used remain constant, so that it takes the form of a Laspeyres index. Each January, however, the weights are updated on the basis of evidence from the EFS, so that the index is in fact a set of chain-linked Laspeyres indices, the chaining taking place in January each year. Despite the formal appearance as a Laspeyres index, the RPI measured over a period of years has the characteristics of a Paasche index, due to the annual change in the weights.

Another departure from principle is the fact that about 14% of households are left out when expenditure weights are calculated. These consist of most pensioner households (10%) and the very rich (4%), because they tend to have significantly different spending patterns from the rest of the population and their inclusion would make the index too unrepresentative. A separate RPI is calculated for pensioners, while the very rich have to do without one.

A change in the quality of goods purchased can also be problematic, as alluded to earlier. If a manufacturer improves the quality of a product and charges more, is it fair to say that the price has gone up? Sometimes it is possible to measure improvement (if the power of a vacuum cleaner is increased, for example), but other cases are more difficult, such as if the punctuality of a train service is improved. By how much has quality improved? In many circumstances the statistician has to make a judgement about the best procedure to adopt.

> ### Prices in the long run
>
> Table 10.19 shows how prices have changed over the longer term. The 'inflation-adjusted' column shows what the item would have cost if it had risen in line with the overall retail price index. It is clear that some relative prices have changed substantially and you can try to work out the reasons.
>
> **Table 10.19 80 years of prices: 1914–1994**
>
> | Item | 1914 price | Inflation-adjusted price | 1994 price |
> |---|---|---|---|
> | Car | £730 | £36 971 | £6995 |
> | London–Manchester 1st class rail fare | £2.45 | £124.08 | £130 |
> | Pint of beer | 1p | 53p | £1.38 |
> | Milk (quart) | 1.5p | 74p | 70p |
> | Bread | 2.5p | £1.21 | 51p |
> | Butter | 6p | £3.06 | 68p |
> | Double room at Savoy Hotel, London | £1.25 | £63.31 | £195 |

**Exercise 10.6**

The index of energy prices for the years 1992–1995 was:

| 1991 | 1992 | 1993 | 1994 | 1995 |
|---|---|---|---|---|
| 100 | 103.5 | 107.8 | 112.2 | 119.8 |

Use these data to calculate a chain index from 1991 to 2003, setting 1991 = 100.

**Discounting and present values**

Deflating makes expenditures in different years comparable by correcting for the effect of inflation. The future sum is deflated (reduced) because of the increase in the general price level. Discounting is a similar procedure for comparing amounts across different years, correcting for time preference. For example, suppose that by investing £1000 today a firm can receive £1100 in a year's time. To decide if the investment is worthwhile, the two amounts need to be compared.

If the prevailing interest rate is 12%, then the firm could simply place its £1000 in the bank and earn £120 interest, giving it £1120 at the end of the year. Hence the firm should not invest in this particular project; it does better keeping money in the bank. The investment is not undertaken because

$$£1000 \times (1 + r) > £1100$$

where $r$ is the interest rate, 12%. Alternatively, this inequality may be expressed as

$$£1000 > \frac{£1100}{(1 + r)}$$

The expression on the right-hand side of the inequality sign is the present value (*PV*) of £1100 received in one year's time. Here, $r$ is the rate of discount

**Table 10.20 The cash flows from an investment project**

| Year | Outlay or income | | Discount factor | Discounted income |
|------|------|------|------|------|
| 2001 | Outlay | −1000 | | |
| 2002 | Income | 300 | 0.893 | 267.86 |
| 2003 | | 400 | 0.797 | 318.88 |
| 2004 | | 450 | 0.712 | 320.30 |
| 2005 | | 200 | 0.636 | 127.10 |
| Total | | | | 1034.14 |

and is equal to the rate of interest in this example because this is the rate at which the firm can transform present into future income, and vice versa. In what follows, we use the terms interest rate and discount rate interchangeably. The term $1/(1 + r)$ is known as the discount factor. Multiplying an amount by the discount factor results in the present value of the sum.

We can also express the inequality as follows (by subtracting £1000 from each side):

$$0 > -£1000 + \frac{£1100}{(1 + r)}$$

The right-hand side of this expression is known as the net present value (*NPV*) of the project. It represents the difference between the initial outlay and the present value of the return generated by the investment. Since this is negative the investment is not worthwhile (the money would be better placed on deposit in a bank). The general rule is to invest if the *NPV* is positive.

Similarly, the present value of £1100 to be received in two years' time is

$$PV = \frac{£1100}{(1 + r)^2} = \frac{£1100}{(1 + 0.12)^2} = £876.91$$

when $r = 12\%$. In general, the *PV* of a sum $S$ to be received in $t$ years is

$$PV = \frac{S}{(1 + r)^t}$$

The *PV* may be interpreted as the amount a firm would be prepared to pay today to receive an amount $S$ in $t$ years' time. Thus a firm would not be prepared to make an outlay of more than £876.91 in order to receive £1100 in two years' time. It would gain more by putting the money on deposit and earning 12% interest per annum.

Most investment projects involve an initial outlay followed by a *series* of receipts over the following years, as illustrated by the figures in Table 10.20. In order to decide if the investment is worthwhile, the present value of the income stream needs to be compared to the initial outlay. The *PV* of the income stream is obtained by adding together the present value of each year's income. Thus we calculate[2]

---

[2] This present value example has only four terms but in principle there can be any number of terms stretching into the future.

$$(10.16) \qquad PV = \frac{S_1}{(1+r)} + \frac{S_2}{(1+r)^2} + \frac{S_3}{(1+r)^3} + \frac{S_4}{(1+r)^4}$$

or more concisely, using $\Sigma$ notation:

$$(10.17) \qquad PV = \Sigma \frac{S_t}{(1+r)^t}$$

Columns 3 and 4 of the table show the calculation of the present value. The discount factors, $1/(1+r)^t$, are given in column 3. Multiplying column 2 by column 3 gives the individual elements of the $PV$ calculation (as in equation (10.16) above) and their sum is 1034.14, which is the present value of the returns. Since the $PV$ is greater than the initial outlay of 1000 the investment generates a return of at least 12% and so is worthwhile.

**An alternative investment criterion: the internal rate of return**

The investment rule can be expressed in a different manner, using the internal rate of return (*IRR*). This is the rate of discount which makes the *NPV* equal to zero, i.e. the present value of the income stream is equal to the initial outlay. An *IRR* of 10% equates £1100 received next year to an outlay of £1000 today. Since the *IRR* is less than the market interest rate (12%) this indicates that the investment is not worthwhile: it only yields a rate of return of 10%. The rule 'invest if the *IRR* is greater than the market rate of interest' is equivalent to the rule 'invest if the net present value is positive, using the interest rate to discount future revenues'.

In general it is mathematically difficult to find the *IRR* of a project with a stream of future income, except by trial and error methods. The *IRR* is the value of $r$ which sets the *NPV* equal to zero, i.e. it is the solution to

$$(10.18) \qquad NPV = -S_0 + \Sigma \frac{S_t}{(1+r)^t} = 0$$

where $S_0$ is the initial outlay. Fortunately, most spreadsheet programs have an internal routine for its calculation. This is illustrated in Figure 10.1 which shows the calculation of the *IRR* for the data in Table 10.20 above.

Cell C11 contains the formula '= IRR(C4:C8)' – this can be seen just above the column headings – which is the function used in *Excel* to calculate the internal rate of return. The *IRR* for this project is therefore 13.7% which is indeed above the market interest rate of 12%. The final two columns show that the *PV* of the income stream, when discounted using the internal rate of return, is equal to the initial outlay. The discount factors in the penultimate column are calculated using $r = 13.7\%$.

The *IRR* is easy to calculate if the income stream is a constant monetary sum. If the initial outlay is $S_0$ and a sum $S$ is received each year in perpetuity (like a bond), then the *IRR* is simply

$$IRR = \frac{S}{S_0}$$

For example, if an outlay of £1000 yields a permanent income stream of £120 p.a. then the *IRR* is 12%. This should be intuitively obvious, since investing £1000 at an interest rate of 12% would give you an annual income of £120.

**Figure 10.1**
**Calculation of IRR**

*Note*: Note that the first term in the series is the initial outlay (cell C4) and that it is entered as a *negative* number. If a positive value is entered, the *IRR* function will not work.

**Nominal and real interest rates**

If an income stream has already been deflated to real terms then the present value should be obtained by discounting by the **real interest rate**, not the nominal (market) rate. Table 10.21 illustrates the principle. Column 1 repeats the income flows in cash terms from Table 10.20. Assuming an inflation rate of $i = 7\%$ per annum gives the price index shown in column 2, based on 2001 = 100. This is used to deflate the cash series to real terms, shown in column 3. This is in constant (2001) prices. If we were presented only with the real income series and could not obtain the original cash flows we would have to discount the real series by the real interest rate $r_r$, defined by

$$(10.19) \qquad 1 + r_r = \frac{1 + r}{1 + i}$$

With a (nominal) interest rate of 12% and an inflation rate of 7% this gives

$$(10.20) \qquad 1 + r_r = \frac{1 + 0.12}{1 + 0.07} = 1.0467$$

**Table 10.21** Discounting a real income stream

| Year | | | Price index | Real income | Real discount factor | Discounted sums |
|------|---|---|---|---|---|---|
| 2001 | Outlay | −1000 | 100 | | | |
| 2002 | Income | 300 | 107.0 | 280.37 | 0.955 | 267.86 |
| 2003 | | 400 | 114.5 | 349.38 | 0.913 | 318.88 |
| 2004 | | 450 | 122.5 | 367.33 | 0.872 | 320.30 |
| 2005 | | 200 | 131.1 | 152.58 | 0.833 | 127.10 |
| Total | | | | | | 1034.14 |

so that the real interest rate is 4.67% and in this example is the same every year. The discount factors used to discount the real income flows are shown in column 4 of the table, based on the real interest rate, the discounted sums are in column 5 and the present value of the series is £1034.14. This is the same as was found earlier, by discounting the cash figures by the nominal interest rate. Thus one can discount *either* the nominal (cash) values using the nominal discount rate, *or* the real flows by the real interest rate. Make sure you do not confuse the nominal and real interest rates.

The real interest rate can be approximated by subtracting the inflation rate from the nominal interest rate, i.e. 12% − 7% = 5%. This gives a reasonably accurate approximation for low values of the interest and inflation rates (below about 10% p.a.). Because of the simplicity of the calculation, this method is often preferred.

**Exercise 10.7**

(a) An investment of £100 000 yields returns of £25 000, £35 000, £30 000 and £15 000 in each of the subsequent four years. Calculate the present value of the income stream and compare to the initial outlay, using an interest rate of 10% per annum.

(b) Calculate the internal rate of return on this investment.

**Exercise 10.8**

(a) An investment of £50 000 yields cash returns of £20 000, £25 000, £30 000 and £10 000 in each subsequent year. The rate of inflation is a constant 5% and the rate of interest is constant at 9%. Use the rate of inflation to construct a price index and discount the cash flows to real terms.

(b) Calculate the real discount rate.

(c) Use the real discount rate to calculate the present value of the real income flows.

(d) Compare the result where the nominal cash flows and nominal interest rate are used.

# Inequality indices

A separate set of index numbers is used specifically in the measurement of inequality, such as inequality in the distribution of income. We have already seen how we can measure the dispersion of a distribution via the variance and standard deviation. This is based upon the deviations of the observations about the mean. An alternative idea is to measure the difference between *every pair* of observations, and this forms the basis of a statistic known as the Gini coefficient. This would probably have remained an obscure measure, due to the complexity of calculation, were it not for Konrad Lorenz, who showed that there is an attractive visual interpretation of it, now known as the Lorenz curve, and a relatively simple calculation of the Gini coefficient, based on this curve.

We start off by constructing the Lorenz curve, based on data for the UK income distribution in 2003, and proceed then to calculate the Gini coefficient. We then use these measures to look at inequality both over time (in the UK) and across different countries.

We then examine another manifestation of inequality, in terms of market shares of firms. For this analysis we look at the calculation of concentration ratios and at their interpretation.

## The Lorenz curve

Table 10.22 shows the data for the distribution of income in the UK based on data from the *Family Resources Survey* 2002–03, published by the ONS. The data report the total weekly income of each household, which means that income is recorded after any cash benefits from the state (e.g. a pension) have been received but before any taxes have been paid.

The table indicates a substantial degree of inequality. For example, the poorest 22% of households earn £200 per week, or less, while the richest 10% earn more than five times as much. Although these figures give some idea of the extent of inequality, they relate only to relatively few households at the extremes of the distribution. A **Lorenz curve** is a way of graphically presenting the whole distribution. A typical Lorenz curve is shown in Figure 10.2.

Households are ranked along the horizontal axis, from poorest to richest, so that the median household, for example, is halfway along the axis. On the

**Table 10.22** The distribution of gross income in the UK, 2002–03

| Range of weekly household income | Mid-point of interval | Numbers of households |
|---|---|---|
| 0– | 50 | 1 000 |
| 100– | 150 | 5 213 |
| 200– | 250 | 5 037 |
| 300– | 350 | 3 548 |
| 400– | 450 | 2 850 |
| 500– | 550 | 2 458 |
| 600– | 650 | 1 996 |
| 700– | 750 | 1 583 |
| 800– | 850 | 1 198 |
| 900– | 950 | 838 |
| 1000– | 1250 | 2 989 |
| Total | | 28 710 |

**Figure 10.2**
**Typical Lorenz curve**

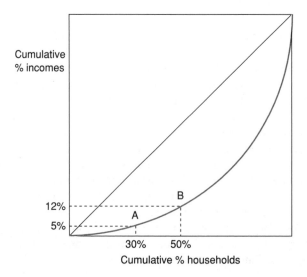

Table 10.23 Calculation of the Lorenz curve coordinates

| Range of income | Mid-point | Households | Total income | % Households | % Cumulative households x | % Income | % Cumulative income y |
|---|---|---|---|---|---|---|---|
| (1) | (2) | (3) | (4) | (5) | (6) | (7) | (8) |
| 0– | 50 | 1 000 | 50 000 | 3.5% | 3.5% | 0.4% | 0.4% |
| 100– | 150 | 5 213 | 781 950 | 18.2% | 21.6% | 5.6% | 5.9% |
| 200– | 250 | 5 037 | 1 259 250 | 17.5% | 39.2% | 9.0% | 14.9% |
| 300– | 350 | 3 548 | 1 241 800 | 12.4% | 51.5% | 8.9% | 23.8% |
| 400– | 450 | 2 850 | 1 282 500 | 9.9% | 61.5% | 9.2% | 33.0% |
| 500– | 550 | 2 458 | 1 351 900 | 8.6% | 70.0% | 9.7% | 42.6% |
| 600– | 650 | 1 996 | 1 297 400 | 7.0% | 77.0% | 9.3% | 51.9% |
| 700– | 750 | 1 583 | 1 187 250 | 5.5% | 82.5% | 8.5% | 60.4% |
| 800– | 850 | 1 198 | 1 018 300 | 4.2% | 86.7% | 7.3% | 67.6% |
| 900– | 950 | 838 | 796 100 | 2.9% | 89.6% | 5.7% | 73.3% |
| 1000– | 1250 | 2 989 | 3 736 250 | 10.4% | 100.0% | 26.7% | 100.0% |
| Totals | | 28 710 | 14 002 700 | 100.0% | | 100.0% | |

*Notes*:
Column 4 = column 2 × column 3
Column 5 = column 3 ÷ 28 710
Column 6 = column 5 cumulated
Column 7 = column 4 ÷ 14 002 700
Column 8 = column 7 cumulated

vertical axis is measured the cumulative share of income, which goes from 0% to 100%. A point such as A on the diagram indicates that the poorest 30% of households earn 5% of total income. Point B shows that the poorest half of the population earn only 12% of income (and hence the other half earn 88%). Joining up all such points maps out the Lorenz curve.

A few things are immediately obvious about the Lorenz curve:

- Since 0% of households earn 0% of income, and 100% of households earn 100% of income, the curve must run from the origin up to the opposite corner.
- Since households are ranked from poorest to richest, the Lorenz curve must lie below the 45° line, which is the line representing complete equality. The further away from the 45° line is the Lorenz curve, the greater is the degree of inequality.
- The Lorenz curve must be concave from above: as we move to the right we encounter successively richer individuals, so the cumulative income grows faster.

Table 10.23 shows how to generate a Lorenz curve for the data given in Table 10.22. The task is to calculate the {x, y} coordinates for the Lorenz curve. These are given in columns 6 and 8 respectively of the table. Column 5 of the table calculates the proportion of households in each income category (i.e. the relative frequencies, as in Chapter 1), and these are then cumulated in column 6. These are the figures which are used along the horizontal axis. Column 4 calculates the total income going to each income class (by multiplying the class frequency by the mid-point). The proportion of total income going to each class is then calculated in column 7 (class income divided by total income). Column 8 cumulates the values in column 7.

**Figure 10.3**
**Lorenz curve for income data**

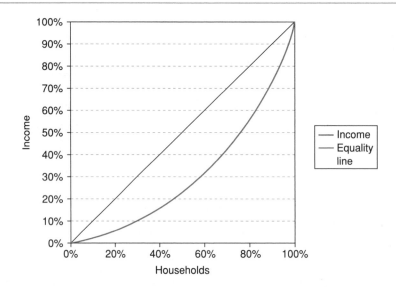

Using columns 6 and 8 of the table we can see, for instance, that the poorest 3.5% of the population have about 0.4% of total income; the poorer half have about 23% of income; and the top 10% have about 26% of total income.

Figure 10.3 shows the Lorenz curve plotted, using the data in columns 6 and 8 of the table above. This shows a fairly smooth Lorenz curve, with perhaps a greater degree of inequality at the bottom of the distribution than at the top.

## The Gini coefficient

The Gini coefficient is a numerical representation of the degree of inequality in a distribution and can be derived directly from the Lorenz curve. The Lorenz curve is illustrated once again in Figure 10.4 and the Gini coefficient is simply the ratio of area A to the sum of areas A and B.

**Figure 10.4**
**Calculation of the Gini coefficient from the Lorenz curve**

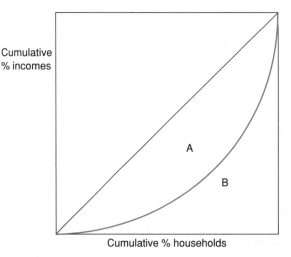

Denoting the Gini coefficient by $G$, we have

**(10.21)**    $G = \dfrac{A}{A + B}$

and it should be obvious that $G$ must lie between 0 and 1. When there is total equality the Lorenz curve coincides with the 45° line, area A then disappears, and $G = 0$. With total inequality (one household having all the income), area B disappears, and $G = 1$. Neither of these extremes is likely to occur in real life; instead one will get intermediate values, but the lower the value of $G$, the less inequality there is (though see the *caveats* listed below). One could compare two countries, for example, simply by examining the values of their Gini coefficients.

The Gini coefficient may be calculated from the following formulae for areas A and B:

**(10.22)**    $\begin{aligned} B = \tfrac{1}{2}\{(x_1 - x_0) &\times (y_1 + y_0) \\ + (x_2 - x_1) &\times (y_2 + y_1) \\ &\vdots \\ + (x_k - x_{k-1}) &\times (y_k + y_{k-1})\} \end{aligned}$

where $x_0 = y_0 = 0$ and $x_k = y_k = 100$ (i.e. the coordinates of the two end-points of the Lorenz curve) and the other $x$ and $y$ values are the coordinates of the intermediate points. $k$ is the number of classes for income in the frequency table. Area A is then given by:[3]

**(10.23)**    $A = 5000 - B$

and the Gini coefficient is then calculated as:

**(10.24)**    $G = \dfrac{A}{A + B}$ or $\dfrac{A}{5000}$

Thus for the data in Table 10.23 we have:

**(10.25)**    $\begin{aligned} B = \tfrac{1}{2} \times \{ (3.5 - 0) &\times (0.4 + 0) \\ + (21.6 - 3.5) &\times (5.9 + 0.4) \\ + (39.2 - 21.6) &\times (14.9 + 5.9) \\ + (51.5 - 39.2) &\times (23.8 + 14.9) \\ + (61.5 - 51.5) &\times (33.0 + 23.8) \\ + (70.0 - 61.5) &\times (42.6 + 33.0) \\ + (77.0 - 70.0) &\times (51.9 + 42.6) \\ + (82.5 - 77.0) &\times (60.4 + 51.9) \\ + (86.7 - 82.5) &\times (67.6 + 60.4) \\ + (89.6 - 86.7) &\times (73.3 + 67.6) \\ + (100 - 89.6) &\times (100 + 73.3) \} \end{aligned}$

$= 3098.43$

---

[3] The value 5000 is correct if one uses percentages, as here (it is $100 \times 100 \times \tfrac{1}{2}$, the area of the triangle). If one uses percentages expressed as decimals, then $A = 0.5 - B$.

Therefore area A = 5000 − 3098.43 = 1901.57 and we obtain

$$(10.26) \qquad G = \frac{1901.57}{5000} = 0.3803$$

or approximately 38%.

This method implicitly assumes that the Lorenz curve is made up of straight line segments connecting the observed points, which is in fact not true – it should be a smooth curve. Since the straight lines will lie inside the true Lorenz curve, area B is *over*-estimated and so the calculated Gini coefficient is biased downwards. The true value of the Gini coefficient is slightly greater than 38% therefore. The bias will be greater (a) the fewer the number of observations and (b) the more concave is the Lorenz curve (i.e. the greater is inequality). The bias is unlikely to be substantial however, so is best left untreated.

An alternative method of calculating *G* is simply to draw the Lorenz curve on gridded paper and count squares. This has the advantage that you can draw a smooth line joining the observations and avoid the bias problem mentioned above. This alternative method can prove reasonably quick and accurate, but has the disadvantage that you can't use a computer to do it!

**Is inequality increasing?**

The Gini coefficient is only useful as a comparative measure, for looking at trends in inequality over time, or for comparing different countries or regions. Table 10.24, taken from the *Statbase* website, shows the value of the Gini coefficient for the UK over the past eight years and shows how it was affected by the tax system. The results are based on *equivalised* income, i.e. after making a correction for differences in family size.[4] For this reason there is a slight difference from the Gini coefficient calculated above, which uses unadjusted data. Using equivalised income appears to make little difference in this case (compare the 'gross income' column with the earlier calculation).

The table shows essentially two things:

1 There appears to have been some increase in inequality in the late 1990s which begins to reverse itself in the early 2000s. This is true whatever definition of income one uses.

**Table 10.24  Gini coefficients for the UK, 1995/6–2002/03**

|  | Original income | Gross income | Disposable income | Post-tax income |
|---|---|---|---|---|
| 1995/96 | 52 | 36 | 33 | 37 |
| 1996/97 | 53 | 37 | 34 | 38 |
| 1997/98 | 53 | 37 | 34 | 38 |
| 1998/99 | 53 | 38 | 35 | 39 |
| 1999/00 | 53 | 38 | 35 | 40 |
| 2000/01 | 51 | 38 | 35 | 39 |
| 2001/02 | 53 | 39 | 36 | 40 |
| 2002/03 | 51 | 37 | 33 | 37 |

*Note*: Gross income is original income plus certain state benefits, such as pensions. Taking off direct taxes gives disposable income and subtracting other taxes gives post-tax income.

[4] This is because a larger family needs more income to have the same living standard as a smaller one.

**Table 10.25  Gini coefficients in past times**

| Year | Gini |
|------|------|
| 1688 | 0.55 |
| 1801–03 | 0.56 |
| 1867 | 0.52 |
| 1913 | 0.43–0.63 |

2  The biggest reduction in inequality comes through cash benefits paid out by the state, rather than through taxes. In fact, the tax system appears to *increase* inequality rather than to reduce it, primarily because of the effects of indirect taxes.

The recent increase in inequality is a reversal of the historical trend. The figures presented in Table 10.25, from L. Soltow,[5] provide estimates of the Gini coefficient in earlier times. These figures suggest that a substantial decline in the Gini coefficient has occurred in the last century or so, perhaps related to the process of economic development. It is difficult to compare Soltow's figures directly with the modern ones because of such factors as the quality of data and different definitions of income.

**A simpler formula for the Gini coefficient**

Kravis, Heston and Summers[6] provide estimates of 'world' GDP by decile and these figures, presented in Table 10.26, will be used to illustrate another method of calculating the Gini coefficient.

These figures show that the poorer half of the world population earns only about 10% of world income and that a third of world income goes to the richest 10% of the population. This suggests a higher degree of inequality than for a single country such as the UK, as one might expect.

When the class intervals contain equal numbers of households (for example, when the data are given for deciles of the income distribution, as here) formula (10.22) for area B simplifies to:

$$(10.27) \qquad B = \frac{100}{2k}(y_0 + 2y_1 + 2y_2 + \ldots + 2y_{k-1} + y_k) = \frac{100}{k}\left(\sum_{i=0}^{i=k} y_i - 50\right)$$

where $k$ is the number of intervals (e.g. 10 in the case of deciles, 5 for quintiles). Thus you simply sum the $y$ values, subtract 50,[7] and divide by the

**Table 10.26  The world distribution of income by decile**

| Decile | 1 | 2 | 3 | 4 | 5 | 6 | 7 | 8 | 9 | 10 |
|--------|-----|-----|-----|-----|------|------|------|------|------|-------|
| % GDP | 1.5 | 2.1 | 2.4 | 2.4 | 3.3 | 5.2 | 8.4 | 17.1 | 24.1 | 33.5 |
| Cumulative % | 1.5 | 3.6 | 6.0 | 8.4 | 11.7 | 16.9 | 25.3 | 42.4 | 66.5 | 100.0 |

[5] Long run changes in British income inequality, *Economic History Review*, vol 21, 17–29, 1968.
[6] Real GDP per capita for more than one hundred countries, *Economic Journal*, vol 88, 215–42, 1978.
[7] If using decimal percentages, subtract 0.5.

number of classes $k$. The $y$ values for the Kravis *et al.* data appear in the final row of Table 10.26, and their sum is 282.3. We therefore obtain

$$(10.28) \quad B = \frac{100}{10}(282.3 - 50) = 2323$$

Hence

$$(10.29) \quad A = 5000 - 2323 = 2677$$

and

$$(10.30) \quad G = \frac{2677}{5000} = 0.5354$$

or about 53%. This is surprisingly similar to the figure for original income in the UK, but, of course, differences in definition, measurement, etc. may make direct comparison invalid. While the Gini coefficient may provide some guidance when comparing inequality over time or across countries, one needs to take care in its interpretation.

**Exercise 10.9**

(a) The same data as used in the text are presented below, but with fewer class intervals:

| Range of income | Mid-point of interval | Numbers of households |
|---|---|---|
| 0– | 100 | 6 213 |
| 200– | 300 | 8 585 |
| 400– | 500 | 5 308 |
| 600– | 700 | 3 579 |
| 800– | 900 | 2 036 |
| 1000– | 1250 | 2 989 |
| Total | | 28 710 |

Draw the Lorenz curve for these data.

(b) Calculate the Gini coefficient for these data and compare to that calculated earlier.

**Exercise 10.10**

Given shares of total income of 8%, 15%, 22%, 25% and 30% by each quintile of a country's population, calculate the Gini coefficient.

# Concentration ratios

Another type of inequality is the distribution of market shares of the firms in an industry. We all know that Microsoft currently dominates the software market with a large market share. In contrast, an industry such as bakery has many different suppliers and there is little tendency to dominance. The concentration ratio is a commonly used measure to examine the distribution of market shares among firms competing in a market. Of course, it would be possible to measure this using the Lorenz curve and Gini coefficient, but the concentration ratio has the advantage that it can be calculated on the basis of less information and also tends to focus attention on the largest firms in the industry. The concentration ratio is often used as a measure of the competitiveness of a particular market but, as with all statistics, it requires careful interpretation.

## Inequality and development

Table 10.27 presents figures for the income distribution in selected countries around the world. They are in approximately ascending order of national income. The table shows that countries have very different experiences of inequality, even for similar levels of income (compare Bangladesh and Kenya, for example). Hungary, the only (former) communist country, shows the greatest equality, although whether income accurately measures people's access to resources in such a regime is perhaps debatable. Note that countries with fast growth (such as Korea and Hong Kong) do not have to have a high degree of inequality. Developed countries seem to have uniformly low Gini coefficients.

**Table 10.27** Income distribution figures in selected countries

| | Year | Quintiles | | | | | Top 10% | Gini |
|---|---|---|---|---|---|---|---|---|
| | | 1 | 2 | 3 | 4 | 5 | | |
| Bangladesh | 1981–82 | 6.6 | 10.7 | 15.3 | 22.1 | 45.3 | 29.5 | 0.36 |
| Kenya | 1976 | 2.6 | 6.3 | 11.5 | 19.2 | 60.4 | 45.8 | 0.51 |
| Côte d'Ivoire | 1985–86 | 2.4 | 6.2 | 10.9 | 19.1 | 61.4 | 43.7 | 0.52 |
| El Salvador | 1976–77 | 5.5 | 10.0 | 14.8 | 22.4 | 47.3 | 29.5 | 0.38 |
| Brazil | 1972 | 2.0 | 5.0 | 9.4 | 17.0 | 66.6 | 50.6 | 0.56 |
| Hungary | 1982 | 6.9 | 13.6 | 19.2 | 24.5 | 35.8 | 20.5 | 0.27 |
| Korea, Rep. | 1976 | 5.7 | 11.2 | 15.4 | 22.4 | 45.3 | 27.5 | 0.36 |
| Hong Kong | 1980 | 5.4 | 10.8 | 15.2 | 21.6 | 47.0 | 31.3 | 0.38 |
| New Zealand | 1981–82 | 5.1 | 10.8 | 16.2 | 23.2 | 44.7 | 28.7 | 0.37 |
| UK | 1979 | 7.0 | 11.5 | 17.0 | 24.8 | 39.7 | 23.4 | 0.31 |
| Netherlands | 1981 | 8.3 | 14.1 | 18.2 | 23.2 | 36.2 | 21.5 | 0.26 |
| Japan | 1979 | 8.7 | 13.2 | 17.5 | 23.1 | 37.5 | 22.4 | 0.27 |

*Source*: World Development Report 1999.

A market is said to be concentrated if most of the demand is met by a small number of suppliers. The limiting case is monopoly where the whole of the market is supplied by a single firm. We shall measure the degree of concentration by the **five-firm concentration ratio**, which is the proportion of the market held by the largest five firms, and it is denoted $C_5$. The larger is this proportion, the greater the degree of concentration and potentially the less competitive is that market. Table 10.28 gives the (imaginary) sales figures of the ten firms in a particular industry.

For convenience the firms have already been ranked by size from A (the largest) to J (smallest). The output of the five largest firms is 482, out of a total of 569, so the five-firm concentration ratio is $C_5 = 84.7\%$, i.e. 84.7% of the market is supplied by the five largest firms.

**Table 10.28** Sales figures for an industry (millions of units)

| Firm | A | B | C | D | E | F | G | H | I | J |
|---|---|---|---|---|---|---|---|---|---|---|
| Sales | 180 | 115 | 90 | 62 | 35 | 25 | 19 | 18 | 15 | 10 |

Without supporting evidence it is hard to interpret this figure. Does it mean that the market is not competitive and the consumer being exploited? Some industries, such as the computer industry, have a very high concentration ratio yet it is hard to deny that they are very competitive. On the other hand, some industries with no large firms have restrictive practices, entry barriers, etc. which mean that they are not very competitive (lawyers might be one example). A further point is that there may be a *threat* of competition from outside the industry which keeps the few firms acting competitively.

Concentration ratios can be calculated for different numbers of largest firms, e.g. the three-firm or four-firm concentration ratio. Straightforward calculation reveals them to be 67.7% and 78.6% respectively for the data given in Table 10.28. There is little reason in general to prefer one measure to the others, and they may give different pictures of the degree of concentration in an industry.

The concentration ratio calculated above relates to the quantity of output produced by each firm, but it is possible to do the same with sales revenue, employment, investment or any other variable for which data are available. The interpretation of the results will be different in each case. For example, the largest firms in an industry, while producing the majority of output, might not provide the greater part of employment if they use more capital-intensive methods of production. Concentration ratios obviously have to be treated with caution, therefore, and are probably best combined with case studies of the particular industry before conclusions are reached about the degree of competition.

**Exercise 10.11**

Total sales in an industry are $400m. The largest five firms have sales of $180m, $70m, $40m, $25m and $15m. Calculate the three- and five-firm concentration ratios.

## Summary

- An index number summarises the variation of a variable over time or across space in a convenient way.

- Several variables can be combined into one index, providing an average measure of their individual movements. The retail price index is an example.

- The Laspeyres price index combines the prices of many individual goods using base-year quantities as weights. The Paasche index is similar but uses current-year weights to construct the index.

- Laspeyres and Paasche quantity indices can also be constructed, combining a number of individual quantity series using prices as weights. Base-year prices are used in the Laspeyres index, current-year prices in the Paasche.

- A price index series multiplied by a quantity index series results in an index of expenditures. Rearranging this demonstrates that deflating (dividing) an expenditure series by a price series results in a volume (quantity) index. This is the basis of deflating a series in cash (or nominal) terms to one measured in real terms (i.e. adjusted for price changes).

- Two series covering different time periods can be spliced together (as long as there is an overlapping year) to give one continuous chain index.

- Discounting the future is similar to deflating but corrects for the rate of time preference rather than inflation. A stream of future income can thus be discounted and summarised in terms of its present value.

- An investment can be evaluated by comparing the discounted present value of the future income stream to the initial outlay. The internal rate of return of an investment is a similar but alternative way of evaluating an investment project.

- The Gini coefficient is a form of index number that is used to measure inequality (e.g. of incomes). It can be given a visual representation using a Lorenz curve diagram.

- For measuring the inequality of market shares in an industry, the concentration ratio is commonly used.

| Key terms and concepts | | | |
|---|---|---|---|
| | weighted average | Laspeyres index | Paasche index |
| | base year | reference year | deflating a data series |
| | chain index | retail price index | discounting |
| | present value | internal rate of return | Lorenz curve |
| | Gini coefficient | concentration ratio | |

## Problems

Some of the more challenging problems are indicated by highlighting the **problem number** in colour.

**Problem 10.1**   The data below show exports and imports for the UK, 1987–92, in £bn at current prices.

|         | 1987  | 1988  | 1989  | 1990  | 1991  | 1992  |
|---------|-------|-------|-------|-------|-------|-------|
| Exports | 120.6 | 121.2 | 126.8 | 133.3 | 132.1 | 135.5 |
| Imports | 122.1 | 137.4 | 147.6 | 148.3 | 140.2 | 148.3 |

(a)  Construct index number series for exports and imports, setting the index equal to 100 in 1987 in each case.

(b)  Is it possible, using only the two indices, to construct an index number series for the balance of trade? If so, do so; if not, why not?

**Problem 10.2**   The following data show the gross trading profits of companies, 1987–92, in the UK, in £m.

| 1987   | 1988   | 1989   | 1990   | 1991   | 1992   |
|--------|--------|--------|--------|--------|--------|
| 61 750 | 69 180 | 73 892 | 74 405 | 78 063 | 77 959 |

(a)  Turn the data into an index number series with 1987 as the reference year.

(b)  Transform the series so that 1990 is the reference year.

(c)  What increase has there been in profits between 1987 and 1992? Between 1990 and 1992?

**Problem 10.3**   The following data show energy prices and consumption in 1984–88 (analogous to the data in the chapter for the years 1999–2003).

| Prices | Coal (£/tonne) | Petroleum (£/tonne) | Electricity (£/MWh) | Gas (£/therm) |
|---|---|---|---|---|
| 1984 | 49.60 | 149.70 | 28.89 | 0.2634 |
| 1985 | 51.00 | 151.75 | 30.02 | 0.2841 |
| 1986 | 49.64 | 72.98 | 30.07 | 0.2378 |
| 1987 | 47.50 | 78.10 | 28.92 | 0.2196 |
| 1988 | 43.10 | 55.04 | 30.02 | 0.2175 |

| Quantities | Coal (m tonnes) | Petroleum (m tonnes) | Electricity (m MWh) | Gas (m therms) |
|---|---|---|---|---|
| 1984 | 12.72 | 10.26 | 78.64 | 6044 |
| 1985 | 14.62 | 9.12 | 79.53 | 6185 |
| 1986 | 14.58 | 9.67 | 80.09 | 5647 |
| 1987 | 15.12 | 8.61 | 83.89 | 6182 |
| 1988 | 15.77 | 9.61 | 88.13 | 5636 |

(a) Construct a Laspeyres price index using 1984 as the base year.

(b) Construct a Paasche price index. Compare this result with the Laspeyres index. Do they differ significantly?

(c) Construct Laspeyres and Paasche quantity indices. Check that they satisfy the conditions that $E^n = P_L \times Q_P$ etc.

**Problem 10.4**   The prices of different house types in south-east England are given in the table below:

| Year | Terraced houses | Semi-detached | Detached | Bungalows | Flats |
|---|---|---|---|---|---|
| 1991 | 59 844 | 77 791 | 142 630 | 89 100 | 47 676 |
| 1992 | 55 769 | 73 839 | 137 053 | 82 109 | 43 695 |
| 1993 | 55 571 | 71 208 | 129 414 | 82 734 | 42 746 |
| 1994 | 57 296 | 71 850 | 130 159 | 83 471 | 44 092 |

(a) If the numbers of each type of house in 1991 were 1898, 1600, 1601, 499 and 1702 respectively, calculate the Laspeyres price index for 1991–94, based on 1991 = 100.

(b) Calculate the Paasche price index, based on the following numbers of dwellings:

| Year | Terraced houses | Semi-detached | Detached | Bungalows | Flats |
|---|---|---|---|---|---|
| 1992 | 1903 | 1615 | 1615 | 505 | 1710 |
| 1993 | 1906 | 1638 | 1633 | 511 | 1714 |
| 1994 | 1911 | 1655 | 1640 | 525 | 1717 |

(c) Compare Paasche and Laspeyres price series.

**Problem 10.5**   (a) Using the data in Problem 10.3, calculate the expenditure shares on each fuel in 1984 and the individual price index number series for each fuel, with 1984 = 100.

(b) Use these data to construct the Laspeyres price index using the expenditures shares approach. Check that it gives the same answer as in Problem 10.3(a).

**Problem 10.6** The following table shows the weights in the retail price index and the values of the index itself, for 1990 and 1994.

|  | Food | Alcohol and tobacco | Housing | Fuel and light | Household items | Clothing | Personal goods | Travel | Leisure |
|---|---|---|---|---|---|---|---|---|---|
| *Weights* |  |  |  |  |  |  |  |  |  |
| 1990 | 205 | 111 | 185 | 50 | 111 | 69 | 39 | 152 | 78 |
| 1994 | 187 | 111 | 158 | 45 | 123 | 58 | 37 | 162 | 119 |
| *Prices* |  |  |  |  |  |  |  |  |  |
| 1990 | 121.0 | 120.7 | 163.7 | 115.9 | 116.9 | 115.0 | 122.7 | 121.2 | 117.1 |
| 1994 | 139.5 | 162.1 | 156.8 | 133.9 | 132.4 | 116.0 | 152.4 | 150.7 | 145.7 |

(a) Calculate the Laspeyres price index for 1994, based on 1990 = 100.

(b) Draw a bar chart of the expenditure weights in 1990 and 1994 to show how spending patterns have changed. What major changes have occurred? Do individuals seem to be responding to changes in relative prices?

(c) The pensioner price index is similar to the general index calculated above, except that it excludes housing. What effect does this have on the index? What do you think is the justification for this omission?

(d) If consumers spent, on average, £188 per week in 1990 and £240 per week in 1994, calculate the real change in expenditure on food.

(e) Do consumers appear rational, i.e. do they respond as one would expect to relative price changes? If not, why not?

**Problem 10.7** Construct a chain index from the following data series:

|  | 1998 | 1999 | 2000 | 2001 | 2002 | 2003 | 2004 |
|---|---|---|---|---|---|---|---|
| Series 1 | 100 | 110 | 115 | 122 | 125 |  |  |
| Series 2 |  |  | 100 | 107 | 111 | 119 | 121 |

What problems arise in devising such an index and how do you deal with them?

**Problem 10.8** Construct a chain index for 1995–2004 using the following data, setting 1998 = 100.

| 1995 | 1996 | 1997 | 1998 | 1999 | 2000 | 2001 | 2002 | 2003 | 2004 |
|---|---|---|---|---|---|---|---|---|---|
| 87 | 95 | 100 | 105 |  |  |  |  |  |  |
|  |  |  | 98 | 93 | 100 | 104 | 110 |  |  |
|  |  |  |  |  |  |  | 100 | 106 | 112 |

**Problem 10.9** Industry is complaining about the rising price of energy. It demands to be compensated for any rise over 2% in energy prices between 1999 and 2000. How much would this compensation cost? Which price index should be used to calculate the compensation and what difference would it make?

**Problem 10.10** Using the data in Problem 10.6 above, calculate how much the average consumer would need to be compensated for the rise in prices between 1990 and 1994.

**Problem 10.11** The following data show expenditure on the National Health Service (in cash terms), the GDP deflator, the NHS pay and prices index, population, and population of working age:

| Year | NHS expenditure (£m) (1) | GDP deflator 1973 = 100 (2) | NHS pay and price index 1973 = 100 (3) | Population (000) (4) | Population of working age (000) (5) |
|---|---|---|---|---|---|
| 1987 | 21 495 | 442 | 573 | 56 930 | 34 987 |
| 1988 | 23 601 | 473 | 633 | 57 065 | 35 116 |
| 1989 | 25 906 | 504 | 678 | 57 236 | 35 222 |
| 1990 | 28 534 | 546 | 728 | 57 411 | 35 300 |
| 1991 | 32 321 | 585 | 792 | 57 801 | 35 467 |

(In all the following answers, set your index to 1987 = 100.)

(a) Turn the expenditure cash figures into an index number series.

(b) Calculate an index of 'real' NHS expenditure using the GDP deflator. How does this alter the expenditure series?

(c) Calculate an index of the volume of NHS expenditure using the NHS pay and prices index. How and why does this differ from the answer arrived at in (b)?

(d) Calculate indices of real and volume expenditure *per capita*. What difference does this make?

(e) Suppose that those not of working age cost twice as much to treat, on average, as those of working age. Construct an index of the need for health care and examine how health care expenditures have changed relative to need.

(f) How do you think the needs index calculated in (e) could be improved?

**Problem 10.12** (a) If $w$ represents the wage rate and $p$ the price level, what is $w/p$?

(b) If $\Delta w$ represents the annual growth in wages and $i$ is the inflation rate, what is $\Delta w - i$?

(c) What does $\ln(w) - \ln(p)$ represent? (ln = natural logarithm.)

**Problem 10.13** A firm is investing in a project and wishes to receive a rate of return of at least 15% on it. The stream of net income is:

| Year | 1 | 2 | 3 | 4 |
|---|---|---|---|---|
| Income | 600 | 650 | 700 | 400 |

(a) What is the present value of this income stream?

(b) If the investment costs £1600 should the firm invest? What is the net present value of the project?

**Problem 10.14** A firm uses a discount rate of 12% for all its investment projects. Faced with the following choice of projects, which yields the higher *NPV*?

| Project | Outlay | Income stream | | | | | |
|---|---|---|---|---|---|---|---|
| | | 1 | 2 | 3 | 4 | 5 | 6 |
| A | 5600 | 1000 | 1400 | 1500 | 2100 | 1450 | 700 |
| B | 6000 | 800 | 1400 | 1750 | 2500 | 1925 | 1200 |

**Problem 10.15**  Calculate the internal rate of return for the project in Problem 10.13. Use either trial and error methods or a computer to solve.

**Problem 10.16**  Calculate the internal rates of return for the projects in Problem 10.14.

**Problem 10.17**  (a)  Draw a Lorenz curve and calculate the Gini coefficient for the wealth data in Chapter 1 (Table 1.3).
(b)  Why is the Gini coefficient typically larger for wealth distributions than for income distributions?

**Problem 10.18**  (a)  Draw a Lorenz curve and calculate the Gini coefficient for the 1979 wealth data contained in Problem 1.5 (Chapter 1). Draw the Lorenz curve on the same diagram as you used in Problem 10.17.
(b)  How does the answer compare to 2001?

**Problem 10.19**  The following table shows the income distribution by quintile for the UK in 1991, for various definitions of income:

| Quintile | Income measure | | | |
|---|---|---|---|---|
| | Original | Gross | Disposable | Post-tax |
| 1 (bottom) | 2.0% | 6.7% | 7.2% | 6.6% |
| 2 | 7.0% | 10.0% | 11.0% | 11.0% |
| 3 | 16.0% | 16.0% | 16.0% | 16.0% |
| 4 | 26.0% | 23.0% | 23.0% | 23.0% |
| 5 | 50.0% | 44.0% | 42.0% | 44.0% |

(a)  Use equation (10.27) to calculate the Gini coefficient for each of the four categories of income.
(b)  For the 'original income' category, draw a smooth Lorenz curve on a piece of gridded paper and calculate the Gini coefficient using the method of counting squares. How does your answer compare to that for part (a)?

**Problem 10.20**  For the Kravis, Heston and Summers data (Table 10.26), combine the deciles into quintiles and calculate the Gini coefficient from the quintile data. How does your answer compare with the answer given in the text, based on deciles? What do you conclude about the degree of bias?

**Problem 10.21**  Calculate the three-firm concentration ratio for employment in the following industry:

| Firm | A | B | C | D | E | F | G | H |
|---|---|---|---|---|---|---|---|---|
| Employees | 3350 | 290 | 440 | 1345 | 821 | 112 | 244 | 352 |

**Problem 10.22**  Compare the degrees of concentration in the following two industries. Can you say which is likely to be more competitive?

| Firm | A | B | C | D | E | F | G | H | I | J |
|---|---|---|---|---|---|---|---|---|---|---|
| Sales | 337 | 384 | 696 | 321 | 769 | 265 | 358 | 521 | 880 | 334 |
| Sales | 556 | 899 | 104 | 565 | 782 | 463 | 477 | 846 | 911 | 227 |

**Problem 10.23**   The World Development Report contains data on the income distributions of many
**(Project)**   countries around the world (by quintile). Use these data to compare income distributions across countries, focusing particularly on the differences between poor countries,
middle-income and rich countries. Can you see any pattern emerging? Are there countries which do not fit into this pattern? Write a brief report summarising your findings.

**Reference**   L. Soltow, Long run changes in British income inequality, *Economic History Review*,
vol. 21(1), pp. 17–29, 1968.

## Answers to exercises

**Exercise 10.1**   (a)  100, 111.9, 140.7, 163.4, 188.1.

(b)  61.2, 68.5, 86.1, 100, 115.1.

(c)  115.1/61.2 = 1.881.

**Exercise 10.2**

|  | 1995 | 1996 | 1997 | 1998 | 1999 |
|---|---|---|---|---|---|
| (a)  1995 = 100 | 100 | 86.3 | 85.5 | 88.1 | 88.1 |
| (b)  1997 = 100 | 116.9 | 100.9 | 100 | 103.0 | 103.0 |
| (c)  Using '96 basket | 100 | 85.8 | 85.2 | 87.9 | 87.8 |

**Exercise 10.3**   The Paasche index is:

| 1995 | 1996 | 1997 | 1998 | 1999 |
|---|---|---|---|---|
| 100 | 85.7 | 85.1 | 87.8 | 87.3 |

**Exercise 10.4**   (a)  Expenditure shares in 1995 are:

|  | Expenditure | Share |
|---|---|---|
| Coal | 108.5 | 1.3% |
| Petroleum | 592.3 | 7.3% |
| Electricity | 4122.5 | 50.5% |
| Gas | 3342.9 | 40.9% |

giving the Laspeyres index for 1996 as

$$P_1^n = \frac{35.41}{37.27} \times 0.013 + \frac{98.33}{92.33} \times 0.073 + \frac{39.16}{40.07} \times 0.505 + \frac{0.464}{0.677} \times 0.409$$

$$= 0.8633 \text{ or } 86.33.$$

The expenditure shares in 1996 are 1.0%, 7.5%, 50.6%, 30.7% which allows the
1996 Paasche index to be calculated as

$$P_1^n = \frac{35.41}{37.27} \times 0.011 + \frac{98.33}{92.93} \times 0.083 + \frac{39.16}{40.07} \times 0.564 + \frac{0.464}{0.677} \times 0.342$$

$$= 0.8575 \text{ or } 85.75.$$

Later years can be calculated in similar fashion.

**Exercise 10.5**   (a/b) The Laspeyres and Paasche quantity indexes are:

|  | Laspeyres | Paasche |
|---|---|---|
| 1995 | 100 | 100 |
| 1996 | 104.27 | 103.93 |
| 1997 | 105.55 | 105.57 |
| 1998 | 105.88 | 106.29 |
| 1999 | 110.49 | 110.49 |

(c)   The expenditure index is 100, 89.72, 90.31, 93.67, 97.33.

(d)   The Paasche quantity index times Laspeyres price index (or vice versa) gives the expenditure index.

**Exercise 10.6**   The full index is (using Laspeyres indexes):

|  | Chain index |  |  |
|---|---|---|---|
| 2002 |  | 111.9 | 144.1 |
| 2003 |  | 111.3 | 160.4 |

| Year | Chain 1 | Chain 2 | Chain 3 | Full |
|---|---|---|---|---|
| 1991 | 100 |  |  | 100 |
| 1992 | 103.5 |  |  | 103.5 |
| 1993 | 107.8 |  |  | 107.8 |
| 1994 | 112.2 |  |  | 112.2 |
| 1995 | 119.8 | 100 |  | 119.8 |
| 1996 |  | 86.3 |  | 103.4 |
| 1997 |  | 85.5 |  | 102.5 |
| 1998 |  | 88.1 |  | 105.6 |
| 1999 |  | 88.1 | 100 | 105.5 |
| 2000 |  |  | 104.6 | 110.4 |
| 2001 |  |  | 116.7 | 128.8 |
| 2002 |  |  | 111.9 | 144.1 |
| 2003 |  |  | 111.3 | 160.4 |

**Exercise 10.7**   (a) The discounted figures are:

| Year | Investment/yield | Discount factor | Discounted yield |
|---|---|---|---|
| 0 | −100 000 |  |  |
| 1 | 25 000 | 0.9091 | 22 727.3 |
| 2 | 35 000 | 0.8264 | 28 925.6 |
| 3 | 30 000 | 0.7513 | 22 539.4 |
| 4 | 15 000 | 0.6830 | 10 245.2 |
| Total |  |  | 84 437.5 |

The present value is less than the initial outlay.

(b) The internal rate of return is 2.12%.

**Exercise 10.8**   (a)   Deflating to real income gives:

| Year | Investment/yield | Price index | Real income |
|---|---|---|---|
| 0 | −50 000 | 100 | −50 000.0 |
| 1 | 20 000 | 105 | 19 047.6 |
| 2 | 25 000 | 110.250 | 22 675.7 |
| 3 | 30 000 | 115.763 | 25 915.1 |
| 4 | 10 000 | 121.551 | 8 227.0 |

(b)     The real discount rate is 1.09/1.05 = 1.038 or 3.8% p.a.

(c/d)

| Nominal values | Discount factor | Discounted value | Real values | Discount factor | Discounted value |
|---|---|---|---|---|---|
| –50 000 | | | –50 000.0 | | |
| 20 000 | 0.917 | 18 348.6 | 19 047.6 | 0.963 | 18 348.6 |
| 25 000 | 0.842 | 21 042.0 | 22 675.7 | 0.928 | 21 042.0 |
| 30 000 | 0.772 | 23 165.5 | 25 915.1 | 0.894 | 23 165.5 |
| 10 000 | 0.708 | 7 084.3 | 8 227.0 | 0.861 | 7 084.3 |
| Totals | | 69 640.4 | | | 69 640.38 |

The present value is the same in both cases and exceeds the initial outlay.

**Exercise 10.9** (b)

| Range of income | Mid-point | Number of households | Total income | % Households | % Cumulative households | % Income | % Cumulative income |
|---|---|---|---|---|---|---|---|
| | | | | | $x$ | | $y$ |
| 0 | 100 | 6 213 | 621 300 | 21.6% | 21.6% | 4.5% | 4.5% |
| 200 | 300 | 8 585 | 2 575 500 | 29.9% | 51.5% | 18.5% | 23.0% |
| 400 | 500 | 5 308 | 2 654 000 | 18.5% | 70.0% | 19.1% | 42.0% |
| 600 | 700 | 3 579 | 2 505 300 | 12.5% | 82.5% | 18.0% | 60.0% |
| 800 | 900 | 2 036 | 1 832 400 | 7.1% | 89.6% | 13.2% | 73.2% |
| 1000 | 1250 | 2 989 | 3 736 250 | 10.4% | 100.0% | 26.8% | 100.0% |
| Totals | | 28 710 | 13 924 750 | 100.0% | | 100.0% | |

The Gini coefficient is then calculated as follows: B = 0.5 × {21.6 × (4.5 + 0) + 29.9 × (23.0 + 4.5) + 18.5 × (42.0 + 23.0) + 12.5 × (60.0 + 42.0) + 7.1 × (73.2 + 60.0) + 10.4 × (100 + 73.2)} = 3068.5. Area A = 5000 – 3068.5 = 1931.5. Hence Gini = 1931.5/5000 = 0.386, very similar to the value in the text using more categories of income.

**Exercise 10.10**   B = 100/5 × (246 – 50) = 3920. Hence A = 1080 and Gini = 0.216.

**Exercise 10.11**   $C_3$ = 290/400 = 72.5% and $C_5$ = 82.5%.

| **Appendix** | **Deriving the expenditure share form of the Laspeyres price index** |
|---|---|

We can obtain the expenditure share version of the formula from the standard formula given in equation (10.1):

$$P_L^n = \frac{\sum p_n q_0}{\sum p_0 q_0} = \frac{\sum \frac{p_n}{p_0} p_0 q_0}{\sum \frac{p_0}{p_0} p_0 q_0}$$

$$= \frac{\sum \frac{p_n}{p_0} \frac{p_0 q_0}{\sum p_0 q_0}}{\sum \frac{p_0}{p_0} \frac{p_0 q_0}{\sum p_0 q_0}} = \sum \frac{p_n}{p_0} \frac{p_0 q_0}{\sum p_0 q_0}$$

$$= \sum \frac{p_n}{p_0} \times s_0$$

which is equation (10.3) in the text.

# Important formulae used in this book

| Formula | Description | Notes |
|---|---|---|
| $\mu = \dfrac{\Sigma x}{N}$ | Mean of a population | Use when all individual observations are available |
| $\mu = \dfrac{\Sigma fx}{\Sigma f}$ | Mean of a population | Use with grouped data. $f$ represents the class frequencies |
| $\bar{x} = \dfrac{\Sigma x}{n}$ | Mean of a sample | $n$ is the number of observations in the sample |
| $\Xi = \dfrac{\Sigma fx}{\Sigma f}$ | Mean of a sample | Use with grouped data |
| $m = x_L + (x_U - x_L)\left\{\dfrac{\dfrac{N+1}{2} - F}{f}\right\}$ | Median (where data are grouped) | $x_L$ and $x_U$ represent the lower and upper limits of the interval containing the median. $F$ represents the cumulative frequency up to (but excluding) the interval |
| $\sigma^2 = \dfrac{\Sigma(x - \mu)^2}{N}$ | Variance of a population | |
| $\sigma^2 = \dfrac{\Sigma f(x - \mu)^2}{\Sigma f}$ | Population variance (grouped data) | |
| $s^2 = \dfrac{\Sigma(x - \bar{x})^2}{n - 1}$ | Sample variance | |
| $s^2 = \dfrac{\Sigma f(x - \bar{x})^2}{n - 1}$ | Sample variance (grouped data) | |
| $c.v. = \dfrac{\sigma}{\mu}$ | Coefficient of variation | |
| $z = \dfrac{x - \mu}{\sigma}$ | $z$ score | Measures the distance from observation $x$ to the mean $\mu$ measured in standard deviations |
| $\dfrac{\Sigma f(x - \mu)^3}{N\sigma^3}$ | Coefficient of skewness | |

| Formula | Description | Notes |
|---|---|---|
| $g = \sqrt[T-1]{\dfrac{x_T}{x_1}} - 1$ | Rate of growth | Measures the average rate of growth between years 1 and $T$ |
| $\sqrt[n]{\prod x}$ | Geometric mean (of $n$ observations on $x$) | |
| $P_L^n = \dfrac{\sum p_n q_0}{\sum p_0 q_0} \times 100$ | Laspeyres price index for year $n$ with base year 0 | |
| $P_L^n = \dfrac{\sum p_n}{\sum p_0} \times s_0 \times 100$ | Laspeyres price index using expenditure weights $s$ | |
| $P_P^n = \dfrac{\sum p_n q_n}{\sum p_0 q_n} \times 100$ | Paasche price index for year $n$ | |
| $P_P^n = \dfrac{1}{\sum \dfrac{p_0}{p_n} \times s_n} \times 100$ | Paasche price index using expenditure weights $s$ | |
| $Q_L^n = \dfrac{\sum q_n p_0}{\sum q_0 p_0} \times 100$ | Laspeyres quantity index | |
| $Q_P^n = \dfrac{\sum q_n p_n}{\sum q_0 p_n} \times 100$ | Paasche quantity index | |
| $E^n = \dfrac{\sum p_n q_n}{\sum p_0 q_0} \times 100$ | Expenditure index | |
| $PV = \dfrac{S}{(1 + r)^t}$ | Present value | The value now of a sum $S$ to be received in $t$ years' time, using discount rate $r$ |
| $NPV = -S_0 + \sum \dfrac{S_t}{(1 + r)^t}$ | Net present value | The value of an investment $S_0$ now, yielding $S_t$ per annum, discounted at a constant rate $r$ |
| $nCr = \dfrac{n!}{r!(n - r)!}$ | Combinatorial formula | $n! = n \times (n - 1) \times \ldots \times 1$ |
| $Pr(r) = nCr \times P^r \times (1 - P)^{n-r}$ | Binomial distribution | In shorthand notation, $r \sim B(n, P)$ |
| $Pr(x) = \dfrac{1}{\sigma\sqrt{2\pi}} e^{-\frac{1}{2}\left\{\frac{x-\mu}{\sigma}\right\}^2}$ | Normal distribution | In shorthand notation, $x \sim N(\mu, \sigma^2)$ |
| $\bar{x} \pm 1.96\sqrt{s^2/n}$ | 95% confidence interval for the mean | Large samples, using Normal distribution |

| Formula | Description | Notes |
|---|---|---|
| $\bar{x} \pm t_v\sqrt{s^2/n}$ | 95% confidence interval for the mean | Small samples, using $t$ distribution. $t_v$ is the critical value of the $t$ distribution for $v = n - 1$ degrees of freedom |
| $p \pm 1.96\sqrt{\dfrac{p(1-p)}{n}}$ | 95% confidence interval for a proportion | Large samples only |
| $(\bar{x}_1 - \bar{x}_2) \pm 1.96\sqrt{\dfrac{s_1^2}{n_1} + \dfrac{s_2^2}{n_2}}$ | 95% confidence interval for the difference of two means | Large samples |
| $(\bar{x}_1 - \bar{x}_2) \pm t_v\sqrt{\dfrac{S^2}{n_1} + \dfrac{S^2}{n_2}}$ | 95% confidence interval for the difference of two means | Small samples. The pooled variance is given by $$S^2 = \dfrac{(n_1 - 1)s_1^2 + (n_2 - 1)s_2^2}{n_1 + n_2 - 2}$$ $v = n_1 + n_2 - 2$ |
| $z = \dfrac{\bar{x} - \mu}{\sqrt{s^2/n}}$ | Test statistic for $H_0$: mean $= \mu$ | Large samples. For small samples, distributed as $t$ with $v = n - 1$ degrees of freedom |
| $z = \dfrac{p - \pi}{\sqrt{\dfrac{\pi(1 - \pi)}{n}}}$ | Test statistic for $H_0$: true proportion $= \pi$ | Large samples |
| $z = \dfrac{(\bar{x}_1 - \bar{x}_2) - (\mu_1 - \mu_2)}{\sqrt{\dfrac{s_1^2}{n_1} + \dfrac{s_2^2}{n_2}}}$ | Test statistic for $H_0$: $\mu_1 - \mu_2 = 0$ | Large samples |
| $t = \dfrac{(\bar{x}_1 - \bar{x}_2) - (\mu_1 - \mu_2)}{\sqrt{\dfrac{S^2}{n_1} + \dfrac{S^2}{n_2}}}$ | Test statistic for $H_0$: $\mu_1 - \mu_2 = 0$ | Small samples. $S^2$ as defined above. Degrees of freedom $v = n_1 + n_2 - 2$ |
| $z = \dfrac{(p_1 - p_2) - (\pi_1 - \pi_2)}{\sqrt{\dfrac{\hat{\pi}(1 - \hat{\pi})}{n_1} + \dfrac{\hat{\pi}(1 - \hat{\pi})}{n_2}}}$ | Test statistic for $H_0$: $\pi_1 - \pi_2 = 0$ | Large samples $$\hat{\pi} = \dfrac{n_1 p_1 + n_2 p_2}{n_1 + n_2}$$ |
| $fpc = 1 - n/N$ | Finite population correction for the variance of $\bar{x}$ | |
| $\chi^2 = \sum \dfrac{(O - E)^2}{E}$ | Test statistic for independence in a contingency table | $v = (r - 1) \times (c - 1)$, where $r$ is the number of rows, $c$ the number of columns |

| Formula | Description | Notes |
|---|---|---|
| $F = \dfrac{s_1^2}{s_2^2}$ | Test statistic for $H_0$: $\sigma_1^2 = \sigma_2^2$ | $v = n_1 - 1, n_2 - 1$. Place larger sample variance in the numerator to ensure rejection region is in right-hand tail of the $F$ distribution |
| $r = \dfrac{n\Sigma XY - \Sigma X \Sigma Y}{\sqrt{(n\Sigma X^2 - (\Sigma X)^2)(n\Sigma Y^2 - (\Sigma Y)^2)}}$ | Correlation coefficient | $-1 \leq r \leq 1$ |
| $t = \dfrac{r\sqrt{n-2}}{\sqrt{1-r^2}}$ | Test statistic for $H_0$: $\rho = 0$ | $v = n - 2$ |
| $r_s = 1 - \dfrac{6\Sigma d^2}{n(n^2-1)}$ | Spearman's rank correlation coefficient | $-1 \leq r_s \leq 1$. $d$ is the difference in ranks between the two variables |
| $b = \dfrac{n\Sigma XY - \Sigma X \Sigma Y}{n\Sigma X^2 - (\Sigma X)^2}$ | Slope of the regression line (simple regression) | |
| $a = \bar{Y} - b\bar{X}$ | Intercept (simple regression) | |
| $TSS = \Sigma Y^2 - n\bar{Y}^2$ | Total sum of squares | |
| $ESS = \Sigma Y^2 - a\Sigma Y - b\Sigma XY$ | Error sum of squares | |
| $RSS = TSS - ESS$ | Regression sum of squares | |
| $R^2 = \dfrac{RSS}{TSS}$ | Coefficient of determination | |
| $s_e^2 = \dfrac{ESS}{n-2}$ | Variance of the error term in regression | Replace $n - 2$ by $n - k - 1$ in multiple regression |
| $s_b^2 = \dfrac{s_e^2}{\Sigma(X-\bar{X})^2}$ | Variance of the slope coefficient in simple regression | |
| $s_a^2 = s_e^2 \times \sqrt{\dfrac{1}{n} + \dfrac{\bar{X}^2}{\Sigma(X-\bar{X})^2}}$ | Variance of the intercept in simple regression | |
| $b \pm t_v \times s_b$ | Confidence interval estimate for $b$ in simple regression | $t_v$ is the critical value of the $t$ distribution with $v = n - 2$ degrees of freedom |
| $t = \dfrac{b - \beta}{s_b}$ | Test statistic for $H_0$: $\beta = 0$ | $v = n - 2$ in simple regression, $n - k - 1$ in multiple regression |

| Formula | Description | Notes |
|---------|-------------|-------|
| $F = \dfrac{RSS/1}{ESS/(n-2)}$ | Test statistic for $H_0$: $R^2 = 0$ | $v = k, n - k - 1$ in multiple regression |
| $\hat{Y} \pm t_v \times s_e \sqrt{\dfrac{1}{n} + \dfrac{(X_P - \bar{X})^2}{\Sigma(X - \bar{X})^2}}$ | Confidence interval for a prediction (simple regression) at $X = X_P$ | $v = n - 2$ |
| $\hat{Y} \pm t_v \times s_e \sqrt{1 + \dfrac{1}{n} + \dfrac{(X_P - \bar{X})^2}{\Sigma(X - \bar{X})^2}}$ | Confidence interval for an observation on $Y$ at $X = X_P$ | $v = n - 2$ |
| $F = \dfrac{(ESS_P - ESS_1)/n_2}{ESS_1/(n_1 - k - 1)}$ | Chow test for a prediction | First $n_1$ observations used for estimation, last $n_2$ for prediction |
| $DW = \dfrac{\Sigma(e_t - e_{t-1})^2}{\Sigma e_t^2}$ | Durbin–Watson statistic for testing autocorrelation | |
| $F = \dfrac{(ESS_R - ESS_U)/q}{ESS_U/(n - k - 1)}$ | Test statistic for testing $q$ restrictions in the regression model | $v = q, n - k - 1$ |

# Appendix: Tables

## Table A1  Random number table

This table contains 1000 random numbers within the range 0–99. Each number within the range has an equal probability of occurrence. The range may be extended by combining successive entries in the table. Thus 7399 (or 7323) becomes the first of 500 random numbers in the range 0–9999. To obtain a sample of random numbers, choose an arbitrary starting point in the table and go down the columns collecting successive values until the required sample is obtained. If the population has been numbered, this method can be used to select a random sample from the population. Alternatively, the method can simulate sampling experiments such as the tossing of a coin (an even number representing a head and an odd number a tail).

| 73 | 23 | 41 | 53 | 38 | 87 | 71 | 79 | 3 | 55 | 24 | 7 | 7 | 17 | 19 | 70 |
|----|----|----|----|----|----|----|----|----|----|----|----|----|----|----|----|
| 99 | 13 | 91 | 13 | 90 | 72 | 84 | 15 | 64 | 90 | 56 | 68 | 38 | 40 | 73 | 78 |
| 97 | 16 | 58 | 2 | 67 | 3 | 92 | 83 | 50 | 53 | 59 | 60 | 33 | 75 | 44 | 95 |
| 73 | 10 | 29 | 14 | 9 | 92 | 35 | 47 | 21 | 47 | 82 | 25 | 71 | 68 | 87 | 53 |
| 99 | 79 | 29 | 68 | 44 | 90 | 65 | 33 | 55 | 85 | 7 | 57 | 77 | 84 | 83 | 5 |
| 71 | 97 | 98 | 60 | 62 | 18 | 49 | 80 | 4 | 51 | 8 | 74 | 81 | 64 | 29 | 45 |
| 41 | 26 | 41 | 30 | 82 | 38 | 52 | 81 | 89 | 64 | 17 | 10 | 49 | 28 | 72 | 99 |
| 60 | 87 | 77 | 81 | 91 | 57 | 6 | 1 | 30 | 47 | 93 | 82 | 81 | 67 | 4 | 3 |
| 95 | 84 | 74 | 92 | 15 | 10 | 37 | 52 | 8 | 10 | 96 | 38 | 69 | 9 | 65 | 41 |
| 59 | 19 | 2 | 61 | 40 | 67 | 80 | 25 | 31 | 18 | 1 | 36 | 54 | 31 | 56 | 27 |
| 35 | 3 | 54 | 83 | 62 | 28 | 21 | 23 | 91 | 46 | 73 | 85 | 11 | 63 | 63 | 49 |
| 66 | 18 | 31 | 17 | 72 | 15 | 8 | 46 | 10 | 3 | 64 | 22 | 64 | 62 | 85 | 16 |
| 3 | 4 | 42 | 8 | 4 | 6 | 40 | 73 | 97 | 0 | 37 | 34 | 91 | 56 | 48 | 98 |
| 28 | 20 | 23 | 98 | 86 | 41 | 41 | 13 | 53 | 61 | 16 | 92 | 95 | 31 | 79 | 36 |
| 74 | 49 | 86 | 5 | 74 | 82 | 12 | 58 | 80 | 14 | 94 | 4 | 88 | 95 | 9 | 32 |
| 80 | 80 | 2 | 47 | 91 | 14 | 76 | 84 | 0 | 57 | 17 | 69 | 87 | 29 | 52 | 39 |
| 65 | 67 | 0 | 39 | 11 | 10 | 54 | 80 | 74 | 56 | 55 | 91 | 94 | 52 | 32 | 18 |
| 67 | 44 | 89 | 50 | 7 | 73 | 70 | 52 | 18 | 28 | 89 | 43 | 54 | 60 | 20 | 10 |
| 48 | 33 | 61 | 66 | 2 | 71 | 74 | 91 | 31 | 45 | 63 | 2 | 97 | 62 | 30 | 90 |
| 3 | 18 | 54 | 19 | 17 | 87 | 3 | 91 | 41 | 64 | 78 | 10 | 99 | 24 | 1 | 20 |
| 69 | 35 | 12 | 53 | 97 | 30 | 96 | 69 | 59 | 55 | 65 | 64 | 30 | 3 | 11 | 17 |
| 15 | 0 | 33 | 86 | 93 | 73 | 52 | 57 | 77 | 77 | 83 | 10 | 64 | 54 | 85 | 18 |
| 87 | 79 | 51 | 68 | 5 | 23 | 50 | 15 | 68 | 67 | 14 | 59 | 42 | 61 | 83 | 2 |
| 69 | 52 | 34 | 86 | 34 | 34 | 78 | 51 | 48 | 65 | 57 | 91 | 8 | 74 | 72 | 36 |
| 11 | 1 | 11 | 43 | 51 | 85 | 6 | 47 | 72 | 43 | 34 | 54 | 20 | 56 | 31 | 81 |
| 59 | 14 | 78 | 32 | 94 | 24 | 19 | 44 | 16 | 49 | 65 | 16 | 30 | 86 | 0 | 65 |
| 18 | 86 | 62 | 47 | 96 | 46 | 73 | 67 | 79 | 40 | 45 | 82 | 96 | 61 | 34 | 60 |
| 99 | 63 | 2 | 81 | 58 | 93 | 81 | 37 | 53 | 20 | 64 | 87 | 3 | 27 | 19 | 55 |
| 34 | 55 | 14 | 29 | 10 | 59 | 7 | 69 | 13 | 8 | 54 | 97 | 56 | 7 | 57 | 16 |
| 88 | 90 | 6 | 98 | 32 | 55 | 37 | 17 | 35 | 93 | 31 | 66 | 67 | 84 | 15 | 14 |

## Table A1 Continued

| | | | | | | | | | | | | | | | |
|---|---|---|---|---|---|---|---|---|---|---|---|---|---|---|---|
| 78 | 30 | 30 | 78 | 41 | 59 | 79 | 77 | 21 | 89 | 76 | 59 | 30 | 9 | 64 | 9 |
| 67 | 10 | 37 | 14 | 62 | 3 | 85 | 2 | 16 | 74 | 40 | 85 | 30 | 83 | 29 | 5 |
| 93 | 50 | 83 | 76 | 42 | 86 | 92 | 41 | 27 | 73 | 31 | 70 | 25 | 40 | 11 | 88 |
| 35 | 68 | 98 | 18 | 67 | 22 | 95 | 34 | 19 | 27 | 21 | 90 | 66 | 20 | 32 | 48 |
| 32 | 52 | 29 | 78 | 68 | 96 | 94 | 44 | 38 | 95 | 27 | 85 | 53 | 76 | 63 | 78 |
| 92 | 68 | 75 | 77 | 26 | 39 | 61 | 33 | 88 | 66 | 77 | 76 | 25 | 67 | 90 | 1 |
| 40 | 73 | 28 | 5 | 50 | 73 | 92 | 32 | 82 | 23 | 78 | 30 | 26 | 52 | 28 | 94 |
| 57 | 41 | 64 | 50 | 78 | 35 | 12 | 60 | 25 | 4 | 5 | 82 | 82 | 57 | 68 | 43 |
| 82 | 41 | 67 | 79 | 30 | 43 | 15 | 72 | 98 | 48 | 6 | 22 | 46 | 92 | 43 | 41 |
| 60 | 11 | 21 | 44 | 43 | 51 | 76 | 89 | 4 | 90 | 48 | 31 | 19 | 89 | 97 | 45 |
| 94 | 8 | 20 | 67 | 32 | 42 | 39 | 6 | 38 | 25 | 97 | 10 | 18 | 85 | 9 | 60 |
| 21 | 59 | 27 | 39 | 13 | 81 | 2 | 47 | 83 | 12 | 17 | 54 | 84 | 68 | 56 | 29 |
| 63 | 62 | 36 | 6 | 57 | 96 | 6 | 36 | 24 | 13 | 70 | 32 | 90 | 92 | 81 | 86 |
| 91 | 42 | 57 | 99 | 55 | 31 | 58 | 21 | 21 | 65 | 70 | 4 | 37 | 28 | 59 | 9 |
| 91 | 27 | 61 | 86 | 36 | 57 | 11 | 35 | 92 | 15 | 79 | 30 | 19 | 85 | 39 | 49 |
| 97 | 39 | 12 | 28 | 35 | 37 | 90 | 93 | 88 | 20 | 99 | 76 | 81 | 61 | 95 | 70 |
| 64 | 89 | 32 | 80 | 9 | 66 | 73 | 71 | 84 | 69 | 70 | 12 | 10 | 56 | 59 | 56 |
| 45 | 34 | 1 | 32 | 80 | 99 | 39 | 52 | 25 | 87 | 76 | 91 | 22 | 26 | 46 | 67 |
| 21 | 65 | 14 | 1 | 78 | 35 | 35 | 63 | 21 | 66 | 34 | 3 | 47 | 51 | 24 | 37 |
| 85 | 64 | 69 | 93 | 47 | 82 | 55 | 87 | 22 | 56 | 53 | 85 | 43 | 66 | 23 | 66 |
| 21 | 37 | 62 | 29 | 44 | 39 | 4 | 4 | 99 | 3 | 6 | 82 | 67 | 53 | 14 | 0 |
| 23 | 8 | 62 | 9 | 19 | 31 | 81 | 92 | 63 | 10 | 65 | 78 | 79 | 96 | 65 | 33 |
| 84 | 14 | 92 | 85 | 9 | 16 | 51 | 70 | 26 | 60 | 7 | 7 | 55 | 66 | 5 | 51 |
| 70 | 37 | 11 | 7 | 93 | 63 | 48 | 12 | 35 | 95 | 32 | 5 | 64 | 5 | 63 | 28 |
| 80 | 27 | 32 | 92 | 81 | 27 | 55 | 98 | 71 | 22 | 66 | 64 | 78 | 79 | 34 | 73 |
| 66 | 13 | 16 | 48 | 74 | 51 | 78 | 83 | 42 | 31 | 97 | 72 | 25 | 75 | 34 | 40 |
| 1 | 51 | 47 | 84 | 82 | 27 | 77 | 40 | 99 | 13 | 66 | 52 | 56 | 27 | 2 | 19 |
| 84 | 26 | 0 | 38 | 55 | 30 | 45 | 80 | 50 | 20 | 17 | 78 | 87 | 4 | 88 | 86 |
| 95 | 28 | 57 | 33 | 51 | 39 | 18 | 12 | 37 | 6 | 89 | 63 | 22 | 50 | 10 | 22 |
| 45 | 76 | 48 | 43 | 18 | 24 | 19 | 1 | 65 | 93 | 16 | 48 | 8 | 60 | 32 | 76 |

### Table A2 The standard Normal distribution

| z | 0.00 | 0.01 | 0.02 | 0.03 | 0.04 | 0.05 | 0.06 | 0.07 | 0.08 | 0.09 |
|---|------|------|------|------|------|------|------|------|------|------|
| 0.0 | .5000 | .4960 | .4920 | .4880 | .4840 | .4801 | .4761 | .4721 | .4681 | .4641 |
| 0.1 | .4602 | .4562 | .4522 | .4483 | .4443 | .4404 | .4364 | .4325 | .4286 | .4247 |
| 0.2 | .4207 | .4168 | .4129 | .4090 | .4052 | .4013 | .3974 | .3936 | .3897 | .3859 |
| 0.3 | .3821 | .3783 | .3745 | .3707 | .3669 | .3632 | .3594 | .3557 | .3520 | .3483 |
| 0.4 | .3446 | .3409 | .3372 | .3336 | .3300 | .3264 | .3228 | .3192 | .3156 | .3121 |
| 0.5 | .3085 | .3050 | .3015 | .2981 | .2946 | .2912 | .2877 | .2843 | .2810 | .2776 |
| 0.6 | .2743 | .2709 | .2676 | .2643 | .2611 | .2578 | .2546 | .2514 | .2483 | .2451 |
| 0.7 | .2420 | .2389 | .2358 | .2327 | .2296 | .2266 | .2236 | .2206 | .2177 | .2148 |
| 0.8 | .2119 | .2090 | .2061 | .2033 | .2005 | .1977 | .1949 | .1922 | .1894 | .1867 |
| 0.9 | .1841 | .1814 | .1788 | .1762 | .1736 | .1711 | .1685 | .1660 | .1635 | .1611 |
| 1.0 | .1587 | .1562 | .1539 | .1515 | .1492 | .1469 | .1446 | .1423 | .1401 | .1379 |
| 1.1 | .1357 | .1335 | .1314 | .1292 | .1271 | .1251 | .1230 | .1210 | .1190 | .1170 |
| 1.2 | .1151 | .1131 | .1112 | .1093 | .1075 | .1056 | .1038 | .1020 | .1003 | .0985 |
| 1.3 | .0968 | .0951 | .0934 | .0918 | .0901 | .0885 | .0869 | .0853 | .0838 | .0823 |
| 1.4 | .0808 | .0793 | .0778 | .0764 | .0749 | .0735 | .0721 | .0708 | .0694 | .0681 |
| 1.5 | .0668 | .0655 | .0643 | .0630 | .0618 | .0606 | .0594 | .0582 | .0571 | .0559 |
| 1.6 | .0548 | .0537 | .0526 | .0516 | .0505 | .0495 | .0485 | .0475 | .0465 | .0455 |
| 1.7 | .0446 | .0436 | .0427 | .0418 | .0409 | .0401 | .0392 | .0384 | .0375 | .0367 |
| 1.8 | .0359 | .0351 | .0344 | .0336 | .0329 | .0322 | .0314 | .0307 | .0301 | .0294 |
| 1.9 | .0287 | .0281 | .0274 | .0268 | .0262 | .0256 | .0250 | .0244 | .0239 | .0233 |
| 2.0 | .0228 | .0222 | .0217 | .0212 | .0207 | .0202 | .0197 | .0192 | .0188 | .0183 |
| 2.1 | .0179 | .0174 | .0170 | .0166 | .0162 | .0158 | .0154 | .0150 | .0146 | .0143 |
| 2.2 | .0139 | .0136 | .0132 | .0129 | .0125 | .0122 | .0119 | .0116 | .0113 | .0110 |
| 2.3 | .0107 | .0104 | .0102 | .0099 | .0096 | .0094 | .0091 | .0089 | .0087 | .0084 |
| 2.4 | .0082 | .0080 | .0078 | .0075 | .0073 | .0071 | .0069 | .0068 | .0066 | .0064 |
| 2.5 | .0062 | .0060 | .0059 | .0057 | .0055 | .0054 | .0052 | .0051 | .0049 | .0048 |
| 2.6 | .0047 | .0045 | .0044 | .0043 | .0041 | .0040 | .0039 | .0038 | .0037 | .0036 |
| 2.7 | .0035 | .0034 | .0033 | .0032 | .0031 | .0030 | .0029 | .0028 | .0027 | .0026 |
| 2.8 | .0026 | .0025 | .0024 | .0023 | .0023 | .0022 | .0021 | .0021 | .0020 | .0019 |
| 2.9 | .0019 | .0018 | .0018 | .0017 | .0016 | .0016 | .0015 | .0015 | .0014 | .0014 |
| 3.0 | .0013 | .0013 | .0013 | .0012 | .0012 | .0011 | .0011 | .0011 | .0010 | .0010 |

## Table A3 Percentage points of the *t* distribution

The table gives critical values of the *t* distribution cutting off an area $\alpha$ in each tail, shown by the top row of the table.

| | | | | Area ($\alpha$) in each tail | | | | | |
|---|---|---|---|---|---|---|---|---|---|
| $v$ | 0.4 | 0.25 | 0.1 | 0.05 | 0.025 | 0.01 | 0.005 | 0.0025 | 0.001 | 0.0005 |
| 1 | 0.325 | 1.000 | 3.078 | 6.314 | 12.706 | 31.821 | 63.657 | 127.320 | 318.310 | 636.620 |
| 2 | 0.289 | 0.816 | 1.886 | 2.920 | 4.303 | 6.965 | 9.925 | 14.089 | 22.327 | 31.598 |
| 3 | 0.277 | 0.765 | 1.638 | 2.353 | 3.182 | 4.541 | 5.841 | 7.453 | 10.214 | 12.924 |
| 4 | 0.271 | 0.741 | 1.533 | 2.132 | 2.776 | 3.747 | 4.604 | 5.598 | 7.173 | 8.610 |
| 5 | 0.267 | 0.727 | 1.476 | 2.015 | 2.571 | 3.365 | 4.032 | 4.773 | 5.893 | 6.869 |
| 6 | 0.265 | 0.718 | 1.440 | 1.943 | 2.447 | 3.143 | 3.707 | 4.317 | 5.208 | 5.959 |
| 7 | 0.263 | 0.711 | 1.415 | 1.895 | 2.365 | 2.998 | 3.499 | 4.029 | 4.785 | 5.408 |
| 8 | 0.262 | 0.706 | 1.397 | 1.860 | 2.306 | 2.896 | 3.355 | 3.833 | 4.501 | 5.041 |
| 9 | 0.261 | 0.703 | 1.383 | 1.833 | 2.262 | 2.821 | 3.250 | 3.690 | 4.297 | 4.781 |
| 10 | 0.260 | 0.700 | 1.372 | 1.812 | 2.228 | 2.764 | 3.169 | 3.581 | 4.144 | 4.587 |
| 11 | 0.260 | 0.697 | 1.363 | 1.796 | 2.201 | 2.718 | 3.106 | 3.497 | 4.025 | 4.437 |
| 12 | 0.259 | 0.695 | 1.356 | 1.782 | 2.179 | 2.681 | 3.055 | 3.428 | 3.930 | 4.318 |
| 13 | 0.259 | 0.694 | 1.350 | 1.771 | 2.160 | 2.650 | 3.012 | 3.372 | 3.852 | 4.221 |
| 14 | 0.258 | 0.692 | 1.345 | 1.761 | 2.145 | 2.624 | 2.977 | 3.326 | 3.787 | 4.140 |
| 15 | 0.258 | 0.691 | 1.341 | 1.753 | 2.131 | 2.602 | 2.947 | 3.286 | 3.733 | 4.073 |
| 16 | 0.258 | 0.690 | 1.337 | 1.746 | 2.120 | 2.583 | 2.921 | 3.252 | 3.686 | 4.015 |
| 17 | 0.257 | 0.689 | 1.333 | 1.740 | 2.110 | 2.567 | 2.898 | 3.222 | 3.646 | 3.965 |
| 18 | 0.257 | 0.688 | 1.330 | 1.734 | 2.101 | 2.552 | 2.878 | 3.197 | 3.610 | 3.922 |
| 19 | 0.257 | 0.688 | 1.328 | 1.729 | 2.093 | 2.539 | 2.861 | 3.174 | 3.579 | 3.883 |
| 20 | 0.257 | 0.687 | 1.325 | 1.725 | 2.086 | 2.528 | 2.845 | 3.153 | 3.552 | 3.850 |
| 21 | 0.257 | 0.686 | 1.323 | 1.721 | 2.080 | 2.518 | 2.831 | 3.135 | 3.527 | 3.819 |
| 22 | 0.256 | 0.686 | 1.321 | 1.717 | 2.074 | 2.508 | 2.819 | 3.119 | 3.505 | 3.792 |
| 23 | 0.256 | 0.685 | 1.319 | 1.714 | 2.069 | 2.500 | 2.807 | 3.104 | 3.485 | 3.767 |
| 24 | 0.256 | 0.685 | 1.318 | 1.711 | 2.064 | 2.492 | 2.797 | 3.091 | 3.467 | 3.745 |
| 25 | 0.256 | 0.684 | 1.316 | 1.708 | 2.060 | 2.485 | 2.787 | 3.078 | 3.450 | 3.725 |
| 26 | 0.256 | 0.684 | 1.315 | 1.706 | 2.056 | 2.479 | 2.779 | 3.067 | 3.435 | 3.707 |
| 27 | 0.256 | 0.684 | 1.314 | 1.703 | 2.052 | 2.473 | 2.771 | 3.057 | 3.421 | 3.690 |
| 28 | 0.256 | 0.683 | 1.313 | 1.701 | 2.048 | 2.467 | 2.763 | 3.047 | 3.408 | 3.674 |
| 29 | 0.256 | 0.683 | 1.311 | 1.699 | 2.045 | 2.462 | 2.756 | 3.038 | 3.396 | 3.659 |
| 30 | 0.256 | 0.683 | 1.310 | 1.697 | 2.042 | 2.457 | 2.750 | 3.030 | 3.385 | 3.646 |
| 40 | 0.255 | 0.681 | 1.303 | 1.684 | 2.021 | 2.423 | 2.704 | 2.971 | 3.307 | 3.551 |
| 60 | 0.254 | 0.679 | 1.296 | 1.671 | 2.000 | 2.390 | 2.660 | 2.915 | 3.232 | 3.460 |
| 120 | 0.254 | 0.677 | 1.289 | 1.658 | 1.980 | 2.358 | 2.617 | 2.860 | 3.160 | 3.373 |
| $\infty$ | 0.253 | 0.674 | 1.282 | 1.645 | 1.960 | 2.326 | 2.576 | 2.807 | 3.090 | 3.291 |

## Table A4 Critical values of the $\chi^2$ distribution

The values in the table give the critical values of $\chi^2$ which cut off the area in the right-hand tail given at the top of the column.

$\chi^{2^*}$

| | | | | Area in right-hand tail | | | |
|---|---|---|---|---|---|---|---|
| $v$ | 0.995 | 0.990 | 0.975 | 0.950 | 0.900 | 0.750 | 0.500 |
| 1 | $392704.10^{-10}$ | $157088.10^{-9}$ | $982069.10^{-9}$ | $393214.10^{-8}$ | 0.0157908 | 0.1015308 | 0.454936 |
| 2 | 0.0100251 | 0.0201007 | 0.0506356 | 0.102587 | 0.210721 | 0.575364 | 1.38629 |
| 3 | 0.0717218 | 0.114832 | 0.215795 | 0.351846 | 0.584374 | 1.212534 | 2.36597 |
| 4 | 0.206989 | 0.297109 | 0.484419 | 0.710723 | 1.063623 | 1.92256 | 3.35669 |
| 5 | 0.411742 | 0.554298 | 0.831212 | 1.145476 | 1.61031 | 2.67460 | 4.35146 |
| 6 | 0.675727 | 0.872090 | 1.23734 | 1.63538 | 2.20413 | 3.45460 | 5.34812 |
| 7 | 0.989256 | 1.239043 | 1.68987 | 2.16735 | 2.83311 | 4.25485 | 6.34581 |
| 8 | 1.34441 | 1.64650 | 2.17973 | 2.73264 | 3.48954 | 5.07064 | 7.34412 |
| 9 | 1.73493 | 2.08790 | 2.70039 | 3.32511 | 4.16816 | 5.89883 | 8.34283 |
| 10 | 2.15586 | 2.55821 | 3.24697 | 3.94030 | 4.86518 | 6.73720 | 9.34182 |
| 11 | 2.60322 | 3.05348 | 3.81575 | 4.57481 | 5.57778 | 7.58414 | 10.3410 |
| 12 | 3.07382 | 3.57057 | 4.40379 | 5.22603 | 6.30380 | 8.43842 | 11.3403 |
| 13 | 3.56503 | 4.10692 | 5.00875 | 5.89186 | 7.04150 | 9.29907 | 12.3398 |
| 14 | 4.07467 | 4.66043 | 5.62873 | 6.57063 | 7.78953 | 10.1653 | 13.3393 |
| 15 | 4.60092 | 5.22935 | 6.26214 | 7.26094 | 8.54676 | 11.0365 | 14.3389 |
| 16 | 5.14221 | 5.81221 | 6.90766 | 7.96165 | 9.31224 | 11.9122 | 15.3385 |
| 17 | 5.69722 | 6.40776 | 7.56419 | 8.67176 | 10.0852 | 12.7919 | 16.3382 |
| 18 | 6.26480 | 7.01491 | 8.23075 | 9.39046 | 10.8649 | 13.6753 | 17.3379 |
| 19 | 6.84397 | 7.63273 | 8.90652 | 10.1170 | 11.6509 | 14.5620 | 18.3377 |
| 20 | 7.43384 | 8.26040 | 9.59078 | 10.8508 | 12.4426 | 15.4518 | 19.3374 |
| 21 | 8.03365 | 8.89720 | 10.28293 | 11.5913 | 13.2396 | 16.3444 | 20.3372 |
| 22 | 8.64272 | 9.54249 | 10.9823 | 12.3380 | 14.0415 | 17.2396 | 21.3370 |
| 23 | 9.26043 | 10.19567 | 11.6886 | 13.0905 | 14.8480 | 18.1373 | 22.3369 |
| 24 | 9.88623 | 10.8564 | 12.4012 | 13.8484 | 15.6587 | 19.0373 | 23.3367 |
| 25 | 10.5197 | 11.5240 | 13.1197 | 14.6114 | 16.4734 | 19.9393 | 24.3266 |
| 26 | 11.1602 | 12.1981 | 13.8439 | 15.3792 | 17.2919 | 20.8434 | 25.3365 |
| 27 | 11.8076 | 12.8785 | 14.5734 | 16.1514 | 18.1139 | 21.7494 | 26.3363 |
| 28 | 12.4613 | 13.5647 | 15.3079 | 16.9279 | 18.9392 | 22.6572 | 27.3362 |
| 29 | 13.1211 | 14.2565 | 16.0471 | 17.7084 | 19.7677 | 23.5666 | 28.3361 |
| 30 | 13.7867 | 14.9535 | 16.7908 | 18.4927 | 20.5992 | 24.4776 | 29.3360 |
| 40 | 20.7065 | 22.1643 | 24.4330 | 26.5093 | 29.0505 | 33.6603 | 39.3353 |
| 50 | 27.9907 | 29.7067 | 32.3574 | 34.7643 | 37.6886 | 42.9421 | 49.3349 |
| 60 | 35.5345 | 37.4849 | 40.4817 | 43.1880 | 46.4589 | 52.2938 | 59.3347 |
| 70 | 43.2752 | 45.4417 | 48.7576 | 51.7393 | 55.3289 | 61.6983 | 69.3345 |
| 80 | 51.1719 | 53.5401 | 57.1532 | 60.3915 | 64.2778 | 71.1445 | 79.3343 |
| 90 | 59.1963 | 61.7541 | 65.6466 | 69.1260 | 73.2911 | 80.6247 | 89.3342 |
| 100 | 67.3276 | 70.0649 | 74.2219 | 77.9295 | 82.3581 | 90.1332 | 99.3341 |

| $v$ | 0.250 | 0.100 | 0.050 | 0.025 | 0.010 | 0.005 | 0.001 |
|---|---|---|---|---|---|---|---|
| 1 | 1.32330 | 2.70554 | 3.84146 | 5.02389 | 6.63490 | 7.87944 | 10.828 |
| 2 | 2.77259 | 4.60517 | 5.99146 | 7.37776 | 9.21034 | 10.5966 | 13.816 |
| 3 | 4.10834 | 6.25139 | 7.81473 | 9.34840 | 11.3449 | 12.8382 | 16.266 |
| 4 | 5.38527 | 7.77944 | 9.48773 | 11.1433 | 13.2767 | 14.8603 | 18.467 |
| 5 | 6.62568 | 9.23636 | 11.0705 | 12.8325 | 15.0863 | 16.7496 | 20.515 |
| 6 | 7.84080 | 10.6446 | 12.5916 | 14.4494 | 16.8119 | 18.5476 | 22.458 |
| 7 | 9.03715 | 12.0170 | 14.0671 | 16.0128 | 18.4753 | 20.2777 | 24.322 |
| 8 | 10.2189 | 13.3616 | 15.5073 | 17.5345 | 20.0902 | 21.9550 | 26.125 |
| 9 | 11.3888 | 14.6837 | 16.9190 | 19.0228 | 21.6660 | 23.5894 | 27.877 |
| 10 | 12.5489 | 15.9872 | 18.3070 | 20.4832 | 23.2093 | 25.1882 | 29.588 |
| 11 | 13.7007 | 17.2750 | 19.6751 | 21.9200 | 24.7250 | 26.7568 | 31.264 |
| 12 | 14.8454 | 18.5493 | 21.0261 | 23.3367 | 26.2170 | 28.2995 | 32.909 |
| 13 | 15.9839 | 19.8119 | 22.3620 | 24.7356 | 27.6882 | 29.8195 | 34.528 |
| 14 | 17.1169 | 21.0641 | 23.6848 | 26.1189 | 29.1412 | 31.3194 | 36.123 |
| 15 | 18.2451 | 22.3071 | 24.9958 | 27.4884 | 30.5779 | 32.8013 | 37.697 |
| 16 | 19.3689 | 23.5418 | 26.2962 | 28.8454 | 31.9999 | 34.2672 | 29.252 |
| 17 | 20.4887 | 24.7690 | 27.5871 | 30.1910 | 33.4087 | 35.7185 | 40.790 |
| 18 | 21.6049 | 25.9894 | 28.8693 | 31.5264 | 34.8053 | 37.1565 | 42.312 |
| 19 | 22.7178 | 27.2036 | 30.1435 | 32.8523 | 36.1909 | 38.5823 | 43.820 |
| 20 | 23.8277 | 28.4120 | 31.4104 | 34.1696 | 37.5662 | 39.9968 | 45.315 |
| 21 | 24.9348 | 29.6151 | 32.6706 | 35.4789 | 38.9322 | 41.4011 | 46.797 |
| 22 | 26.40393 | 30.8133 | 33.9244 | 36.7807 | 40.2894 | 42.7957 | 48.268 |
| 23 | 27.1413 | 32.0069 | 35.1725 | 38.0756 | 41.6384 | 44.1813 | 49.728 |
| 24 | 28.2412 | 33.1962 | 36.4150 | 39.3641 | 42.9798 | 45.5585 | 51.179 |
| 25 | 29.3389 | 34.3816 | 37.6525 | 40.6465 | 44.3141 | 46.9279 | 52.618 |
| 26 | 30.4346 | 35.5632 | 38.8851 | 41.9232 | 45.6417 | 48.2899 | 54.052 |
| 27 | 31.5284 | 36.7412 | 40.1133 | 43.1945 | 46.9629 | 49.6449 | 55.476 |
| 28 | 32.6205 | 37.9150 | 41.3371 | 44.4608 | 48.2782 | 50.9934 | 56.892 |
| 29 | 33.7109 | 39.0875 | 42.5570 | 45.7223 | 49.5879 | 52.3356 | 58.301 |
| 30 | 34.7997 | 40.2560 | 43.7730 | 46.9792 | 50.8922 | 53.6720 | 59.703 |
| 40 | 45.6160 | 51.8051 | 55.7585 | 59.3417 | 63.6907 | 66.7660 | 73.402 |
| 50 | 56.3336 | 63.1671 | 67.5048 | 71.4202 | 76.1539 | 79.4900 | 86.661 |
| 60 | 66.9815 | 74.3970 | 79.0819 | 83.2977 | 88.3794 | 91.9517 | 99.607 |
| 70 | 77.5767 | 85.5270 | 90.5312 | 95.0232 | 100.425 | 104.215 | 112.317 |
| 80 | 88.1303 | 96.5782 | 101.879 | 106.629 | 112.329 | 116.321 | 124.839 |
| 90 | 98.6499 | 107.565 | 113.145 | 118.136 | 124.116 | 128.299 | 137.208 |
| 100 | 109.141 | 118.498 | 124.342 | 129.561 | 135.807 | 140.169 | 149.449 |

## Table A5(a) Critical values of the F distribution (upper 5% points)

The entries in the table give the critical values of $F$ cutting off 5% in the right-hand tail of the distribution. $v_1$ gives the degrees of freedom in the numerator, $v_2$ those in the denominator.

| $v_2$ \ $v_1$ | 1 | 2 | 3 | 4 | 5 | 6 | 7 | 8 | 9 |
|---|---|---|---|---|---|---|---|---|---|
| 1 | 161.45 | 199.50 | 215.71 | 224.58 | 230.16 | 230.99 | 236.77 | 238.88 | 240.54 |
| 2 | 18.513 | 19.000 | 19.164 | 19.247 | 19.296 | 19.330 | 19.353 | 19.371 | 19.385 |
| 3 | 10.128 | 9.5521 | 9.2766 | 9.1172 | 9.0135 | 8.9406 | 8.8867 | 8.8452 | 8.8123 |
| 4 | 7.7086 | 6.9443 | 6.5914 | 6.3882 | 6.2561 | 6.1631 | 6.0942 | 6.0410 | 5.9988 |
| 5 | 6.6079 | 5.7861 | 5.4095 | 5.1922 | 5.0503 | 4.9503 | 4.8759 | 4.8183 | 4.7725 |
| 6 | 5.9874 | 5.1433 | 4.7571 | 4.5337 | 4.3874 | 4.2839 | 4.2067 | 4.1468 | 4.0990 |
| 7 | 5.5914 | 4.7374 | 4.3468 | 4.1203 | 3.9715 | 3.8660 | 3.7870 | 3.7257 | 3.6767 |
| 8 | 5.3177 | 4.4590 | 4.0662 | 3.8379 | 3.6875 | 3.5806 | 3.5005 | 3.4381 | 3.3881 |
| 9 | 5.1174 | 4.2565 | 3.8625 | 3.6331 | 3.4817 | 3.3738 | 3.2927 | 3.2296 | 3.1789 |
| 10 | 4.9646 | 4.1028 | 3.7083 | 3.4780 | 3.3258 | 3.2172 | 3.1355 | 3.0717 | 3.0204 |
| 11 | 4.8443 | 3.9823 | 3.5874 | 3.3567 | 3.2039 | 3.0946 | 3.0123 | 2.9480 | 2.8962 |
| 12 | 4.7472 | 3.8853 | 3.4903 | 3.2592 | 3.1059 | 2.9961 | 2.9134 | 2.8486 | 2.7964 |
| 13 | 4.6672 | 3.8056 | 3.4105 | 3.1791 | 3.0254 | 2.9153 | 2.8321 | 2.7669 | 2.7144 |
| 14 | 4.6001 | 3.7389 | 3.3439 | 3.1122 | 2.9582 | 2.8477 | 2.7642 | 2.6987 | 2.6458 |
| 15 | 4.5431 | 3.6823 | 3.2874 | 3.0556 | 2.9013 | 2.7905 | 2.7066 | 2.6408 | 2.5876 |
| 16 | 4.4940 | 3.6337 | 3.2389 | 3.0069 | 2.8524 | 2.7413 | 2.6572 | 2.5911 | 2.5377 |
| 17 | 4.4513 | 3.5915 | 3.1968 | 2.9647 | 2.8100 | 2.6987 | 2.6143 | 2.5480 | 2.4943 |
| 18 | 4.4139 | 3.5546 | 3.1599 | 2.9277 | 2.7729 | 2.6613 | 2.5767 | 2.5102 | 2.4563 |
| 19 | 4.3807 | 3.5219 | 3.1274 | 2.8951 | 2.7401 | 2.6283 | 2.5435 | 2.4768 | 2.4227 |
| 20 | 4.3512 | 3.4928 | 2.0984 | 2.8661 | 2.7109 | 2.5990 | 2.5140 | 2.4471 | 2.3928 |
| 21 | 4.3248 | 3.4668 | 3.0725 | 2.8401 | 2.6848 | 2.5727 | 2.4876 | 2.4205 | 2.3660 |
| 22 | 4.3009 | 3.4434 | 3.0491 | 2.8167 | 2.6613 | 2.5491 | 2.4638 | 2.3965 | 2.3419 |
| 23 | 4.2793 | 3.4221 | 3.0280 | 2.7955 | 2.6400 | 2.5277 | 2.4422 | 2.3748 | 2.3201 |
| 24 | 4.2597 | 3.4028 | 3.0088 | 2.7763 | 2.6307 | 2.5082 | 2.4226 | 2.3551 | 2.3002 |
| 25 | 4.2417 | 3.3852 | 2.9912 | 2.7587 | 2.6030 | 2.4904 | 2.4047 | 2.3371 | 2.2821 |
| 26 | 4.2252 | 3.3690 | 2.9752 | 2.7426 | 2.5868 | 2.4741 | 2.3883 | 2.3205 | 2.2655 |
| 27 | 4.2100 | 3.3541 | 2.9604 | 2.7278 | 2.5719 | 2.4591 | 2.3732 | 2.3053 | 2.2501 |
| 28 | 4.1960 | 3.3404 | 2.9467 | 2.7141 | 2.5581 | 2.4453 | 2.3593 | 2.2913 | 2.2360 |
| 29 | 4.1830 | 3.3277 | 2.9340 | 2.7014 | 2.5454 | 2.4324 | 2.3463 | 2.2783 | 2.2229 |
| 30 | 4.1709 | 3.3158 | 2.9223 | 2.6896 | 2.5336 | 2.4205 | 2.3343 | 2.2662 | 2.2107 |
| 40 | 4.0847 | 3.2317 | 2.8387 | 2.6060 | 2.4495 | 2.3359 | 2.2490 | 2.1802 | 2.1240 |
| 60 | 4.0012 | 3.1504 | 2.7581 | 2.5252 | 2.3683 | 2.2541 | 2.1665 | 2.0970 | 2.0401 |
| 120 | 3.9201 | 3.0718 | 2.6802 | 2.4472 | 2.2899 | 2.1750 | 2.0868 | 2.0164 | 1.9588 |
| ∞ | 3.8415 | 2.9957 | 2.6049 | 2.3719 | 2.2141 | 2.0986 | 2.0096 | 1.9384 | 1.8799 |

| $v_1$<br>$v_2$ | 10 | 12 | 15 | 20 | 24 | 30 | 40 | 60 | 120 | ∞ |
|---|---|---|---|---|---|---|---|---|---|---|
| 1 | 241.88 | 243.91 | 245.95 | 248.01 | 249.05 | 250.10 | 251.14 | 252.20 | 253.25 | 254.31 |
| 2 | 19.396 | 19.413 | 19.429 | 19.446 | 19.454 | 19.462 | 19.471 | 19.479 | 19.487 | 19.496 |
| 3 | 8.7855 | 8.7446 | 8.7029 | 8.6602 | 8.6385 | 8.6166 | 8.5944 | 8.5720 | 8.5494 | 8.5264 |
| 4 | 5.9644 | 5.9117 | 5.8578 | 5.8025 | 5.7744 | 5.7459 | 5.7170 | 5.6877 | 5.6581 | 5.6281 |
| 5 | 4.7351 | 4.6777 | 4.6188 | 4.5581 | 4.5272 | 4.4957 | 4.4638 | 4.4314 | 4.3985 | 4.3650 |
| 6 | 4.0600 | 3.9999 | 3.9381 | 3.8742 | 3.8415 | 3.8082 | 3.7743 | 3.7398 | 3.7047 | 3.6689 |
| 7 | 3.6365 | 3.5747 | 3.5107 | 3.4445 | 3.4105 | 3.3758 | 3.3404 | 3.3043 | 3.2674 | 3.2298 |
| 8 | 3.3472 | 3.2839 | 3.2184 | 3.1503 | 3.1152 | 3.0794 | 3.0428 | 3.0053 | 2.9669 | 2.9276 |
| 9 | 3.1373 | 3.0729 | 3.0061 | 2.9365 | 2.9005 | 2.8637 | 2.8259 | 2.7872 | 2.7475 | 2.7067 |
| 10 | 2.9782 | 2.9130 | 2.8450 | 2.7740 | 2.7372 | 2.6996 | 2.6609 | 2.6211 | 2.5801 | 2.5379 |
| 11 | 2.8536 | 2.7876 | 2.7186 | 2.6464 | 2.6090 | 2.5705 | 2.5309 | 2.4901 | 2.4480 | 2.4045 |
| 12 | 2.7534 | 2.6866 | 2.6169 | 2.5436 | 2.5055 | 2.4663 | 2.4259 | 2.3842 | 2.3410 | 2.2962 |
| 13 | 2.6710 | 2.6037 | 2.5331 | 2.4589 | 2.4202 | 2.3803 | 2.3392 | 2.2966 | 2.2524 | 2.2064 |
| 14 | 2.6022 | 2.5342 | 2.4630 | 2.3879 | 2.3487 | 2.3082 | 2.2664 | 2.2229 | 2.1778 | 2.1307 |
| 15 | 2.5437 | 2.4753 | 2.4034 | 2.3275 | 2.2878 | 2.2468 | 2.2043 | 2.1601 | 2.1141 | 2.0658 |
| 16 | 2.4935 | 2.4247 | 2.3522 | 2.2756 | 2.2354 | 2.1938 | 2.1507 | 2.1058 | 2.0589 | 2.0096 |
| 17 | 2.4499 | 2.3807 | 2.3077 | 2.2304 | 2.1898 | 2.1477 | 2.1040 | 2.0584 | 2.0107 | 1.9604 |
| 18 | 2.4117 | 2.3421 | 2.2686 | 2.1906 | 2.1497 | 2.1071 | 2.0629 | 2.0166 | 1.9681 | 1.9168 |
| 19 | 2.3779 | 2.3080 | 2.2341 | 2.1555 | 2.1141 | 2.0712 | 2.0264 | 1.9795 | 1.9302 | 1.8780 |
| 20 | 2.3479 | 2.2776 | 2.2033 | 2.1242 | 2.0825 | 2.0391 | 1.9938 | 1.9464 | 1.8963 | 1.8432 |
| 21 | 2.3210 | 2.2504 | 2.1757 | 2.0960 | 2.0540 | 2.0102 | 1.9645 | 1.9165 | 1.8657 | 1.8117 |
| 22 | 2.2967 | 2.2258 | 2.1508 | 2.0707 | 2.0283 | 1.9842 | 1.9380 | 1.8894 | 1.8380 | 1.7831 |
| 23 | 2.2747 | 2.2036 | 2.1282 | 2.0476 | 2.0050 | 1.9605 | 1.9139 | 1.8648 | 1.8128 | 1.7570 |
| 24 | 2.2547 | 2.1834 | 2.1077 | 2.0267 | 1.9838 | 1.9390 | 1.8920 | 1.8424 | 1.7896 | 1.7330 |
| 25 | 2.2365 | 2.1649 | 2.0889 | 2.0075 | 1.9643 | 1.9192 | 1.8718 | 1.8217 | 1.7684 | 1.7110 |
| 26 | 2.2197 | 2.1479 | 2.0716 | 1.9898 | 1.9464 | 1.9010 | 1.8533 | 1.8027 | 1.7488 | 1.6906 |
| 27 | 2.2043 | 2.1323 | 2.0558 | 1.9736 | 1.9299 | 1.8842 | 1.8361 | 1.7851 | 1.7306 | 1.6717 |
| 28 | 2.1900 | 2.1179 | 2.0411 | 1.9586 | 1.9147 | 1.8687 | 1.8203 | 1.7689 | 1.7138 | 1.6541 |
| 29 | 2.1768 | 2.1045 | 2.0275 | 1.9446 | 1.9005 | 1.8543 | 1.8055 | 1.7537 | 1.6981 | 1.6376 |
| 30 | 2.1646 | 2.0921 | 2.0148 | 1.9317 | 1.8874 | 1.8409 | 1.7918 | 1.7396 | 1.6835 | 1.6223 |
| 40 | 2.0772 | 2.0035 | 1.9245 | 1.8389 | 1.7929 | 1.7444 | 1.6928 | 1.6373 | 1.5766 | 1.5089 |
| 60 | 1.9926 | 1.9174 | 1.8364 | 1.7480 | 1.7001 | 1.6491 | 1.5943 | 1.5343 | 1.4673 | 1.3893 |
| 120 | 1.9105 | 1.8337 | 1.7505 | 1.6587 | 1.6084 | 1.5543 | 1.4952 | 1.4290 | 1.3519 | 1.2539 |
| ∞ | 1.8307 | 1.7522 | 1.6664 | 1.5705 | 1.5173 | 1.4591 | 1.3940 | 1.3180 | 1.2214 | 1.0000 |

## Table A5(b) Critical values of the F distribution (upper 2.5% points)

The entries in the table give the critical values of F cutting off 2.5% in the right-hand tail of the distribution. $v_1$ gives the degrees of freedom in the numerator, $v_2$ in the denominator.

2.5%

$F^*$

| $v_2$ \ $v_1$ | 1 | 2 | 3 | 4 | 5 | 6 | 7 | 8 | 9 |
|---|---|---|---|---|---|---|---|---|---|
| 1 | 647.79 | 799.50 | 864.16 | 899.58 | 921.85 | 937.11 | 948.22 | 956.66 | 963.28 |
| 2 | 38.506 | 39.000 | 39.165 | 39.248 | 39.298 | 39.331 | 39.355 | 39.373 | 39.387 |
| 3 | 17.443 | 16.044 | 15.439 | 15.101 | 14.885 | 14.735 | 14.624 | 14.540 | 14.473 |
| 4 | 12.218 | 10.649 | 9.9792 | 9.6045 | 9.3645 | 9.1973 | 9.0741 | 8.9796 | 8.9047 |
| 5 | 10.007 | 8.4336 | 7.7636 | 7.3879 | 7.1464 | 6.9777 | 6.8531 | 6.7572 | 6.6811 |
| 6 | 8.8131 | 7.2599 | 6.5988 | 6.2272 | 5.9876 | 5.8198 | 5.6955 | 5.5996 | 5.5234 |
| 7 | 8.0727 | 6.5415 | 5.8898 | 5.5226 | 5.2852 | 5.1186 | 4.9949 | 4.8993 | 4.8232 |
| 8 | 7.5709 | 6.0595 | 5.4160 | 5.0526 | 4.8173 | 4.6517 | 4.5286 | 4.4333 | 4.3572 |
| 9 | 7.2093 | 5.7147 | 5.0781 | 4.7181 | 4.4844 | 4.3197 | 4.1970 | 4.1020 | 4.0260 |
| 10 | 6.9367 | 5.4564 | 4.8256 | 4.4683 | 4.2361 | 4.0721 | 3.9498 | 3.8549 | 3.7790 |
| 11 | 6.7241 | 5.2559 | 4.6300 | 4.2751 | 4.0440 | 3.8807 | 3.7586 | 3.6638 | 3.5879 |
| 12 | 6.5538 | 5.0959 | 4.4742 | 4.1212 | 3.8911 | 3.7283 | 3.6065 | 3.5118 | 3.4358 |
| 13 | 6.4143 | 4.9653 | 4.3472 | 3.9959 | 3.7667 | 3.6043 | 3.4827 | 3.3880 | 3.3120 |
| 14 | 6.2979 | 4.8567 | 4.2417 | 3.8919 | 3.6634 | 3.5014 | 3.3799 | 3.2853 | 3.2093 |
| 15 | 6.1995 | 4.7650 | 4.1528 | 3.8043 | 3.5764 | 3.4147 | 3.2934 | 3.1987 | 3.1227 |
| 16 | 6.1151 | 4.6867 | 4.0768 | 3.7294 | 3.5021 | 3.3406 | 3.2194 | 3.1248 | 3.0488 |
| 17 | 6.0420 | 4.6189 | 4.0112 | 3.6648 | 3.4379 | 3.2767 | 3.1556 | 3.0610 | 2.9849 |
| 18 | 5.9781 | 4.5597 | 3.9539 | 3.6083 | 3.3820 | 3.2209 | 3.0999 | 3.0053 | 2.9291 |
| 19 | 5.9216 | 4.5075 | 3.9034 | 3.5587 | 3.3327 | 3.1718 | 3.0509 | 2.9563 | 2.8801 |
| 20 | 5.8715 | 4.4613 | 3.8587 | 3.5147 | 3.2891 | 3.1283 | 3.0074 | 2.9128 | 2.8365 |
| 21 | 5.8266 | 4.4199 | 3.8188 | 3.4754 | 3.2501 | 3.0895 | 2.9686 | 2.8740 | 2.7977 |
| 22 | 5.7863 | 4.3828 | 3.7829 | 3.4401 | 3.2151 | 3.0546 | 2.9338 | 2.8392 | 2.7628 |
| 23 | 5.7498 | 4.3492 | 3.7505 | 3.4083 | 3.1835 | 3.0232 | 2.9023 | 2.8077 | 2.7313 |
| 24 | 5.7166 | 4.3187 | 3.7211 | 3.3794 | 3.1548 | 2.9946 | 2.8738 | 2.7791 | 2.7027 |
| 25 | 5.6864 | 4.2909 | 3.6943 | 3.3530 | 3.1287 | 2.9685 | 2.8478 | 2.7531 | 2.6766 |
| 26 | 5.6586 | 4.2655 | 3.6697 | 3.3289 | 3.1048 | 2.9447 | 2.8240 | 2.7293 | 2.6528 |
| 27 | 5.6331 | 4.2421 | 3.6472 | 3.3067 | 3.0828 | 2.9228 | 2.8021 | 2.7074 | 2.6309 |
| 28 | 5.6096 | 4.2205 | 3.6264 | 3.2863 | 3.0626 | 2.9027 | 2.7820 | 2.6872 | 2.6106 |
| 29 | 5.5878 | 4.2006 | 3.6072 | 3.2674 | 3.0438 | 2.8840 | 2.7633 | 2.6686 | 2.5919 |
| 30 | 5.5675 | 4.1821 | 3.5894 | 3.2499 | 3.0265 | 2.8667 | 2.7460 | 2.6513 | 2.5746 |
| 40 | 5.4239 | 4.0510 | 3.4633 | 3.1261 | 2.9037 | 2.7444 | 2.6238 | 2.5289 | 2.4519 |
| 60 | 5.2856 | 3.9253 | 3.3425 | 3.0077 | 2.7863 | 2.6274 | 2.5068 | 2.4117 | 2.3344 |
| 120 | 5.1523 | 3.8046 | 3.2269 | 2.8943 | 2.6740 | 2.5154 | 2.3948 | 2.2994 | 2.2217 |
| ∞ | 5.0239 | 3.6889 | 3.1161 | 2.7858 | 2.5665 | 2.4082 | 2.2875 | 2.1918 | 2.1136 |

| $v_1$ | 10 | 12 | 15 | 20 | 24 | 30 | 40 | 60 | 120 | ∞ |
|---|---|---|---|---|---|---|---|---|---|---|
| $v_2$ | | | | | | | | | | |
| 1 | 968.63 | 976.71 | 984.87 | 993.10 | 997.25 | 1001.4 | 1005.6 | 1009.8 | 1014.0 | 1018.3 |
| 2 | 39.398 | 39.415 | 39.431 | 39.448 | 39.456 | 39.465 | 39.473 | 39.481 | 39.400 | 39.498 |
| 3 | 14.419 | 14.337 | 14.253 | 14.167 | 14.124 | 14.081 | 14.037 | 13.992 | 13.947 | 13.902 |
| 4 | 8.8439 | 8.7512 | 8.6565 | 8.5599 | 8.5109 | 8.4613 | 8.4111 | 8.3604 | 8.3092 | 8.2573 |
| 5 | 6.6192 | 6.5245 | 6.4277 | 6.3286 | 6.2780 | 6.2269 | 6.1750 | 6.1225 | 6.069? | 6.0153 |
| 6 | 5.4613 | 5.3662 | 5.2687 | 5.1684 | 5.1172 | 5.0652 | 5.0125 | 4.9589 | 4.9044 | 4.8491 |
| 7 | 4.7611 | 4.6658 | 4.5678 | 4.4667 | 4.4150 | 4.3624 | 4.3089 | 4.2544 | 4.1989 | 4.1423 |
| 8 | 4.2951 | 4.1997 | 4.1012 | 3.9995 | 3.9472 | 3.8940 | 3.8398 | 3.7844 | 3.7279 | 3.6702 |
| 9 | 3.9639 | 3.8682 | 3.7694 | 3.6669 | 3.6142 | 3.5604 | 3.5055 | 3.4493 | 3.3918 | 3.3329 |
| 10 | 3.7168 | 3.6209 | 3.5217 | 3.4185 | 3.3654 | 3.3110 | 3.2554 | 3.1984 | 3.1399 | 3.0798 |
| 11 | 3.5257 | 3.4296 | 3.3299 | 3.2261 | 3.1725 | 3.1176 | 3.0613 | 3.0035 | 2.9441 | 2.8828 |
| 12 | 3.3736 | 3.2773 | 3.1772 | 3.0728 | 3.0187 | 2.9633 | 2.9063 | 2.8478 | 2.7874 | 2.7249 |
| 13 | 3.2497 | 3.1532 | 3.0527 | 2.9477 | 2.8932 | 2.8372 | 2.7797 | 2.7204 | 2.6590 | 2.5955 |
| 14 | 3.1469 | 3.0502 | 2.9493 | 2.8437 | 2.7888 | 2.7324 | 2.6742 | 2.6142 | 2.5519 | 2.4872 |
| 15 | 3.0602 | 2.9633 | 2.8621 | 2.7559 | 2.7006 | 2.6437 | 2.5850 | 2.5242 | 2.4611 | 2.3953 |
| 16 | 2.9862 | 2.8890 | 2.7875 | 2.6808 | 2.6252 | 2.5678 | 2.5085 | 2.4471 | 2.3831 | 2.3163 |
| 17 | 2.9222 | 2.8249 | 2.7230 | 2.6158 | 2.5598 | 2.5020 | 2.4422 | 2.3801 | 2.3153 | 2.2474 |
| 18 | 2.8664 | 2.7689 | 2.6667 | 2.5590 | 2.5027 | 2.4445 | 2.3842 | 2.3214 | 2.2558 | 2.1869 |
| 19 | 2.8172 | 2.7196 | 2.6171 | 2.5089 | 2.4523 | 2.3937 | 2.3329 | 2.2696 | 2.2032 | 2.1333 |
| 20 | 2.7737 | 2.6758 | 2.5731 | 2.4645 | 2.4076 | 2.3486 | 2.2873 | 2.2234 | 2.1562 | 2.0853 |
| 21 | 2.7348 | 2.6368 | 2.5338 | 2.4247 | 2.3675 | 2.3082 | 2.2465 | 2.1819 | 2.1141 | 2.0422 |
| 22 | 2.6998 | 2.6017 | 2.4984 | 2.3890 | 2.3315 | 2.2718 | 2.2097 | 2.1446 | 2.0760 | 2.0032 |
| 23 | 2.6682 | 2.5699 | 2.4665 | 2.3567 | 2.2989 | 2.2389 | 2.1763 | 2.1107 | 2.0415 | 1.9677 |
| 24 | 2.6396 | 2.5411 | 2.4374 | 2.3273 | 2.2693 | 2.2090 | 2.1460 | 2.0799 | 2.0099 | 1.9353 |
| 25 | 2.6135 | 2.5149 | 2.4110 | 2.3005 | 2.2422 | 2.1816 | 2.1183 | 2.0516 | 1.9811 | 1.9055 |
| 26 | 2.5896 | 2.4908 | 2.3867 | 2.2759 | 2.2174 | 2.1565 | 2.0928 | 2.0257 | 1.9545 | 1.8781 |
| 27 | 2.5676 | 2.4688 | 2.3644 | 2.2533 | 2.1946 | 2.1334 | 2.0693 | 2.0018 | 1.9299 | 1.8527 |
| 28 | 2.5473 | 2.4484 | 2.3438 | 2.2324 | 2.1735 | 2.1121 | 2.0477 | 1.9797 | 1.9072 | 1.8291 |
| 29 | 2.5286 | 2.4295 | 2.3248 | 2.2131 | 2.1540 | 2.0923 | 2.0276 | 1.9591 | 1.8861 | 1.8072 |
| 30 | 2.5112 | 2.4120 | 2.3072 | 2.1952 | 2.1359 | 2.0739 | 2.0089 | 1.9400 | 1.8664 | 1.7867 |
| 40 | 2.3882 | 2.2882 | 2.1819 | 2.0677 | 2.0069 | 1.9429 | 1.8752 | 1.8028 | 1.7242 | 1.6371 |
| 60 | 2.2702 | 2.1692 | 2.0613 | 1.9445 | 1.8817 | 1.8152 | 1.7440 | 1.6668 | 1.5810 | 1.4821 |
| 120 | 2.1570 | 2.0548 | 1.9450 | 1.8249 | 1.7597 | 1.6899 | 1.6141 | 1.5299 | 1.4327 | 1.3104 |
| ∞ | 2.0483 | 1.9447 | 1.8326 | 1.7085 | 1.6402 | 1.5660 | 1.4835 | 1.3883 | 1.2684 | 1.0000 |

## Table A5(c)  Critical values of the F distribution (upper 1% points)

The entries in the table give the critical values of $F$ cutting off 1% in the right-hand tail of the distribution. $v_1$ gives the degrees of freedom in the numerator, $v_2$ in the denominator.

| $v_2$ \ $v_1$ | 1 | 2 | 3 | 4 | 5 | 6 | 7 | 8 | 9 |
|---|---|---|---|---|---|---|---|---|---|
| 1 | 4052.2 | 4999.5 | 5403.4 | 5624.6 | 5763.6 | 5859.0 | 5928.4 | 5981.1 | 6022.5 |
| 2 | 98.503 | 99.000 | 99.166 | 99.249 | 99.299 | 99.333 | 99.356 | 99.374 | 99.388 |
| 3 | 34.116 | 30.817 | 29.457 | 28.710 | 28.237 | 27.911 | 27.672 | 27.489 | 27.345 |
| 4 | 21.198 | 18.000 | 16.694 | 15.977 | 15.522 | 15.207 | 14.976 | 14.799 | 14.659 |
| 5 | 16.258 | 13.274 | 12.060 | 11.392 | 10.967 | 10.672 | 10.456 | 10.289 | 10.158 |
| 6 | 13.745 | 10.925 | 9.7795 | 9.1483 | 8.7459 | 8.4661 | 8.2600 | 8.1017 | 7.9761 |
| 7 | 12.246 | 9.5466 | 8.4513 | 7.8466 | 7.4604 | 7.1914 | 6.9928 | 6.8400 | 6.7188 |
| 8 | 11.259 | 8.6491 | 7.5910 | 7.0061 | 6.6318 | 6.3707 | 6.1776 | 6.0289 | 5.9106 |
| 9 | 10.561 | 8.0215 | 6.9919 | 6.4221 | 6.0569 | 5.8018 | 5.6129 | 5.4671 | 5.3511 |
| 10 | 10.044 | 7.5594 | 6.5523 | 5.9943 | 5.6363 | 5.3858 | 5.2001 | 5.0567 | 4.9424 |
| 11 | 9.6460 | 7.2057 | 6.2167 | 5.6683 | 5.3160 | 5.0692 | 4.8861 | 4.7445 | 4.6315 |
| 12 | 9.3302 | 6.9266 | 5.9525 | 5.4120 | 5.0643 | 4.8206 | 4.6395 | 4.4994 | 4.3875 |
| 13 | 9.0738 | 6.7010 | 5.7394 | 5.2053 | 4.8616 | 4.6204 | 4.4410 | 4.3021 | 4.1911 |
| 14 | 8.8618 | 6.5149 | 5.5639 | 5.0354 | 4.6950 | 4.4558 | 4.2779 | 4.1399 | 4.0297 |
| 15 | 8.6831 | 6.3589 | 5.4170 | 4.8932 | 4.5556 | 4.3183 | 4.1415 | 4.0045 | 3.8948 |
| 16 | 8.5310 | 6.2262 | 5.2922 | 4.7726 | 4.4374 | 4.2016 | 4.0259 | 3.8896 | 3.7804 |
| 17 | 8.3997 | 6.1121 | 5.1850 | 4.6690 | 4.3359 | 4.1015 | 3.9267 | 3.7910 | 3.6822 |
| 18 | 8.2854 | 6.0129 | 5.0919 | 4.5790 | 4.2479 | 4.0146 | 3.8406 | 3.7054 | 3.5971 |
| 19 | 8.1849 | 5.9259 | 5.0103 | 4.5003 | 4.1708 | 3.9386 | 3.7653 | 3.6305 | 3.5225 |
| 20 | 8.0960 | 5.8489 | 4.9382 | 4.4307 | 4.1027 | 3.8714 | 3.6987 | 3.5644 | 3.4567 |
| 21 | 8.0166 | 5.7804 | 4.8740 | 4.3688 | 4.0421 | 3.8117 | 3.6396 | 3.5056 | 3.3981 |
| 22 | 7.9454 | 5.7190 | 4.8166 | 4.3134 | 3.9880 | 3.7583 | 3.5867 | 3.4530 | 3.3458 |
| 23 | 7.8811 | 5.6637 | 4.7649 | 4.2636 | 3.9392 | 3.7102 | 3.5390 | 3.4057 | 3.2986 |
| 24 | 7.8229 | 5.6136 | 4.7181 | 4.2184 | 3.8951 | 3.6667 | 3.4959 | 3.3629 | 3.2560 |
| 25 | 7.7698 | 5.5680 | 4.6755 | 4.1774 | 3.8550 | 3.6272 | 3.4568 | 3.3439 | 3.2172 |
| 26 | 7.7213 | 5.5263 | 4.6366 | 4.1400 | 3.8183 | 3.5911 | 3.4210 | 3.2884 | 3.1818 |
| 27 | 7.6767 | 5.4881 | 4.6009 | 4.1056 | 3.7848 | 3.5580 | 3.3882 | 3.2558 | 3.1494 |
| 28 | 7.6356 | 5.4529 | 4.5681 | 4.0740 | 3.7539 | 3.5276 | 3.3581 | 3.2259 | 3.1195 |
| 29 | 7.5977 | 5.4204 | 4.5378 | 4.0449 | 3.7254 | 3.4995 | 3.3303 | 3.1982 | 3.0920 |
| 30 | 7.5625 | 5.3903 | 4.5097 | 4.0179 | 3.6990 | 3.4735 | 3.3045 | 3.1726 | 3.0665 |
| 40 | 7.3141 | 5.1785 | 4.3126 | 3.8283 | 3.5138 | 3.2910 | 3.1238 | 2.9930 | 2.8876 |
| 60 | 7.0771 | 4.9774 | 4.1259 | 3.6490 | 3.3389 | 3.1187 | 2.9530 | 2.8233 | 2.7185 |
| 120 | 6.8509 | 4.7865 | 3.9491 | 3.4795 | 3.1735 | 2.9559 | 2.7918 | 2.6629 | 2.5586 |
| ∞ | 6.6349 | 4.6052 | 3.7816 | 3.3192 | 3.0173 | 2.8020 | 2.6393 | 2.5113 | 2.4073 |

| $v_1$ | 10 | 12 | 15 | 20 | 24 | 30 | 40 | 60 | 120 | ∞ |
|---|---|---|---|---|---|---|---|---|---|---|
| $v_2$ | | | | | | | | | | |
| 1 | 6055.8 | 6106.3 | 6157.3 | 6208.7 | 6234.6 | 6260.6 | 6286.8 | 6313.0 | 6339.4 | 6365.9 |
| 2 | 99.399 | 99.416 | 99.433 | 99.449 | 99.458 | 99.466 | 99.474 | 99.482 | 99.491 | 99.499 |
| 3 | 27.229 | 27.052 | 26.872 | 26.690 | 26.598 | 26.505 | 26.411 | 26.316 | 26.221 | 26.125 |
| 4 | 14.546 | 14.374 | 14.198 | 14.020 | 13.929 | 13.838 | 13.745 | 13.652 | 13.558 | 13.463 |
| 5 | 10.051 | 9.8883 | 9.7222 | 9.5526 | 9.4665 | 9.3793 | 9.2912 | 9.2020 | 9.1118 | 9.0204 |
| 6 | 7.8741 | 7.7183 | 7.5590 | 7.3958 | 7.3127 | 7.2285 | 7.1432 | 7.0567 | 6.9690 | 6.8800 |
| 7 | 6.6201 | 6.4691 | 6.3143 | 6.1554 | 6.0743 | 5.9920 | 5.9084 | 5.8236 | 5.7373 | 5.6495 |
| 8 | 5.8143 | 5.6667 | 5.5151 | 5.3591 | 5.2793 | 5.1981 | 5.1156 | 5.0316 | 4.9461 | 4.8588 |
| 9 | 5.2565 | 5.1114 | 4.9621 | 4.8080 | 4.7290 | 4.6486 | 4.5666 | 4.4831 | 4.3978 | 4.3105 |
| 10 | 4.8491 | 4.7059 | 4.5581 | 4.4054 | 4.3269 | 4.2469 | 4.1653 | 4.0819 | 3.9965 | 3.9090 |
| 11 | 4.5393 | 4.3974 | 4.2509 | 4.0990 | 4.0209 | 3.9411 | 3.8596 | 3.7761 | 3.6904 | 3.6024 |
| 12 | 4.2961 | 4.1553 | 4.0096 | 3.8584 | 3.7805 | 3.7008 | 3.6192 | 3.5355 | 3.4494 | 3.3608 |
| 13 | 4.1003 | 3.9603 | 3.8154 | 3.6646 | 3.5868 | 3.5070 | 3.4253 | 3.3413 | 3.2548 | 3.1654 |
| 14 | 3.9394 | 3.8001 | 3.6557 | 3.5052 | 3.4274 | 3.3476 | 3.2656 | 3.1813 | 3.0942 | 3.0040 |
| 15 | 3.8049 | 3.6662 | 3.5222 | 3.3719 | 3.2940 | 3.2141 | 3.1319 | 3.0471 | 2.9595 | 2.8684 |
| 16 | 3.6909 | 3.5527 | 3.4089 | 3.2587 | 3.1808 | 3.1007 | 3.0182 | 2.9330 | 2.8447 | 2.7528 |
| 17 | 3.5931 | 3.4552 | 3.3117 | 3.1615 | 3.0835 | 2.0032 | 2.9205 | 2.8348 | 2.7459 | 2.6530 |
| 18 | 3.5082 | 3.3706 | 3.2273 | 3.0771 | 2.9990 | 2.9185 | 2.8354 | 2.7493 | 2.6597 | 2.5660 |
| 19 | 3.4338 | 3.2965 | 3.1533 | 3.0031 | 2.9249 | 2.8442 | 2.7608 | 2.6742 | 2.5839 | 2.4893 |
| 20 | 3.3682 | 3.2311 | 3.0880 | 2.9377 | 2.8594 | 2.7785 | 2.6947 | 2.6077 | 2.5168 | 2.4212 |
| 21 | 3.3098 | 3.1730 | 3.0300 | 2.8796 | 2.8010 | 2.7200 | 2.6359 | 2.5484 | 2.4568 | 2.3603 |
| 22 | 3.2576 | 3.1209 | 2.9779 | 2.8274 | 2.7488 | 2.6675 | 2.5831 | 2.4951 | 2.4029 | 2.3055 |
| 23 | 3.2106 | 3.0740 | 2.9311 | 2.7805 | 2.7017 | 2.6202 | 2.5355 | 2.4471 | 2.3542 | 2.2558 |
| 24 | 3.1681 | 3.0316 | 2.8887 | 2.7380 | 2.6591 | 2.5773 | 2.4923 | 2.4035 | 2.3100 | 2.2107 |
| 25 | 3.1294 | 2.9931 | 2.8502 | 2.6993 | 2.6203 | 2.5383 | 2.4530 | 2.3637 | 2.2696 | 2.1694 |
| 26 | 3.0941 | 2.9578 | 2.8150 | 2.6640 | 2.5848 | 2.5026 | 2.4170 | 2.3273 | 2.2325 | 2.1315 |
| 27 | 3.0618 | 2.9256 | 2.7827 | 2.6316 | 2.5522 | 2.4699 | 2.3840 | 2.2938 | 2.1985 | 2.0965 |
| 28 | 3.0320 | 2.8959 | 2.7530 | 2.6017 | 2.5223 | 2.4397 | 2.3535 | 2.2629 | 2.1670 | 2.0642 |
| 29 | 3.0045 | 2.8685 | 2.7256 | 2.5742 | 2.4946 | 2.4118 | 2.3253 | 2.2344 | 2.1379 | 2.0342 |
| 30 | 2.9791 | 2.8431 | 2.7002 | 2.5487 | 2.4689 | 2.3860 | 2.2992 | 2.2079 | 2.1108 | 2.0062 |
| 40 | 2.8005 | 2.6648 | 2.5216 | 2.3689 | 2.2880 | 2.2034 | 2.1142 | 2.0194 | 1.9172 | 1.8047 |
| 60 | 2.6318 | 2.4961 | 2.3523 | 2.1978 | 2.1154 | 2.0285 | 1.9360 | 1.8363 | 1.7263 | 1.6006 |
| 120 | 2.4721 | 2.3363 | 2.1915 | 2.0346 | 1.9500 | 1.8600 | 1.7628 | 1.6557 | 1.5330 | 1.3805 |
| ∞ | 2.3209 | 2.1847 | 2.0385 | 1.8783 | 1.7908 | 1.6964 | 1.5923 | 1.4730 | 1.3246 | 1.0000 |

## Table A5(d) Critical values of the $F$ distribution (upper 0.5% points)

The entries in the table give the critical values of $F$ cutting off 0.5% in the right-hand tail of the distribution. $v_1$ gives the degrees of freedom in the numerator, $v_2$ in the denominator.

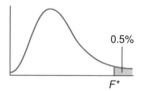

0.5%

$F^*$

| $v_2$ \ $v_1$ | 1 | 2 | 3 | 4 | 5 | 6 | 7 | 8 | 9 |
|---|---|---|---|---|---|---|---|---|---|
| 1 | 16211 | 20000 | 21615 | 22500 | 23056 | 23437 | 23715 | 23925 | 24091 |
| 2 | 198.50 | 199.00 | 199.17 | 199.25 | 199.30 | 199.33 | 199.36 | 199.37 | 199.39 |
| 3 | 55.552 | 49.799 | 47.467 | 46.195 | 45.392 | 44.838 | 44.434 | 44.126 | 43.882 |
| 4 | 31.333 | 26.284 | 24.259 | 23.155 | 22.456 | 21.975 | 21.622 | 21.352 | 21.139 |
| 5 | 22.785 | 18.314 | 16.530 | 15.556 | 14.940 | 14.513 | 14.200 | 13.961 | 13.772 |
| 6 | 18.635 | 14.544 | 12.917 | 12.028 | 11.464 | 11.073 | 10.786 | 10.566 | 10.391 |
| 7 | 16.236 | 12.404 | 10.882 | 10.050 | 9.5221 | 9.1553 | 8.8854 | 8.6781 | 8.5138 |
| 8 | 14.688 | 11.042 | 9.5965 | 8.8051 | 9.3018 | 7.9520 | 7.6941 | 7.4959 | 7.3386 |
| 9 | 13.614 | 10.107 | 8.7171 | 7.9559 | 7.4712 | 7.1339 | 6.8849 | 6.6933 | 6.5411 |
| 10 | 12.826 | 9.4270 | 8.0807 | 7.3428 | 6.8724 | 6.5446 | 6.3025 | 6.1159 | 5.9676 |
| 11 | 12.226 | 8.9122 | 7.6004 | 6.8809 | 6.4217 | 6.1016 | 5.8648 | 5.6821 | 5.5368 |
| 12 | 11.754 | 8.5096 | 7.2258 | 6.5211 | 6.0711 | 5.7570 | 5.5245 | 5.3451 | 5.2021 |
| 13 | 11.374 | 8.1865 | 6.9258 | 6.2335 | 5.7910 | 5.4819 | 5.2529 | 5.0761 | 4.9351 |
| 14 | 11.060 | 7.9216 | 6.6804 | 5.9984 | 5.5623 | 5.2574 | 5.0313 | 4.8566 | 4.7173 |
| 15 | 10.798 | 7.7008 | 6.4760 | 5.8029 | 5.3721 | 5.0708 | 4.8473 | 4.6744 | 3.5364 |
| 16 | 10.575 | 7.5138 | 6.3034 | 5.6378 | 5.2117 | 4.9134 | 4.6920 | 4.5207 | 4.3838 |
| 17 | 10.384 | 7.3536 | 6.1556 | 5.4967 | 5.0746 | 4.7789 | 4.5594 | 4.3894 | 4.2535 |
| 18 | 10.218 | 7.2148 | 6.0278 | 5.3746 | 3.9560 | 4.6627 | 4.4448 | 3.2759 | 4.1410 |
| 19 | 10.073 | 7.0935 | 5.9161 | 5.2681 | 4.8526 | 4.5614 | 4.3448 | 4.1770 | 4.0428 |
| 20 | 9.9439 | 6.9865 | 5.8177 | 5.1743 | 4.7616 | 4.4721 | 4.2569 | 4.0900 | 3.9564 |
| 21 | 9.8295 | 6.8914 | 5.7304 | 5.0911 | 4.6809 | 4.3931 | 4.1789 | 4.0128 | 3.8799 |
| 22 | 9.7271 | 6.8064 | 5.6524 | 5.0168 | 4.6088 | 4.3225 | 4.1094 | 3.9440 | 3.8116 |
| 23 | 9.6348 | 6.7300 | 5.5823 | 4.9500 | 3.5441 | 4.2591 | 4.0469 | 3.8822 | 3.7502 |
| 24 | 9.5513 | 6.6609 | 5.5190 | 4.8898 | 4.4857 | 4.2019 | 3.9905 | 3.8264 | 3.6949 |
| 25 | 9.4753 | 6.5982 | 5.4615 | 4.8351 | 4.4327 | 4.1500 | 3.9394 | 3.7758 | 3.6447 |
| 26 | 9.4059 | 6.5409 | 5.4091 | 4.7852 | 4.3844 | 4.1027 | 3.8928 | 3.7297 | 3.5989 |
| 27 | 9.3423 | 6.4885 | 5.3611 | 4.7396 | 4.3402 | 4.0594 | 3.8501 | 3.6875 | 3.5571 |
| 28 | 9.2838 | 6.4403 | 5.3170 | 4.6977 | 4.2996 | 4.0197 | 3.8110 | 3.6487 | 3.5186 |
| 29 | 9.2297 | 6.3958 | 5.2764 | 4.6591 | 4.2622 | 3.9831 | 3.7749 | 3.6131 | 3.4832 |
| 30 | 9.1797 | 6.3547 | 5.2388 | 4.6234 | 4.2276 | 3.9492 | 3.7416 | 3.5801 | 3.4504 |
| 40 | 8.8279 | 6.0664 | 4.9758 | 4.3738 | 3.9860 | 3.7129 | 3.5088 | 3.3498 | 3.2220 |
| 60 | 8.4946 | 5.7950 | 4.7290 | 4.1399 | 3.7599 | 3.4918 | 3.2911 | 3.1344 | 3.0083 |
| 120 | 8.1788 | 5.5393 | 4.4972 | 3.9207 | 3.5482 | 3.2849 | 3.0874 | 2.9330 | 2.8083 |
| ∞ | 7.894 | 5.2983 | 4.2794 | 3.7151 | 3.3499 | 3.0913 | 2.8968 | 2.7444 | 2.6210 |

| $v_1$ | 10 | 12 | 15 | 20 | 24 | 30 | 40 | 60 | 120 | ∞ |
|---|---|---|---|---|---|---|---|---|---|---|
| $v_2$ | | | | | | | | | | |
| 1 | 24224 | 24426 | 24630 | 24836 | 24940 | 25044 | 25148 | 25253 | 25359 | 25464 |
| 2 | 199.40 | 199.42 | 199.43 | 199.45 | 199.46 | 199.47 | 199.47 | 199.48 | 199.49 | 199.50 |
| 3 | 43.686 | 43.387 | 43.085 | 42.778 | 42.622 | 42.466 | 42.308 | 42.149 | 41.989 | 41.828 |
| 4 | 20.967 | 20.705 | 20.438 | 20.167 | 20.030 | 19.892 | 19.752 | 19.611 | 19.468 | 19.325 |
| 5 | 13.618 | 13.384 | 13.146 | 12.903 | 12.780 | 12.656 | 12.530 | 12.402 | 12.274 | 12.144 |
| 6 | 10.250 | 10.034 | 9.8140 | 9.5888 | 9.4742 | 9.3582 | 9.2408 | 9.1219 | 9.0015 | 8.8793 |
| 7 | 8.3803 | 8.1764 | 7.9678 | 7.7540 | 7.6450 | 7.5345 | 7.4224 | 7.3088 | 7.1933 | 7.0760 |
| 8 | 7.2106 | 7.0149 | 6.8143 | 6.6082 | 6.5029 | 6.3961 | 6.2875 | 6.1772 | 6.0649 | 5.9506 |
| 9 | 6.4172 | 6.2274 | 6.0325 | 5.8318 | 5.7292 | 5.6248 | 5.5186 | 5.4104 | 5.3001 | 5.1875 |
| 10 | 5.8467 | 5.6613 | 5.4707 | 5.2740 | 5.1732 | 5.0706 | 4.9659 | 4.8592 | 4.7501 | 4.6385 |
| 11 | 5.4183 | 5.2363 | 5.0489 | 4.8552 | 4.7557 | 4.6543 | 4.5508 | 4.4450 | 4.3367 | 4.2255 |
| 12 | 5.0855 | 4.9062 | 4.7213 | 4.5299 | 4.4314 | 4.3309 | 4.2282 | 5.1229 | 4.0149 | 3.9039 |
| 13 | 4.8199 | 4.6429 | 4.4600 | 4.2703 | 4.1726 | 4.0727 | 3.9704 | 3.8655 | 3.7577 | 3.6465 |
| 14 | 4.6034 | 4.4281 | 4.2468 | 4.0585 | 3.9614 | 3.8619 | 3.7600 | 3.6552 | 3.5473 | 3.4359 |
| 15 | 4.4235 | 4.2497 | 4.0698 | 3.8826 | 3.7859 | 3.6867 | 3.5850 | 3.4803 | 3.3722 | 3.2602 |
| 16 | 4.2719 | 4.0994 | 3.9205 | 3.7342 | 3.6378 | 3.5389 | 3.4372 | 3.3324 | 3.2240 | 3.1115 |
| 17 | 4.1424 | 3.9709 | 3.7929 | 3.6073 | 3.5112 | 3.4124 | 3.3108 | 3.2058 | 3.0971 | 2.9839 |
| 18 | 4.0305 | 3.8599 | 3.6827 | 3.4977 | 3.4017 | 3.3030 | 3.2014 | 3.0962 | 2.9871 | 2.8732 |
| 19 | 3.9329 | 3.7631 | 4.5866 | 3.4020 | 3.3062 | 3.2075 | 3.1058 | 3.0004 | 2.8908 | 2.7762 |
| 20 | 3.8470 | 3.6779 | 3.5020 | 3.3178 | 3.2220 | 3.1234 | 3.0215 | 2.9159 | 2.8058 | 2.6904 |
| 21 | 3.7709 | 3.6024 | 3.4270 | 3.2431 | 3.1474 | 3.0488 | 2.9467 | 2.7408 | 2.7302 | 2.6140 |
| 22 | 3.7030 | 3.5350 | 3.3600 | 3.1764 | 3.0807 | 2.9821 | 2.8799 | 2.7736 | 2.6625 | 2.5455 |
| 23 | 3.6420 | 3.4745 | 3.2999 | 3.1165 | 3.0208 | 2.9221 | 2.8197 | 2.7132 | 2.6015 | 2.4837 |
| 24 | 3.5870 | 3.4199 | 3.2456 | 3.0624 | 2.9667 | 2.8679 | 2.7654 | 2.6585 | 2.5463 | 2.4276 |
| 25 | 3.5370 | 3.3704 | 3.1963 | 3.0133 | 2.9176 | 2.8187 | 2.7160 | 2.6088 | 2.4961 | 2.3765 |
| 26 | 3.4916 | 3.3252 | 3.1515 | 2.9685 | 2.8728 | 2.7738 | 2.6709 | 2.5633 | 2.4501 | 2.3297 |
| 27 | 3.4499 | 3.2839 | 3.1104 | 2.9275 | 2.8318 | 2.7327 | 2.6296 | 2.5217 | 2.4079 | 2.2867 |
| 28 | 3.4117 | 3.2460 | 3.0727 | 2.8899 | 2.7941 | 2.6949 | 2.5916 | 2.4834 | 2.3690 | 2.2470 |
| 29 | 3.3765 | 3.2110 | 3.0379 | 2.8551 | 2.7594 | 2.6600 | 2.5565 | 2.4479 | 2.3331 | 2.2102 |
| 30 | 3.3440 | 3.1787 | 3.0057 | 2.8230 | 2.7272 | 2.6278 | 2.5241 | 2.4151 | 2.2998 | 2.1760 |
| 40 | 3.1167 | 2.9531 | 2.7811 | 2.5984 | 2.5020 | 2.4015 | 2.2958 | 2.1838 | 2.0636 | 1.9318 |
| 60 | 2.9042 | 2.7419 | 2.5705 | 2.3872 | 2.2898 | 2.1874 | 2.0789 | 1.9622 | 1.8341 | 1.6885 |
| 120 | 2.7052 | 2.5439 | 2.3727 | 2.1881 | 2.0890 | 1.9840 | 1.8709 | 1.7469 | 1.6055 | 1.4311 |
| ∞ | 2.5188 | 2.3583 | 2.1868 | 1.9998 | 1.8983 | 1.7891 | 1.6691 | 1.5325 | 1.3637 | 1.0000 |

### Table A6 Critical values of Spearman's rank correlation coefficient

Entries in the table show critical values of Spearman's rank correlation coefficient. The value at the top of each column shows the significance level for a two-tail test. For a one-tail test, the significance level is half that shown.

| N | 10% | 5% | 2% | 1% |
|---|---|---|---|---|
| 5 | 0.900 | – | – | – |
| 6 | 0.829 | 0.886 | 0.943 | – |
| 7 | 0.714 | 0.786 | 0.893 | – |
| 8 | 0.643 | 0.738 | 0.833 | 0.881 |
| 9 | 0.600 | 0.683 | 0.783 | 0.833 |
| 10 | 0.564 | 0.648 | 0.745 | 0.818 |
| 11 | 0.523 | 0.623 | 0.763 | 0.794 |
| 12 | 0.497 | 0.591 | 0.703 | 0.780 |
| 13 | 0.475 | 0.566 | 0.673 | 0.746 |
| 14 | 0.457 | 0.545 | 0.646 | 0.716 |
| 15 | 0.441 | 0.525 | 0.623 | 0.689 |
| 16 | 0.425 | 0.507 | 0.601 | 0.666 |
| 17 | 0.412 | 0.490 | 0.582 | 0.645 |
| 18 | 0.399 | 0.476 | 0.564 | 0.625 |
| 19 | 0.388 | 0.462 | 0.549 | 0.608 |
| 20 | 0.377 | 0.450 | 0.534 | 0.591 |
| 21 | 0.368 | 0.438 | 0.521 | 0.576 |
| 22 | 0.359 | 0.428 | 0.508 | 0.562 |
| 23 | 0.351 | 0.418 | 0.496 | 0.549 |
| 24 | 0.343 | 0.409 | 0.485 | 0.537 |
| 25 | 0.336 | 0.400 | 0.475 | 0.526 |
| 26 | 0.329 | 0.392 | 0.465 | 0.515 |
| 27 | 0.323 | 0.385 | 0.456 | 0.505 |
| 28 | 0.317 | 0.377 | 0.448 | 0.496 |
| 29 | 0.311 | 0.370 | 0.440 | 0.487 |
| 30 | 0.305 | 0.364 | 0.432 | 0.478 |

Source: *Annals of Statistics*, 1936 and 1949

**Table A7** **Critical values for the Durbin–Watson test at 5% significance level**

| Sample size | Number of explanatory variables | | | | | | | | | |
|---|---|---|---|---|---|---|---|---|---|---|
| | 1 | | 2 | | 3 | | 4 | | 5 | |
| $n$ | $d_L$ | $d_U$ | $d_L$ | $d_U$ | $d_L$ | $d_U$ | $d_L$ | $d_U$ | $d_L$ | $d_U$ |
| 10 | 0.879 | 1.320 | 0.697 | 1.641 | 0.525 | 2.016 | 0.376 | 2.414 | 0.243 | 2.822 |
| 11 | 0.927 | 1.324 | 0.758 | 1.604 | 0.595 | 1.928 | 0.444 | 2.283 | 0.316 | 2.645 |
| 12 | 0.971 | 1.331 | 0.812 | 1.579 | 0.658 | 1.864 | 0.512 | 2.177 | 0.379 | 2.506 |
| 13 | 1.010 | 1.340 | 0.861 | 1.562 | 0.715 | 1.816 | 0.574 | 2.094 | 0.445 | 2.390 |
| 14 | 1.045 | 1.350 | 0.905 | 1.551 | 0.767 | 1.779 | 0.632 | 2.030 | 0.505 | 2.296 |
| 15 | 1.077 | 1.361 | 0.946 | 1.543 | 0.814 | 1.750 | 0.685 | 1.977 | 0.562 | 2.220 |
| 20 | 1.201 | 1.411 | 1.100 | 1.537 | 0.998 | 1.676 | 0.894 | 1.828 | 0.792 | 1.991 |
| 25 | 1.288 | 1.454 | 1.206 | 1.550 | 1.123 | 1.654 | 1.038 | 1.767 | 0.953 | 1.886 |
| 30 | 1.352 | 1.489 | 1.284 | 1.567 | 1.214 | 1.650 | 1.143 | 1.739 | 1.071 | 1.833 |
| 35 | 1.402 | 1.519 | 1.343 | 1.584 | 1.283 | 1.653 | 1.222 | 1.726 | 1.160 | 1.803 |
| 40 | 1.442 | 1.544 | 1.391 | 1.600 | 1.338 | 1.659 | 1.285 | 1.721 | 1.230 | 1.786 |
| 50 | 1.503 | 1.585 | 1.462 | 1.628 | 1.421 | 1.674 | 1.378 | 1.721 | 1.335 | 1.771 |
| 100 | 1.654 | 1.694 | 1.634 | 1.715 | 1.613 | 1.736 | 1.592 | 1.758 | 1.571 | 1.780 |
| 200 | 1.758 | 1.778 | 1.748 | 1.789 | 1.738 | 1.799 | 1.728 | 1.810 | 1.718 | 1.820 |

# Answers to problems

## Chapter 1

**Problem 1.1**   (a)  Comparison is complicated by different numbers, but there are relatively more women in the 'Other' education category, relatively less in the 'higher' category.

        (b)  A higher proportion of women are 'inactive' or unemployed.

        (c)  The bar chart shows slightly more 'inactive' women.

        (d)  Relatively fewer women have no qualifications, A levels and higher education, but relatively more have other qualifications.

**Problem 1.3**   (a)  Higher education, 88%.

        (b)  Those in work, 20%.

**Problem 1.5**   The difference between bar chart and histogram should be similar to those for the 200 distribution. Overall shape similar (heavily skewed to right). Comparison difficult because of different wealth levels (due to inflation) and because grouping into classes can affect precise shape of graph.

**Problem 1.7**   (a)  Mean 16.399 (£000); median 8.92; mode 0–1 (£000) group has the greatest frequency density. They differ because of skewness in the distribution.

        (b)  Q1 = 3.295, Q3 = 18.339, IQR = 15.044; variance = 652.88; s.d. = 25.552; cv = 1.56.

        (c)  $95{,}469.32/25.55^3 = 5.72 > 0$ as expected.

        (d)  Comparison in text.

        (e)  This would increase the mean substantially (to 31.12), but the median and mode would be unaffected.

**Problem 1.9**   57.62 pence/litre.

**Problem 1.11**   (a)  $z = 1.5$ and $-1.5$ respectively.

        (b)  Using Chebyshev's theorem with $k = 1.5$, we have that at least $(1 - 1/1.5^2) = 0.56$ (56%) lies within 1.5 standard deviations of the mean, so at most 0.44 (44 students) lies outside the range.

        (c)  Chebyshev's theorem applies to *both* tails, so we cannot answer this part. You cannot halve the figure of 0.44 because the distribution may be skewed.

**Problem 1.13**   (a)  Strong upward trend for 1974–89, but substantial falls in 1972–74 and 1989–91. The market appears quite volatile, therefore. Note that this shows the *volume* of car registrations. *If* the 1972–76 pattern is repeated, one might expect car registrations to turn up again in 1992–93.

(b) This figure shows the substantial volatility of the series, around an average not much above zero. 1989–91 looks less like 1971–73 on this graph. The log graphs are very similar to the levels graphs. There is not always an advantage to drawing these. Here, the time period is relatively short and the growth rate rather small.

**Problem 1.15** (a) 1.81% p.a. (but 4.88% p.a. between 1975 and 1989).

(b) 0.187 (around the arithmetic mean).

(c) Registrations appear more volatile, as measured by the cv (10.33 for car registrations, 0.815 for investment). Possible reasons: investment covers several categories and fluctuations in one may offset those in another; the registrations series is shorter, so a big random fluctuation has a larger effect; investment is nominal and the price influence may help to smooth out the series.

**Problem 1.17** (a) Non-linear, upward trend. Likely to be positively autocorrelated. Variation around the trend is likely to grow over time (heteroscedasticity).

(b) Similar to (a), except trend would be shallower after deflating. Probably less heteroscedasticity because price variability has been removed, which may also increase the autocorrelation of the series.

(c) Unlikely to show a trend in the *very* long run, but there might be one over, say, five years, if inflation is increasing. Likely to be homoscedastic, with some degree of autocorrelation.

**Problem 1.19** (a) Using $S_t = S_0(1 - r)^t$, hence $S_0 = S_t/(1 + r)^t$. Setting $S_t = 1000$, $r = 0.07$ gives $S_0 = 712.99$. Price after two years: £816.30. If $r$ rose to 10% the bond would fall to $1000/1.1^3 = 751.31$.

(b) The income stream should be discounted to the present using

$$\frac{200}{1 + r} + \frac{200}{(1 + r)^2} + \ldots + \frac{200}{(1 + r)^5} = 820.04$$

so the bond should sell for £820.04. It is worth more than the previous bond because the return is obtained earlier.

**Problem 1.21** (a) 17.9% p.a. for BMW, 14% p.a. for Mercedes.

(b) Depreciated values are

| | | | | | |
|---|---|---|---|---|---|
| BMW 525i | 22 275 | 18 284 | 15 008 | 12 319 | 10 112 | 8 300 |
| Merc 200E | 21 900 | 18 833 | 16 196 | 13 928 | 11 977 | 10 300 |

which are close to actual values. Depreciation is initially slower than the average, then speeds up, for both cars.

**Problem 1.23** $E(x + k) = \dfrac{\Sigma(x + k)}{n} = \dfrac{\Sigma x + nk}{n} = \dfrac{\Sigma x}{n} + k = E(x) + k$

**Problem 1.25** The mistake is comparing non-comparable averages. A first-time buyer would have an above average mortgage and purchase a below average priced house, hence the amount of buyer's equity would be small.

## Answers to problems on $\Sigma$ notation

**Problem 1A.1**   20, 90, 400, 5, 17, 11.

**Problem 1A.3**   88, 372, 16, 85.

**Problem 1A.5**   113, 14, 110.

**Problem 1A.7**   $\dfrac{\Sigma f(x-k)}{\Sigma f} = \dfrac{\Sigma fx - k\Sigma f}{\Sigma f} = \dfrac{\Sigma fx}{\Sigma f} - k$

## Answers to problems on logarithms

**Problem 1C.1**   −0.8239, 0.17609, 1.17609, 2.17609, 3.17609, 1.92284, 0.96142, impossible!

**Problem 1C.3**   −1.89712, 0.40547, 2.70705, 5.41610, impossible!

**Problem 1C.5**   0.15, 12.58925, 125.8925, 1,258.925, $10^{12}$.

**Problem 1C.7**   15, 40.77422, 2.71828, 22 026.4658.

**Problem 1C.9**   3.16228, 1.38692, 1.41421, 0.0005787, 0.008.

## Chapter 2

**Problem 2.1**   (a)  4/52 or 1/13.

(b)  12/52 or 3/13.

(c)  1/2.

(d)  $4/52 \times 3/52 \times 2/52 = 3/17\ 576$ (0.017%).

(e)  $(4/52)^3 = 0.000455$.

**Problem 2.3**   (a)  0.25, 0.4, 5/9.

(b)  'Probabilities' are 0.33, 0.4, 0.5, which sum to 1.23. These cannot be real probabilities, therefore. The difference leads to an (expected) gain to the bookmaker.

(c)  Suppose the true probabilities of winning are proportional to the odds, i.e. 0.33/1.23, 0.4/1.23, 0.5/1.23, or 0.268, 0.325, 0.407. If £1 were bet on each horse, then the bookie would expect to pay out $0.268 \times 3 + 0.325 \times 1.5 + 0.407 \times 0.8 = 1.6171$, plus one of the £1 stakes, £2.62 in total. He would thus gain 38 pence on every £3 bet, or about 12.7%.

**Problem 2.5**   A number of factors might help: statistical ones such as the ratio of exports to debt interest, the ratio of GDP to external debt, the public sector deficit, etc., and political factors such as the policy stance of the government.

**Problem 2.7**   (a)   is the more probable, since it encompasses her being active *or* not active in the feminist movement. Many people get this wrong, which shows how one's pre-conceptions can mislead.

**Problem 2.9**   The advertiser is a trickster and guesses at random. Every correct guess ($P = 0.5$) nets a fee, every wrong one costs nothing except reimbursing the fee. The trickster would thus keep half the money sent in. You should be wary of such advertisements!

**Problem 2.11**   (a)   E(winnings) = $0.5^{20} \times$ £1bn + $(1 - 0.5^{20}) \times$ –£100 = £853.67.

   (b)   Despite the positive expected value, most would not play because of their aversion to risk. Would you?

**Problem 2.13**   (a), (b) and (d) are independent, though legend says that rain on St Swithins day means rain for the next forty!

**Problem 2.15**   (a)   There are 15 ways in which a 4–2 score could be arrived at, of which this is one. Hence the probability is 1/15.

   (b)   Six of the routes through the tree diagram involve a 2–2 score at some stage, so the probability is 6/15.

**Problem 2.17**   Pr(guessing all six) = $6/50 \times 5/49 \times \ldots \times 1/45$ = 1/15 890 700. Pr(six from ten guesses) = $10/50 \times 9/49 \times \ldots \times 5/45$ = 151 200/11 441 304 000. This is exactly 210 times the first answer, so there is no discount for bulk gambling!

**Problem 2.19**

|           | Prior | Likelihood | Prior × likelihood | Posterior |
|-----------|-------|------------|--------------------|-----------|
| Fair coin | 0.5   | 0.25       | 0.125              | 0.2       |
| Two heads | 0.5   | 1.00       | 0.500              | 0.8       |
| Total     |       |            | 0.625              |           |

**Problem 2.21**   (a)   Using Bayes' theorem the probability is $p/(p + (1 - p)) = p$.

   (b)   Again using Bayes' theorem we obtain $p^2/(p^2 + (1 - p)^2)$.

   (c)   If $p < 0.5$ then (b) < (a). The agreement of the second witness *reduces* the probability that the defendant is guilty. Intuitively this seems unlikely. The fallacy is that they can lie in many different ways, so Bayes' theorem is not applicable here.

**Problem 2.23**   (a)   EVs are 142, 148.75 and 146 respectively. Hence B is chosen.

   (b)   The minima are 100, 130, 110, so B has the greatest minimum. The maxima are 180, 170, 200 so C is chosen.

(c) The regret table is

|   | Low | Middle | High | Max. |
|---|---|---|---|---|
| A | 30 | 5 | 20 | 30 |
| B | 0 | 0 | 30 | 30 |
| C | 20 | 15 | 0 | 20 |

so C has the minimax regret figure.

(d) The EV assuming perfect information is 157.75, against an EV of 148.75 for project B, so the value of information is 9.

**Problem 2.25** The probability of *no* common birthday is $365/365 \times 364/365 \times 363/365 \times \ldots \times 341/365 = 0.43$. Hence the probability of at least one birthday in common is 0.57, or greater than one-half. Most people underestimate this probability by a large amount. (This result could form the basis of a useful source of income at parties . . . )

# Chapter 3

**Problem 3.1** The graph looks like a pyramid, centred on the value of 7, which is the mean of the distribution. The probabilities of scores of 2, 3, . . . , 12 are (out of 36): 1, 2, 3, 4, 5, 6, 5, 4, 3, 2, 1 respectively. The probability that the sum is nine or greater is therefore 10/36. The variance is 5.83.

**Problem 3.3** The distribution should be sharply peaked (at or just after the timetabled departure time) and should be skewed to the right.

**Problem 3.5** Similar to the train departure time, except that it is a discrete distribution. The mode would be 0 accidents, and the probability above 1 accident per day very low indeed.

**Problem 3.7** The probabilities are 0.33, 0.40, 0.20, 0.05, 0.008, 0.000, 0.000 of 0–6 sixes respectively.

**Problem 3.9** (a) $Pr(0) = 0.9^{15} = 0.21$, $Pr(1) = 15 \times 0.9^{14} \times 0.1 = 0.34$, hence $Pr(0 \text{ or } 1) = 0.55$.

(b) By taking a larger sample or tightening the acceptance criteria, e.g. only accepting if the sample is defect free.

(c) 7%.

(d) The assumption of a large batch means that the probability of a defective component being selected does not alter significantly as the sample is drawn.

**Problem 3.11** The $y$-axis coordinates are:

0.05   0.13   0.24   0.35   0.40   0.35   0.24   0.13   0.05

This gives the outline of the central part of the Normal distribution.

**Problem 3.13** (a) 5%.

(b) 30.85%.

(c) 93.32%.

(d) 91.04%.

(e) Zero! (You must have an *area* for a probability.)

---

**Problem 3.15** (a) $z = 0.67$, area = 25%.

(b) $z = -1$, area = 15.87%.

(c) $z_L = -0.67$, $z_U = 1.67$, area = 70.11%.

(d) Zero again!

---

**Problem 3.17** (a) $I \sim N(100, 16^2/10)$.

(b) $z = 1.98$, Pr = 2.39%.

(c) 2.39% (same as (b)).

(d) 95.22%. This is much greater than the previous answer. This question refers to the distribution of sample means, which is less dispersed than the population.

(e) Since the marginal student has an IQ of 108 (see previous question) nearly all university students will have an IQ above 110 and so, to an even greater extent, the sample mean will be above 110. Note that the distribution of students' IQ is not Normal but skewed to the right, since it is taken from the upper tail of a Normal distribution. The small sample size means we cannot safely use the Central Limit Theorem here.

(f) 105, *not* 100. The expected value of the last 9 is 100, so the average is 105.

---

**Problem 3.19** (a) $r \sim B(10, \frac{1}{2})$.

(b) $r \sim N(5, 2.5)$.

(c) Binomial: Pr = 82.8%; Normal: 73.57% (82.9% using the continuity correction).

---

**Problem 3.21** (a) By the Binomial, Pr(no errors) = $0.99^{100}$ = 36.6%. By the Poisson, $nP = 1$, so $Pr(x = 0) = (1^0 \times e^{-1})/0! = 36.8\%$.

(b) $Pr(r = 1) = 100 \times 0.99^{99} \times 0.01 = 0.370$; $Pr(r = 2) = 100C2 \times 0.99^{98} \times 0.01^2 = 0.185$. Hence $Pr(r \leq 2) = 0.921$. Poisson method: $Pr(x = 1) = 1^1 \times e^{-1}/1! = 0.368$; $Pr(x = 2) = 1^2 \times e^{-1}/2! = 0.184$. Hence $Pr(x \leq 2) = 0.920$. Hence the probability of more than two errors is about 8% using either method. Using the Normal method we would have $x \sim N(1, 0.99)$. So the probability of $x > 2.5$ (taking account of the continuity correction) is given by $z = (2.5 - 1)/\sqrt{0.99} = 1.51$, giving an answer of 6.55%, a significant underestimate of the true value.

---

**Problem 3.23** (a) Normal.

(b) Uniform distribution between 0 and 1 (look up the =*RAND*() function in your software documentation).

(c) Mean = 0.5, variance = 5/12 = 0.42 for parent, mean = 0.5, variance = 0.42/5 for sample means (Normal distribution).

---

# Chapter 4

**Problem 4.1** (a) It gives the reader some idea of the reliability of an estimate.

(b) The population variance (or its sample estimate) and the sample size.

**Problem 4.3** An estimator is the rule used to find the estimate or a parameter. A good estimator does not *guarantee* a good estimate, only that it is correct *on average* (if the estimator is unbiased) and close to the true value (if precise).

**Problem 4.5** $E(w_1x_1 + w_2x_2) = w_1E(x_1) + w_2E(x_2) = w_1\mu + w_2\mu = \mu$ if $w_1 + w_2 = 1$.

**Problem 4.7** $40 \pm 2.57 \times \sqrt{10^2/36} = [35.71, 44.28]$. If $n = 20$, the $t$ distribution should be used, giving $40 \pm 2.861 \times \sqrt{10^2/20} = [33.60, 46.40]$.

**Problem 4.9** $40 \pm 2.57 \times \sqrt{0.4 \times 0.6/50} = [0.22, 0.58]$.

**Problem 4.11** $(25 - 22) \pm 1.96 \times \sqrt{12^2/80 + 18^2/100} = [-1.40, 7.40]$.

**Problem 4.13** $(0.67 - 0.62) \pm 2.57\sqrt{\dfrac{0.67 \times 0.33}{150} + \dfrac{0.62 \times 0.38}{120}} = [-0.10, 0.20]$.

**Problem 4.15** $30 \pm 2.131 \times \sqrt{5^2/16} = [27.34, 32.66]$.

**Problem 4.17** $(45 - 52) \pm 2.048\sqrt{40.32/12 + 40.32/18} = [-2.15, -11.85]$. 40.32 is the pooled variance.

# Chapter 5

**Problem 5.1** (a) False, you can alter the sample size.

(b) True.

(c) False, you need to consider the Type II error probability also.

(d) True.

(e) False, it's the probability of a Type I error.

(f) False, the confidence level is $1 - \Pr(\text{Type I error})$ or the probability of accepting $H_0$ when true.

**Problem 5.3** $H_0$: fair coin, $(\Pr(H) = \frac{1}{2})$, $H_1$: two heads $(\Pr(H) = 1)$. $\Pr(\text{Type I error}) = (\frac{1}{2})^2 = \frac{1}{4}$; $\Pr(\text{Type II error}) = 0$.

**Problem 5.5** (a) Rejecting a good batch or accepting a bad batch.

(b) $H_0$: $\mu = 0.01$ and $H_1$: $\mu = 0.10$ are the hypotheses. Under $H_0$, $\Pr(0$ or 1 defective in sample$) = 0.911$, hence 8.9% chance of rejecting a good batch. Under $H_1$, $\Pr(0$ or $1) = 0.034$, hence 3.4% chance of accepting a bad batch. One could also use the Normal approximation to the Binomial, giving probabilities of 7.78% and 4.95%.

(c)  Pr(Type I error) = 26%; Pr(Type II error) = 4.2%.

(d) (i)  Try to avoid faulty batches, hence increase the risk of rejecting good batches, the significance level of the test.

(ii)  Since there are alternative suppliers it can increase the risk of rejecting good batches (which upsets its supplier).

(iii) Avoid accepting bad batches.

**Problem 5.7**  $z = 1.83$, hence Prob-value is 3.36%.

**Problem 5.9**  100%. You will always reject $H_0$ when false.

**Problem 5.11**  $z = 1 < 1.96$, the critical value at the 95% confidence level.

**Problem 5.13**  $z = 0.59$, not significant, do not reject.

**Problem 5.15**  $z = (115 - 105)/\sqrt{21^2/49 + 23^2/63} = 2.4 > 1.64$, the critical value, hence reject with 95% confidence.

**Problem 5.17**  $z = \dfrac{0.57 - 0.47}{\sqrt{\dfrac{0.51 \times (1 - 0.51)}{180} + \dfrac{0.51 \times (1 - 0.51)}{225}}} = 2.12.$

This is significant using either a one- or a two-tail test. Whether you used a one- or a two-tail test reveals something about your prejudices! The proportions passing are the actual outcomes for 1992 in the UK, based on 1.85 million tests altogether. You might have an interesting class discussion about what these statistics prove! To redress the balance you might investigate the relationship between gender and road accidents.

**Problem 5.19**  (a)  $t = -5/\sqrt{10^2/20} = -2.24 < -2.093$, the critical value, hence reject $H_0$.

(b)  The parent distribution is Normal.

**Problem 5.21**  $S^2 = 38.8$, and $t = 8.29$, so $H_0$ is rejected.

**Problem 5.23**  (a)  $t_{20} = 1.18$.

(b)  $t_{10} = 1.63$. Neither is significant at the 5% level, though the latter is closer. Note that only one worker performs worse, but this one does substantially worse, perhaps due to other factors.

**Problem 5.25**  (a)  It would be important to check *all* the predictions of the astrologer. Too often, correct predictions are highlighted ex-post and incorrect ones ignored.

(b)  Like astrology, a fair test is important, where it is possible to pass or fail, with known probabilities. Then performance can be judged.

(c)  Samples of both taken-over companies and independent companies should be compared, with as little difference between samples as possible.

# Chapter 6

**Problem 6.1** The 95% c.i. for the variance is

$$\frac{39 \times 20^2}{59.34} \leq \sigma^2 \leq \frac{39 \times 20^2}{24.43}$$

where 24.43 and 59.34 are the limits cutting off 2.5% in each tail of the $\chi^2$ distribution, so the c.i. for $\sigma$ is [16.21, 25.29].

**Problem 6.3** $\chi^2 = 0.70 < 3.84$, the 95% critical value, hence no apparent difference between quarters I/III and II/IV.

**Problem 6.5** Using the data as presented, with expected values of 565, yields $\chi^2(3) = 1.33$, not significant. However, adding the dissatisfied customers (24, 42, 20, 54) and constructing a contingency table yields $\chi^2(3) = 22.94$, highly significant. The differences between the small numbers of dissatisfied customers add most to the test statistic. The former result should be treated with suspicion since it is fairly obvious that there would be small numbers of dissatisfied customers.

**Problem 6.7** $\chi^2(4) = 8.12$ which is not significant at the 5% significance level. There appears to be no relationship between size and profitability.

**Problem 6.9** (a) The correct observed and expected values are

47.0 (54.9)    72.0 (64.1)
86.0 (76.6)    80.0 (89.4)
 4.0 (5.5)      8.0 (6.5)

and this yields a $\chi^2$ value of 5.05 against a critical value of 5.99 (5% significance level, 2 degrees of freedom).

(b) Omitting the non-responses leads to a $2 \times 2$ contingency table with a test statistic of 4.22, against a critical value of 3.84, yielding a significant result.

**Problem 6.11** $F = 55/48 = 1.15 < 2.76$, the 1% critical value for 24 and 29 degrees of freedom. There is no significant difference, therefore.

**Problem 6.13** (a) Between sum of squares = 335.8; within sum of squares = 2088; total sum of squares = 2424. $F = (335.8/3)/(2088/21) = 1.126 < 3.07$, the critical value for 3, 21 degrees of freedom.

(b) A significant result would indicate some difference between the classes, but this could be due to any number of factors which have not been controlled for, e.g. different teachers, different innate ability, different gender ratios, etc.

# Chapter 7

**Problem 7.1** (b) We would expect similar slopes to those using Todaro's data, but the graphs for growth and the income ratio don't look promising.

(c) There seems to exist a psychological propensity to overestimate the degree of correlation. See (d) to see if you did.

(d) $r = -0.73, -0.25, -0.22$ for GNP, growth, the income ratio respectively. Note that $r < 0$ for the income ratio, in contrast to the result in the text.

(e) $t = -3.7, -0.89, -0.78$, so only the first is significant. The critical value is 1.78 (for a one-tail test).

**Problem 7.3** (a) Very high and positive.

(b) A medium degree of negative correlation (bigger countries can provide more for themselves).

(c) Theoretically negative, but empirically the association tends to be weak, especially using the real interest rate. There might be lags in (a) and (c). (b) would best be estimated in cross-section.

**Problem 7.5** Rank correlations are:

|  | Birth rate |
| --- | --- |
| GNP | -0.77 |
| Growth | -0.27 |
| Inc. ratio | -0.37 |

These are similar to the ordinary $r$ values. Only the first is significant at 5%.

**Problem 7.7** (a)

|  | GNP | Growth | Income ratio |
| --- | --- | --- | --- |
| $a$ | 47.18 | 42.88 | 45.46 |
| $b$ | -0.006 | -1.77 | -1.40 |
| $R^2$ | 0.53 | 0.061 | 0.047 |

These results are quite different from what was found before! GNP appears the best, not worst, explanatory variable.

(b)–(c)

|  | GNP | Growth | Income ratio |
| --- | --- | --- | --- |
| $s_e$ | 7.83 | 11.11 | 11.20 |
| $s_b$ | 0.0017 | 1.99 | 1.82 |
| $t$ | -3.71 | -0.89 | -0.77 |
| $F$ | 13.74 | 0.78 | 0.59 |

Only in the case of GNP is the $t$ ratio significant. The same is true for the $F$ statistic.

(d) You should be starting to have serious doubts! Two samples produce quite different results. We should think more carefully about how to model the birth rate and what data to apply it to.

(e)   Using all 26 observations gives:

|     | GNP   | Growth | IR    |
| --- | ----- | ------ | ----- |
| $a$ | 42.40 | 43.06  | 36.76 |
| $b$ | −0.01 | −2.77  | −0.20 |
| $R$ | 0.31  | 0.28   | 0.002 |
| $F$ | 11.02 | 9.52   | 0.04  |
| $S_b$ | 0.00 | 0.90   | 1.01  |
| $t$ | −3.32 | −3.08  | −0.20 |

The results seem quite sensitive to the data employed. We should try to ensure that we get a *representative* sample for estimation.

**Problem 7.9**   (a)   27.91 (34.71).

(b)   37.58 (32.61).

(c)   35.67 (33.76).

(Predictions in brackets are obtained from Todaro's data.) Again, different samples, different results, which doesn't inspire confidence.

# Chapter 8

**Problem 8.1**   (a)   $B = 46.77 - 0.0064\text{GNP} - 0.55\text{growth} + 0.34\text{IR}$

s.e.        (0.002)      (1.66)        (1.54)

$R^2 = 0.54$, $F = 3.91$

(i)   Calculating elasticities: GNP: $-0.0064 \times 17\,050/551 = -0.19$; growth: $-0.55 \times 27.9/551 = -0.03$; IR: $0.34 \times 61.1/551 = 0.04$. All seem quite small, although the first suggests a 10% rise in GNP should lower the birth rate by 2%.

(ii)   Only GNP appears significant. Note that the $R^2$ value is only just greater than in the simple regression on GNP.

(iii)   The $F$ statistic is just significant at the 5% level (3.71 is the critical value).

(b)   It looks like the growth and income ratio variables should be dropped.

(c)   We need restricted and unrestricted ESS values for this test. $\text{ESS}_R = 736.17$ (from Problem 9.7 (Chapter 9): $\text{ESS} = s_e^2(n-2)$). $\text{ESS}_U = 726.96$ (from above regression). Hence $F = \dfrac{(736.17 - 726.96)/2}{726.96/3} = 0.019$, less than the critical value so the variables can be omitted.

(d)   $B = 43.61 - 0.005\text{GNP} - 2.026\text{growth} + 0.69\text{IR}$

(0.0017)    (0.845)      (0.81)

$R^2 = 0.48$, $F = 6.64$, $n = 26$

The GNP and IR coefficients are of similar orders of magnitude and significance levels. The growth coefficient changes markedly and is now significant. The $F$ statistic for exclusion is 3.365, against a critical value of 3.44 at 5%, suggesting both could be excluded, in spite of the significant $t$ ratio on the growth variable.

(e)   Not much progress has been made. More planning of the research is needed.

(f)   Women's education, religion and health expenditures are possibilities.

**Problem 8.3**   28.29 from 14 countries; 27.93 from all 26 countries.

**Problem 8.5** (a) A set of dummy variables, one for each class.

(b) Difficult, because crime is so heterogeneous. One could use the number of recorded offences, but this would equate murder with bicycle theft. It would be better to model the different types of crime separately.

(c) A proxy variable could be constructed, using such factors as the length of time for which the bank governor is appointed, whether appointed by the government, etc. This would be somewhat arbitrary, but possibly better than nothing.

**Problem 8.7** (a) Time-series data, since the main interest is in *movements* of the exchange rate in response to changes in the money supply.

(b) Cross-section (cross-country) data would be affected by enormous cultural and social differences, which would be hard to measure. Regional (within-country) data might not yield many observations and might simply vary randomly. Time-series data might be better, but it would still be difficult to measure the gradual change in cultural and social influences. Best would be cross-section data on couples (both divorced and still married).

(c) Cross-section data would be of more interest. There would be many observations, with substantial variation across hospitals. This rich detail would not be so easily observable in time-series data.

**Problem 8.9** Suitable models would be:

(a) $C = b_0 + b_1 P + b_2 F + b_3 L + b_4 W$ where $C$: total costs; $P$: passenger miles flown; $F$: freight miles flown; $L$: % of long-haul flights; $W$: wage rates faced by the firm. This would be estimated using cross-section data, each airline constituting an observation. $P^2$ and $F^2$ terms could be added, to allow the cost function to be non-linear. Alternatively, it could be estimated in logs to get elasticity estimates. One would expect $b_1, b_2, b_4 > 0$, $b_3 < 0$.

(b) $IM = b_0 + b_1 GNP + b_2 FEMED + b_3 HLTHEXP$ where $IM$: infant mortality (deaths per thousand births); $FEMED$: a measure of female education (e.g. the literacy rate); $HLTHEXP$: health expenditure (ideally on women, as % of GNP). One would expect $b_1, b_2, b_3 < 0$. This would be a cross-country study. There is likely to be a 'threshold' effect of GNP, so a non-linear (e.g. log) form should be estimated.

(c) $BP = b_0 + b_1 \Delta GNP + b_2 R$ where $BP$: profits; $\Delta GNP$: growth; $R$: the interest rate. This would be estimated on time-series data. BP and growth should be measured in real terms, but the nominal interest rate might be appropriate. Bank profits depend upon the spread of interest rates, which tends to be greater when the rate is higher.

**Problem 8.11** (a) Higher $U$ reduces the demand for imports; higher OECD income raises the demand for UK exports; higher materials prices (the UK imports materials) lowers demand, but the effect on expenditure (and hence the BoP) depends upon the elasticity. Here, higher $P$ leads to a greater BoP deficit, implying inelastic demand; higher $C$ (lower competitiveness) worsens the BoP.

(b) (iii).

(c) $U$: linear; $Y$: non-linear.

(d) Since $B$ is sometimes negative, a log transformation cannot be performed. This means elasticity estimates cannot be obtained directly. Since $B$ is sometimes positive, sometimes negative, an elasticity estimate would be hard to interpret.

(e) 1.80, a surplus.

# Chapter 9

**Problem 9.1**   GNP versus GDP; gross or net national product; factor cost or market prices; coverage (UK, GB, England and Wales); current or constant prices are some of the issues.

**Problem 9.3**   The following are measures of UK and US GDP, both at year 2000 prices. The UK figures are £bn, the US figures are $bn. Your own figures may be slightly different, but should be highly correlated with these numbers.

|    | 1995 | 1996 | 1997 | 1998 | 1999 | 2000 | 2001 | 2002 | 2003 |
|----|------|------|------|------|------|------|------|------|------|
| UK | 821.4 | 843.6 | 875.0 | 897.7 | 929.7 | 961.9 | 979.2 | 997.5 | 1 023.2 |
| US | 8031.7 | 8328.9 | 8703.5 | 9066.9 | 9470.3 | 9817.0 | 9890.7 | 10 074.8 | 10 381.3 |

**Problem 9.5**   $n = 1.96^2 \times 400/2^2 = 385$.

# Chapter 10

**Problem 10.1**   (a)

|         | 1987 | 1988 | 1989 | 1990 | 1991 | 1992 |
|---------|------|------|------|------|------|------|
| Exports | 100 | 100.5 | 105.1 | 110.5 | 109.5 | 112.4 |
| Imports | 100 | 112.5 | 120.9 | 121.5 | 114.8 | 121.5 |

(b)  No. Using the indices, information about the *levels* of imports and exports is lost.

**Problem 10.3**   (a)–(c)

| Year | $E$ | $P_L$ | $P_P$ | $Q_L$ | $Q_P$ |
|------|------|------|------|------|------|
| 1984 | 100 | 100 | 100 | 100 | 100 |
| 1985 | 104.0 | 104.2 | 104.3 | 99.8 | 99.9 |
| 1986 | 85.9 | 85.9 | 86.7 | 99.0 | 100.0 |
| 1987 | 85.8 | 83.0 | 85.0 | 101.0 | 103.3 |

**Problem 10.5**   (a)

| Year | Coal | Petroleum | Electricity | Gas |
|------|------|-----------|-------------|-----|
| 1984 | 100 | 100 | 100 | 100 |
| 1985 | 102.8 | 101.4 | 103.9 | 107.9 |
| 1986 | 100.1 | 48.8 | 104.1 | 90.3 |
| 1987 | 95.8 | 52.2 | 100.1 | 83.4 |
| 1988 | 86.9 | 36.8 | 103.9 | 82.6 |
| Shares | 0.105 | 0.255 | 0.377 | 0.264 |

(b)  Answer as in Problem 3(a).

**Problem 10.7**   The chain index is 100, 110, 115, 123.1, 127.7, 136.9, 139.2, using 2000 as the common year. Using one of the other years to chain yields a slightly different index. There is no definitive right answer.

**Problem 10.9** Expenditure on energy in 1999 was £7948.31m. The Laspeyres index increased from 100 to 104.63 between 1999 and 2000, an increase of 4.63%. Hence industry should be compensated 2.63% of 7948.31 = £209.0m. A similar calculation using the Paasche index yields compensation of £213.8m.

**Problem 10.11** The index number series are as follows:

| Year | Cash expenditure | Real expenditure | Volume of expenditure | Real expenditure per capita | Volume of expenditure per capita | Needs index | Spending deflated by need |
|------|------|------|------|------|------|------|------|
| | (a) | (b) | (c) | (d) | (d) | (e) | (e) |
| 1987 | 100.0 | 100.0 | 100.0 | 100.0 | 100.0 | 100.0 | 100.0 |
| 1988 | 109.8 | 102.6 | 99.4 | 102.4 | 99.2 | 100.2 | 99.2 |
| 1989 | 120.5 | 105.7 | 101.9 | 105.1 | 101.3 | 100.5 | 101.4 |
| 1990 | 132.7 | 107.5 | 104.5 | 106.6 | 103.6 | 100.8 | 103.6 |
| 1991 | 150.4 | 113.6 | 108.8 | 111.9 | 107.1 | 101.6 | 107.1 |

(a) $109.8 = 23\ 601/21\ 495 \times 100$; $120.5 = 25\ 906/21\ 495 \times 100$; etc.

(b) This series is obtained by dividing column 1 by column 2 (and setting 1987 as the reference year). Clearly, much of the increase in column 1 is due to inflation.

(c) This series is column 1 divided by column 3. Since the NHS price index rose faster than the GDP deflator, the volume of expenditure rises more slowly than the real figure.

(d) Per capita figures are obtained by dividing by the population, column 4.

(f) Needs index could be improved by finding the true cost of treating people of different ages.

**Problem 10.13** (a) 1702.20.
(b) Yes, 102.20.

**Problem 10.15** 18.3%.

**Problem 10.17** (a) Area A = 0.303, B = 0.197, Gini = 0.607.
(b) The old have had a lifetime to accumulate wealth whereas the young haven't. This does not apply to income.

**Problem 10.19** (a) The Gini coefficients are 44.8%, 35.4%, 33.6% and 34.0% respectively.
(b) These differ from the values given in Table 2.24 (from *Economic Trends*), substantially so in the case of original and post-tax income. The figures based on quintiles are all lower than the figures in *Economic Trends*, as expected, although the bias is large in some cases. Drawing a smooth, freehand Lorenz curve based on the quintiles data for original income results in a Gini coefficient of around 46%, closer to the calculated figure than the *Economic Trends* figure. The results seem puzzling.

**Problem 10.21** 79.3%.

# Index